THE SYSTEM OF NATURE
Volumes 1 & 2

M. DE MIRABAUD

Paul Henri Thiery,
Baron d'Holbach

Introduction by
Robert D. Richardson, Jr.

THE SYSTEM OF NATURE

M. DE MIRABAUD

Paul Henri Thiery,
Baron d'Holbach

Introduction by
Robert D. Richardson, Jr.

INTRODUCTION

Paul Henri Thiery, Baron d'Holbach (1723-1789), was the center of the radical wing of the *philosophes*. He was friend, host, and patron to a wide circle that included Diderot, D'Alembert, Helvetius, and Hume. Holbach wrote, translated, edited, and issued a stream of books and pamphlets, often under other names, that has made him the despair of bibliographers but has connected his name, by innuendo, gossip, and association, with most of what was written in defense of atheistic materialism in late eighteenth-century France.

Holbach is best known for *The System of Nature* (1770) and deservedly, since it is a clear and reasonably systematic exposition of his main ideas. His initial position determines all the rest of his argument. "There is not, there can be nothing out of that Nature which includes all beings." Conceiving of nature as strictly limited to matter and motion, both of which have always existed, he flatly denies that there is any such thing as spirit or a supernatural. Mythology began, Holbach claims, when men were still in a state of nature and at the point when wise, strong, and for the most part benign men were arising as leaders and lawgivers. These leaders "formed discourses by which they spoke to the imaginations of their willing auditors," using the medium of poetry, because it "seem[ed] best adapted to strike the mind." Through poetry, then, and by means of "its images, its fictions, its numbers, its rhyme, its harmony... the entire of nature, as well as all its parts, was personified, by its beautiful allegories." Thus mythology is given an essentially political origin. These early poets are literally legislators of mankind. "The first institutors of nations, and their immediate successors in authority, only spoke to the people by fables, allegories, enigmas, of which they reserved to themselves the right of giving an explanation." Holbach is rather condescending about the process, but since mythology is a representation of nature itself, he is far more tolerant of mythology than he is of the next step. "Natural philosophers and poets were transformed by leisure into metaphysicians and theologians," and at this point a fatal error was introduced: the theologians made a distinction between the power of nature and nature itself, separated the two, made the power of nature prior to nature, and called it God. Thus man was left with an abstract and chimerical being on one side and a despoiled inert nature, destitute of power, on the other. In Holbach's critique the point at which theology split off from mythology marks the moment of nature's alienation from itself and paves the way for man's alienation from nature.

Holbach is thus significant for Romantic interest in myth in two ways. First, he provides a clear statement of what can be loosely called the antimythic position, that rationalist condescension and derogation of all myth and all religion that was never far from the surface during the Romantic era. Holbach was and is a reminder that the Romantic affirmation of myth was never easy, uncritical, or unopposed. Any new endorsement of myth had to be made in the teeth of Holbach and the other skeptics. The very vigor of the Holbachian critique of myth impelled the Romantics to think more deeply and defend more carefully any new claim for myth. Secondly, although Holbach's argument generally drove against myth and religion both, he did make an important, indeed a saving distinction between mythology and theology. Mythology is the more or less harmless personification of the power in and of nature; theology concerns itself with what for Holbach was the nonexistent power beyond or behind nature. By exploiting this distinction it would become possible for a Shelley, for example, to take a strong antitheological— even an anti-Christian—position without having to abandon myth.

Holbach was one of William Godwin's major sources for his ideas about political justice, and Shelley, who discussed Holbach with Godwin, quotes extensively from *The System of Nature* in *Queen Mab*. Furthermore, Volney's *Ruins*, another important book for Shelley, is directly descended from *The System of Nature*. On the other side, Holbach was a standing challenge to such writers as Coleridge and Goethe and was reprinted and retranslated extensively in America, where his work was well known to the rationalist circle around Jefferson and Barlow.

Issued in 1770 as though by Jean Baptiste de Mirabaud (a former perpetual secretary to the Académie française who had died ten years before), *La Système de la nature* was translated and reprinted frequently. The Samuel Wilkinson translation we have chosen to reprint was the most often reprinted or pirated version in English. A useful starting point for Holbach's work is Jerome Vercruysse, *Bibliographie descriptive des écrits du baron d'Holbach* (Paris, 1971). The difficult subject of the essentially clandestine evolution of biblical criticism as an anti-Christian and antimyth critique in the early part of the eighteenth century, before the well-documented era of the biblical critic Eichhorn in Germany, is illuminated in Ira Wade, *The Clandestine Organization and Diffusion of Philosophic Ideas in France from 1700- 1750* (Princeton Univ. Press, 1938).

Robert D. Richardson, Jr.
University of Denver

CONTENTS

Preface
PART I - Laws of Nature.—Of man.—The faculties of the soul. —Doctrine of immortality.—On happiness.
CHAP. I. Nature and her laws.
CHAP. II. Of motion and its origin.
CHAP. III. Of matter—of its various combinations—of its diversified motion—or of the course of Nature.
CHAP. IV. Laws of motion common to every being of Nature— attraction and repulsion—inert force-necessity.
CHAP. V. Order and confusion—intelligence—chance.
CHAP. VI. Moral and physical distinctions of man—his origin.
CHAP. VII. The soul and the spiritual system.
CHAP. VII. The soul and the spiritual system.
CHAP. VIII. The intellectual faculties derived from the faculty of feeling.
CHAP. IX. The diversity of the intellectual faculties; they depend on physical causes, as do their moral qualities.—The natural principles of society—morals—politics.
CHAP. X. The soul does not derive its ideas from itself—it has no innate ideas.
CHAP. XI. Of the system of man's free-agency.
CHAP. XII. An examination of the opinion which pretends that the system of fatalism is dangerous.
CHAP. XIII. Of the immortality of the soul—of the doctrine of a future state—of the fear of death.
CHAP. XIV. Education, morals, and the laws suffice to restrain man—of the desire of immortality—of suicide.
CHAP. XV. Of man's true interest, or of the ideas he forms to himself of happiness.—Man cannot be happy without virtue.
CHAP. XVI. The errors of man.—Upon what constitutes happiness.—The true source of his evils.—Remedies that may be applied.
CHAP. XVII. Those ideas which are true, or founded upon Nature, are the only remedies for the evil of man.—Recapitulation.— Conclusions of the First Part.

PART II - Of the Divinity.—Proofs of his existence.— Of his attributes.—Of his influence over the happiness of man.
CHAP. I. The origin of man's ideas upon the Divinity.
CHAP. II. Of mythology.—Of theology
CHAP. III. Of the confused and contradictory ideas of theology.
CHAP. IV. Examination of the proofs of the existence of the Divinity, as given by Clarke.

CHAP. V. Examination of the proofs offered by Descartes, Malebranche, Newton, &c.
CHAP. VI. Of Pantheism; or of the natural ideas of the Divinity.
CHAP. VII. Of Theism—Of the System of Optimism—Of Final Causes
CHAP. VIII. Examination of the Advantages which result from Man's Notions on the Divinity;—of their Influence upon Morals;—upon Politics;—upon Science;—upon the Happiness of Nations, and that of individuals.
CHAP. IX. Theological Notions cannot be the Basis of Morality.—Comparison between Theological Ethics and Natural Morality—Theology prejudicial to the Human Mind.
CHAP. X. Man can form no Conclusion from the Ideas which are offered him of the Divinity.—Of their want of just Inference.—Of the Inutility of his Conduct.
CHAP. XI Defence of the Sentiments contained in this Work.—Of Impiety.—
Do there exist Atheists?
CHAP. XII. Is what is termed Atheism, compatible with Morality?
CHAP. XIII. Of the motives which lead to what is falsely called Atheism.—Can this System be dangerous?—Can it be embraced by the Illiterate?
CHAP. XIV. A summary of the Code of Nature.
A Brief Sketch of the Life and Writings of M. de Mirabaud

THE SYSTEM OF NATURE
Volume I

M. DE MIRABAUD

Paul Henri Thiery,
Baron d'Holbach

Introduction by
Robert D. Richardson, Jr.

PREFACE

The source of man's unhappiness is his ignorance of Nature. The pertinacity with which he clings to blind opinions imbibed in his infancy, which interweave themselves with his existence, the consequent prejudice that warps his mind, that prevents its expansion, that renders him the slave of fiction, appears to doom him to continual error. He resembles a child destitute of experience, full of ideal notions: a dangerous leaven mixes itself with all his knowledge: it is of necessity obscure, it is vacillating and false:—He takes the tone of his ideas on the authority of others, who are themselves in error, or else have an interest in deceiving him. To remove this Cimmerian darkness, these barriers to the improvement of his condition; to disentangle him from the clouds of error that envelope him; to guide him out of this Cretan labyrinth, requires the clue of Ariadne, with all the love she could bestow on Theseus. It exacts more than common exertion; it needs a most determined, a most undaunted courage—it is never effected but by a persevering resolution to act, to think for himself; to examine with rigour and impartiality the opinions he has adopted. He will find that the most noxious weeds have sprung up beside beautiful flowers; entwined themselves around their stems, overshadowed them with an exuberance of foliage, choaked the ground, enfeebled their growth, diminished their petals; dimmed the brilliancy of their colours; that deceived by their apparent freshness of their verdure, by the rapidity of their exfoliation, he has given them cultivation, watered them, nurtured them, when he ought to have plucked out their very roots.

Man seeks to range out of his sphere: notwithstanding the reiterated checks his ambitious folly experiences, he still attempts the impossible; strives to carry his researches beyond the visible world; and hunts out misery in imaginary regions. He would be a metaphysician before he has become a practical philosopher. He quits the contemplation of realities to meditate on chimeras. He neglects experience to feed on conjecture, to indulge in hypothesis. He dares not cultivate his reason, because from his earliest days he has been taught to consider it criminal. He pretends to know his date in the indistinct abodes of another life, before he has considered of the means by which he is to render himself happy in the world he inhabits: in short, man disdains the study of Nature, except it be partially: he pursues phantoms that resemble an *ignis-fatuus*, which at once dazzle, bewilders, and affright: like the benighted traveller led astray by these deceptive exhalations of a swampy soil, he frequently quits the plain, the simple road of truth, by pursuing of which, he can alone ever reasonably hope to reach the goal of happiness.

The most important of our duties, then, is to seek means by which we may destroy delusions that can never do more than mislead us. The remedies for these evils must be sought for in Nature herself; it is only in the abundance of her resources, that we can rationally expect to find antidotes to the mischiefs brought upon us by an ill directed, by an overpowering enthusiasm. It is time these remedies were sought; it is time to look the evil boldly in the face, to examine its foundations, to scrutinize its superstructure: reason, with its faithful guide experience, must attack in their entrenchments those prejudices, to which the human race has but too long been the victim. For this purpose reason must be restored to its proper rank,—it must be rescued from the evil company with which it is associated. It has been too long degraded —too long neglected—cowardice has rendered it subservient to delirium, the slave to falsehood. It must no longer be held down by the massive claims of ignorant prejudice.

Truth is invariable—it is requisite to man—it can never harm him—his very necessities, sooner or later, make him sensible of this; oblige him to acknowledge it. Let us then discover it to mortals—let us exhibit its charms—let us shed it effulgence over the darkened road; it is the only mode by which man can become disgusted with that disgraceful superstition which leads him into error, and which but too often usurps his homage by treacherously covering itself with the mask of truth—its lustre can wound none but those enemies to the human race whose power is bottomed solely on the ignorance, on the darkness in which they have in almost every claimed contrived to involve the mind of man.

Truth speaks not to those perverse beings:—her voice can only be heard by generous souls accustomed to reflection, whose sensibilities make them lament the numberless calamities showered on the earth by political and religious tyranny—whose enlightened minds contemplate with horror the immensity, the ponderosity of that series of misfortunes which error has in all ages overwhelmed mankind.

To error must be attributed those insupportable chains which tyrants, which priests have forged for most nations. To error must be equally attributed that abject slavery into which the people of almost every country have fallen. Nature designed they should pursue their happiness by the most perfect freedom.—To error must be attributed those religious terrors which, in almost every climate, have either petrified man with fear, or caused him to destroy himself for coarse or fanciful beings. To error must be attributed those inveterate hatreds, those barbarous persecutions, those numerous massacres, those dreadful tragedies, of which, under pretext of serving the interests of heaven, the earth has been but too frequently made the theatre. It is error consecrated by religious enthusiasm, which produces that ignorance, that uncertainty in which man ever finds himself with regard to his most evident duties, his clearest rights, the most demonstrable truths. In short, man is almost everywhere a poor degraded captive, devoid of greatness of soul, of reason, or of virtue, whom his inhuman gaolers have never permitted to see the light of day.

Let us then endeavour to disperse those clouds of ignorance, those mists of darkness, which impede man on his journey, which obscure his progress, which prevent his marching through life with a firm, with a steady grip. Let us try to inspire him with courage—with respect for his reason—with an inextinguishable love for truth—with a remembrance of Gallileo—to the end that he may learn to know himself—to know his legitimate rights—that he may learn to consult his experience, and no longer be the dupe of an imagination led astray by authority—that he may renounce the prejudices of his childhood—that he may learn to found his morals on his nature, on his wants, on the real advantage of society—that he may dare to love himself—that he may learn to pursue his true happiness by promoting that of others—in short, that he may no longer occupy himself with reveries either useless or dangerous—that he may become a virtuous, a rational being, in which case he cannot fail to become happy.

If he must have his chimeras, let him at least learn to permit others to form theirs after their own fashion; since nothing can be more immaterial than the manner of men's thinking on subjects not accessible to reason, provided those thoughts be not suffered to embody themselves into actions injurious to others: above all, let him be fully persuaded that it is of the utmost importance to the inhabitants of this world to be JUST, KIND, and PEACEABLE.

Far from injuring the cause of virtue, an impartial examination of the principles of this work will shew that its object is to restore truth to its proper temple, to build up an altar whose foundations shall be consolidated by morality, reason, and justice: from this sacred pane, virtue guarded by truth, clothed with experience, shall shed forth her radiance on delighted mortals; whose homage flowing consecutively shall open to the world a new aera, by rendering general the belief that happiness, the true end of man's existence, can never be attained but BY PROMOTING THAT OF HIS FELLOW CREATURE.

In short, man should learn to know, that happiness is simply an emanative quality formed by reflection; that each individual ought to be the sun of his own system, continually shedding around him his genial rays; that these, re-acting, will keep his own existence constantly supplied with the requisite heat to enable him to put forth kindly fruit._

MIRABAUD'S SYSTEM OF NATURE

Translated from the Original,
BY SAMUEL WILKINSON.

PART I.
LAWS OF NATURE—OF MAN—THE FACULTIES OF THE SOUL—DOCTRINE OF IMMORTALITY—ON HAPPINESS.
CHAP. I.

Nature and her Laws.

Man has always deceived himself when he abandoned experience to follow imaginary systems.—He is the work of nature.—He exists in Nature.—He is submitted to the laws of Nature.—He cannot deliver himself from them:—cannot step beyond them even in thought. It is in vain his mind would spring forward beyond the visible world: direful and imperious necessity ever compels his return—being formed by Nature, he is circumscribed by her laws; there exists nothing beyond the great whole of which he forms a part, of which he experiences the influence. The beings his fancy pictures as above nature, or distinguished from her, are always chimeras formed after that which he has already seen, but of which it is utterly impossible he should ever form any finished idea, either as to the place they occupy, or their manner of acting—for him there is not, there can be nothing out of that Nature which includes all beings.

Therefore, instead of seeking out of the world he inhabits for beings who can procure him a happiness denied to him by Nature, let him study this Nature, learn her laws, contemplate her energies, observe the immutable rules by which she acts.—Let him apply these discoveries to his own felicity, and submit in silence to her precepts, which nothing can alter.—Let him cheerfully consent to be ignorant of causes hid from him under the most impenetrable veil.—Let him yield to the decrees of a universal power, which can never be brought within his comprehension, nor ever emancipate him from those laws imposed on him by his essence.

The distinction which has been so often made between the *physical* and the *moral* being, is evidently an abuse of terms. Man is a being purely physical: the moral man is nothing more than this physical being considered under a certain point of view; that is to say, with relation to some of his modes of action, arising out of his individual organization. But is not this organization itself the work of Nature? The motion or impulse to action, of which he is susceptible, is that not physical? His visible actions, as well as the invisible motion interiorly excited by his will or his thoughts, are equally the natural effects, the necessary consequences, of his peculiar construction, and the impulse he receives from those beings by whom he is always surrounded. All that the human mind has successively invented, with a view to change or perfect his being, to render himself happy, was never more than the necessary consequence of man's peculiar essence, and that of the beings who act upon him. The object of all his institutions, all his reflections, all his knowledge, is only to procure that happiness toward which he is continually impelled by the peculiarity of his nature. All that he does, all that he thinks, all that he is, all that he will be, is nothing more than what Universal Nature has made him. His ideas, his actions, his will, are the necessary effects of those properties infused into him by Nature, and of those circumstances in which she has placed him. In short, art is nothing but Nature acting with the tools she has furnished.

Nature sends man naked and destitute into this world which is to be his abode: he quickly learns to cover his nakedness—to shelter himself from the inclemencies of the weather, first with artlessly constructed huts, and the skins of the beasts of the forest; by degrees he mends their appearance, renders them more convenient: he establishes manufactories to supply his immediate wants; he digs clay, gold, and other fossils from the bowels of the earth; converts them into bricks for his house, into vessels for his use, gradually improves their shape, and augments their beauty. To a being exalted above our terrestrial globe, man would not appear less subjected to the laws of Nature when naked in the forest painfully seeking his sustenance, than when living in civilized society surrounded with ease, or enriched with greater experience, plunged in luxury, where he every day invents a thousand new wants and discovers a thousand new modes of supplying them. All the steps taken by man to regulate his existence, ought only to be considered as a long succession of causes and effects, which are nothing more than the development of the first impulse given him by nature.

The same animal, by virtue of his organization, passes successively from the most simple to the most complicated wants; it is nevertheless the consequence of his nature. The butterfly whose beauty we admire, whose colours are so rich, whose appearance is so brilliant, commences as an inanimate unattractive egg; from this, heat produces a worm, this becomes a chrysalis, then changes into that beautiful insect adorned with the most vivid tints: arrived at this stage he reproduces, he generates; at last despoiled of his ornaments, he is obliged to disappear, having fulfilled the task imposed on him by Nature, having performed the circle of transformation marked out for beings of his order.

The same course, the same change takes place in the vegetable world. It is by a series of combinations originally interwoven with the energies of the aloe, that this plant is insensibly regulated, gradually expanded, and at the end of a number of years produces those flowers which announce its dissolution.

It is equally so with man, who in all his motion, all the changes he undergoes, never acts but according to the laws peculiar to his organization, and to the matter of which he is composed.

The *physical man*, is he who acts by the causes our faculties make us understand.

The *moral man*, is he who acts by physical causes, with which our prejudices preclude us from becoming perfectly acquainted.

The *wild man* is a child destitute of experience, incapable of proceeding in his happiness, because he has not learnt how to oppose resistance to the impulses he receives from those beings by whom he is surrounded.

The *civilized man*, is he whom experience and sociality have enabled to draw from nature the means of his own happiness, because he has learned to oppose resistance to those impulses he receives from exterior beings, when experience has taught him they would be destructive to his welfare.

The *enlightened man* is man in his maturity, in his perfection; who is capable of advancing his own felicity, because he has learned to examine, to think for himself, and not to take that for truth upon the authority of others, which experience has taught him a critical disquisition will frequently prove erroneous.

The *happy man* is he who knows how to enjoy the benefits bestowed upon him by nature: in other words, he who thinks for himself; who is thankful for the good he possesses; who does not envy the welfare of others, nor sigh after imaginary benefits always beyond his grasp.

The *unhappy man* is he who is incapacitated to enjoy the benefits of nature; that is, he who suffers others to think for him; who neglects the absolute good he possesses, in a fruitless search after ideal benefits; who vainly sighs after that which ever eludes his pursuit.

It necessarily results, that man in his enquiry ought always to contemplate experience, and natural philosophy: These are what he should consult in his religion,—in his morals,—in his legislation,—in his political government,—in the arts,—in the sciences,—in his pleasures,—above all, in his misfortunes. Experience teaches that Nature acts by simple, regular, and invariable laws. It is by his senses, man is bound to this universal Nature; it is by his perception he must penetrate her secrets; it is from his senses he must draw experience of her laws. Therefore, whenever he neglects to acquire experience or quits its path, he stumbles into an abyss; his imagination leads him astray.

All the errors of man are physical: he never deceives himself but when he neglects to return back to nature, to consult her laws, to call practical knowledge to his aid. It is for want of practical knowledge he forms such imperfect ideas of matter, of its properties, of its combinations, of its power, of its mode of action, and of the energies which spring from its essence. Wanting this experience, the whole universe, to him, is but one vast scene of error. The most ordinary results appear to him the most astonishing phenomena; he wonders at every thing, understands nothing, and yields the guidance of his actions to those interested in betraying his interests. He is ignorant of Nature, and he has mistaken her laws; he has not contemplated the necessary routine which she has marked out for every thing she holds. Mistaken the laws of

Nature, did I say? He has mistaken himself: the consequence is, that all his systems, all his conjectures, all his reasonings, from which he has banished experience, are nothing more than a tissue of errors, a long chain of inconsistencies.

Error is always prejudicial to man: it is by deceiving himself, the human race is plunged into misery. He neglected Nature; he did not comprehend her laws; he formed gods of the most preposterous and ridiculous kinds: these became the sole objects of his hope, and the creatures of his fear: he was unhappy, he trembled under these visionary deities; under the supposed influence of visionary beings created by himself; under the terror inspired by blocks of stone; by logs of wood; by flying fish; or the frowns of men, mortal as himself, whom his disturbed fancy had elevated above that Nature of which alone he is capable of forming any idea. His very posterity laughs at his folly, because experience has convinced them of the absurdity of his groundless fears—of his misplaced worship. Thus has passed away the ancient mythology, with all the trifling and nonsensical attributes attached to it by ignorance.

Not understanding that Nature, equal in her distributions, entirely destitute of malice, follows only necessary and immutable laws, when she either produces beings or destroys them, when she causes those to suffer, whose construction creates sensibility; when she scatters among them good and evil; when she subjects them to incessant change—he did not perceive it was in the breast of Nature herself, that it was in her exuberance he ought to seek to satisfy his deficiencies; for remedies against his pains; for the means of rendering himself happy: he expected to derive these benefits from fantastic beings, whom he supposed to be above Nature; whom he mistakingly imagined to be the authors of his pleasures, and the cause of his misfortunes. From hence it appears that to his ignorance of Nature, man owes the creation of those illusive powers; under which he has so long trembled with fear; that superstitious worship, which has been the source of all his misery, and the evils entailed upon posterity.

For want of clearly comprehending his own peculiar nature, his proper course, his wants, and his rights, man has fallen in society, from FREEDOM into SLAVERY. He had forgotten the purpose of his existence, or else he believed himself obliged to suppress the natural desires of his heart, to sacrifice his welfare to the caprice of chiefs, either elected by himself, or submitted to without examination. He was ignorant of the true policy of association—of the object of government; he disdained to listen to the voice of Nature, which loudly proclaimed the price of all submission to be protection and happiness: the end of all government is the benefit of the governed, not the exclusive advantage of the governors. He gave himself up without enquiry to men like himself, whom his prejudices induced him to contemplate as beings of a superior order, as Gods upon earth, they profited by his ignorance, took advantage of his prejudices, corrupted him, rendered him vicious, enslaved him, and made him miserable. Thus man, intended by Nature for the full enjoyment of liberty, to patiently search out her laws, to investigate her secrets, to cling to his experience; has, from a neglect of her salutary admonitions, from an inexcusable ignorance of his own peculiar essence, fallen into servility: has been wickedly governed.

Having mistaken himself, he has remained ignorant of the indispensable affinity that subsists between him, and the beings of his own species: having mistaken his duty to himself, it consequently follows, he has mistaken his duty to others. He made a calculation in error of what his happiness required; he did not perceive, what he owed to himself, the excesses he ought to avoid, the desires he ought to resist, the impulses he ought to follow, in order to consolidate his felicity, to promote his comfort, and to further his advantage. In short, he was ignorant of his true interests; hence his irregularities, his excesses, his shameful extravagance, with that long train of vices, to which he has abandoned himself, at the expense of his preservation, at the hazard of his permanent prosperity.

It is, therefore, ignorance of himself that has hindered man from enlightening his morals. The corrupt authorities to which he had submitted, felt an interest in obstructing the practice of his duties, even when he knew them. Time, with the influence of ignorance, aided by his corruption, gave them a strength not to be resisted by his enfeebled voice. His duties continued unperformed, and he fell into contempt both with himself and with others.

The ignorance of Man has endured so long, he has taken such slow, such irresolute steps to ameliorate his condition, only because he has neglected to study Nature, to scrutinize her laws, to search out her expedients, to discover her properties, that his sluggishness finds its account, in permitting himself to be guided by example, rather than to follow experience, which demands activity; to be led by routine, rather than by his reason, which enjoins reflection; to take that for truth upon the authority of others, which would require a diligent and patient investigation. From hence may be traced the hatred man betrays for every thing that deviates from those rules to which he has been accustomed; hence his stupid, his scrupulous respect for antiquity, for the most silly, the most absurd and ridiculous institutions of his fathers: hence those fears that seize him, when the most beneficial changes are proposed to him, or the most likely attempts are made to better his condition. He dreads to examine, because he has been taught to hold it irreverent of something immediately connected with his welfare; his credulity suffers him to believe the interested advice, and spurns at those who wish to show him the danger of the road he is travelling.

This is the reason why nations linger on in the most shameful lethargy, suffering under abuses handed down from century to century, trembling at the very idea of that which alone can repair their calamities.

It is for want of energy, for want of consulting experience, that medicine, natural philosophy, agriculture, painting, in fact, all the useful sciences, have so long remained under the fetters of authority, have progressed so little: those who profess these sciences, prefer treading the beaten paths, however imperfect, rather than strike out new ones,—they prefer the phrensy of their imagination, their voluntary conjectures, to that laboured experience which alone can extract her secrets from Nature.

Man, in short, whether from sloth or from terror, having abnegated the evidence of his senses, has been guided in all his actions, in all his enterprizes, by imagination, by enthusiasm, by habit, by preconceived opinions, but above all, by the influence of authority, which knew well how to deceive him, to turn his ignorance to esteem, his sloth to advantage. Thus imaginary, unsubstantial systems, have supplied the place of experience—of mature reflection—of reason. Man, petrified with his fears, intoxicated with the marvellous, stupified with sloth, surrendered his experience: guided by his credulity, he was unable to fall back upon it; he became consequently inexperienced; from thence he gave birth to the most ridiculous opinions, or else adopted all those vague chimeras, all those idle notions offered to him by men whose interest it was to continue him in that lamentable state of ignorance.

Thus the human race has continued so long in a state of infancy, because man has been inattentive to Nature; has neglected her ways, because he has disdained experience—because he has thrown by his reason—because he has been enraptured with the marvellous and the supernatural,— because he has unnecessarily TREMBLED. These are the reasons there is so much trouble in conducting him from this state of childhood to that of manhood. He has had nothing but the most trifling hypotheses, of which he has never dared to examine either the principles or the proofs, because he has been accustomed to hold them sacred, to consider them as the most perfect truths, and which he is not permitted to doubt, even for an instant. His ignorance made him credulous; his curiosity made him swallow the wonderful: time confirmed him in his opinions, and he passed his conjectures from race to race for realities; a tyrannical power maintained him in his notions, because by those alone could society be enslaved. It was in vain that some faint glimmerings of Nature occasionally attempted the recall of his reason—that slight corruscations of experience sometimes threw his darkness into light, the interest of the few was founded on his enthusiasm; their pre-eminence depended on his love of the marvellous; their very existence rested on the firmness of his ignorance; they consequently suffered no opportunity to escape, of smothering even the transient flame of intelligence. The many were thus first deceived into credulity, then forced into submission. At length the whole science of man became a confused mass of darkness, falsehood, and contradictions, with here and there a feeble ray of truth, furnished by that Nature, of which he can never entirely divest himself; because, without his perception, his necessities are continually bringing him back to her resources.

Let us then, if possible, raise ourselves above these clouds of prepossession! Let us quit the heavy atmosphere in which we are enucleated; let us in a more unsullied medium—in a more elastic current, contemplate the opinions of men, and observe their various systems. Let us learn to distrust a disordered conception; let us take that faithful monitor, experience, for our guide; let us consult Nature, examine her laws, dive into her stores; let us draw from herself, our ideas of the beings she contains; let us recover our senses, which interested error has taught us to suspect; let us consult that reason, which, for the vilest purposes has been so infamously calumniated, so cruelly dishonoured; let us examine with attention the visible world; let us try, if it will not enable us to form a supportable judgment of the invisible territory of the intellectual world: perhaps it may be found there has been no sufficient reason for distinguishing them—that it is not without motives, well worthy our enquiry, that two empires have been separated, which are equally the inheritance of nature.

The universe, that vast assemblage of every thing that exists, presents only matter and motion: the whole offers to our contemplation, nothing but an immense, an uninterrupted succession of causes and effects; some of these causes are known to us, because they either strike immediately on our senses, or have been brought under their cognizance, by the examination of long experience; others are unknown to us, because they act upon us by effects, frequently very remote from their primary cause. An immense variety of matter, combined under an infinity of forms, incessantly communicates, unceasingly receives a diversity of impulses. The different qualities of this matter, its innumerable combinations, its various methods of action, which are the necessary consequence of these associations, constitute for man what he calls the ESSENCE of beings: it is from these varied essences that spring the orders, the classes, or the systems, which these beings respectively possess, of which the sum total makes up that which is known by the term *nature*.

Nature, therefore, in its most significant meaning, is the great whole that results from the collection of matter, under its various combinations, with that contrariety of motion, which the universe presents to our view. Nature, in a less extended sense, or considered in each individual, is the whole that results from its essence; that is to say, the peculiar qualities, the combination, the impulse, and the various modes of action, by which it is discriminated from other beings. It is thus that MAN is, as a whole, or in his nature, the result of a certain combination of matter, endowed with peculiar properties, competent to give, capable of receiving, certain impulses, the arrangement of which is called *organization*; of which the essence is, to feel, to think, to act, to move, after a manner distinguished from other beings, with which he can be compared. Man, therefore, ranks in an order, in a system, in a class by himself, which differs from that of other animals, in whom we do not perceive those properties of which he is possessed. The different systems of beings, or if they will, their *particular natures*, depend on the general system of the great whole, or that Universal Nature, of which they form a part; to which every thing that exists is necessarily submitted and attached.

Having described the proper definition that should be applied to the word NATURE, I must advise the reader, once for all, that whenever in the course of this work the expression occurs, that "Nature produces such or such an effect," there is no intention of personifying that nature which is purely an abstract being; it merely indicates that the effect spoken of necessarily springs from the peculiar properties of those beings which compose the mighty macrocosm. When, therefore, it is said, *Nature demands that man should pursue his own happiness*, it is to prevent circumlocution—to avoid tautology; it is to be understood, that it is the property of a being that feels, that thinks, that acts, to labour to its own happiness; in short, that is called *natural*, which is conformable to the essence of things, or to the laws, which Nature prescribes to the beings she contains, in the different orders they occupy, under the various circumstances through which they are obliged to pass. Thus health is *natural* to man in a certain state; disease is *natural* to him under other circumstances; dissolution, or if they will, death, is a *natural* state for a body, deprived of some of those things, necessary to maintain the existence of the animal, &c. By ESSENCE is to be understood, that which constitutes a being, such as it is; the whole of the properties or qualities by which it acts as it does. Thus, when it is said, it is the *essence* of a stone to fall, it is the same as saying that its descent is the necessary effect of its gravity—of its density—of the cohesion of its parts—of the elements of which it is composed. In short, the *essence* of a being is its particular, its individual nature.

CHAP. II.
Of Motion, and its Origin.

Motion is an effect by which a body either changes, or has a tendency to change, its position: that is to say, by which it successively corresponds with different parts of space, or changes its relative distance to other bodies. It is motion alone that establishes the relation between our senses and exterior or interior beings: it is only by motion that these beings are impressed upon us—that we know their existence—that we judge of their properties—that we distinguish the one from the other—that we distribute them into classes.

The beings, the substances, or the various bodies of which Nature is the assemblage, are themselves effects of certain combinations or causes which become causes in their turn. A CAUSE is a being which puts another in motion, or which produces some change in it. The EFFECT is the change produced in one body, by the motion or presence of another.

Each being, by its essence, by its peculiar nature, has the faculty of producing, is capable of receiving, has the power of communicating, a variety of motion. Thus some beings are proper to strike our organs; these organs are competent to receiving the impression, are adequate to undergoing changes by their presence. Those which cannot act on any of our organs, either immediately and by themselves, or immediately by the intervention of other bodies, exist not for us; since they can neither move us, nor consequently furnish us with ideas: they can neither be known to us, nor of course be judged of by us. To know an object, is to have felt it; to feel it, it is requisite to have been moved by it. To see, is to have been moved, by something acting on the visual organs; to hear, is to have been struck, by something on our auditory nerves. In short, in whatever mode a body may act upon us, whatever impulse we may receive from it, we can have no other knowledge of it than by the change it produces in us.

Nature, as we have already said, is the assemblage of all the beings, consequently of all the motion of which we have a knowledge, as well as of many others of which we know nothing, because they have not yet become accessible to our senses. From the continual action and re-action of these beings, result a series of causes and effects; or a chain of motion guided by the constant and invariable laws peculiar to each being; which are necessary or inherent to its particular nature—which make it always act or move after a determinate manner. The different principles of this motion are unknown to us, because we are in many instances, if not in all, ignorant of what constitutes the essence of beings. The elements of bodies escape our senses; we know them only in the mass: we are neither acquainted with their intimate combination, nor the proportion of these combinations; from whence must necessarily result their mode of action, their impulse, or their different effects.

Our senses bring us generally acquainted with two sorts of motion in the beings that surround us: the one is the motion of the mass, by which an entire body is transferred from one place to another. Of the motion of this genus we are perfectly sensible.—Thus, we see a stone fall, a ball roll, an arm move, or change its position. The other is an internal or concealed motion, which always depends on the peculiar energies of a body: that is to say, on its *essence*, or the combination, the action, and re-action of the minute—of the insensible particles of matter, of which that body is composed. This motion we do not see; we know it only by the alteration or change, which after some time we discover in these bodies or mixtures. Of this genus is that concealed motion which fermentation produces in the particles that compose flour, which, however scattered, however separated, unite, and form that mass which we call BREAD. Such also is the imperceptible motion by which we see a plant or animal enlarge, strengthen, undergo changes, and acquire new qualities, without our eyes being competent to follow its progression, or to perceive the causes which have produced these effects. Such also is the internal motion that takes place in man, which is called his INTELLECTUAL FACULTIES, his THOUGHTS, his PASSIONS, his will. Of these we have no other mode of judging, than by their action; that is, by those sensible effects which either accompany or follow them. Thus, when we see a man run away, we judge him to be interiorly actuated by the passion of fear.

Motion, whether visible or concealed, is styled ACQUIRED, when it is impressed on one body by another; either by a cause to which we are a stranger, or by an exterior agent which our senses enable us to discover. Thus we call that *acquired motion*, which the wind gives to the sails of a ship. That motion which is excited in a body, that contains within itself the causes of those changes we see it undergo, is called SPONTANEOUS. Then it is said, this body acts or moves by its own peculiar energies. Of this kind is the motion of the man who walks, who talks, who thinks. Nevertheless, if we examine the matter a little closer, we shall be convinced, that, strictly speaking, there is no such thing as spontaneous motion in any of the various bodies of Nature; seeing they are perpetually acting one upon the other; that all their changes are to be attributed to the causes, either visible or concealed, by which they are moved. The will of man is secretly moved or determined by some exterior cause that produces a change in him: we believe he moves of himself, because we neither see the cause that determined him, the mode in which it acted, nor the organ that it put in motion.

That is called SIMPLE MOTION, which is excited in a body by a single cause. COMPOUND MOTION, that which is produced by two or more different causes; whether these causes are equal or unequal, conspiring differently, acting together or in succession, known or unknown.

Let the motion of beings be of whatsoever nature it may, it is always the necessary consequence of their essence, or of the properties which compose them, and of those causes of which they experience the action. Each being can only move and act after a particular manner; that is to say, conformably to those laws which result from its peculiar essence, its particular combination, its individual nature: in short, from its specific energies, and those of the bodies from which it receives an impulse. It is this that constitutes the invariable laws of motion: I say *invariable*, because they can never change, without producing confusion in the essence of things. It is thus that a heavy body must necessarily fall, if it meets with no obstacle sufficient to arrest its descent; that a sensible body must naturally seek pleasure, and avoid pain; that fire must necessarily burn, and diffuse light.

Each being, then, has laws of motion, that are adapted to itself, and constantly acts or moves according to these laws; at least when no superior cause interrupts its action. Thus, fire ceases to burn combustible matter, as soon as sufficient water is thrown into it, to arrest its progress. Thus, a sensible being ceases to seek pleasure, as soon as he fears that pain will be the result.

The communication of motion, or the medium of action, from one body to another, also follows certain and necessary laws; one being can only communicate motion to another, by the affinity, by the resemblance, by the conformity, by the analogy, or by the point of contact, which it has with that other being. Fire can only propagate when it finds matter analogous to itself: it extinguishes when it encounters bodies which it cannot embrace; that is to say, that do not bear towards it a certain degree of relation or affinity.

Every thing in the universe is in motion: the essence of matter is to act: if we consider its parts, attentively, we shall discover there is not a particle that enjoys absolute repose. Those which appear to us to be without motion, are, in fact, only in relative or apparent rest; they experience such an imperceptible motion, and expose it so little on their surfaces, that we cannot perceive the changes they undergo. All that appears to us to be at rest, does not, however, remain one instant in the same state. All beings are continually breeding, increasing, decreasing, or dispersing, with more or less dullness or rapidity. The insect called EPHEMERON, is produced and perishes in the same day; of consequence, it experiences the greatest changes of its being very rapidly, in our eyes. Those combinations which form the most solid bodies, which appear to enjoy the most perfect repose, are nevertheless decomposed, and dissolved in the course of time. The hardest stones, by degrees, give way to the contact of air. A mass of iron, which time, and the action of the atmosphere, has gnawed into rust, must have been in motion, from the moment of its formation, in the bowels of the earth, until the instant we behold it in this state of dissolution.

Natural philosophers, for the most part, seem not to have sufficiently reflected on what they call the *nisus*; that is to say, the incessant efforts one body is making on another, but which, notwithstanding appear, to our superficial observation, to enjoy the most perfect repose. A stone of five hundred weight seems to rest quiet on the earth, nevertheless, it never ceases for an instant, to press with force upon the earth, which resists or repulses it in its turn. Will the assertion be ventured, that the stone and earth do not act? Do they wish to be undeceived? They have nothing to do but interpose their hand betwixt the earth and the stone; it will then be discovered, that notwithstanding its seeming repose, the stone has power adequate to bruise it; because the hand has not energies sufficient, within itself, to resist effectually both the stone and earth.—Action cannot exist in bodies without re-action. A body that experiences an impulse, an attraction, or a pressure of any kind, if it resists, clearly demonstrates by such resistance that it re-acts; from whence it follows, there is a concealed force, called by these philosophers *vis inertia*, that displays itself against another force; and this clearly demonstrates, that this inert force is capable of both acting and re-acting. In short, it will be found, on close investigation, that those powers which are called *dead*, and those which are termed *live* or *moving*, are powers of the same kind; which only display themselves after a different manner. Permit us to go a greater distance yet. May we not say, that in those bodies, or masses, of which their whole become evident from appearances to us to be at rest, there is notwithstanding, a continual action, and counter-action, constant efforts, uninterrupted or communicated force, and continued opposition? In short, a *nisus*, by which the constituting portions of these bodies press one upon another, mutually resisting each other, acting and re-acting incessantly? that this reciprocity of action, this simultaneous re-action, keeps them united, causes their particles to form a mass, a body, and a combination, which, viewed in its whole, has the appearance of complete rest, notwithstanding no one of its particles really ceases to be in motion for a single instant? These collective masses appear to be at rest, simply by the equality of the motion—by the responsory impulse of the powers acting in them.

Thus it appears that bodies enjoying perfect repose, really receive, whether upon their surface, or in their interior, a continual communicated force, from those bodies by which they are either surrounded or penetrated, dilated or contracted, rarified or condensed: in fact, from those which compose them; whereby their particles are incessantly acting and re-acting, or in continual motion, the effects of which are displayed by extraordinary changes. Thus heat rarifies and dilates metals, which is evidence deducible that a bar of iron, from the change of the atmosphere alone, must be in continual motion; that there is not a single particle in it that can be said to enjoy rest even for a single moment. In those hard bodies, indeed, the particles of which are in actual contact, and which are closely united, how is it possible to conceive, that air, cold, or heat, can act upon one of these particles, even exteriorly, without the motion being communicated to those which are most intimate and minute in their union? Without motion, how should we be able to comprehend the manner in which our sense of smelling is affected, by emanations escaping from the most solid bodies, of which all the particles appear to be at perfect rest? How could we, even by the assistance of a telescope, see the most distant stars, if there was not a progressive motion of light from these stars to the retina of our eye?

Observation and reflection ought to convince us, that every thing in Nature is in continual motion—that there is not a single part, however small, that enjoys repose—that Nature acts in all—that she would cease to be Nature if she did not act. Practical knowledge teaches us, that without unceasing motion, nothing could be preserved—nothing could be produced—nothing could act in this Nature. Thus the idea of Nature necessarily includes that of motion. But it will be asked, and not a little triumphantly, from whence did she derive her motion? Our reply is, we know not, neither do they—that *we* never shall, that *they* never will. It is a secret hidden from us, concealed from them, by the most impenetrable veil. We also reply, that it is fair to infer, unless they can logically prove to the contrary, that it is in herself, since she is the great whole, out of which nothing can exist. We say this motion is a manner of existence, that flows, necessarily, out of the nature of matter; that matter moves by its own peculiar energies; that its motion is to be attributed to the force which is inherent in itself; that the variety of motion, and the phenomena which result, proceed from the diversity of the properties—of the qualities—of the combinations, which are originally found in the primitive matter, of which Nature is the assemblage.

Natural philosophers, for the most part, have regarded as inanimate, or as deprived of the faculty of motion, those bodies which are only moved by the intervention of some agent or exterior cause; they have considered themselves justified in concluding, that the matter which forms these bodies is perfectly inert in its nature. They have not forsaken this error, although they must have observed, that whenever a body is left to itself, or disengaged from those obstructions which oppose themselves to its descent, it has a tendency to fall or to approach the centre of the earth, by a motion uniformly accelerated; they have rather chosen to suppose a visionary exterior cause, of which they themselves had but an imperfect idea, than admit that these bodies held their motion from their own peculiar nature.

These philosophers, also, notwithstanding they saw above them an infinite number of globes that moved with great rapidity round a common centre, still adhered to their favourite opinions; and never ceased to suppose some whimsical causes for these movements, until the immortal NEWTON clearly demonstrated that it was the effect of the gravitation of these celestial bodies towards each other. Experimental philosophers, however, and amongst them the great Newton himself, have held the cause of gravitation as inexplicable. Notwithstanding the great weight of this authority, it appears manifest that it may be deduced from the motion of matter, by which bodies are diversely determined. Gravitation is nothing more than a mode of moving—a tendency towards a centre: to speak strictly, all motion is relative gravitation; since that which falls relatively to us, rises, with relation to other bodies. From this it follows, that every motion in our microcosm is the effect of gravitation; seeing that there is not in the universe either top or bottom, nor any absolute centre. It should appear, that the weight of bodies depends on their configuration, as well external as internal, which gives them that form of action which is called gravitation. Thus, for instance, a piece of lead, spherically formed, falls quickly and direct: reduce this ball into very thin plates, it will be sustained in the air for a much longer time: apply to it the action of fire, this lead will rise in the atmosphere: here, then, the same metal, variously modified, has very different modes of action.

A very simple observation would have sufficed to make the philosophers, antecedent to Newton, feel the inadequateness of the causes they admitted to operate with such powerful effect. They had a sufficiency to convince themselves, in the collision of two bodies, which they could contemplate, and in the known laws of that motion, which these always communicate by reason of their greater or less compactness; from whence they ought to have inferred, that the density of *subtle* or *ethereal* matter, being considerably less than that of the planets, it could only communicate to them a very feeble motion, quite insufficient to produce that velocity of action, of which they could not possibly avoid being the witnesses.

If Nature had been viewed uninfluenced by prejudice, they must have been long since convinced that matter acts by its own peculiar activity; that it needs no exterior communicative force to set it in motion. They might have perceived that whenever mixed bodies were placed in a situation to act on each other, motion was instantly excited; and that these mixtures acted with a force capable of producing the most surprising results.

If particles of iron, sulphur, and water be mixed together, these bodies thus capacitated to act on each other, are heated by degrees, and ultimately produce a violent combustion. If flour be wetted with water, and the mixture closed up, it will be found, after some lapse of time, (by the aid of a microscope) to have produced organized beings that enjoy life, of which the water and the flour were believed incapable: it is thus that inanimate matter can pass into life, or animate matter, which is in itself only an assemblage of motion.

Reasoning from analogy, which the philosophers of the present day do not hold incompatible, the production of a man, independent of the ordinary means, would not be more astonishing than that of an insect with flour and water. Fermentation and putrid substances, evidently produce living animals. We have here the principle; with proper materials, principles can always be brought into action. That generation which is styled *uncertain* is only so for those who do not reflect, or who do not permit themselves, attentively, to observe the operations of Nature.

The generative of motion, and its developement, as well as the energy of matter, may be seen everywhere; more particularly in those unitions in which fire, air, and water, find themselves combined. These elements, or rather these mixed bodies, are the most volatile, the most fugitive of beings; nevertheless in the hands of Nature, they are the essential agents employed to produce the most striking phenomena. To these we must ascribe the effects of thunder, the eruption of volcanoes, earthquakes, &c. Science offers to our consideration an agent of astonishing force, in gunpowder, the instant it comes in contact with fire. In short, the most terrible effects result from the combination of matter, which is generally believed to be dead and inert.

These facts prove, beyond a doubt, that motion is produced, is augmented, is accelerated in matter, without the help of any exterior agent: therefore it is reasonable to conclude that motion is the necessary consequence of immutable laws, resulting from the essence, from the properties existing in the different elements, and the various combinations of these elements. Are we not justified, then, in concluding, from these precedents, that there may be an infinity of other combinations, with which we are unacquainted, competent to produce a great variety of motion in matter, without being under the necessity of having recourse, for the explanation, to agents who are more difficult to comprehend than even the effects which are attributed to them?

Had man but paid proper attention to what passed under his review, he would not have sought out of Nature, a power distinguished from herself, to set her in action, and without which he believes she cannot move. If, indeed, by Nature is meant a heap of dead matter, destitute of peculiar qualities purely passive, we must unquestionably seek out of this Nature the principle of her motion. But if by Nature be understood, what it really is, a whole, of which the numerous parts are endowed with various properties, which oblige them to act according to these properties; which are in a perpetual ternateness of action and reaction; which press, which gravitate towards a common center, whilst others depart from and fly off towards the periphery, or circumference; which attract and repel; which by continual approximation and constant collision, produce and decompose all the bodies we behold; then, I say, there is no necessity to have recourse to supernatural powers, to account for the formation of things, and those extraordinary appearances which are the result of motion.

Those who admit a cause exterior to matter, are obliged to believe that this cause produced all the motion by which matter is agitated in giving it existence. This belief rests on another, namely, that matter could begin to exist; an hypothesis that, until this moment, has never been satisfactorily demonstrated. To produce from nothing, or the CREATION, is a term that cannot give us the least idea of the formation of the universe; it presents no sense, upon which the mind can rely. In fact, the human mind is not adequate to conceive a moment of non-existence, or when all shall have passed away; even admitting this to be a truth, it is no truth for us, because by the very nature of our organization, we cannot admit positions as facts, of which no evidence can be adduced that has relation to our senses; we may, indeed, consent to believe it, because others say it; but will any rational being be satisfied with such an admission? Can any moral good spring from such blind assurance? Is it consistent with sound doctrine, with philosophy, or with reason? Do we, in fact, pay any respect to the intellectual powers of another, when we say to him, "I will believe this, because in all the attempts you have ventured, for the purpose of proving what you say, you have entirely failed; and have been at last obliged to acknowledge you know nothing about the matter?" What moral reliance ought we to have on such people? Hypothesis may succeed hypothesis; system may destroy system: a new set of ideas may overturn the ideas of a former day. Other Gallileos may be condemned to death—other Newtons may arise—we may reason— argue—dispute—quarrel—punish and destroy: nay, we may even exterminate those who differ from us in opinion; but when we have done all this, we shall be obliged to fall back upon our original darkness— to confess, that that which has no relation with our senses, that which cannot manifest itself to us by some of the ordinary modes by which other things are manifested, has no existence for us—is not comprehensible by us—can never entirely remove our doubt—can never seize on our stedfast belief; seeing it is that of which we cannot form even a notion; in short, that it is that, which as long as we remain what we are, must be hidden from us by a veil, which no power, no faculty, no energy we possess, is able to remove. All who are not enslaved by prejudice agree to the truth of the position, that *nothing can be made of nothing*. Many theologians have acknowledged Nature to be an active whole. Almost all the ancient philosophers were agreed to regard the world as eternal. OCELLUS LUCANUS, speaking of the universe, says, "*it has always been, and it always will be.*" VATABLE and GROTIUS assure us, that to render the Hebrew phrase in the first chapter of GENESIS correctly, we must say, "*when God made heaven and earth, matter was without form.*" If this be true, and every Hebraist can judge for himself, then the word which has been rendered *created*, means only to fashion, form, arrange. We know that the Greek words *create* and *form*, have always indicated the same thing. According to ST. JEROME, *creare* has the same meaning as *condere*, to found, to build. The Bible does not anywhere say in a clear manner, that the world was made of nothing. TERTULLIAN and the father PETAU both admit, that "*this is a truth established more by reason than by authority.*" ST. JUSTIN seems to have contemplated matter as eternal, since he commends PLATO for having said, that "*God, in the creation of the world, only gave impulse to matter, and fashioned it.*" BURNET and PYTHAGORAS were entirely of this opinion, and even our Church Service may be adduced in support; for although it admits by implication a beginning, it expressly denies an end: "*As it was in the beginning, is now, and ever shall be, world without end.*" It is easy to perceive that that which cannot cease to exist, must have always been.

    Motion becomes still more obscure, when creation, or the formation of matter, is attributed to a SPIRITUAL being; that is to say, to a being which has no analogy, no point of contact, with it—to a being which has neither extent or parts, and cannot, therefore, be susceptible of motion, as we understand the term; this being only the change of one body, relatively to another body, in which the body moved presents successively different parts to different points of space. Moreover, as all the world are nearly agreed that matter can never be totally annihilated, or cease to exist; by what reasoning, I would ask, do they comprehend—how understand—that that which cannot cease to be, could ever have had a beginning?

If, therefore, it be asked, whence came matter? it is very reasonable to say it has always existed. If it be inquired, whence proceeds the motion that agitates matter? the same reasoning furnishes the answer; namely, that as motion is coeval with matter, it must have existed from all eternity, seeing that motion is the necessary consequence of its existence—of its essence—of its primitive properties, such as its extent, its gravity, its impenetrability, its figure, &c. By virtue of these essential constituent properties, inherent in all matter, and without which it is impossible to form an idea of it, the various matter of which the universe is composed must from all eternity have pressed against, each other—have gravitated towards a center—have clashed— have come in contact—have been attracted—have been repelled—have been combined—have been separated: in short, must have acted and moved according to the essence and energy peculiar to each genus, and to each of its combinations.

Existence supposes properties in the thing that exists: whenever it has properties, its mode of action must necessarily flow from those properties which constitute, its mode of being. Thus, when a body is ponderous, it must fall; when it falls, it must come in collision with the bodies it meets in its descent; when it is dense, when it is solid, it must, by reason of this density, communicate motion to the bodies with which it clashes; when it has analogy, when it has affinity with these bodies, it must be attracted, must be united with them; when it has no point of analogy with them, it must be repulsed.

From which it may be fairly inferred, that in supposing, as we are under the necessity of doing, the existence of matter, we must suppose it to have some kind of properties; from which its motion, or modes of action, must necessarily flow. To form the universe, DESCARTES asked but matter and motion: a diversity of matter sufficed for him; variety of motion was the consequence of its existence, of its essence, of its properties: its different modes of action would be the necessary consequence of its different modes of being. Matter without properties would be a mere nothing; therefore, as soon as matter exists, it must act; as soon as it is various, it must act variously; if it cannot commence to exist, it must have existed from all eternity; if it has always existed, it can never cease to be: if it can never cease to be, it can never cease to act by its own energy. Motion is a manner of being, which matter derives from its peculiar existence.

The existence, then, of matter is a fact: the existence of motion is another fact. Our visual organs point out to us matter with different essences, forming a variety of combinations, endowed with various properties that discriminate them. Indeed, it is a palpable error to believe that matter is a homogeneous body, of which the parts differ from each other only by their various modifications. Among the individuals of the same species that come under our notice, no two resemble exactly; and it is therefore evident that the difference of situation alone will, necessarily, carry a diversity more or less sensible, not only in the modifications, but also in the essence, in the properties, in the entire system of beings. This truth was well understood by the profound and subtle LEIBNITZ.

If this principle be properly digested, and experience seems always to produce evidence of its truth, we must be convinced that the matter or primitive elements which enter into the composition of bodies, are not of the same nature, and consequently, can neither have the same properties, nor the same modifications; and if so, they cannot have the same mode of moving and acting. Their activity or motion, already different, can be diversified to infinity, augmented or diminished, accelerated or retarded, according to the combinations, the proportions, the pressure, the density, the volume of the matter, that enters their composition. The endless variety to be produced, will need no further illustration than the commonest book of arithmetic furnishes us, where it will be found, that to ring all the changes that can be produced on twelve bells only, would occupy a space of more than ninety-one years. The element of fire is visibly more active and more inconstant than that of earth. This is more solid and ponderous than fire, air, or water. According to the quantity of these elements, which enter the composition of bodies, these must act diversely, and their motion must in some measure partake the motion peculiar to each of their constituent parts. Elementary fire appears to be in Nature the principle of activity; it may be compared to a fruitful leaven, that puts the mass into fermentation and gives it life. Earth appears to be the principle of solidity in bodies, from its impenetrability, and by the firm coherence of its parts. Water is a medium, to facilitate the combination of bodies, into which it enters itself, as a constituent part. Air is a fluid whose business it seems to be, to furnish the other elements with the space requisite to expand, to exercise their motion, and which is, moreover, found proper to combine with them. These elements, which our senses never discover in a pure state—which are continually and reciprocally set in motion by each other—which are always acting and re-acting, combining and separating, attracting and repelling—are sufficient to explain to us the formation of all the beings we behold. Their motion is uninterruptedly and reciprocally produced from each other; they are alternately causes and effects. Thus, they form a vast circle of generation and destruction—of combination and decomposition, which, it is quite reasonable to suppose, could never have had a beginning, and which, consequently can never have an end. In short, Nature is but an immense chain of causes and effects, which unceasingly flow from each other. The motion of particular beings depends on the general motion, which is itself maintained by individual motion. This is strengthened or weakened, accelerated or retarded, simplified or complicated, procreated or destroyed, by a variety of combinations and circumstances, which every moment change the directions, the tendency, the modes of existing, and of acting, of the different beings that receive its impulse.

If it were true, as has been asserted by some philosophers, that every thing has a tendency to form one unique or single mass, and in that unique mass the instant should arrive when all was in *nisus*, all would eternally remain in this state; to all eternity there would be no more than one Being and one effort: this would be eternal and universal death.

If we desire to go beyond this, to find the principle of action in matter, to trace the origin of things, it is for ever to fall back upon difficulties; it is absolutely to abridge the evidence of our senses; by which only we can understand, by which alone we can judge of the causes acting upon them, or the impulse by which they are set in action.

Let us, therefore, content ourselves with saying WHAT is supported by our experience, and by all the evidence we are capable of understanding; against the truth of which not a shadow of proof, such as our reason can admit, has ever been adduced—which has been maintained by philosophers in every age—which theologians themselves have not denied, but which many of them have upheld; namely, that *matter always existed; that it moves by virtue of its essence; that all the phenomena of Nature is ascribable to the diversified motion of the variety of matter she contains; and which, like the phoenix, is continually regenerating out of its own ashes.*

CHAP. III.

Of Matter.—Of its various Combinations.—Of its diversified Motion, or of the Course of Nature.

We know nothing of the elements of bodies, but we know some of their properties or qualities; and we distinguish their various matter by the effect or change produced on our senses; that is to say, by the variety of motion their presence excites in us. In consequence, we discover in them, extent, mobility, divisibility, solidity, gravity, and inert force. From these general and primitive properties flow a number of others, such as density, figure, colour, ponderosity, &c. Thus, relatively to us, matter is all that affects our senses in any manner whatever; the various properties we attribute to matter, by which we discriminate its diversity, are founded on the different impressions we receive on the changes they produce in us.

A satisfactory definition of matter has not yet been given. Man, deceived and led astray by his prejudices, formed but vague, superficial, and imperfect notions concerning it. He looked upon it as an unique being, gross and passive, incapable of either moving by itself, of forming combinations, or of producing any thing by its own energies. Instead of this unintelligible jargon, he ought to have contemplated it as a *genus* of beings, of which the individuals, although they might possess some common properties, such as extent, divisibility, figure, &c. should not, however, be all ranked in the same class, nor comprised under the same general denomination.

An example will serve more fully to explain what we have asserted, throw its correctness into light, and facilitate the application. The properties common to all matter, are extent, divisibility, impenetrability, figure, mobility, or the property of being moved in mass. FIRE, beside these general properties, common to all matter, enjoys also the peculiar property of being put into activity by a motion that produces on our organs of feeling the sensation of heat; and by another, that communicates to our visual organs the sensation of light. Iron, in common with matter in general, has extent and figure; is divisible, and moveable in mass: if fire be combined with it in a certain proportion, the iron acquires two new properties; namely, those of exciting in us similar sensations of heat and light, which were excited by the element of fire, but which the iron had not, before its combination with the igneous matter. These distinguishing properties are inseparable from matter, and the phenomena that result, may, in the strictest sense of the word, be said to result necessarily.

If we contemplate a little the paths of Nature—if, for a time, we trace the beings in this Nature, under the different states through which, by reason of their properties, they are compelled to pass; we shall discover, that it is to motion, and motion only, that is to be ascribed all the changes, all the combinations, all the forms, in short, all the various modifications of matter. That it is by motion every thing that exists is produced, experiences change, expands, and is destroyed. It is motion that alters the aspect of beings; that adds to, or takes away from their properties; which obliges each of them, by a consequence of its nature, after having occupied a certain rank or order, to quit it, to occupy another, and to contribute to the generation, maintenance, and decomposition of other beings, totally different in their bulk, rank, and essence.

In what experimental philosophers have styled the THREE ORDERS OF NATURE, that is to say, the *mineral*, the *vegetable*, and *animal* worlds, they have established, by the aid of motion, a transmigration, an exchange, a continual circulation in the particles of matter. Nature has occasion in one place, for those particles which, for a time, she has placed in another. These particles, after having, by particular combinations, constituted beings endued with peculiar essences, with specific properties, with determinate modes of action, dissolve and separate with more or less facility; and combining in a new manner, they form new beings. The attentive observer sees this law execute itself, in a manner more or less prominent, through all the beings by which he is surrounded. He sees nature full of *erratic germe*, some of which expand themselves, whilst others wait until motion has placed them in their proper situation, in suitable wombs or matrices, in the necessary circumstances, to unfold, to increase, to render them more perceptible by the addition of other substances of matter analogous to their primitive being. In all this we see nothing but the effect of motion, necessarily guided, modified, accelerated or slackened, strengthened or weakened, by reason of the various properties that beings successively acquire and lose; which, every moment, infallibly produces alterations in bodies more or less marked. Indeed, these bodies cannot be, strictly speaking, the same in any two successive moments of their existence; they must, every instant, either acquire or lose: in short, they are obliged to undergo continual variations in their essences, in their properties, in their energies, in their masses, in their qualities, in their mode of existence.

Animals, after they have been expanded in, and brought out of, the wombs that are suitable to the elements of their machine, enlarge, strengthen, acquire new properties, new energies, new faculties; either by deriving nourishment from plants analogous to their being, or by devouring other animals whose substance is suitable to their preservation; that is to say, to repair the continual deperdition or loss of some portion of their own substance, that is disengaging itself every instant. These same animals are nourished, preserved, strengthened, and enlarged, by the aid of air, water, earth, and fire. Deprived of air, or of the fluid that surrounds them, that presses on them, that penetrates them, that gives them their elasticity, they presently cease to live. Water, combined with this air, enters into their whole mechanism of which it facilitates the motion. Earth serves them for a basis, by giving solidity to their texture: it is conveyed by air and water, which carry it to those parts of the body with which it can combine. Fire itself, disguised and enveloped under an infinity of forms, continually received into the animal, procures him heat, continues him in life, renders him capable of exercising his functions. The aliments, charged with these various principles, entering into the stomach, re-establish the nervous system, and restore, by their activity, and the elements which compose them, the machine which begins to languish, to be depressed, by the loss it has sustained. Forthwith the animal experiences a change in his whole system; he has more energy, more activity; he feels more courage; displays more gaiety; he acts, he moves, he thinks, after a different manner; all his faculties are exercised with more ease. This igneous matter, so congenial to generation—so restorative in its effect—so necessary to life, was the JUPITER of the ancients: from all that has preceded, it is clear, that what are called the elements, or primitive parts of matter, variously combined, are, by the agency of motion, continually united to, and assimilated with, the substance of animals— that they visibly modify their being—have an evident influence over their actions, that is to say, upon the motion they undergo, whether visible or concealed.

The same elements, which under certain circumstances serve to nourish, to strengthen, to maintain the animal, become, under others, the principles of his weakness, the instruments of his dissolution—of his death: they work his destruction, whenever they are not in that just proportion which renders them proper to maintain his existence: thus, when water becomes too abundant in the body of the animal, it enervates him, it relaxes the fibres, and impedes the necessary action of the other elements: thus, fire admitted in excess, excites in him disorderly motion destructive of his machine: thus, air, charged with principles not analogous to his mechanism, brings upon him dangerous diseases and contagion. In fine, the aliments modified after certain modes, in the room of nourishing, destroy the animal, and conduce to his ruin: the animal is preserved no longer than these substances are analogous to his system. They ruin him when they want that just equilibrium that renders them suitable to maintain his existence.

Plants that serve to nourish and restore animals are themselves nourished by earth; they expand on its bosom, enlarge and strengthen at its expense, continually receiving into their texture, by their roots and their pores, water, air, and igneous matter: water visibly reanimates them whenever their vegetation or genus of life languishes; it conveys to them those analogous principles by which they are enabled to reach perfection: air is requisite to their expansion, and furnishes them with water, earth, and the igneous matter with which it is charged. By these means they receive more or less of the inflammable matter; the different proportions of these principles, their numerous combinations, from whence result an infinity of properties, a variety of forms, constitute the various families and classes into which botanists have distributed plants: it is thus we see the cedar and the hyssop develop their growth; the one rises to the clouds, the other creep humbly on the earth. Thus, by degrees, from an acorn springs the majestic oak, accumulating, with time, its numerous branches, and overshadowing us with its foliage. Thus, a grain of corn, after having drawn its own nourishment from the juices of the earth, serves, in its turn, for the nourishment of man, into whose system it conveys the elements or principles by which it has been itself expanded, combined, and modified in such a manner, as to render this vegetable proper to assimilate and unite with the human frame; that is to say, with the fluids and solids of which it is composed.

The same elements, the same principles, are found in the formation of minerals, as well as in their decomposition, whether natural or artificial. We find that earth, diversely modified, wrought, and combined, serves to increase their bulk, and give them more or less density and gravity. Air and water contribute to make their particles cohere; the igneous matter, or inflammable principle, tinges them with colour, and sometimes plainly indicates its presence, by the brilliant scintillation which motion elicits from them. These stones and metals, these bodies, so compact and solid, are disunited, are destroyed, by the agency of air, water, and fire; which the most ordinary analysis is sufficient to prove, as well as a multitude of experience, to which our eyes are the daily evidence.

Animals, plants, and minerals, after a lapse of time, give back to Nature; that is to say, to the general mass of things, to the universal magazine, the elements, or principles, which they have borrowed: The earth retakes that portion of the body of which it formed the basis and the solidity; the air charges itself with these parts, that are, analogous to it, and with those particles which are light and subtle; water carries off that which is suitable to liquescency; fire, bursting its chains, disengages itself, and rushes into new combinations with other bodies.

The elementary particles of the animal, being thus dissolved, disunited, and dispersed; assume new activity, and form new combinations: thus, they serve to nourish, to preserve, or destroy new beings; among others, plants, which arrived at their maturity, nourish and preserve new animals; these in their turn yielding to the same fate as the first.

Such is the constant, the invariable course, of Nature; such is the eternal circle of mutation, which all that exists is obliged to describe. It is thus motion generates, preserves for a time, and successively, destroys, one part of the universe by the other; whilst the sum of existence remains eternally the same. Nature, by its combinations, produces suns, which place themselves in the centre of so many systems: she forms planets, which, by their peculiar essence, gravitate and describe their revolutions round these suns: by degrees the motion is changed altogether, and becomes eccentric: perhaps the day may arrive when these wondrous masses will disperse, of which man, in the short space of his existence, can only have a faint and transient glimpse.

It is clear, then, that the continual motion inherent in matter, changes and destroys all beings; every instant depriving them of some of their properties, to substitute others: it is motion, which, in thus changing their actual essence, changes also their order, their direction, their tendency, and the laws which regulate their mode of acting and being: from the stone formed in the bowels of the earth, by the intimate combination and close coherence of similar and analogous particles, to the sun, that vast reservoir of igneous particles, which sheds torrents of light over the firmament; from the benumbed oyster, to the thoughtful and active man; we see an uninterrupted progression, a perpetual chain of motion and combination; from which is produced, beings that only differ from each other by the variety of their elementary matter—by the numerous combinations of these elements, from whence springs modes of action and existence, diversified to infinity. In generation, in nutrition, in preservation, we see nothing more than matter, variously combined, of which each has its peculiar motion, regulated by fixed and determinate laws, which oblige them to submit to necessary changes. We shall find, in the formation, in the growth, in the instantaneous life, of animals, vegetables, and minerals, nothing but matter; which combining, accumulating, aggregating, and expanding by degrees, forms beings, who are either feeling, living, vegetating, or else destitute of these faculties; which, having existed some time under one particular form, are obliged to contribute by their ruin to the production of other forms.

Thus, to speak strictly, nothing in Nature is either born, or dies, according to the common acceptation of those terms. This truth was felt by many of the ancient philosophers. PLATO says, that according to tradition, "the living were born of the dead, the same as the dead did come of the living; and that this is the constant routine of Nature." He adds from himself, "who knows, if to live, be not to die; and if to die, be not to live?" This was the doctrine of PYTHAGORAS, a man of great talent and no less note. EMPEDOCLES asserts, "there is neither birth nor death, for any mortal; but only a combination, and a separation of that which was combined, and that this is what amongst men they call birth, and death." Again he remarks, "those are infants, or short-sighted persons, with very contracted understandings, who imagine any thing is born, which did not exist before, or that any thing can die or perish totally."

CHAP. IV.

Laws of Motion, common to every Being of Nature.—Attraction and Repulsion.—Inert Force.—Necessity.

Man is never surprised at those effects, of which he thinks he knows the cause; he believes he does know the cause, as soon as he sees them act in an uniform and determinate manner, or when the motion excited is simple: the descent of a stone, that falls by its own peculiar weight, is an object of contemplation to the philosopher only; to whom the mode by which the most immediate causes act, and the most simple motion, are no less impenetrable mysteries than the most complex motion, and the manner by which the most complicated causes give impulse. The uninformed are seldom tempted either to examine the effects which are familiar to them, or to recur to first principles. They think they see nothing in the descent of a stone, which ought to elicit their surprise, or become the object of their research: it requires a NEWTON to feel that the descent of heavy bodies is a phenomenon, worthy his whole, his most serious attention; it requires the sagacity of a profound experimental philosopher, to discover the laws by which heavy bodies fall, by which they communicate to others their peculiar motion. In short, the mind that is most practised in philosophical observation, has frequently the chagrin to find, that the most simple and most common effects escape all his researches, and remain inexplicable to him.

When any extraordinary, any unusual, effect is produced, to which our eyes have not been accustomed; or when we are ignorant of the energies of the cause, the action of which so forcibly strikes our senses, we are tempted to meditate upon it, and take it into our consideration. The European, accustomed to the use of GUNPOWDER, passes it by, without thinking much of its extraordinary energies; the workman, who labours to manufacture it, finds nothing marvellous in its properties, because he daily handles the matter that forms its composition. The American, to whom this powder was a stranger, who had never beheld its operation, looked upon it as a divine power, and its energies as supernatural. The uninformed, who are ignorant of the true cause of THUNDER, contemplate it as the instrument of divine vengeance. The experimental philosopher considers it as the effect of the electric matter, which, nevertheless, is itself a cause which he is very far from perfectly understanding.—It required the keen, the penetrating mind of a FRANKLIN, to throw light on the nature of this subtle fluid—to develop the means by which its effects might be rendered harmless—to turn to useful purposes, a phenomenon that made the ignorant tremble—that filled their minds with terror, their hearts with dismay, as indicating the anger of the gods: impressed with this idea, they prostrated themselves, they sacrificed to JUPITER, to deprecate his wrath.

Be this as it may, whenever we see a cause act, we look upon its effect as natural: when this cause becomes familiar to the sight, when we are accustomed to it, we think we understand it, and its effects surprise us no longer. Whenever any unusual effect is perceived, without our discovering the cause, the mind sets to work, becomes uneasy; this uneasiness increases in proportion to its extent: as soon as it is believed to threaten our preservation, we become completely agitated; we seek after the cause with an earnestness proportioned to our alarm; our perplexity augments in a ratio equivalent to the persuasion we are under: how essentially requisite it is, we should become acquainted with the cause that has affected us in so lively a manner. As it frequently happens that our senses can teach us nothing respecting this cause which so deeply interests us—which we seek with so much ardour, we have recourse to our imagination; this, disturbed with alarm, enervated by fear, becomes a suspicious, a fallacious guide: we create chimeras, fictitious causes, to whom we give the credit, to whom we ascribe the honour of those phenomena by which we have been so much alarmed. It is to this disposition of the human mind that must be attributed, as will be seen in the sequel, the religious errors of man, who, despairing of the capacity to trace the natural causes of those perplexing phenomena to which he was the witness, and sometimes the victim, created in his brain (heated with terror) imaginary causes, which have become to him a source of the most extravagant folly.

In Nature, however, there can be only natural causes and effects; all motion excited in this Nature, follows constant and necessary laws: the natural operations, to the knowledge of which we are competent, of which we are in a capacity to judge, are of themselves sufficient to enable us to discover those which elude our sight; we can at least judge of them by analogy. If we study Nature with attention, the modes of action which she displays to our senses will teach us not to be disconcerted by those which she refuses to discover. Those causes which are the most remote from their effects, unquestionably act by intermediate causes; by the aid of these, we can frequently trace out the first. If in the chain of these causes we sometimes meet with obstacles that oppose themselves to our research, we ought to endeavour by patience and diligence to overcome them; when it so happens we cannot surmount the difficulties that occur, we still are never justified in concluding the chain to be broken, or that the cause which acts is SUPER-NATURAL. Let us, then, be content with an honest avowal, that Nature contains resources of which we are ignorant; but never let us substitute phantoms, fictions, or imaginary causes, senseless terms, for those causes which escape our research; because, by such means we only confirm ourselves in ignorance, impede our enquiries, and obstinately remain in error.

In spite of our ignorance with respect to the meanderings of Nature, (for of the essence of being, of their properties, their elements, their combinations, their proportions, we yet know the simple and general laws, according to which bodies move;) we see clearly, that some of these laws, common to all beings, never contradict themselves; although, on some occasions, they appear to vary, we are frequently competent to discover that the cause becoming complex, from combination with other causes, either impedes or prevents its mode of action being such as in its primitive state we had a right to expect. We know that active, igneous matter, applied to gunpowder, must necessarily cause it to explode: whenever this effect does not follow the combination of the igneous matter with the gunpowder—whenever our senses do not give us evidence of the fact, we are justified in concluding, either that the powder is damp, or that it is united with some other substance that counteracts its explosion. We know that all the actions of man have a tendency to render him happy: whenever, therefore, we see him labouring to injure or destroy himself, it is just to infer that he is moved by some cause opposed to his natural tendency; that he is deceived by some prejudice; that, for want of experience, he is blind to consequences: that he does not see whither his actions will lead him.

If the motion excited in beings was always simple; if their actions did not blend and combine with each other, it would be easy to know, and we should be assured, in the first instance, of the effect a cause would produce. I know that a stone, when descending, ought to describe a perpendicular: I also know, that if it encounters any other body which changes its course, it is obliged to take an oblique direction, but if its fall be interrupted by several contrary powers, which act upon it alternately, I am no longer competent to determine what line it will describe. It may be a parabola, an ellipsis, spiral, circular, &c. this will depend on the impulse, it receives, and the powers by which it is impelled.

The most complex motion, however, is never more than the result of simple motion combined: therefore as soon as we know the general laws of beings and their action, we have only to decompose, to analyse them, in order to discover those of which they are combined; experience teaches us the effects we are to expect. Thus it is clear, the simplest motion causes that necessary junction of different matter, of which all bodies are composed: that matter, varied in its essence, in its properties, in its combinations, has each its several modes of action or motion, peculiar to itself; the whole motion of a body is consequently the sum total of each particular motion that is combined.

Amongst the matter we behold, some is constantly disposed to unite, whilst other is incapable of union; that which is suitable to unite, forms combinations, more or less intimate, possessing more or less durability: that is to say, with more or less capacity to preserve their union, to resist dissolution. Those bodies which are called SOLIDS, receive into their composition a great number of homogeneous, similar, and analogous particles, disposed to unite themselves with energies conspiring or tending to the same point. The primitive beings, or elements of bodies, have need of supports, of props; that is to say, of the presence of each other, for the purpose of preserving themselves; of acquiring consistence or solidity: a truth, which applies with equal uniformity to what is called *physical*, as to what is termed *moral*.

It is upon this disposition in matter and bodies, with relation to each other, that is founded those modes of action which natural philosophers designate by the terms *attraction, repulsion, sympathy, antipathy, affinities, relations*; that moralists describe under the names of *love, hatred, friendship, aversion*. Man, like all the beings in nature, experiences the impulse of attraction and repulsion; the motion excited in him differing from that of other beings, only, because it is more concealed, and frequently so hidden, that neither the causes which excite it, nor their mode of action are known. This system of attraction and repulsion is very ancient, although it required a NEWTON to develop it. That love, to which the ancients attributed the unfolding, or disentanglement of chaos, appears to have been nothing more than a personification of the principle of attraction. All their allegories and fables upon chaos, evidently indicate nothing more than the accord or union that exists between analogous and homogeneous substances; from whence resulted the existence of the universe: whilst discord or repulsion, which they called SOIS, was the cause of dissolution, confusion, and disorder; there can scarcely remain a doubt, but this was the origin of the doctrines of the TWO PRINCIPLES. According to DIOGENES LAERTIUS, the philosopher, EMPEDOCLES, asserted, that "*there is a kind of affection by which the elements unite themselves; and a sort of discord, by which they separate or remove themselves.*"

However it may be, it is sufficient for us to know that by an invariable law, certain bodies are disposed to unite with more or less facility; whilst others cannot combine or unite themselves: water combines itself readily with salt, but will not blend with oil. Some combinations are very strong, cohering with great force, as metals; others are extremely feeble, their cohesion slight and easily decomposed, as in fugitive colours. Some bodies, incapable of uniting by themselves, become susceptible of union by the agency of other bodies, which serve for common bonds or MEDIUMS. Thus, oil and water, naturally heterogeneous, combine and make soap, by the intervention of alkaline salt. From matter diversely combined, in proportions varied almost to infinity, result all physical and moral bodies; the properties and qualities of which are essentially different, with modes of action more or less complex: which are either understood with facility, or difficult of comprehension, according to the elements or matter that has entered into their composition, and the various modifications this matter has undergone.

It is thus, from the reciprocity of their attraction, the primitive imperceptible particles of matter, which constitute bodies, become perceptible, form compound substances, aggregate masses; by the union of similar and analogous matter, whose essences fit them to cohere. The same bodies are dissolved, their union broken, whenever they undergo the action of matter inimical to their junction. Thus by degrees are formed, plants, metals, animals, men; each grows, expands, and increases in its own system or order; sustaining itself in its respective existence, by the continual attraction of analogous matter; to which it becomes united, and by which it is preserved and strengthened. Thus, certain aliments become fit for the sustenance of man, whilst others destroy his existence: some are pleasant to him, strengthen his habit; others are repugnant to him, weaken his system: in short, never to separate physical from moral laws, it is thus that men, mutually attracted to each other by their reciprocal wants, form those unions which we designate by the terms, MARRIAGE, FAMILIES, SOCIETIES, FRIENDSHIPS, CONNEXIONS: it is thus that virtue strengthens and consolidates them; that vice relaxes or totally dissolves them.

Of whatever nature may be the combination of beings, their motion has always one direction or tendency: without direction we could not have any idea of motion: this direction is regulated by the properties of each being; as soon as they have any given properties, they necessarily act in obedience to them: that is to say, they follow the law invariably determined by these same properties; which, of themselves, constitute the being such as he is found, and settle his mode of action, which is always the consequence of his manner of existence. But what is the general direction, or common tendency, we see in all beings? What is the visible and known end of all their motion? It is to conserve their actual existence—to preserve themselves—to strengthen their several bodies—to attract that which is favorable to them—to repel that which is injurious them—to avoid that which can harm them—to resist impulsions contrary to their manner of existence, and to their natural tendency.

To exist, is to experience the motion peculiar to a determinate essence: to conserve this existence, is to give and receive that motion from which results its maintenance:—it is to attract matter suitable to corroborate its being—to avoid that by which it may be either endangered or enfeebled. Thus, all beings of which we have any knowledge, have a tendency to conserve themselves, each after its peculiar manner: the stone, by the firm adhesion of its particles, opposes resistance to its destruction. Organized beings conserve themselves by more complicated means, but which are, nevertheless, calculated to maintain their existence against that by which it may be injured. Man, both in his physical and in his moral capacity, is a living, feeling, thinking, active being; who, every instant of his duration, strives equally to avoid that which may be injurious, and to procure that which is pleasing to him, or that which is suitable to his mode of existence; all his actions tending solely to conserve himself. ST. AUGUSTINE admits this tendency in all whether organized or not.

Conservation, then, is the common point to which all the energies, all the powers, all the faculties of beings, seem continually directed. Natural philosophers call this direction or tendency, SELF-GRAVITATION: NEWTON calls it INERT FORCE: moralists denominate it in man, SELF-LOVE which is nothing more than the tendency he has to preserve himself—a desire of happiness—a love of his own welfare—a wish for pleasure—a promptitude in seizing on every thing that appears favourable to his conservation—a marked aversion to all that either disturbs his happiness, or menaces his existence—primitive sentiments, that are common to all beings of the human species; which all their faculties are continually striving to satisfy;

which all their passions, their wills, their actions, have eternally for their object and their end. This self- gravitation, then, is clearly a necessary disposition in man, and in all other beings; which, by a variety means, contribute to the preservation of the existence they have received, as long as nothing deranges the order of their machine, or its primitive tendency.

Cause always produces effect; there can be no effect without cause. Impulse is always followed by some motion, more or less sensible; by some change, more or less remarkable in the body which receives it. But motion, and its various modes of displaying itself, is, as has been already shewn, determined by the nature, the essence, the properties, the combinations of the beings acting. It must, then, be concluded that motion, or the modes by which beings act, arises from some cause; that as this cause is not able to move or act, but in conformity with the manner of its being or its essential properties, it must equally be concluded, that all the phenomena we perceive are necessary; that every being in Nature, under the circumstances in which it is placed, and with the given properties it possesses, cannot act otherwise than it does.

Necessity is the constant and infallible relation of causes with their effects. Fire consumes, of necessity, combustible matter plated within its circuit of action: man, by fatality, desires either that which really is, or appears to be serviceable to his welfare. Nature, in all the extraordinary appearances she exhibits, necessarily acts after her own peculiar essence: all the beings she contains, necessarily act each after its own a individual nature: it is by motion that the whole has relation with its parts; and these parts with the whole: it is thus that in the general system every thing is connected: it is itself but an immense chain of causes and effects, which flow without ceasing, one from the other. If we reflect, we shall be obliged to acknowledge that every thing we see is necessary; that it cannot be otherwise than it is; that all the beings we behold, as well as those which escape our sight, act by invariable laws. According to these laws, heavy bodies fall— light bodies ascend—analogous substances attract each other—beings tend to preserve themselves—man cherishes himself; loves that which he thinks advantageous—detests that which he has an idea may prove unfavourable to him.—In fine, we are obliged to admit, there can be no perfectly independent energy—no separated cause—no detached action, in a nature where all the beings are in a reciprocity of action—who, without interruption, mutually impel and resist each other—who is herself nothing more than an eternal circle of motion, given and received according to necessary laws; which under the same given incidents, invariably produce the same effect.

Two examples will serve to throw the principle here laid down, into light—one shall be taken from physics, the other from morals.

In a whirlwind of dust, raised by elemental force, confused as it appears to our eyes, in the most frightful tempest excited by contrary winds, when the waves roll high as mountains, there is not a single particle of dust, or drop of water, that has been placed by CHANCE, that has not a cause for occupying the place where it is found; that does not, in the most rigorous sense of the word, act after the manner in which it ought to act; that is, according to its own peculiar essence, and that of the beings from whom it receives this communicated force. A geometrician exactly knew the different energies acting in each case, with the properties of the particles moved, could demonstrate that after the causes given, each particle acted precisely as it ought to act, and that it could not have acted otherwise than it did.

In those terrible convulsions that sometimes agitate political societies, shake their foundations, and frequently produce the overthrow of an empire; there is not a single action, a single word, a single thought, a single will, a single passion in the agents, whether they act as destroyers, or as victims, that is not the necessary result of the causes operating; that does not act, as, of necessity, it must act, from the peculiar essence of the beings who give the impulse, and that of the agents who receive it, according to the situation these agents fill in the moral whirlwind. This could be evidently proved by an understanding capacitated to rate all the action and re-action, of the minds and bodies of those who contributed to the revolution.

In fact, if all be connected in Nature, if all motion be produced, the one from the other, notwithstanding their secret communications frequently elude our sight; we ought to feel convinced of this truth, that there is no cause, however minute, however remote, that does not sometimes produce the greatest and most immediate effects on man. It may, perhaps, be in the parched plains of Lybia, that are amassed the first elements of a storm or tempest, which, borne by the winds, approach our climate, render our atmosphere dense, and thus operating on the temperament, may influence the passions of a man, whose circumstances shall have capacitated him to influence many others, who shall decide after his will the fate of many nations.

Man, in fact, finds himself in Nature, and makes a part of it: he acts according to laws, which are appropriate to him; he receives in a manner more or less distinct, the action and impulse of the beings who surround him; who themselves act after laws that are peculiar to their essence. Thus he is variously modified; but his actions are always the result of his own energy, and that of the beings who act upon him, and by whom he is modified. This is what gives such variety to his determinations—what generally produces such contradiction in his thoughts, his opinions, his will, his actions; in short, in that motion, whether concealed or visible, by which he is agitated. We shall have occasion, in the sequel, to place this truth, at present so much contested, in a clearer light: it will be sufficient for our purpose at present to prove, generally, that every thing in Nature is necessary—that nothing to be found in it can act otherwise than it does.

Motion, alternately communicated and received, establishes the connection or relation between the different orders of beings: when they are in the sphere of reciprocal action, attraction approximates them; repulsion dissolves and separates them; the one strengthens and preserves them; the other enfeebles and destroys them. Once combined, they have a tendency to conserve themselves in that mode of existence, by virtue of their *inert force*; in this they cannot succeed, because they are exposed to the continual influence of all other beings, who perpetually and successively act upon them; their change of form, their dissolution, is requisite to the preservation of Nature herself: this is the sole end we are able to assign her—to which we see her tend without intermission—which she follows without interruption, by the destruction and reproduction of all subordinate beings, who are obliged to submit to her laws—to concur, by their mode of action, to the maintenance of her active existence, so essentially requisite to the GREAT WHOLE.

It is thus each being is an individual, who, in the great family, performs his necessary portion of the general labour—who executes the unavoidable task assigned to him. All bodies act according to laws, inherent in their peculiar essence, without the capability to swerve, even for a single instant, from those according to which Nature herself acts. This is the central power, to which all other powers, essences, and energies, are submitted: she regulates the motions of beings, by the necessity of her own peculiar essence: she makes them concur by various modes to the general plan: this appears to be nothing more than the life, action, and maintenance of the whole, by the continual change of its parts. This object she obtains, in removing them, one by the other; by that which establishes, and by that which destroys, the relation subsisting between them; by that which gives them, and that which deprives them of, their forms, combinations, proportions, and qualities, according to which they act for a time, after a given mode; these are afterwards taken from them, to make them act after a different manner. It is thus that Nature makes them expand and change, grow and decline, augment and diminish, approximate and remove, forms and destroys them, according as she finds it requisite to maintain the whole; towards the conservation which this Nature is herself essentially necessitated to have a tendency.

This irresistible power, this universal necessity, this general energy, then, is only a consequence of the nature of things; by virtue of which every thing acts, without intermission, after constant and immutable laws: these laws not varying more for the whole than for the beings of which it is composed. Nature is an active living whole, to which all its parts necessarily concur; of which, without their own knowledge, they maintain the activity, the life, and the existence. Nature acts and exists necessarily: all that she contains, necessarily conspires to perpetuate her active existence. This is the decided opinion of PLATO, when he says, "*matter and necessity are the same thing; this necessity is the mother of the world.*" In point of fact, we cannot go beyond this aphorism, MATTER ACTS, BECAUSE IT EXISTS; AND EXISTS, TO ACT. If it be enquired how, or for why, matter exists? We answer, we know not: but reasoning by analogy, of what we do not know by that which we do, we should be of opinion it exists necessarily, or because it contains within itself a sufficient reason for its existence. In supposing it to be created or produced by a being distinguished from it, or less known than itself, (which it may be, for any thing we know to the contrary,) we must still admit, that this being is necessary, and includes a sufficient reason for his own existence. We have not then removed any of the difficulty, we have not thrown a clearer light upon the subject, we have not advanced a single step; we have simply laid aside a being, of which we know some few of the properties, but of which we are still extremely ignorant, to have recourse to a power, of which it is utterly impossible we can, as long as we are men, form any distinct idea; of which, notwithstanding it may be a truth, we cannot, by any means we possess, demonstrate the existence. As, therefore, these must be at best but speculative points of belief, which each individual, by reason of its obscurity, may contemplate with different optics, under various aspects, they surely ought to be left free for each to judge after his own fashion: the Hindoo can have no just cause of enmity against the Christian for his faith: this has no moral right to question the Mussulman upon his; the numerous sects of each of the various persuasions spread over the face of the earth, ought to make it a creed to look with an eye of complacency on the deviation of the others; and rest upon that great moral axiom, which is strictly conformable to Nature, which contains the whole of man's happiness—"*Do not unto another, that which do you not wish another should do unto you*," for it is evident, according to their own doctrines, out of all the variety of systems, one only can be right.

We shall see in the sequel, how much man's imagination labours to form an idea, of the energies of that Nature he has personified, and distinguished from herself: in short, we shall examine some of the ridiculous and pernicious inventions, which, for want of understanding Nature, have been imagined to impede her course, to suspend her eternal laws, to place obstacles to the necessity of things.

CHAP. V.
Order and Confusion.—Intelligence.—Chance.

The observation of the necessary, regular, and periodical motion in the universe, generated in the mind of man the idea of ORDER; this term, in its original signification, represents nothing more than a mode of considering, a facility of perceiving, together and separately, the different relations of a whole; in which is discovered, by its manner of existing and acting, a certain affinity or conformity with his own. Man, in extending this idea to the universe, carried with him those methods of considering things which are peculiar to himself: he has consequently supposed there really existed in Nature affinities and relations, which he classed under the name of ORDER; and others which appeared to him not to conform to those, which he has ranked under the term of CONFUSION.

It is easy to comprehend, that this idea of order and confusion can have no absolute existence in Nature, where every thing is necessary; where the whole follows constant and invariable laws, which oblige each being, in every moment of its duration, to submit to other laws, which flow from its own peculiar mode of existence. Therefore it is in his imagination, only, man finds a model of that which he terms order or confusion; which, like all his abstract, metaphysical ideas, supposes nothing beyond his reach. Order, however, is never more than the faculty of conforming himself with the beings by whom he is environed, or with the whole of which he forms a part.

Nevertheless, if the idea of order be applied to Nature, it will be found to be nothing but a series of action or motion, which he judges to conspire to one common end. Thus, in a body that moves, order is the chain of action, the series of motion, proper to constitute it what it is, and to maintain it in its actual state. Order, relatively to the whole of Nature, is the concatenation of causes and effects, necessary to her *active* existence—to maintaining her constantly together; but, as it has been proved in the chapter preceding, every individual being is obliged to concur to this end, in the different ranks they occupy; from whence it is a necessary deduction, that what is called the ORDER OF NATURE, can never be more than a certain manner of considering the necessity of things, to which all, of which man has any knowledge, is submitted. That which is styled CONFUSION, is only a relative term, used to designate that series of necessary action, that chain of requisite motion, by which an individual being is necessarily changed or disturbed in its mode of existence—by which it is instantaneously obliged to alter its manner of action; but no one of these actions, no part of this motion is capable, even for a single instant, of contradicting or deranging the general order of Nature; from which all beings derive their existence, their properties, the motion appropriate to each.

What is termed confusion in a being, is nothing more than its passage into a new class, a new mode of existence; which necessarily carries with it a new series of action, a new chain of motion, different from that of which this being found itself susceptible in the preceding rank it occupied. That which is called order, in Nature, is a mode of existence, or a disposition of its particles, strictly *necessary*. In every other assemblage of causes and effects, of worlds, as well as in that which we inhabit, some sort of arrangement, some kind of order would necessarily be established. Suppose the most incongruous, the most heterogeneous substances were put into activity, and assembled by a concatenation of extraordinary circumstances; they would form amongst themselves, a complete order, a perfect arrangement. This is the true notion of a property, which may be defined, an aptitude to constitute a being, such as it is actually found, such as it is with respect to the whole of which it makes a part.

Order, then, is nothing but necessity, considered relatively to the series of actions, or the connected chain of causes and effects, that it produces in the universe. What is the motion in our planetary system; but a series of phenomena, operated upon according to necessary laws, that regulate the bodies of which it is composed? In conformity to these laws, the sun occupies the centre; the planets gravitate towards it, and revolve round it, in regulated periods: the satellites of these planets gravitate towards those which are in the centre of their sphere of action, and describe round them their periodical route. One of these planets, the earth which man inhabits, turns on its own axis; and by the various aspects which its revolution obliges it to present to the sun, experiences those regular variations which are called SEASONS. By a sequence of the sun's action upon different parts of this globe, all its productions undergo vicissitudes: plants, animals, men, are in a sort of morbid drowsiness during *Winter*: in *Spring*, these beings re-animate, to come as it were out of a long lethargy. In short, the mode in which the earth receives the sun's beams, has an influence on all its productions; these rays, when darted obliquely, do not act in the same manner as when they fall perpendicularly; their periodical absence, caused by the revolution of this sphere on itself, produces *night* and *day*. However, in all this, man never witnesses more than necessary effects, flowing from the nature of things, which, whilst that remains the same, can never be opposed with propriety. These effects are owing to gravitation, attraction, centrifugal power, &c.

On the other hand, this *order*, which man admires as a supernatural effect, is sometimes disturbed, or changed into what he calls *confusion*: this confusion is, however, always a necessary consequence of the laws of Nature; in which it is requisite to the support of the whole that some of her parts should be deranged and thrown out of the ordinary course. It is thus, COMETS present themselves so unexpectedly to man's wondering eyes; their eccentric motion disturbs the tranquillity of his planetary system; they excite the terror of the misinstructed to whom every thing unusual is marvellous. The natural philosopher, himself, conjectures that in former ages, these comets have overthrown the surface of this mundane ball, and caused great revolutions on the earth. Independent of this extraordinary *confusion*, he is exposed to others more familiar to him: sometimes, the seasons appear to have usurped each other's place; to have quitted their regular order: sometimes the opposing elements seem to dispute among themselves the dominion of the world; the sea bursts its limits; the solid earth is shaken and rent asunder; mountains are in a state of conflagration; pestilential diseases destroy both men and animals; sterility desolates a country: then affrighted man utters piercing cries, offers up his prayers to recall order; tremblingly raises his hands towards the Being he supposes to be the author of all these calamities; nevertheless, the whole of this afflicting confusion are necessary effects, produced by natural causes; which act according to fixed laws, determined by their own peculiar essence, and the universal essence of Nature: in which every thing must necessarily be changed, moved, and dissolved; where that which is called ORDER, must sometimes be disturbed and altered into a new mode of existence; which to his deluded mind, to his imagination, led astray by ignorance and want of reflection, appears CONFUSION.

There cannot possibly exist what is generally termed *a confusion of Nature*: man finds order in every thing that is conformable to his own mode of being; confusion in every thing by which it is opposed: nevertheless, in Nature, all is in order; because none of her parts are ever able to emancipate themselves from those invariable rules which flow from their respective essences: there *is* not, there *cannot* be confusion in a whole, to the maintenance of which what is *called* confusion is absolutely requisite; of which the general course can never be discomposed, although individuals may be, and necessarily are; where all the effects produced are the consequence of natural causes, that under the circumstances in which they are placed, act only as they infallibly are obliged to act.

It therefore follows, there can be neither monsters nor prodigies; wonders nor miracles in Nature: those which are designated MONSTERS, are certain combinations, with which the eyes of man are not familiarized; but which, therefore, are not less the necessary effects of natural causes. Those which he terms PRODIGIES, WONDERS, or SUPERNATURAL effects, are phenomena of Nature, with whose mode of action he is unacquainted; of which his ignorance does not permit him to ascertain the principles; whose causes he cannot trace; but which his impatience, his heated imagination, aided by a desire to explain, makes him foolishly attribute to imaginary causes; which, like the idea of order, have no existence but in himself; and which, that he may conceal his own ignorance, that he may obtain more respect with the uninformed, he places beyond Nature, out of which his experience is every instant demonstrably proving that none of these things can have existence.

As for those effects which are called MIRACLES, that is to say, contrary to the unalterable laws of Nature, it must be felt such things are impossible; because, nothing can, for an instant, suspend the necessary course of beings, without the whole of Nature was arrested; without she was disturbed in her tendency. There have neither been wonders nor miracles in Nature; except for those, who have not sufficiently studied the laws, who consequently do not feel, that those laws can never be contradicted, even in the most minute parts, without the whole being destroyed, or at least without changing her essence, her mode of action; that it is the height of folly to recur to supernatural causes to explain the phenomena man beholds, before he becomes fully acquainted with natural causes—with the powers and capabilities which Nature herself contains.

Order and *Confusion*, then, are only relative terms, by which man designates the state in which particular beings find themselves. He says, a being is in order, when all the motion it undergoes conspires to favor its tendency to its own preservation; when it is conducive to the maintenance of its actual existence: that it is in confusion when the causes which move it disturb the harmony of its existence, or have a tendency to destroy the equilibrium necessary to the conservation of its actual state. Nevertheless, confusion, as we have shown, is nothing but the passage of a being into a new order; the more rapid the progress, the greater the confusion for the being that is submitted to it: that which conducts man to what is called death, is, for him, the greatest of all possible confusion. Yet this death is nothing more than a passage into a new mode of existence: it is the eternal, the invariable, the unconquerable law of Nature, to which the individuals of his order, each in his turn, is obliged to submit.

The human body is said to be in order, when its various component parts act in that mode, from which results the conservation of the whole; from which emanates that which is the tendency of his actual existence; in other words, when all the impulse he receives, all the motion he communicates, tends to preserve his health, to render him happy, by promoting the happiness of his fellow men. He is said to be in health when the fluids and solids of his body concur to render him robust, to keep his mind in vigour; when each lends mutual aid towards this end. He is said to be in *confusion*, or in ill health, whenever this tendency is disturbed; when any of the essential parts of his body cease to concur to his preservation, or to fulfil its peculiar functions. This it is that happens in a state of sickness, in which, however, the motion excited in the human machine is as necessary, is regulated by laws as certain, as natural, as invariable, as that which concurs to produce health. Sickness merely produces in him a new order of motion, a new series of action, a new chain of things. Man dies: to him, this appears the greatest confusion he can experience; his body is no longer what it was—its parts no longer concur to the same end—his blood has lost its circulation—he is deprived of feeling—his ideas have vanished—he thinks no more—his desires have fled—death is the epoch, the cessation of his human existence.—His frame becomes an inanimate mass, by the subtraction of those principles by which it was animated; that is, which made it act after a determinate manner: its tendency has received a new direction; its action is changed; the motion excited in its ruins conspires to a new end. To that motion, the harmony of which he calls order, which produced life, sentiment, thought, passions, health, succeeds a series of motion of another species; that, nevertheless, follows laws as necessary as the first; all the parts of the dead man conspire to produce what is called dissolution, fermentation, putrefaction: these new modes of being, of acting, are just as natural to man, reduced to this state, as sensibility, thought, the periodical motion of the blood, &c. were to the living man: his essence having changed, his mode of action can no longer be the same. To that regulated motion, to that necessary action, which conspired to the production of life, succeeds that determinate motion, that series of action which concurs to produce the dissolution of the dead carcass; the dispersion of its parts; the formation of new combinations, from which result new beings; and which, as we have before seen, is the immutable order of active Nature.

How then can it be too often repeated, that relatively to the great whole, all the motion of beings, all their modes of action, can never be but in order, that is to say, are always conformable to Nature; that in all the stages through which beings are obliged to pass, they invariably act after a mode necessarily subordinate to the universal whole? To say more, each individual being always acts in order; all its actions, the whole system of its motion, are the necessary consequence of its peculiar mode of existence; whether that be momentary or durable. Order, in political society, is the effect of a necessary series of ideas, of wills, of actions, in those who compose it; whose movements are regulated in a manner, either calculated to maintain its indivisibility, or to hasten its dissolution. Man constituted, or modified, in the manner we term virtuous, acts necessarily in that mode, from whence results the welfare of his associates: the man we stile wicked, acts necessarily in that mode, from whence springs the misery of his fellows: his Nature, being essentially different, he must necessarily act after a different mode: his individual order is at variance, but his relative order is complete: it is equally the essence of the one, to promote happiness, as it is of the other to induce misery.

Thus, order and confusion in individual beings, is nothing more than the manner of man's considering the natural and necessary effects, which they produce relatively to himself. He fears the wicked man; he says that he will carry confusion into society, because he disturbs its tendency and places obstacles to its happiness. He avoids a falling stone, because it will derange in him the order necessary to his conservation. Nevertheless, order and confusion, are always, as we have shewn, consequences, equally necessary to either the transient or durable state of beings. It is in order that fire burns, because it is of its essence to burn; on the other hand, it is in order, that an intelligent being should remove himself from whatever can disturb his mode of existence. A being, whose organization renders him sensible, must in virtue of his essence, fly from every thing that can injure his organs, or that can place his existence in danger.

Man calls those beings *intelligent*, who are organized after his own manner; in whom he sees faculties proper for their preservation; suitable to maintain their existence in the order that is convenient to them; that can enable them to take the necessary measures towards this end, with a consciousness of the motion they undergo. From hence, it will be perceived, that the faculty called intelligence, consists in a possessing capacity to act comfortably to a known end, in the being to which it is attributed. He looks upon these beings as deprived of intelligence, in which he finds no conformity with himself; in whom he discovers neither the same construction, nor the same faculties: of which he knows neither the essence, the end to which they tend, the energies by which they act, nor the order that is necessary to them. The whole cannot have a distinct name, or end, because there is nothing out of itself, to which it can have a tendency. If it be in himself, that he arranges the idea of *order*, it is also in himself, that he draws up that of *intelligence*. He refuses to ascribe it to those beings, who do not act after his own manner: he accords it to all those whom he supposes to act like himself: the latter he calls intelligent agents: the former blind causes; that is to say, intelligent agents who act by *chance*: thus chance is an empty word without sense, but which is always opposed to that of intelligence, without attaching any determinate, or any certain idea.

Man, in fact, attributes to *chance* all those effects, of which the connection they have with their causes is not seen. Thus he uses the word *chance*, to cover his ignorance of those natural causes, which produce visible effects, by means which he cannot form an idea of; or that act by a mode of which he does not perceive the order; or whose system is not followed by actions conformable to his own. As soon as he sees, or believes he sees, the order of action, or the manner of motion, he attributes this order to an *intelligence*; which is nothing more than a quality borrowed from himself—from his own peculiar mode of action—from the manner in which he is himself affected.

Thus an *intelligent being* is one who thinks, who wills, and who acts, to compass an end. If so, he must have organs, an aim conformable to those of man: therefore, to say Nature is governed by an intelligence, is to affirm that she is governed by a being, furnished with organs; seeing that without this organic construction, he can neither have sensations, perceptions, ideas, thought, will, plan, nor action which he understands.

Man always makes himself the center of the universe: it is to himself that he relates all he beholds. As soon as he believes he discovers a mode of action that has a conformity with his own, or some phenomenon that interests his feelings, he attributes it to a cause that resembles himself—that acts after his manner—that has faculties similar to those he possesses—whose interests are like his own—whose projects are in unison with and have the same tendency as those he himself indulges: in short, it is from himself, or the properties which actuate him, that he forms the model of this cause. It is thus that man beholds, out of his own species, nothing but beings who act differently from himself; yet believes that he remarks in Nature an order similar to his own ideas—

views conformable to those which he himself possesses. He imagines that Nature is governed by a cause whose intelligence is conformable to his own, to whom he ascribes the honor of the order which he believes he witnesses—of those views that fall in with those that are peculiar to himself—of an aim which quadrates with that which is the great end of all his own actions. It is true that man, feeling his incapability of producing the vast, the multiplied effects of which he witnesses the operation, when contemplating the universe, was under the necessity of making a distinction between himself and the cause which he supposed to be the author of such stupendous effects; he believed he removed every difficulty, by amplifying in this cause all those faculties of which he was himself in possession; adding others of which his own self-love made him desirous, or which he thought would render his being more perfect: thus, he gave JUPITER wings, with the faculty of assuming any form he might deem convenient: it was thus, by degrees, he arrived at forming an idea of that intelligent cause, which he has placed above Nature, to preside over action—to give her that motion of which he has chosen to believe she was in herself incapable. He obstinately persists in regarding this Nature as a heap of dead, inert matter, without form, which has not within itself the power of producing any of those great effects, those regular phenomena, from which emanates what he styles *the order of the Universe.* ANAXAGORAS is said to have been the first who supposed the universe created and governed by an intelligence: ARISTOTLE reproaches him with having made an automaton of this intelligence; or in other words, with ascribing to it the production of things, only when he was at a loss to account for their appearance. From whence it may be deduced, that it is for want of being acquainted with the powers of Nature, or the properties of matter, that man has multiplied beings without necessity—that he has supposed the universe under the government of an intelligent cause, which he is, and perhaps always will be, himself the model: in fine, this cause has been personified under such a variety of shapes, sexes, and names, that a list of the deities he has at various times supposed to guide this Nature, or to whom he has submitted her, makes a large volume that occupies some years of his youthful education to understand. He only rendered this cause more inconceivable, when he extended in it his own faculties too much. He either annihilates, or renders it altogether impossible, when he would attach to it incompatible qualities, which he is obliged to do, to enable him to account for the contradictory and disorderly effects he beholds in the world. In fact, he sees confusion in the world; yet, notwithstanding his confusion contradicts the plan, the power, the wisdom, the bounty of this intelligence, and the miraculous order which he ascribes to it; he says, the extreme beautiful arrangement of the whole, obliges him to suppose it to be the work of a sovereign intelligence: unable, however, to reconcile this seeming confusion with the benevolence he attaches to this cause, he had recourse to another effort of his imagination; he made a new cause, to whom he ascribed all the evil, all the misery, resulting from this confusion: still, his own person served for the model; to which he added those deformities which he had learned to hold in disrespect: in multiplying these counter or destroying causes, he peopled Pandemonium.

It will no doubt be argued, that as Nature contains and produces intelligent beings, either she must be herself intelligent, or else she must be governed by an intelligent cause. We reply, intelligence is a faculty peculiar to organized beings, that it is to say, to beings constituted and combined after a determinate manner; from whence results certain modes of action, which are designated under various names; according to the different effects which these beings produce: wine has not the properties called *wit* and *courage*; nevertheless, it is sometimes seen that it communicates those qualities to men, who are supposed to be in themselves entirely devoid of them. It cannot be said Nature is intelligent after the manner of any of the beings she contains; but she can produce intelligent beings by assembling matter suitable to their particular organization, from whose peculiar modes of action will result the faculty called intelligence; who shall be capable of producing certain effects which are the necessary consequence of this property. I therefore repeat, that to have intelligence, designs and views, it is requisite to have ideas; to the production of ideas, organs or senses are necessary: this is what is neither said of Nature nor of the causes he has supposed to preside over her actions. In short experience warrants the assertion, it does more, it proves beyond a doubt, that matter, which is regarded as inert and dead, assumes sensible action, intelligence, and life, when it is combined and organized after particular modes.

From what has been said, it must rationally be concluded that *order* is never more than the necessary or uniform connection of causes with their effects; or that series of action which flows from the peculiar properties of beings, so long as they remain in a given state; that *confusion* is nothing more than the change of this state; that in the universe, all is necessarily in order, because every thing acts and moves according to the various properties of the different beings it contains; that in Nature there cannot be either confusion or real evil, since every thing follows the laws of its natural existence; that there is neither *chance* nor any thing fortuitous in this Nature, where no effect is produced without a sufficient, without a substantial cause; where all causes act necessarily according to fixed and certain laws, which are themselves dependant on the essential properties of these causes or beings, as well as on the combination, which constitutes either their transitory or permanent state; that intelligence is a mode of acting, a method of existence natural to some particular beings; that if this intelligence should be attributed to Nature, it would then be nothing more than the faculty of conserving herself in active existence by necessary means. In refusing to Nature the intelligence he himself enjoys—in rejecting the intelligent cause which is supposed to be the contriver of this Nature, or the principle of that *order* he discovers in her course, nothing is given to *chance*, nothing to a blind cause, nothing to a power which is indistinguishable; but every thing he beholds is attributed to real, to known causes; or to those which by analogy are easy of comprehension. All that exists is acknowledged to be a consequence of the inherent properties of eternal matter, which by contact, by blending, by combination, by change of form, produces order and confusion; with all those varieties which assail his sight, it is himself who is blind, when he imagines blind causes:—man only manifested his ignorance of the powers of motion, of the laws of Nature, when he attributed, any of its effects to *chance*. He did not shew a more enlightened feeling when he ascribed them to an intelligence, the idea of which he borrowed from himself, but which is never in conformity with the effects which he attributes to its intervention—he only imagined words to supply the place of things—he made JUPITER, SATURN, JUNO, and a thousand others, operate that which he found himself inadequate to perform; he distinguished them from Nature, gave them an amplification of his own properties, and believed he understood them by thus obscuring ideas, which he never dared either define or analyze.

CHAP. VI.

Moral and Physical Distinctions of Man.—His Origin.

Let us now apply the general laws we have scrutinized, to those beings of Nature who interest us the most. Let us see in what man differs from the other beings by which he is surrounded. Let us examine if he has not certain points in conformity with them, that oblige him, notwithstanding the different properties they respectively possess, to act in certain respects according to the universal laws to which every thing is submitted. Finally, let us enquire if the ideas he has formed of himself in meditating on his own peculiar mode of existence, be chimerical, or founded in reason.

Man occupies a place amidst that crowd, that multitude of beings, of which Nature is the assemblage. His essence, that is to say, the peculiar manner of existence, by which he is distinguished from other beings, renders him susceptible of various modes of action, of a variety of motion, some of which are simple and visible, others concealed and complicated. His life itself is nothing more than a long series, a succession of necessary and connected motion; which operates perpetual changes in his machine; which has for its principle either causes contained within himself, such as blood, nerves, fibres, flesh, bones; in short, the matter, as well solid as fluid, of which his body is composed—or those exterior causes, which, by acting upon him, modify him diversely; such as the air with which he is encompassed, the aliments by which he is nourished, and all those objects from which he receives any impulse whatever, by the impression they make on his senses.

Man, like all other beings in Nature, tends to his own destruction—he experiences inert force—he gravitates upon himself—he is attracted by objects that are contrary or repugnant to his existence—he seeks after some—he flies, or endeavours to remove himself from others. It is this variety of action, this diversity of modification of which the human being is susceptible, that has been designated under such different names, by such varied nomenclature. It will be necessary, presently, to examine these closely and go more into detail.

However marvellous, however hidden, however secret, however complicated may be the modes of action, which the human frame undergoes, whether interiorly or exteriorly; whatever may be, or appear to be the impulse he either receives or communicates, examined closely, it will be found that all his motion, all his operations, all his changes, all his various states, all his revolutions, are constantly regulated by the same laws, which Nature has prescribed to all the beings she brings forth—which she developes—which she enriches with faculties—of which she increases the bulk—which she conserves for a season—which she ends by decomposing, by destroying: obliging them to change their form.

Man, in his origin, is an imperceptible point, a speck, of which the parts are without form; of which the mobility, the life, escapes his senses; in short, in which he does not perceive any sign of those qualities, called SENTIMENT,

FEELING, THOUGHT, INTELLIGENCE, FORCE, REASON, &c. Placed in the womb suitable to his expansion, this point unfolds, extends, increases, by the continual addition of matter he attracts, that is analogous to his being, which consequently assimilates itself with him. Having quitted this womb, so appropriate to conserve his existence, to unfold his qualities, to strengthen his habits; so competent to give, for a season, consistence to the weak rudiments of his frame; he travels through the stage of infancy; he becomes adult: his body has then acquired a considerable extension of bulk, his motion is marked, his action is visible, he is sensible in all his parts; he is a living, an active mass; that is to say, a combination that feels and thinks; that fulfils the functions peculiar to beings of his species. But how has he become sensible? Because he has been by degrees nourished, enlarged, repaired by the continual attraction that takes place within himself, of that kind of matter which is pronounced inert, insensible, inanimate; which is, nevertheless, continually combining itself with his machine; of which it forms an active whole, that is living, that feels, judges, reasons, wills, deliberates, chooses, elects; that has the capability of labouring, more or less efficaciously, to his own individual preservation; that is to say, to the maintenance of the harmony of his existence.

All the motion and changes that man experiences in the course of his life, whether it be from exterior objects or from those substances contained within himself, are either favorable or prejudicial to his existence; either maintain its order, or throw it into confusion; are either in conformity with, or repugnant to, the essential tendency of his peculiar mode of being. He is compelled by Nature to approve of some, to disapprove of others; some of necessity render him happy, others contribute to his misery; some become the objects of his most ardent desire, others of his determined aversion: some elicit his confidence, others make him tremble with fear.

In all the phenomena man presents, from the moment he quits the womb of his mother, to that wherein he becomes the inhabitant of the silent tomb, he perceives nothing but a succession of necessary causes and effects, which are strictly conformable to those laws that are common to all the beings in Nature. All his modes of action—all his sensations— all his ideas—all his passions—every act of his will—every impulse which he either gives or receives, are the necessary consequences of his own peculiar properties, and those which he finds in the various beings by whom he is moved. Every thing he does—every thing that passes within himself—his concealed motion—his visible action, are the effects of inert force—of self-gravitation—the attractive or repulsive powers contained in his machine—of the tendency he has, in common with other beings, to his own individual preservation; in short, of that energy which is the common property of every being he beholds. Nature, in man, does nothing more than shew, in a decided manner, what belongs to the peculiar nature by which he is distinguished from the beings of a different system or order.

The source of those errors into which man has fallen, when he has contemplated himself, has its rise, as will presently be shown, in the opinion he has entertained, that he moved by himself—that he always acts by his own natural energy—that in his actions, in the will that gave him impulse, he was independent of the general laws of Nature; and of those objects which, frequently, without his knowledge, always in spite of him, in obedience to these laws, are continually acting upon him. If he had examined himself attentively, he must have acknowledged, that none of the motion he underwent was spontaneous—he must have discovered, that even his birth depended on causes, wholly out of the reach of his own powers—that, it was without his own consent he entered into the system in which he occupies a place—that, from the moment in which he is born, until that in which he dies, he is continually impelled by causes, which, in spite of himself, influence his frame, modify his existence, dispose of his conduct. Would not the slightest reflection have sufficed to prove to him, that the fluids, the solids, of which his body is composed, as well as that concealed mechanism, which he believes to be independent of exterior causes, are, in fact, perpetually under the influence of these causes; that without them he finds himself in a total incapacity to act? Would he not have seen, that his temperament, his constitution, did in no wise depend on himself— that his passions are the necessary consequence of this temperament— that his will is influenced, his actions determined by these passions; consequently by opinions, which he has not given to himself, of which he is not the master? His blood, more or less heated or abundant; his nerves more or less braced, his fibres more or less relaxed, give him dispositions either transitory or durable—are not these, at every moment decisive of his ideas; of his thoughts: of his desires: of his fears: of his motion, whether visible or concealed? The state in which he finds himself, does it not necessarily depend on the air which surrounds him diversely modified; on the various properties of the aliments which nourish him; on the secret combinations that form themselves in his machine, which either preserve its order, or throw it into confusion? In short, had man fairly studied himself, every thing must have convinced him, that in every moment of his duration, he was nothing more than a passive instrument in the hands of necessity.

Thus it must appear, that where all is connected, where all the causes are linked one to the other, where the whole forms but one immense chain, there cannot be any independent, any isolated energy; any detached power. It follows then, that Nature, always in action, marks out to man each point of the line he is bound to describe; establishes the route, by which he must travel. It is Nature that elaborates, that combines the elements of which he must be composed;—It is Nature that gives him his being, his tendency, his peculiar mode of action. It is Nature that develops him, expands him, strengthens him, increases his bulk—preserves him for a season, during which he is obliged to fulfil the task imposed on him. It is Nature, that in his journey through life, strews on the road those objects, those events; those adventures, that modify him in a variety of ways, that give him impulses which are sometimes agreeable and beneficial, at others prejudicial and disagreeable. It is Nature, that in giving him feeling, in supplying him with sentiment, has endowed him with capacity to choose, the means to elect those objects, to take those methods that are most conducive, most suitable, most natural, to his conservation. It is Nature, who when he has run his race, when he has finished his career, when he has described the circle marked out for him, conducts him in his turn to his destruction; dissolves the union of his elementary particles, and obliges him to undergo the constant, the universal law; from the operation of which nothing is exempted. It is thus, motion places man in the matrix of his mother; brings him forth out of her womb; sustains him for a season; at length destroys him; obliges him to return into the bosom of Nature; who speedily reproduces him, scattered under an infinity of forms; in which each of his particles run over again, in the same manner, the different stages, as necessary as the whole had before run over those of his preceding existence.

The beings of the human species, as well as all other beings, are susceptible of two sorts of motion: the one, that of the mass, by which an entire body, or some of its parts, are visibly transferred from one place to another; the other, internal and concealed, of some of which man is sensible, while some takes place without his knowledge, and is not even to be guessed at, but by the effect it outwardly produces. In a machine so extremely complex as man, formed by the combination of such a multiplicity of matter, so diversified in its properties, so different in its proportions, so varied in its modes of action, the motion necessarily becomes of the most complicated kind; its dullness, as well as its rapidity, frequently escapes the observation of those themselves, in whom it takes place.

Let us not, then, be surprised, if, when man would account to himself for his existence, for his manner of acting, finding so many obstacles to encounter, he invented such strange hypotheses to explain the concealed spring of his machine—if then this motion appeared to him, to be different from that of other bodies, he conceived an idea, that he moved and acted in a manner altogether distinct from the other beings in Nature. He clearly perceived that his body, as well as different parts of it, did act; but, frequently, he was unable to discover what brought them into action: from whence he received the impulse: he then conjectured he contained within himself a moving principle distinguished from his machine, which secretly gave an impulse to the springs which set this machine in motion; that moved him by its own natural energy; that consequently he acted according to laws totally distinct from those which regulated the motion of other beings: he was conscious of certain internal motion, which he could not help feeling; but how could he conceive, that this invisible motion was so frequently competent to produce such striking effects? How could he comprehend, that a fugitive idea, an imperceptible act of thought, was so frequently capacitated to bring his whole being into trouble and confusion? He fell into the belief, that he perceived within himself a substance distinguished from that self, endowed with a secret force; in which he supposed existed qualities distinctly differing from those, of either the visible causes that acted on his organs, or those organs themselves. He did not sufficiently understand, that the primitive cause which makes a stone fall, or his arm move, are perhaps as difficult of comprehension, as arduous to be explained, as those internal impulses, of which his thought or his will are the effects. Thus, for want of meditating Nature—of considering her under her true point of view—of remarking the conformity—of noticing the simultaneity, the unity of the motion of this fancied motive-power with that of his body—of his material organs —he conjectured he was not only a distinct being, but that he was set apart, with different energies, from all the other beings in Nature; that he was of a more simple essence having nothing in common with any thing by which he was surrounded; nothing that connected him with all that he beheld.

It is from thence has successively sprung his notions of SPIRITUALITY, IMMATERIALITY, IMMORTALITY; in short, all those vague unmeaning words he has invented by degrees, in order to subtilize and designate the attributes of the unknown power, which he believes he contains within himself; which he conjectures to be the concealed principle of all his visible actions when man once imbibes an idea that he cannot comprehend, he meditates upon it until he has given it a complete personification: Thus he saw, or fancied he saw, the igneous matter pervade every thing; he conjectured that it was the only principle of life and activity; he proceeded to embody it; he gave it his own form; called it JUPITER, and ended by worshipping this image of his own creation, as the power from whom he derived every good he experienced, every evil he sustained. To crown the bold conjectures he ventured to make on this internal motive- power, he supposed, that different from all other beings, even from the body that served to envelope it, it was not bound to undergo dissolution; that such was its perfect simplicity, that it could not be decomposed, nor even change its form; in short, that it was by its essence exempted from those revolutions to which he saw the body subjected, as well as all the compound beings with which Nature is filled.

Thus man, in his own ideas, became double; he looked upon himself as a whole, composed by the inconceivable assemblage of two different, two distinct natures, which have no point of analogy between themselves: he distinguished two substances in himself; one evidently submitted to the influence of gross beings, composed of coarse inert matter: this he called BODY;—the other, which he supposed to be simple, of a purer essence, was contemplated as acting from itself: giving motion to the body, with which it found itself so miraculously united: this he called SOUL, or SPIRIT; the functions of the one, he denominated *physical, corporeal, material*; the functions of the other he styled *spiritual, intellectual.* Man, considered relatively to the first, was termed the PHYSICAL MAN; viewed with relation to the last, he was designated the MORAL MAN. These distinctions, although adopted by the greater number of the philosophers of the present day, are, nevertheless, only founded on gratuitous suppositions. Man has always believed he remedied his ignorance of things, by inventing words to which he could never attach any true sense or meaning. He imagined he understood matter, its properties, its faculties, its resources, its different combinations, because he had a superficial glimpse of some of its qualities: he has, however, in reality, done nothing more than obscure the faint ideas he has been capacitated to form of this matter, by associating it with a substance much less intelligible than itself. It is thus, speculative man, in forming words, in multiplying beings, has only plunged himself into greater difficulties than those he endeavoured to avoid; and thereby placed obstacles to the progress of his knowledge: whenever he has been deficient of facts, he has had recourse to conjecture, which he quickly changed into fancied realities. Thus, his imagination, no longer guided by experience, hurried on by his new ideas, was lost, without hope of return, in the labyrinth of an ideal, of an intellectual world, to which he had himself given birth; it was next to impossible to withdraw him from this delusion, to place him in the right road, of which nothing but experience can furnish him the clue. Nature points out to man, that in himself, as well as in all those objects which act upon him, there is never more than matter endowed with various properties, diversely modified, that acts by reason of these properties: that man is an organized whole, composed of a variety of matter; that like all the other productions of Nature, he follows general and known laws, as well as those laws or modes of action which are peculiar to himself and unknown.

Thus, when it shall be inquired, what is man?

We say, he is a material being, organized after a peculiar manner; conformed to a certain mode of thinking—of feeling; capable of modification in certain modes peculiar to himself—to his organization— to that particular combination of matter which is found assembled in him.

If, again, it be asked, what origin we give to beings of the human species?

We reply, that, like all other beings, man is a production of Nature, who resembles them in some respects, and finds himself submitted to the same laws; who differs from them in other respects, and follows particular laws, determined by the diversity of his conformation.

If, then, it be demanded, whence came man?

We answer, our experience on this head does not capacitate us to resolve the question: but that it cannot interest us, as it suffices for us to know that man exists; that he is so constituted, as to be competent to the effects we witness.

But it will be urged, has man always existed? Has the human species existed from all eternity; or is it only an instantaneous production of Nature? Have there been always men like ourselves? Will there always be such? Have there been, in all times, males and females? Was there a first man, from whom all others are descended? Was the animal anterior to the egg, or did the egg precede the animal? Is this species without beginning? Will it also be without end? The species itself, is it indestructible, or does it pass away like its individuals? Has man always been what he now is; or has he, before he arrived at the state in which we see him, been obliged to pass under an infinity of successive developements? Can man at last flatter himself with having arrived at a fixed being, or must the human species again change? If man is the production of Nature, it will perhaps be asked, Is this Nature competent to the production of new beings, to make the old species disappear? Adopting this supposition, it may be inquired, why Nature does not produce under our own eyes new beings—new species?

It would appear on reviewing these questions, to be perfectly indifferent, as to the stability of the argument we have used, which side was taken; that, for want of experience, hypothesis must settle a curiosity that always endeavours to spring forward beyond the boundaries prescribed to our mind. This granted, the contemplator of Nature will say, that he sees no contradiction, in supposing the human species, such as it is at the present day, was either produced in the course of time, or from all eternity: he will not perceive any advantage that can arise from supposing that it has arrived by different stages, or successive developements, to that state in which it is actually found. Matter is eternal, it is necessary, but its forms are evanescent and contingent. It may be asked of man, is he any thing more than matter combined, of which the former varies every instant?

Notwithstanding, some reflections seem to favor the supposition, to render more probable the hypothesis, that man is a production formed in the course of time; who is peculiar to the globe he inhabits, who is the result of the peculiar laws by which it is directed; who, consequently, can only date his formation as coeval with that of his planet. Existence is essential to the universe, or the total assemblage of matter essentially varied that presents itself to our contemplation; the combinations, the forms, however, are not essential. This granted, although the matter of which the earth is composed has always existed, this earth may not always have had its present form—its actual properties; perhaps it may be a mass detached in the course of time from some other celestial body;—perhaps it is the result of the spots, or those encrustations which astronomers discover in the sun's disk, which have had the faculty to diffuse themselves over our planetary system;— perhaps the sphere we inhabit may be an extinguished or a displaced comet, which heretofore occupied some other place in the regions of space;—which, consequently, was then competent to produce beings very different from those we now behold spread over its surface; seeing that its then position, its nature, must have rendered its productions different from those which at this day it offers to our view.

Whatever may be the supposition adopted, plants, animals, men, can only be regarded as productions inherent in and natural to our globe, in the position and in the circumstances in which it is actually found: these productions it would be reasonable to infer would be changed, if this globe by any revolution should happen to shift its situation. What appears to strengthen this hypothesis, is, that on our ball itself, all the productions vary, by reason of its different climates: men, animals, vegetables, minerals, are not the same on every part of it: they vary sometimes in a very sensible manner, at very inconsiderable distances. The elephant is indigenous to, or native of the torrid zone: the rein deer is peculiar to the frozen climates of the North; Indostan is the womb that matures the diamond; we do not find it produced in our own country: the pine-apple grows in the common atmosphere of America; in our climate it is never produced in the open ground, never until art has furnished a sun analogous to that which it requires—the European in his own climate finds not this delicious fruit. Man in different climates varies in his colour, in his size, in his conformation, in his powers, in his industry, in his courage, and in the faculties of his mind. But, what is it that constitutes climate? It is the different position of parts of the same globe, relatively to the sun; positions that suffice to make a sensible variety in its productions.

There is, then, sufficient foundation to conjecture that if by any accident our globe should become displaced, all its productions would of necessity be changed; seeing that causes being no longer the same, or no longer acting after the same manner, the effects would necessarily no longer be what they now are, all productions, that they may be able to conserve themselves, or maintain their actual existence, have occasion to co-order themselves with the whole from which they have emanated. Without this they would no longer be in a capacity to subsist: it is this faculty of co-ordering themselves,—this relative adaption, which is called the ORDER OF THE UNIVERSE: the want of it is called CONFUSION. Those productions which are treated as MONSTROUS, are such as are unable to co-order themselves with the general or particular laws of the beings who surround them, or with the whole in which they find themselves placed: they have had the faculty in their formation to accommodate themselves to these laws; but these very laws are opposed to their perfection: for this reason they are unable to subsist. It is thus that by a certain analogy of conformation, which exists between animals of different species, mules are easily produced; but these mules, unable to co-order themselves with the beings that surround them, are not able to reach perfection, consequently cannot propagate their species. Man can live only in air, fish only in water: put the man into the water, the fish into the air, not being able to co-order themselves with the fluids which surround them, these animals will quickly be destroyed. Transport by imagination, a man from our planet into SATURN, his lungs will presently be rent by an atmosphere too rarified for his mode of being, his members will be frozen with the intensity of the cold; he will perish for want of finding elements analogous to his actual existence: transport another into MERCURY, the excess of heat, beyond what his mode of existence can bear, will quickly destroy him.

Thus, every thing seems to authorise the conjecture, that the human species is a production peculiar to our sphere, in the position in which it is found: that when this position may happen to change, the human species will, of consequence, either be changed or will be obliged to disappear; seeing that there would not then be that with which man could co-order himself with the whole, or connect himself with that which can enable him to subsist. It is this aptitude in man to co-order himself with the whole, that not only furnishes him with the idea of order, but also makes him exclaim "*whatever is, is right*;" whilst every thing is only that which it can be, as long as the whole is necessarily what it is; whilst it is positively neither good nor bad, as we understand those terms: it is only requisite to displace a man, to make him accuse the universe of confusion.

These reflections would appear to contradict the ideas of those, who are willing to conjecture that the other planets, like our own, are inhabited by beings resembling ourselves. But if the LAPLANDER differs in so marked a manner from the HOTTENTOT, what difference ought we not rationally to suppose between an inhabitant of our planet and one of SATURN or of VENUS?

However it may be, if we are obliged to recur by imagination to the origin of things, to the infancy of the human species, we may say that it is probable that man was a necessary consequence of the disentangling of our globe; or one of the results of the qualities, of the properties, of the energies, of which it is susceptible in its present position— that he was born male and female—that his existence is co-ordinate with that of the globe, under its present position— that as long as this co-ordination shall subsist, the human specie will conserve himself, will propagate himself, according to the impulse, after the primitive laws, which he has originally received—that if this co-ordination should happen to cease; if the earth, displaced, should cease to receive the same impulse, the same influence, on the part of those causes which actually act upon it, or which give it energy; that then the human species would change, to make place for new beings, suitable to co-order themselves with the state that should succeed to that which we now see subsist.

In thus supposing the changes in the position of our globe, the primitive man did, perhaps, differ more from the actual man, than the quadruped differs from the insect. Thus man, the same as every thing else that exists on our planet, as well as in all the others, may be regarded as in a state of continual vicissitude: thus the last term of the existence of man is to us as unknown and as indistinct as the first: there is, therefore, no contradiction in the belief that the species vary incessantly—that to us it is as impossible to know what he will become, as to know what he has been.

With respect to those who may ask why Nature does not produce new beings? we may enquire of them in turn, upon what foundation they suppose this fact? What it is that authorizes them to believe this sterility in Nature? Know they if, in the various combinations which she is every instant forming, Nature be not occupied in producing new beings, without the cognizance of these observers? Who has informed them that this Nature is not actually assembling, in her immense elaboratory, the elements suitable to bring to light, generations entirely new, that will have nothing in common with those of the species at present existing? What absurdity then, or what want of just inference would there be, to imagine that the man, the horse, the fish, the bird, will be no more? Are these animals so indispensably requisite to Nature, that without them she cannot continue her eternal course? Does not all change around us? Do we not ourselves change? Is it not evident that the whole universe has not been, in its anterior eternal duration, rigorously the same that it now is? that it is impossible, in its posterior eternal duration, it can be rigidly in the same state that it now is for a single instant? How, then, pretend to divine that, to which the infinite succession of destruction, of reproduction, of combination, of dissolution, of metamorphosis, of change, of transposition, may be able eventually to conduct it by their consequence? Suns encrust themselves, and are extinguished; planets perish and disperse themselves in the vast plains of air; other suns are kindled, and illumine their systems; new planets form themselves, either to make revolutions round these suns, or to describe new routes; and man, an infinitely small portion of the globe, which is itself but an imperceptible point in the immensity of space, vainly believes it is for himself this universe is made; foolishly imagines he ought to be the confident of Nature; confidently flatters himself he is eternal: and calls himself KING OF THE UNIVERSE!!!

O man! wilt thou never conceive, that thou art but an ephemeron? All changes in the great macrocosm: nothing remains the same an instant, in the planet thou inhabitest: Nature contains no one constant form, yet thou pretendest thy species can never disappear; that thou shalt be exempted from the universal law, that wills all shall experience change! Alas! In thy actual being, art not thou submitted to continual alterations? Thou, who in thy folly, arrogantly assumest to thyself the title of KING OF NATURE! Thou, who measurest the earth and the heavens! Thou, who in thy vanity imaginest, that the whole was made, because thou art intelligent! There requires but a very slight accident, a single atom to be displaced, to make thee perish; to degrade thee; to ravish from thee this intelligence of which thou appearest so proud.

If all the preceding conjectures be refused by those opposed to us; if it be pretended that Nature acts by a certain quantum of immutable and general laws; if it be believed that men, quadrupeds, fish, insects, plants, are from all eternity, and will remain eternally, what they now are: if I say it be contended, that from all eternity the stars have shone, in the immense regions of space, have illuminated the firmament; if it be insisted, we must no more demand why man is such as he appears, then ask why Nature is such as we behold her, or why the world exists? We are no longer opposed to such arguments. Whatever may be the system adopted, it will perhaps reply equally well to the difficulties with which our opponents endeavour to embarrass the way: examined closely, it will be perceived they make nothing against those truths, which we have gathered from experience. It is not given to man to know every thing—it is not given him to know his origin—it is not given him to penetrate into the essence of things, nor to recur to first principles—but it is given him, to have reason, to have honesty, to ingenuously allow he is ignorant of that which he cannot know, and not to substitute unintelligible words, absurd suppositions, for his uncertainty. Thus, we say to those, who to solve difficulties far above their reach, pretend that the human species descended from a first man and a first woman, created diversely according to different creeds;—that we have some ideas of Nature, but that we have none of creation;—that the human mind is incapable of comprehending the period when all was nothing;—that to use words we cannot understand, is only in other terms to acknowledge our ignorance of the powers of Nature;—that we are unable to fathom the means by which she has been capacitated to produce the phenomena we behold.

Let us then conclude, that man has no just, no solid reason to believe himself a privileged being in Nature; because he is subject to the same vicissitudes, as all her other productions. His pretended prerogatives have their foundation in error, arising from mistaken opinions concerning his existence. Let him but elevate himself by his thoughts above the globe he inhabits, he will look upon his own species with the same eyes he does all other beings in Nature: He will then clearly perceive that in the same manner that each tree produces its fruit, by reason of its energies, in consequence of its species: so each man acts by reason of his particular energy; that he produces fruit, actions, works, equally necessary: he will feel that the illusion which he anticipates in favour of himself, arises from his being, at one and the same time, a spectator and a part of the universe. He will acknowledge, that the idea of excellence which he attaches to his being, has no other foundation than his own peculiar interest; than the predilection he has in favour of himself—that the doctrine he has broached with such seeming confidence, bottoms itself on a very suspicious foundation, namely IGNORANCE and SELF-LOVE.

CHAP. VII.
The Soul and the Spiritual System.

Man, after having gratuitously supposed himself composed of two distinct independent substances, that have no common properties, relatively with each other; has pretended, as we have seen, that that which actuated him interiorly, that motion which is invisible, that impulse which is placed within himself, is essentially different from those which act exteriorly. The first he designated, as we have already said, by the name of a SPIRIT or a SOUL. If however it be asked, what is a spirit? The moderns will reply, that the whole fruit of their metaphysical researches is limited to learning that this motive-power, which they state to be the spring of man's action, is a substance of an unknown nature; so simple, so indivisible, so deprived of extent, so invisible, so impossible to be discovered by the senses, that its parts cannot be separated, even by abstraction or thought. The question then arises, how can we conceive such a substance, which is only the negation of every thing of which we have a knowledge? How form to ourselves an idea of a substance, void of extent, yet acting on our senses; that is to say, on those organs which are material, which have extent? How can a being without extent be moveable; how put matter in action? How can a substance devoid of parts, correspond successively with different parts of space? But a very cogent question presents itself on this occasion: if this distinct substance that is said to form one of the component parts of man, be really what it is reported, and if it be not, it is not what it is described; if it be unknown, if it be not pervious to the senses; if it be invisible, by what means did the metaphysicians themselves become acquainted with it? How did they form ideas of a substance, that taking their own account of it, is not, under any of its circumstances, either directly or by analogy, cognizable to the mind of man? If they could positively achieve this, there would no longer be any mystery in Nature: it would be as easy to conceive the time when all was nothing, when all shall have passed away, to account for the production of every thing we behold, as to dig in a garden or read a lecture.— Doubt would vanish from the human species; there could no longer be any difference of opinion, since all must necessarily be of one mind on a subject so accessible to every enquirer.

But it will be replied, the materialist himself admits, the natural philosophers of all ages have admitted, elements and atoms, beings simple and indivisible, of which bodies are composed:—granted; they have no more: they have also admitted that many of these atoms, many of these elements, if not all, are unknown to them: nevertheless, these simple beings, these atoms of the materialist, are not the same thing with the spirit, or the soul of the metaphysician. When the natural philosopher talks of atoms—when he describes them as simple beings, he indicates nothing more than that they are homogeneous, pure, without mixture: but then he allows that they have extent, consequently parts, are separable by thought, although no other natural agent with which he is acquainted is capable of dividing them: that the simple beings of this genus are susceptible of motion—can impart action—receive impulse—are material—are placed in Nature—are indestructible;—that consequently, if he cannot know them from themselves, he can form some idea of them by analogy: thus he has done that intelligibly, which the metaphysician would do unintelligibly: the latter, with a view to render man immortal, finding difficulties to his wish, from seeing that the body decayed—that it has submitted to the great, the universal law— has, to solve the difficulty, to remove the impediment, given him a soul, distinct from the body, which he says is exempted from the action of the general law: to account for this, he has called it a spiritual being, whose properties are the negation of all known properties, consequently inconceivable: had he, however, had recourse to the atoms of the former—had he made this substance the last possible term of the division of matter—it would at least have been intelligible; it would also have been immortal, since, according to the reasonings of all men, whether metaphysicians, theologians, or natural philosophers, an atom is an indestructible element, that must exist to all eternity.

All men are agreed in this position, that motion is the successive change of the relations of one body with other bodies, or with the different parts of space. If that which is called *spirit* be susceptible of communicating or receiving motion—if it acts—if it gives play to the organs of body—to produce these effects, it necessarily follows that this being changes successively its relation, its tendency, its correspondence, the position of its parts, either relatively to the different points of space, or to the different organs of the body which it puts in action: but to change its relation with space, with the organs to which it gives impulse, it follows of necessity that this spirit most have extent, solidity, consequently distinct parts: whenever a substance possesses these qualities, it is what we call MATTER, it can no longer be regarded as a simple pure being, in the sense attached to it by the moderns, or by theologians.

Thus it will be seen, that those who, to conquer insurmountable difficulties, have supposed in man an immaterial substance, distinguished from his body, have not thoroughly understood themselves; indeed they have done nothing more than imagined a negative quality, of which they cannot have any correct idea: matter alone is capable of acting on our senses; without this action nothing would be capable of making itself known to us. They have not seen that a being without extent is neither in a capacity to move itself, nor has the capability of communicating motion to the body; since such a being, having no parts, has not the faculty of changing its relation, or its distance, relatively to other bodies, nor of exciting motion in the human body, which is itself material. That which is called our soul moves itself with us; now motion is a property of matter—this soul gives impulse to the arm; the arm, moved by it, makes an impression, a blow, that follows the general law of motion: in this case, the force remaining the same, if the mass was two-fold, the blow should be double. This soul again evinces its materiality in the invincible obstacles it encounters on the part of the body. If the arm be moved by its impulse when nothing opposes it, yet this arm can no longer move, when it is charged with a weight beyond its strength. Here then is a mass of matter that annihilates the impulse given by a spiritual cause, which spiritual cause having no analogy with matter, ought not to find more difficulty in moving the whole world, than in moving a single atom, nor an atom, than the universe. From this, it is fair to conclude, such a substance is a chimera—a being of the imagination. That it required a being differently endowed, differently constituted, to set matter in motion— to create all the phenomena we behold: nevertheless, it is a being the metaphysicians have made the contriver, the Author of Nature. As man, in all his speculations, takes himself for the model, he no sooner imagined a spirit within himself, than giving it extent, he made it universal; then ascribed to it all those causes with which his ignorance prevents him from becoming acquainted, thus he identified himself with the Author of Nature—then availed himself of the supposition to explain the connection of the soul with the body: his self-complacency prevented his perceiving that he was only enlarging the circle of his errors, by pretending to understand that which it is more than possible he will never be permitted to know; his self-love prevented him from feeling, that whenever he punished another for not thinking as he did, that he committed the greatest injustice, unless he was satisfactorily able to prove that other wrong, and himself right: that if he himself was obliged to have recourse to hypothesis—to gratuitous suppositions, whereon to found his doctrine, that from the very fallibility of his nature, these might be erroneous: thus GALLILEO was persecuted, because the metaphysicians, the theologians of his day, chose to make others believe what it was evident they did not themselves understand.

As soon as I feel an impulse, or experience motion, I am under the necessity to acknowledge extent, solidity, density, impenetrability in the substance I see move, or from which I receive impulse: thus, when action is attributed to any cause whatever, I am obliged to consider it MATERIAL. I may be ignorant of its individual nature, of its mode of action, or of its generic properties; but I cannot deceive myself in general properties, which are common to all matter: this ignorance will only be increased, when I shall take that for granted of a being, of which from that moment I am precluded by what I admit from forming any idea, which moreover deprives it completely either of the faculty of moving itself, giving an impulse, or acting. Thus, according to the received idea of the term, a spiritual substance that moves itself, that gives motion to matter, and that acts, implies a contradiction, that necessarily infers a total impossibility.

The partizans of spirituality believe they answer the difficulties they have accumulated, by asserting that "*the soul is entire—is whole under each point of its extent.*" If an absurd answer will solve difficulties, they certainly have done it. But let us examine this reply:—it will be found that this indivisible part which is called soul, however insensible or however minute, must yet remain something: then an infinity of unextended substances, or the same substance having no dimensions, repeated an infinity of times, would constitute a substance that has extent: this cannot be what they mean, because according to this principle, the human soul would then be as infinite as the Author of Nature; seeing that they have stated this to be a being without extent, who is an infinity of times whole in each part of the universe. But when there shall appear as much solidity in the answer as there is a want of it, it must be acknowledged that in whatever manner the spirit or the soul finds itself in its extent, when the body moves forward the soul does not remain behind; if so, it has a quality in common with the body, peculiar to matter; since it is conveyed from place to place jointly with the body. Thus, when even the soul should be admitted to be immaterial, what conclusion must be drawn? Entirely submitted to the motion of the body, without this body it would remain dead and inert. This soul would only be part of a two-fold machine, necessarily impelled forward by a concatenation, or connection with the whole. It would resemble a bird, which a child conducts at its pleasure, by the string with which it is bound.

Thus, it is for want of consulting experience, by not attending to reason, that man has darkened his ideas upon the concealed principle of his motion. If, disentangled from prejudice—if, destitute of gratuitous suppositions—if, throwing aside error, he would contemplate his soul, or the moving principle that acts within him, he would be convinced that it forms a part of its body, that it cannot be distinguished from it, but by abstraction; that it is only the body itself, considered relatively with some of its functions, or with those faculties of which its nature, or its peculiar organization, renders it susceptible:—he will perceive that this soul is obliged to undergo the same changes as the body; that it is born with it; that it expands itself with it; that like the body, it passes through a state of infancy, a period of weakness, a season of inexperience; that it enlarges itself, that it strengthens itself, in the same progression; that like the body, it arrives at an adult age or reaches maturity; that it is then, and not till then, it obtains the faculty of fulfilling certain functions; that it is in this stage, and in no other, that it enjoys reason; that it displays more or less wit, judgment, and manly activity; that like the body, it is subject to those vicissitudes which exterior causes obliges it to undergo by their influence; that, conjointly with the body, it suffers, enjoys, partakes of its pleasures, shares its pains, is sound when the body is healthy, and diseased when the body is oppressed with sickness; that like the body, it is continually modified by the different degrees of density in the atmosphere; by the variety of the seasons, and by the various properties of the aliments received into the stomach: in short, he would be obliged to acknowledge that at some periods it manifests visible signs of torpor, stupefaction, decrepitude, and death.

In despite of this analogy, or rather this continual identity, of the soul with the body, man has been desirous of distinguishing their essence; he has therefore made the soul an inconceivable being: but in order that he might form to himself some idea of it, he was, notwithstanding, obliged to have recourse to material beings, and to their manner of acting. The word *spirit*, therefore, presents to the mind no other ideas than those of breathing, of respiration, of wind. Thus, when it is said the *soul is a spirit*, it really means nothing more than that its mode of action is like that of breathing: which though invisible in itself, or acting without being seen, nevertheless produces very visible effects. But breath, it is acknowledged, is a material cause; it is allowed to be air modified; it is not, therefore, a simple or pure substance, such as the moderns designate under the name of SPIRIT.

It is rather singular that in the Hebrew, the Greek, and the Latin, the synonymy, or corresponding term for spirit should signify *breath*. The metaphysicians themselves can best say why they have adopted such a word, to designate the substance they have distinguished from matter: some of them, fearful they should not have distinct beings enough, have gone farther, and compounded man of three substances, BODY, SOUL, and INTELLECT.

Although the word *spirit* is so very ancient among men, the sense attached to it by the moderns is quite new: the idea of spirituality, as admitted at this day, is a recent production of the imagination. Neither PYTHAGORAS nor PLATO, however heated their brain, however decided their taste for the marvellous, appear to have understood by spirit an immaterial substance, or one without extent, devoid of parts; such as that of which the moderns have formed the human soul, the concealed author of motion. The ancients, by the word spirit, were desirous to define matter of an extreme subtilty, of a purer quality than that which acted grossly on our senses. In consequence, some have regarded the soul as an ethereal substance; others as igneous matter; others again have compared it to light. DEMOCRITUS made it consist in motion, consequently gave it a manner of existence. ARISTOXENES, who was himself a musician, made it harmony. ARISTOTLE regarded the soul as the moving faculty, upon which depended the motion of living bodies.

The earliest doctors of Christianity had no other idea of the soul, than that it was material. TERTULLIAN, ARNOBIUS, CLEMENT of ALEXANDRIA, ORIGEN, SAINT JUSTIN, IRENAEUS, have all of them discoursed upon it; but have never spoken of it other than as a corporeal substance—as matter. It was reserved for their successors at a great distance of time, to make the human soul and the soul of the world *pure spirits*; that is to say, immaterial substances, of which it is impossible they could form any accurate idea: by degrees this incomprehensible doctrine of spirituality, conformable without doubt to the views of those who make it a principle to annihilate reason, prevailed over the others: But it might be fairly asked, if the pretended proofs of this doctrine owe themselves to a man, who on a much more comprehensible point has been proved in error; if, on that which time has shewn was accessible to man's reason, the great champion in support of this dogma was deceived; are we not bound to examine, with the most rigorous investigation, the reasonings, the evidence, of one who was the decided, the proven child of enthusiasm and error? Yet DESCARTES, to whose sublime errors the world is indebted for the Newtonian system, although before him the soul had been considered spiritual, was the first who established that, "*that which thinks ought to be distinguished from matter;*" from whence he concludes rather hastily, that the soul, or that which thinks in man, is a spirit; or a simple indivisible substance. Perhaps it would have been more logical, more consistent with reason, to have said, since man, who is matter, who has no idea but of matter, enjoys the faculty of thought, matter can think; that is, it is susceptible of that particular modification called thought.

However this may be, this doctrine was believed divine, supernatural, because it was inconceivable to man. Those who dared believe even that which was believed before; namely, *that the soul was material*, were held as rash inconsiderate madmen, or else treated as enemies to the welfare and happiness of the human race. When man had once renounced experience; when he had abjured his reason; when he had joined the banner of this enthusiastic novelty; he did nothing more, day after day, than subtilize the delirium, the ravings of his imagination: he pleased himself by continually sinking deeper into the most unfathomable depths of error: he felicitated himself on his discoveries; on his pretended knowledge; in an exact ratio as his understanding became enveloped in the mists of darkness, environed with the clouds of ignorance. Thus, in consequence of man's reasoning upon false principles; of having relinquished the evidence of his senses; the moving principle within him, the concealed author of motion, has been made a mere chimera, a mere being of the imagination, because he has divested it of all known properties; because he has attached to it nothing but properties which, from the very nature of his existence, he is incapacitated to comprehend.

The doctrine of spirituality, such as it now exists, offers nothing but vague ideas; or rather is the absense of all ideas. What does it present to the mind, but a substance which possesses nothing of which our senses enable us to have a knowledge? Can it be truth that a man is able to figure to himself a being not material, having neither extent nor parts, which, nevertheless, acts upon matter without having any point of contact, any kind of analogy with it; and which itself receives the impulse of matter by means of material organs, which announce to it the presence of other beings? Is it possible to conceive the union of the soul with the body; to comprehend how this material body can bind, enclose, constrain, determine a fugitive being which escapes all our senses? Is it honest, is it plain dealing, to solve these difficulties, by saying there is a mystery in them; that they are the effects of a power, more inconceivable than the human soul; than its mode of acting, however concealed from our view? When to resolve these problems, man is obliged to have recourse to miracles or to make the Divinity interfere, does he not avow his own ignorance? When, notwithstanding the ignorance he is thus obliged to avow by availing himself of the divine agency, he tells us, this immaterial substance, this soul, shall experience the action of the element of fire, which he allows to be material;

when he confidently says this soul shall be burnt; shall suffer in purgatory; have we not a right to believe, that either he has a design to deceive us, or else that he does not himself understand that which he is so anxious we should take upon his word?

Let us not then be surprised at those subtile hypotheses, as ingenious as they are unsatisfactory, to which theological prejudice has obliged the most profound modern speculators to recur; when they have undertaken to reconcile the spirituality of the soul, with the physical action of material beings, on this incorporeal substance; its re-action upon these beings; its union with the body. When the human mind permits itself to be guided by authority without proof, to be led forward by enthusiasm; when it renounces the evidence of its senses; what can it do more than sink into error? Let those who doubt this, read the metaphysical romances of LEIBNITZ, DESCARTES, MALEBRANCHE, CUDWORTH, and many others: let them coolly examine the ingenious, but fanciful systems entitled *the pre-established harmony of occasional causes; physical pre-motion, &c.*

If man wishes to form to himself clear, perspicuous ideas of his soul, let him throw himself back on his experience—let him renounce his prejudices—let him avoid theological conjecture—let him tear the bandages which he has been taught to think necessary, but with which he has been blind-folded, only to confound his reason. If it be wished to draw man to virtue, let the natural philosopher, let the anatomist, let the physician, unite their experience; let them compare their observations, in order to show what ought to be thought of a substance, so disguised, so hidden by absurdities, as not easily to be known. Their discoveries may perhaps teach moralists the true motive-power that ought to influence the actions of man—legislators, the true motives that should actuate him, that should excite him to labour to the welfare of society—sovereigns, the means of rendering their subjects truly happy; of giving solidity to the power of the nations committed to their charge. Physical souls have physical wants, and demand physical happiness. These are real, are preferable objects, to that variety of fanciful chimeras, each in its turn giving place to the other, with which the mind of man has been fed during so many ages. Let us, then, labour to perfect the morality of man; let us make it agreeable to him; let us excite in him an ardent thirst for its purity: we shall presently see his morals become better, himself become happier; his soul become calm and serene; his will determined to virtue, by the natural, by the palpable motives held out to him. By the diligence, by the care which legislators shall bestow on natural philosophy, they will form citizens of sound understandings; robust and well constituted; who, finding themselves happy, will be themselves accessary to that useful impulse so necessary for their soul. When the body is suffering, when nations are unhappy, the soul cannot be in a proper state. *Mens sana in corpore sano*, a sound mind in a sound body, will be always able to make a good citizen.

The more man reflects, the more he will be convinced that the soul, very far from being distinguished from the body, is only the body itself, considered relatively to some of its functions, or to some of the modes of existing or acting, of which it is susceptible whilst it enjoys life. Thus, the soul is man, considered relatively to the faculty he has of feeling, of thinking, of acting in a mode resulting from his peculiar nature; that is to say, from his properties, from his particular organization: from the modifications, whether durable or transitory, which the beings who act upon him cause his machine to undergo.

Those who have distinguished the soul from the body, appear only to have distinguished their brain from themselves. Indeed, the brain is the common center, where all the nerves, distributed through every part of the body, meet and blend themselves: it is by the aid of this interior organ that all those operations are performed which are attributed to the soul: it is the impulse, or the motion, communicated to the nerve, which modifies the brain: in consequence, it re-acts, or gives play to the bodily organs; or rather it acts upon itself, and becomes capable of producing within itself a great variety of motion, which has been designated *intellectual faculties*.

From this it may be seen that some philosophers have been desirous to make a spiritual substance of the brain. It is evidently nothing but ignorance that has given birth to and accredited this system, which embraces so little, either of the natural or the rational. It is from not having studied himself, that man has supposed he was compounded with an agent, essentially different from his body: in examining this body, he will find that it is quite useless to recur to hypothesis for the explanation of the various phenomena it presents to his contemplation; that hypothesis can do nothing more than lead him out of the right road to the information after which he seeks. What obscures this question, arises from this, that man cannot see himself: indeed, for this purpose, that would be requisite which is impossible; namely, that he could he at one and the same moment both within and without himself: he may be compared to an Eolian harp, that issues sounds of itself, and should demand what it is that causes it to give them forth? It does not perceive that the sensitive quality of its chords causes the air to brace them; that being so braced, it is rendered sonorous by every gust of wind with which it happens to come in contact.

When a theologian, obstinately bent on admitting into man two substances essentially different, is asked why he multiplies beings without necessity? he will reply, because *"thought cannot be a property of matter."* If, then, it be enquired of him, *cannot God give to matter the faculty of thought?* he will answer, *"no! seeing that God cannot do impossible things!"* According to his principles, it is as impossible that spirit or thought can produce matter, as it is impossible that matter can produce spirit or thought: it might, therefore, be concluded against him, that the world was not made by a spirit, any more than a spirit was made by the world. But in this case, does not the theologian, according to his own assertion, acknowledge himself to be the true atheist?

Does he not, in fact, circumscribe the attributes of the Deity, and deny his power, to suit his own purpose? Yet these men demand implicit belief in doctrines, which they are obliged to maintain by the most contradictory assertions.

The more experience we collect, the more we shall be convinced that the word *spirit*, in its present received usage, conveys no one sense that is tangible, either to ourselves or to those that invented it; consequently cannot be of the least use, either in physics or morals. What modern metaphysicians believe and understand by the word, is nothing more than an *occult* power, imagined to explain *occult* qualities and actions, but which, in fact, explains nothing. Savage nations admit of spirits, to account to themselves for those effects, which to them appear marvellous, as long as their ignorance knows not the cause to which they ought to be attributed. In attributing to spirits the phenomena of Nature, as well as those of the human body, do we, in fact, do any thing more than reason like savages? Man has filled Nature with spirits, because he has almost always been ignorant of the true causes of those effects by which he was astonished. Not being acquainted with the powers of Nature, he has supposed her to be animated by a *great spirit*: not understanding the energy of the human frame, he has in like manner conjectured it to be animated by a *minor spirit*: from this it would appear, that whenever he wished to indicate the unknown cause of a phenomena, he knew not how to explain in a natural manner, he had recourse to the word *spirit*. In short, *spirit* was a term by which he solved all his doubts, and cleared up his ignorance to himself. It was according to these principles that when the AMERICANS first beheld the terrible effects of gunpowder, they ascribed the cause to wrathful spirits, to their enraged divinities: it was by adopting these principles, that our ancestors believed in a plurality of gods, in ghosts, in genii, &c. Pursuing the same track, we ought to attribute to spirits gravitation, electricity, magnetism, &c. &c. It is somewhat singular, that priests have in all ages so strenuously upheld those systems which time has exploded; that they have appeared to be either the most crafty or the most ignorant of men. Where are now the priests of Apollo, of Juno, of the Sun, and a thousand others? Yet these are the men, who in all times have persecuted those who have been the first to give natural explanations of the phenomena of Nature, as witness ANAXAGORAS, ARISTOTLE, GALLILEO, DESCARTES, &c. &c.

CHAP. VIII.
The Intellectual Faculties derived from the Faculty of Feeling.

To convince ourselves that the faculties called *intellectual*, are only certain modes of existence, or determinate manners of acting, which result from the peculiar organization of the body, we have only to analyze them; we shall then see that all the operations which are attributed to the soul, are nothing more than certain modifications of the body; of which a substance that is without extent, that has no parts, that is immaterial, is not susceptible.

The first faculty we behold in the living man, and that from which all his others flow, is *feeling*: however inexplicable this faculty may appear, on a first view, if it be examined closely, it will be found to be a consequence of the essence, or a result of the properties of organized beings; the same as *gravity, magnetism, elasticity, electricity,* &c. result from the essence or nature of some others. We shall also find these last phenomena are not less inexplicable than that of feeling. Nevertheless, if we wish to define to ourselves a clear and precise idea of it, we shall find that feeling is a particular manner of being moved—a mode of receiving an impulse peculiar to certain organs of animated bodies, which is occasioned by the presence of a material object that acts upon these organs, and transmit the impulse or shock to the brain.

Man only feels by the aid of nerves dispersed through his body; which is itself, to speak correctly, nothing more than a great nerve; or may be said to resemble a large tree, of which the branches experience the action of the root, communicated through the trunk. In man the nerves unite and lose themselves in the brain; that intestine is the true seat of feeling: like the spider in the centre of his web, it is quickly warned of all the changes that happen to the body, even at the extremities to which it sends its filaments and branches. Experience enables us to ascertain, that man ceases to feel in those parts of his body of which the communication with the brain is intercepted; he feels very little, or not at all, whenever this organ is itself deranged or affected in too lively a manner. A proof of this is afforded in the transactions of the Royal Academy of Sciences at Paris: they inform us of a man who had his scull taken off, in the room of which his brain was recovered with skin; in proportion as a pressure was made by the hand on his brain, the man fell into a kind of insensibility, which deprived him of all feeling. BARTOLIN says, the brain of a man is twice as big as that of an ox. This observation had been already made by ARISTOTLE. In the dead body of an idiot dissected by WILLIS, the brain was found smaller than ordinary: he says the greatest difference he found between the parts of the body of this idiot, and those of wiser men, was, that the plexus of the intercostal nerves, which is the mediator between the brain and the heart, was extremely small, accompanied by a less number of nerves than usual. According to WILLIS, the ape is, of all animals, that which has the largest brain, relatively to his size: he is also, after man, that which has the most intelligence: this is further confirmed, by the name he bears in the soil, to which he is indigenous, which is *ourang outang*, or the man beast. There is, therefore, every reason to believe that it is entirely in the brain, that consists the difference, that is found not only between man and beasts, but also between the man of wit, and the fool: between the thinking man, and he who is ignorant; between the man of sound understanding, and the madman: a multitude of experience, serves to prove, that those persons who are most accustomed to use their intellectual faculties, have their brain more extended than others: the same has been remarked of watermen, that they have arms much longer than other men.

However this may be, the sensibility of the brain, and all its parts, is a fact: if it be asked, whence comes this property? We shall reply, it is the result of an arrangement, of a combination, peculiar to the animal: it is thus that milk, bread, wine, change themselves in the substance of man, who is a sensible being: this insensible matter becomes sensible, in combining itself with a sensible whole. Some philosophers think that sensibility is a universal quality of matter: in this case, it would be useless to seek from whence this property is derived, as we know it by its effects. If this hypothesis be admitted, in like manner as two kinds of motion are distinguished in Nature, the one called *live* force, the other *dead*, or *inert* force, two sorts of sensibility will be distinguished, the one active or alive, the other inert or dead. Then to animalize a substance, is only to destroy the obstacles that prevent its being active or sensible. In fact, sensibility is either a quality which communicates itself like motion, and which is acquired by combination; or this sensibility is a property inherent in all matter: in both, or either case, an unextended being, without parts, such as the human soul is said to be, can neither be the cause of it nor submitted to its operation; but we may fairly conclude, that all the parts of Nature enjoy the capability to arrive at animation; the obstacle is only in the state, not in the quality. Life is the perfection of Nature: she has no parts which do not tend to it— which do not attain it by the same means. Life in an insect, a dog, a man, has no other difference, than that this act is more perfect, relatively to ourselves in proportion to the structure of the organs: if, therefore, it be asked, what is requisite to animate a body? we reply, it needs no foreign aid; it is sufficient that the power of Nature be joined to its organization.

The conformation, the arrangement, the texture, the delicacy of the organs, as well exterior as interior, which compose men and animals, render their parts extremely mobile, or make their machine susceptible of being moved with great facility. In a body, which is only a heap of fibres, a mass of nerves, contiguous one to the other, united in a common center, always ready to act; in a whole, composed of fluids and solids, of which the parts are in equilibrium, the smallest touching each other, are active in their motion, communicating reciprocally, alternately and in succession, the impression, oscillations, and shocks they receive; in such a composition, it is not surprising that the slightest impulse propagates itself with celerity; that the shocks excited in its remotest parts, make themselves quickly felt in the brain, whose delicate texture renders it susceptible of being itself very easily modified. Air, fire, water, agents the most inconstant, possessing the most rapid motion, circulate continually in the fibres, incessantly penetrate the nerves: without doubt these contribute to that incredible celerity with which the brain is acquainted with what passes at the extremities of the body.

Notwithstanding the great mobility with which man's organization renders him susceptible, although exterior as well as interior causes are continually acting upon him, he does not always feel in a distinct, in a decided manner, the impulse given to his senses: indeed, he does not feel it, until it has produced some change, or given some shock to his brain. Thus, although completely environed by air, he does not feel its action, until it is so modified, as to strike with a sufficient degree of force on his organs; to penetrate his skin, through which his brain is warned of its presence. Thus, during a profound and tranquil sleep, undisturbed by any dream, man ceases to feel. In short, notwithstanding the continued motion that agitates his frame, man does not appear to feel, when this motion acts in a convenient order; he does not perceive a state of health, but he discovers a state of grief or sickness; because, in the first, his brain does not receive too lively an impulse, whilst in the others, his nerves are contracted, shocked, and agitated, with violent, with disorderly motion: these communicating with his brain, give notice that some cause acts strongly upon them—impels them in a manner that bears no analogy with their natural habit: this constitutes, in him, that peculiar mode of existing which he calls *grief*.

On the other hand, it sometimes happens that exterior objects produce very considerable changes on his body, without his perceiving them at the moment. Often, in the heat of battle, the soldier perceives not that he is dangerously wounded, because, at the time, the rapidity, the multiplicity of impetuous motion that assails his brain, does not permit him to distinguish the particular change a part of his body has undergone by the wound. In short, when a great number of causes are simultaneously acting on him with too much vivacity, he sinks under their accumulated pressure,—he swoons—he loses his senses—he is deprived of feeling.

In general, feeling only obtains, when the brain can distinguish distinctly, the impressions made on the organs with which it has communication; it is the distinct shock, the decided modification man undergoes, that constitutes *conscience*. Doctor Clarke, says to this effect: "Conscience is the act of reflecting, by means of which I know that I think, and that my thoughts, or my actions belong to me, and not to another." From this it will appear, that *feeling* is a mode of being, a marked change, produced on our brain, occasioned by the impulse communicated to our organs, whether by interior or exterior agents, by which it is modified either in a durable or transient manner: it is not always requisite that man's organs should be moved by an exterior object, to enable him to feel that he should be conscious of the changes effected in him: he can feel them within himself by means of an interior impulse; his brain is then modified, or rather he renews within himself the anterior modifications. We are not to be astonished that the brain should be necessarily warned of the shocks, of the impediments, of the changes that may happen to so complicated a machine as the human body, in which, notwithstanding all the parts are contiguous to the brain, and concentrate themselves in this brain, and are by their essence in a continual state of action and re-action.

When a man experiences the pains of the gout, he is conscious of them; in other words, he feels interiorly, that it has produced very marked, very distinct changes in him, without his perceiving, that he has received an impulse from any exterior cause; nevertheless, if he will recur to the true source of these changes, he will find that they have been wholly produced by exterior agents: they have been the consequence, either of his temperament; of the organization received from his parents; of the aliments with which his frame has been nourished; besides a thousand trivial, inappreciable causes, which congregating themselves by degrees produce in him the gouty humour; the effect of which is to make him feel in an acute and very lively manner. The pain of the gout engenders in his brain an idea, so modifies it that it acquires the faculty of representing to itself, of reiterating as it were, this pain when even he shall be no longer tormented with the gout: his brain, by a series of motion interiorly excited, is again placed in a state analogous to that in which it was when he really experienced this pain: but if he had never felt it, he would never have been in a capacity to form to himself any just idea of its excruciating torments.

The visible organs of man's body, by the intervention of which his brain is modified, take the name of *senses*. The various modifications which his brain receives by the aid of these senses, assumes a variety of names. *Sensation*, *perception*, and *idea*, are terms that designate nothing more than the changes produced in this interior organ, in consequence of impressions made on the exterior organs by bodies acting on them: these changes considered by themselves, are called *sensations*; they adopt the term *perception* when the brain is warned of their presence; *ideas* is that state of them in which the brain is able to ascribe them to the objects by which they have been produced.

Every *sensation*, then, is nothing more than the shock given to the organs, every *perception* is this shock propagated to the brain; every *idea* is the image of the object to which the sensation and the perception is to be ascribed. From whence it will be seen, that if the senses be not moved, there can neither be sensations, perceptions, nor ideas: this will be proved to those, who can yet permit themselves to doubt so demonstrable and striking a truth.

It is the extreme mobility of which man is capable, owing to his peculiar organization, that distinguishes him from other beings that are called insensible or inanimate; the different degrees of this mobility, of which the individuals of his species are susceptible, discriminate them from each other; make that incredible variety, that infinity of difference which is to be found, as well in their corporeal faculties, as in those which are mental or intellectual. From this mobility, more or less remarkable in each human being, results wit, sensibility, imagination, taste, &c.: for the present, however, let us follow the operation of the senses; let us examine in what manner they are acted upon, and are modified by exterior objects:—we will afterwards scrutinize the re-action of the interior organ or brain.

The eyes are very delicate, very movable organs, by means of which the sensation of light or colour is experienced: these give to the brain a distinct perception, in consequence of which, man forms an idea, generated by the action of luminous or coloured bodies: as soon as the eyelids are opened, the retina is affected in a peculiar manner; the fluid, the fibres, the nerves, of which they are composed, are excited by shocks which they communicate to the brain; to which they delineate the images of the bodies from which they have received the impulse; by this means, an idea is acquired of the colour, the size, the form, the distance of these bodies: it is thus that may he explained the mechanism of *sight*.

The mobility and the elasticity of which the skin is rendered susceptible, by the fibres and nerves which form its texture, accounts for the rapidity with which this envelope to the human body is affected when applied to any other body; by their agency, the brain has notice of its presence, of its extent, of its roughness, of its smoothness, of its surface, of its pressure of its ponderosity, &c. Qualities from which the brain derives distinct perceptions, which breed in it a diversity of ideas; it is this that constitutes the *touch* or *feeling*.

The delicacy of the membrane by which the interior of the nostrils is covered, renders them easily susceptible of irritation, even by the invisible and impalpable corpuscles that emanate from odorous bodies: by these means sensations are excited, the brain has perceptions, and generates ideas: it is this that forms the sense of *smelling*.

The mouth, filled with nervous, sensible, movable, irritable glands, saturated with juices suitable to the dissolution of saline substances, is affected in a very lively manner by the aliments which pass through it for the nourishment of the body; these glands transmit to the brain the impressions received: perceptions are of consequence; ideas follow: it is from this mechanism that results *taste*.

The ear, whose conformation fits it to receive the various impulses of air, diversely modified, communicates to the brain the shocks or sensations; these breed the perception of sound, and generate the idea of sonorous bodies: it is this that constitutes *hearing*.

Such are the only means by which man receives sensations, perceptions, and ideas. These successive modifications of his brain are effects produced by objects that give impulse to his senses; they become themselves causes, producing in his soul new modifications, which are denominated *thought, reflection, memory, imagination, judgment, will, action*; the basis, however, of all these is *sensation*.

To form a precise notion of *thought*, it will be requisite to examine, step by step, what passes in man during the presence of any object whatever.

Suppose for a moment this object to be a peach: this fruit makes, at the first view, two different impressions on his eyes; that is to say, it produces two modifications, which are transmitted to the brain, which on this occasion experiences two new perceptions, or has two new ideas or modes of existence, designated by the terms *colour* and *rotundity*; in consequence, he has an idea of a body possessing roundness and colour: if he places his hand on this fruit, the organ of feeling having been set in action, his hand experiences three new impressions, which are called *softness, coolness, weight*, from whence result three new perceptions in the brain, he has consequently three new ideas: if he approximates this peach to his nose, the organ of *smelling* receives an impulse, which, communicated to the brain, a new perception arises, by which he acquires a new idea, called *odour*: if he carries this fruit to his mouth, the organ of taste becomes affected in a very lively manner: this impulse communicated to the brain, is followed by a perception that generates in him the idea of *flavour*. In re-uniting all these impressions, or these various modifications of his organs, which it have been consequently transmitted to his brain; that is to say, in combining the different sensations, perceptions, and ideas, that result from the impulse he has received, he has an idea of a whole, which he designates by the name of a peach, with which he can then occupy his thoughts.

From this it is sufficiently proved that thought has a commencement, a duration, an end; or rather a generation, a succession, a dissolution, like all the other modifications of matter; like them, thought is excited, is determined, is increased, is divided, is compounded, is simplified, &c. If, therefore, the soul, or the principle that thinks, be indivisible; how does it happen, that this soul has the faculty of memory, or of forgetfulness; is capacitated to think successively, to divide, to abstract, to combine, to extend its ideas, to retain them, or to lose them? How can it cease to think? If forms appear divisible in matter, it is only in considering them by abstraction, after the method, of geometricians; but this divisibility of form exists not in Nature, in which there is neither a point, an atom, nor form perfectly regular; it must therefore be concluded, that the forms of matter are not less indivisible than thought.

What has been said is sufficient to show the generation of sensations, of perceptions, of ideas, with their association, or connection in the brain: it will be seen that these various modifications are nothing more than the consequence of successive impulses, which the exterior organs transmit to the interior organ, which enjoys the faculty of thought, that is to say, to feel in itself the different modifications it has received, or to perceive the various ideas which it has generated; to combine them, to separate them, to extend them, to abridge them, to compare them, to renew them, &c. From whence it will be seen, that thought is nothing more than the perception of certain modifications, which the brain either gives to itself, or has received from exterior objects.

Indeed, not only the interior organ perceives the modifications it receives from without, but again it has the faculty of modifying itself; of considering the changes which take place in it, the motion by which it is agitated in its peculiar operations, from which it imbibes new perceptions and new ideas. It is the exercise of this power to fall back upon itself, that is called *reflection*.

From this it will appear, that for man to think and to reflect, is to feel, or perceive within himself the impressions, the sensations, the ideas, which have been furnished to his brain by those objects which give impulse to his senses, with the various changes which his brain produced on itself in consequence.

Memory is the faculty which the brain has of renewing in itself the modifications it has received, or rather, to restore itself to a state similar to that in which it has been placed by the sensations, the perceptions, the ideas, produced by exterior objects, in the exact order it received them, without any new action on the part of these objects, or even when these objects are absent; the brain perceives that these modifications assimilate with those it formerly experienced in the presence of the objects to which it relates, or attributes them. Memory is faithful, when these modifications are precisely the same; it is treacherous, when they differ from those which the organs have exteriorly experienced.

Imagination in man is only the faculty which the brain has of modifying itself, or of forming to itself new perceptions, upon the model of those which it has anteriorly received through the action of exterior objects on the senses. The brain, then, does nothing more than combine ideas which it has already formed, which it recalls to itself, from which it forms a whole, or a collection of modifications, which it has not received, which exists no-where but in itself, although the individual ideas, or the parts of which this ideal whole is composed, have been previously communicated to it, in consequence of the impulse given to the senses by exterior objects: it is thus man forms to himself the idea of *centaurs*, or a being composed of a man and a horse, of *hyppogriffs*, or a being composed of a horse with wings and a griffin, besides a thousand other objects, equally ridiculous. By memory, the brain renews in itself the sensations, the perceptions, and the ideas which it has received or generated; represents to itself the objects which have actually moved its organs. By imagination it combines them variously: forms objects in their place which have not moved its organs, although it is perfectly acquainted with the elements or ideas of which it composes them. It is thus that man, by combining a great number of ideas borrowed from himself, such as justice, wisdom, goodness, intelligence, &c. by the aid of imagination, has formed various ideal beings, or imaginary wholes, which he has called JUPITER, JUNO, BRAMAH, SATURN, &c.

Judgment is the faculty which the brain possesses of comparing with each other the modifications it receives, the ideas it engenders, or which it has the power of awakening within itself, to the end that it may discover their relations, or their effects.

Will is a modification of the brain, by which it is disposed to action, that is to say, to give such an impulse to the organs of the body, as can induce to act in a manner, that will procure for itself what is requisite to modify it in a mode analogous to its own existence, or to enable it to avoid that by which it can be injured. To *will* is to be disposed to *action*. The exterior objects, or the interior ideas, which give birth to this disposition are called *motives*, because they are the springs or movements which determine it to act, that is to say, which give play to the organs of the body. Thus, *voluntary actions* are the motion of the body, determined by the modification of the brain. Fruit hanging on a tree, through the agency of the visual organs, modifies the brain in such a manner as to dispose the arm to stretch itself forth to cull it; again, it modifies it in another manner, by which it excites the hand to carry it to the mouth.

All the modifications which the interior organ or the brain receives, all the sensations, all the perceptions, all the ideas that are generated by the objects which give impulse to the senses, or which it renews within itself by its own peculiar faculties, are either favourable or prejudicial to man's mode of existence, whether that be transitory or habitual: they dispose the interior organ to action, which it exercises by reason of its own peculiar energy: this action is not, however, the same in all the individuals of the human species, depending much on their respective temperaments. From hence the PASSIONS have their birth: these are more or less violent; they are, however, nothing more than the motion of the will, determined by the objects which give it activity; consequently composed of the analogy or of the discordance which is found between these objects, man's peculiar mode of existence, and the force of his temperament. From this it results, that the passions are modes of existence or modifications of the brain; which either attract or repel those objects by which man is surrounded; that consequently they are submitted in their action to the physical laws of attraction and repulsion.

The faculty of perceiving or of being modified, as well by itself as exterior objects which the brain enjoys is sometimes designated by the term *understanding*. To the assemblage of the various faculties of which this interior organ is susceptible, is applied the name of *intelligence*. To a determined mode in which the brain exercises the faculties peculiar to itself, is given the appellation of *reason*. The dispositions or the modifications of the brain, some of them constant, others transitory, which give impulse to the beings of the human species, causing them to act, are styled *wit, wisdom, goodness, prudence, virtue, &c.*

In short, as there will be an opportunity presently to prove, all the intellectual faculties—that is to say, all the modes of action attributed to the soul, may be reduced to the modifications, to the qualities, to the modes of existence, to the changes produced by the motion of the brain; which is visibly in man the seat of feeling, the principle of all his actions. These modifications are to be attributed to the objects that strike on his senses; of which the impression is transmitted to the brain, or rather to the ideas, which the perceptions caused by the action of these objects on his senses have there generated, and which it has the faculty to re-produce. This brain moves itself in its turn, re-acts upon itself, gives play to the organs, which concentrate themselves in it, or which are rather nothing more than an extension of its own peculiar substance. It is thus the concealed motion of the interior organ, renders itself sensible by outward and visible signs. The brain, affected by a modification which is called FEAR, diffuses a paleness over the countenance, excites a tremulous motion in the limbs called trembling. The brain, affected by a sensation of GRIEF, causes tears to flow from the eyes, even without being moved by any exterior object; an idea which it retraces with great strength, suffices to give it very little modifications, which visibly have an influence on the whole frame.

In all this, nothing more is to be perceived than the same substance which acts diversely on the various parts of the body. If it be objected that this mechanism does not sufficiently explain the principles of the motion or the faculties of the soul; we reply, that it is in the same situation as all the other bodies of Nature, in which the most simple motion, the most ordinary phenomena, the most common modes of action are inexplicable mysteries, of which we shall never be able to fathom the first principles. Indeed, how can we flatter ourselves we shall ever be enabled to compass the true principle of that gravity by which a stone falls? Are we acquainted with the mechanism which produces attraction in some substances, repulsion in others? Are we in a condition to explain the communication of motion from one body to another? But it may be fairly asked,—Are the difficulties that occur, when attempting to explain the manner in which the soul acts, removed by making it a *spiritual being*, a substance of which we have not, nor cannot form one idea, which consequently must bewilder all the notions we are capable of forming to ourselves of this being? Let us then be contented to know that the soul moves itself, modifies itself, in consequence of material causes, which act upon it which give it activity: from whence the conclusion may he said to flow consecutively, that all its operations, all its faculties, prove that it is itself *material*.

CHAP. IX.
The Diversity of the Intellectual Faculties: they depend on Physical Causes, as do their Moral Qualities.—The Natural Principles of Society.—Morals.—Politics.

Nature is under the necessity of diversifying all her works. Elementary matter, different in its essence, must necessarily form different beings, various in their combinations, in their properties, in their modes of action, in their manner of existence. There is not, neither can there be, two beings, two combinations, which are mathematically and rigorously the same; because the place, the circumstances, the relations; the proportions, the modifications, never being exactly alike, the beings that result can never bear a perfect resemblance to each other: their modes of action must of necessity vary in something, even when we believe we find between them the greatest conformity.

In consequence of this principle, which every thing we see conspires to prove to be a truth, there are not two individuals of the human species who have precisely the same traits—who think exactly in the same manner—who view things under the same identical point of sight—who have decidedly the same ideas; consequently no two of them have uniformly the same system of conduct. The visible organs of man, as well as his concealed organs, have indeed some analogy, some common points of resemblance, some general conformity; which makes them appear, when viewed in the gross, to be affected in the same manner by certain causes: but the difference is infinite in the detail. The human soul may be compared to those instruments, of which the chords, already diversified in themselves, by the manner in which they have been spun, are also strung upon different notes: struck by the same impulse, each chord gives forth the sound that is peculiar to itself; that is to say, that which depends on its texture, its tension, its volume, on the momentary state in which it is placed by the circumambient air. It is this that produces the diversified spectacle, the varied scene, which the moral world offers to our view: it is from this that results the striking contrariety that is to be found in the minds, in the faculties, in the passions, in the energies, in the taste, in the imagination, in the ideas, in the opinions of man. This diversity is as great as that of his physical powers: like them it depends on his temperament, which is as much varied as his physiognomy. This variety gives birth to that continual series of action and reaction, which constitutes the life of the moral world: from this discordance results the harmony which at once maintains and preserves the human race.

The diversity found among the individuals of the human species, causes inequalities between man and man: this inequality constitutes the support of society. If all men were equal in their bodily powers, in their mental talents, they would not have any occasion for each other: it is the variation of his faculties, the inequality which this places him in, with regard to his fellows, that renders morals necessary to man: without these, he would live by himself, he would remain an isolated being. From whence it may be perceived, that this inequality of which man so often complains without cause—this impossibility which each man finds when in an isolated state, when left to himself, when unassociated with his fellow men, to labour efficaciously to his own welfare, to make his own security, to ensure his own conservation; places him in the happy situation of associating with his like, of depending on his fellow associates, of meriting their succour, of propitiating them to his views, of attracting their regard, of calling in their aid to chase away, by common and united efforts, that which would have the power to trouble or derange the order of his existence. In consequence of man's diversity, of the inequality that results, the weaker is obliged to seek the protection of the stronger; this, in his turn, recurs to the understanding, to the talents, to the industry of the weaker, whenever his judgment points out he can be useful to him: this natural inequality furnishes the reason why nations distinguish those citizens who have rendered their country eminent services. It is in consequence of his exigencies that man honors and recompenses those whose understanding, good deeds, assistance, or virtues, have procured for him real or supposed advantages, pleasures, or agreeable sensations of any sort: it is by this means that genius gains an ascendancy over the mind of man, and obliges a whole people to acknowledge its powers. Thus, the diversity and inequality of the faculties, as well corporeal as mental or intellectual, renders man necessary to his fellow man, makes him a social being, and incontestibly proves to him the necessity of morals.

According to this diversity of faculties, the individuals of the human species are divided into different classes, each in proportion to the effects produced, or the different qualities that may be remarked: all these varieties in man flow from the individual properties of his soul, or from the particular modification of his brain. It is thus, that wit, imagination, sensibility, talents, &c. diversify to infinity the differences that are to be found in man. It is thus, that some are called good, others wicked; some are denominated virtuous, others vicious; some are ranked as learned, others as ignorant; some are considered reasonable, others unreasonable, &c.

If all the various faculties attributed to the soul are examined, it will be found that like those of the body they are to be ascribed to physical causes, to which it will be very easy to recur. It will be found that the powers of the soul are the same as those of the body; that they always depend on the organization of this body, on its peculiar properties, on the permanent or transitory modifications that it undergoes; in a word, on its temperament.

Temperament is, in each individual, the habitual state in which he finds the fluids and the solids of which his body is composed. This temperament varies, by reason of the elements or matter that predominate in him, in consequence of the different combinations, of the various modifications, which this matter, diversified in itself, undergoes in his machine. Thus, in one, the blood is superabundant; in another, the bile; in a third, phlegm, &c.

It is from Nature—from his parents—from causes, which from the first moment of his existence have unceasingly modified him, that man derives his temperament. It is in his mother's womb that he has attracted the matter which, during his whole life, shall have an influence on his intellectual faculties—on his energies—on his passions—on his conduct. The very nourishment he takes, the quality of the air he respires, the climate he inhabits, the education he receives, the ideas that are presented to him, the opinions he imbibes, modify this temperament. As these circumstances can never be rigorously the same in every point for any two men, it is by no means surprising that such an amazing variety, so great a contrariety, should be found in man; or that there should exist as many different temperaments, as there are individuals in the human species.

Thus, although man may bear a general resemblance, he differs essentially, as well by the texture of his fibres and the disposition of his nerves, as by the nature, the quality, the quantity of matter that gives them play, that sets his organs in motion. Man, already different from his fellow, by the elasticity of his fibres, the tension of his nerves, becomes still more distinguished by a variety of other circumstances: he is more active, more robust, when he receives nourishing aliments, when he drinks wine, when he takes exercise: whilst another, who drinks nothing but water, who takes less juicy nourishment, who languishes in idleness, shall be sluggish and feeble.

All these causes have necessarily an influence on the mind, on the passions, on the will; in a word, on what are called the intellectual faculties. Thus, it may he observed, that a man of a sanguine constitution, is commonly lively, ingenious, full of imagination, passionate, voluptuous, enterprising; whilst the phlegmatic man is dull, of a heavy understanding, slow of conception, inactive, difficult to be moved, pusillanimous, without imagination, or possessing it in a less lively degree, incapable of taking any strong measures, or of willing resolutely.

If experience was consulted, in the room of prejudice, the physician would collect from morals, the key to the human heart: in curing the body, he would sometimes be assured of curing the mind. Man, in making a spiritual substance of his soul, has contented himself with administering to it spiritual remedies, which either have no influence over his temperament, or do it an injury. The doctrine of the spirituality of the soul has rendered morals a conjectural science, that does not furnish a knowledge of the true motives which ought to be put in activity, in order to influence man to his welfare. If, calling experience to his assistance, man sought out the elements which form the basis of his temperament, or of the greater number of the individuals composing a nation, he would then discover what would be most proper for him,—that which could be most convenient to his mode of existence— which could most conduce to his true interest—what laws would be necessary to his happiness— what institutions would be most useful for him—what regulations would be most beneficial. In short, morals and politics would be equally enabled to draw from *materialism*, advantages which the dogma of spirituality can never supply, of which it even precludes the idea. Man will ever remain a mystery, to those who shall obstinately persist in viewing him with eyes prepossessed by metaphysics; he will always be an enigma to those who shall pertinaciously attribute his actions to a principle, of which it is impossible to form to themselves any distinct idea. When man shall be seriously inclined to understand himself, let him sedulously endeavour to discover the matter that enters into his combination, which constitutes his temperament; these discoveries will furnish him with the clue to the nature of his desires, to the quality of his passions, to the bent of his inclinations—will enable him to foresee his conduct on given occasions—will indicate the remedies that may be successfully employed to correct the defects of a vicious organization, of a temperament, as injurious to himself as to the society of which he is a member.

Indeed, it is not to be doubted that man's temperament is capable of being corrected, of being modified, of being changed, by causes as physical as the matter of which it is constituted. We are all in some measure capable of forming our own temperament: a man of a sanguine constitution, by taking less juicy nourishment, by abating its quantity, by abstaining from strong liquor, &c. may achieve the correction of the nature, the quality, the quantity, the tendency, the motion of the fluids, which predominate in his machine. A bilious man, or one who is melancholy, may, by the aid of certain remedies, diminish the mass of this bilious fluid; he may correct the blemish of his humours, by the assistance of exercise; he may dissipate his gloom, by the gaiety which results from increased motion. An European transplanted into Hindostan, will, by degrees, become quite a different man in his humours, in his ideas, in his temperament, in his character.

Although but few experiments have been made with a view to learn what constitutes the temperament of man, there are still enough if he would but deign to make use of them—if he would vouchsafe to apply to useful purposes the little experience he has gleaned. It would appear, speaking generally, that the igneous principle which chemists designate under the name of *phlogiston*, or inflammable matter, is that which in man yields him the most active life, furnishes him with the greatest energy, affords the greatest mobility to his frame, supplies the greatest spring to his organs, gives the greatest elasticity to his fibres, the greatest tension to his nerves, the greatest rapidity to his fluids. From these causes, which are entirely material, commonly result the dispositions or faculties called sensibility, wit, imagination, genius, vivacity, &c. which give the tone to the passions, to the will, to the moral actions of man. In this sense, it is with great justice we apply the expressions, 'warmth of soul,' 'ardency of imagination,' 'fire of genius,' &c.

It is this fiery element, diffused unequally, distributed in various proportions through the beings of the human species, that sets man in motion, gives him activity, supplies him with animal heat, and which, if we may be allowed the expression, renders him more or less alive. This igneous matter, so active, so subtle, dissipates itself with great facility, then requires to be reinstated in his system by means of aliments that contain it, which thereby become proper to restore his machine, to lend new warmth to the brain, to furnish it with the elasticity requisite to the performance of those functions which are called intellectual. It is this ardent matter contained in wine, in strong liquor, that gives to the most torpid, to the dullest, to the most sluggish man, a vivacity of which, without it, he would be incapable—which urges even the coward on to battle. When this fiery element is too abundant in man, whilst he is labouring under certain diseases, it plunges him into delirium; when it is in too weak or in too small a quantity, he swoons, he sinks to the earth. This igneous matter diminishes in his old age—it totally dissipates at his death. It would not be unreasonable to suppose, that what physicians call the nervous fluid, which so promptly gives notice to the brain of all that happens to the body, is nothing more than electric matter; that the various proportions of this matter diffused through his system, is the cause of that great diversity to be discovered in the human being, and in the faculties he possesses.

If the intellectual faculties of man, or his moral qualities, be examined according to the principles here laid down, the conviction must be complete that they are to be attributed to material causes, which have an influence more or less marked, either transitory or durable, over his peculiar organization. But where does he derive this organization, except it be from the parents from whom he receives the elements of a machine necessarily analogous to their own? From whence does he derive the greater or less quantity of igneous matter, or vivifying heat, that decides upon, that gives the tone to his mental qualities? It is from the mother who bore him in her womb, who has communicated to him a portion of that fire with which she was herself animated, which circulated through her veins with her blood;—it is from the aliments that have nourished him,—it is from the climate he inhabits,—it is from the atmosphere that surrounds: all these causes have an influence over his fluids, over his solids, and decide on his natural dispositions. In examining these dispositions, from whence his faculties depend, it will ever be found, that they are *corporeal*, that they are *material*.

The most prominent of these dispositions in man, is that physical sensibility from which flows all his intellectual or moral qualities. To feel, according to what has been said, is to receive an impulse, to be moved, to have a consciousness of the changes operated on his system. To have sensibility is nothing more than to be so constituted as to feel promptly, and in a very lively manner, the impressions of those objects which act upon him. A sensible soul is only man's brain, disposed in a mode to receive the motion communicated to it with facility, to re-act with promptness, by giving an instantaneous impulse to the organs. Thus the man is called sensible, whom the sight of the distressed, the contemplation of the unhappy, the recital of a melancholy tale, the witnessing of an afflicting catastrophe, or the idea of a dreadful spectacle, touches in so lively a manner as to enable the brain to give play to his lachrymal organs, which cause him to shed tears; a sign by which we recognize the effect of great grief, of extreme anguish in the human being. The man in whom musical sounds excite a degree of pleasure, or produce very remarkable effects, is said to have a *sensible* or a fine ear. In short, when it is perceived that eloquence—the beauty of the arts—the various objects that strike his senses, excite in him very lively emotions, he is said to possess a soul full of sensibility.

Wit, is a consequence of this physical sensibility; indeed, wit is nothing more than the facility which some beings, of the human species possess, of seizing with promptitude, of developing with quickness, a whole, with its different relations to other objects. *Genius*, is the facility with which some men comprehend this whole, and its various relations when they are difficult to be known, but useful to forward great and mighty projects. Wit may be compared to a piercing eye which perceives things quickly. Genius is an eye that comprehends at one view, all the points of an extended horizon: or what the French term *coup d'oeil*. True wit is that which perceives objects with their relations such as they really are. False wit is that which catches at relations, which do not apply to the object, or which arises from some blemish in the organization. True wit resembles the direction on a hand-post.

Imagination is the faculty of combining with promptitude ideas or images; it consists in the power man possesses of re-producing with ease the modifications of his brain: of connecting them, of attaching them to the objects to which they are suitable. When imagination does this, it gives pleasure; its fictions are approved, it embellishes Nature, it is a proof of the soundness of the mind, it aids truth: when on the contrary, it combines ideas, not formed to associate themselves with each other—when it paints nothing but disagreeable phantoms, it disgusts, its fictions are censured, it distorts Nature, it advocates falsehood, it is the proof of a disordered, of a deranged mind: thus poetry, calculated to render Nature more pathetic, more touching, pleases when it creates ideal beings, but which move us agreeably: we, therefore, forgive the illusions it has held forth, on account of the pleasure we have reaped from them. The hideous chimeras of superstition displease, because they are nothing more than the productions of a distempered imagination, that can only awaken the most afflicting sensations, fills us with the most disagreeable ideas.

Imagination, when it wanders, produces fanaticism, superstitious terrors, inconsiderate zeal, phrenzy, and the most enormous crimes: when it is well regulated, it gives birth to a strong predilection for useful objects, an energetic passion for virtue, an enthusiastic love of our country, and the most ardent friendship: the man who is divested of imagination, is commonly one in whose torpid constitution phlegm predominates over the igneous fluid, over that sacred fire, which is the great principle of his mobility, of that warmth of sentiment, which vivifies all his intellectual faculties. There must be enthusiasm for transcendent virtues as well as for atrocious crimes; enthusiasm places the soul in a state similar to that of drunkenness; both the one and the other excite in man that rapidity of motion which is approved, when good results, when its effects are beneficial; but which is censured, is called folly, delirium, crime, fury; when it produces nothing but disorder and confusion.

The mind is out of order, it is incapable of judging sanely—the imagination is badly regulated, whenever man's organization is not so modified, as to perform its functions with precision. At each moment of his existence, man gathers experience; every sensation he has, furnishes a fact that deposits in his brain an idea which his memory recalls with more or less fidelity: these facts connect themselves, these ideas are associated; their chain constitutes *experience*; this lays the foundation of *science*. Knowledge is that consciousness which arises from reiterated experience—from experiments made with precision of the sensations, of the ideas, of the effects which an object is capable of producing, either in ourselves or in others. All science, to be just, must be founded on truth. Truth itself rests on the constant, the faithful relation of our senses. Thus, *truth* is that conformity, that perpetual affinity, which man's senses, when well constituted, when aided by experience, discover to him, between the objects of which he has a knowledge, and the qualities with which he clothes them. In short, truth is nothing more than the just, the precise association of his ideas. But how can he, without experience, assure himself of the accuracy, of the justness of this association? How, if he does not reiterate this experience, can he compare it? how prove its truth? If his senses are vitiated, how is it possible they can convey to him with precision, the sensations, the facts, with which they store his brain? It is only by multiplied, by diversified, by repeated experience, that he is enabled to rectify the errors of his first conceptions.

Man is in error every time his organs, either originally defective in their nature, or vitiated by the durable or transitory modifications which they undergo, render him incapable of judging soundly of objects. Error consists in the false association of ideas, by which qualities are attributed to objects which they do not possess. Man is in error, when he supposes those beings really to have existence, which have no local habitation but in his own imagination: he is in error, when he associates the idea of happiness with objects capable of injuring him, whether immediately or by remote consequences which he cannot foresee.

But how can he foresee effects of which he has not yet any knowledge? It is by the aid of experience: by the assistance which this experience affords, it is known that analogous, that like causes, produce analogous, produce like effects. Memory, by recalling these effects, enables him to form a judgment of those he may expect, whether it be from the same causes, or from causes that bear a relation to those of which he has already experienced the action. From this it will appear, that *prudence, foresight*, are faculties that are ascribable to, that grow out of experience. If he has felt that fire excited in his organs painful sensation, this experience suffices him to know, to foresee, that fire so applied, will consequently excite the same sensations. If he has discovered that certain actions, on his part, stirred up the hatred, elicited the contempt of others, this experience sufficiently enables him to foresee, that every time he shall act in a similar manner, he will be either hated or despised.

The faculty man has of gathering experience, of recalling it to himself, of foreseeing effects by which he is enabled to avoid whatever may have the power to injure him, to procure that which may be useful to the conservation of his existence, which may contribute to that which is the sole end of all his actions, whether corporeal or mental,—his felicity —constitutes that, which, in one word, is designated under the name of *Reason*. Sentiment, imagination, temperament, may be capable of leading him astray—may have the power to deceive him; but experience and reflection will rectify his errors, point out his mistakes, place him in the right road, teach him what can really conduce to, what can truly conduct him to happiness. From this, it will appear, that *reason* is man's nature, modified by experience, moulded by judgment, regulated by reflection: it supposes a moderate, sober temperament; a just, a sound mind; a well-regulated, orderly imagination; a knowledge of truth, grounded upon tried, upon reiterated experience; in fact, prudence and foresight: this will serve to prove, that although nothing is more commonly asserted, although the phrase is repeated daily, nay, hourly, that *man is a reasonable being*, yet there are but a very small number of the individuals who compose the human species, of whom it can with truth be said; who really enjoy the faculty of reason, or who combine the dispositions, the experience, by which it is constituted. It ought not, then to excite surprise, that the individuals of the human race, who are in a capacity to make true experience, are so few in number. Man, when he is born, brings with him into the world organs susceptible of receiving impulse, amassing ideas, of collecting experience; but whether it be from the vice of his system, the imperfection of his organization, or from those causes by which it is modified, his experience is false, his ideas are confused, his images are badly associated, his judgment is erroneous, his brain is saturated with vicious, with wicked systems, which necessarily have an influence over his conduct, which are continually disturbing his mind, and confounding his reason.

Man's senses, as it has been shewn, are the only means by which he is enabled to ascertain whether his opinions are true or false, whether his conduct is useful to himself and beneficial to others, whether it is advantageous or disadvantageous. But that his senses may be competent to make a faithful relation—that they may be in a capacity to impress true ideas on his brain, it is requisite they should be sound; that is to say, in the state necessary to maintain his existence; in that order which is suitable to his preservation—that condition which is calculated to ensure his permanent felicity. It is also indispensable that his brain itself should be healthy, or in the proper circumstances to enable it to fulfil its functions with precision, to exercise its faculties with vigour. It is necessary that memory should faithfully delineate its anterior sensations, should accurately retrace its former ideas; to the end, that he may be competent to judge, to foresee the effects he may have to hope, the consequences he may have to fear, from those actions to which he may be determined by his will. If his organic system be vicious, if his interior or exterior organs be defective, whether by their natural conformation or from those causes by which they are regulated, he feels but imperfectly—in a manner less distinct than is requisite; his ideas are either false or suspicious, he judges badly, he is in a delusion, in a state of ebriety, in a sort of intoxication that prevents his grasping the true relation of things. In short, if his memory is faulty, if it is treacherous, his reflection is void, his imagination leads him astray, his mind deceives him, whilst the sensibility of his organs, simultaneously assailed by a crowd of impressions, shocked by a variety of impulsions, oppose him to prudence, to foresight, to the exercise of his reason. On the other hand, if the conformation of his organs, as it happens with those of a phlegmatic temperament, of a dull habit, does not permit him to move, except with feebleness, in a sluggish manner, his experience is slow, frequently unprofitable. The tortoise and the butterfly are alike incapable of preventing their destruction. The stupid man, equally with him who is intoxicated, are in that state which renders it impossible for them to arrive at or attain the end they have in view.

But what is the end? What is the aim of man in the sphere he occupies? It is to preserve himself; to render his existence happy. It becomes then of the utmost importance, that he should understand the true means which reason points out, which prudence teaches him to use, in order that he may with certainty, that he may constantly arrive at the end which he proposes to himself. These he will find are his natural faculties—his mind—his talents—his industry—his actions, determined by those passions of which his nature renders him susceptible, which give more or less activity to his will. Experience and reason again shew him, that the men with whom he is associated are necessary to him, are capable of contributing to his happiness, are in a capacity to administer to his pleasures, are competent to assist him by those faculties which are peculiar to them; experience teaches him the mode he must adopt to induce them to concur in his designs, to determine them to will and incline them to act in his favour. This points out to him the actions they approve—those which displease them—the conduct which attracts them—that which repels them—the judgment by which they are swayed—the advantages that occur—the prejudicial effects that result to him from their various modes of existence and from their diverse manner of acting. This experience furnishes him with the ideas of virtue and of vice, of justice and of injustice, of goodness and of wickedness, of decency and of indecency, of probity and of knavery: In short, he learns to form a judgment of men—to estimate their actions—to distinguish the various sentiments excited in them, according to the diversity of those effects which they make him experience. It is upon the necessary diversity of these effects that is founded the discrimination between good and evil—between virtue and vice; distinctions which do not rest, as some thinkers have believed, on the conventions made between men; still less, as some metaphysicians have asserted, upon the chimerical will of supernatural beings: but upon the solid, the invariable, the eternal relations that subsist between beings of the human species congregated together, and living in society: which relations will have existence as long as man shall remain, as long as society shall continue to exist.

Thus *virtue* is every thing that is truly beneficial, every thing that is constantly useful to the individuals of the human race, living together in society; *vice* every thing that is really prejudicial, every thing that is permanently injurious to them. The greatest virtues are those which procure for man the most durable advantages, from which he derives the most solid happiness, which preserves the greatest degree of order in his association: the greatest vices, are those which most disturb his tendency to happiness, which perpetuate error, which most interrupt the necessary order of society.

The *virtuous man*, is he whose actions tend uniformly to the welfare, constantly to the happiness, of his fellow creatures. The *vicious man*, is he whose conduct tends to the misery, whose propensities form the unhappiness of those with whom he lives; from whence his own peculiar misery most commonly results.

Every thing that procures for a man true and permanent happiness is reasonable; every thing that disturbs his individual felicity, or that of the beings necessary to his happiness, is foolish and unreasonable. The man who injures others, is wicked; the man who injures himself, is an imprudent being, who neither has a knowledge of reason, of his own peculiar interests, nor of truth.

Man's *duties* are the means pointed out to him by experience, the circle which reason describes for him, by which he is to arrive at that goal he proposes to himself; these duties are the necessary consequence of the relations subsisting between mortals, who equally desire happiness, who are equally anxious to preserve their existence. When it is said these duties *compel him*, it signifies nothing more than that, without taking these means, he could not reach the end proposed to him by his nature. Thus, *moral obligation* is the necessity of employing the natural means to render the beings with whom he lives happy; to the end that he may determine them in turn to contribute to his own individual happiness: his obligation toward himself, is the necessity he is under to take those means, without which he would be incapable to conserve himself, or render his existence solidly and permanently happy. Morals, like the universe, is founded upon necessity, or upon the eternal relation of things.

Happiness is a mode of existence of which man naturally wishes the duration, or in which he is willing to continue. It is measured by its duration, by its vivacity. The greatest happiness is that which has the longest continuance: transient happiness, or that which has only a short duration, is called *Pleasure*; the more lively it is, the more fugitive, because man's senses are only susceptible of a certain quantum of motion. When pleasure exceeds this given quantity, it is changed into *anguish*, or into that painful mode of existence, of which he ardently desires the cessation: this is the reason why pleasure and pain frequently so closely approximate each other as scarcely to be discriminated. Immoderate pleasure is the forerunner of regret. It is succeeded by ennui, it is followed by weariness, it ends in disgust: transient happiness frequently converts itself into durable misfortune. According to these principles it will be seen that man, who in each moment of his duration seeks necessarily after happiness, ought, when he is reasonable, to manage, to husband, to regulate his pleasures; to refuse himself to all those of which the indulgence would be succeeded by regret; to avoid those which can convert themselves into pain; in order that he may procure for himself the most permanent felicity.

Happiness cannot be the same for all the beings of the human species; the same pleasures cannot equally affect men whose conformation is different, whose modification is diverse. This no doubt, is the true reason why the greater number of moral philosophers are so little in accord upon those objects in which they have made man's happiness consist, as well as on the means by which it may be obtained. Nevertheless, in general, happiness appears to be a state, whether momentary or durable, in which man readily acquiesces, because he finds it conformable to his being. This state results from the accord, springs out of the conformity, which is found between himself and those circumstances in which he has been placed by Nature; or, if it be preferred, *happiness is the co-ordination of man, with the causes that give him impulse.*

The ideas which man forms to himself of happiness depend not only on his temperament, on his individual conformation, but also upon the habits he has contracted. *Habit* is, in man, a mode of existence—of thinking—of acting, which his organs, as well interior as exterior, contract, by the frequent reiteration of the same motion; from whence results the faculty of performing these actions with promptitude, of executing them with facility.

If things be attentively considered, it will be found that almost the whole conduct of man—the entire system of his actions—his occupations —his connexions—his studies—his amusements—his manners—his customs —his very garments—even his aliments, are the effect of habit. He owes equally to habit, the facility with which he exercises his mental faculties of thought—of judgment—of wit—of reason—of taste, &c. It is to habit he owes the greater part of his inclinations—of his desires—of his opinions—of his prejudices—of the ideas, true or false, he forms to himself of his welfare. In short, it is to habit, consecrated by time, that he owes those errors into which everything strives to precipitate him; from which every thing is calculated to prevent him emancipating himself. It is habit that attaches him either to virtue or to vice: experience proves this: observation teaches incontrovertibly that the first crime is always accompanied by more pangs of remorse than the second; this again, by more than the third; so on to those that follow. A first action is the commencement of a habit; those which succeed confirm it: by force of combatting the obstacles that prevent the commission of criminal actions, man arrives at the power of vanquishing them with ease; of conquering them with facility. Thus he frequently becomes wicked from habit.

Man is so much modified by habit, that it is frequently confounded with his nature: from hence results, as will presently be seen, those opinions or those ideas, which he has called *innate*: because he has been unwilling to recur back to the source from whence they sprung: which has, as it were, identified itself with his brain. However this may be, he adheres with great strength of attachment to all those things to which he is habituated; his mind experiences a sort of violence, an incommodious revulsion, a troublesome distaste, when it is endeavoured to make him change the course of his ideas: a fatal predilection frequently conducts him back to the old track in despite of reason.

It is by a pure mechanism that may be explained the phenomena of habit, as well physical as moral; the soul, notwithstanding its spirituality, is modified exactly in the same manner as the body. Habit, in man, causes the organs of voice to learn the mode of expressing quickly the ideas consigned to his brain, by means of certain motion, which, during his infancy, the tongue acquires the power of executing with facility: his tongue, once habituated to move itself in a certain manner, finds much trouble, has great pain, to move itself after another mode; the throat yields with difficulty to those inflections which are exacted by a language different from that to which he has, been accustomed. It is the same with regard to his ideas; his brain, his interior organ, his soul, inured to a given manner of modification, accustomed to attach certain ideas to certain objects, long used to form to itself a system connected with certain opinions, whether true or false, experiences a painful sensation, whenever he undertakes to give it a new impulse, or alter the direction of its habitual motion. It is nearly as difficult to make him change his opinions as his language.

Here, then, without doubt, is the cause of that almost invincible attachment which man displays to those customs—those prejudices—those institutions of which it is in vain that reason, experience, good sense prove to him the inutility, or even the danger. Habit opposes itself to the clearest, the most evident demonstrations; these can avail nothing against those passions, those vices, which time has rooted in him— against the most ridiculous systems—against the most absurd notions— against the most extravagant hypotheses—against the strangest customs: above all, when he has learned to attach to them the ideas of utility, of common interest, of the welfare of society. Such is the source of that obstinacy, of that stubbornness, which man evinces for his religion, for ancient usages, for unreasonable customs, for laws so little accordant with justice, for abuses, which so frequently make him suffer, for prejudices of which he sometimes acknowledges the absurdity, yet is unwilling to divest himself of them. Here is the reason why nations contemplate the most useful novelties as mischievous innovations—why they believe they would be lost, if they were to remedy those evils to which they have become habituated; which they have learned to consider as necessary to their repose; which they have been taught to consider dangerous to be cured.

Education is only the art of making man contract, in early life, that is to say, when his organs are extremely flexible, the habits, the opinions, the modes of existence, adopted by the society in which he is placed. The first moments of his infancy are employed in collecting experience; those who are charged with the care of rearing him, or who are entrusted to bring him up, teach him how to apply it: it is they who develope reason in him: the first impulse they give him commonly decides upon his condition, upon his passions, upon the ideas he forms to himself of happiness, upon the means he shall employ to procure it, upon his virtues, and upon his vices. Under the eyes of his masters, the infant acquires ideas: under their tuition he learns to associate them, —to think in a certain manner,—to judge well or ill. They point out to him various objects, which they accustom him either to love or to hate, to desire or to avoid, to esteem or to despise. It is thus opinions are transmitted from fathers, mothers, nurses, and masters, to man in his infantine state. It is thus, that his mind by degrees saturates itself with truth, or fills itself with error; after which he regulates his conduct, which renders him either happy or miserable, virtuous or vicious, estimable or hateful. It is thus he becomes either contented or discontented with his destiny, according to the objects towards which they have directed his passions—towards which they have bent the energies of his mind; that is to say, in which they have shewn him his interest, in which they have taught him to place his felicity: in consequence, he loves and searches after that which they have taught him to revere—that which they have made the object of his research; he has those tastes, those inclinations, those phantasms, which, during the whole course of his life, he is forward to indulge, which he is eager to satisfy, in proportion to the activity they have excited in him, and the capacity with which he has been provided by Nature.

Politics ought to be the art of regulating the passions of man—of directing them to the welfare of society—of diverting them into a genial current of happiness—of making them flow gently to the general benefit of all: but too frequently it is nothing more than the detestable art of arming the passions of the various members of society against each other,—of making them the engines to accomplish their mutual destruction,—of converting them into agents which embitter their existence, create jealousies among them, and fill with rancorous animosities that association from which, if properly managed, man ought to derive his felicity. Society is commonly so vicious because it is not founded upon Nature, upon experience, and upon general utility; but on the contrary, upon the passions, upon the caprices, and upon the particular interests of those by whom it is governed. In short, it is for the most part the advantage of the few opposed to the prosperity of the many.

Politics, to be useful, should found its principles upon Nature; that is to say, should conform itself to the essence of man, should mould itself to the great end of society: but what is society? and what is its end? It is a whole, formed by the union of a great number of families, or by a collection of individuals, assembled from a reciprocity of interest, in order that they may satisfy with greater facility their reciprocal wants—that they may, with more certainty, procure the advantages they desire—that they may obtain mutual succours—above all, that they may gain the faculty of enjoying, in security, those benefits with which Nature and industry may furnish them: it follows, of course, that politics, which are intended to maintain society, and to consolidate the interests of this congregation, ought to enter into its views, to facilitate the means of giving them efficiency, to remove all those obstacles that have a tendency to counteract the intention with which man entered into association.

Man, in approximating to his fellow man, to live with him in society, has made, either formally or tacitly, a covenant; by which he engages to render mutual services, to do nothing that can be prejudicial to his neighbour. But as the nature of each individual impels him each instant to seek after his own welfare, which he has mistaken to consist in the gratification of his passions, and the indulgence of his transitory caprices, without any regard to the convenience of his fellows; there needed a power to conduct him back to his duty, to oblige him to conform himself to his obligations, and to recall him to his engagements, which the hurry of his passions frequently make him forget. This power is the *law*; it is, or ought to be, the collection of the will of society, reunited to fix the conduct of its members, to direct their action in such a mode, that it may concur to the great end of his association— the general good.

But as society, more especially when very numerous, is incapable of assembling itself, unless with great difficulty, as it cannot with tumult make known its intentions, it is obliged to choose citizens in whom it places a confidence, whom it makes the interpreter of its will, whom it constitutes the depositaries of the power requisite to carry it into execution. Such is the origin of all *government*, which to be legitimate can only be founded on the free consent of society. Those who are charged with the care of governing, call themselves sovereigns, chiefs, legislators: according to the form which society has been willing to give to its government: these sovereigns are styled monarchs, magistrates, representatives, &c. Government only borrows its power from society: being established for no other purpose than its welfare, it is evident society can revoke this power whenever its interest shall exact it; change the form of its government; extend or limit the power which it has confided to its chiefs, over whom, by the immutable laws of Nature, it always conserves a supreme authority: because these laws enjoin, that the part shall always remain subordinate to the whole.

Thus sovereigns are the ministers of society, its interpreters, the depositaries of a greater or of a less portion of its power; but they are not its absolute masters, neither are they the proprietors of nations. By a *covenant*, either expressed or implied, they engage themselves to watch over the maintenance, to occupy themselves with the welfare of society; it is only upon these conditions society consents to obey them. The price of obedience is protection. There is or ought to be a reciprocity of interest between the governed and the governor: whenever this reciprocity is wanting, society is in that state of confusion of which we spoke in the fifth chapter: it is verging on destruction. No society upon earth was ever willing or competent to confer irrevocably upon its chiefs the power, the right, of doing it injury. Such a concession, such a compact, would be annulled, would be rendered void by Nature; because she wills that each society, the same as each individual of the human species shall tend to its own conservation; it has not therefore the capacity to consent to its permanent unhappiness. *Laws*, in order that they may be just, ought invariably to have for their end, the general interest of society; that is to say, to assure to the greater number of citizens those advantages for which man originally associated. These advantages are *liberty, property, security*.

Liberty, to man, is the faculty of doing, for his own peculiar happiness, every thing which does not injure or diminish the happiness of his associates: in associating, each individual renounced the exercise of that portion of his natural liberty which would be able to prejudice or injure the liberty of his fellows. The exercise of that liberty which is injurious to society is called *licentiousness*.

Property, to man, is the faculty of enjoying those advantages which spring from labour; those benefits which industry or talent has procured to each member of society.

Security, to man, is the certitude, the assurance, that each individual ought to have, of enjoying in his person, of finding for his property the protection of the laws, as long as he shall faithfully observe, as long as he shall punctually perform, his engagements with society.

Justice, to man, assures to all the members of society, the possession of these advantages, the enjoyment of those rights, which belong to them. From this, it will appear, that without justice, society is not in a condition to procure the happiness of any man. Justice is also called *equity*, because by the assistance of the laws made to command the whole, she reduces all its members to a state of equality; that is to say, she prevents them from prevailing one over the other, by the inequality which Nature or industry may have made between their respective powers.

Rights, to man, are every thing which society, by equitable laws, permits each individual to do for his own peculiar felicity. These rights are evidently limited by the invariable end of all association: society has, on its part, rights over all its members, by virtue of the advantages which it procures for them; all its members, in turn, have a right to claim, to exact from society, or secure from its ministers those advantages for the procuring of which they congregated, in favour of which they renounced a portion of their natural liberty. A society, of which the chiefs, aided by the laws, do not procure any good for its members, evidently loses its right over them: those chiefs who injure society lose the right of commanding. It is not our country, without it secures the welfare of its inhabitants; a society without equity contains only enemies; a society oppressed is composed only of tyrants and slaves; slaves are incapable of being citizens; it is liberty, property, and security, that render our country dear to us; it is the true love of his country that forms the citizen.

For want of having a proper knowledge of these truths, or for want of applying them when known, some nations have become unhappy—have contained nothing but a vile heap of slaves, separated from each other, detached from society, which neither procures for them any good, nor secures to them any one advantage. In consequence of the imprudence of some nations, or of the craft, cunning, and violence of those to whom they have confided the power of making laws, and carrying them into execution, their sovereigns have rendered themselves absolute masters of society. These, mistaking the true source of their power, pretended to hold it from heaven, to be accountable for their actions to God alone, to owe nothing, not to have any obligation to society, in a word, to be gods upon earth, to possess the right of governing arbitrarily. From thence politics became corrupted: they were only a mockery. Such nations, disgraced and grown contemptible, did not dare resist the will of their chiefs; their laws were nothing more than the expression of the caprice of these chiefs; public welfare was sacrificed to their peculiar interests; the force of society was turned against itself; its members withdrew to attach themselves to its oppressors, to its tyrants; these to seduce them, permitted them to injure it with impunity and to profit by its misfortunes. Thus liberty, justice, security, and virtue, were banished from many nations; politics was no longer any thing more than the art of availing itself of the forces of a people and of the treasure of society; of dividing it on the subject of its interest, in order to subjugate it by itself; at length a stupid, a mechanical habit, made them cherish their oppressors, and love their chains.

Man when he has nothing to fear, presently becomes wicked; he who believes be has not occasion for his fellow, persuades himself he may follow the inclinations of his heart without caution or discretion. Thus fear is the only obstacle society can effectually oppose to the passions of its chiefs; without it they will quickly become corrupt, and will not scruple to avail themselves of the means society has placed in their hands, to make them accomplices in their iniquity. To prevent these abuses, it is requisite society should set bounds to its confidence; should limit the power which it delegates to its chiefs; should reserve to itself a sufficient portion of authority to prevent them from injuring it; it must establish prudent checks: it must cautiously divide the power it confers, because re-united, it will by such reunion be infallibly oppressed. The slightest reflection, the most scanty review, will make men feel that the burthen of governing and weight of administration, is too ponderous and overpowering to be borne by an individual; that the scope of his jurisdiction, that the range of his surveillance, and multiplicity of his duties must always render him negligent; that the extent of his power has ever a tendency to render him mischievous. In short, the experience of all ages will convince nations that man is continually tempted to the abuse of power: that as an abundance of strong liquor intoxicates his brain, so unlimited power corrupts his heart; that therefore the sovereign ought to be subject to the law, not the law to the sovereign.

Government has necessarily an equal influence over the philosophy, as over the morals of nations. In the same manner that its care produces labour, activity, abundance, salubrity and justice; its negligence induces idleness, sloth, discouragement, penury, contagion, injustice, vices and crimes. It depends upon government either to foster industry, mature genius, give a spring to talents, or stifle them. Indeed government, the disturber of dignities, of riches, of rewards, and punishments; the master of those objects in which man from his infancy has learned to place his felicity, and contemplate as the means of his happiness; acquires a necessary influence over his conduct: it kindles his passions; gives them direction; makes him instrumental to whatever purpose it pleases; it modifies him; determines his manners; which in a whole people, as in the individual, is nothing more than the conduct, the general system of wills, of actions that necessarily result from his education, government, laws, and religious opinions—his institutions, whether rational or irrational. In short, manners are the habits of a people: these are good whenever society draws from them true felicity and solid happiness; they are bad, they are detestable in the eye of reason, when the happiness of society does not spring from them; they are unwholesome when they have nothing more in their favour than the suffrage of time, and the countenance of prejudice which rarely consults experience, which is almost ever at variance with good sense: notwithstanding they may have the sanction of the law, custom, religion, public opinion, or example, they may be unworthy and may be disgraceful, provided society is in disorder; that crime abounds; that virtue shrinks beneath the basilisk eye of triumphant vice; they may then be said to resemble the UPAS, whose luxuriant yet poisonous foliage, the produce of a rank soil, becomes more baneful to those who are submitted to its vortex, in proportion as it extends its branches. If experience he consulted, it will be found there is no action, however abominable, that has not received the applause, that has not obtained the approbation of some people. Parricide, the sacrifice of children, robbery, usurpation, cruelty, intolerance, and prostitution, have all in their turn been licensed actions; have been advocated; have been deemed laudable and meritorious deeds with some nations of the earth. Above all, *superstition* has consecrated the most unreasonable, the most revolting customs.

Man's passions result from and depend on the motion of attraction or repulsion, of which he is rendered susceptible by Nature; who enables him, by his peculiar essence, to be attracted by those objects which appear useful to him, to be repelled by those which he considers prejudicial; it follows that government, by holding the magnet, can put these passions into activity, has the power either of restraining them, or of giving them a favorable or an unfavorable direction. All his passions are constantly limited by either loving or hating, seeking or avoiding, desiring or fearing. These passions, so necessary to the conservation of man, are a consequence of his organization; they display themselves with more or less energy, according to his temperament; education and habit develope them; government gives them play, conducts them towards those objects, which it believes itself interested in making desirable to its subjects. The various names which have been given to these passions, are relative to the different objects by which they are excited, such as pleasure, grandeur, or riches, which produce voluptuousness, ambition, vanity and avarice. If the source of those passions which predominate in nations be attentively examined it will be commonly found in their governments. It is the impulse received from their chiefs that renders them sometimes warlike, sometimes superstitious, sometimes aspiring after glory, sometimes greedy after wealth, sometimes rational, and sometimes unreasonable; if sovereigns, in order to enlighten and render happy their dominions, were to employ only the *tenth* part of the vast expenditures which they lavish, only a *tythe* of the pains which they employ to render them brutish, to stupify them, to deceive them, and to afflict them; their subjects would presently be as wise, would quickly be as happy, as they are now remarkable for being blind, ignorant, and miserable.

Let the vain project of destroying, the delusive attempt at rooting his passions from the heart of man, be abandoned; let an effort be made to direct them towards objects that may be useful to himself, beneficial to his associates. Let education, let government, let the laws, habituate him to restrain his passions within those just bounds that experience fixes and reason prescribes. Let the ambitious have honours, titles, distinctions, and power, when they shall have usefully served their country; let riches be given to those who covet them, when they shall have rendered themselves necessary to their fellow citizens; let commendations, let eulogies, encourage those who shall be actuated by the love of glory. In short, let the passions of man have a free, an uninterrupted course, whenever there shall result from their exercise, real, substantial, and durable advantages to society. Let education kindle only those, which are truly beneficial to the human species; let it favour those alone which are really necessary to the maintenance of society. The passions of man are dangerous, only because every thing conspires to give them an evil direction.

Nature does not make man either good or wicked: she combines machines more or less active, mobile, and energetic; she furnishes him with organs and temperament, of which his passions, more or less impetuous, are the necessary consequence; these passions have always his happiness for their object, his welfare for their end: in consequence they are legitimate, they are natural, they can only be called bad or good, relatively, to the influence they have on the beings of his species. Nature gives man legs proper to sustain his weight, and necessary to transport him from one place to another; the care of those who rear them strengthens them, habituates him to avail himself of him, accustoms him to make either a good or a bad use of them. The arm which he has received from Nature is neither good nor bad; it is necessary to a great number of the actions of life; nevertheless, the use of this arm becomes criminal, if he has contracted the habit of using it to rob, to assassinate, with a view to obtain that money which he has been taught from his infancy to desire, and which the society in which he lives renders necessary to him, but which his industry will enable him to obtain without doing injury to his fellow man.

The heart of man is a soil which Nature has made equally suitable to the production of brambles, or of useful grain—of deleterious poison, or of refreshing fruit, by virtue of the seeds which may he sown in it—by the cultivation that may be bestowed upon it, In his infancy, those objects are pointed out to him which he is to estimate or to despise, to seek after or to avoid, to love or to hate. It is his parents, his instructors, who render him either virtuous or wicked, wise or unreasonable, studious or dissipated, steady or trifling, solid or vain. Their example, their discourse, modify him through his whole life, teaching him what are the things he ought either to desire or to avoid; what the objects he ought to fear or to love: he desires them, in consequence; and he imposes on himself the task of obtaining them, according to the energy of his temperament, which ever decides the force of his passions. It is thus that education, by inspiring him with opinions, by infusing into him ideas, whether true or false, gives him those primitive impulsions after which he acts, in a manner either advantageous or prejudicial both to himself and to others. Man, at his birth, brings with him into the world nothing but the necessity of conserving himself, of rendering his existence happy: instruction, example, the customs of the world, present him with the means, either real or imaginary, of achieving it; habit procures for him the facility of employing these means: he attaches himself strongly to those he judges best calculated, most proper to secure to him the possession of those objects which they have taught him, which he has learned to desire as the preferable good attached to his existence. Whenever his education—whenever the examples which have been afforded him—whenever the means with which he has been provided, are approved by reason, are the result of experience, every thing concurs to render him virtuous; habit strengthens these dispositions in him; he becomes, in consequence, a useful member of society; to the interests of which, every thing ought to prove to him his own permanent well-being, his own durable felicity, is necessarily allied. If, on the contrary, his education—his institutions—the examples which are set before him—the opinions which are suggested to him in his infancy, are of a nature to exhibit to his mind virtue as useless and repugnant—vice as useful and congenial to his own individual happiness, he will become vicious; he will believe himself interested in injuring society, in rendering his associates unhappy; he will be carried along by the general current: he will renounce virtue, which to him will no longer be any thing more than a vain idol, without attractions to induce him to follow it; without charms to tempt his adoration; because it will appear to exact, that he should immolate at its shrine, that he should sacrifice at its altar all those objects which he has been constantly taught to consider the most dear to himself; to contemplate as benefits the most desirable.

In order that man may become virtuous, it is absolutely requisite that he should have an interest, that he should find advantages in practising virtue. For this end, it is necessary that education should implant in him reasonable ideas; that public opinion should lean towards virtue, as the most desirable good; that example should point it out as the object most worthy esteem; that government should faithfully recompense, should regularly reward it; that honor should always accompany its practice; that vice should constantly be despised; that crime should invariably be punished. Is virtue in this situation amongst men? does the education of man infuse into him just, faithful ideas of happiness—true notions of virtue—dispositions really favourable to the beings with whom he is to live? The examples spread before him, are they suitable to innocence and manners? are they calculated to make him respect decency—to cause him to love probity—to practice honesty—to value good faith—to esteem equity—to revere conjugal fidelity—to observe exactitude in fulfilling his duties? Religion, which alone pretends to regulate his manners, does it render him sociable—does it make him pacific—does it teach him to be humane? The arbiters, the sovereigns of society, are they faithful in recompensing, punctual in rewarding, those who have best served their country? in punishing those who have pillaged, who have robbed, who have plundered, who have divided, who have ruined it? Justice, does she hold her scales with a firm, with an even hand, between all the citizens of the state? The laws, do they never support the strong against the weak— favor the rich against the poor—uphold the happy against the miserable? In short, is it an uncommon spectacle to behold crime frequently justified, often applauded, sometimes crowned with success, insolently triumphing, arrogantly striding over that merit which it disdains, over that virtue which it outrages? Well then, in societies thus constituted, virtue can only be heard by a very small number of peaceable citizens, a few generous souls, who know how to estimate its value, who enjoy it in secret. For the others, it is only a disgusting object; they see in it nothing but the supposed enemy to their happiness, or the censor of their individual conduct.

If man, according to his nature, is necessitated to desire his welfare, he is equally obliged to love and cherish the means by which he believes it is to be acquired: it would be useless, it would perhaps be unjust, to demand that a man should be virtuous, if he could not be so without rendering himself miserable. Whenever he thinks vice renders him happy, he must necessarily love vice; whenever he sees inutility recompensed, crime rewarded—whenever he witnesses either or both of them honored,— what interest will he find in occupying himself with the happiness of his fellow-creatures? what advantage will he discover in restraining the fury of his passions? Whenever his mind is saturated with false ideas, filled with dangerous opinions, it follows, of course, that his whole conduct will become nothing more than a long chain of errors, a tissue of mistakes, a series of depraved actions.

We are informed, that the savages, in order to flatten the heads of their children, squeeze them between two boards, by that means preventing them from taking the shape designed for them by Nature. It is pretty nearly the same thing with the institutions of man; they commonly conspire to counteract Nature, to constrain and divert, to extinguish the impulse Nature has given him, to substitute others which are the source of all his misfortunes. In almost all the countries of the earth, man is bereft of truth, is fed with falsehoods, and amused with marvellous chimeras: he is treated like those children whose members are, by the imprudent care of their nurses, swathed with little fillets, bound up with rollers, which deprive them of the free use of their limbs, obstruct their growth, prevent their activity, and oppose themselves to their health.

Most of the superstitious opinions of man have for their object only to display to him his supreme felicity in those illusions for which they kindle his passions: but as the phantoms which are presented to his imagination are incapable of being considered in the same light by all who contemplate them, he is perpetually in dispute concerning these objects; he hates his fellow, he persecutes his neighbour, his neighbour in turn persecutes him, and he believes that in doing this he is doing well: that in committing the greatest crimes to sustain his opinions he is acting right. It is thus superstition infatuates man from his infancy, fills him with vanity, and enslaves him with fanaticism: if he has a heated imagination, it drives him on to fury; if he has activity, it makes him a madman, who is frequently as cruel himself, as he is dangerous to his fellow-creatures, as he is incommodious to others: if, on the contrary, he be phlegmatic, and of a slothful habit, he becomes melancholy and useless to society.

Public opinion every instant offers to man's contemplation false ideas of honor, and wrong notions of glory: it attaches his esteem not only to frivolous advantages, but also to prejudicial interests and injurious actions; which example authorizes, which prejudice consecrates, which habit precludes him from viewing with the disgust and horror which they merit. Indeed, habit familiarizes his mind with the most absurd ideas, the most unreasonable customs, the most blameable actions; with prejudices the most contrary to his own interests, and detrimental to the society in which he lives. He finds nothing strange, nothing singular, nothing despicable, nothing ridiculous, except those opinions and objects to which he is himself unaccustomed. There are countries in which the most laudable actions appear very blameable and ridiculous— where the foulest and most diabolical actions pass for very honest and perfectly rational conduct. In some nations they kill the old men; in some the children strangle their fathers. The Phoenicians and Carthaginians immolated their children to their gods. Europeans approve duels; he who refuses to cut the throat of another, or to blow out the brains of his neighbour, is contemplated by them as dishonoured. The Spaniards and Portuguese think it meritorious to burn an heretic. In some countries women prostitute themselves without dishonour; in others it is the height of hospitality for a man to present his wife to the embraces of the stranger: the refusal to accept this, excites his scorn and calls forth his resentment.

Authority commonly believes itself interested in maintaining the received opinions: those prejudices and errors which it considers requisite to the maintenance of its power and the consolidation of its interests, are sustained by force, which is never rational. Princes themselves, filled with deceptive images of happiness, mistaken notions of power, erroneous opinions of grandeur, and false ideas of glory, are surrounded with flattering courtiers, who are interested in keeping up the delusion of their masters: these contemptible men have acquired ideas of virtue, only that they may outrage it: by degrees they corrupt the people, these become depraved, lend themselves to their debaucheries, pander to the vices of the great, then make a merit of imitating them in their irregularities. A court is too frequently the true focus of the corruption of a people.

This is the true source of moral evil. It is thus that every thing conspires to render man vicious, and give a fatal impulse to his soul: from whence results the general confusion of society, which becomes unhappy, from the misery of almost every one of its members. The strongest motive-powers are put in action to inspire man with a passion for futile objects which are indifferent to him; which make him become dangerous to his fellow man, by the means which he is compelled to employ, in order to obtain them. Those who have the charge of guiding his steps, either impostors themselves, or the dupes to their own prejudices, forbid him to hearken to reason; they make truth appear dangerous to him; they exhibit error as requisite to his welfare, not only in this world, but in the next. In short, habit strongly attaches him to his irrational opinions, to his perilous inclinations, and to his blind passion for objects either useless or dangerous. Here, then, is the reason why for the most part man finds himself necessarily determined to evil; the reason why the passions, inherent in his Nature and necessary to his conservation, become the instruments of his destruction, and the bane of that society, which properly conducted, they ought to preserve; the reason why society becomes a state of warfare; why it does nothing but assemble enemies, who are envious of each other, and are always rivals for the prize. If some virtuous beings are to be found in these societies, they must be sought for in the very small number of those, who born with a phlegmatic temperament have moderate passions, who therefore, either do not desire at all, or desire very feebly, those objects with which their associates are continually inebriated.

Man's nature, diversely cultivated, decides upon his faculties, as well corporeal as intellectual; upon his qualities, as well moral as physical. The man who is of a sanguine, robust constitution, must necessarily have strong passions; he who is of a bilious, melancholy habit, will as necessarily have fantastical and gloomy passions; the man of a gay turn, of a sprightly imagination, will have cheerful passions; while the man in whom phlegm abounds, will have those which are gentle, or which have a very slight degree of violence. It appears to be upon the equilibrium of the humours, that depends the state of the man who is called *virtuous*; his temperament seems to be the result of a combination, in which the elements or principles are balanced with such precision that no one passion predominates over another, or carries into his machine more disorder than its neighbour.

Habit, as we have seen, is man's nature modified: this latter furnishes the matter; education, domestic example, national manners, give it the form: these, acting on his temperament, make him either reasonable, or irrational—enlightened, or stupid—a fanatic, or a hero—an enthusiast for the public good, or an unbridled criminal—a wise man, smitten with the advantages of virtue, or a libertine, plunged into every kind of vice. All the varieties of the moral man, depend on the diversity of his ideas; which are themselves arranged and combined in his brain by the intervention of his senses. His temperament is the produce of physical substances, his habits are the effect of physical modifications; the opinions, whether good or bad, injurious or beneficial, true or false, which form themselves in his mind, are never more than the effect of those physical impulsions which the brain receives by the medium of the senses.

CHAP. X.
The Soul does not derive its ideas from itself—It has no innate Ideas.

What has preceded suffices to prove, that the interior organ of man, which is called his *soul*, is purely material. He will be enabled to convince himself of this truth, by the manner in which he acquires his ideas,—from those impressions which material objects successively make on his organs, which are themselves acknowledged to be material. It has been seen, that the faculties which are called intellectual, are to be ascribed to that of feeling; the different qualities of those faculties which are called moral, have been explained after the necessary laws of a very simple mechanism: it now remains, to reply to those who still obstinately persist in making the soul a substance distinguished from the body, or who insist on giving it an essence totally distinct. They seem to found their distinction upon this, that this interior organ has the faculty of drawing its ideas from within itself; they will have it, that man, at his birth, brings with him ideas into the world, which, according to this wonderful notion, they have called *innate*. The Jews have a similar doctrine which they borrowed from the Chaldeans: their rabbins taught, that each soul, before it was united to the seed that must form an infant in the womb of a woman, is confided to the care of an angel, which causes him to behold heaven, earth, and hell: this, they pretend, is done by the assistance of a lamp, which extinguishes itself as soon as the infant comes into the world. Some ancient philosophers have held, that the soul originally contains the principles of several notions or doctrines: the Stoics designated this by the term PROLEPSIS, *anticipated opinions*; the Greek mathematicians, KOINAS ENNOIAS, *universal ideas*. They have believed that the soul, by a special privilege, in a nature where every thing is connected, enjoyed the faculty of moving itself without receiving any impulse; of creating to itself ideas, of thinking on a subject, without being determined to such action, by any exterior object; which by moving its organs should furnish it with an image of the subject of its thoughts. In consequence of these gratuitous suppositions, of these extraordinary pretensions, which it is only requisite to expose, in order to confute some very able speculators, who were prepossessed by their superstitious prejudices; have ventured the length to assert, that without model, without prototype to act on the senses, the soul is competent to delineate to itself, the whole universe with all the beings it contains. DESCARTES and his disciples have assured us, that the body went absolutely for nothing, in the sensations, in the perceptions, in the ideas of the soul; that it can feel, that it can perceive, that it can understand, that it can taste, that it can touch, even when there should exist nothing that is corporeal or material exterior to ourselves. But what shall be said of a BERKELEY, who has endeavoured, who has laboured to prove to man, that every thing in this world is nothing more than a chimerical illusion; that the universe exists nowhere but in himself; that it has no identity but in his imagination; who has rendered the existence of all things problematical by the aid of sophisms, insolvable even to those who maintain the doctrine of the spirituality of the soul.

Extravagant as this doctrine of the BISHOP OF CLOYNE may appear, it cannot well be more so than that of MALEBRANCHE, the champion of innate ideas; who makes the divinity the common bond between the soul and the body: or than that of those metaphysicians, who maintain that the soul is a substance heterogeneous to the body; who by ascribing to this soul the thoughts of man, have in fact rendered the body superfluous. They have not perceived they were liable to one solid objection, which is, that if the ideas of man are innate, if he derives them from a superior being, independent of exterior causes, if he sees every thing in God; how comes it that so many false ideas are afloat, that so many errors prevail, with which the human mind is saturated? From whence comes these opinions, which according to the theologians are so displeasing to God? Might it not be a question to the Malebranchists, was it in the Divinity that SPINOZA beheld his system?

Nevertheless, to justify such monstrous opinions, they assert that ideas are only the objects of thought. But according to the last analysis, these ideas can only reach man from exterior objects, which in giving impulse to his senses modify his brain; or from the material beings contained within the interior of his machine, who make some parts of his body experience those sensations which he perceives, which furnish him with ideas, which he relates, faithfully or otherwise, to the cause that moves him. Each idea is an effect, but however difficult it may be to recur to the cause, can we possibly suppose it is not ascribable to a cause? If we can only form ideas of material substances, how can we suppose the cause of our ideas can possibly be immaterial? To pretend that man without the aid of exterior objects, without the intervention of his senses, is competent to form ideas of the universe, is to assert, that a blind man is in a capacity to form a true idea of a picture, that represents some fact of which he has never heard any one speak.

It is very easy to perceive the source of those errors, into which men, otherwise extremely profound and very enlightened have fallen, when they have been desirous to speak of the soul: to describe its operations. Obliged either by their own prejudices, or by the fear of combatting the opinions of some imperious theologian, they have become the advocates of the principle, that the soul was a pure spirit: an immaterial substance; of an essence directly different from that of the body; from every thing we behold: this granted, they have been incompetent to conceive how material objects could operate, in what manner gross and corporeal organs were enabled to act on a substance, that had no kind of analogy with them; how they were in a capacity to modify it by conveying its ideas; in the impossibility of explaining this phenomenon, at the same time perceiving that the soul had ideas, they concluded that it must draw them from itself, and not from those beings, which according to their own hypothesis, were incapable of acting on it, or rather, of which they could not conceive the manner of action; they therefore imagined that all the modifications, all the actions of this soul, sprung from its own peculiar energy, were imprinted on it from its first formation, by the Author of Nature: that these did not in any manner depend upon the beings of which we have a knowledge, or which act upon it, by the gross means of our senses.

There are, however, some phenomena, which, considered superficially, appear to support the opinion of these philosophers; to announce a faculty in the human soul of producing ideas within itself, without any exterior aid; these are *dreams*, in which the interior organ of man, deprived of objects that move it visibly, does not, however, cease to have ideas—to be set in activity—to be modified in a manner that is sufficiently sensible—to have an influence upon his body. But if a little reflection be called in, the solution to this difficulty will be found: it will be perceived that, even during sleep, his brain is supplied with a multitude of ideas, with which the eye or time before has stocked it; these ideas were communicated to it by exterior or corporeal objects, by which they have been modified: it will be found that these modifications renew themselves, not by any spontaneous, not by any voluntary motion on its part, but by a chain of involuntary movements which take place in his machine, which determine, which excite those that give play to the brain; these modifications renew themselves with more or less fidelity, with a greater or lesser degree of conformity to those which it has anteriorly experienced. Sometimes in dreaming, he has memory, then he retraces to himself the objects which have struck him faithfully;—at other times, these modifications renew themselves without order, and without connection, very differently from those, which real objects have before excited in his interior organ. If in a dream he believes he sees a friend, his brain renews in itself the modifications or the ideas which this friend had formerly excited—in the same order that they arranged themselves when his eyes really beheld him—this is nothing more than an effect of memory. If in his dream he fancies he sees a monster which has no model in nature, his brain is then modified in the same manner that it was by the particular, by the detached ideas, with which it then does nothing more than compose an ideal whole; by assembling, and associating, in a ridiculous manner, the scattered ideas that were consigned to its keeping; it is then, that in dreaming he has imagination.

Those dreams that are troublesome, extravagant, whimsical, or unconnected, are commonly the effect of some confusion in his machine; such as painful indigestion—an overheated blood—a prejudicial fermentation, &c.—these material causes excite in his body a disorderly motion, which precludes the brain from being modified in the same manner it was on the day before; in consequence of this irregular motion the brain is disturbed, it only represents to itself confused ideas that want connection. When in a dream, he believes he sees a Sphinx, a being supposed by the poets to have a head and face like a woman, a body like a dog, wings like a bird, and claws like a lion, who put forth riddles and killed those who could not expound them; either, he has seen the representation of one when he was awake, or else the disorderly motion of the brain is such that it causes it to combine ideas, to connect parts, from which there results a whole without model, of which the parts were not formed to be united. It is thus, that his brain combines the head of a woman, of which it already has the idea, with the body of a lioness, of which it also has the image. In this his head acts in the same manner, as when by any defect in the interior organ, his disordered imagination paints to him some objects, notwithstanding he is awake. He frequently dreams, without being asleep: his dreams never produce any thing so strange but that they have some resemblance, with the objects which have anteriorly acted on his senses; which have already communicated ideas to his brain. The watchful theologians have composed, at their leisure, in their waking hours, those phantoms, of which they avail themselves, to terrify or frighten man; they have done nothing more than assemble the scattered traits which they have found in the most terrible beings of their own species; by exaggerating the powers, by enlarging the rights claimed by tyrants, they have formed ideal beings, before whom man trembles, and is afraid.

Thus, it is seen, that dreams, far from proving that the soul acts by its own peculiar energy, that it draws its ideas from its own recesses; prove, on the contrary, that in sleep it is intirely passive, that it does not even renew its modifications, but according to the involuntary confusion, which physical causes produce in the body, of which every thing tends to shew the identity, the consubstantiality with the soul. What appears to have led those into a mistake, who maintained that the soul drew its ideas from itself, is this, they have contemplated these ideas, as if they were real beings, when, in point of fact, they are nothing more than the modifications produced in the brain of man, by objects to which this brain is a stranger; they are these objects, who are the true models, who are the real archetypes to which it is necessary to recur: here is the source of all their errors.

In the individual who dreams, the soul does not act more from itself, than it does in the man who is drunk, that is to say, who is modified by some spirituous liquor: or than it does in the sick man, when he is delirious, that is to say, when he is modified by those physical causes which disturb his machine, which obstruct it in the performance of its functions; or than it, does in him, whose brain is disordered: dreams, like these various states, announce nothing more than a physical confusion in the human machine, under the influence of which the brain ceases to act, after a precise and regular manner: this disorder may be traced to physical causes, such as the aliments—the humours—the combinations—the fermentations, which are but little analogous to the salutary state of man; from hence it will appear, that his brain is necessarily confused, whenever his body is agitated in an extraordinary manner.

Do not let him, therefore, believe that his soul acts by itself, or without a cause, in any one moment of his existence; it is, conjointly with the body, submitted to the impulse of beings, who act on him necessarily, according to their various properties. Wine taken in too great a quantity, necessarily disturbs his ideas, causes confusion in his corporeal functions, occasions disorder in his mental faculties.

If there really existed a being in Nature, with the capability of moving itself by its own peculiar energies, that is to say, able to produce motion, independent of all other causes, such a being would have the power of arresting itself, or of suspending the motion of the universe; which is nothing more than an immense chain of causes linked one to another, acting and re-acting by necessary immutable laws, and which cannot be changed, which are incapable of being suspended, unless the essences of every thing in it were changed, without the properties of every thing were annihilated. In the general system of the world, nothing more can be perceived than a long series of motion, received and communicated in succession, by beings capacitated to give impulse to each other: it is thus, that each body is moved by the collision of some other body. The invisible motion of some soul is to be attributed to causes concealed within himself; he believes that it is moved by itself, because he does not see the springs which put it in motion, or because he conceives those powers are incapable of producing the effects he so much admires: but, does he more clearly conceive, how a spark in exploding gunpowder, is capable of producing the terrible effects he witnesses? The source of his errors arise from this, that he regards his body as gross and inert, whilst this body is a sensible machine, which has necessarily an instantaneous conscience the moment it receives an impression; which is conscious of its own existence by the recollection of impressions successively experienced; memory by resuscitating an impression anteriorly received, by detaining it, or by causing an impression which it receives to remain, whilst it associates it with another, then with a third, gives all the mechanism of *reasoning*.

An idea, which is only an imperceptible modification of the brain, gives play to the organ of speech, which displays itself by the motion it excites in the tongue: this, in its turn, breeds ideas, thoughts, and passions, in those beings who are provided with organs susceptible of receiving analagous motion; in consequence of which, the wills of a great number of men are influenced, who, combining their efforts, produce a revolution in a state, or even have an influence over the entire globe. It is thus, that an ALEXANDER decided the fate of Asia, it is thus, that a MAHOMET changed the face of the earth; it is thus, that imperceptible causes produce the most terrible, the most extended effects, by a series of necessary motion imprinted on the brain of man.

The difficulty of comprehending the effects produced on the soul of man, has made him attribute to it those incomprehensible qualities which have been examined. By the aid of imagination, by the power of thought, this soul appears to quit his body, to carry itself with the greatest ease, to transport itself with the utmost facility towards the most distant objects; to run over, to approximate in the twinkling of an eye, all the points of the universe: he has therefore believed, that a being who is susceptible of such rapid motion, must be of a nature very distinguished from all others; he has persuaded himself that this soul in reality does travel, that it actually springs over the immense space necessary to meet these various objects; he did not perceive, that to do it in an instant, it had only to run over itself to approximate the ideas consigned to its keeping, by means of the senses.

Indeed, it is never by any other means than by his senses, that beings become known to man, or furnish him with ideas; it is only in consequence of the impulse given to his body, that his brain is modified, or that his soul thinks, wills, and acts. If, as ARISTOTLE asserted more than two thousand years ago,—"*nothing enters the mind of man but through the medium of his senses*,"—it follows as a consequence, that every thing that issues from it must find some sensible object to which it can attach its ideas, whether immediately, as a man, a tree, a bird, &c. or in the last analysis or decomposition, such as pleasure, happiness, vice, virtue, &c. This principle, so true, so luminous, so important in its consequence, has been set forth in all its lustre, by a great number of philosophers; among the rest, by the great LOCKE. Whenever, therefore, a word or its idea does not connect itself with some sensible object to which it can be related, this word or this idea is unmeaning, and void of sense; it were better for man that the idea was banished from his mind, struck out of his language: this principle is only the converse of the axiom of ARISTOTLE,—"*if the direct be evident, the inverse must be so likewise.*" How has it happened, that the profound LOCKE, who, to the great mortification of the metaphysicians, has placed this principle of ARISTOTLE in the clearest point of view? how is it, that all those who, like him, have recognized the absurdity of the system of innate ideas, have not drawn the immediate, the necessary consequences? How has it come to pass, that they have not had sufficient courage to apply so clear a principle to all those fanciful chimeras with which the human mind has for such a length of time been so vainly occupied? did they not perceive that their principle sapped the very foundations of those metaphysical speculations, which never occupy man but with those objects of which, as they are inaccessible to his senses, he consequently can never form to himself any accurate idea? But prejudice, when it is generally held sacred, prevents him from seeing the most simple application of the most self-evident principles. In metaphysical researches, the greatest men are frequently nothing more than children, who are incapable of either foreseeing or deducing the consequence of their own data.

LOCKE, as well as all those who have adopted his system, which is so demonstrable,—or to the axiom of ARISTOTLE, which is so clear, ought to have concluded from it that all those wonderful things with which metaphysicians have amused themselves, are mere chimeras; mere wanderings of the imagination; that an immaterial spirit or substance, without extent, without parts, is, in fact, nothing more than an absence of ideas; in short, they ought to have felt that the ineffable intelligence which they have supposed to preside at the helm of the world, is after all nothing more than a being of their own imagination, on which man has never been in accord, whom he has pictured under all the variety of forms, to which he has at different periods, in different climes, ascribed every kind of attribute, good or bad; but of which it is impossible his senses can ever prove either the existence or the qualities.

For the same reason, moral philosophers ought to have concluded, that what is called moral sentiment, *moral instinct*, that is, innate ideas of virtue, anterior to all experience of the good or bad effects resulting from its practice, are mere chimerical notions, which, like a great many others, have for their guarantee and base only metaphysical speculation. Before man can judge, he must feel; before he can distinguish good from evil, he must compare. *Morals*, is a science of facts: to found them, therefore, on an hypothesis inaccessible to his senses, of which he has no means of proving the reality, is to render them uncertain; it is to cast the log of discord into his lap, to cause him unceasingly to dispute upon that which he can never understand. To assert that the ideas of morals are *innate*, or the effect of *instinct*, is to pretend that man knows how to read before he has learned the letters of the alphabet; that he is acquainted with the laws of society before they are either made or promulgated.

To undeceive him, with respect to innate ideas or modifications, imprinted on his soul, at the moment of his birth, it is simply requisite to recur to their source; he will then see that those with which he is familiar, which have, as it were, identified themselves with his existence, have all come to him through the medium of some of his senses; that they are sometimes engraven on his brain with great difficulty,—that they have never been permanent,—that they have perpetually varied in him: he will see that these pretended inherent ideas of his soul, are the effect of education, of example, above all, of habit, which by reiterated motion has taught his brain to associate his ideas either in a confused or a perspicuous manner; to familiarize itself with systems either rational or absurd. In short, he takes those for innate ideas of which he has forgotten the origin; he no longer recals to himself, either the precise epoch, or the successive circumstances when these ideas were first consigned to his brain: arrived at a certain age he believes he has always had the same notions; his memory, crowded with experience, loaded with a multitude of facts, is no longer able to distinguish the particular circumstances which have contributed to give his brain its present modifications; its instantaneous mode of thinking; its actual opinions. For example, not one of his race, perhaps, recollects the first time the word God struck his ears—the first ideas that it formed in him—the first thoughts that it produced in him; nevertheless, it is certain that from thence he has searched for some being with whom to connect the idea which he has either formed to himself, or which has been suggested to him: accustomed to hear God continually spoken of, he has, when in other respects, the most enlightened, regarded this idea as if it were infused into him by Nature; whilst it is visibly to be attributed to those delineations of it, which his parents or his instructors have made to him; which he has, in consequence, modified according to his own particular organization, and the circumstances in which he has been placed; it is thus, that each individual forms to himself a God, of which he is himself the model, or which he modifies after his own fashion.

His ideas of morals, although more real than those of metaphysics, are not however innate: the moral sentiments he forms on the will, or the judgment he passes on the actions of man, are founded on experience; which alone can enable him to discriminate those which are either useful or prejudicial, virtuous or vicious, honest or dishonest, worthy his esteem, or deserving his censure. His moral sentiments are the fruit of a multitude of experience that is frequently very long and very complicated. He gathers it with time; it is more or less faithful, by reason of his particular organization and the causes by which he is modified; he ultimately applies this experience with greater or less facility; to this is to be attributed his habit of judging. The celerity with which he applies his experience when he judges of the moral actions of his fellow man, is what has been termed *moral instinct*.

That which in natural philosophy is called *instinct*, is only the effect of some want of the body, the consequence of some attraction or some repulsion in man or animals. The child that is newly born, sucks for the first time; the nipple of the breast is put into his mouth: by the natural analogy, that is found between the conglomerate glands, filled with nerves; which line his mouth, and the milk which flows from the bosom of the nurse, through the medium of the nipple, causes the child to press it with his mouth, in order to express the fluid appropriate to nourish his tender age; from all this the infant gathers experience; by degrees the idea of a nipple, of milk, of pleasure, associate themselves in his brain: every time he sees the nipple, he seizes it, promptly conveys it to his mouth, and applies it to the use for which it is designed.

What has been said, will enable us to judge of those prompt and sudden sentiments, which have been designated *the force of blood*. Those sentiments of love, which fathers and mothers have for their children— those feelings of affection, which children, with good inclinations, bear towards their parents, are by no means *innate sentiments*; they are nothing more, than the effect of experience, of reflection, of habit, in souls of sensibility. These sentiments do not even exist in a great number of human beings. We but too often witness tyrannical parents, occupied with making enemies of their children, who appear to have been formed, only to be the victims of their irrational caprices or their unreasonable desires.

From the instant in which man commences, until that in which he ceases to exist, he feels—he is moved either agreeably or unpleasantly—he collects facts—he gathers experience; these produce ideas in his brain, that are either cheerful or gloomy. Not one individual has all this experience present to his memory at the same time, it does not ever represent to him the whole clew at once: it is, however, this experience that mechanically directs him, without his knowledge, in all his actions; it was to designate the rapidity with, which he applied this experience, of which he so frequently loses the connection—of which he is so often at a loss to render himself an account, that he imagined the word *instinct*: it appears to be the effect of magic, the operation of a supernatural power, to the greater number of individuals: it is a word devoid of sense to many others; but to the philosopher it is the effect of a very lively feeling to him it consists in the faculty of combining, promptly, a multitude of experience—of arranging with facility—of comparing with quickness, a long and numerous train of extremely complicated ideas. It is want that causes the inexplicable instinct we behold in animals which have been denied souls without reason, whilst they are susceptible of an infinity of actions that prove they think— judge—have memory—are capable of experience—can combine ideas—can apply them with more or less facility to satisfy the wants engendered by their particular organization; in short, that prove they have passions that are capable of being modified. Nothing but the height of folly can refuse intellectual faculties to animals; they feel, choose, deliberate, express love, show hatred; in many instances their senses are much keener than those of man. Fish will return periodically to the spot where it is the custom to throw them bread.

It is well known the embarrassments which animals have thrown in the way of the partizans of the doctrine of spirituality; they have been fearful, if they allowed them to have a spiritual soul, of elevating them to the condition of human creatures; on the other hand, in not allowing them to have a soul, they have furnished their adversaries with authority to deny it in like manner to man, who thus finds himself debased to the condition of the animal. Metaphysicians have never known how to extricate themselves from this difficulty. DESCARTES fancied he solved it by saying that beasts have no souls, but are mere machines. Nothing can be nearer the surface, than the absurdity of this principle. Whoever contemplates Nature without prejudice, will readily acknowledge that there is no other difference between the man and the beast, than that which is to be attributed to the diversity of his organization.

In some beings of the human species, who appear to be endowed with a greater sensibility of organs than others, may be seen an instinct, by the assistance of which they very promptly judge of the concealed dispositions of their fellows, simply by inspecting the lineaments of their face. Those who are denominated *physiognomists*, are only men of very acute feelings; who have gathered an experience of which others, whether from the coarseness of their organs, from the little attention they have paid, or from some defect in their senses, are totally incapable: these last do not believe in the science of physiognomy, which appears to them perfectly ideal. Nevertheless, it is certain, that the action of this soul, which has been made spiritual, makes impressions that are extremely marked upon the exterior of the body; these impressions, continually reiterated, their image remains: thus the habitual passions of man paint themselves on his countenance; by which the attentive observer, who is endowed with acute feeling, is enabled to judge with great rapidity of his mode of existence, and even to foresee his actions, his inclinations, his desires, his predominant passions, &c. Although the science of physiognomy appears chimerical to a great number of persons, yet there are few who have not a clear idea of a tender regard—of a cruel eye—of an austere aspect—of a false, dissimulating look—of an open countenance, &c. Keen practised optics acquire without doubt the faculty of penetrating the concealed motion of the soul, by the visible traces it leaves upon features that it has continually modified. Above all, the eyes of man very quickly undergo changes according to the motion which is excited in him: these delicate organs are visibly altered by the smallest shock communicated to his brain. Serene eyes announce a tranquil soul; wild eyes indicate a restless mind; fiery eyes pourtray a choleric, sanguine temperament; fickle or inconstant eyes give room to suspect a soul either alarmed or dissimulating. It is the study of this variety of shades that renders man practised and acute: upon the spot he combines a multitude of acquired experience, in order to form his judgment of the person he beholds. His judgment, thus rapidly formed, partakes in nothing of the supernatural, in nothing of the wonderful: such a man is only distinguished by the fineness of his organs, and by the celerity with which his brain performs its functions.

It is the same with some beings of the human species, in whom may be discovered an extraordinary sagacity, which, to the uninformed, appears miraculous. The most skilful practitioners in medicine, are, no doubt, men endowed with very acute feelings, similar to that of the physiognomists, by the assistance of which they judge with great facility of diseases, and very promptly draw their prognostics. Indeed, we see men who are capable of appreciating in the twinkling of an eye a multitude of circumstances, who have sometimes the faculty of foreseeing the most distant events; yet, this species of prophetic talent has nothing in it of the supernatural; it indicates nothing more than great experience, with an extremely delicate organization, from which they derive the faculty of judging with extreme faculty of causes, of foreseeing their very remote effects. This faculty, however, is also found in animals, who foresee much better than man, the variations of the atmosphere with the various changes of the weather. Birds have long been the prophets, and even the guides of several nations who pretend to be extremely enlightened.

It is, then, to their organization, exercised after a particular manner, that must be attributed those wonderous faculties which distinguish some beings, that astonish others. To have *instinct*, only signifies to judge quickly, without requiring to make a long, reasoning on the subject. Man's ideas upon vice and upon virtue, are by no means innate; they are, like all others, acquired: the judgment he forms, is founded upon experience, whether true or false,—this depends upon his conformation, and upon the habits that have modified him. The infant has no ideas either of the Divinity or of virtue; it is from those who instruct him that he receives these ideas; he makes more or less use of them, according to his natural organization, or as his dispositions have been more or less exercised. Nature gives man legs, the nurse teaches him their use, his agility depends upon their natural conformation, and the manner in which he exercises them.

What is called *taste*, in the fine arts, is to be attributed, in the same manner, only to the acuteness of man's organs, practised by the habit of seeing, of comparing, of judging certain objects; from whence results, to some of his species, the faculty of judging with great rapidity, in the twinkling of an eye, the whole with its various relations. It is by the force of seeing, of feeling, of experiencing objects, that he attains to a knowledge of them; it is in consequence of reiterating this experience, that he acquires the power, that he gains the habit of judging with celerity. But this experience is by no means innate, he did not possess it before he was born; he is neither able to think, to judge, nor to have ideas, before he has feeling; he is neither in a capacity to love, nor to hate; to approve, nor to blame, before he has been moved, either agreeably or disagreeably. Nevertheless, this is precisely what must be supposed by those who are desirous to make man admit of innate ideas, of opinions; infused by Nature, whether in morals, metaphysics, or any other science. That his mind should have the faculty of thought, that it should occupy itself with an object, it is requisite it should be acquainted with its qualities; that it may have a knowledge of these qualities, it is necessary some of his senses should have been struck by them: those objects, therefore, of which he does not know any of the qualities, are nullities; or at least they do not exist for him.

It will be asserted, perhaps, that the universal consent of man, upon certain propositions, such as *the whole is greater than its part*, upon all geometrical demonstrations, appear to warrant the supposition of certain primary notions that are innate, not acquired. It may be replied, that these notions are always acquired; that they are the fruit of an experience more or less prompt; that it is requisite to have compared the whole with its part, before conviction can ensue, that the whole is the greater of the two. Man when he is born, does not bring with him the idea that two and two make four; but he is, nevertheless, speedily convinced of its truth. Before forming any judgment whatever, it is absolutely necessary to have compared facts.

It is evident, that those who have gratuitously supposed innate ideas, or notions inherent in man, have confounded his organization, or his natural dispositions, with the habit by which he is modified; with the greater or less aptitude he has of making experience, and of applying it in his judgment. A man who has taste in painting, has, without doubt, brought with him into the world eyes more acute, more penetrating than another; but these eyes would by no means enable him to judge with promptitude, if he had never had occasion to exercise them; much less, in some respects, can those dispositions which are called *natural*, be regarded as innate. Man is not, at twenty years of age, the same as he was when he came into the world; the physical causes that are continually acting upon him, necessarily have an influence upon his organization, and so modify it, that his natural dispositions themselves are not at one period what they are at another. La Motte Le Vayer says, "We think quite otherwise of things at one time than at another; when young than when old—when hungry than when our appetite is satisfied—in the night than in the day—when peevish than when cheerful. Thus, varying every hour, by a thousand other circumstances, which keep us in a state of perpetual inconstancy and instability." Every day may be seen children, who, to a certain age—display a great deal of ingenuity, a strong aptitude for the sciences, who finish by falling into stupidity. Others may be observed, who, during their infancy, have shown dispositions but little favourable to improvement, yet develope themselves in the end, and astonish us by an exhibition of those qualities of which we hardly thought them susceptible: there arrives a moment in which the mind takes a spring, makes use of a multitude of experience which it has amassed, without its having been perceived; and, if I may be allowed the expression, without their own knowledge.

Thus, it cannot be too often repeated, all the ideas, all the notions, all the modes of existence, and all the thoughts of man, are acquired. His mind cannot act, cannot exercise itself, but upon that of which it has knowledge; it can understand either well or ill, only those things which it has previously felt. Such of his ideas that do not suppose some exterior material object for their model, or one to which he is able to relate them, which are therefore called *abstract ideas*, are only modes in which his interior organ considers its own peculiar modifications, of which it chooses some without respect to others. The words which he uses to designate these ideas, such as *bounty, beauty, order, intelligence, virtue*, &c. do not offer any one sense, if he does not relate them to, or if he does not explain them by, those objects which his senses have shewn him to be susceptible of those qualities, or of those modes of existence, of that manner of acting, which is known to him. What is it that points out to him the vague idea of *beauty*, if he does not attach it to some object that has struck his senses in a peculiar manner, to which, in consequence, he attributes this quality? What is it that represents the word *intelligence*, if he does not connect it with a certain mode of being and of acting? Does the word *order* signify any thing, if he does not relate it to a series of actions, to a chain of motion, by which he is affected in a certain manner? Is not the word *virtue* void of sense, if he does not apply it to those dispositions of his fellows which produce known effects, different from those which result from contrary inclinations? What do the words *pain* and *pleasure* offer to his mind in the moment when his organs neither suffer nor enjoy, if it be not the modes in which he has been affected, of which his brain conserves the remembrance, of those impressions, which experience has shewn him to be either useful or prejudicial? But when he bears the words spirituality, immateriality, incorporeality, &c. pronounced, neither his senses nor his memory afford him any assistance; they do not furnish him with any means by which he can form an idea of their qualities, or of the objects to which he ought to apply them; in that which is not matter he can only see vacuum and emptiness, which as long as he remains what he is, cannot, to his mind, be susceptible of any one quality.

All the errors, all the disputes of men, have their foundation in this, that they have renounced experience, have surrendered the evidence of their senses, to give themselves up to the guidance of notions which they have believed infused or innate; although in reality they are no more than the effect of a distempered imagination, of prejudices, in which they have been instructed from their infancy, with which habit has familiarized them, which authority has obliged them to conserve. Languages are filled with abstract words, to which are attached confused and vague ideas; of which, when they come to be examined, no model can be found in Nature; no object to which they can be related. When man gives himself the trouble to analyze things, he is quite surprised to find, that those words which are continually in the mouths of men, never present any fixed or determinate idea: he hears them unceasingly speaking of spirits—of the soul and its faculties—of duration—of space—of immensity—of infinity—of perfection—of virtue—of reason— of sentiment—of instinct—of taste, &c. without his being able to tell precisely, what they themselves understand by these words. Nevertheless, they do not appear to have been invented, but for the purpose of representing the images of things; or to paint, by the assistance of the senses, those known objects on which the mind is able to meditate, which it is competent to appreciate, to compare, and to judge.

For man to think of that which has not acted on any of his senses, is to think on words; it is for his senses to dream; it is to seek in his own imagination for objects to which he can attach his wandering ideas: to assign qualities to these objects is, unquestionably, to redouble his extravagance, to set no limits to his folly. If a word be destined to represent to him an object that has not the capacity to act on any one of his organs; of which, it is impossible for him to prove either the existence or the qualities; his imagination, by dint of racking itself, will nevertheless, in some measure, supply him with the ideas he wants; he composes some kind of a picture, with the images or colours he is always obliged to borrow, from the objects of which he has a knowledge: thus the Divinity has been represented by some under the character of a venerable old man; by others, under that of a puissant monarch; by others, as an exasperated, irritated being, &c. It is evident, however, that man, with some of his qualities, has served for the model of these pictures: but if he be informed of objects that are represented as pure spirits—that have neither body nor extent—that are not contained in space—that are beyond nature,—here then he is plunged into emptiness; his mind no longer has any ideas—it no longer knows upon what it meditates. This, as will be seen in the sequel, no doubt, is the source of those unformed notions which some men have formed of the Divinity; they themselves frequently annihilate him, by assembling incompatible and contradictory attributes. In giving him morals—in composing him of known qualities,—they make him a man;—in assigning him the negative attributes of every thing they know, they render him inaccessible to their senses—they destroy all antecedent ideas—they make him a mere nothing. From this it will appear, that those sublime sciences which are called *Theology, Psychology, Metaphysics*, have been mere sciences of words: morals and politics, with which they very frequently mix, have, in consequence, become inexplicable enigmas, which there is nothing short of the study of Nature can enable us to expound.

Man has occasion for truth; it consists in a knowledge of the true relations he has with those beings competent to have an influence on his welfare; these relations are to be known only by experience: without experience there can be no reason; without reason man is only a blind creature, who conducts himself by chance. But, how is he to acquire experience upon ideal objects, which his senses neither enable him to know nor to examine? How is he to assure himself of the existence, how ascertain the qualities of beings he is not able to feel? How can he judge whether there objects be favorable or prejudicial to him? How is he to know, without the evidence of his senses, what he ought to love, what he should hate, what to seek after, what to shun, what to do, what to leave undone? It is, however, upon this knowledge that his condition in this world rests; it is upon this knowledge that morals is founded. From whence it may be seen, that, by causing him to blend vague metaphysical notions with morals, or the science of the certain and invariable relations which subsist between mankind; or by weakly establishing them upon chimerical ideas, which have no existence but in his imagination; these morals, upon which the welfare of society so much depends, are rendered uncertain, are made arbitrary, are abandoned to the caprices of fancy, are not fixed upon any solid basis.

Beings essentially different by their natural organization, by the modifications they experience, by the habits they contract, by the opinions they acquire, must of necessity think differently. His temperament, as we have seen, decides the mental qualities of man: this temperament itself is diversely modified in him: from whence it consecutively follows, his imagination cannot possibly be the same; neither can it create to him the same images. Each individual is a connected whole, of which all the parts have a necessary correspondence. Different eyes must see differently, must give extremely varied ideas of the objects they contemplate, even when these objects are real. What, then, must be the diversity of these ideas, if the objects meditated upon do not act upon the senses? Mankind have pretty nearly the same ideas, in the gross, of those substances that act upon his organs with vivacity; he is sufficiently in unison upon some qualities which he contemplates very nearly in the same manner; I say, very nearly, because the intelligence, the notion, the conviction of any one proposition, however simple, however evident, however clear it may be supposed, is not, nor cannot be, strictly the same, in any two men. Indeed, one man not being another man, the first cannot, for example, have rigorously and mathematically the same notion of unity as the second; seeing that an identical effect cannot be the result of two different causes. Thus, when men are in accord in their ideas, in their modes of thinking, in their judgment, in their passions, in their desires, in, their tastes, their consent does not arise from their seeing or feeling the same objects precisely in the same manner, but pretty nearly; language is not, nor cannot be, sufficiently copious to designate the vast variety of shades, the multiplicity of imperceptible differences, which is to be found in their modes of seeing and thinking. Each man, then, has, to say thus, a language which is peculiar to himself alone, and this language is incommunicable to others. What harmony, what unison, then, can possibly exist between them, when they discourse with each other, upon objects only known to their imagination? Can this imagination in one individual ever be the same as in another? How can they possibly understand each other, when they assign to those objects qualities that can only be attributed to the particular manner in which their brain is affected.

For one man to exact from another that he shall think like himself, is to insist that he shall be organized precisely in the same manner—that he shall have been modified exactly the same in every moment of his existence: that he shall have received the same temperament, the same nourishment, the same education: in a word, that he shall require that other to be himself. Wherefore is it not exacted that all men shall have the same features? Is man more the master of his opinions? Are not his opinions the necessary consequence of his Nature, and of those peculiar circumstances which, from his infancy, have necessarily had an influence upon his mode of thinking, and his manner of acting? If man be a connected whole, whenever a single feature differs from his own, ought he not to conclude that it is not possible his brain can either think, associate ideas, imagine, or dream precisely in the same manner with that other.

The diversity in the temperament of man, is the natural, the necessary source of the diversity of his passions, of his taste, of his ideas of happiness, of his opinions of every kind. Thus, this same diversity will be the fatal source of his disputes, of his hatreds, of his injustice, every time he shall reason upon unknown objects, but to which he shall attach the greatest importance. He will never understand either himself or others, in speaking of a spiritual soul, or of immaterial substances distinguished from Nature; he will, from that moment, cease to speak the same language, and he will never attach the same ideas to the same words. What, then, shall be, the common standard that shall decide which is the man that thinks with the greatest justice? What the scale by which to measure who has the best regulated imagination? What balance shall be found sufficiently exact to determine whose knowledge is most certain, when he agitates subjects, which experience cannot enable him to examine, that escape all his senses, that have no model, that are above reason? Each individual, each legislator, each speculator, each nation, has ever formed to himself different ideas of these things; each believes, that his own peculiar reveries ought to be preferred to those of his neighbours; which always appear to him an absurd, ridiculous, and false as his own can possibly have appeared to his fellow; each clings to his own opinion, because each retains his own peculiar mode of existence; each believes his happiness depends upon his attachment to his prejudices, which he never adopts but because he believes them beneficial to his welfare. Propose to a man to change his religion for yours, he will believe you a madman; you will only excite his indignation, elicit his contempt; he will propose to you, in his turn, to adopt his own peculiar opinions; after much reasoning, you will treat each other as absurd beings, ridiculously opiniated, pertinaciously stubborn: and he will display the least folly, who shall first yield. But if the adversaries become heated in the dispute, which always happens, when they suppose the matter important, or when they would defend the cause of their own self-love; from thence their passions sharpen, they grow angry, quarrels are provoked, they hate each other, and end by reciprocal injury. It is thus, that for opinions, which no man can demonstrate, we see the Brahmin despised; the Mahommedan hated; the Pagan held in contempt; that they oppress and disdain each with the most rancorous animosity: the Christian burns the Jew at what is called an *auto-de-fe*, because he clings to the faith of his fathers: the Roman Catholic condemns the Protestant to the flames, and makes a conscience of massacring him in cold blood: this re-acts in his turn; sometimes the various sects of Christians league together against the incredulous Turk, and for a moment suspend their own bloody disputes that they may chastise the enemies to the true faith: then, having glutted their revenge, return with redoubled fury, to wreak over again their infuriated vengeance on each other.

If the imaginations of men were the same, the chimeras which they bring forth would be every where the same; there would be no disputes among them on this subject, if they all dreamt in the same manner; great numbers of human beings would be spared, if man occupied his mind with objects capable of being known, of which the existence was proved, of which he was competent to discover the true qualities, by sure, by reiterated experience. *Systems of Philosophy* are not subject to dispute but when their principles are not sufficiently proved; by degrees experience, in pointing out the truth and detecting their errors, terminates these quarrels. There is no variance among *geometricians* upon the principles of their science; it is only raised, when their suppositions are false, or their objects too much complicated. *Theologians* find so much difficulty in agreeing among themselves, simply, because, in their contests, they divide without ceasing, not known and examined propositions, but prejudices with which they have been imbued in their youth—in the schools—by each other's books, &c. They are perpetually reasoning, not upon real objects, of which the existence is demonstrated, but upon imaginary systems of which they have never examined the reality; they found these disputes, not upon averred experience, or constant facts, but upon gratuitious suppositions, which each endeavours to convince the other are without solidity. Finding these ideas of long standing, that few people, refuse to admit them, they take them for incontestible truths, that ought to be received merely upon being announced; whenever they attach great importance to them, they irritate themselves against the temerity of those who have the audacity to doubt, or even to examine them.

If prejudice had been laid aside, it would perhaps have been discovered that many of those objects, which have given birth to the most shocking, the most sanguinary disputes among men, were mere phantoms; which a little examination would have shown to be unworthy their notice: *the priests of Apollo* would have been harmless, if man had examined for himself, without prejudice, the tenets they held forth: he would have found, that he was fighting, that he was cutting his neighbour's throat, for words void of sense; or, at the least, he would have learned to doubt his right to act in the manner he did; he would have renounced that dogmatical, that imperious tone he assumed, by which he would oblige his fellow to unite with him in opinion. The most trifling reflection would have shewn him the necessity of this diversity in his notions, of this contrariety in his imagination, which depends upon his Natural conformation diversely modified: which necessarily has an influence over his thoughts, over his will, and over his actions. In short, if he had consulted morals, if he had fallen back upon reason, every thing would have conspired to prove to him, that beings who call themselves rational, were made to think variously; on that account were designed to live peaceable with each other, to love each other, to lend each other mutual succours whatever may be their opinions upon subjects, either impossible to be known, or to be contemplated under the same point of view: every thing would have joined in evidence to convince him of the unreasonable tyranny, of the unjust violence, of the useless cruelty of those men of blood, who persecute, who destroy mankind, in order that they may mould him to their own peculiar opinions; every thing would have conducted mortals to *mildness*, to *indulgence*, to *toleration*; virtues, unquestionably of more real importance, much more necessary to the welfare of society, than the marvellous speculations by which it is divided, by which it is frequently hurried on to sacrifice to a maniacal fury, the pretended enemies to these revered flights of the imagination.

From this it must be evident, of what importance it is to *morals* to examine the ideas, to which it has been agreed to attach so much worth; to which man is continually sacrificing his own peculiar happiness; to which he is immolating the tranquillity of nations, at the irrational command of fanatical cruel guides. Let him fall back on his experience; let him return to Nature; let him occupy himself with reason; let him consult those objects that are real, which are useful to his permanent felicity; let him study Nature's laws; let him study himself; let him consult the bonds which unite him to his fellow mortals; let him examine the fictitious bonds that enchain him to the most baneful prejudices. If his imagination must always feed itself with illusions, if he remains steadfast in his own opinions, if his prejudices are dear to him, let him at least permit others to ramble in their own manner, or seek after truth as best suits their inclination; but let him always recollect, that all the opinions—all the ideas—all the systems—all the wills— all the actions of man, are the necessary consequence of his nature, of his temperament, of his organization, and of those causes, either transitory or constant, which modify hint: in short, that *man is not more a free agent to think than to act:* a truth that will be again proved in the following chapter.

CHAP. XI
Of the System of Man's free agency.

Those who have pretended that the *soul* is distinguished from the body, is immaterial, draws its ideas from its own peculiar source, acts by its own energies without the aid of any exterior object; by a consequence of their own system, have enfranchised it from those physical laws, according to which all beings of which we have a knowledge are obliged to act. They have believed that the foul is mistress of its own conduct, is able to regulate its own peculiar operations; has the faculty to determine its will by its own natural energy; in a word, they have pretended man is a *free agent*.

It has been already sufficiently proved, that the soul is nothing more than the body, considered relatively to some of its functions, more concealed than others: it has been shewn, that this soul, even when it shall be supposed immaterial, is continually modified conjointly with the body; is submitted to all its motion; that without this it would remain inert and dead: that, consequently, it is subjected to the influence of those material, to the operation those physical causes, which give impulse to the body; of which the mode of existence, whether habitual or transitory, depends upon the material elements by which it is surrounded; that form its texture; that constitute its temperament; that enter into it by the means of the aliments; that penetrate it by their subtility; the faculties which are called intellectual, and those qualities which are styled moral, have been explained in a manner purely physical; entirely natural: in the last place, it has been demonstrated, that all the ideas, all the systems, all the affections, all the opinions, whether true or false, which man forms to himself, are to be attributed to his physical powers; are to be ascribed to his material senses. Thus man is a being purely physical; in whatever manner he is considered, he is connected to universal Nature: submitted to the necessary, to the immutable laws that she imposes on all the beings she contains, according to their peculiar essences; conformable to the respective properties with which, without consulting them, she endows each particular species. Man's life is a line that Nature commands him to describe upon the surface of the earth: without his ever being able to swerve from it even for an instant. He is born without his own consent; his organizations does in no wise depend upon himself; his ideas come to him involuntarily; his habits are in the power of those who cause him to contract them; he is unceasingly modified by causes, whether visible or concealed, over which he has no controul; give the hue to his way of thinking, and determine his manner of acting. He is good or bad—happy or miserable—wise or foolish—reasonable or irrational, without his will going for anything in these various states. Nevertheless, in despite of the shackles by which he is bound, it is pretended he is a free agent, or that independent of the causes by which he is moved, he determines his own will; regulates his own condition.

However slender the foundation of this opinion, of which every thing ought to point out to him the error; it is current at this day for an incontestible truth, and believed enlightened; it is the basis or religion, which has been incapable of imagining how man could either merit reward or deserve punishment if he was not a free agent. Society has been believed interested in this system, because an idea has gone abroad, that if all the actions of man were to be contemplated as necessary, the right of punishing those who injure their associates would no longer exist. At length human vanity accommodated itself to an hypothesis which, unquestionable, appears to distinguish man from all other physical beings, by assigning to him the special privilege of a total independence of all other causes; but of which a very little reflection would have shewn him the absurdity or even the impossibility.

As a part, subordinate to the great whole, man is obliged to experience its influence. To be a free agent it were needful that each individual was of greater strength than the entire of Nature; or, that he was out of this Nature: who, always in action herself, obliges all the beings she embraces, to act, and to concur to her general motion; or, as it has been said elsewhere, to conserve her active existence, by the motion that all beings produce in consequence of their particular energies, which result from their being submitted to fixed, eternal, and immutable laws. In order that man might be a free agent, it were needful that all beings should lose their essences; it is equally necessary that he himself should no longer enjoy physical sensibility; that he should neither know good nor evil; pleasure nor pain; but if this was the case, from that moment he would no longer be in a state to conserve himself, or render his existence happy; all beings would become indifferent to him; he would no longer have any choice; he would cease to know what he ought to love; what it was right he should fear; he would not have any acquaintance with that which he should seek after; or with that which it is requisite he should avoid. In short, man would be an unnatural being; totally incapable of acting in the manner we behold. It is the actual essence of man to tend to his well-being; to be desirous to conserve his existence; if all the motion of his machine springs as a necessary consequence from this primitive impulse; if pain warns him of that which he ought to avoid; if pleasure announces to him that which he should desire; if it is in his essence to love that which either excites delight, or, that from which he expects agreeable sensations; to hate that which makes him either fear contrary impressions; or, that which afflicts him with uneasiness; it must necessarily be, that he will be attracted by that which he deems advantageous; that his will shall he determined by those objects which he judges useful; that he will he repelled by those beings which he believes prejudicial, either to his habitual, or to his transitory mode of existence; by that which he considers disadvantageous. It is only by the aid of experience, that man acquires the faculty of understanding what he ought to love; of knowing what he ought to fear. Are his organs sound? his experience will he true: are they unsound? it will be false: in the first instance he will have reason, prudence, foresight; he will frequently foresee very remote effects; he will know, that what he sometimes contemplates as a good, may possibly become an evil, by its necessary or probable consequences: that what must be to him a transient evil, may by its result procure him a solid and durable good. It is thus experience enables him to foresee that the amputation of a limb will cause him painful sensation, he consequently is obliged to fear this operation, and he endeavours to avoid the pain; but if experience has also shewn him, that the transitory pain this amputation will cause him may be the means of saving his life; the preservation, of his existence being of necessity dear to him, he is obliged to submit himself to the momentary pain with a view to procuring a permanent good, by which it will be overbalanced.

The will, as we have elsewhere said, is a modification of the brain, by which it is disposed to action or prepared to give play to the organs. This will is necessarily determined by the qualities, good or bad, agreeable or painful, of the object or the motive that acts upon his senses; or of which the idea remains with him, and is resuscitated by his memory. In consequence, he acts necessarily; his action is the result of the impulse he receives either from the motive, from the object, or from the idea, which has modified his brain, or disposed his will. When he does not act according to this impulse, it is because there comes some new cause, some new motive, some new idea, which modifies his brain in a different manner, gives him a new impulse, determines his will in another way; by which the action of the former impulse is suspended: thus, the sight of an agreeable object, or its idea, determines his will to set him in action to procure it; but if a new object or a new idea more powerfully attracts him, it gives a new direction to his will, annihilates the effect of the former, and prevents the action by which it was to be procured. This is the mode in which reflection, experience, reason, necessarily arrests or suspends the action of man's will; without this, he would, of necessity, have followed the anterior impulse which carried him towards a then desirable object. In all this he always acts according to necessary laws, from which he has no means of emancipating himself.

If, when tormented with violent thirst, he figures to himself an idea, or really perceives a fountain, whose limpid streams might cool his feverish habit, is he sufficient master of himself to desire or not to desire the object competent to satisfy so lively a want? It will no doubt be conceded, that it is impossible he should not be desirous to satisfy it; but it will be said,—If at this moment it is announced to him, the water he so ardently desires is poisoned, he will, notwithstanding his vehement thirst, abstain from drinking it; and it has, therefore, been falsely concluded that he is a free agent. The fact, however, is, that the motive in either case is exactly the same: his own conservation. The same necessity that determined him to drink, before he knew the water was deleterious, upon this new discovery, equally determines him not to drink; the desire of conserving himself, either annihilates or suspends the former impulse; the second motive becomes stronger than the preceding; that is, the fear of death, or the desire of preserving himself, necessarily prevails over the painful sensation caused by his eagerness to drink. But, (it will be said) if the thirst is very parching, an inconsiderate man, without regarding the danger, will risque swallowing the water. Nothing is gained by this remark: in this case, the anterior impulse only regains the ascendency; he is persuaded, that life may possibly be longer preserved, or that he shall derive a greater good by drinking the poisoned water, than by enduring the torment, which, to his mind, threatens instant dissolution: thus, the first becomes the strongest, and necessarily urges him on to action. Nevertheless, in either case, whether he partakes of the water, or whether he does not, the two actions will be equally necessary; they will be the effect of that motive which finds itself most puissant; which consequently acts in a most coercive manner upon his will.

This example will serve to explain the whole phaenomena of the human will. This will, or rather the brain, finds itself in the same situation as a bowl, which although it has received an impulse that drives it forward in a straight line, is deranged in its course, whenever a force, superior to the first, obliges it to change its direction. The man who drinks the poisoned water, appears a madman; but the actions of fools are as necessary as those of the most prudent individuals. The motives that determine the voluptuary, that actuate the debauchee to risk their health, are as powerful, their actions are as necessary, as those which decide the wise man to manage his. But, it will be insisted, the debauchee may be prevailed on to change his conduct; this does not imply that he is a free agent; but, that motives may be found sufficiently powerful to annihilate the effect of those that previously acted upon him; then these new motives determine his will to the new mode of conduct he may adopt, as necessarily as the former did to the old mode.

Man is said to *deliberate* when the action of the will is suspended; this happens when two opposite motives act alternately upon him. To deliberate, is to hate and to love in succession; it is to be alternately attracted and repelled; it is to be moved sometimes by one motive, sometimes by another. Man only deliberates when he does not distinctly understand the quality of the objects from which he receives impulse, or when experience has not sufficiently apprised him of the effects, more or less remote, which his actions will produce. He would take the air, but the weather is uncertain; he deliberates in consequence; he weighs the various motives that urge his will to go out or to stay at home; he is at length determined by that motive which is most probable; this removes his indecision, which necessarily settles his will either to remain within or to go abroad: this motive is always either the immediate or ultimate advantage he finds or thinks he finds in the action to which he is persuaded.

Man's will frequently fluctuates between two objects, of which either the presence or the ideas move him alternately: he waits until he has contemplated the objects or the ideas they have left in his brain; which solicit him to different actions; he then compares these objects or ideas: but even in the time of deliberation, during the comparison, pending these alternatives of love and hatred, which succeed each other sometimes with the utmost rapidity, he is not a free agent for a single instant; the good or the evil which he believes he finds successively in the objects, are the necessary motives of these momentary wills; of the rapid motion of desire or fear that he experiences as long as his uncertainty continues. From this it will be obvious, that deliberation is necessary; that uncertainty is necessary; that whatever part he takes, in consequence of this deliberation, it will always necessarily be that which he has judged, whether well or ill, is most probable to turn to his advantage.

When the soul is assailed by two motives that act alternately upon it, or modify it successively, it deliberates; the brain is in a sort of equilibrium, accompanied with perpetual oscillations, sometimes towards one object, sometimes towards the other, until the most forcible carries the point, and thereby extricates it, from this state of suspense, in which consists the indecision of his will. But when the brain is simultaneously assailed by causes equally strong, that move it in opposite directions; agreeable to the general law of all bodies, when they are struck equally by contrary powers, it stops, it is in *nisu*; it is neither capable to will nor to act; it waits until one of the two causes has obtained sufficient force to overpower the other, to determine its will, to attract it in such a manner that it may prevail over the efforts of the other cause.

This mechanism, so simple, so natural, suffices to demonstrate, why uncertainty is painful; why suspense is always a violent state for man. The brain, an organ so delicate, so mobile, experiences such rapid modifications, that it is fatigued; or when it is urged in contrary directions, by causes equally powerful, it suffers a kind of compression, that prevents the activity which is suitable to the preservation of the whole, which is necessary to procure what is advantageous to its existence. This mechanism will also explain the irregularity, the indecision, the inconstancy of man; and account for that conduct, which frequently appears an inexplicable mystery, which indeed it is, under the received systems. In consulting experience, it will be found that the soul is submitted to precisely the same physical laws as the material body. If the will of each individual, during a given time, was only moved by a single cause or passion, nothing would be more easy than to foresee his actions; but his heart is frequently assailed by contrary powers, by adverse motives, which either act on him simultaneously or in succession; then his brain, attracted in opposite directions, is either fatigued, or else tormented by a state of compression, which deprives it of activity. Sometimes it is in a state of incommodious inaction; sometimes it is the sport of the alternate shocks it undergoes. Such, no doubt, is the state in which man finds himself, when a lively passion solicits him to the commission of crime, whilst fear points out to him the danger by which it is attended: such, also, is the condition of him whom remorse, by the continued labour of his distracted soul, prevents from enjoying the objects he has criminally obtained.

If the powers or causes, whether exterior or interior, acting on the mind of man, tend towards opposite points, his soul, is well as all other bodies, will take a mean direction between the two; in consequence of the violence with which his soul is urged, his condition becomes sometimes so painful that his existence is troublesome: he has no longer a tendency to his own peculiar conservation; he seeks after death, as a sanctuary against himself—as the only remedy to his despair: it is thus we behold men, miserable and discontented, voluntarily destroy themselves, whenever life becomes insupportable. Man is competent to cherish his existence, no longer than life holds out charms to him; when he is wrought upon by painful sensations, or drawn by contrary impulsions, his natural tendency is deranged, he is under the necessity to follow a new route; this conducts him to his end, which it even displays to him as the most desirable good. In this manner may be explained, the conduct of those melancholy beings, whose vicious temperaments, whose tortured consciences, whose chagrin, whose *ennui*, sometimes determine them to renounce life.

The various powers, frequently very complicated, that act either successively or simultaneously upon the brain of man, which modify him so diversely in the different periods of his existence, are the true causes of that obscurity in morals, of that difficulty which is found, when it is desired to unravel the concealed springs of his enigmatical conduct. The heart of man is a labyrinth, only because it very rarely happens that we possess the necessary gift of judging it; from whence it will appear, that his circumstances, his indecision, his conduct, whether ridiculous, or unexpected, are the necessary consequences of the changes operated in him; are nothing but the effect of motives that successively determine his will; which are dependent on the frequent variations experienced by his machine. According to these variations, the same motives have not, always, the same influence over his will, the same objects no longer enjoy the faculty of pleasing him; his temperament has changed, either for the moment, or for ever. It follows as a consequence, that his taste, his desires, his passions, will change; there can be no kind of uniformity in his conduct, nor any certitude in the effects to be expected.

Choice by no means proves the free-agency of man; he only deliberates when he does not yet know which to choose of the many objects that move him, he is then in an embarrassment, which does not terminate, until his will as decided by the greater advantage he believes be shall find in the object he chooses, or the action he undertakes. From whence it may he seen that choice is necessary, because he would not determine for an object, or for an action, if he did not believe that he should find in it some direct advantage. That man should have free-agency, it were needful that he should he able to will or choose without motive; or, that he could prevent motives coercing his will. Action always being the effect of his will once determined, as his will cannot be determined but by a motive, which is not in his own power, it follows that he is never the master of the determination of his own peculiar will; that consequently he never acts as a free agent. It has been believed that man was a free agent, because he had a will with the power of choosing; but attention has not been paid to the fact, that even his will is moved by causes independent of himself, is owing to that which is inherent in his own organization, or which belongs to the nature of the beings acting on him. Indeed, man passes a great portion of his life without even willing. His will attends the motive by which it is determined. If he was to render an exact account of every thing he does in the course of each day, from rising in the morning to lying down at night, he would find, that not one of his actions have been in the least voluntary; that they have been mechanical, habitual, determined by causes he was not able to foresee, to which he was either obliged to, yield, or with which he was allured to acquiesce; he would discover, that all the motives of his labours, of his amusements, of his discourses, of his thoughts, have been necessary; that they have evidently either seduced him or drawn him along. Is he the master of willing, not to withdraw his hand from the fire when he fears it will be burnt? Or has he the power to take away from fire the property which makes him fear it? Is he the master of not choosing a dish of meat which he knows to be agreeable, or analogous to his palate; of not preferring it to that which he knows to be disagreeable or dangerous? It is always according to his sensations, to his own peculiar experience, or to his suppositions, that he judges of things either well or ill; but whatever way be his judgment, it depends necessarily on his mode of feeling, whether habitual or accidental, and the qualities he finds in the causes that move him, which exist in despite of himself.

All the causes which by his will is actuated, must act upon him in a manner sufficiently marked, to give him some sensation, some perception, some idea, whether complete or incomplete, true or false; as soon as his will is determined, he must have felt, either strongly or feebly; if this was not the case he would have determined without motive: thus, to speak correctly, there are no causes which are truly indifferent to the will: however faint the impulse he receives, whether on the part of the objects themselves, or on the part of their images or ideas, as soon as his will acts, the impulse has been competent to determine him. In consequence of a slight, of a feeble impulse, the will is weak, it is this weakness of the will that is called *indifference*. His brain with difficulty perceives the sensation, it has received; it consequently acts with less vigour, either to obtain or remove the object or the idea that has modified it. If the impulse is powerful, the will is strong, it makes him act vigorously, to obtain or to remove the object which appears to him either very agreeable or very incommodious.

It has been believed man was a free agent, because it has been imagined that his soul could at will recall ideas, which sometimes suffice to check his most unruly desires. Thus, the idea of a remote evil frequently prevents him from enjoying a present and actual good: thus, remembrance, which is an almost insensible, a slight modification of his brain, annihilates, at each instant, the real objects that act upon his will. But he is not master of recalling to himself his ideas at pleasure; their association is independent of him; they are arranged in his brain, in despite of him, without his own knowledge, where they have made an impression more or less profound; his memory itself depends upon his organization; its fidelity depends upon the habitual or momentary state in which he finds himself; when his will is vigorously determined to some object or idea that excites a very lively passion in him, those objects or ideas that would be able to arrest his action no longer present themselves to his mind; in those moments his eyes are shut to the dangers that menace him, of which the idea ought to make him forbear; he marches forward headlong towards the object by whose image he is hurried on; reflection cannot operate upon him in any way; he sees nothing but the object of his desires; the salutary ideas which might be able to arrest his progress disappear, or else display themselves either too faintly or too late to prevent his acting. Such is the case with all those who, blinded by some strong passion, are not in a condition to recal to themselves those motives, of which the idea alone, in cooler moments, would be sufficient to deter them from proceeding; the disorder in which they are, prevents their judging soundly; render them incapable of foreseeing the consequence of their actions; precludes them from applying to their experience; from making use of their reason; natural operations, which suppose a justness in the manner of associating their ideas; but to which their brain is then not more competent, in consequence of the momentary delirium it suffers, than their hand is to write whilst they are taking violent exercise.

Man's mode of thinking is necessarily determined by his manner of being; it must, therefore, depend on his natural organization, and the modification his system receives independently of his will. From this we are obliged to conclude, that his thoughts, his reflections, his manner of viewing things, of feeling, of judging, of combining ideas, is neither voluntary nor free. In a word, that his soul is neither mistress of the motion excited in it, nor of representing to itself, when wanted, those images or ideas that are capable of counterbalancing the impulse it receives. This is the reason why man, when in a passion, ceases to reason; at that moment reason is as impossible to be heard, as it is during an extacy, or in a fit of drunkenness. The wicked are never more than men who are either drunk or mad: if they reason, it is not until tranquillity is re-established in their machine; then, and not till then, the tardy ideas that present themselves to their mind, enable them to see the consequence of their actions, and give birth to ideas, that bring on them that trouble, which is designated *shame, regret, remorse.*

The errors of philosophers on the free-agency of man, have arisen from their regarding his will as the *primum mobile*, the original motive of his actions; for want of recurring back, they have not perceived the multiplied, the complicated causes, which, independently of him, give motion to the will itself, or which dispose and modify his brain, whilst he himself is purely passive in the motion he receives. Is he the master of desiring or not desiring an object that appears desirable to him? Without doubt it will be answered, No: but he is the master of resisting his desire, if he reflects on the consequences. But, I ask, is he capable of reflecting on these consequences when his soul is hurried along by a very lively passion, which entirely depends upon his natural organization, and the causes by which he is modified? Is it in his power to add to these consequences all the weight necessary to counterbalance his desire? Is he the master of preventing the qualities which render an object desirable from residing in it? I shall be told, he ought to have learned to resist his passions; to contract a habit of putting a curb on his desires. I agree to it without any difficulty: but in reply, I again ask, Is his nature susceptible of this modification? Does his boiling blood, his unruly imagination, the igneous fluid that circulates in his veins, permit him to make, enable him to apply true experience in the moment when it is wanted? And, even when his temperament has capacitated him, has his education, the examples set before him, the ideas with which he has been inspired in early life, been suitable to make him contract this habit of repressing his desires? Have not all these things rather contributed to induce him to seek with avidity, to make him actually desire those objects which you say he ought to resist.

The *ambitious man* cries out,—You will have me resist my passion, but have they not unceasingly repeated to me, that rank, honours, power, are the most desirable advantages in life? Have I not seen my fellow- citizens envy them—the nobles of my country sacrifice every thing to obtain them? In the society in which I live, am I not obliged to feel, that if I am deprived of these advantages, I must expect to languish in contempt, to cringe under the rod of oppression?

The *miser* says,—You forbid me to love money, to seek after the means of acquiring it: alas! does not every thing tell me, that in this world money is the greatest blessing; that it is amply sufficient to render me happy? In the country I inhabit, do I not see all my fellow-citizens covetous of riches? but do I not also witness that they are little scrupulous in the means of obtaining wealth? As soon as they are enriched by the means which you censure, are they not cherished, considered, and respected? By what authority, then, do you object to my amassing treasure? what right have you to prevent my using means, which although you call them sordid and criminal, I see approved by the sovereign? Will you have me renounce my happiness?

The *voluptuary* argues,—You pretend that I should resist my desires; but was I the maker of my own temperament, which unceasingly invites me to pleasure? You call my pleasures disgraceful; but in the country in which I live, do I not witness the most dissipated men enjoying the most distinguished rank? Do I not behold, that no one is ashamed of adultery but the husband it has outraged? do not I see men making trophies of their debaucheries, boasting of their libertinism, rewarded, with applause?

The *choleric* man vociferates,—You advise me to put a curb on my passions; to resist the desire of avenging myself: but can I conquer my nature? Can I alter the received opinions of the world? Shall I not be for ever disgraced, infallibly dishonoured in society, if I do not wash out, in the blood of my fellow-creature, the injuries I have received?

The *zealous enthusiast* exclaims,—You recommend to me mildness, you advise me to be tolerant, to be indulgent to the opinions of my fellow- men; but is not my temperament violent? Do I not ardently love my God? Do they not assure me that zeal is pleasing to him; that sanguinary inhuman persecutors have been his friends? That those who do not think as I do are his enemies? I wish to render myself acceptable in his sight, I therefore adopt the means you reprobate.

In short, the actions of man are never free; they are always the necessary consequence of his temperament, of the received ideas, of the notions, either true or false, which he has formed to himself of happiness: of his opinions, strengthened by example, forfeited by education, consolidated by daily experience. So many crimes are witnessed on the earth, only because every thing conspires to render man vicious, to make him criminal; very frequently, the superstitions he has adopted, his government, his education, the examples set before him, irresistibly drive him on to evil: under these circumstances morality preaches virtue to him in vain. In those societies where vice is esteemed, where crime is crowned, where venality is constantly recompenced, where the most dreadful disorders are punished, only in those who are too weak to enjoy the privilege of committing them with impunity; the practice of virtue is considered nothing more than a painful sacrifice of fancied happiness. Such societies chastise, in the lower orders, those excesses which they respect in the higher ranks; and frequently have the injustice to condemn those in penalty of death, whom public prejudices, maintained by constant example, have rendered criminal.

Man, then, is not a free agent in any one instant of his life; he is necessarily guided in each step by those advantages, whether real or fictitious, that he attaches to the objects by which his passions are roused: these passions themselves are necessary in a being who, unceasingly tends towards his own happiness; their energy is necessary, since that depends on his temperament; his temperament is necessary, because it depends on the physical elements which enter into his composition; the modification of this temperament is necessary, as it is the infallible result, the inevitable consequence of the impulse he receives from the incessant action of moral and physical beings.

In despite of these proofs of the want of free-agency in man, so clear to unprejudiced minds, it will, perhaps, be insisted upon with no small feeling of triumph, that if it be proposed to any one to move or not to move his hand, an action in the number of those called *indifferent*, he evidently appears to be the master of choosing; from which it is concluded, evidence has been offered of his free-agency. The reply is, this example is perfectly simple; man in performing some action which he is resolved on doing, does not by any means prove his free-agency: the very desire of displaying this quality, excited by the dispute, becomes a necessary motive which decides his will either for the one or the other of these actions: what deludes him in this instance, or that which persuades him he is a free agent at this moment, is, that he does not discern the true motive which sets him in action; which is neither more nor less than the desire of convincing his opponent: if in the heat of the dispute he insists and asks, "Am I not the master of throwing myself out of the window?" I shall answer him, no; that whilst he preserves his reason, there is not even a probability that the desire of proving his free-agency, will become a motive sufficiently powerful, to make him sacrifice his life to the attempt; if, notwithstanding this, to prove he is a free agent, he should actually precipitate himself from the window, it would not be a sufficient warrantry to conclude he acted freely, but rather that it was the violence of his temperament which spurred him on to this folly. Madness is a state that depends upon the heat of the blood, not upon the will. A fanatic or a hero, braves death as necessarily as a more phlegmatic man or a coward flies from it. There is, in point of fact, no difference between the man who is cast out of the window by another, and the man who throws himself out of it, except that the impulse in the first instance comes immediately from without, whilst that which determines the fall in the second case, springs from within his own peculiar machine, having its more remote cause also exterior. When Mutius Scaevola held his hand in the fire, he was as much acting under the influence of necessity, caused by interior motives, that urged him to this strange action, as if his arm had been held by strong men; pride, despair, the desire of braving his enemy, a wish to astonish him, an anxiety to intimidate him, &c. were the invisible chains that held his hand bound to the fire. The love of glory, enthusiasm for their country, in like manner, caused Codrus and Decius to devote themselves for their fellow citizens. The Indian Calanus and the philosopher Peregrinus were equally obliged to burn themselves, by the desire of exciting the astonishment of the Grecian assembly.

It is said that free-agency is the absence of those obstacles competent to oppose themselves to the actions of man, or to the exercise of his faculties: it is pretended that he is a free agent, whenever, making use of these faculties, he produces the effect he has proposed to himself. In reply to this reasoning, it is sufficient to consider that it in no wise depends upon himself to place or remove the obstacles that either determine or resist him; the motive that causes his action is no more in his own power than the obstacle that impedes him, whether this obstacle or motive be within his own machine or exterior of his person: he is not master of the thought presented to his mind which determines his will; this thought is excited by some cause independent of himself.

To be undeceived on the system of his free-agency, man has simply to recur to the motive by which his will is determined, he will always find this motive is out of his own controul. It is said, that in consequence of an idea to which the mind gives birth, man acts freely if he encounters no obstacle. But the question is, what gives birth to this idea in his brain? has he the power either to prevent it from presenting itself, or from renewing itself in his brain? Does not this idea depend either upon objects that strike him exteriorly and in despite of himself, or upon causes that without his knowledge act within himself and modify his brain? Can he prevent his eyes, cast without design upon any object whatever, from giving him an idea of this object, from moving his brain? He is not more master of the obstacles; they are the necessary effects of either interior or exterior causes, which always act according to their given properties. A man insults a coward, who is necessarily irritated against his insulter, but his will cannot vanquish the obstacle that cowardice places to the object of his desire, which is, to resent the insult; because his natural conformation, which does not depend upon himself, prevents his having courage. In this case the coward is insulted in despite of himself, and against his will is obliged patiently to brook the insult he has received.

The partizans of the system of free-agency appear ever to have confounded constraint with necessity. Man believes he acts as a free agent, every time he does not see any thing that places obstacles to his actions; he does not perceive that the motive which causes him to will is always necessary, is ever independent of himself. A prisoner loaded with chains is compelled to remain in prison, but he is not a free agent, he is not able to resist the desire to emancipate himself; his chains prevent him from acting, but they do not prevent him from willing; he would save himself if they would loose his fetters, but he would not save himself as a free agent, fear or the idea of punishment would be sufficient motives for his action.

Man may therefore cease to be restrained, without, for that reason, becoming a free agent: in whatever manner he acts, he will act necessarily; according to motives by which he shall be determined. He may be compared to a heavy body, that finds itself arrested in its descent by any obstacle whatever: take away this obstacle, it will gravitate or continue to fall; but who shall say this dense body is free to fall or not? Is not its descent the necessary effect of its own specific gravity? The virtuous Socrates submitted to the laws of his country, although they were unjust; notwithstanding the doors of his gaol were left open to him he would not save himself; but in this he did not act as a free agent; the invisible chains of opinion, the secret love of decorum, the inward respect for the laws, even when they were iniquitous, the fear of tarnishing his glory, kept him in his prison: they were motives sufficiently powerful, with this enthusiast for virtue, to induce him to wait death with tranquillity; it was not in his power to save himself, because he could find no potential motive to bring him to depart, even for an instant, from those principles to which his mind was accustomed.

Man, says he, frequently acts against his inclination, from whence he has falsely concluded he is a free agent; when he appears to act contrary to his inclination, he is determined to it by some motive sufficiently efficacious to vanquish this inclination. A sick man, with a view to his cure, arrives at conquering his repugnance to the most disgusting remedies: the fear of pain, the dread of death, then become necessary and intelligent motives; consequently, this sick man cannot be said, with truth, by any means, to act freely.

When it is said, that man is not a free agent, it is not pretended to compare him to a body moved by a simple impulsive cause: he contains within himself causes inherent to his existence; he is moved by an interior organ, which has its own peculiar laws; which is itself necessarily determined, in consequence of ideas formed from perceptions, resulting from sensations, which it receives from exterior objects. As the mechanism of these sensations, of these perceptions, and the manner they engrave ideas on the brain of man, are not known to him, because he is unable to unravel all these motions; because he cannot perceive the chain of operations in his soul, or the motive-principle that acts within him, he supposes himself a free agent; which, literally translated, signifies that he moves himself by himself; that he determines himself without cause; when he rather ought to say, he is ignorant how or for why he acts in the manner he does. It is true the soul enjoys an activity peculiar to itself, but it is equally certain that this activity would never be displayed if some motive or some cause did not put it in a condition to exercise itself, at least it will not be pretended that the soul is able either to love or to hate without being moved, without knowing the objects, without having some idea of their qualities. Gunpowder has unquestionably a particular activity, but this activity will never display itself, unless fire be applied to it; this, however, immediately sets in motion.

It is the great complication of motion in man, it is the variety of his action, it is the multiplicity of causes that move him, whether simultaneously or in continual succession, that persuades him he is a free agent: if all his motions were simple, if the causes that move him did not confound themselves with each other, if they were distinct, if his machine was less complicated, he would perceive that all his actions were necessary, because he would be enabled to recur instantly to the cause that made him act. A man who should be always obliged to go towards the west would always go on that side, but he would feel extremely well, that in so going he was not a free agent: if he had another sense, as his actions or his motion augmented by a sixth would be still more varied, much more complicated, he would believe himself still more a free agent than he does with his five senses.

It is, then, for want of recurring to the causes that move him, for want of being able to analyse, from not being competent to decompose the complicated motion of his machine, that man believes himself a free agent; it is only upon his own ignorance that he founds the profound yet deceitful notion he has of his free-agency, that he builds those opinions which he brings forward as a striking proof of his pretended freedom of action. If, for a short time, each man was willing to examine his own peculiar actions, to search out their true motives, to discover their concatenation, he would remain convinced that the sentiment he has of his natural free-agency is a chimera that must speedily be destroyed by experience.

Nevertheless, it must be acknowledged that the multiplicity, the diversity of the causes which continually act upon man, frequently without even his knowledge, render it impossible, or at least extremely difficult, for him to recur to the true principles of his own peculiar actions, much less the actions of others; they frequently depend upon causes so fugitive, so remote from their effects, and which, superficially examined, appear to have so little analogy, so slender a relation with them, that it requires singular sagacity to bring them into light. This is what renders the study of the moral man a task of such difficulty; this is the reason why his heart is an abyss, of which it is frequently impossible for him to fathom the depth. He is, then, obliged to content himself with a knowledge of the general and necessary laws by which the human heart is regulated; for the individuals of his own species these laws are pretty nearly the same, they vary only in consequence of the organization that is peculiar to each, and of the modification it undergoes; this, however, is not, cannot be rigorously the same in any two. It suffices to know that by his essence man tends to conserve himself, to render his existence happy: this granted, whatever may be his actions, if he recurs back to this first principle, to this general, this necessary tendency of his will, he never can be deceived with regard to his motives. Man, without doubt, for want of cultivating reason, being destitute of experience, frequently deceives himself upon the means of arriving at this end; sometimes the means he employs are unpleasant to his fellows, because they are prejudicial to their interests; or else those of which he avails himself appear irrational, because they remove him from the end to which he would approximate: but whatever may be these means, they have always necessarily and invariably for object, either an existing or imaginary happiness; are directed to preserve himself in a state analogous to his mode of existence, to his manner of feeling, to his way of thinking; whether durable or transitory. It is from having mistaken this truth, that the greater number of moral philosophers have made rather the romance, than the history of the human heart; they have attributed the actions of man to fictitious causes; at least they have not sought out the necessary motives of his conduct. Politicians and legislators have been in the same state of ignorance; or else impostors have found it much shorter to employ imaginary motive-powers, than those which really have existence: they have rather chosen to make man wander out of his way, to make him tremble under incommodious phantoms, than guide him to virtue by the direct road to happiness; notwithstanding the conformity of the latter with the natural desires of his heart. So true it is, that *error can never possibly be useful, to the human species.*

However this may be, man either sees or believes he sees, much more distinctly, the necessary relation of effects with their causes in natural philosophy than in the human heart; at least he sees in the former sensible causes constantly produce sensible effects, ever the same, when the circumstances are alike. After this, he hesitates not to look upon physical effects as necessary, whilst he refuses to acknowledge necessity in the acts of the human will; these he has, without any just foundation, attributed to a motive-power that acts independently by its own peculiar energy, that is capable of modifying itself without the concurrence of exterior causes, and which is distinguished from all material or physical beings. *Agriculture* is founded upon the assurance afforded by experience, that the earth, cultivated and sown in a certain manner, when it has otherwise the requisite qualities, will furnish grain, fruit, and flowers, either necessary for subsistence or pleasing to the senses. If things were considered without prejudice, it would be perceived, that in morals education is nothing more than *the agriculture of the mind*; that like the earth, by reason of its natural disposition, of the culture bestowed upon it, of the seeds with which it is sown, of the seasons, more or less favorable, that conduct it to maturity, we may be assured that the soul will produce either virtue or vice; *moral fruit* that will be either salubrious for man or baneful to society. *Morals* is the science of the relations that subsist between the minds, the wills, and the actions of men; in the same manner that *geometry* is the science of the relations that are found between bodies. Morals would be a chimera, it would have no certain principles, if it was not founded upon the knowledge of the motives which must necessarily have an influence upon the human will, and which must necessarily determine the actions of human beings.

If in the moral as well as in the physical world, a cause of which the action is not interrupted be necessarily followed by a given effect, it flows consecutively that a *reasonable education*, grafted upon truth, founded upon wise laws,—that honest principles instilled during youth, virtuous examples continually held forth, esteem attached solely to merit, recompense awarded to none but good actions, contempt regularly visiting vice, shame following falsehood as its shadow, rigorous chastisements applied without distinction to crime, are causes that would necessarily act on the will of man; that would determine the greater number of his species to exhibit virtue, to love it for its own sake, to seek after it as the most desirable good, as the surest road to the happiness he so ardently desires. But if, on the contrary, superstition, politics, example, public opinion, all labour to countenance wickedness, to train man viciously; if, instead of fanning his virtues, they stifle good principles; if, instead of directing his studies to his advantage, they render his education either useless or unprofitable; if this education itself, instead of grounding him in virtue, only inoculates him with vice; if, instead of inculcating reason, it imbues him with prejudice; if, instead of making him enamoured of truth, it furnishes him with false notions; if, instead of storing his mind with just ideas drawn from experience, it fills him with dangerous opinions; if, instead of fostering mildness and forbearance, it kindles in his breast only those passions which are incommodious to himself and hurtful to others; it must be of necessity, that the will of the greater number shall determine them to evil; shall render them unworthy, make them baneful to society. Many authors have acknowledged the importance of a good education, that youth was the season to feed the human heart with wholesome diet; but they have not felt, that a good education is incompatible, nay, impossible, with the superstition of man, since this commences with giving his mind a false bias: that it is equally inconsistent with arbitrary government, because this always dreads lest he should become enlightened, and is ever sedulous to render him servile, mean, contemptible, and cringing; that it is incongruous with laws that are not founded in equity, that are frequently bottomed on injustice; that it cannot obtain with those received customs that are opposed to good sense; that it cannot exist whilst public opinion is unfavourable to virtue; above all, that it is absurd to expect it from incapable instructors, from masters with weak minds, who have only the ability to infuse into their scholars those false ideas with which they are themselves infected. Here, without doubt, is the real source from whence springs that universal corruption, that wide-spreading depravity, of which moralists, with great justice, so loudly complain; without, however, pointing out those causes of the evil, which are true as they are necessary: instead of this, they search for it in human nature, say it is corrupt, blame man for loving himself, and for seeking after his own happiness, insist that he must have supernatural assistance, some marvellous interference, to enable him to become good: this is a very prejudicial doctrine for him, it is directly subversive of his true happiness; by teaching him to hold himself in contempt, it tends necessarily to discourage him; it either makes him sluggish, or drives him to despair whilst waiting for this grace: is it not easy to be perceived, that he would always have it if he was well educated; if he was honestly governed? There cannot well exist a wilder or a stranger system of morals, than that of the theologians who attribute all moral evil to an original sin, and all moral good to the pardon of it. It ought not to excite surprise if such a system is of no efficacy; what can reasonably be the result of such an hypothesis? Yet, notwithstanding the supposed, the boasted free-agency of man, it is insisted that nothing less than the Author of Nature himself is necessary to destroy the wicked desires of his heart: but, alas! no power whatever is found sufficiently efficacious to resist those unhappy propensities, which, under the fatal constitution of things, the most vigorous motives, as before observed, are continually infusing into the will of man; no agency seems competent to turn the course of that unhappy direction these are perpetually giving to the stream of his natural passions. He is, indeed, incessantly exhorted to resist these passions, to stifle them, and to root them out of his heart; but is it not evident they are necessary to his welfare? Can it not be perceived they are inherent in his nature? Does not experience prove them to be useful to his conservation, since they have for object, only to avoid that which may be injurious to him; to procure that which may be advantageous to his mode of existence? In short, is it not easy to be seen, that these passions, well directed, that is to say, carried towards objects that are truly useful, that are really interesting to himself, which embrace the happiness of others, would necessarily contribute to the substantial, to the permanent well-being of society? Theologians themselves have felt, they have acknowledged the necessity of the passions: many of the fathers of the church have broached this doctrine; among the rest Father Senault has written a book expressly on the subject: the passions of man are like fire, at once necessary to the wants of life, suitable to ameliorate the condition of humanity, and equally capable of producing the most terrible ravages, the most frightful devastation.

Every thing becomes an impulse to the will; a single word frequently suffices to modify a man for the whole course of his life, to decide for ever his propensities; an infant who has burned his finger by having approached it too near the flame of a lighted taper, is warned from thence, that he ought to abstain from indulging a similar temptation; a man, once punished and despised for having committed a dishonest action, is not often tempted to continue so unfavourable a course. Under whatever point of man is considered, he never acts but after the impulse given to his will, whether it be by the will of others, or by more perceptible physical causes. The particular organization decides the nature of the impulse; souls act upon souls that are analogous; inflamed, fiery imaginations, act with facility upon strong passions; upon imaginations easy to be inflamed, the surprising progress of enthusiasm; the hereditary propagation of superstition; the transmission of religious errors from race to race, the excessive ardour with which man seizes on the marvellous, are effects as necessary as those which result from the action and re-action of bodies.

In despite of the gratuitous ideas which man has formed to himself on his pretended free-agency; in defiance of the illusions of this suppose intimate sense, which, contrary to his experience, persuades him that he is master of his will,—all his institutions are really founded upon necessity: on this, as on a variety of other occasions, practice throws aside speculation. Indeed, if it was not believed that certain motives embraced the power requisite to determine the will of man, to arrest the progress of his passions, to direct them towards an end, to modify him; of what use would be the faculty of speech? What benefit could arise from education itself? What does education achieve, save give the first impulse to the human will, make man contract habits, oblige him to persist in them, furnish him with motives, whether true or false, to act after a given manner? When the father either menaces his son with punishment, or promises him a reward, is he not convinced these things will act upon his will? What does legislation attempt, except it be to present to the citizens of a state those motives which are supposed necessary to determine them to perform some actions that are considered worthy; to abstain from committing others that are looked upon as unworthy? What is the object of morals, if it be not to shew man that his interest exacts he should suppress the momentary ebullition of his passions, with a view to promote a more certain happiness, a more lasting well-being, than can possibly result from the gratification of his transitory desires? Does not the religion of all countries suppose the human race, together with the entire of Nature, submitted to the irresistible will of a necessary being, who regulates their condition after the eternal laws of immutable wisdom? Is not God the absolute master of their destiny? Is it not this divine being who chooses and rejects? The anathemas fulminated by religion, the promises it holds forth, are they not founded upon the idea of the effects they will necessarily produce upon mankind? Is not man brought into existence without his own knowledge? Is he not obliged to play a part against his will? Does not either his happiness or his misery depend on the part he plays?

All religion has been evidently founded upon *Fatalism*. Among the Greeks they supposed men were punished for their necessary faults, as may be seen in Orestes, in Oedipus, &c. who only committed crimes predicted by the oracles. It is rather singular that the theological defenders of the doctrine of *free-agency*, which they endeavour to oppose to that of *predestination*,—which according to them is irreconcileable with *Christianity*, inasmuch as it is a false and dangerous system,—should not have been aware that the doctrines of *the fall of angels, original sin, the small number of the elect, the system of grace*, &c. were most incontestibly supporting, by the most cogent arguments, a *true system of fatalism*.

Education, then, is only necessity shewn to children: *legislation* is necessity shewn to the members of the body politic: *morals* is the necessity of the relations subsisting between men, shewn to reasonable beings: in short, man grants *necessity* in every thing for which he believes he has certain, unerring experience: that of which he does not comprehend the necessary connection of causes with their effects he styles *probability*: he would not act as he does, if he was not convinced, or, at least, if he did not presume he was, that certain effects will necessarily follow his actions. The *moralist* preaches reason, because he believes it necessary to man: the *philosopher* writes, because he believes truth must, sooner or later, prevail over falsehood: *tyrants* and *fanatical priests* necessarily hate truth, despise reason, because they believe them prejudicial to their interests: the *sovereign*, who strives to terrify crime by the severity of his laws, but who nevertheless, from motives of state policy sometimes renders it useful and even necessary to his purposes, presumes the motives he employs will be sufficient to keep his subjects within bounds. All reckon equally upon the power or upon the necessity of the motives they make use of; each individual flatters himself, either with or without reason, that these motives will have an influence on the conduct of mankind. The education of man is commonly so defective, so inefficacious, so little calculated to promote the end he has in view, because it is regulated by prejudice: even when this education is good, it is but too often speedily counteracted, by almost every thing that takes place in society. Legislation and politics are very frequently iniquitous, and serve no better purpose than to kindle passions in the bosom of man, which once set afloat, they are no longer competent to restrain. The great art of the moralist should be, to point out to man, to convince those who are entrusted with the sacred office of regulating his will, that their interests are identified; that their reciprocal happiness depends upon the harmony of their passions; that the safety, the power, the duration of empires, necessarily depend on the good sense diffused among the individual members; on the truth of the notions inculcated in the mind of the citizens, on the moral goodness that is sown in their hearts, on the virtues that are cultivated in their breasts; religion should not be admissible, unless it truly fortified, unless it really strengthened these motives. But in the miserable state into which error has plunged a considerable portion of the human species, man, for the most part, is seduced to be wicked: he injures his fellow-creature as a matter of conscience, because the strongest motives are held out to him to be persecuting; because his institutions invite him to the commission of evil, under the lure of promoting his own immediate happiness. In most countries superstition renders him a useless being, makes him an abject slave, causes him to tremble under its terrors, or else turns him into a furious fanatic, who is at once cruel, intolerant, and inhuman: in a great number of states arbitrary power crushes him, obliges him to become a cringing sycophant, renders him completely vicious: in those despotic states the law rarely visits crime with punishment, except in those who are too feeble to oppose its course? or when it has become incapable of restraining the violent excesses to which a bad government gives birth. In short, rational education is neglected; a prudent culture of the human mind is despised; it depends, but too frequently, upon bigotted, superstitious priests, who are interested in deceiving man, and who are sometimes impostors; or else upon parents or masters without understanding, who are devoid of morals, who impress on the ductile mind of their scholars those vices with which they are themselves tormented; who transmit to them the false opinions, which they believe they have an interest in making them adopt.

All this proves the necessity of falling back to man's original errors, and recurring to the primitive source of his wanderings, if it be seriously intended to furnish him with suitable remedies for such enormous maladies: it is useless to dream of correcting his mistakes, of curing him of his depravity, until the true causes that move his will are unravelled; until more real, more beneficial, more certain motives are substituted for those which are found so inefficacious; which prove so dangerous both to society and to himself. It is for those who guide the human will, who regulate the condition of nations, who hold the real happiness of man in their grasp, to seek after these motives,—with which reason will readily furnish them—which experience will enable them to apply with success: even a good book, by touching the heart of a great prince, may become a very powerful cause that shall necessarily have an influence over the conduct of a whole people, and decide upon the felicity of a portion of the human race.

From all that has been advanced in this chapter, it results, that in no one moment of his existence man is a free agent: he is not the architect of his own conformation; this he holds from Nature, he has no controul over his own ideas, or over the modification of his brain; these are due to causes, that, in despite of him, very frequently without his own knowledge, unceasingly act upon him; he is not the master of not loving that which he finds amiable; of not coveting that which appears to him desirable; he is not capable of refusing to deliberate, when he is uncertain of the effects certain objects will produce upon him; he cannot avoid choosing that which he believes will be most advantageous to him: in the moment when his will is determined by his choice, he is not competent to act otherwise than he does: in what instance, then, is he the master of his own actions? In what moment is he a free agent?

That which a man is about to do is always a consequence of that which he has been—of that which he is—of that which he has done up to the moment of the action: his total and actual existence, considered under all its possible circumstances, contains the sum of all the motives to the action he is about to commit; this is a principle, the truth of which no thinking, being will be able to refuse accrediting: his life is a series of necessary moments; his conduct, whether good or bad, virtuous or vicious, useful or prejudicial, either to himself or to others, is a concatenation of action, a chain of causes and effects, as necessary as all the moments of his existence. To *live*, is to exist in a necessary mode during the points of its duration, which succeed each other necessarily: to *will*, is to acquiesce or not in remaining such as he is: to be *free*, is to yield to the necessary motives that he carries within himself.

If he understood the play of his organs, if he was able to recal to himself all the impulsions they have received, all the modifications they have undergone, all the effects they have produced, he would perceive, that all his actions are submitted to that *fatality* which regulates his own particular system, as it does the entire system of the universe: no one effect in him, any more than in Nature, produce itself by *chance*; this, as has been before proved, is a word void of sense. All that passes in him, all that is done by him, as well as all that happens in Nature, or that is attributed to her, is derived from necessary laws, which produce necessary effects; from whence necessarily flow others.

Fatality is the eternal, the immutable, the necessary order established in Nature, or the indispensible connection of causes that act with the effects they operate. Conforming to this order, heavy bodies fall, light bodies rise; that which is analogous in matter, reciprocally attracts; that which is heterogeneous, mutually repels; man congregates himself in society, modifies each his fellow, becomes either virtuous or wicked; either contributes to his mutual happiness, or reciprocates his misery; either loves his neighbour, or hates his companion necessarily; according to the manner in which the one acts upon the other. From whence it may be seen, that the same necessity which regulates the physical, also regulates the moral world: in which every thing is in consequence submitted to fatality. Man, in running over, frequently without his own knowledge, often in despite of himself, the route which Nature has marked out for him, resembles a swimmer who is obliged to follow the current that carries him along; he believes himself a free agent, because he sometimes consents, sometimes does not consent, to glide with the stream; which, notwithstanding, always hurries him forward; he believes himself the master of his condition, because he is obliged to use his arms under the fear of sinking.

The false ideas he has formed to himself upon free-agency, are in general thus founded: there are certain events which he judges *necessary*; either because he sees they are effects that are constantly, are invariably linked to certain causes, which nothing seems to prevent; or because he believes he has discovered the chain of causes and effects that is put in play to produce those events: whilst he contemplates as *contingent*, other events, of whose causes he is ignorant; the concatenation of which he does not perceive; with whose mode of acting he is unacquainted: but in Nature, where every thing is connected by one common bond, there exists no effect without a cause. In the moral as well as in the physical world, every thing that happens is a necessary consequence of causes, either visible or concealed; which are, of necessity, obliged to act after their peculiar essences. *In man, free-agency is nothing more than necessity contained within himself.*

CHAP. XII.
An examination of the Opinion which pretends that the System of Fatalism is dangerous.

For a being whose essence obliges him to have a constant tendency to his own conservation, to continually seek to render himself happy, experience is indispensible: without it he cannot discover truth, which is nothing more, as has been already said, than a knowledge of the constant relations which subsist between man, and those objects that act upon him; according to his experience he denominates those that contribute to his permanent welfare useful and salutary; those that procure him pleasure, more or less durable, he calls agreeable. Truth itself becomes the object of his desires, only when he believes it is useful; he dreads it, whenever he presumes it will injure him. But has truth the power to injure him? Is it possible that evil can result to man from a correct understanding of the relations he has with other beings? Can it be true, that he can be harmed by becoming acquainted with those things, of which, for his own happiness, he is interested in having a knowledge? No: unquestionably not. It is upon its utility that truth founds its worth; upon this that it builds its rights; sometimes it may be disagreeable to individuals—it may even appear contrary to their interests—but it will ever be beneficial to them in the end; it will always be useful to the whole human species; it will eternally benefit the great bulk of mankind; whose interests must for ever remain distinct from those of men, who, duped by their own peculiar passions, believe their advantage consists in plunging others into error.

Utility, then, is the touchstone of his systems, the test of his opinions, the criterion of the actions of man; it is the standard of the esteem, the measure of the love he owes to truth itself: the most useful truths are the most estimable: those truths which are most interesting for his species, he styles *eminent*; those of which the utility limits itself to the amusement of some individuals who have not correspondent ideas, similar modes of feeling, wants analogous to his own, he either disdains, or else calls them *barren*.

It is according to this standard, that the principles laid down in this work, ought to be judged. Those who are acquainted with the immense chain of mischief produced on the earth by erroneous systems of superstition, will acknowledge the importance of opposing to them systems more accordant with truth, schemes drawn from Nature, sciences founded on experience. Those who are, or believe they are, interested in maintaining the established errors, will contemplate, with horror, the truths here presented to them: in short, those infatuated mortals, who do not feel, or who only feel very faintly, the enormous load of misery brought upon mankind by metaphysical speculation; the heavy yoke of slavery under which prejudice makes him groan, will regard all our principles as useless; or, at most, as sterile truths, calculated to amuse the idle hours of a few speculators.

No astonishment, therefore, need be excited at the various judgments formed by man: his interests never being the same, any more than his notions of utility, he condemns or disdains every thing that does not accord with his own peculiar ideas. This granted, let us examine, if in the eyes of the disinterested man, who is not entangled by prejudice— who is sensible to the happiness of his species—who delights in truth— the *doctrine of fatalism* be useful or dangerous? Let us see if it is a barren speculation, that his not any influence upon the felicity of the human race? At has been already shewn, that it will furnish morals with efficacious arguments, with real motives to determine the will, supply politics with the true lever to raise the proper activity in the mind of man. It will also be seen that it serves to explain in a simple manner the mechanism of man's actions; to develope in an easy way the arcana of the most striking phenomena of the human heart: on the other hand, if his ideas are only the result of unfruitful speculations, they cannot interest the happiness of the human species. Whether he believes himself a free agent, or whether he acknowledges the necessity of things, he always equally follows the desires imprinted on his soul; which are to preserve his existence and render himself happy. A rational education, honest habits, wise systems, equitable laws, rewards uprightly distributed, punishments justly inflicted, will conduct man to happiness by making him virtuous; while thorny speculations, filled with difficulties, can at most only have an influence over persons unaccustomed to think.

After these reflections, it will be very easy to remove the difficulties that are unceasingly opposed to the system of fatalism, which so many persons, blinded by their superstitious prejudices, are desirous to have considered as dangerous—as deserving of punishment—as calculated to disturb public tranquility—as tending to unchain the passions—to undermine the opinions man ought to have; and to confound his ideas of vice and of virtue.

The opposers of necessity, say, that if all the actions of man are necessary, no right whatever exists to punish bad ones, or even to he angry with those who commit them: that nothing ought to be imputed to them; that the laws would he unjust if they should decree punishment for necessary actions; in short, that under this system man could neither have merit nor demerit. In reply, it may he argued, that, to impute an action to any one, is to attribute that action to him; to acknowledge him for the author: thus, when even an action was supposed to be the effect of an agent, and that agent *necessity*, the imputation would lie: the merit or demerit, that is ascribed to an action are ideas originating in the effects, whether favourable or pernicious, that result to those who experience its operation; when, therefore, it should be conceded, that the agent was necessity, it is not less certain, that the action would be either good or bad; estimable or contemptible, to those who must feel its influence; in short that it would be capable of either eliciting their love, or exciting their anger. Love and anger are modes of existence, suitable to modify, beings of the human species: when, therefore, man irritates himself against his fellow, he intends to excite his fear, or even to punish him, in order to deter him from committing that which is displeasing to him. Moreover his anger is necessary; it is the result of his Nature; the consequence of his temperament. The painful sensation produced by a stone that falls on the arm, does not displease the less, because it comes from a cause deprived of will; which acts by the necessity of its Nature. In contemplating man as acting necessarily, it is impossible to avoid distinguishing that mode of action or being which is agreeable, which elicits approbation, from that which is afflicting, which irritates, which Nature obliges him to blame and to prevent. From this it will he seen, that the system of fatalism, does not in any manner change the actual state of things, and is by no means calculated to confound man's ideas of virtue and vice.

Man's Nature always revolts against that which opposes it: there are men so choleric, that they infuriate themselves even against insensible and inanimate objects; reflection on their own impotence to modify these objects ought to conduct them back to reason. Parents are frequently very much to be blamed for correcting their children with anger: they should be contemplated as beings who are not yet modified; or who have, perhaps, been very badly modified by themselves: nothing is more common in life, than to see men punish faults of which they are themselves the cause.

Laws are made with a view to maintain society; to uphold its existence; to prevent man associated, from injuring his neighbour; they are therefore competent to punish those who disturb its harmony, or those who commit actions that are injurious to their fellows; whether these associates may be the agents of necessity, or whether they are free agents, it suffices to know they are susceptible of modification, and are therefore submitted to the operation of the law. Penal laws are, or ought to be, those motives which experience has shewn capable of restraining the inordinate passions of man, or of annihilating the impulse these passions give to his will; from whatever necessary cause man may derive these passions, the legislator proposes to arrest their effect, when he takes suitable means, when he adopts proper methods, he is certain of success. The Judge, in decreeing to crime, gibbets, tortures, or any other chastisement whatever, does nothing more than is done by the architect, who in building a house, places gutters to carry off the rain, and prevent it from sapping the foundation.

Whatever may be the cause that obliges man to act, society possesses the right to crush the effects, as much as the man whose land would be ruined by a river, has to restrain its waters by a bank: or even, if he is able, to turn its course. It is by virtue of this right that society has the power to intimidate, the faculty to punish, with a view to its own conservation, those who may be tempted to injure it; or those who commit actions which are acknowledged really to interrupt its repose; to be inimical to its security; repugnant to its happiness.

It will, perhaps, he argued, that society does not, usually, punish those faults in which the will has no share; that, in fact, it punishes the will alone; that this it is which decides the nature of the crime, and the degree of its atrocity; that if this will be not free, it ought not to be punished. I reply, that society is an assemblage of sensible beings, susceptible of reason, who desire their own welfare; who fear evil, and seek after good. These dispositions enable their will to be so modified or determined, that they are capable of holding such a conduct as will conduce to the end they have in view. Education, the laws, public opinion, example, habit, fear, are the causes that must modify associated man, influence his will, regulate his passions, restrain the actions of him who is capable of injuring the end of his association, and thereby make him concur to the general happiness. These causes are of a nature to make impressions on every man, whose organization, whose essence, whose sanity, places him in a capacity to contract the habits, to imbibe the modes of thinking, to adopt the manner of acting, with which society is willing to inspire him. All the individuals of the human species are susceptible of fear, from whence it flows as a natural consequence, that the fear of punishment, or the privation of the happiness he desires, are motives that must necessarily more or less influence his will, and regulate his actions. If the man is to be found who is so badly constituted as to resist, whose organization is so vicious as to be insensible to those motives which operate upon all his fellows, he is not fit to live in society; he would contradict the very end of his association: he would he its enemy; he would place obstacles to its natural tendency; his rebellious disposition, his unsociable will, not being susceptible of that modification which is convenient to his own true interests and to the interests of his fellow-citizens; these would unite themselves against such an enemy; and the law which is, or ought to be the expression of the general will, would visit with condign punishment that refractory individual upon whom the motives presented to him by society, had not the effect which it had been induced to expect: in consequence, such an unsociable man would be chastised; he would be rendered miserable, and according to the nature of his crime he would be excluded from society as a being but little calculated to concur in its views.

If society has the right to conserve itself, it has also the right to take the means: these means are the laws which present or ought to present to the will of man those motives which are most suitable to deter him from committing injurious actions. If these motives fail of the proper effect, if they are unable to influence him, society, for its own peculiar good, is obliged to wrest from him the power of doing it further injury. From whatever source his actions may arise, therefore, whether they are the result of free-agency, or whether they are the offspring of necessity, society coerces him if, after having furnished him with motives, sufficiently powerful to act upon reasonable beings, it perceives that these motives have not been competent to vanquish his depraved nature. It punishes him with justice, when the actions from which it dissuades him are truly injurious to society; it has an unquestionable right to punish, when it only commands those things that are conformable to the end proposed by man in his association; or defends the commission of those acts, which are contrary to this end; which are hostile to the nature of beings associated for their reciprocal advantage. But, on the other hand, the law has not acquired the right to punish him: if it has failed to present to him the motives necessary to have an influence over his will, it has not the right to coerce him if the negligence of society has deprived him of the means of subsisting; of exercising his talents; of exerting his industry; of labouring for its welfare. It is unjust, when it punishes those to whom it has, neither given an education, nor honest principles; whom it has not enabled to contract habits necessary to the maintenance of society: it is unjust when it punishes them for faults which the wants of their nature, or the constitution of society has rendered necessary to them: it is unjust, it is irrational, whenever it chastises them for having followed those propensities, which example, which public opinion, which the institutions, which society itself conspires to give them. In short, the law is defective when it does not proportion the punishment to the real evil which society has sustained. The last degree of injustice, the acme of folly is, when society is so blinded as to inflict punishment on those citizens who have served it usefully.

The *penal* laws, in exhibiting terrifying objects to man, who must be supposed susceptible of fear, presents him with motives calculated to have an influence over his will. The idea of pain, the privation of liberty, the fear of death, are, to a being well constituted, in the full enjoyment of his faculties, very puissant obstacles, that strongly oppose themselves to the impulse of his unruly desires: when these do not coerce his will, when they fail to arrest his progress, he is an irrational being; a madman; a being badly organized; against whom society has the right to guarantee itself; against whom it has a right to take measures for its own security. Madness is, without doubt, an involuntary, a necessary state; nevertheless, no one feels it unjust to deprive the insane of their liberty, although their actions can only be imputed to the derangement of their brain. The wicked are men whose brain is either constantly or transitorily disturbed; still they must he punished by reason of the evil they commit; they must always be placed in the impossibility of injuring society: if no hope remains of bringing them back to a reasonable conduct—if every prospect of recalling them to their duty has vanished—if they cannot be made to adopt a mode of action conformable to the great end of association—they must be for ever excluded its benefits.

It will not be requisite to examine here, how far the punishments which society inflicts upon those who offend against it, may be reasonably carried. Reason should seem to indicate that the law ought to shew to the necessary crimes of man, all the indulgence that is compatible with the conservation of society. The system of fatalism, as we have seen, does not leave crime unpunished; but it is, at least, calculated to moderate the barbarity with which a number of nations punish the victims to their anger. This cruelty becomes still more absurd, when experience has shewn its inutility: the habit of witnessing ferocious punishments familiarizes criminals with the idea. If it be true that society possesses the right of taking away the life of its members—if it be really a fact, that the death of a criminal, thenceforth useless, can be advantageous for society, which it will be necessary to examine, humanity, at least, exacts that this death should not be accompanied with useless tortures; with which laws, perhaps in this instance too rigorous, frequently seem to delight in overwhelming their victim. This cruelty seems to defeat its own end, it only serves to make the culprit, who is immolated to the public vengeance, suffer without any advantage to society; it moves the compassion of the spectator, interests him in favor of the miserable offender who groans under its weight; it impresses nothing upon the wicked, but the sight of those cruelties destined for himself; which but too frequently renders him more ferocious, more cruel, more the enemy of his associates: if the example of death was less frequent, even without being accompanied with tortures, it would be more efficacious. If experience was consulted, it would be found that the greater number of criminals only look upon death as a *bad quarter of an hour*. It is an unquestionable fact, that a thief seeing one of his comrades, display a want of firmness under the punishment, said to him: *"Is not this what I have often told you, that in our business, we have one evil more than the rest of mankind?"* Robberies are daily committed, even at the foot of the scaffolds where criminals are punished. In those nations, where the penalty of death is so lightly inflicted, has sufficient attention been paid to the fact, that society is yearly deprived of a great number of individuals who would be able to render it very useful service, if made to work, and thus indemnify the community for the injuries they have committed? The facility with which the lives of men are taken away, proves the incapacity of counsellors; is an evidence of the negligence of legislators: they find it a much shorter road, that it gives them less trouble to destroy the citizens than to seek after the means to render them better.

What shall be said for the unjust cruelty of some nations, in which the law, that ought to have for its object the advantage of the whole, appears to be made only for the security of the most powerful? How shall we account for the inhumanity of those societies, in which punishments the most disproportionate to the crime, unmercifully take away the lives of men, whom the most urgent necessity, the dreadful alternative of famishing in a land of plenty, has obliged to become criminal? It is thus that in a great number of civilized nations, the life of the citizen is placed in the same scales with money; that the unhappy wretch who is perishing from hunger, who is writhing under the most abject misery, is put to death for having taken a pitiful portion of the superfluity of another whom he beholds rolling in abundance! It is this that, in many otherwise very enlightened societies, is called *justice*, or making the punishment commensurate with the crime.

Let the man of humanity, whose tender feelings are alive to the welfare of his species—let the moralist, who preaches virtue, who holds out forbearance to man—let the philosopher, who dives into the secrets of Nature—let the theologian himself say, if this dreadful iniquity, this heinous sin, does not become yet more crying, when the laws decree the most cruel tortures for crimes to which the most irrational customs gave birth—which bad institutions engender—which evil examples multiply? Is not this something like building a sorry, inconvenient hovel, and then punishing the inhabitant, because he does not find all the conveniences of the most complete mansion, of the most finished structure? Man, as at cannot be too frequently repeated, is so prone to evil, only because every thing appears to urge him on to the commission of it, by too frequently shewing him vice triumphant: his education is void in a great number of states, perhaps defective in nearly all; in many places he receives from society no other principles, save those of an unintelligible superstition; which make but a feeble barrier against those propensities that are excited by dissolute manners; which are encouraged by corrupt examples: in vain the law cries out to him: "abstain from the goods of thy neighbour;" his wants, more powerful, loudly declare to him that he must live: unaccustomed to reason, having never been submitted to a wholesome discipline, he conceives he must do it at the expence of a society who has done nothing for him: who condemns him to groan in misery, to languish in indigence: frequently deprived of the common necessaries requisite to support his existence, which his essence, of which he is not the master, compels him to conserve. He compensates himself by theft, he revenges himself by assassination, he becomes a plunderer by profession, a murderer by trade; he plunges into crime, and seeks at the risque of his life, to satisfy those wants, whether real or imaginary, to which every thing around him conspires to give birth. Deprived of education, he has not been taught to restrain the fury of his temperament—to guide his passions with discretion—to curb his inclinations. Without ideas of decency, destitute of the true principles of honour, he engages in criminal pursuits that injure his country: which at the same time has been to him nothing more than a step-mother. In the paroxysm of his rage, in the exacerbation of his mind, he loses sight of his neighbour's rights, he overlooks the gibbet, he forgets the torture; his unruly desires have become too potent—they have completely absorbed his mind; by a criminal indulgence they have given an inveteracy to his habits which preclude him from changing them; laziness has made him torpid: remorse has gnawed his peace; despair has rendered him blind; he rushes on to death; and society is compelled to punish him rigorously, for those fatal, those necessary dispositions, which it has perhaps itself engendered in his heart by evil example: or which at least, it has not taken the pains seasonably to root out; which it has neglected to oppose by suitable motives—by those calculated to give him honest principles— to excite him to industrious habits, to imbue him with virtuous inclinations. Thus, society frequently punishes those propensities of which it is itself the author, or which its negligence has suffered to spring up in the mind of man: it acts like those unjust fathers, who chastise their children for vices which they have themselves made them contract.

However unjust, however unreasonable this conduct may be, or appear to be, it is not the less necessary: society, such as it is, whatever may be its corruption, whatever vices may pervade its institutions, like every thing else in Nature, is willing to subsist; tends to conserve itself: in consequence, it is obliged to punish those excesses which its own vicious constitution has produced: in despite of its peculiar prejudices, notwithstanding its vices, it feels cogently that its own immediate security demands that it should destroy the conspiracies of those who make war against its tranquillity: if these, hurried on by the foul current of their necessary propensities, disturb its repose—if, borne on the stream of their ill-directed desires, they injure its interests, this following the natural law, which obliges it to labour to its own peculiar conservation, removes them out of its road; punishes them with more or less rigor, according to the objects to which it attaches the greatest importance, or which it supposes best suited to further its own peculiar welfare: without doubt, it deceives itself frequently, both upon these objects and the means; but it deceives itself necessarily, for want of the knowledge calculated to enlighten it, with regard to its true interests; for want of those, who regulate its movements possessing proper vigilance—suitable talents—the requisite virtue. From this it will appear, that the injustice of a society badly constituted, and blinded by its prejudices, is as necessary, as the crimes of those by whom it is hostilely attacked—by whose vices it is distracted. The body politic, when in a state of insanity, cannot act more consistently with reason, than one of its members whose brain is disturbed by madness.

It will still be said that these maxims, by submitting every thing to necessity, must confound, or even destroy the notions man forms of justice and injustice; of good and evil; of merit and demerit: I deny it. Although man, in every thing he does, acts necessarily, his actions are good, they are just, they are meritorious, every time they tend to the real utility of his fellows; of the society of which he makes a part: they are, of necessity, distinguished from those which are really prejudicial to the welfare of his associates. Society is just, it is good, it is worthy our reverence, when it procures for all its members, their physical wants, when it affords them protection, when it secures their liberty, when it puts them in possession of their natural rights. It is ill this that consists all the happiness of which the social compact is susceptible: society is unjust, it is bad, it is unworthy our esteem, when it is partial to a few, when it is cruel to the greater number: it is then that it multiplies its enemies, obliges them to revenge themselves by criminal actions which it is under the necessity to punish. It is not upon the caprices of political society that depend the true notions of justice and injustice—the right ideas of moral good and evil—a just appreciation of merit and demerit; it is upon *utility*, upon the necessity of things, which always forces man to feel that there exists a mode of acting on which he implicitly relies, which he is obliged to venerate, which he cannot help approving either in his fellows, in himself, or in society: whilst there is another mode to which he cannot lend his confidence, which his nature makes him to hate, which his feelings compel him to condemn. It is upon his own peculiar essence that man founds his ideas of pleasure and of pain—of right and of wrong—of vice and of virtue: the only difference between these is, that pleasure and pain make them instantaneously felt in his brain; he becomes conscious of their existence upon the spot; in the place of which, the advantages that accrue to him from justice, the benefit that he derives from virtue, frequently do not display themselves but after a long train of reflections—after multiplied experience and complicated attention; which many, either from a defect in their conformation, or from the peculiarity of the circumstances under which they are placed, are prevented from making, or at least from making correctly.

By a necessary consequence of this truism, the system of fatalism, although it has frequently been so accused, does not tend to encourage man in crime, to make remorse vanish from his mind. His propensities are to be ascribed to his nature; the use he makes of his passions depends upon his habits, upon his opinions, upon the ideas he has received in his education; upon the examples held forth by the society in which he lives. These things are what necessarily decide his conduct. Thus, when his temperament renders him susceptible of strong passions, he is violent in his desires, whatever may be his speculations.

Remorse is the painful sentiment excited in him by grief, caused either by the immediate or probable future effect of his indulged passions: if these effects were always useful to him, he would not experience remorse; but, as soon as he is assured that his actions render him hateful, that his passions make him contemptible; or, as soon as he fears he shall be punished in some mode or other, he becomes restless, discontented with himself—he reproaches himself with his own conduct—he feels ashamed—he fears the judgement of those beings whose affection he has learned to esteem—in whose good-will he finds his own comfort deeply interested. His experience proves to him that the wicked man is odious to all those upon whom his actions have any influence: if these actions are concealed at the moment of commission, he knows it very rarely happens they remain so for ever. The smallest reflection convinces him that there is no wicked man who is not ashamed of his own conduct—who is truly contented with himself—who does not envy the condition of the good man—who is not obliged to acknowledge that he has paid very dearly for those advantages he is never able to enjoy, without experiencing the most troublesome sensations, without making the most bitter reproaches against himself; then he feels ashamed, despises himself, hates himself, his conscience becomes alarmed, remorse follows in it train. To be convinced of the truth of this principle it is only requisite to cast our eyes on the extreme precautions that tyrants and villains, who are otherwise sufficiently powerful not to dread the punishment of man, take to prevent exposure;—to what lengths they push their cruelties against some, to what meannesses they stoop to others of those who are able to hold them up to public scorn. Have they not, then, a consciousness of their own iniquities? Do they not know that they are hateful and contemptible? Have they not remorse? Is their condition happy? Persons well brought up acquire these sentiments in their education; which are either strengthened or enfeebled by public opinion, by habit, or by the examples set before them. In a depraved society, remorse either does not exist, or presently disappears; because, in all his actions, it is ever the judgment of his fellow-man that man is obliged necessarily to regard. He never feels either shame or remorse for actions he sees approved, that are practised by the world. Under corrupt governments, venal souls, avaricious being, mercenary individuals, do not blush either at meanness, robbery, or rapine, when it is authorized by example; in licentious nations, no one blushes at adultery except the husband, at whose expence it is committed; in superstitious countries, man does not blush to assassinate his fellow for his opinions. It will be obvious, therefore, that his remorse, as well as the ideas, whether right or wrong, which man has of decency, virtue, justice, &c. are the necessary consequence of his temperament, modified by the society in which he lives: assassins and thieves, when they live only among themselves, have neither shame nor remorse.

Thus, I repeat, all the actions of man are necessary those which are always useful, which constantly contribute to the real, tend to the permanent happiness of his species, are called *virtues*, and are necessarily pleasing to all who experience their influence; at least, if their passions or false opinions do not oblige them to judge in that manner which is but little accordant with the nature of things: each man acts, each individual judges, necessarily, according to his own peculiar mode of existence—after the ideas, whether true or false, which he has formed with regard to his happiness. There are necessary actions which man is obliged to approve; there are others, that, in despite of himself, he is compelled to censure; of which the idea generates shame when his reflection permits him to contemplate them under the same point of view that they are regarded by his associates. The virtuous man and the wicked man act from motives equally necessary: they differ simply in their organization—in the ideas they form to themselves of happiness: we love the one necessarily—we detest the other from the same necessity. The law of his nature, which wills that a sensible being shall constantly labour to preserve himself, has not left to man the power to choose, or the free-agency to prefer pain to pleasure—vice to utility—crime to virtue. It is, then, the essence of man himself that obliges him to discriminate those actions which are advantageous to him, form those which are prejudicial to his interest, from those which are baneful to his felicity.

This distinction subsists even in the most corrupt societies, in which the ideas of virtue, although completely effaced from their conduct, remain the same in their mind. Let us suppose a matt, who had decidedly determined for villainy, who should say to himself—"It is folly to be virtuous in a society that is depraved, in a community that is debauched." Let us suppose also, that he has sufficient address, the unlooked-for good fortune to escape censure or punishment, during a long series of years; I say, that in despite of all these circumstances, apparently so advantageous for himself, such a man has neither been happy nor contented with his own conduct, He has been in continual agonies—ever at war with his own actions—in a state of constant agitation. How much pain, how much anxiety, has he not endured in this perpetual conflict with himself? How many precautions, what excessive labour, what endless solicitude, has he not been compelled to employ in this continued struggle; how many embarrassments, how many cares, has he not experienced in this eternal wrestling with his associates, whose penetration he dreads, whose scorn he fears will follow a true knowledge of his pursuits. Demand of him what he thinks of himself, he will shrink from the question. Approach the bedside of this villain at the moment he is dying; ask him if he would be willing to recommence, at the same price, a life of similar agitation? If he is ingenuous, he will avow that he has tasted neither repose nor happiness; that each crime filled him with inquietude—that reflection prevented him from sleeping—that the world has been to him only one continued scene of alarm—an uninterrupted concatenation of terror—an everlasting, anxiety of mind; — that to live peaceably upon bread and water, appears to him to be a much happier, a more easy condition, than to possess riches, credit, reputation, honours, on the same terms that he has himself acquired them. If this villain, notwithstanding all his success, finds his condition so deplorable, what must be thought of the feelings of those who have neither the same resources nor the same advantages to succeed in their criminal projects.

Thus, the system of necessity is a truth not only founded upon certain experience, but, again, it establishes morals upon an immoveable basis. Far from sapping the foundations of virtue, it points out its necessity; it clearly shows the invariable sentiments it must excite—sentiments so necessary, so strong, so congenial to his existence, that all the prejudices of man—all the vices of his institutions—all the effect of evil example, have never been able entirely to eradicate them from his mind. When he mistakes the advantages of virtue, it ought to be ascribed to the errors that are infused into him—to the irrationality of his institutions: all his wanderings are the fatal consequences of error,— the necessary result of prejudices which have identified themselves with his existence. Let it not, therefore, any longer be imputed to his nature that he has become wicked, but to those baneful opinions which he has imbibed with his mother's milk,—that have rendered him ambitious, avaricious, envious, haughty, arrogant, debauched, intolerant, obstinate, prejudiced, incommodious to his fellows, mischievous to himself. It is education that carries into his system the germ of those vices which necessarily torment him during the whole course of his life.

Fatalism is reproached with discouraging man—with damping the ardour of his soul—with plunging him into apathy—with destroying the bonds that should connect him with society. Its opponents say, "If every thing is necessary, we must let things go on, and not be disturbed by any thing." But does it depend on man to be sensible or not? Is he master of feeling or not feeling pain? If Nature has endowed him with a humane, with a tender soul, is it possible he should not interest himself in a very lively manner, in the welfare of beings whom he knows are necessary to his own peculiar happiness? His feelings are necessary: they depend on his own peculiar nature, cultivated by education. His imagination, prompt to concern itself with the felicity of his race, causes his heart to be oppressed at the sight of those evils his fellow-creature is obliged to endure,—makes his soul tremble in the contemplation of the misery arising from the despotism that crushes him—from the superstition that leads him astray—from the passions that distract him in a state of warfare against his neighbour. Although he knows that death is the fatal, the necessary period to the form of all beings, his soul is not affected in a less lively manner at the loss of a beloved wife,—at the demise of a child calculated to console his old age,—at the final separation from an esteemed friend who had become dear to his heart. Although he is not ignorant that it is the essence of fire to burn, he does not believe he is dispensed from using his utmost efforts to arrest the progress of a conflagration. Although he is intimately convinced that the evils to which he is a witness, are the necessary consequence of primitive errors with which his fellow-citizens are imbued, he feels he ought to display truth to them, if Nature has given him the necessary courage; under the conviction, that if they listen to it, it will, by degrees, become a certain remedy for their sufferings, that it will produce those necessary effects which it is of its essence to operate.

If the speculations of man modify his conduct, if they change his temperament, he ought not to doubt that the system of necessity would have the most advantageous influence over him; not only is it suitable to calm the greater part of his inquietude, but it will also contribute to inspire him with a useful submission, a rational resignation, to the decrees of a destiny with which his too great sensibility frequently causes him to be overwhelmed. This happy apathy, without doubt, would be, desirable to those whose souls, too tender to brook the inequalities of life, frequently render them the deplorable sport of their fate; or whose organs, too weak to make resistance to the buffettings of fortune, incessantly expose them to be dashed in pieces under the rude blows of adversity.

But, of all the important advantages the human race would be enabled to derive from the doctrine of fatalism, if man was to apply it to his conduct, none would be of greater magnitude, none of more happy consequence, none that would more efficaciously corroborate his happiness, than that general indulgence, that universal toleration, that must necessarily spring from the opinion, that *all is necessary*. In consequence, of the adoption of this principle, the fatalist, if he had a sensible soul, would commiserate the prejudices of his fellow-man— would lament over his wanderings—would seek to undeceive him—would try by gentleness to lead him into the right path, without ever irritating himself against his weakness, without ever insulting his misery.

Indeed, what right have we to hate or despise man for his opinions? His ignorance, his prejudices, his imbecility, his vices, his passions, his weakness, are they not the inevitable consequence of vicious institutions? Is he not sufficiently punished by the multitude of evils that afflict him on every side? Those despots who crush him with an iron sceptre, are they not continual victims to their own peculiar restlessness—mancipated to their perpetual diffidence—eternal slaves to their suspicions? Is there one wicked individual who enjoys a pure, an unmixed, a real happiness? Do not nations unceasingly suffer from their follies? Are they not the incessant dupes to their prejudices? Is not the ignorance of chiefs, the ill-will they bear to reason, the hatred they have for truth, punished by the imbecility of their citizens, by the ruin of the states they govern? In short, the fatalist would grieve to witness necessity each moment exercising its severe decrees upon mortals who are ignorant of its power, or who feel its castigation, without being willing to acknowledge the hand from whence it proceeds; he will perceive that ignorance is necessary, that credulity is the necessary result of ignorance—that slavery and bondage are necessary consequences of ignorant credulity—that corruption of manners springs necessarily from slavery—that the miseries of society, the unhappiness of its members, are the necessary offspring of this corruption. The fatalist, in consequence, of these ideas, will neither he a gloomy misanthrope, nor a dangerous citizen; he will pardon in his brethren those wanderings, he will forgive them those errors—which their vitiated nature, by a thousand causes, has rendered necessary—he will offer them consolation—he will endeavour to inspire them with courage—he will be sedulous to undeceive them in their idle notions, in their chimerical ideas; but he will never display against them bitterness of soul—he will never show them that rancorous animosity which is more suitable, to make them revolt from his doctrines, than to attract them to reason;—he will not disturb the repose of society—he will not raise the people to insurrection against the sovereign authority; on the contrary, he will feel that the miserable blindness of the great, and the wretched perverseness, the fatal obstinacy of so many conductors of the people, are the necessary consequence of that flattery that is administered to them in their infancy—that feeds their hopes with allusive falsehoods—of the depraved malice of those who surround them—who wickedly corrupt them, that they may profit by their folly— that they may take advantage of their weakness: in short, that these things are the inevitable effect of that profound ignorance of their true interest, in which every thing strives to keep them.

The fatalist has no right to be vain of his peculiar talents; no privilege to be proud of his virtues; he knows that these qualities are only the consequence of his natural organization, modified by circumstances that have in no wise depended upon himself. He will neither have hatred nor feel contempt for those whom Nature and circumstances have not favoured in a similar manner. It is the fatalist who ought to be humble, who should be modest from principle: is he not obliged to acknowledge, that he possesses nothing that he has not previously received?

In fact, will not every thing conduct to indulgence the fatalist whom experience has convinced of the necessity of things? Will he not see with pain, that it is the essence of a society badly constituted, unwisely governed, enslaved to prejudice, attached to unreasonable customs, submitted to irrational laws, degraded under despotism, corrupted by luxury, inebriated by false opinions, to be filled with trifling members; to be composed of vicious citizens; to be made up of cringing slaves, who are proud of their chains; of ambitious men, without idea of true glory; of misers and prodigals; of fanatics and libertines! Convinced of the necessary connection of things, he will not be surprised to see that the supineness of their chiefs carries discouragement into their country, or that the influence of their governors stirs up bloody wars by which it is depopulated, and causes useless expenditures that impoverish it; that all these excesses united, is the reason why so many nations contain only men wanting happiness, without understanding to attain it; who are devoid of morals, destitute of virtue. In all this he will contemplate nothing more than the necessary action and re-action of physics upon morals, of morals upon physics. In short, all who acknowledge fatality, will remain persuaded that a nation badly governed is a soil very fruitful in venomous reptiles—very abundant in poisonous plants; that these have such a plentiful growth as to crowd each other and choak themselves. It is in a country cultivated by the hands of a Lycurgus, that he will witness the production of intrepid citizens, of noble-minded individuals, of disinterested men, who are strangers to irregular pleasures. In a country cultivated by a Tiberius, he will find nothing but villains with depraved hearts, men with mean contemptible souls, despicable informers, execrable traitors. It is the soil, it is the circumstances in which man finds himself placed, that renders him either a useful object or a prejudicial being: the wise man avoids the one, as he would those dangerous reptiles whose nature it is to sting and communicate their deadly venom; he attaches himself to the other, esteems him, loves him, as he does those delicious fruits with whose rich maturity his palate is pleasantly gratified, with whose cooling juices he finds himself agreeably refreshed: he sees the wicked without anger—he cherishes the good with pleasure—he delights in the bountiful: he knows full well that the tree which is languishing without culture in the arid, sandy desert, that is stunted for want of attention, leafless for want of moisture, that has grown crooked from neglect, become barren from want of loam, whose tender bark is gnawed by rapacious beasts of prey, pierced by innumerable insects, would perhaps have expanded far and wide its verdant boughs from a straight and stately stem, have brought forth delectable fruit, have afforded from its luxuriant foliage under its lambent leaves an umbrageous refreshing retreat from the scorching rays of a meridian sun, have offered beneath its swelling branches, under its matted tufts a shelter from the pitiless storm, it its seed had been fortunately sown in a more fertile soil, placed in a more congenial climate, had experienced the fostering cares of a skilful cultivator.

Let it not then be said, that it is degrading man reduce his functions to a pure mechanism; that it is shamefully to undervalue him, scandalously to abuse him, to compare him to a tree; to an abject vegetation. The philosopher devoid of prejudice does not understand this language, invented by those who are ignorant of what constitutes the true dignity of man. A tree is an object which, in its station, joins the useful with the agreeable; it merits our approbation when it produces sweet and pleasant fruit; when it affords a favourable shade. All machines are precious, when they are truly useful, when they faithfully perform the functions for which they are designed. Yes, I speak it with courage, reiterate it with pleasure, the honest man, when he has talents, when he possesses virtue, is, for the beings of his species, a tree that furnishes them with delicious fruit, that affords them refreshing shelter: the honest man is a machine of which the springs are adapted to fulfil its functions in a manner that must gratify the expectation of all his fellows. No, I should not blush, I should not feel degraded, to be a machine of this sort; and my heart would leap with joy, if I could foresee that the fruit of my reflections would one day be useful to my race, consoling to my fellow-man.

Is not Nature herself a vast machine, of which the human species is but a very feeble spring? I see nothing contemptible either in her or her productions; all the beings who come out of her hands are good, are noble, are sublime, whenever they co-operate to the production of another, to the maintenance of harmony in the sphere where they must act. Of whatever nature the soul may be, whether it is made mortal, or whether it be supposed immortal; whether it is regarded as a spirit, or whether it be looked upon as a portion of the body; it will be found noble, it will be estimated great, it will be ranked good, it will be considered sublime, in a Socrates, in an Aristides, in a Cato: it will be thought abject, it will be viewed as despicable, it will be called corrupt, in a Claudius, in a Sejanus, in a Nero: its energies will be admired, we shall be delighted with its manner, fascinated with its efforts, in a Shakespeare, in a Corneille, in a Newton, in a Montesquieu: its baseness will be lamented, when we behold mean, contemptible men, who flatter tyranny, or who servilely cringe at the foot of superstition.

All that has been said in the course of this work, proves clearly that every thing is necessary; that every thing is always in order, relatively to Nature; where all beings do nothing more than follow the laws that are imposed on their respective classes. It is part of her plan, that certain portions of the earth shall bring forth delicious fruits, shall blossom beauteous flowers; whilst others shall only furnish brambles, shall yield nothing but noxious vegetables: she has been willing that some societies should produce wise men, great heroes; that others should only give birth to abject souls, contemptible men, without energy, destitute of virtue. Passions, winds, tempests, hurricanes, volcanoes, wars, plagues, famines, diseases, death, are as necessary to her eternal march as the beneficent heat of the sun, the serenity of the atmosphere, the gentle showers of spring, plentiful years, peace, health, harmony, life: vice and virtue, darkness and light, and science are equally necessary; the one are not benefits, the other are not evils, except for those beings whose happiness they influence by either favouring or deranging their peculiar mode of existence. *The whole cannot be miserable, but it may contain unhappy individuals.*

Nature, then, distributes with the same hand that which is called *order*, and that which is called *disorder*; that which is called *pleasure*, and that which is called *pain*: in short, she diffuses by the necessity of her existence, good and evil in the world we inhabit. Let not man, therefore, either arraign her bounty, or tax her with malice; let him not imagine that his feeble cries, his weak supplications, can never arrest her colossal power, always acting after immutable laws; let him submit silently to his condition; and when he suffers, let him not seek a remedy by recurring to chimeras that his own distempered imagination has created; let him draw from the stores of Nature herself, the remedies which she offers for the evil she brings upon him: if she sends him diseases, let him search in her bosom for those salutary productions to which she has given birth, which will cure them: if she gives him errors, she also furnishes him with experience to counteract them; in truth, she supplies him with an antidote suitable to destroy their fatal effects. If she permits man to groan under the pressure of his vices, beneath the load of his follies, she also shews him in virtue, a sure remedy for his infirmities: if the evils that some societies experience are necessary, when they shall have become too incommodious they will be irresistibly obliged to search for those remedies which Nature will always point out to them. If this Nature has rendered existence insupportable, to some unfortunate beings, whom she appears to have selected for her victims, still death, is a door that will surely be opened to them—that will deliver them from their misfortunes, although in their puny, imbecile, wayward judgment, they may be deemed impossible of cure.

Let not man, then, accuse Nature with being inexorable to him, since there does not exist in her whole circle an evil for which she has not furnished the remedy, to those who have the courage to seek it, who have the fortitude to apply it. Nature follows general and necessary laws in all her operations; physical calamity and moral evil are not to be ascribed to her want of kindness, but to the necessity of things. Physical calamity is the derangement produced in man's organs by physical causes which he sees act: moral evil is the derangement produced in him by physical causes of which the action is to him a secret. These causes always terminate by producing sensible effects, which are capable of striking his senses; neither the thoughts nor the will of man ever shew themselves, but by the marked effects they produce either in himself or upon those beings whom Nature has rendered susceptible of feeling their impulse. He suffers, because it is of the essence of some beings to derange the economy of his machine; he enjoys, because the properties of some beings are analogous to his own mode of existence; he is born, because it is of the nature of some matter to combine itself under a determinate form; he lives, he acts, he thinks, because it is of the essence of certain combinations to maintain themselves in existence by given means for a season; at length he dies, because a necessary law prescribes that all the combinations which are formed, shall either be destroyed or dissolve themselves. From all this it results, that Nature is impartial to all its productions; she submits man, like all other beings, to those eternal laws from which she has not even exempted herself; if she was to suspend these laws, even for an instant, from that moment disorder would reign in her, system; her harmony would be disturbed.

Those who wish to study Nature, must take experience for their guide; this, and this only, can enable them to dive into her secrets, to unravel by degrees, the frequently imperceptible woof of those slender causes, of which she avails herself to operate the greatest phenomena: by the aid of experience, man often discovers in her properties, perceives modes of action entirely unknown to the ages which have preceded him; those effects which his grandfathers contemplated as marvellous, which they regarded as supernatural efforts, looked upon as miracles, have become familiar to him in the present day, and are at this moment contemplated as simple and natural consequences, of which he comprehends the mechanism—of which he understands the cause—of which he can unfold the manner of action. Man, in fathoming Nature, has arrived at discovering the true causes of earthquakes; of the periodical motion of the sea; of subterraneous conflagrations; of meteors; of the electrical fluid, the whole of which were considered by his ancestors, and are still so by the ignorant, by the uninformed, as indubitable signs of heaven's wrath. His posterity, in following up, in rectifying the experience already made, will perhaps go further, and discover those causes which are totally veiled from present eyes. The united efforts of the human species will one day perhaps penetrate even into the sanctuary of Nature, and throw into light many of those mysteries which up to the present time she seems to have refused to all his researches.

In contemplating man under his true aspect; in quitting authority to follow experience; in laying aside error to consult reason; in submitting every thing to physical laws, from which his imagination has vainly exerted its utmost power to withdraw them; it will be found that the phenomena of the moral world follow exactly the same general rules as those of the physical; that the greater part of those astonishing effects, which ignorance, aided by his prejudices, make him consider as inexplicable, and regard as wonderful, are natural consequences flowing from simple causes. He will find that the eruption of a volcano and the birth of a Tamerlane are to Nature the same thing; in recurring to the primitive causes of those striking events which he beholds with consternation, which he contemplates with fearful alarm, in falling back to the sources of those terrible revolutions, those frightful convulsions, those dreadful explosions that distract mankind, lay waste the fairest works of Nature, ravage nations, and tear up society by the roots; he will find that the wills that compassed the most surprising changes, that operated the most extensive alterations in the state of things, that brought about the most unlooked-for events, were moved by physical causes, whose exility made him treat them as contemptible; whose want of consequence in his own purblind eyes led him to believe them utterly incapable to give birth to the phenomena whose magnitude strikes him with such awe, whose stupendous range fills him with such amazement.

If man was to judge of causes by their effects, there would be no small causes in the universe. In a Nature where every thing is connected, where every thing acts and re-acts, moves and changes, composes and decomposes, forms and destroys, there is not an atom which does not play an important part—that does not occupy a necessary station; there is not an imperceptible particle, however minute, which, placed in convenient circumstances, does not operate the most prodigious effects. If man was in a capacity to follow the eternal chain, to pursue the concatenated links, that connect with their causes all the effects he witnesses, without losing sight of any one of its rings,—if he could unravel the ends of those insensible threads that give impulse to the thoughts, decision to the will, direction to the passions of those men who are called mighty, according to their actions, he would find, they are true atoms which Nature employs to move the moral world; that it is the unexpected but necessary function of these indiscernible particles of matter, it is their aggregation, their combination, their proportion, their fermentation, which modifying the individual by degrees, in despite of himself, frequently without his own knowledge, make him think, will, and act, in a determinate, but necessary mode. If, then, the will and the actions of this individual have an influence over a great number of other men, here is the moral world in a state of the greatest combustion, and those consequences ensue which man contemplates with fearful wonder. Too much acrimony in the bile of a fanatic—blood too much inflamed in the heart of a conqueror—a painful indigestion in the stomach of a monarch—a whim that passes in the mind of a woman—are sometimes causes sufficient to bring on war—to send millions of men to the slaughter—to root out an entire people—to overthrow walls—to reduce cities into ashes—to plunge nations into slavery—to put a whole people into mourning—to breed famine in a land—to engender pestilence — to propagate calamity—to extend misery—to spread desolation far and wide upon the surface of our globe, through a long series of ages.

The dominant passion of an individual of the human species, when it disposes of the passions of many others, arrives at combining their will, at uniting their efforts, and thus decides the condition of man. It is after this manner that an ambitious, crafty, and voluptuous Arab, gave to his countrymen an impulse of which the effect was the subjugation and desolation of vast countries in Asia, in Africa, and in Europe; whose consequences were sufficiently potential to erect a new, extensive, but slavish empire; to give a novel system of religion to millions of human beings; to overturn the altars of their former gods; in short, to alter the opinions, to change the customs of a considerable portion of the population of the earth. But in examining the primitive sources of this strange revolution, what were the concealed causes that had an influence over this man—that excited his peculiar passions, and modified his temperament? What was the matter from the combination of which resulted a crafty, ambitious, enthusiastic, and eloquent man; in short, a personage competent to impose on his fellow-creatures—capable of making them concur in his most extravagant views. They were, undoubtedly, the insensible particles of his blood; the imperceptible texture of his fibres; the salts, more or less acrid, that stimulated his nerves; the proportion of igneous fluid that circulated in his system. From whence came these elements? It was from the womb of his mother; from the aliments which nourished him; from the climate in which he had his birth; from the ideas he received; from the air which he respired; without reckoning a thousand inappreciable, a thousand transitory causes, that in the instance given had modified, had determined the passions of this important being, who had thereby acquired the capacity to change the face of this mundane sphere.

To causes so weak in their principles, if in the origin the slightest obstacle had been opposed, these wonderful events, which have astounded man, would never have been produced. The fit of an ague, the consequence of bile a little too much inflamed, had sufficed, perhaps, to have rendered abortive all the vast projects, of the legislator of the Mussulmen. Spare diet, a glass of water, a sanguinary evacuation, would sometimes have been sufficient to have saved kingdoms.

It will be seen, then, that the condition of the human species, as well as that of each of its individuals, every instant depends on insensible causes, to which circumstances, frequently fugitive, give birth; that opportunity develops, that convenience puts in action: man attributes their effects to chance, whilst these causes operate necessarily, act according to fixed rules: he has frequently neither the sagacity nor the honesty to recur to their true principles; he regards such feeble motives with contempt, because he has been taught to consider them as incapable of producing such stupendous events. They are, however, these motives, weak as they may appear to be, these springs, so pitiful in his eyes, is which according to her necessary laws, suffice in the hands of Nature to move the universe. The conquests of a Gengis-Khan have nothing in them that is more strange to the eye of a philosopher than the explosion of a mine, caused in its principle by a feeble spark, which commences with setting fire to a single grain of powder; this presently communicates itself to many millions of other contiguous grains, of which the united force, the multiplied powers, terminate by blowing up mountains, overthrowing fortifications, or converting populous, well- built cities, into heaps of ruins.

Thus, imperceptible causes, concealed in the bosom of Nature, until the moment their action is displayed, frequently decide the fate of man. The happiness or the wretchedness, the prosperity or the misery of each individual, as well as that of whole nations, are attached to powers which it is impossible for him to foresee, which he cannot appreciate, of which he is incapable to arrest the action. Perhaps at this moment atoms are amassing, insensible particles are combining, of which the assemblage shall form a sovereign, who will be either the scourge or the saviour of a mighty empire. Man cannot answer for his own destiny one single instant; he has no cognizance of what is passing within himself; he is ignorant of the causes which act in the interior of his machine; he knows nothing of the circumstances that will give them activity: he is unacquainted with what may develope their energy; it is, nevertheless, on these causes, impossible to be unravelled by him, that depends his condition in life. Frequently, an unforeseen rencontre gives birth to a passion in his soul, of which the consequences shall, necessarily, have an influence over his felicity. It is thus that the most virtuous man, by a whimsical combination of unlooked-for circumstances, may become in an instant the most criminal of his species.

This truth, without doubt, will be found frightful—this fact will unquestionably appear terrible: but at bottom, what has it more revolting than that which teaches him that an infinity of accidents, as irremediable as they are unforeseen, may every instant wrest from him that life to which he is so strongly attached? Fatalism reconciles the good man easily to death: it makes him contemplate it as a certain means of withdrawing himself from wickedness; this system shews death, even to the happy man himself, as a medium between him and those misfortunes which frequently terminate by poisoning his happiness; that end with embittering the most fortunate existence.

Let man, then, submit to necessity: in despite of himself it will always hurry him forward: let him resign himself to Nature, let him accept the good with which she presents him: let him oppose to the necessary evil which she makes him experience, those necessary remedies which she consents to afford him; let him not disturb his mind with useless inquietude; let him enjoy with moderation, because he will find that pain is the necessary companion of excess: let him follow the paths of virtue, because every thing will prove to him, even in this world of perverseness, that it is absolutely necessary to render him estimable in the eyes of others, to make him contented with himself.

Feeble, vain mortal, thou pretendest to be a free agent. Alas! dost thou not see all the threads which enchain thee? Dost thou not perceive that they are atoms which form thee; that they are atoms which move thee; that they are circumstances independent of thyself, that modify thy being; that they are circumstances over which thou hast not any controul, that rule thy destiny? In the puissant Nature that environs thee, shalt thou pretend to be the only being who is able to resist her power? Dost thou really believe that thy weak prayers will induce her to stop in her eternal march; that thy sickly desires can oblige her to change her everlasting course?

CHAP. XIII.

Of the Immortality of the Soul;—of the Doctrine of a future State;—of the Fear of Death.

The reflections presented to the reader in this work, tend to shew what ought to be thought of the human soul, as well as of its operations and faculties: every thing proves, in the most convincing manner, that it acts, that it moves according to laws similar to those prescribed to the other beings of Nature; that it cannot be distinguished from the body; that it is born with it; that it grows up with it; that it is modified in the same progression; in short, every thing ought to make man conclude that it perishes with it. This soul, as well as the body, passes through a state of weakness and infancy; it is in this stage of its existence, that it is assailed by a multitude of modifications; that it is stored with an infinity of ideas, which it receives from exterior objects through the medium of the organs; that it amasses facts, that it collects experience, whether true or false, that it forms to itself a system of conduct, according to which it thinks, in conformity with which it acts, from whence results either its happiness or its misery, its reason or its delirium, its virtues or its vices; arrived with the body at its full powers, having in conjunction with it reached maturity, it does not cease for a single instant to partake in common of its sensations, whether these are agreeable or disagreeable; it participates in all its pleasures; it shares in all its pains; in consequence it conjointly approves or disapproves its state; like it, it is either sound or diseased; active or languishing; awake or asleep. In old age man extinguishes entirely, his fibres become rigid, his nerves loose their elasticity, his senses are obtunded, his sight grows dim, his ears lose their quickness, his ideas become unconnected, his memory fails, his imagination cools: what then becomes of his soul? Alas! it sinks down with the body; it gets benumbed as this loses its feeling; becomes sluggish as this decays in activity; like it, when enfeebled by years it fulfils its functions with pain; this substance, which is deemed spiritual, which is considered immaterial, which it is endeavoured to distinguish from matter, undergoes the same revolutions, experiences the same vicissitudes, submits to the same modifications, as does the body itself.

In despite of this proof of the materiality of the soul, of its identity with the body, so convincing to the unprejudiced, some thinkers have supposed, that although the latter is perishable, the former does not perish: that this portion of man enjoys the especial privilege of *immortality*; that it is exempt from dissolution: free from those changes of form all the beings in Nature undergo: in consequence of this, man has persuaded himself, that this privileged soul does not die: its immortality, above all, appears indubitable to those who suppose it spiritual: after having made it a simple being, without extent, devoid of parts, totally different from any thing of which he has a knowledge, he pretended that it was not subjected to the laws of decomposition common to all beings, of which experience shews him the continual operation.

Man, feeling within himself a concealed force, that insensibly produced action, that imperceptibly gave direction to the motion of his machine, believed that the entire of Nature, of whose energies he is ignorant, with whose modes of acting he is unacquainted, owed its motion to an agent analogous to his own soul; who acted upon the great macrocosm, in the same manner that this soul acted upon his body. Man, having supposed himself double, made Nature double also: he distinguished her from her own peculiar energy; he separated her from her mover, which by degrees he made spiritual. Thus Nature, distinguished from herself, was regarded as the soul of the world; and the soul of man was considered as opinions emanating from this universal soul. This notion upon the origin of the soul is of very remote antiquity. It was that of the Egyptians, of the Chaldeans, of the Hebrews, of the greater number of the *wise men of the east.* It should appear that Moses believed with the Egyptians the divine emanation of souls: according to him, *"God formed man of the dust of the ground, and breathed into his nostrils the breath of life; and man became a living soul:"* nevertheless, the Catholic, at this day, rejects this system of *divine emanation,* seeing that it supposes the Divinity divisible: which would have, been inconvenient to the Romish idea of purgatory, or to the system of everlasting punishment. Although Moses, in the above quotation, seems to indicate that the soul was a portion of the Divinity, it does not appear that the doctrine of the *immortality of the soul* was established in any one of the books attributed to him. It was during the Babylonish captivity, that the Jews learned the doctrine of future rewards and punishments, taught by Zoroaster to the Persians, but which the Hebrew legislator did not understand, or, at least, he left his people ignorant on the subject. It was in those schools, that Pherecydes, Pythagoras, and Plato, drew up a doctrine so flattering to the vanity of human nature—so gratifying to the imagination of mortals. Man thus believed himself a portion of the Divinity; immortal, like the Godhead, in one part of himself: nevertheless, subsequent religions have renounced these advantages, which they judged incompatible with the other parts of their systems; they held forth that the Sovereign of Nature, or her contriver was not the soul of man, but, that, in virtue of his omnipotence, he created human souls, in proportion as he produced the bodies which they must animate; and they taught, that these souls once produced, by an effect of the same omnipotence, enjoyed immortality.

However it may be with these variations upon the origin of souls, those who supposed them emanating from the Divinity, believed that after the death of the body, which served them for an envelope, they returned, by refunding to their first source. Those who, without adopting the opinion of divine emanation, admired the spirituality, believed the immortality of the soul, were under the necessity to suppose a region, to find out an abode for these souls, which their imagination painted to them, each according to his fears, his hopes, his desires, and his prejudices.

Nothing is more popular than the doctrine of the *immortality of the soul;* nothing is more universally diffused than the expectation of another life.

Nature having inspired man with the most ardent love for his existence, the desire of preserving himself for ever was a necessary consequence; this desire was presently converted into certainty: from that desire of existing eternally which Nature has implanted in him, he made an argument, to prove that man would never cease to exist. Abady says, "our soul has no useless desires, it naturally desires an eternal life;" and by a very strange logic, he concludes that this desire could not fail to be fulfilled. Cicero, before Abady, had declared the immortality of the soul to be an innate idea in man; yet, strange to tell, in another part of his works he considers Pherecydes as the inventor of the doctrine. However this may be, man, thus disposed, listened with avidity to those who announced to him systems so conformable to his wishes. Nevertheless, he ought not to regard as supernatural the desire of existing, which always was, and always will be, of the essence man; it ought not to excite surprise, if he received with eagerness an hypothesis that flattered his hopes, by promising that his desire would one day be gratified; but let him beware how he concludes that this desire itself is an indubitable proof of the reality of this future life, with which at present he seems to be so much occupied. The passion for existence is in man only a natural consequence of the tendency of a sensible being, whose essence it is to be willing to conserve himself: in the human being it follows the energy of his soul—keeps pace with the force of his imagination—always ready to realize that which he strongly desires. He desires the life of the body, nevertheless this desire is frustrated; wherefore should not the desire for the life of the soul be frustrated like the other? The partizans of the doctrine of the immortality of the soul reason thus: "All men desire to live for ever, therefore they will live for ever." Suppose the argument retorted on them; would it be believed? If it was asserted, "All men naturally desire to be rich; therefore all men will one day be rich," how many partizans would this doctrine find?

The most simple reflection upon the nature of his soul, ought to convince man that the idea of its immortality is only an illusion of the brain. Indeed what is his soul, save the principle of sensibility? What is it, to think, to enjoy, to suffer; is it not to feel? What is life, except it be the assemblage of modifications, the congregation of motion, peculiar to an organized being? Thus, as soon as the body ceases to live, its sensibility can no longer exercise itself; when its sensibility is no more, it can no longer have ideas, nor in consequence thoughts. Ideas, as we have proved, can only reach man through his senses; now, how will they have it, that once deprived of his senses, he is yet capable of receiving sensations, of having perceptions, of forming ideas? As they have made the soul of man a being separated from the animated body, wherefore have they not made life a being distinguished from the living body? Life in a body is the totality of this motion; feeling and thought make a part of this motion: thus it is reasonable to suppose, that in the dead man these motions will cease, like all the others.

Indeed, by what reasoning will it be proved, that this soul, which cannot feel, think, will, or act, but by aid of man's organs, can suffer pain, be susceptible of pleasure, or even have a consciousness of its own existence, when the organs which should warn it of their presence are decomposed or destroyed? Is it not evident, that the soul depends on the arrangement of the various parts of the body; on the order with which these parts conspire to perform their functions; on the combined motion of the whole? Thus the organic structure once destroyed, can it be reasonably doubted the soul will be destroyed also? Is it not seen, that during the whole course of human life this soul is stimulated, changed, deranged, disturbed, by all the changes man's organs experience? And yet it will be insisted, that this soul acts, thinks, subsists, when these same organs have entirely disappeared!

An organized being may be compared to a clock, which once broken, is no longer suitable to the use for which it was designed. To say, that the soul shall feel, shall think, shall enjoy, shall suffer after the death of the body; is to pretend that a clock, shivered into a thousand pieces, will continue to strike the hour; shall yet have the faculty of marking the progress of time. Those who say, that the soul of man is able to subsist, notwithstanding the destruction of the body, evidently support the position, that the modification of a body will be enabled to conserve itself after the subject is destroyed: this on any other occasion would be considered as completely absurd.

It will be said that the conservation of the soul after the death of the body, is an effect of the Divine Omnipotence: but this is supporting an absurdity by a gratuitous hypothesis. It surely is not meant by Divine Omnipotence, of whatever nature it may be supposed, that a thing shall exist and not exist at the same time: unless this be granted, it will be rather difficult to prove, that a soul shall feel and think without the intermediates necessary to thought.

Let them then, at least, forbear asserting, that reason is not wounded by the doctrine of the immortality of the soul; or by the expectation of a future life. These notions, formed to flatter man, to disturb the imagination of the uninformed, who do not reason, cannot appear either convincing or probable to enlightened minds. Reason, exempted from the illusions of prejudice, is, without doubt, wounded by the supposition of a soul, that feels, that thinks, that is afflicted, that rejoices, that has ideas, without having organs; that is to say, destitute of the only known medium, wanting all the natural means, by which, according to what we can understand, it is possible for it to feel sensations, have perceptions, or form ideas. If it he replied, other means are able to exist, which are *supernatural* or *unknown*, it may be answered, that these means of transmitting ideas to the soul, separated from the body, are not better known to, or more within the reach of, those who suppose it, that they are of other men. It is, at least, very certain, it cannot admit even of a controversy, that all those who reject the system of innate ideas, cannot, without contradicting their own principles, admit the doctrine of the immortality of the soul.

In defiance of the consolation that so many persons pretend to find in the notion of an eternal existence; in despite of that firm persuasion which such numbers of men assure us they have, that their souls will survive their bodies, they seem so very much alarmed at the dissolution of this body, that they do not contemplate their end, which they ought to desire as the period of so many miseries, but with the greatest inquietude; so true it is, that the real, the present, even accompanied with pain, has much more influence over mankind, than the most beautiful chimeras of the future; which he never views but through the clouds of uncertainty. Indeed the most religious men, notwithstanding the conviction they express of a blessed eternity, do not find these flattering hopes sufficiently consoling to repress their fears; to prevent their trembling, when they think on the necessary dissolution of their bodies. Death was always, for mortals, the most frightful point of view; they regard it as a strange phenomenon, contrary to the order of things, opposed to Nature; in a word, as an effect of the celestial vengeance, as the *wages of sin*. Although every thing proves to man that death is inevitable, he is never able to familiarize himself with its idea; he never thinks on it without shuddering; the assurance of possessing an immortal soul but feebly indemnifies him for the grief he feels in the deprivation of his perishable body. Two causes contribute to strengthen his fears, to nourish his alarm; the one is, that this death, commonly accompanied with pain, wrests from him an existence that pleases him—with which he is acquainted—to which he is accustomed; the other is the uncertainty of the state that must succeed his actual existence.

The illustrious Bacon has said, that "men fear death for the same reason that children dread being alone in darkness." Man naturally challenges every thing with which he is unacquainted; he is desirous to see clearly to the end, that he may guarantee himself against those objects which may menace his safety; that he may also be enabled to procure for himself those which may be useful to him; the man who exists cannot form to himself any idea of non-existence; as this circumstance disturbs him, for want of experience, his imagination sets to work; this points out to him, either well or ill, this uncertain state: accustomed to think, to feel, to be stimulated into activity, to enjoy society, he contemplates as the greatest misfortune, a dissolution that will strip him of these objects, that will deprive him of those sensations which his present nature has rendered necessary to him; he views with dismay a situation that will prevent his being warned of his own existence—that shall bereave him of his pleasures—to plunge him into nothing. In supposing it even exempt from pain, he always looks upon this nothing as an afflicting solitude—as an heap of profound darkness; he sees himself in a state of general desolation; destitute of all assistance; and he feels keenly all the rigour of this frightful situation. But does not a profound sleep help to give him a true idea of this nothing? Does not that deprive him of every thing? Does it not appear to annihilate the universe to him, and him to the universe? Is death any thing more than a profound, a permanent steep? It is for want of being able to form an idea of death that man dreads it; if he could figure to himself a true image of this state of annihilation, he would from thence cease to fear it; but he is not able to conceive a state in which there is no feeling; he therefore believes, that when he shall no longer exist, he will have the same feelings, the same consciousness of things, which, during his existence, appear so sad to his mind; which his fancy paints in such gloomy colours. Imagination pictures to him his funeral pomp—the grave they are digging for him—the lamentations that will accompany him to his last abode-the epicedium that surviving friendship may dictate; he persuades himself that these melancholy objects will affect him as painfully even after his decease, as they do in his present condition, in which he is in full possession of his senses.

Mortal, led astray by fear! after thy death thine eyes will see no more; thine ears will hear no longer; in the depth of thy grave thou wilt no more be witness to this scene, which thine imagination, at present, represents to thee under such dismal colours; thou wilt no longer take part in what shall he done in the world; thou wilt no more be occupied with what may befal thine inanimate remains, than thou wast able to be the day previous to that which ranked thee among the beings of thy species. To die is to cease to think; to lack feeling; no longer to enjoy; to find a period to suffering; thine ideas will perish with thee; thy sorrows will not follow thee to the silent tomb. Think of death, not to feed thy fears—not to nourish thy melancholy—but to accustom thyself to look upon it with a peaceable eye; to cheer thee up against those false terrors with which the enemies to thy repose labour to inspire thee! The fears of death are vain illusions, that must disappear as soon as we learn to contemplate this necessary event under its true point of view. A great man has defined philosophy to be *a meditation on death;* he is not desirous by that to have it understood that man ought to occupy himself sorrowfully with his end, with a view to nourish his fears; on the contrary, he wishes to invite him to familiarize himself with an object that Nature has rendered necessary to him; to accustom himself to expect it with a serene countenance. If life is a benefit, if it be necessary to love it, it is no less necessary to quit it; reason ought to teach him a calm resignation to the decrees of fate: his welfare exacts that he should contract the habit of contemplating with placidity, of viewing without alarm, an event that his essence has rendered inevitable: his interest demands that he should not brood gloomily over his misfortune; that he should not, by continual dread, embitter his life; the charms of which he must inevitably destroy, if he can never view its termination but with trepidation. Reason and his interest then, concur to assure him against those vague terrors with which his imagination inspires him, in this respect. If he was to call them to his assistance, they would reconcile him to an object that only startles him, because he has no knowledge of it; because it is only shewn to him with those hideous accompaniments with which it is clothed by superstition. Let him then, endeavour to despoil death of these vain illusions, and he will perceive that it is only the sleep of life; that this sleep will not be disturbed with disagreeable dreams; that an unpleasant awakening is never likely to follow it. To die is to sleep; it is to enter into that state of insensibility in which he was previous to his birth; before he had senses; before he was conscious of his actual existence. Laws, as necessary as those which gave him birth, will make him return into the bosom of Nature, from whence he was drawn, in order to reproduce him afterwards under some new form, which it would he useless for him to know: without consulting him, Nature places him for a season in the order of organized beings; without his consent, she will oblige him to quit it, to occupy some other order.

Let him not complain then, that Nature is callous; she only makes him undergo a law from which she does not exempt any one being she contains. Man complains of the short duration of life—of the rapidity with which time flies away; yet the greater number of men do not know how to employ either time or life. If all are born and perish—if every thing is changed and destroyed—if the birth of a being is never more than the first step towards its end; how is it possible to expect that man, whose machine is so frail, of which the parts are so complicated, the whole of which possesses such extreme mobility, should be exempted from the common law; which decrees, that even the solid earth he inhabits shall experience change—shall undergo alteration—perhaps be destroyed! Feeble, frail mortal! Thou pretendest to exist for ever; whit thou, then, that for thee alone eternal Nature shall change her undeviating course? Dost thou not behold in those eccentric comets with which thine eyes are sometimes astonished, that the planets themselves are subject to death? Live then in peace for the season that Nature permits thee; if thy mind be enlightened by reason thou wilt die without terror!

Notwithstanding the simplicity of these reflections; nothing is more rare than the sight of men truly fortified against the fears of death: the wise man himself turns pale at its approach; he has occasion to collect the whole force of his mind, to expect it with serenity. It cannot then, furnish matter for surprise, if the idea of death is so revolting to the generality of mortals; it terrifies the young—it redoubles the chagrin of the middle-aged—it even augments the sorrow of the old, who are worn down with infirmity: indeed the aged, although enfeebled by time, dread it much more than the young, who are in the full vigour of life; the man of many lustres is more accustomed to live years as they roll over his head, confirm his attachment to existence; nevertheless, long unwearied exertions weaken the powers of his mind; labour, sickness, and pain, waste his animal strength; he has less energy; his volition becomes faint, superstitious terrors easily appal him; at length disease consumes him; sometimes with excruciating tortures: the unhappy wretch, thus plunged into misfortune, has, notwithstanding, scarcely ever dared to contemplate death; which he ought to consider as the period to all his anguish.

If the source of this pusillanimity be sought, it will be found in his nature, which attaches him to life; in that deficiency of energy in his soul, which hardly any thing tends to corroborate, but which every thing strives to enfeeble: which superstition, instead of strengthening, contributes to bruise. Almost all human institutions, nearly all the opinions of man, conspire to augment his fears; to render his ideas of death more terrible; to make them more revolting to his feelings. Indeed, superstition pleases itself with exhibiting death under the most frightful traits: it represents it to man under the most disgusting colours; as a dreadful moment, which not only puts an end to his pleasures, but gives him up without defence to the strange rigour of a pitiless decree, which nothing can soften. According to this superstition, the most virtuous man has reason to tremble for the severity of his fate; is never certain of being happy; the most dreadful torments, endless punishments, await the victim to involuntary weakness; to the necessary faults of a short-lived existence; his infirmities, his momentary offences, the propensities that have been planted in his heart, the errors of his mind, the opinions he has imbibed, even in the society in which he was born without his own consent, the ideas he has formed, the passions he has indulged above all, his not being able to comprehend all the extravagant dogmas offered to his acceptance, are to be implacably avenged with the most severe and never-ending penalties. Ixion is for ever fastened to his wheel; Sisyphus must to all eternity roll his stone without ever being able to reach the apex of his mountain; the vulture must perpetually prey on the liver of the unfortunate Prometheus: those who dare to think for themselves—those who have refused to listen to their enthusiastic guides—those who have not reverenced the oracles—those who have had the audacity to consult their reason—those who have boldly ventured to detect impostors—those who have doubted the divine mission of the Phythonissa—those who believe that Jupiter violated decency in his visit to Danae—those who look upon Apollo as no better than a strolling musician—those who think that Mahomet was an arch knave—are to smart everlastingly in flaming oceans of burning sulpher; are to float to all eternity in the most excruciating agonies on seas of liquid brimstone, wailing and gnashing their teeth: what wonder, then, if man dreads to be cast into these hideous gulfs; if his mind loathes the horrific picture; if he wishes to defer for a season these dreadful punishments; if he clings to an existence, painful as it may be, rather than encounter such revolting cruelties.

Such, then, are the afflicting objects with which superstition occupies its unhappy, its credulous disciples; such are the fears which the tyrant of human thoughts points out to them as salutary. In defiance Of the exility of the effect which these notions produce oil the greater number, even of those who say they are, or who believe themselves persuaded, they are held forth as the most powerful rampart that can be opposed to the irregularities of man. Nevertheless, as will be seen presently, it will be found that these systems, or rather these chimeras, so terrible to behold, operate little or nothing on the larger portion of mankind, who dream of them but seldom, never in the moment that passion, interest, pleasure, or example, hurries them along. If these fears act, it is commonly on those, who have but little occasion to abstain from evil; they make honest hearts tremble, but fail of effect on the perverse.

They torment sensible souls, but leave those that are hardened in repose; they disturb tractable, gentle minds, but cause no trouble to rebellious spirits: thus they alarm none but those who are already sufficiently alarmed; they coerce only those who are already restrained.

These notions, then, impress nothing on the wicked; when by accident they do act on them, it is only to redouble the wickedness of their natural character—to justify them in their own eyes—to furnish them with pretexts to exercise it without fear—to follow it without scruple. Indeed, the experience of a great number of ages has shewn to what excess of wickedness, to what lengths, the passions of man have carried him, when they have been authorized by the priesthood—when they have been unchained by superstition—or, at least, when he has been enabled to cover himself with its mantle. Man has never been more ambitious, never more covetous, never more crafty, never more cruel, never more seditious, than when he has persuaded himself that superstition permitted or commanded him to be so: thus, superstition did nothing more than lend an invincible force to his natural passions, which under its sacred auspices he could exercise with impunity, indulge without remorse; still more, the greatest villains, in giving free vent to the detestable propensities of their natural wickedness, have under its influence believed, that, by displaying an over-heated zeal, they merited well of heaven; that they exempted themselves by new crimes, from that chastisement which they thought their anterior conduct had richly merited.

These, then, are the effects which what are called the *salutary* notions of superstition, produce on mortals. These reflections will furnish an answer to those who say that, "If heaven was promised equally to the wicked as to the righteous, there would be found none incredulous of another life." We reply, that, in point of fact, superstition does accord heaven to the wicked, since it frequently places in this happy abode the most useless, the most depraved of men. Is not Mahomet himself enthroned in the empyrean by this superstition? If the calendar of the Romish saints was examined, would it be found to contain none but righteous, none but good men? Does not Mahometanism cut off from all chance of future existence, consequently from all hope of reaching heaven, the female part of mankind? Have the Jews exalted no one to the celestial regions, save the virtuous? When the Jew is condemned to the devouring flames, do not the men who thus torture an unhappy wretch, whose only crime is adherence to the religion of his forefathers, expect to be rewarded for the deed with everlasting happiness? Are they not promised eternal salvation for their orthodoxy? Was Constantine, was St. Cyril, was St. Athanasius, was St. Dominic, worthy beatification? Were Jupiter, Thor, Mercury, Woden, and a thousand others, deserving of celestial diadems? Is erring, feeble man, with all his imbecilities, competent to form a judgment of the heavenly deserts of his fellows? Can be, with his dim optics, with his limited vision, fathom the human heart? Can he sound its depths, trace its meanderings, dive into its recesses, with sufficient precision, to determine who amongst his race is or is not possessed of the requisite merit to enjoy a blessed eternity? Thus wicked men are held up as models by superstition, which as we shall see, sharpens the passions of evil-disposed men, by legitimating those crimes, at which, without this sanction, they would shudder; which they would fear to commit; or for which, at least, they would feel shame; for which they would experience remorse. In short, the ministers of superstition furnish to the most profligate men the power of indulging their inflamed passions, and then hold forth to them means of diverting from their own heads the thunderbolt that should strike their crimes, by spreading before them fresh incentives to intolerant persecution, with the promise of a never-fading happiness.

With respect to the incredulous, without doubt, there may be amongst them wicked men, as well as amongst the most credulous; but incredulity no more supposes wickedness, than credulity supposes righteousness. On the contrary, the man who thinks, who meditates, knows far better the true motives to goodness, than he who suffers himself to be blindly guided by uncertain motives, or by the interest of others. Sensible men have the greatest advantage in examining opinions, which it is pretended must have an influence over their eternal happiness: if these are found false, if they appear injurious to their present life, they will not therefore conclude, that they have not another life either to fear or to hope; that they are permitted to deliver themselves up with impunity to vice, which would do an injury to themselves, that would draw upon them the contempt of their neighbour, which would subject them to the anger of society: the man who does not expect another life, is only more interested in prolonging his existence in this; in rendering himself dear to his fellows, by cultivating virtue; by performing all his duties with more strictness, in the only life of which be has any knowledge: he has made a great stride towards felicity, in disengaging himself from those terrors which afflict others, which frequently prevent their acting. Such a man has nothing to fear, but every thing to hope; if, contrary to what he is able to judge, there should be an hereafter existence, will not his actions have been so regulated by virtue, will he not have so comported himself in his present existence, as to stand a fair chance of enjoying in their fullest extent those felicities prepared for his species?

Superstition, in fact, takes a pride in rendering man slothful, in moulding him to credulity, in making him pusillanimous. It is its principle to afflict him without intermission; to redouble in him the horrors of death: ever ingenious in tormenting him, it has extended his inquietudes beyond even his own existence; its ministers, the more securely to dispose of him in this world, invented, in future regions, a variety of rewards and punishments, reserving to themselves the privilege of awarding these heavenly recompences to those who yielded most implicitly to their arbitrary laws; of decreeing punishment to those refractory beings who rebelled against their power: thus, according to them, Tantalus for divulging their secrets, must eternally fear, engulphed in burning sulphur, the stone ready to fall on his devoted head; whilst Romulus was beatified and worshipped as a god under the name of Quirinus. The same system of superstition caused the philosopher Callisthenes to be put to death, for opposing the worship of Alexander; and elevated the monk Athanasius to be a saint in heaven. Far from holding forth consolation to mortals, far from cultivating man's reason, far from teaching him to yield under the hands of necessity, superstition, in a great many countries, strives to render death still more bitter to him; to make its yoke sit heavy; to fill up its retinue with a multitude of hideous phantoms; to paint it in the most frightful colours; to render its approach terrible: by this means it has crowded the world with enthusiasts, whom it seduces by vague promises; with contemptible slaves, whom it coerces with the fear of imaginary evils: it has at length persuaded man, that his actual existence is only a journey, by which he will arrive at a more important life: this doctrine, whether it be rational or irrational, prevents him from occupying himself with his true happiness; from even dreaming of ameliorating his institutions, of improving his laws, of advancing the progress of science, of perfectioning his morals. Vain and gloomy ideas have absorbed his attention: he consents to groan under fanatical tyranny—to writhe under political inflictions—to live in error—to languish in misfortune—in the hope, when he shall be no more, of being one day happier; in the firm confidence, that after he has disappeared, his calamities, his patience, will conduct him to a never-ending felicity: he has believed himself submitted to cruel priests, who are willing to make him purchase his future welfare at the expence of every thing most dear to his peace, most valuable to his existence here below: they have pictured heaven as irritated against him, as disposed to appease itself by punishing him eternally, for any efforts he should make to withdraw himself from, their power. It is thus the doctrine of a future life has been made fatal to the human species: it plunged whole nations into sloth, made them languid, filled them with indifference to their present welfare, or else precipitated them, into the most furious enthusiasm, which hurried them on to such lengths that they tore each other in pieces in order to merit the promised heaven.

It will be asked, perhaps, by what road has man been conducted to form to himself these gratuitous ideas of another world? I reply, that it is a truth man has no idea of a future life, they are the ideas of the past and the present that furnish his imagination with the materials of which he constructs the edifice of the regions of futurity. Hobbes says, "We believe that, that which is will always be, and that the same causes will have the same effects." Man in his actual state, has two modes of feeling, one that he approves, another that he disapproves: thus, persuaded that these two modes of feeling must accompany him, even beyond his present existence, he placed in the regions of eternity two distinguished abodes, one destined to felicity, the other to misery: the one must contain those who obey the calls of superstition, who believe in its dogmas; the other is a prison, destined to avenge the cause of heaven, on all those who shall not faithfully believe the doctrines promulgated by the ministers of a vast variety of superstitions. Has sufficient attention been paid to the fact that results as a necessary consequence from this reasoning; which on examination will be found to have rendered the first place entirely useless, seeing, that by the number and contradiction of these various systems, let man believe which ever he may, let him follow it in the most faithful manner, still he must he ranked as an infidel, as a rebel to the Divinity, because he cannot believe in all; and those from which he dissents, by a consequence of their own creed, condemn him to the prison-house?

Such is the origin of the ideas upon a future life, so diffused among mankind. Every where may be seen an Elysium and a Tartarus; a Paradise and a Hell; in a word, two distinguished abodes, constructed according to the imagination of the enthusiasts who have invented them, who have accommodated them to their own peculiar prejudices, to the hopes, to the fears, of the people who believe in them. The Indian figures the first of these abodes as one of in-action, of permanent repose, because, being the inhabitant of a hot climate, he has learned to contemplate rest as the extreme of felicity: the Mussulman promises himself corporeal pleasures, similar to those that actually constitute the object of his research in this life: each figures to himself, that on which he has learned to set the greatest value.

Of whatever nature these pleasures may be, man apprehended that a body was needful, in order that his soul might be enabled to enjoy the pleasures, or to experience the pains in reserve for him: from hence the doctrine of the *resurrection*; but as he beheld this body putrify, as he saw it dissolve, as he witnessed its decomposition, after death, he was at a loss how to form anew what he conceived so necessary to his system he therefore had recourse to the Divine Omnipotence, by whose interposition he now believes it will he effected. This opinion, so incomprehensible, is said to have originated in Persia, among the Magi, and finds a great number of adherents, who have never given it a serious examination: but the doctrine of the resurrection appears perfectly useless to all those, who believe in the existence of a soul that feels, thinks, suffers, and enjoys, after a separation from the body: indeed, there are already sects who begin to maintain, that the body is not necessary; that therefore it will not be resurrected. Like Berkeley, they conceive that "the soul has need neither of body nor any exterior being, either to experience sensations, or to have ideas:" the Malebranchists, in particular, must suppose that the rejected souls will see every thing in the Divinity; will feel themselves burn, without having occasion for bodies for that purpose. Others, incapable of elevating themselves to these sublime notions, believed, that under divers forms, man animated successively different animals of various species; that he never ceased to be an inhabitant of the earth; such was the opinion of those who adopted the doctrine of Metempsychosis.

As for the miserable abode of souls, the imagination of fanatics, who were desirous of governing the people, strove to assemble the most frightful images, to render it still more terrible: fire is of all beings that which produces in man the most pungent sensation; not finding any thing more cruel, the enemies to the several dogmas were to be everlastingly punished with this torturing element: fire, therefore, was the point at which their imagination was obliged to stop. The ministers of the various systems agreed pretty generally, that fire would one day avenge their offended divinities: thus they painted the victims to the anger of the gods, or rather those who questioned their own creeds, as confined in fiery dungeons, as perpetually rolling in a vortex of bituminous flames, as plunged in unfathomable gulphs of liquid sulphur, making the infernal caverns resound with their useless groanings, with their unavailing gnashing of teeth.

But it will, perhaps, be enquired, how could man reconcile himself to the belief of an existence accompanied with eternal torments; above all, as many according to their own superstitions had reason to fear it for themselves? Many causes have concurred to make him adopt so revolting an opinion: in the first place, very few thinking men have ever believed such an absurdity, when they have deigned to make use of their reason; or, when they have accredited it, this notion was always counterbalanced by the idea of the goodness, by a reliance on the mercy, which they attributed to their respective divinities: in the second place, those who were blinded by their fears, never rendered to themselves any account of these strange doctrines, which they either received with awe from their legislators, or which were transmitted to them by their fathers: in the third place, each sees the object of his terrors only at a favourable distance: moreover, superstition promises him the means of escaping the tortures he believes he has merited. At length, like those sick people whom we see cling with fondness, even to the most painful life, man preferred the idea of an unhappy, though unknown existence, to that of non-existence, which he looked upon as the most frightful evil that could befal him; either because he could form no idea of it, or because his imagination painted to him this non-existence this nothing, as the confused assemblage of all evils. A known evil, of whatever magnitude, alarmed him less (above all, when there remained the hope of being able to avoid it), than an evil of which he knew nothing, upon which, consequently, his imagination was painfully employed, but to which he knew not how to oppose a remedy.

It will be seen, then, that *superstition*, far from consoling man upon the necessity of death, only redoubles his terrors, by the evils with which it pretends his decease will be followed; these terrors are so strong, that the miserable wretches who believe strictly in these formidable doctrines, pass their days in affliction, bathed in the most bitter tears. What shall be said of an opinion so destructive to society, yet adopted by so many nations, which announces to them, that a severe fate may at each instant take them unprovided; that at each moment they are liable to pass under the most rigorous judgment? What idea can be better suited to terrify man—what more likely to discourage him—what more calculated to damp the desire of ameliorating his condition—than the afflicting prospect of a world always on the brink of dissolution; of a Divinity seated upon the ruins of Nature, ready to pass judgment on the human species? Such are, nevertheless, the fatal opinions with which the mind of nations has been fed for thousands of years: they are so dangerous, that if by a happy want of just inference, he did not derogate in his conduct from these afflicting ideas, he would fall into the most abject stupidity. How could man occupy himself with a perishable world, ready every moment to crumble into atoms? How dream of rendering himself happy on earth, when it is only the porch to an eternal kingdom? Is it then, surprising, that the superstitions to which similar doctrines serve for a basis, have prescribed to their disciples a total detachment from things below—an entire renunciation of the most innocent pleasures; have given birth to a sluggishness, to a pusillanimity, to an abjection of soul, to an insociability, that renders him useless to himself, dangerous to others? If necessity did not oblige man to depart in his practice from these irrational systems— if his wants did not bring him back to reason, in despite of these superstitious doctrines—the whole world would presently become a vast desert, inhabited by some few isolated savages, who would not even have courage to multiply themselves. What are these, but notions which he must necessarily put aside, in order that human association may subsist?

Nevertheless, the doctrine of a future life, accompanied with rewards and punishments, has been regarded for a great number of ages as the most powerful, or even as the only motive capable of coercing the passions of man; as the sole means that can oblige him to be virtuous: by degrees, this doctrine has become the basis of almost all religions and political systems, so much so, that at this day it is said, this prejudice cannot be attacked without absolutely rending asunder the bonds of society. The founders of superstition have made use of it to attach their credulous disciples; legislators have looked upon it as the curb best calculated to keep mankind under discipline; religion considers it necessary to his happiness; many philosophers themselves have believed with sincerity, that this doctrine was requisite to terrify man, was the only means to divert him from crime: notwithstanding, when the doctrine of the immortality of the soul first came out of the school of Plato; when it first diffused itself among the Greeks, it caused the greatest ravages; it determined a multitude of men, who were discontented with their condition, to terminate their existence: Ptolemy Philadelphus, king of Egypt, seeing the effect this doctrine, which at the present day is looked upon as so salutary, produced on the brains of his subjects, prohibited the teaching of it under the penalty of death.

It must, indeed, be allowed that this doctrine has been of the greatest utility to those who have given superstitions to nations, who at the same time made themselves its ministers; it was the foundation of their power, the source of their wealth, the permanent cause of that blindness, the solid basis of those terrors, which it was their interest to nourish in the human race. It was by this doctrine the priest became first the rival, then the master of kings: it is by this dogma that nations are filled with enthusiasts inebriated with superstition, always more disposed to listen to its menaces, than to the counsels of reasons, to the orders of the sovereign, to the cries of Nature, or to the laws of society. Politics itself was enslaved to the caprice of the priest; the temporal monarch was obliged to bend under the yoke of the monarch of superstition; the one only disposed of this perishable world, the other extended his power into the world to come; much more important for man than the earth, on which he is only a pilgrim, a mere passenger. Thus the doctrine of another life placed the government itself in a state of dependance upon the priest; the monarch was nothing more than his first subject; he was never obeyed, but when the two were in accord. Nature in vain cried out to man, to be careful of his present happiness; the priest ordered him to be unhappy, in the expectation of future felicity; reason in vain exhorted him to be peaceable; the priest breathed forth fanaticism, fulminated fury, obliged him to disturb the public tranquillity, every time there was a question of the supposed interests of the invisible monarch of another life, and the real interests of his ministers in this.

Such is the fruit that politics has gathered from the doctrine of a future life; the regions of the world to come have enabled the priesthood to conquer the present world. The expectation of celestial happiness, and the dread of future tortures, only served to prevent man from seeking after the means to render himself happy here below. Thus error, under whatever aspect it is considered, will never be more than a source of evil for mankind. The doctrine of another life, in presenting to mortals an ideal happiness, will render them enthusiasts; in overwhelming them with fears, it will make useless beings; generate cowards; form atrabilarious or furious men; who will lose sight of their present abode, to occupy themselves with the pictured regions of a world to come, with those dreadful evils which they must fear after their death.

If it be insisted that the doctrine of future rewards and punishments is the most powerful curb to restrain the passions of man, we shall reply by calling in daily experience. If we only cast our eyes around, if for a moment we examine what passes in review before us, we shall see this assertion contradicted; we shall find that these marvellous speculations do not in any manner diminish the number of the wicked, because they are incapable of changing the temperament of man, of annihilating those passions which the vices of society engender in his heart. In those nations who appear the most thoroughly convinced of this future punishment, may be seen assassins, thieves, crafty knaves, oppressors, adulterers, voluptuaries; all these pretend they are firmly persuaded of the reality of an hereafter; yet in the whirlwind of dissipation, in the vortex of pleasure, in the fury of their passions, they no longer behold this formidable future existence, which in those moments has no kind of influence over their earthly conduct.

In short, in many of those countries where the doctrine of another life is so firmly established, that each individual irritates himself against whoever may have the temerity to combat the opinion, or even to doubt it, we see that it is utterly incapable of impressing any thing on rulers who are unjust, who are negligent of the welfare of their people, who are, debauched, on courtezans who are lewd in their habits, on covetous misers, on flinty extortioners who fatten on the substance of a nation, on women without modesty, on a vast multitude of drunken, intemperate, vicious men, on great numbers even amongst those priests, whose function it is to preach this future state, who are paid to announce the vengeance of heaven, against vices which they themselves encourage by their example. If it be enquired of them, how they dare to give themselves up to such scandalous actions, which they ought to know are certain to draw upon them eternal punishment? They will reply, that the madness of their passions, the force of their habits, the contagion of example, or even the power of circumstances, have hurried them along; have made them forget the dreadful consequences in which their conduct is likely to involve them; besides, they will say, that the treasures of the divine mercy are infinite; that repentance suffices to efface the foulest transgressions; to cleanse the blackest guilt; to blot out the most enormous crimes: in this multitude of wretched beings, who each after his own manner desolates society with his criminal pursuits, you will find only a small number who are sufficiently intimidated by the fears of the miserable hereafter, to resist their evil propensities. What did I say? These propensities are in themselves too weak to carry them forward without the aid of the doctrine of another life; without this, the law and the fear of censure would have been motives sufficient to prevent them from rendering themselves criminal.

It is indeed, fearful, timorous souls, upon whom the terrors of another life make a profound impression; human beings of this sort come into the world with moderate passions, are of a weakly organization, possess a cool imagination; it is not therefore surprising, that in such men, who are already restrained by their nature, the fear of future punishment counterbalances the weak efforts of their feeble passions; but it is by no means the same with those determined sinners, with those hardened criminals, with those men who are habitually vicious, whose unseemly excesses nothing can arrest, who in their violence shut their eyes to the fear of the laws of this world, despising still more those of the other. Nevertheless, how many persons say they are, and even believe themselves, restrained by the fears of the life to come? But, either they deceive us, or they impose upon themselves, by attributing to these fears, that which is only the effect of motives much nearer at hand; such as the feebleness of their machine, the mildness of their temperament, the slender energy of their souls, their natural timidity, the ideas imbibed in their education, the fear of consequences immediately resulting from criminal actions, the physical evils attendant on unbridled irregularities: these are the true motives that restrain them; not the notions of a future life: which men, who say they are most firmly persuaded of its existence, forget whenever a powerful interest solicits them to sin. If for a time man would pay attention to what passes before his eyes, he would perceive that he ascribes to the fear of the gods that which is in reality only the effect of peculiar weakness, of pusillanimity, of the small interest found to commit evil: these men would not act otherwise than they do, if they had not this fear before them; if, therefore he reflected, he would feel that it is always necessity that makes men act as they do.

Man cannot be restrained, when he does not find within himself motives sufficiently powerful to conduct him back to reason. There is nothing, either in this world or in the other, that can render him virtuous, when an untoward organization—a mind badly cultivated—a violent imagination—inveterate habits—fatal examples—powerful interests— invite him from every quarter to the commission of crime. No speculations are capable of restraining the man who braves public opinion, who despises the law, who is careless of its censure, who turns a deaf ear to the cries of conscience, whose power in this world places him out of the reach of punishment; in the violence of his transports, he will fear still less a distant futurity, of which the idea always recedes before that which he believes necessary to his immediate interests, consistent with his present happiness. All lively passions blind man to every thing that is not its immediate object; the terrors of a future life, of which his passions always possess the secret to diminish to him the probability, can effect nothing upon the wicked man, who does not fear even the much nearer punishment of the law; who sets at nought the assured hatred of those by whom he is surrounded. Man, when he delivers himself up to crime, sees nothing certain except the supposed advantage which attends it; the rest always appear to him either false or problematical.

If man would but open his eyes, even for a moment, he would clearly perceive, that to effect any thing upon hearts hardened by crime, he must not reckon upon the chastisement of an avenging Divinity, which the self-love natural to man always shews him as pacified in the long run. He who has arrived at persuading himself he cannot be happy without crime, will always readily deliver himself up to it, notwithstanding the menaces of religion. Whoever is sufficiently blind not to read his infamy in his own heart, to see his own vileness in the countenances of his associates, his own condemnation in the anger of his fellow-men, his own unworthiness in the indignation of the judges established to punish the offences he may commit: such a man, I say, will never feel the impression his crimes shall make on the features of a judge, that is either hidden from his view, or that he only contemplates at a distance. The tyrant who with dry eyes can hear the cries of the distressed, who with callous heart can behold the tears of a whole people, of whose misery he is the cause, will not see the angry countenance of a more powerful master: like another Menippus, he may indeed destroy himself from desperation, to avoid reiterated reproach; which only proves, that when a haughty, arrogant despot pretends to be accountable for his actions to the Divinity alone, it is because he fears his nation more than he does his God.

On the other hand, does not superstition itself, does not even religion, annihilate the effects of those fears which it announces as salutary? Does it not furnish its disciples with the means of extricating themselves from the punishments with which it has so frequently menaced them? Does it not tell them, that a steril repentance will, even at the moment of death, disarm the celestial wrath; that it will purify the filthy souls of sinners? Do not even the priests, in some superstitions, arrogate to themselves the right of remitting to the dying the punishment due to the crimes committed during the course of a disorderly life? In short, do not the most perverse men, encouraged in iniquity, countenanced in debauchery, upheld in crime, reckon, even to the last moment, either upon the assistance of superstition, or upon the aid of religion, that promises them the infallible means of reconciling themselves to the Divinity, whom they have irritated; of avoiding the rigorous punishments pronounced against their enormities?

In consequence of these notions, so favourable to the wicked, so suitable to tranquillize their fears, we see that the hope of an easy expiation, far from correcting man, engages him to persist, until death, in the most crying disorders. Indeed, in despite of the numberless advantages which he is assured flows from the doctrine of a life to come, in defiance of its pretended efficacy to repress the passions of men, do not the priests themselves, although so interested in the maintenance of this system, every day complain of its insufficiency? They acknowledge, that mortals, who from their infancy they have imbued with these ideas, are not less hurried forward by their evil propensities—less sunk in the vortex of dissipation—less the slaves to their pleasures—less captivated by bad habits—less driven along by the torrent of the world—less seduced by their present interest—which make them forget equally the recompense and the chastisement of a future existence. In a word, the interpreters of superstition, the ministers of religion themselves, allow that their disciples, for the greater part, conduct themselves in this world as if they had nothing either to hope or fear in another.

In short, let it be supposed for a moment, that the doctrine of eternal punishments was of some utility; that it really restrained a small number of individuals; what are these feeble advantages compared to the numberless evils that flow from it? Against one timid man whom this idea restrains, there are thousands upon whom it operates nothing; there are thousands whom it makes irrational; whom it renders savage persecutors; whom it converts into fanatics; there are thousands whose mind it disturbs; whom it diverts from their duties towards society; there are an infinity whom it grievously afflicts, whom it troubles without producing any real good for their associates.

Notwithstanding so many are inclined to consider those who do not fall in with this doctrine as the enemies of society; it will be found on examination that the wisest the most enlightened men of antiquity, as well as many of the moderns, have believed not only that the soul is material and perishes with the body, but also that they have attacked without subterfuge the opinion of future everlasting punishments; it will also be found that many of the systems, set up to establish the immortality of the soul, are in themselves the best evidence that can be adduced of the futility of this doctrine; if for a moment we only follow up the natural the just inferences that are to be drawn from them. This sentiment was far from being, as some have supposed, peculiar to the Epicureans, it has been adopted by philosophers of all sects, by Pythagoreans, by Stoics, by Peripatetics, by Academics; in short by the most godly the most virtuous men of Greece and of Rome.

Pythagoras, according to Ovid, speaks strongly to the fact. Timaeus of Locris, who was a Pythagorean, admits that the doctrine of future punishments was fabulous, solely destined for the imbecility of the uninformed; but little calculated for those who cultivate their reason.

Aristotle expressly says, that "man has neither good to hope nor evil to fear after death."

Zeno, according to Cicero, supposed the soul to be an igneous substance, from whence he concluded it destroyed itself.

Cicero, the philosophical orator, who was of the sect of Academics, although he is not on all occasions, in accord with himself, treats openly as fables the torments of Hell; and looks upon death as the end of every thing for man.

Seneca, the philosopher, is filled with passages which contemplate death as a state of total annihilation, particularly in speaking of it to his brother: and nothing can be more decisive of his holding this opinion, than what he writes to Marcia, to console him.

Seneca, the tragedian, explains himself in the same manner as the philosopher.

The Platonists, who made the soul immortal, could not have an idea of future punishments, because the soul according to them was a portion of the divinity which after the dissolution of the body it returned to rejoin.

Epictetus has the same idea. In a passage reported by Arrian, he says, "but where are you going? It cannot be to a place of suffering: you will only return to the place from whence you came; you are about to be again peaceably associated with the elements from which you are derived. That which in your composition, is of the nature of fire, will return to the element of fire; that which is of the nature of earth, will rejoin itself to the earth; that which is air, will re-unite itself with air; that which is water, will resolve itself into water; there is no Hell, no Acheron, no Cocytus, no Phlegethon."

In another place he says, "the hour of death approaches; but do not aggravate your evil, nor render things worse than they are: represent them to yourself under their true point of view. The time is come when the materials of which you are composed, go to resolve themselves into the elements from whence they were originally borrowed. What is there that is terrible or grievous in that? Is there any thing in the world that perishes totally?"

The sage and pious Antoninus says, "he who fears death, either fears to be deprived of all feeling, or dreads to experience different sensations. If you lose all feeling, you will no longer be subject either to pain or to misery. If you are provided with other senses of a different nature, you will become a creature of a different species." This great emperor further says, "that we must expect death with tranquillity, seeing, that it is only a dissolution of the elements of which each animal is composed."

To the evidence of so many great men of *Pagan antiquity*, may be joined, that of the author of Ecclesiastes, who speaks of death, and of the condition of the human soul, like an *epicurean*; he says, "for that which befalleth the sons of men, befalleth beasts; even one thing befalleth them: as the one dieth, so dieth the other; yea, they have all one breath: so that a man hath no pre-eminence above a beast; for all is vanity. All go unto one place; all are of the dust, and all turn to dust again." And further, "wherefore I perceive that there is nothing better than that a man should rejoice in his own works; for that is his portion: for who shall bring him to see what shall be after him."

In short, how can the utility or the necessity of this doctrine be reconciled with the fact, that the great *legislator of the Jews*, who is supposed to have been inspired by the Divinity, should have remained silent on a subject, that is said to be of so much importance? In the third chapter of Genesis it, is said, "In the sweat of thy face shalt thou eat bread, till thou return unto the ground; for out of it wast thou taken: for dust thou art, and unto dust shalt thou return."

CHAP. XIV.

Education, Morals, and the Laws suffice to restrain Man.—Of the desire of Immortality.—Of Suicide.

It is not then in an ideal world, existing no where perhaps, but in the imagination of man, that he must seek to collect motives calculated to make him act properly in this; it is in the visible world that will be found incitements to divert him from crime; to rouse him to virtue. It is in Nature,—in experience,—in truth, that he must search out remedies for the evils of his species; for motives suitable to infuse into the human heart, propensities truely useful to society; calculated to promote its advantage; to conduce to the end for which it was designed.

If attention has been paid to what has been said In the course of this work, it will he seen that above all it is *education* that will best furnish the true means of rectifying the errors, of recalling the wanderings of mankind. It is this that should scatter the Seeds in his heart; cultivate the tender shoots; make a profitable use of his dispositions; turn to account those faculties, which depend on his organization: which should cherish the fire of his imagination, kindle it for useful objects; damp it, or extinguish it for others; in short, it is this which should make sensible souls contract habits which are advantageous for society and beneficial to the individual. Brought up in this manner, man would not have occasion for celestial punishments, to teach him the value of virtue; he would not need to behold burning gulphs of brimstone under his feet, to induce him to feel horror for crime; Nature without these fables, would teach much better what he owes to himself; the law would point out what he owes to the body politic, of which he is a member. It is thus, that education grounded upon utility, would form valuable citizens to the state; the depositaries of power would distinguish those whom education should have thus formed, by reason of the advantages which they would procure for their country; they would punish those who should be found injurious to it; it would make the citizens see, that the promises of reward which education held forth, the punishments denounced by morals, are by no means vain; that in a state well constituted, *virtue* is the true, the only road to happiness; *talents* the way to gain respect; that *inutility* conducts to misfortune: that *crime* leads to contempt.

A just, enlightened, virtuous, and vigilant government, who should honestly propose the public good, would have no occasion either for fables or for falsehoods, to govern reasonable subjects; it would blush to make use of imposture, to deceive its citizens; who, instructed in their duties, would find their interest in submitting to equitable laws; who would be capable of feeling the benefit these have the power of conferring on them; it would feel, that habit is sufficient to inspire them with horror, even for those concealed crimes that escape the eyes of society; it would understand that the visible punishments of this world impose much more on the generality of men, than those of an uncertain and distant futurity: in short, it would ascertain that the sensible benefits within the compass of the sovereign power to distribute, touch the imagination of mortals more keenly, than those vague recompences which are held forth to them in a future existence: above all, it would discover that those on whom these distant advantages do operate, would be still more attached to virtue by receiving their reward both here and hereafter.

Man is almost every where so wicked, so corrupt, so rebellious to reason, only because he is not governed according to his Nature, nor properly instructed in her necessary laws: he is almost in every climate fed with superstitious chimeras; submitted to masters who neglect his instruction or who seek to deceive him. On the face of this globe, may be frequently witnessed unjust sovereigns, who, enervated by luxury, corrupted by flattery, depraved by licentiousness, made wicked by impunity, devoid of talents, without morals, destitute of virtue, are incapable of exerting any energy for the benefit of the states they govern; they are consequently but little occupied with the welfare of their people; indifferent to their duties; of which indeed they are often ignorant. Such governors suffer their whole attention to be absorbed by frivolous amusement; stimulated by the desire of continually finding means to feed their insatiable ambition they engage in useless depopulating wars; and never occupy their mind with those objects which are the most important to the happiness of their nation: yet these weak men feel interested in maintaining the received prejudices, and visit with severity those who consider the means of curing them: in short themselves deprived of that understanding, which teaches man that it is his interest to be kind, just, and virtuous; they ordinarily reward only those crimes which their imbecility makes them imagine as useful to them; they generally punish those virtues which are opposed to their own imprudent passions, but which reason would point out as truly beneficial to their interests. Under such masters is it surprising that society should be ravaged; that weak beings should be willing to imitate them; that perverse men should emulate each other in oppressing its members; in sacrificing its dearest interests; in despoiling its happiness? The state of society in such countries, is a state of hostility of the sovereign against the whole, of each of its members the one against the other. Man is wicked, not because he is born so, but because he is rendered so; the great, the powerful, crush with impunity the indigent and the unhappy; these, at the risk of their lives seek to retaliate, to render back the evil they have received: they attack either openly or in secret a country, who to them is a step-mother, who gives all to some of her children, and deprives the others of every thing: they punish it for its partiality, and clearly shew that the motives borrowed from a life hereafter are impotent against the fury of those passions to which a corrupt administration has given birth; that the terror of the punishments in this world are too feeble against necessity; against criminal habits; against dangerous organization uncorrected by education.

In many countries the morals of the people are neglected; the government is occupied only with rendering them timid; with making them miserable. Man is almost every where a slave; it must then follow of necessity, that he is base, interested, dissimulating, without honour, in a word that he has the vices of the state of which he is a citizen. Almost every where he is deceived; encouraged in ignorance; prevented from cultivating his reason; of course he must be stupid, irrational, and wicked almost every where he sees vice applauded, and crime honoured; thence he concludes vice to be a good; virtue, only a useless sacrifice of himself: almost every where he is miserable, therefore he injures his fellow-men in a fruitless attempt to relieve his own anguish: it is in vain to shew him heaven in order to restrain him; his views presently descend again to earth; he is willing to be happy at any price; therefore, the laws which have neither provided for his instruction, for his morals, nor his happiness, menace him uselessly; he plunges on in his pursuits, and these ultimately punish him, for the unjust negligence of his legislators. If politics more enlightened, did seriously occupy itself with the instruction, with the welfare of the people; if laws were more equitable; if each society, less partial, bestowed on its members the care, the education, and the assistance which they have a right to expect; if governments less covetous, and more vigilant, were sedulous to render their subjects more happy, there would not be seen such numbers of malefactors, of robbers, of murderers, who every where infest society; they would not be obliged to destroy life, in order to punish wickedness; which is commonly ascribable to the vices of their own institutions: it would be unnecessary to seek in another life for fanciful chimeras, which always prove abortive against the infuriate passions; against the real wants of man. In short, if the people were instructed, they would be more happy; politics would no longer be reduced to the exigency of deceiving them, in order to restrain them; nor to destroy so many unfortunates, for having procured necessaries, at the expence of their hard-hearted fellow-citizens.

When it shall be desired to enlighten man, let him always have truth laid before him. Instead of kindling his imagination by the idea of those punishments that a future state has in reserve for him, let him be solaced—let him be succoured; or, at least, let him be permitted to enjoy the fruit of his labour—let not his substance be ravished from him by cruel imposts—let him not be discouraged from work, by finding all his labour inadequate to support his existence; let him not be driven into that idleness, that will surely lead him on to crime: let him consider his present existence, without carrying his views to that which may attend him after his death; let his industry be excited—let his talents be rewarded—let him be rendered active, laborious, beneficent, and virtuous, in the world he inhabits; let it be shewn to him, that his actions are capable of having an influence over his fellow-men. Let him not be menaced with the tortures of a future existence when he shall be no more; let him behold society armed against those who disturb its repose; let him see the consequence of the hatred of his associates; let him learn to feel the value of their affection; let him be taught to esteem himself; let him understand, that to obtain it, he must have virtue; above all, that the virtuous man in society has nothing to fear, but every thing to hope.

If it be desired to form honest, courageous, industrious citizens, who may be useful to their country, let them beware of inspiring man from his infancy with an ill-founded dread of death; of amusing his imagination with marvellous fables; of occupying his mind with his destiny in a future life, quite useless to be known, which has nothing in common with his real felicity. Let them speak of immortality to intrepid, noble souls; let them shew it as the price of their labours to energetic minds, who are solely occupied with virtue; who springing forward beyond the boundaries of their actual existence—who, little satisfied with eliciting the admiration, with gaining the love of their contemporaries, are will also to wrest the homage, to secure the affection of future races. Indeed, this is an immortality to which genius, talents, above all virtue, has a just right to pretend; do not therefore let them censure—do not let them endeavour to stifle so noble a passion in man; which is founded upon his nature; which is so calculated to render him happy; from which society gather the most advantageous fruits.

The idea of being buried in total oblivion, of having nothing in common after his death with the beings of his species; of losing all possibility of again having any influence over them, is a thought extremely painful to man; it is above all afflicting to those who possess an ardent imagination. The *desire of immortality*, or of living in the memory of his fellow men, was always the passion of great souls; it was the motive to the actions of all those who have played a great part on the earth. *Heroes* whether virtuous or criminal, *philosophers* as well as *conquerors, men of genius* and *men of talents*, those sublime personages who have done honor to their species, as well as those illustrious villains who have debased and ravaged it, have had an eye to posterity in all their enterprises; have flattered themselves with the hope of acting upon the souls of men, even when they themselves should no longer exist. If man in general does not carry his views so far, he is at least sensible to the idea of seeing himself regenerated in his children; whom he knows are destined to survive him; to transmit his name; to preserve his memory; to represent him in society; it is for them that he rebuilds his cottage; it is for them that he plants the tree which his eyes will never behold in its vigour; it is that they may be happy that he labours. The sorrow which embitters the life of those rich men, frequently so useless to the world, when they have lost the hope of continuing their race, has its source in the fear of being entirely forgotten: they feel that the useless man dies entirely. The idea that his name will be in the mouths of men, the thought that it will be pronounced with tenderness, that it will be recollected with kindness, that it will excite in their hearts favourable sentiments, is an illusion that is useful; is a vision suitable to flatter even those who know that nothing will result from it. Man pleases himself with dreaming that he shall have power, that he shall pass for something in the universe, even after the term of his human existence; he partakes by imagination in the projects, in the actions, in the discussions of future ages, and would be extremely unhappy if he believed himself entirely excluded from their society. The laws in all countries have entered into these views; they have so far been willing to console their citizens for the necessity of dying, by giving them the means of exercising their will, even for a long time after their death: this condescension goes to that length, that the dead frequently regulate the condition of the living during a long series of years.

Every thing serves to prove the desire in man of surviving himself. *Pyramids, mausoleums, monuments, epitaphs,* all shew that he is willing to prolong his existence even beyond his decease. He, is not insensible to the judgment of posterity; it is for him the philosopher writes; it is to astonish him that the monarch erects sumptuous edifices, gorgeous palaces; it is his praises, it is his commendations, that the great man already hears echo in his ears; it is to him that the virtuous citizen appeals from unjust laws; from prejudiced contemporaries—happy chimera! generous illusion! mild vision! its power is so consoling, so bland, that it realizes itself to ardent imaginations; it is calculated to give birth, to sustain, to nurture, to mature enthusiasm of genius, constancy of courage, grandeur of soul, transcendency of talent; its force is so gentle, its influence so pleasing, that it is sometimes able to repress the vices, to restrain the excesses of the most powerful men; who are, as experience has shewn, frequently very much disquieted for the judgment of their posterity; from a conviction that this will sooner or later avenge the living of the foul injustice which they may be inclined to make them suffer.

No man, therefore, can consent to be entirely effaced from the remembrance of his fellows; some men have not the temerity to place themselves above the judgment of the future human species, to degrade themselves in his eyes. Where is the being who is insensible to the pleasure of exciting the tears of those who shall survive him; of again acting upon their souls; of once more occupying their thoughts; of exercising upon them his power even from the bottom of his grave? Let then eternal silence be imposed upon those superstitious beings, upon those melancholy men, upon those furious bigots, who censure a sentiment from which society derives so many real advantages; let not mankind listen to those passionless philosophers who are willing to smother this great, this noble spring of his soul; let him not be seduced by the sarcasms of those voluptuaries, who pretend to despise an immortality, towards which they lack the power to set forward; the desire of pleasing posterity, of rendering his name agreeable to generations yet to come, is a respectable, a laudable motive, when it causes him to undertake those things, of which the utility may be felt, of which the advantages may have an influence not only over his contemporaries, but also over nations who have not yet an existence. Let him not treat as irrational, the enthusiasm of those beneficent beings, of those mighty geniuses, of those stupendous talents, whose keen, whose penetrating regards, have foreseen him even in their day; who have occupied themselves for him; for his welfare; for his happiness; who have desired his suffrage; who have written for him; who have enriched him by their discoveries; who have cured him of some of his errors. Let him render them the homage which they have expected at his hands; let him, at least, reverence their memory for the benefits he has derived from them; let him treat their mouldering remains with respect, for the pleasure he receives from their labours; let him pay to their ashes a tribute of grateful recollection, for the happiness they have been sedulous to procure for him. Let him sprinkle with his tears, let him hallow with his remembrance, let him consecrate with his finest sensibilities, the urns of Socrates, of Phocion; of Archimedes; of Anaxarchus; let him wash out the stain that their punishment has made on the human species; let him expiate by his regret the Athenian ingratitude, the savage barbarity of Nicocreon; let him learn by their example to dread superstitious fanaticism; to hold political intolerance in abhorrence; let him fear to harrass merit; let him be cautious how he insults virtue, in persecuting those who may happen to differ from him in his prejudices.

Let him strew flowers over the tombs of an Homer—of a Tasso—of a Shakespeare—of a Milton—of a Goldsmith; let him revere the immortal shades of those happy geniuses, whose songs yet vibrate on his ears; whose harmonious lays excite in his soul the most tender sentiments; let him bless the memory of all those benefactors to the people, who were the delight of the human race; let him adore the virtues Of a Titus—of a Trajan—of an Antoninus—of a Julian: let him merit in his sphere, the eulogies of future ages; let him always remember, that to carry with him to the grave the regret of his fellow man, he must display talents; evince integrity; practice virtue. The funeral ceremonies of the most powerful monarchs, have rarely been wetted with the tears of the people, they have commonly drained them while living. The names of tyrants excite the horror of those who bear them pronounced. Tremble then cruel kings! ye who plunge your subjects into misery; who bathe them with bitter tears—who ravage nations—who deluge the land with the vital stream—who change the fruitful earth into a barren cemetery; tremble for the sanguinary traits under which the future historian will paint you, to generations yet unborn: neither your splendid monuments—your imposing victories—your innumerable armies, nor your sycophant courtiers, can prevent posterity from avenging their grandfathers; from insulting your odious manes; from treating your execrable memories with scorn; from showering their contempt on your transcendant crimes.

Not only man sees his dissolution with pain, but again, he wishes his death may be an interesting event for others. But, as we have already said, he must have talents—he must have beneficence—he must have virtue, in order, that those who surround him, may interest themselves in his condition; that those who survive him, may give regret to his ashes. Is it, then, surprising if the greater number of men, occupied entirely with themselves, completely absorbed by their own vanity, devoted to their own puerile objects, for ever busied with the care of gratifying their vile passions, at the expence, perhaps, of their family happiness, unheedful of the wants of a wife, unmindful of the necessity of their children, careless of the calls of friendship, regardless of their duty to society, do not by their death excite the sensibilities of their survivors; or that they should be presently forgotten? There is an infinity of monarchs of which history does not tell us any thing, save that they have lived. In despite of the inutility in which men for the most part pass their existence, maugre the little care they bestow, to render themselves dear to the beings who environ them; notwithstanding the numerous actions they commit to displease their associates; the self love of each individual, persuades him, that his death must he an interesting occurrence: few men but think themselves an Euryalus in friendship, all expect to find a Nisus, thus man's over-weening philauty shews him to say thus the order of things are overturned at his decease. O mortal! feeble and vain! Dost thou not know the Sesostris's, the Alexanders, the Caesars are dead? Yet the course of the universe is not arrested; the demise of those famous conquerors, afflicting to some few favoured slaves, was a subject of delight for the whole human race. Dost thou then foolishly believe that thy talents ought to interest thy species, that they are of sufficient extent to put it into mourning at thy decease? Alas! The Corneilles, the Lockes, the Newtons, the Boyles, the Harveys, the Montesquieus, the Sheridans are no more! Regretted by a small number of friends, who have presently consoled themselves by their necessary avocations, their death was indifferent to the greater number of their fellow citizens. Darest thou then flatter thyself, that thy reputation, thy titles, thy riches, thy sumptuous repasts, thy diversified pleasures, will make thy funeral a melancholy event! It will be spoken of by some few for two days, and do not be at all surprised: learn that there have died in former ages, in Babylon, in Sardis, in Carthage, in Athens, in Rome, millions of citizens more illustrious, more powerful, more opulent, more voluptuous, than thou art; of whom, however, no one has taken care to transmit to thee even the names. Be then virtuous, O man! in whatever station thy destiny assigns thee, and thou shalt be happy in thy life time; do thou good and thou shalt be cherished; acquire talents and thou shalt be respected; posterity shall admire thee, if those talents, by becoming beneficial to their interests, shall bring them acquainted with the name under which they formerly designated thy annihilated being. But the universe will not be disturbed by thy loss; and when thou comest to die, whilst thy wife, thy children, thy friends, fondly leaning over thy sickly couch, shall be occupied with the melancholy task of closing thine eyes, thy nearest neighbour shall perhaps be exulting with joy!

Let not then man occupy himself with his condition that may be to come, but let him sedulously endeavour to make himself useful, to those with whom he lives; let him for his own peculiar happiness render himself dutiful to his parents—faithful to his wife—attentive to his children —kind to his relations—true to his friends—lenient to his servants; let him strive to become estimable in the eyes of his fellow citizens; let him faithfully serve a country which assures to him his welfare; let the desire of pleasing posterity, of meriting its applause, excite him to those labours that shall elicit their eulogies: let a legitimate self-love, when he shall be worthy of it, make him taste in advance those commendations which he is willing to deserve; let him learn to love himself—to esteem himself; but never let him consent that concealed vices, that sacred crimes, shall degrade him in his own eyes; shall oblige him to be ashamed of his own conduct.

Thus disposed, let him contemplate his own decease with the same indifference, that it will he looked upon by the greater number of his fellows; let him expect death with constancy; wait for it with calm resignation; let him learn to shake off those vain terrors with which superstition, would overwhelm him; let him leave to the enthusiast his vague hopes; to the fanatic his mad-brained speculations; to the bigot those fears with which he ministers to his own melancholy; but let his heart, fortified by reason, corroborated by a love of virtue, no longer dread a dissolution that will destroy all feeling.

Whatever may be the attachment man has to life, whatever may be his fear of death, it is every day witnessed, that habit, that opinion, that prejudice, are motives sufficiently powerful to annihilate these passions in his breast; to make him brave danger; to cause him to hazard his existence. Ambition, pride, jealousy, love, vanity, avarice, the desire of glory, that deference of opinion which is decorated with the sounding title of *a point of honour*, have the efficacy to make him shut his eyes to danger; to laugh at peril; to push him on to death: vexation, anxiety of mind, disgrace, want of success, softens to him its hard features; makes him regard it as a door that will afford him shelter from the injustice of mankind: indigence, trouble, adversity, familiarizes him with this death, so terrible to the happy. The poor man, condemned to labour, inured to privations, deprived of the comforts of life, views its approach with indifference: the unfortunate, when he is unhappy, when he is without resource, embraces it in despair; the wretched accelerates its march as soon as he sees that happiness is no longer within his grasp.

Man in different ages, in different countries, has formed opinions extremely various upon the conduct of those, who have had the temerity to put an end to their own existence. His ideas upon this subject, as upon all others, have taken their tone from his religion, have been governed by his superstitious systems, have been modified by his political institutions. The Greeks, the Romans, and other nations, which every thing conspired to make intrepid, to render courageous, to lead to magnanimity, regarded as heroes, contemplated as Gods, those who voluntarily cut the thread of life. In Hindoostan, the Brahmin yet knows how to inspire even women with sufficient fortitude to burn themselves upon the dead bodies of their husbands. The Japanese, upon the most trifling occasion, takes no kind of difficulty in plunging a dagger into his bosom.

Among the people of our own country, religion renders man less prodigal of life; it teaches that it is offensive to the Deity that he should destroy himself.

Some moralists, abstracting the height of religious ideas, have held that it is never permitted to man to break the conditions of the covenant that he has made with society. Others have looked upon suicide as cowardice; they have thought that it was weakness, that it displayed pusillanimity, to suffer, himself to be overwhelmed with the shafts of his destiny; and have held that there would be much more courage, more elevation of soul, in supporting his afflictions, in resisting the blows of fate.

If nature be consulted upon this point, it will be found that all the actions of man, that feeble plaything in the hands of necessity, are indispensable; that they depend on causes which move him in despite of himself—that without his knowledge, make him accomplish at each moment of his existence some one of its decrees. If the same power that obliges all intelligent beings to cherish their existence, renders that of man so painful, so cruel, that he finds it insupportable he quits his species; order is destroyed for him, he accomplishes a decree of Nature, that wills he shall no longer exist. This Nature has laboured during thousands of years, to form in the bowels of the earth the iron that must number his days.

If the relation of man with Nature be examined, it will be found that his engagement was neither voluntary on his part, nor reciprocal on the part of Nature. The volition of his will had no share in his birth; it is commonly against his will that he is obliged to finish life; his actions are, as we have proved, only the necessary effects of unknown causes which determine his will. He is, in the hands of Nature, that which a sword is in his own hands; he can fall upon it without its being able to accuse him with breaking his engagements; or of stamping with ingratitude the hand that holds it: man can only love his existence on condition of being happy; as soon as the entire of nature refuses him this happiness; as soon as all that surrounds him becomes incommodious to him, as soon as his melancholy ideas offer nothing but afflicting pictures to his imagination; he already exists no longer; he is suspended in the void; he quits a rank which no longer suits him; in which he finds no one interest; which offers him no protection; which overwhelms him with calamity; in which he can no more be useful either to himself or to others.

If the covenant which unites man to society be considered, it will be obvious that every contract is conditional, must be reciprocal; that is to say, supposes mutual advantages between the contracting parties. The citizen cannot be bound to his country, to his associates, but by the bonds of happiness. Are these bonds cut asunder? He is restored to liberty. Society, or those who represent it, do they use him with harshness, do they treat him with injustice, do they render his existence painful? Does disgrace hold him out to the finger of scorn; does indigence menace him in an obdurate world? Perfidious friends, do they forsake him in adversity? An unfaithful wife, does she outrage his heart? Rebellious, ungrateful children, do they afflict his old age? Has he placed his happiness exclusively on some object which it is impossible for him to procure? Chagrin, remorse, melancholy, and despair, have they disfigured to him the spectacle of the universe? In short, for whatever cause it may be: if he is not able to support his evils, he quits a world, which from henceforth, is for him only a frightful desert he removes himself for ever from a country he thinks no longer willing to reckon him amongst the number of her children—he quits a house that to his mind is ready to bury him under its ruins—he renounces a society, to the happiness of which he can no longer contribute; which his own peculiar felicity alone can render dear to him: and could the man be blamed, who, finding himself useless; who being without resources, in the town where destiny gave him birth, should quit it in chagrin, to plunge himself in solitude? Death appears to the wretched the only remedy for despair; it is then the sword seems the only friend, the only comfort that is left to the unhappy: as long as hope remains the tenant of his bosom—as long as his evils appear to him at all supportable—as long as he flatters himself with seeing them brought to a termination—as long as he finds some comfort in existence, however slender, he will not consent to deprive himself of life: but when nothing any longer sustains in him the love of this existence, then to live, is to him the greatest of evils; to die, the only mode by which he can avoid the excess of despair. This has been the opinion of many great men: Seneca, the moralist, whom Lactantius calls the divine Pagan, who has been praised equally by St. Austin and St. Augustine, endeavours by every kind of argument to make death a matter of indifference to man. Cato has always been commended, because he would not survive the cause of liberty; for that he would not live a slave. Curtius, who rode voluntarily into the gap, to save his country, has always been held forth as a model of heroic virtue. Is it not evident, that those martyrs who have delivered themselves up to punishment, have preferred quitting the world to living in it contrary to their own ideals of happiness? When Samson wished to be revenged on the Philistines, did he not consent to die with them as the only means? If our country is attacked, do we not voluntarily sacrifice our lives in its defence?

That society who has not the ability, or who is not willing to procure man any one benefit, loses all its rights over him; Nature, when it has rendered his existence completely miserable, has in fact, ordered him to quit it: in dying he does no more than fulfil one of her decrees, as he did when he first drew his breath. To him who is fearless of death, there is no evil without a remedy; for him who refuses to die, there yet exists benefits which attach him to the world; in this case let him rally his powers—let him oppose courage to a destiny that oppresses him—let him call forth those resources with which Nature yet furnishes him; she cannot have totally abandoned him, while she yet leaves him the sensation of pleasure; the hopes of seeing a period to his pains.

Man regulates his judgment on his fellows, only by his own peculiar mode of feeling; he deems as folly, he calls delirium all those violent actions which he believes but little commensurate with their causes; or which appear to him calculated to deprive him of that happiness, towards which he supposes a being in the enjoyment of his senses, cannot cease to have a tendency: he treats his associate as a weak creature, when he sees him affected with that which touches him but lightly; or when he is incapable of supporting those evils, which his self-love flatters him, he would himself he able to endure with more fortitude. He accuses with madness whoever deprives himself of life, for objects that he thinks unworthy so dear a sacrifice; he taxes him with phrenzy, because he has himself learned to regard this life as the greatest blessing. It is thus that he always erects himself into a judge of the happiness of others— of their mode of seeing—of their manner of feeling: a miser who destroys himself after the loss of his treasure, appears a fool in the eyes of him who is less attached to riches; he does not feel, that without money, life to this miser is only a continued torture; that nothing in the world is capable of diverting him from his painful sensations: he will proudly tell you, that in his place he had not done so much; but to be exactly in the place of another man, it is needful to have his organization—his temperament—his passions—his ideas; it is in fact needful to be that other; to be placed exactly in the same circumstances; to be moved by the same causes; and in this case all men, like the miser, would sacrifice their life, after being deprived of the only source of their happiness.

He who deprives himself of his existence, does not adopt this extremity, so repugnant to his natural tendency; but when nothing in this world has the faculty of rejoicing him; when no means are left of diverting his affliction; when reason no longer acts; his misfortune whatever it may be, for him is real; his organization, be it strong, or be it weak, is his own, not that of another: a man who is sick only in imagination, really suffers considerably; even troublesome dreams place him in a very uncomfortable situation. Thus when a man kills himself, it ought to be concluded, that life, in the room of being a benefit, had become a very great evil to him; that existence had lost all its charms in his eyes; that the entire of nature was to him destitute of attraction; that it no longer contained any thing that could seduce him; that after the comparison which his disturbed imagination had made of existence with non-existence, the latter appeared to him preferable to the first.

Many will consider these maxims as dangerous; they certainly account why the unhappy cut the thread of life, in a manner not corresponding with the received prejudices; but, nevertheless, it is a temperament soured by chagrin, a bilious constitution, a melancholy habit, a defect in the organization, a derangement in the mind; it is in fact necessity and not reasonable speculations, that breed in man the design of destroying himself. Nothing invites him to this step so long as reason remains with him; or whilst he yet possesses hope, that sovereign balm for every evil: as for the unfortunate, who cannot lose sight of his sorrows—who cannot forget his pains—who has his evils always present to his mind; he is obliged to take counsel from these alone: besides, what assistance, what advantage can society promise to himself, from a miserable wretch reduced to despair; from a misanthrope overwhelmed with grief; from a wretch tormented with remorse, who has no longer any motive to render himself useful to others—who has abandoned himself— who finds no more interest in preserving his life? Frequently, those who destroy themselves are such, that had they lived, the offended laws must have ultimately been obliged to remove them from a society which they disgraced; from a country which they had injured.

As life is commonly the greatest blessing for man, it is to be presumed that he who deprives himself of it, is compelled to it by an invincible force. It is the excess of misery, the height of despair, the derangement of his brain, caused by melancholy, that urges man on to destroy himself. Agitated by contrary impulsions, he is, as we have before said, obliged to follow a middle course that conducts him to his death; if man be not a free-agent, in any one instant of his life, he is again much less so in the act by which it is terminated.

It will be seen then, that he who kills himself, does not, as it is pretended, commit an outrage on nature. He follows an impulse which has deprived him of reason; adopts the only means left him to quit his anguish; he goes out of a door which she leaves open to him; he cannot offend in accomplishing a law of necessity: the iron hand of this having broken the spring that renders life desirable to him; which urged him to self-conservation, shews him he ought to quit a rank or system where he finds himself too miserable to have the desire of remaining. His country or his family have no right to complain of a member, whom it has no means of rendering happy; from whom consequently they have nothing more to hope: to be useful to either, it is necessary he should cherish his own peculiar existence; that he should have an interest in conserving himself—that he should love the bonds by which he is united to others— that he should be capable of occupying himself with their felicity—that he should have a sound mind. That the suicide should repent of his precipitancy, he should outlive himself, he should carry with him into his future residence, his organs, his senses, his memory, his ideas, his actual mode of existing, his determinate manner of thinking.

In short, nothing is more useful for society, than to inspire man with a contempt for death; to banish from his mind the false ideas he has of its consequences. The fear of death can never do more than make cowards; the fear of its consequences will make nothing but fanatics or melancholy beings, who are useless to themselves, unprofitable to others. Death is a resource that ought not by any means to be taken away from oppressed virtue; which the injustice of man frequently reduces to despair. If man feared death less, he would neither be a slave nor superstitious; truth would find defenders more zealous; the rights of mankind would be more hardily sustained; virtue would be intrepidly upheld: error would be more powerfully opposed; tyranny would be banished from nations: cowardice nourishes it, fear perpetuates it. In fact, *man can neither be contented nor happy whilst his opinions shall oblige him to tremble.*

CHAP. XV.
Of Man's true Interest, or of the Ideas he forms to himself of Happiness.—
Man cannot be happy without Virtue.

Utility, as has been before observed, ought to be the only standard of the judgment of man. To be useful, is to contribute to the happiness of his fellow creatures; to be prejudicial, is to further their misery. This granted, let us examine if the principles we have hitherto established be prejudicial or advantageous, useful or useless, to the human race. If man unceasingly seeks after his happiness, he can only approve of that which procures for him his object, or furnishes him the means by which it is to be obtained.

What has been already said will serve in fixing our ideas upon what constitutes this happiness: it has been already shewn that it is only continued pleasure: but in order that an object may please, it is necessary that the impressions it makes, the perceptions it gives, the ideas which it leaves, in short, that the motion it excites in man should be analogous to his organization; conformable to his temperament; assimilated to his individual nature:—modified as it is by habit, determined as it is by an infinity of circumstances, it is necessary that the action of the object by which he is moved, or of which the idea remains with him, far from enfeebling him, far from annihilating his feelings, should tend to strengthen him; it is necessary, that without fatiguing his mind, exhausting his faculties, or deranging his organs, this object should impart to his machine that degree of activity for which it continually has occasion. What is the object that unites all these qualities? Where is the man whose organs are susceptible of continual agitation without being fatigued; without experiencing a painful sensation; without sinking? Man is always willing to be warned of his existence in the most lively manner, as long as he can be so without pain. What do I say? He consents frequently to suffer, rather than not feel. He accustoms himself to a thousand things which at first must have affected him in a disagreeable manner; but which frequently end either by converting themselves into wants, or by no longer affecting him any way: of this truth tobacco, coffee, and above all brandy furnish examples: this is the reason he runs to see tragedies; that he witnesses the execution of criminals. In short, the desire of feeling, of being powerfully moved, appears to be the principle of curiosity; of that avidity with which man seizes on the marvellous; of that earnestness with which he clings to the supernatural; of the disposition he evinces for the incomprehensible. Where, indeed, can he always find objects in nature capable of continually supplying the stimulus requisite to keep him in activity, that shall be ever proportioned to the state of his own organization; which his extreme mobility renders subject to perpetual variation? The most lively pleasures are always the least durable, seeing they are those which exhaust him most.

That man should be uninterruptedly happy, it would be requisite that his powers were infinite; it would require that to his mobility he joined a vigor, attached a solidity, which nothing could change; or else it is necessary that the objects from which he receives impulse, should either acquire or lose properties, according to the different states through which his machine is successively obliged to pass; it would need that the essences of beings should be changed in the same proportion as his dispositions; should be submitted to the continual influence of a thousand causes, which modify him without his knowledge, and in despite of himself. If, at each moment, his machine undergoes changes more or less marked, which are ascribable to the different degrees of elasticity, of density, of serenity of the atmosphere; to the portion of igneous fluid circulating through his blood; to the harmony of his organs; to the order that exists between the various parts of his body; if, at every period of his existence, his nerves have not the same tensions, his fibres the same elasticity, his mind the same activity, his imagination the same ardour, &c. it is evident that the same causes in preserving to him only the same qualities, cannot always affect him in the same manner. Here is the reason why those objects that please him in one season displease him in another: these objects have not themselves sensibly changed; but his organs, his dispositions, his ideas, his mode of seeing, his manner of feeling, have changed:—such is the source of man's inconstancy.

If the same objects are not constantly in that state competent to form the happiness of the same individual, it is easy to perceive that they are yet less in a capacity to please all men; or that the same happiness cannot be suitable to all. Beings already various by their temperament, unlike in their faculties, diversified in their organization, different in their imagination, dissimilar in their ideas, of distinct opinions, of contrary habits, which an infinity of circumstances, whether physical or moral, have variously modified, must necessarily form very different notions of happiness. Those of a MISER cannot be the same as those of a PRODIGAL; those of a VOLUPTUARY, the same as those of one who is PHLEGMATIC; those of an intemperate, the same as those of a rational man, who husbands his health. The happiness of each, is in consequence composed of his natural organization, and of those circumstances, of those habits, of those ideas, whether true or false, that have modified him: this organization and these circumstances, never being the same in any two men, it follows, that what is the object of one man's views, must be indifferent, or even displeasing to another; thus, as we have before said, no one can be capable of judging of that which may contribute to the felicity of his fellow man.

Interest is the object to which each individual according to his temperament and his own peculiar ideas, attaches his welfare; from which it will be perceived that this interest is never more than that which each contemplates as necessary to his happiness. It must, therefore, be concluded, that no man is totally without interest. That of the miser to amass wealth; that of the prodigal to dissipate it: the interest of the ambitious is to obtain power; that of the modest philosopher to enjoy tranquillity; the interest of the debauchee is to give himself up, without reserve, to all sorts of pleasure; that of the prudent man, to abstain from those which may injure him: the interest of the wicked is to gratify his passions at any price: that of the virtuous to merit by his conduct the love, to elicit by his actions the approbation of others; to do nothing that can degrade himself in his own eyes.

Thus, when it is said that *Interest is the only motive of human actions;* it is meant to indicate that each man labours after his own manner, to his own peculiar happiness; that he places it in some object either visible or concealed; either real or imaginary; that the whole system of his conduct is directed to its attainment. This granted, no man can be called disinterested; this appellation is only applied to those of whose motives we are ignorant; or whose interest we approve. Thus the man who finds a greater pleasure in assisting his friends in misfortune than preserving in his coffers useless treasure, is called generous, faithful, and disinterested; in like manner all men are denominated disinterested, who feel their glory far more precious than their fortune. In short, all men are designated disinterested who place their happiness in making sacrifices which man considers costly, because he does not attach the same value to the object for which the sacrifice is made.

Man frequently judges very erroneously of the interest of others, either because the motives that animate them are too complicated for him to unravel; or because to be enabled to judge of them fairly, it is needful to have the same eyes, the same organs the same passions, the same opinions: nevertheless, obliged to form his judgment of the actions of mankind, by their effect on himself, he approves the interest that actuates them whenever the result is advantageous for his species: thus, he admires valour, generosity, the love of liberty, great talents, virtue, &c. he then only approves of the objects in which the beings he applauds have placed their happiness; he approves these dispositions even when he is not in a capacity to feel their effects; but in this judgment he is not himself disinterested; experience, reflection, habit, reason, have given him a taste for morals, and he finds as much pleasure in being witness to a great and generous action, as the man of *virtu* finds in the sight of a fine picture of which he is not the proprietor. He who has formed to himself a habit of practising virtue, is a man who has unceasingly before his eyes the interest that he has in meriting the affection, in deserving the esteem, in securing the assistance of others, as well as to love and esteem himself: impressed with these ideas which have become habitual to him, he abstains even from concealed crimes, since these would degrade him in his own eyes: he resembles a man who having from his infancy contracted the habit of cleanliness, would be painfully affected at seeing himself dirty, even when no one should witness it. The honest man is he to whom truth has shewn his interest or his happiness in a mode of acting that others are obliged to love, are under the necessity to approve for their own peculiar interest.

These principles, duly developed, are the true basis of morals; nothing is more chimerical than those which are founded upon imaginary motives placed out of nature; or upon innate sentiments; which some speculators have regarded as anterior to man's experience; as wholly independant of those advantages which result to him from its use: it is the essence of man to love himself; to tend to his own conservation; to seek to render his existence happy: thus interest, or the desire of happiness, is the only real motive of all his actions; this interest depends upon his natural organization, rests itself upon his wants, is bottomed upon his acquired ideas, springs from the habits he has contracted: he is without doubt in error, when either a vitiated organization or false opinions shew him his welfare in objects either useless or injurious to himself, as well as to others; he marches steadily in the paths of virtue when true ideas have made him rest his happiness on a conduct useful to his species; in that which is approved by others; which renders him an interesting object to his associates. *Morals* would be a vain science if it did not incontestibly prove to man that *his interest consists in being virtuous*. Obligation of whatever kind, can only be founded upon the probability or the certitude of either obtaining a good or avoiding an evil.

Indeed, in no one instant of his duration, can a sensible, an intelligent being, either lose sight of his own preservation or forget his own welfare; he owes happiness to himself; but experience quickly proves to him, that bereaved of assistance, quite alone, left entirely to himself, he cannot procure all those objects which are requisite to his felicity: he lives with sensible, with intelligent beings, occupied like himself with their own peculiar happiness; but capable of assisting him, in obtaining those objects he most desires; he discovers that these beings will not be favorable to his views, but when they find their interest involved; from which he concludes, that his own happiness demands, that his own wants render it necessary he should conduct himself at all times in a manner suitable to conciliate the attachment, to obtain the approbation, to elicit the esteem, to secure the assistance of those beings who are most capacitated to further his designs. He perceives, that it is man who is most necessary to the welfare of man: that to induce him to join in his interests, he ought to make him find real advantages in recording his projects: but to procure real advantages to the beings of the human species, is to have virtue; the reasonable man, therefore, is obliged to feel that it is his interest to be virtuous. *Virtue is only the art of rendering himself happy, by the felicity of others*. The virtuous man is he who communicates happiness to those beings who are capable of rendering his own condition happy; who are necessary to his conservation; who have the ability to procure him a felicitous existence.

Such, then, is the true foundation of all morals; merit and virtue are founded upon the nature of man; have their dependance upon his wants. It is virtue alone that can render him truly happy: without virtue society can neither be useful nor indeed subsist; it can only have real utility when it assembles beings animated with the desire of pleasing each other, and disposed to labour to their reciprocal advantage: there exists no comfort in those families whose members are not in the happy disposition to lend each other mutual succours;

who have not a reciprocity of feeling that stimulates them to assist one another; that induces them to cling to each other, to support the sorrows of life; to unite their efforts, to put away those evils to which nature has subjected them; the conjugal bonds, are sweet only in proportion as they identify the interest of two beings, united by the want of legitimate pleasure; from whence results the maintenance of political society, and the means of furnishing it with citizens. Friendship has charms only when it more particularly associates two virtuous beings; that is to say, animated with the sincere desire of conspiring to their reciprocal happiness. In short, it is only by displaying virtue, that man can merit the benevolence, can win the confidence, can gain the esteem, of all those with whom he has relation; in a word, no man can be independently happy.

Indeed, the happiness of each human individual depends on those sentiments to which he gives birth, on those feelings which he nourishes in the beings amongst whom his destiny has placed him; grandeur may dazzle them; power may wrest from them an involuntary homage; force may compel an unwilling obedience; opulence may seduce mean, may attract venal souls; but it is humanity, it is benevolence, it is compassion, it is equity, that unassisted by these, can without efforts obtain for him, from those by whom he is surrounded, those delicious sentiments of attachments, those soothing feelings of tenderness, those sweet ideas of esteem, of which all reasonable men feel the necessity. To be virtuous then, is to place his interest in that which accords with the interest of others; it is to enjoy those benefits, to partake of that pleasure which he himself diffuses over his fellows. He whom, his nature, his education, his reflections, his habits, have rendered susceptible of these dispositions, and to whom his circumstances have given him the faculty of gratifying them, becomes an interesting object to all those who approach him: he enjoys every instant, he reads with satisfaction the contentment, he contemplates with pleasure the joy which he has diffused over all countenances: his wife, his children, his friends, his servants greet him with gay, serene faces, indicative of that content, harbingers of that peace, which he recognizes for his own work: every thing that environs him is ready to partake his pleasures; to share his pains; cherished, respected, looked up to by others, every thing conducts him to agreeable reflections; he knows the rights he has acquired over their hearts; he applauds himself for being the source of a felicity that captivates all the world; his own condition, his sentiments of self-love, become an hundred times more delicious when he sees them participated by all those with whom his destiny has connected him. The habit of virtue creates for him no wants but those which virtue itself suffices to satisfy; it is thus that *virtue is always its own peculiar reward*, that it remunerates itself with all the advantages which it incessantly procures for others.

It will be said, and perhaps even proved, that under the present constitution of things, virtue far from procuring the welfare of those who practice it frequently plunges man into misfortune; often places continual obstacles to his felicity; that almost every where it is without recompence.

What do I say? A thousand examples could be adduced as evidence, that in almost every country it is hated, persecuted, obliged to lament the ingratitude of human nature. I reply with avowing, that by a necessary consequence of the errors of his race, virtue rarely conducts man to those objects in which the uninformed make their happiness consist. The greater number of societies, too frequently ruled by those whose ignorance makes them abuse their power,—whose prejudices render them enemies of virtue,—who flattered by sycophants, secure in the impunity their actions enjoy, commonly lavish their esteem, bestow their kindness, on none but the most unworthy objects; reward only the most frivolous, recompence none but the most prejudicial qualities; and hardly ever accord that justice to merit which is unquestionably its due. But the truly honest man, is neither ambitious of renumeration, nor sedulous of the suffrages of a society thus badly constituted: contented with domestic happiness, he seeks not to augment relations, which would do no more than increase his danger; he knows that a vitiated community is a whirlwind, with which an honest man cannot co-order himself: he therefore steps aside; quits the beaten path, by continuing in which he would infallibly be crushed. He does all the good of which he is capable in his sphere; he leaves the road free to the wicked, who are willing to wade through its mire; he laments the heavy strokes they inflict on themselves; he applauds mediocrity that affords him security: he pities those nations made miserable by their errors,—rendered unhappy by those passions which are the fatal but necessary consequence; he sees they contain nothing but wretched citizens, who far from cultivating their true interest, far from labouring to their mutual felicity, far from feeling the real value of virtue, unconscious how dear it ought to be to them, do nothing but either openly attack, or secretly injure it; in short, who detests a quality which would restrain their disorderly propensities.

In saying that virtue is its own peculiar reward, it is simply meant to announce, that in a society whose views were guided by truth, trained by experience, conducted by reason, each individual would be acquainted with his real interests; would understand the true end of association; would have sound motives to perform his duties; find real advantages in fulfilling them; in fact, it would be convinced, that to render himself solidly happy, he should occupy his actions with the welfare of his fellows; by their utility merit their esteem, elicit their kindness, and secure their assistance. In a well-constituted society, the government, the laws, education, example, would all conspire to prove to the citizen, that the nation of which he forms a part, is a whole that cannot be happy, that cannot subsist without virtue; experience would, at each step, convince him that the welfare of its parts can only result from that of the whole body corporate; justice would make him feel, that no society, can be advantageous to its members, where the volition of wills in those who act, is not so conformable to the interests of the whole, as to produce an advantageous re-action.

But, alas! by the confusion which the errors of man have carried into his ideas: virtue disgraced, banished, and persecuted, finds not one of those advantages it has a right to expect: man is indeed shewn those rewards for it in a future life, of which he is almost always deprived in his actual existence. It is thought necessary to deceive, considered proper to seduce, right to intimidate him, in order to induce him to follow that virtue which every thing renders incommodious to him; he is fed with distant hopes, in order to solicit him to practice virtue, while contemplation of the world makes it hateful to him; he is alarmed by remote terrors, to deter him from committing evil, which his associates paint as amiable; which all conspires to render necessary. It is thus that politics, thus that superstition, by the formation of chimeras, by the creation of fictitious interests pretend to supply those true, those real motives which nature furnishes,—which experience would point out,—which an enlightened government should hold forth,— which the law ought to enforce,—which instruction should sanction,— which example should encourage,-which rational opinions would render pleasant. Man, blinded by his passions, not less dangerous than necessary, led away by precedent, authorised by custom, enslaved by habit, pays no attention to these uncertain promises, is regardless of the menaces held out; the actual interests of his immediate pleasures, the force of his passions, the inveteracy of his habits, always rise superior to the distant interests pointed out in his future welfare, or the remote evils with which he is threatened; which always appear doubtful, whenever he compares them with present advantages.

Thus *superstition, far from making man virtuous by principle, does nothing more than impose upon him a yoke as severe as it is useless*; it is borne by none but enthusiasts, or by the pusillanimous; who, without becoming better, tremblingly champ the feeble bit put into their mouth; who are either rendered unhappy by their opinions, or dangerous by their tenets; indeed, experience, that faithful monitor, incontestibly proves, that superstition is a dyke inadequate to resist the torrent of corruption, to which so many accumulated causes give an irresistible force: nay more, does not this superstition itself augment the public disorder, by the dangerous passions which it lets loose, by the conduct which it sanctions, by the actions which it consecrates? Virtue, in almost every climate, is confined to some few rational souls, who have sufficient strength of mind to resist the stream of prejudice; who are contented by remunerating themselves with the benefits they difuse over society: whose temperate dispositions are gratified with the suffrages of a small number of virtuous approvers; in short, who are detached from those frivolous advantages which the injustice of society but too commonly accords only to baseness, which it rarely bestows, except to intrigue, with which in general it rewards nothing but crime.

In despite of the injustice that reigns in the world, there are, however, some virtuous men in the bosom even of the most degenerate nations; notwithstanding the general depravity, there are some benevolent beings, still enamoured of virtue; who are fully acquainted with its true value; who are sufficiently enlightened to know that it exacts homage even from its enemies; who to use the language of ECCLESIASTES, "rejoice in their own works_;" who are, at least, happy in possessing contented minds, who are satisfied with concealed pleasures, those internal recompences of which no earthly power is competent to deprive them. The honest man acquires a right to the esteem, has a just claim to the veneration, wins the confidence, gains the love, even of those whose conduct is exposed by a contrast with his own. In short, vice is obliged to cede to virtue; of which it blushingly, though unwillingly, acknowledges the superiority. Independent of this ascendancy so gentle, of this superiority so grand, of this pre-eminence so infallible, when even the whole universe should be unjust to him, when even every tongue should cover him with venom, when even every arm should menace him with hostility, there yet remains to the honest man the sublime advantage of loving his own conduct; the ineffable pleasure of esteeming himself; the unalloyed gratification of diving with satisfaction into the recesses of his own heart; the tranquil delight of contemplating his own actions with that delicious complacency that others ought to do, if they were not hood-winked, No power is adequate to ravish from him the merited esteem of himself; no authority is sufficiently potent to give it to him when he deserves it not; the mightiest monarch cannot lend stability to this esteem, when it is not well founded; it is then a ridiculous sentiment: it ought to be considered, it really is "*vanity and vexation of spirit,*" it is not wisdom, but folly in the extreme; it ought to be censured when it displays itself in a mode that is mortifying to its neighbour, in a manner that is troublesome to others; it is then called ARROGANCE; it is called VANITY; but when it cannot be condemned, when it is known for legitimate when it is discovered to have a solid foundation, when it bottoms itself upon talents, when it rises upon great actions that are useful to the community, when it erects its edifice upon virtue; even though society should not set these merits at their just price, it is NOBLE PRIDE, ELEVATION OF MIND, and GRANDEUR OF SOUL.

Of what consequence then, is it to listen to those superstitious beings, those enemies to man's happiness, who have been desirous of destroying it, even in the inmost recesses of his heart; who have prescribed to him hatred of his follower; who have filled him with contempt for himself; who pretend to wrest from the honest man that self-respect which is frequently the only reward that remains to virtue, in a perverse world. To annihilate in him this sentiment, so full in justice, this love of himself, is to break the most powerful spring, to weaken the most efficacious stimulus, that urges him to act right; that spurs him on to do good to his fellow mortals. What motive, indeed, except it be this, remains for him in the greater part of human societies? Is not virtue discouraged? Is not honesty contemned? Is not audacious crime encouraged? Is not subtle intrigue eulogized? Is not cunning vice rewarded? Is not love of the public weal taxed as folly; exactitude in fulfilling duties looked upon as a bubble? Is not compassion laughed to scorn? ARE NOT TRAITORS DISTINGUISHED BY PUBLIC HONORS? Is not negligence of morals applauded,—sensibility derided,—tenderness scoffed,—conjugal fidelity jeered,—sincerity despised,—enviolable friendship treated with ridicule: while seduction, adultery, hard- heartedness, punic faith, avarice, and fraud, stalk forth unabashed, decked in gorgeous array, lauded by the world? Man must have motives for action: he neither acts well nor ill, but with a view to his own happiness: that which he judges will conduce to this "*consummation so devoutly to be wished,*" he thinks his interest; he does nothing gratuitously; when reward for useful actions is withheld from him, he is reduced either to become as abandoned as others, or else to remunerate himself with his own applause.

This granted; the honest man can never be completely unhappy; he can never be entirely deprived of the recompence which is his due; virtue is competent to repay him for all the benefits he may bestow on others; can amply make up to him all the happiness denied him by public opinion; *but nothing can compensate to him the want of virtue.* It does not follow that the honest man will be exempted from afflictions: like, the wicked, he is subject to physical evils; he may pine in indigence; he may be deprived of friendship; he may be worn down with disease; he may frequently be the subject of calumny; he may be the victim to injustice; he may be treated with ingratitude; he may be exposed to hatred; but in the midst of all his misfortunes, in the very bosom of his sorrows, in the extremity of his vexation, he finds support in himself; he is contented with his own conduct; he respects himself; he feels his own dignity; he knows the equity of his rights; he consoles himself with the confidence inspired by the justness of his cause; he cheers himself amidst the most sullen circumstances. These supports are not calculated for the wicked; they avail him nothing: equally liable with the honest man to infirmities, equally submitted to the caprices of his destiny, equally the sport of a fluctuating world, he finds the recesses of his own heart filled with dreadful alarms; diseased with care; cankered with solitude; corroded with regret; gnawed by remorse; he dies within himself; his conscience sustains him not but loads him with reproach; his mind, overwhelmed, sinks beneath its own turpitude; his reflection is the bitter dregs of hemlock; maddening anguish holds him to the mirror that shews him his own deformity; that recalls unhallowed deeds; gloomy thoughts rush on his too faithful memory; despondence benumbs him; his body, simultaneously assailed on all sides, bends under the storm of—his own unruly passions; at last despair grapples him to her filthy bosom, he flies from himself. The honest man is not an insensible Stoic; virtue does not procure impassibility; honesty gives no exemption from misfortune, but it enables him to bear cheerly up against it; to cast off despair, to keep his own company: if he is infirm, if he is worn with disease, he has less to complain of than the vicious being who is oppressed with sickness, who is enfeebled by years; if he is indigent, he is less unhappy in his poverty; if he is in disgrace, he can endure it with fortitude, he is not overwhelmed by its pressure, like the wretched slave to crime.

Thus the happiness of each individual depends on the cultivation of his temperament; nature makes both the happy and the unhappy; it is culture that gives value to the soil nature has formed; it is instruction that makes the fruit it produces palatable; It is reflection that makes it useful. For man to be happily born, is to have received from nature a sound body, organs that act with precision—a just mind, a heart whose passions are analogous, whose desires are conformable to the circumstances in which his destiny has placed him: nature, then, has done every thing for him, when she has joined to these faculties the quantum of vigour, the portion of energy, sufficient to enable him to obtain those Proper things, which his station, his mode of thinking, his temperament, have rendered desirable. Nature has made him a fatal present, when she has filled his sanguinary vessels with an over-heated fluid; when she has given him an imagination too active; when she has infused into him desires too impetuous; when he has a hankering after objects either impossible or improper to be obtained under his circumstances; or which at least he cannot procure without those incredible efforts, that either place his own welfare in danger or disturb the repose of society. The most happy man, is commonly he who possesses a peaceful soul; who only desires those things which he can procure by labour, suitable to maintain his activity; which he can obtain without causing those shocks, that are either too violent for society, or troublesome to his associates. A philosopher whose wants are easily satisfied, who is a stranger, to ambition, who is contented with the limited circle of a small number of friends, is, without doubt a being much more happily constituted than an ambitious conqueror, whose greedy imagination is reduced to despair by having only one world to ravage. He who is happily born, or whom nature has rendered susceptible of being conveniently modified, is not a being injurious to society: it is generally disturbed by men who are unhappily born, whose organization renders them turbulent; who are discontented with their destiny; who are inebriated with their own licentious passions; who are infatuated with their own vile schemes; who are smitten with difficult enterprises; who set the world in combustion, to gather imaginary benefits in order to attain which they must inflict he heaviest curses on mankind, but in which they make their own happiness consist. An ALEXANDER requires the destruction of empires, nations to be deluged with blood, cities to be laid in ashes, its inhabitants to be exterminated, to content that passion for glory, of which he has formed to himself a false idea; but which his too ardent imagination, his too vehement mind anxiously thirsts after: for a DIOGENES there needs only a tub with the liberty of appearing whimsical; a SOCRATES wants nothing but the pleasure of forming disciples to virtue.

Man by his organization is a being to whom motion is always necessary; he must therefore always desire it: this is the reason why too much facility In procuring the objects of his search, renders them quickly insipid. To feel happiness, it is necessary to make efforts to obtain it; to find charms in its enjoyment, it is necessary that the desire should be whetted by obstacles; he is presently disgusted with those benefits which have cost him but little pains. The expectation of happiness, the labour requisite to procure it, the varied prospects it holds forth, the multiplied pictures which his imagination forms to him, supply his brain with that motion for which it has occasion; this gives impulse to his organs, puts his whole machine into activity, exercises his faculties, sets all his springs in play, in a word, puts him into that agreeable activity, for the want of which the enjoyment of happiness itself cannot compensate him. Action is the true element of the human mind; as soon as it ceases to act, it falls into disgust, sinks into lassitude. His soul has the same occasion for ideas, his stomach has for aliment.

Thus the impulse given him by desire, is itself a great benefit; it is to the mind what exercise is to the body; without it he would not derive any pleasure in the aliments presented to him; it is thirst that renders the pleasure of drinking so agreeable; life is a perpetual circle of regenerated desires and wants satisfied: repose is only a pleasure to him who labours; it is a source of weariness, the cause of sorrow, the spring of vice to him who has nothing to do. To enjoy without interruption is not to enjoy any thing: the man who has nothing to desire is certainly more unhappy than he who suffers.

These reflections, grounded upon experience, drawn from the fountain of truth, ought to prove to man, that good as well as evil depends on the essence of things. Happiness to be felt cannot be continued. Labour is necessary, to make intervals between his pleasures; his body has occasion for exercise, to co-order him with the beings who surround him; his heart must have desires; trouble alone can give him the right relish of his welfare; it is this which puts in the shadows, this which furnishes the true perspective to the picture of human life. By an irrevocable law of his destiny, man is obliged to be discontented with his present condition; to make efforts to change it; to reciprocally envy that felicity which no individual enjoys perfectly. Thus the poor man envies the opulence of his richer neighbour, although this is frequently more unhappy than his needy maligner; thus the rich man views with pain the advantages of a poverty, which he sees active, healthy, and frequently jocund, even in the bosom of penury.

If man was perfectly contented, there would no longer be any activity in the world; it is necessary that he should desire; it is requisite that he should act; it is incumbent he should labour, in order that he may be happy: such is the course of nature of which the life consists in action. Human societies can only subsist, by the continual exchange of those things in which man places his happiness. The poor man is obliged to desire, he is necessitated to labour, that he may procure what he knows is requisite to the preservation of his existence; the primary wants given to him by nature, are to nourish himself, clothe himself, lodge himself, and propagate his species; has he satisfied these? He is quickly obliged to create others entirely new; or rather, his imagination only refines upon the first; he seeks to diversify them; he is willing to give them fresh zest; arrived at opulence, when he has run over the whole circle of wants, when he has completely exhausted their combinations, he falls into disgust. Dispensed from labour, his body amasses humours; destitute of desires, his heart feels a languor; deprived of activity, he is obliged to participate his riches, with beings more active, more laborious than himself: these, following their own peculiar interests, take upon themselves the task of labouring for his advantage; of procuring for him means to satisfy his want; of ministering to his caprices, in order to remove the languor that oppresses him. It is thus the great, the rich excite the energies, give play to the activity, rouse the faculties, spur on the industry of the indigent; these labour to their own peculiar welfare by working for others: thus the desire of ameliorating his condition, renders man necessary to his fellow man; thus wants, always regenerating, never satisfied, are the principles of life,—the soul of activity,—the source of health,—the basis of society. If each individual was competent to the supply of his own exigencies, there would be no occasion for him to congregate in society; but it is his wants, his desires, his whims, that place him in a state of dependence on others: these are the causes that each individual, in order to further his own peculiar interest, is obliged to be useful to those, who have the capability of procuring for him the objects which he himself has not. A nation is nothing more than the union of a great number of individuals, connected with each other by the reciprocity of their wants; by their mutual desire of pleasure. The most happy man is he who has the fewest wants, and who has the most numerous means of satisfying them. The man who would be truly rich, has no need to increase his fortune, it suffices he should diminish his wants.

In the individuals of the human species, as well as in political society, the progression of wants, is a thing absolutely necessary; it is founded upon the essence of man, it is requisite that the natural wants once satisfied, should be replaced by those which he calls *Imaginary, or wants of the Fancy:* these become as necessary to his happiness as the first. Custom, which permits the native American to go quite naked, obliges the more civilized inhabitant of Europe to clothe himself; the poor man contents himself with very simple attire, which equally serve him for winter and for summer, for autumn and for spring; the rich man desires to have garments suitable to each mutation of these seasons; he would experience pain if he had not the convenience of changing his raiment with every variation of his climate; he would be wretched if he was obliged to wear the same habiliments in the heat of summer, which he uses in the winter; in short, he would be unhappy if the expence and variety of his costume did not display to the surrounding multitude his opulence, mark his rank, announce his superiority. It is thus habit multiplies, the wants of the wealthy; it is thus that vanity itself becomes a want which sets a thousand hands in, motion, a thousand heads to work, who are all eager to gratify its cravings; in short, this very vanity procures for the necessitous man, the means of subsisting at the expense of his opulent neighbours He who is accustomed to pomp, who is used to ostentatious splendour, whose habits are luxurious, whenever he is deprived of these insignia of opulence, to which he has attached the idea of happiness, finds himself just as unhappy as the needy wretch who has not wherewith to cover his nakedness. The civilized nations of the present day were in their origin savages composed of erratic tribes,—mere wanderers who were occupied with war; employed in, the chace; painfully obliged to seek precarious subsistence by hunting in those woods which the industry of their successors has cleared; which their labour has covered with yellow waving ears of nutritious corn; in time they have become stationary: they first applied themselves to Agriculture, afterwards to commerce: by degrees they have refined on their primitive wants, extended their sphere of action, given birth to a thousand new wants, imagined a thousand new means to satisfy them; this is the natural course, the necessary progression, the regular march of active beings, who cannot live without feeling; who to be happy, must of necessity diversify their sensations. In proportion as man's wants multiply the means to satisfy them becomes more difficult, he is obliged to depend on a greater number of his fellow creatures; his interest obliges him to rouse their activity; to engage them to concur with his views; consequently he is obliged to procure for them those objects by which they can be excited; he is under the necessity of contenting their desires, which increase like his own, by the very food that satisfies them. The savage needs only put forth his hand to gather the fruit that offers itself spontaneously to his reach: this he finds sufficient for his nourishment. The opulent citizen of a flourishing society is obliged to set innumerable hands to work to produce the sumptuous repast; the four quarters of the globe are ransacked to procure the far-fetched viands become necessary to revive his languid appetite; the merchant, the sailor, the mechanic, leave nothing unattempted to flatter his inordinate vanity. From this it will appear, that in the same proportion the wants of man are multiplied, he is obliged to augment the means to satisfy them. Riches are nothing more than the measure of a convention, by the assistance of which man is enabled to make a great number of his fellows concur in the gratification of his desires; by which he is capacitated to invite them, for their own peculiar interests, to contribute to his pleasures. What, in fact, does the rich man do, except announce to the needy, that he can furnish him with the means of subsistence if he consents to lend himself to his will? What does the man in power, except shew to others, that he is in a state to supply the requisites to render them happy? Sovereigns, nobles, men of wealth, appear to be happy, only because they possess the ability, are masters of the motives sufficient to determine a great number of individuals to occupy themselves with their respective felicity.

The more things are considered the more man will be convinced that his false opinion are the true source of his misery; the clearer it will appear to him that happiness is so rare, only because he attaches it to objects either indifferent or useless to his welfare; which, when enjoyed, convert themselves into real evils; which afflict him; which become the cause of his misfortune.

Riches are indifferent in themselves, it is only by their application, by the purposes they compass, that they either become objects of utility to man, or are rendered prejudicial to his welfare.

Money, useless to the savage who understands not its value, is amassed by the miser, for fear it should be employed uselessly; lest it should be squandered by the prodigal; or dissipated by the voluptuary; who make no other use of it than to purchase infirmities; to buy regret.

Pleasures are nothing for the man who is incapable of feeling them; they become real evils when they are too freely indulged, when they are destructive to his health,—when they derange the economy of his machine,—when they entail diseases on himself and on his posterity,— when they make him neglect his duties,—when they render him despicable in the eyes of others.

Power is nothing in itself, it is useless to man if he does not avail himself of it to promote his own peculiar felicity, by augmenting the happiness of his species; it becomes fatal to him as soon as he abuses it; it becomes odious whenever he employs it to render others miserable; it is always the cause of his own misery whenever he stretches it beyond the due bounds prescribed by nature.

For want of being enlightened on his true interest, the man who enjoys all the means of rendering himself completely happy, scarcely ever discovers the secret of making those means truly subservient to his own peculiar felicity: the art of enjoying, is that which of all others is least understood; man should learn this art before he begins to desire; the earth is covered with individuals who only occupy themselves with the care of procuring the means without ever being acquainted with the end. All the world desire fortune, solicit power, seek after pleasure, yet very few, indeed, are those whom objects render truly happy.

It is quite natural in man, it is extremely reasonable, it is absolutely necessary, to desire those things which can contribute to augment the sum of his felicity. *Pleasure, riches, power,* are objects worthy his ambition, deserving his most strenuous efforts, when he has learned how to employ them; when he has acquired the faculty of making them render his existence really more agreeable. It is impossible to censure him who desires them, to despise him who commands them, but when to obtain them he employs odious means; or when after he has obtained them he makes a pernicious use of them, injurious to himself, prejudicial to others; let him wish for power, let him seek after grandeur, let him be ambitious of reputation, when he can shew just pretensions to them; when he can obtain them, without making the purchase at the expence of his own repose, or that of the beings with whom he lives: let him desire riches, when he knows how to make a use of them that is truly advantageous for himself, really beneficial for others; but never let him employ those means to procure them of which he may be ashamed; with which he may be obliged to reproach himself; which may draw upon him the hatred of his associates; or which may render him obnoxious to the castigation of society: let him always recollect, that his solid happiness should rest its foundations upon its own esteem,—upon the advantages he procures for others; above all, never let him for a moment forget, that of all the objects to which his ambition may point, the most impracticable for a being who lives in society, is that of *attempting to render himself exclusively happy.*

CHAP. XVI

The Errors of Man,—upon what constitutes Happiness.—the true Source of his Evil.—Remedies that may be applied.

Reason by no means forbids man from forming capacious desires; ambition is a passion useful to his species when it has for, its object the happiness of his race. Great minds, elevated souls, are desirous of acting on an extended sphere; geniuses who are powerful, beings who are enlightened, men who are beneficent, distribute very widely their benign influence; they must necessarily, in order to promote their own peculiar felicity, render great numbers happy. So many princes fail to enjoy true happiness only, because their feeble, narrow souls, are obliged to act in a sphere too extensive for their energies: it is thus that by the supineness, the indolence, the incapacity of their chiefs, nations frequently pine in misery; are often submitted to masters, whose exility of mind is as little calculated to promote their own immediate happiness, as it is to further that of their miserable subjects. On the other hand, souls too vehement, too much inflamed, too active, are themselves tormented by the narrow sphere that confines them; their ardour misplaced, becomes the scourge of the human race. Alexander was a monarch who was equally injurious to the earth, equally discontented with his condition, as the indolent despot whom he dethroned. The souls of neither were by any means commensurate with their sphere of action.

The happiness of man will never be more than the result of the harmony that subsists between his desires and his circumstances. The sovereign power to him who knows not how to apply it to the advantage of his citizens, is as nothing; it cannot even conduce to his own peculiar happiness. If it renders him miserable, it is a real evil; if it produces the misfortune of a portion of the human race, it is a detestable abuse. The most powerful princes are ordinarily such strangers to happiness, their subjects are commonly so unfortunate, only because the first possess all the means of rendering themselves happy without ever giving them activity; or because the only knowledge they have of them, is their abuse. A wise man seated on a throne, would be the most happy of mortals. A monarch is a man for whom his power, let it be of whatever extent, cannot procure other organs, other modes of feeling, than the meanest of his subjects; if he has an advantage over them, it is by the grandeur, the variety, the multiplicity of the objects with which he can occupy himself; which by giving perpetual activity to his mind, can prevent it from decay; from falling into sloth. If his soul is virtuous, if his mind is expansive, his ambition finds continual food in the contemplation of the power he possesses, to unite by gentleness, to consolidate by kindness, the will of his subjects with his own; to interest them in his own conservation, to merit their affections,—to draw forth the respect of strangers,—to render luminous the page of history—to elicit the eulogies of all nations—to clothe the orphan,—to dry the widow's tears. Such are the conquests that reason proposes to all those whose destiny it is to govern the fate of empires; they are sufficiently grand to satisfy the most ardent imagination, of a sublimity to gratify the most capacious ambition: for a monarch they are paramount duties.—KINGS are the most happy of men, only because they have the power of making others happy; because they possess the means of multiplying the causes of legitimate content with themselves.

The advantages of the sovereign power are participated by all those who contribute to the government of states. Thus grandeur, rank, reputation, are desirable, are legitimate objects for all who are acquainted with the means of rendering them subservient to their own peculiar felicity; they are useless, they are illegitimate to those ordinary men who have neither the energy nor the capacity to employ them in a mode advantageous to themselves; they are detestable whenever to obtain them man compromises his own happiness, when he implicates the welfare of society: this society itself is in an error every time it respects men who only employ to its destruction, a power, the exercise of which it ought never to approve but when it reaps from it substantial benefits.

Riches, useless to the miser, who is no more than their miserable gaoler; prejudicial to the debauchee, for whom they only procure infirmities; injurious to the voluptuary, to whom they only bring disgust—whom they oppress with satiety; can in the hands of the honest man produce unnumbered means of augmenting the sum of his happiness; but before man covets wealth it is proper he should know how to employ it; money is only a token, a representative of happiness; to enjoy it is so to use it as to make others happy: this is the great secret, this is the talisman, this is the reality. Money, according to the compact of man, procures for him all those benefits he can desire; there is only one, which it will not procure, that is, *the knowledge how to apply it properly.* For man to have money, without the true secret how to enjoy it, is to possess the key of a commodious palace to which he is interdicted entrance; to lavish it, prodigally, is to throw the key into the river; to make a bad use of it, is only to make it the means of wounding himself. Give the most ample treasures to the enlightened man, he will not be overwhelmed with them; if he has a capacious mind, if he has a noble soul, he will only extend more widely his benevolence; he will deserve the affection of a greater number of his fellow men; he will attract the love, he will secure the homage, of all those who surround him; he will restrain himself in his pleasures, in order that he may be enabled truly to enjoy them; he will know that money cannot re-establish a soul worn out with enjoyment; cannot give fresh elasticity to organs enfeebled by excess; cannot give fresh tension to nerves grown flaccid by abuse; cannot invigorate a body enervated by debauchery; cannot corroborate a machine, from thenceforth become incapable of sustaining him, except by the necessity of privations; he will know that the licentiousness of the voluptuary stifles pleasure in its source; that all the treasure in the world cannot renew his senses.

From this, it will be obvious, that nothing is more frivolous than the declamations of a gloomy philosophy against the desire of power; nothing more absurd than the rant of superstition against the pursuit of grandeur; nothing more inconsistent than homilies against the acquisition of riches; nothing more unreasonable than dogmas that forbid the enjoyment of pleasure. These objects are desirable for man, whenever his situation allows him to make pretensions to them; they are useful to society, conducive to public happiness, whenever he has acquired the knowledge of making them turn to his own real advantage; reason cannot censure him, virtue cannot despise him, when in order to obtain them, he never travels out of the road of truth; when in their acquisition, he wounds no one's interest; when he pursues only legitimate means: his associates will applaud him; his contemporaries will esteem him: he will respect himself, when he only employs their agency to secure his own happiness, and that of his fellows. Pleasure is a benefit, it is of the essence of man to love, it is even rational when it renders his existence really valuable to himself—when it does not injure him in his own esteem; when its consequences are not grievous to others. *Riches* are the symbols of the great majority of the benefits of this life; they become a reality in the hands of the man who has the clew to their just application. *Power* is the most sterling of all benefits, when he who is its depositary has received from nature a soul sufficiently noble, a mind sufficiently elevated, a heart sufficiently benevolent, faculties sufficiently energetic, above all, when he has derived from education a true regard for virtue, that sacred love for truth which enables him to extend his happy influence over whole nations; which by this means he places in, a state of legitimate dependence on his will; *man only acquires the right of commanding men, when he renders them happy.*

The right of man over his fellow man can only be founded either upon the actual happiness he secures to him, or that which he gives him reason to hope he will procure for him; without this, the power he exercises would be violence, usurpation, manifest tyranny; it is only upon the faculty of rendering him happy, that legitimate authority builds its structure; without this it is the *"baseless fabric of a vision." No man derives from nature the right of commanding another*; but it is voluntarily accorded to those, from whom he expects his welfare. *Government* is the right of commanding, conferred on the sovereign only for the advantage of those who are governed. Sovereigns are the defenders of the persons, the guardians of the property, the protectors of the liberty of their subjects: this is the price of their obedience; it is only on this condition these consent to obey; government would not be better than a robbery whenever it availed itself of the powers confided to it, to render society unhappy. *The empire of religion* is founded on the opinion man entertains of its having power to render nations happy; government and religion are reasonable institutions; but only so, inasmuch as they equally contribute to the felicity of man: it would be folly in him to submit himself to a yoke from which there resulted nothing but evil. It would be folly to expect that man should bind himself to misery; it would be rank injustice to oblige him to renounce his rights without some corresponding advantage!

The authority which a father exercises over his family is only founded on the advantages which he is supposed to procure for it. Rank, in political society, has only for its basis the real or imaginary utility of some citizens for which the others are willing to distinguish them— agree to respect them— consent to obey them. The rich acquire rights over the indigent, the wealthy claim the homage of the needy, only by virtue of the welfare they are conditioned to procure them. Genius, talents, science, arts, have rights over man, only in consequence of their utility; of the delight they confer; of the advantages they procure for society. In a word, it is happiness, it is the expectation of happiness, it is its image that man cherishes—that he esteems—that he unceasingly adores. Monarchs, the rich, the great, may easily impose on him, may dazzle him, may intimidate him, but they will never be able to obtain the voluntary submission of his heart, which alone can confer upon them legitimate rights, without they make him experience real benefits—without they display virtue. Utility is nothing more than true happiness; to be useful is to be virtuous; to be virtuous is to make others happy.

The happiness which man derives from them is the invariable, the necessary standard of his sentiments, for the beings of his species; for the objects he desires; for the opinions he embraces; for those actions on which he decides. He is the dupe of his prejudices every time he ceases to avail himself of this standard to regulate his judgment. He will never run the risk of deceiving himself, when he shall examine strictly what is the real utility resulting to his species from the religion, from the superstition, from the laws, from the institutions, from the inventions, from the various actions of all mankind.

A superficial view may sometimes seduce him; but experience, aided by reflection, will reconduct him to reason, which is incapable of deceiving him. This teaches him that pleasure is a momentary happiness, which frequently becomes an evil; that evil is a fleeting trouble that frequently becomes a good: it makes him understand the true nature of objects, enables him to foresee the effects he may expect; it makes him distinguish those desires to which his welfare permits him to lend himself, from those to whose seduction he ought to make resistance. In short, it will always convince him that the true interest of intelligent beings, who love happiness, who desire to render their own existence felicitous, demands that they should root out all those phantoms, abolish all those chimerical ideas, destroy all those prejudices, which by traducing virtue, obstruct their felicity in this world.

If he consults experience, he will perceive that it is in illusions, in false opinions, rendered sacred by time, that he ought to search out the source of that multitude of evils which almost every where overwhelms mankind. From ignorance of natural causes, man has created imaginary causes; not knowing to what cause to attribute thunder, he ascribed it to an imaginary being whom he called JUPITER; imposture availing itself of this disposition, rendered these causes terrible to him; these fatal ideas haunted him without rendering him better; made him tremble without either benefit to himself or to others; filled his mind with chimeras that opposed themselves to the progress of his reason; that prevented him from really seeking after his happiness. His vain fears rendered him the slave of those who deceived him, under pretence of consulting his welfare; he committed evil, because they persuaded him his gods demanded sacrifices; he lived in misfortune, because they made him believe these gods condemned him to be miserable; the slave of beings, to which his own imagination had given birth, he never dared to disentangle himself from his chains; the artful ministers of these divinities gave him to understand that stupidity, the renunciation of reason, sloth of mind, abjection of soul, were the sure means of obtaining eternal felicity.

Prejudices, not less dangerous, have blinded man upon the true nature of government. Nations in general are ignorant of the true foundations of authority; they dare not demand happiness from those kings who are charged with the care of procuring it for them: some have believed their sovereigns were gods disguised, who received with their birth the right of commanding the rest of mankind; that they could at their pleasure dispose of the felicity of the people; that they were not accountable for the misery they engendered. By a necessary consequence of these erroneous opinions, politics have almost every where degenerated into the fatal art of sacrificing the interests of the many, either to the caprice of an individual, or to some few privileged irrational beings. In despite of the evils which assailed them, nations fell down in adoration before the idols they themselves had made: foolishly respected the instruments of their misery; had a stupid veneration for those who possessed the sovereign power of injuring them; obeyed their unjust will; lavished their blood; exhausted their treasure; sacrificed their lives, to glut the ambition, to feed the cupidity to minister to the regenerated phantasms, to gratify the never-ending caprices of these men; they bend the knee to established opinion, bowed to rank, yielded to title, to opulence, to pageantry, to ostentation: at length victims to their prejudices, they in vain expected their welfare at the hands of men who were themselves unhappy from their own vices; whose neglect of virtue, had rendered them incapable of enjoying true felicity; who are but little disposed to occupy themselves with their prosperity: under such chiefs their physical and moral happiness were equally neglected or even annihilated.

The same blindness may be perceived in the science of morals. Superstition, which never had any thing but ignorance for its basis, which never had more than a disordered imagination for its guide, did not found ethics upon man's nature; upon his relations with his fellows; upon those duties which necessarily flow from these relations; it preferred, as more in unison with itself, founding them upon imaginary relations which it pretended subsisted between him and those invisible powers it had so gratuitously imagined; that were delivered by oracles which their priests had the address to make him believe spoke the will of the Divinity: thus, TROPHONIUS, from his cave made affrighted mortals tremble; shook the stoutest nerves; made them turn pale with fear; his miserable, deluded supplicants, who were obliged to sacrifice to him, anointed their bodies with oil, bathed in certain rivers, and after they had offered their cake of honey and received their destiny, became so dejected, so wretchedly forlorn, that to this day their descendants, when they behold a malencholy man, exclaim, "*He has consulted the oracle of Trophonius.*" It was these invisible gods, which superstition always paints as furious tyrants, who were declared the arbiters of man's destiny; the models of his conduct: when he was willing to imitate them, when he was willing to conform himself to the lessons of their interpreters, he became wicked, was an unsociable creature, an useless being or else a turbulent maniac—a zealous fanatic. It was these alone who profited by superstition, who advantaged themselves by the darkness in which they contrived to involve the human mind; nations were ignorant of nature; they knew nothing of reason; they understood not truth; they had only a gloomy superstition, without one certain idea of either morals or virtue. When man committed evil against his fellow creature, he believed he had offended these gods; but he also believed himself forgiven, as soon as he had prostrated himself before them; as soon as he had by costly presents gained over the priest to his interest. Thus superstition, far from giving a sure, far from affording a natural, far from introducing a known basis to morals, only rested it on an unsteady foundation; made it consist in ideal duties impossible to be accurately understood. What did I say? It first corrupted him, and his expiations finished by ruining him. Thus when superstition was desirous to combat the unruly passions of man it attempted it in vain; always enthusiastic, ever deprived of experience, it knew nothing of the true remedies: those which it applied were disgusting, only suitable to make the sick revolt against them; it made them pass for divine, because they were not made of man; they were inefficacious, because chimeras could effectuate nothing against those substantive passions to which motives more real, impulsions more powerful, concurred to give birth, which every thing conspired, to flourish in his heart. The voice of superstition or of the gods, could not make itself heard amidst the tumult of society—where all was in confusion—where the priest cried out to man, that he could not render himself happy without injuring his fellow creatures, who happened to differ from him in opinion: these vain clamours only made virtue hateful to him, because they always represented it as the enemy to his happiness; as the bane of human pleasures: he consequently failed in the observation of his duties, because real motives were never held forth to induce him to make the requisite sacrifice; the present prevailed over the future; the visible over the invisible; the known over the unknown: man became wicked because every thing informed him he must be so, in order to obtain the happiness after which he sighed.

Thus the sum of human misery was never diminished; on the contrary, it was accumulating either by his superstition, by his government, by his education, by his opinions or by the institutions he adopted under the idea of rendering his condition more pleasant: it not unfrequently happened that the whole of these acted upon him simultaneously; he was then completely wretched. It cannot be too often repeated, *it is in error that man will find the true spring of those evils with which the human race is afflicted;* it is not nature that renders him miserable; it is not nature that makes him unhappy; it is not an irritated Divinity who is desirous he should live in tears; it is not hereditary depravation that has caused him to be wicked; it is to error, to long cherished, consecrated error, to error identified with his very existence, that these deplorable effects are to be ascribed.

The sovereign good, so much sought after by some philosophers, announced with so much emphasis by others, may be considered as a chimera, like unto that marvellous panacea which some adepts have been willing to pass upon mankind for an universal remedy. All men are diseased; the moment of their birth delivers them over to the contagion of error; but individuals are variously affected by it by a consequence of their natural organization; of their peculiar circumstances. If there is a sovereign remedy, which can be indiscriminately applied to the diseases of man, there is without doubt only ONE, this catholic balsam is TRUTH, Which he must draw from nature.

At the afflicting sight of those errors which blind the greater number of mortals—of those delusions which man is doomed to suck in with his mother's milk; viewing with painful sensations those irregular desires, those disgusting propensities, by which he is perpetually agitated; seeing the terrible effect of those licentious passions which torment him; of those lasting inquietudes which gnaw his repose; of those stupendous evils, as well physical as moral, which assail him on every side: the contemplator of humanity would be tempted to believe that happiness was not made for this world; that any effort to cure those minds which every thing unites to poison, would be a vain enterprize; that it was an Augean stable, requiring the strength of another Hercules. When he considers those numerous superstitions by which man is kept in a continual state of alarm—that divide him from his fellow— that render him vindictive, persecuting, and irrational; when he beholds the many despotic governments that oppress him; when he examines those multitudinous, unintelligible, contradictory laws that torture him; the manifold injustice under which he groans; when he turns his mind to the barbarous ignorance in which he is steeped, almost over the whole surface of the earth; when he witnesses those enormous crimes that debase society; when he unmasks those rooted vices that render it so hateful to almost every individual; he has great difficulty to prevent his mind from embracing the idea that misfortune is the only appendage of the human species; that this world is made solely to assemble the unhappy; that human felicity is a chimera, or at least a point so fugitive, that it is impossible it can be fixed.

Thus superstitious mortals, atrabilious men, beings nourished in melancholy, unceasingly see either nature or its author exasperated against the human race; they suppose that man is the constant object of heaven's wrath; that he irritates it even by his desires: that he renders himself criminal by seeking a felicity which is not made for him: struck with beholding that those objects which he covets in the most lively manner, are never competent to content his heart, they have decried them as abominations, as things prejudicial to his interest, as odious to his gods; they prescribe him abstinence from all search after them; that he should entirely shun them; they have endeavoured to put to the rout all his passions, without any distinction even of those which are the most useful to himself, the most beneficial to those beings with whom he lives: they have been willing that man should render himself insensible; should become his own enemy; that he should separate himself from his fellow creatures; that he should renounce all pleasure; that he should refuse happiness; in short, *that he should cease to be a man, that he should become unnatural.* "Mortals!" have they said, "ye were born to be unhappy; the author of your existence has destined ye for misfortune; enter then into his views, and render yourselves miserable. Combat those rebellious desires which have felicity for their object; renounce those pleasures which it is your essence to love; attach yourselves to nothing in this world; by a society that only serves to inflame your imagination, to make you sigh after benefits you ought not to enjoy; break up the spring of your souls; repress that activity that seeks to put a period to your sufferings; suffer, afflict yourselves, groan, be wretched; such is for you the true road to happiness."

Blind physicians! who have mistaken for a disease the natural state of man! they have not seen that his desires were necessary; that his passions were essential to him; that to defend him from loving legitimate pleasures; to interdict him from desiring them, is to deprive him of that activity which is the vital principle of society; that to tell him to hate, to desire him to despise himself, is to take from him the most substantive motive, that can conduct him to virtue. It is thus, by its supernatural remedies, by its wretched panacea, superstition, far from curing those evils which render man decrepid, which bend him almost to the earth, has only increased them; made them more desperate; in the room of calming his passions, it gives them inveteracy; makes them more dangerous; renders them more venomous; turns that into a curse which nature has given him for his preservation; to be the means of his own happiness. It is not by extinguishing the passions of man that he is to be rendered happier; it is by turning them into proper channels, by directing them towards useful objects, which by being truly advantageous to himself, must of necessity be beneficial to others.

In despite of the errors which blind the human race, in despite of the extravagance of man's superstition, maugre the imbecility of his political institutions, notwithstanding the complaints, in defiance of the murmurs he is continually breathing forth against his destiny, there are yet happy individuals on the earth. Man has sometimes the felicity to behold sovereigns animated by the noble passion to render nations flourishing; full of the laudable ambition to make their people happy; now and then he encounters an ANTONINUS, a TRAJAN, a JULIAN, an ALFRED, a WASHINGTON; he meets with elevated minds who place their glory in encouraging merit—who rest their happiness in succouring indigence—who think it honourable to lend a helping hand to oppressed virtue: he sees genius occupied with the desire of meriting the eulogies of posterity; of eliciting the admiration of his fellow-citizens by serving them usefully, satisfied with enjoying that happiness he procures for others.

Let it not be believed that the man of poverty himself is excluded from happiness: mediocrity and indigence frequently procure for him advantages that opulence and grandeur are obliged to acknowledge; which title and wealth are constrained to envy: the soul of the needy man, always in action, never ceases to form desires which his activity places within his reach; whilst the rich, the powerful, are frequently in the afflicting embarrassment, of either not knowing what to wish for, or else of desiring those objects which their listlessness renders it impossible for them to obtain. The poor man's body, habituated to labour, knows the sweets of repose; this repose of the body, is the most troublesome fatigue to him who is wearied with his idleness; exercise, and frugality, procure for the one vigour, health, and contentment; the intemperance and sloth of the other, furnish him only with disgust—load him with infirmities. Indigence sets all the springs of the soul to work; it is the mother of industry; from its bosom arises genius; it is the parent of talents, the hot-bed of that merit to which opulence is obliged to pay tribute; to which grandeur bows its homage. In short the blows of fate find in the poor man a flexible reed, who bends without breaking, whilst the storms of adversity tear the rich man like the sturdy oak in the forest, up by the very roots.

Thus Nature is not a step-mother to the greater number of her children. He whom fortune has placed in an obscure station is ignorant of that ambition which devours the courtier; knows nothing of the inquietude which deprives the intriguer of his rest; is a stranger to the remorse, an alien to the disgust, is unconscious of the weariness of the man, who, enriched with the spoils of a nation, does not know how to turn them to his profit. The more the body labours, the more the imagination reposes itself; it is the diversity of the objects man runs over that kindles it; it is the satiety of those objects that causes him disgust; the imagination of the indigent is circumscribed by necessity: he receives but few ideas: he is acquainted with but few objects: in consequence, he has but little to desire; he contents himself with that little: whilst the entire of nature with difficulty suffices to satisfy the insatiable desires, to gratify the imaginary wants of the man, plunged in luxury, who has run over and exhausted all common objects. Those, whom prejudice contemplates; as the most unhappy of men, frequently enjoy advantages more real, happiness much greater, than those who oppress them—who despise them—but who are nevertheless often reduced to the misery of envying them. Limited desires are a real benefit: the man of meaner condition, in his humble fortune, desires only bread: he obtains it by the sweat of his brow; he would eat it with pleasure if injustice did not sometimes render it bitter to him. By the delirium of some governments, those who roll in abundance, without for that reason being more happy, dispute with the cultivator even the fruits which the earth yields to the labour of his hands. *Princes* sometimes sacrifice their true happiness, as well as that of their states, to these passions—to those caprices which discourage the people; which plunge their provinces in misery: which make millions unhappy, without any advantage to themselves. *Tyrants* oblige the subjects to curse their existence; to abandon labour; take from them the courage of propagating a progeny who would be as unhappy as their fathers: the excess of oppression sometimes obliges them to revolt; makes them avenge themselves by wicked outrages of the injustice it has heaped on their devoted heads: injustice, by reducing indigence to despair, obliges it to seek in crime, resources, against its misery. An unjust government, produces discouragement in the soul: its vexations depopulate a country; under its influence, the earth remains without culture; from thence is bred frightful famine, which gives birth to contagion and plague. The misery of a people produce revolutions; soured by misfortunes, their minds get into a state of fermentation; the overthrow of an empire, is the necessary effect. It is thus that *physics* and *morals* are always connected, or rather are the *same thing*.

If the bad morals of chiefs do not always produce such marked effects, at least they generate slothfulness, of which their effect is to fill society with mendicants; to crowd it with malefactors; whose vicious course neither superstition nor the terror of the laws can arrest; which nothing can induce to remain the unhappy spectators of a welfare they are not permitted to participate. They seek a fleeting happiness at the expence even of their lives, when injustice has shut up to them the road of labour, those paths of industry which would have rendered them both useful and honest.

Let it not then be said that no government can render all its subjects happy; without doubt it cannot flatter itself with contenting the capricious humours of some idle citizens who are obliged to rack their imagination, to appease the disgust arising from lassitude: but it can, and it ought to occupy itself with ministering to the real wants of the multitude, with giving a useful activity to the whole body politic. A society enjoys all the happiness of which it is susceptible whenever the greater number of its members are wholesomely fed, decently cloathed, comfortably lodged—in short when they can without an excess of toil beyond their strength, procure wherewith to satisfy those wants which nature has made necessary to their existence. Their mind rests contented as soon as they are convinced no power can ravish from them the fruits of their industry; that they labour for themselves; that the sweat of their brow is for the immediate comfort of their own families. By a consequence of human folly in some regions, whole nations are obliged to toil incessantly, to waste their strength, to sweat under their burdens to undulate the air with their sighs, to drench the earth with their tears, in order to maintain the luxury, to gratify the whims, to support the corruption of a small number of irrational beings; of some few useless men to whom happiness has become impossible, because their bewildered imaginations no longer know any bounds. It is thus that superstitious, thus that political errors have changed the fair face of nature into a valley of tears.

For want of consulting reason, for want of knowing the value of virtue, for want of being instructed in their true interest, for want of being acquainted with what constitutes solid happiness, in what consists real felicity, the prince and the, people, the rich and the poor, the great and the little, are unquestionably, frequently very far removed from content; nevertheless if an impartial eye be glanced over the human race, it will be found to comprise a greater number of benefits than of evils. No man is entirely happy, but he is so in detail; those who make the most bitter complaints of the rigour of their fate, are however, held in existence by threads frequently imperceptible; are prevented from the desire of quitting it by circumstances of which they are not aware. In short, habit lightens to man the burden of his troubles; grief suspended becomes true enjoyment; every want is a pleasure in the moment when it is satisfied; freedom from chagrin, the absence of disease, is a happy state which he enjoys secretly, without even perceiving it; hope, which rarely abandons him entirely, helps him to support the most cruel disasters. The PRISONER laughs in his irons. The wearied VILLAGER returns singing to his cottage. In short, the man who calls himself the most unfortunate, never sees death approach without dismay, at least, if despair has not totally disfigured nature in his eyes.

As long as man desires the continuation of his being, he has no right to call himself completely unhappy; whilst hope sustains him, he still enjoys a great benefit. If man was more just, in rendering to himself an account of his pleasures, in estimating his pains, he would acknowledge that the sum of the first exceeds by much the amount of the last; he would perceive that he keeps a very exact ledger of the evil, but a very unfaithful journal of the good: indeed he would avow, that there are but few days entirely unhappy during the whole course of his existence. His periodical wants procure for him the pleasure of satisfying them; his soul is perpetually moved by a thousand objects, of which, the variety, the multiplicity, the novelty, rejoices him, suspends his sorrows, diverts his chagrin. His physical evils, are they violent? They are not of long duration; they conduct him quickly to his end: the sorrows of his mind, when too powerful, conduct him to it equally. At the same time nature refuses him every happiness, she opens to him a door by which he quits life; does he refuse to enter it? It is that he yet finds pleasure in existence. Are nations reduced to despair? Are they completely miserable? They have recourse to arms; at the risque of perishing, they make the most violent efforts to terminate there sufferings.

Thus because he sees so many of his fellows cling to life, man ought to conclude they are not so unhappy as he thinks. Then let him not exaggerate the evils of the human race, but let him impose silence on that gloomy humour that persuades him these evils are without remedy; let him only diminish by degrees the number of his errors, his calamities will vanish in the same proportion; he is not to conclude himself infelicitous because his heart never ceases to form new desires, which he finds it difficult, sometimes impossible to gratify. Since his body daily requires nourishment, let him infer that it is sound, that it fulfils its functions. As long as he has desires, the proper deduction ought to be, that his mind is kept in the necessary activity; he should gather from all this that passions are essential to him, that they constitute the happiness of a being who feels; are indispensable to a man who thinks; are requisite to furnish him with ideas; that they are a vital principle with a creature who must necessarily love that which procures him comfort, who must equally desire that which promises him a mode of existence analogous to his natural energies. As long as he exists, as long as the spring of his soul maintains its elasticity, this soul desires; as long as it desires, he experiences the activity which is necessary to him; as long as he acts, so long he lives. Human life may be compared to a river, of which the waters succeed each other, drive each other forward, and flow on without interruption; these waters, obliged to roll over an unequal bed, encounter at intervals those obstacles which prevent their stagnation; they never cease to undulate; sometimes they recoil, then again rush forward, thus continuing to run with more or less velocity, until they are restored to *the ocean of nature*.

CHAP. XVII.

Those Ideas which are true, or founded upon Nature, are the only Remedies for the Evils of Man.—Recapitulation.—Conclusion of the first Part.

Whenever man ceases to take experience for his guide, he falls into error. His errors become yet more dangerous, assume a more determined inveteracy, when they are clothed with the sanction of superstition; it is then that he hardly ever consents to return into the paths of truth; he believes himself deeply interested in no longer seeing clearly that which lies before him; he fancies he has an essential advantage in no longer understanding himself; he supposes his happiness exacts that he should shut his eyes to truth. If the majority of moral philosophers have mistaken the human heart—if they have deceived themselves upon its diseases—if they have miscalculated the remedies that are suitable—if the remedies they have administered have been inefficacious or even dangerous—it is because they have abandoned nature—because they have resisted experience—because they have not had sufficient steadiness to consult their reason—because they have renounced the evidence of their senses—because they have only followed the caprices of an imagination either dazzled by enthusiasm or disturbed by fear; because they have preferred the illusions it has held forth to the realities of nature, *who never deceives.*

It is for want of having felt that an intelligent being cannot for an instant lose sight of his own peculiar conservation—of his particular interests, either real or fictitious—of his own welfare, whether permanent or transitory; in short, of his happiness, either true or false. It is for want of having considered that desires are natural, that passions are essential, that both the one and the other are motions necessary to the soul of man,—that the physicians of the, human mind have supposed supernatural causes for his wanderings; have only applied to his evils topical remedies, either useless or dangerous. Indeed, in desiring him to stifle his desires, to combat his propensities, to annihilate his passions, they have done no more than give him sterile precepts, at once vague and impracticable; these vain lessons have influenced no one; they have at most restrained some few mortals whom a quiet imagination but feebly solicited to evil; the terrors with which they have accompanied them have disturbed the tranquillity of those persons who were moderate by their nature, without ever arresting the ungovernable temperament of those who were inebriated by their passions, or hurried along; by the torrent of habit. In short, the promises of superstition, as well as the menaces it holds forth, have only formed fanatics, given birth to enthusiasts, who are either dangerous or useless to society, without ever making man truly virtuous; that is to say, useful to his fellow creatures.

These, empirics guided by a blind routine have, not seen that man as long as he exists, is obliged to feel, to desire, to have passions, to satisfy them in proportion to the energy which his organization has given him; they have not perceived that education planted these desires in his heart—that habit rooted them—that his government, frequently vicious, corroborated their growth—that public opinion stamped them with its approbation—that—experience render them necessary—that to tell men thus constituted to destroy their passions, was either to plunge them into despair or else to order them remedies too revolting for their temperament. In the actual state of opulent societies, to say to a man who knows by experience that riches procure every pleasure, that he must not desire them; that he must not make any efforts to obtain them; that he ought to detach himself from them: is to persuade him to render himself miserable. To tell an ambitious man not to desire grandeur, not to covet power, which every thing conspires to point out to him as the height of felicity, is to order him to overturn at one blow the habitual system of his ideas; it is to speak, to a deaf man. To tell a lover of an impetuous temperament to stifle his passions for the object that enchants him, is to make him understand, that he ought to renounce his happiness. To oppose superstition to such substantive, such puissant interests is to combat realities by chimerical speculations.

Indeed, if things were examined without prepossession, it would be found that the greater part of the precepts inculcated by superstition, which fanatical dogmas hold forth, which, supernatural mortals give to man, are as ridiculous as they are impossible to be put into practice. To interdict passion to man, is to desire of him not to be a human creature; to counsel an individual of a violent imagination to moderate his desires, is to advise him to change his temperament—is to request his blood to flow more sluggishly. To tell a man to renounce his habits, is to be willing that a citizen, accustomed to clothe himself, should consent to walk quite naked; it would avail as much, to desire him to change the lineament of his face, to destroy his configuration, to extinguish his imagination, to alter the course of his fluids, as to command him not to have passions which excite an activity analogous with his natural energy; or to lay aside those which confirmed habit has made him contract; which his circumstances, by a long succession of causes and effects, have converted into wants. Such are, however, the so much boasted remedies which the greater number of moral philosophers apply to human depravity. Is it, then surprising they do not produce the desired effect, or that they only reduce man to a state of despair by the effervescence that results from the continual conflict which they excite between the passions of his heart and these fanciful doctrines; between his vices and his virtues; between his habits and those chimerical fears with which superstition is at all times ready to overwhelm him? The vices of society, aided by the objects of which it avails itself to what the desires of man, the pleasures, the riches, the grandeur which his government holds forth to him as so many seductive magnets, the advantage which education, the benefits which example, the interests which public opinion render dear to him, attract him on one side; whilst a gloomy morality, founded upon superstitious illusions, vainly solicit him on the other; thus, superstition plunges him into misery; holds a violent struggle with his heart, without scarcely ever gaining the victory; when by accident it does prevail against so many united forces, it renders him unhappy; it completely destroys the spring of his soul.

Passions are the true counterpoise to passions; then let him not seek to destroy them; but let him endeavour to direct them; let him balance those which are prejudicial, by those which are useful to society. *Reason*, the fruit of experience, is only the art of choosing those passions to which for his own peculiar happiness he ought to listen. *Education* is the true art of disseminating the proper method of cultivating advantageous passions in the heart of man. *Legislation* is the art of restraining dangerous passions; of exciting those which may be conducive to the public welfare. *Superstition* is only the miserable art of planting the unproductive labour—of nourishing in the soul of man those chimeras, those illusions, those impostures, those incertitudes from whence spring passions fatal to himself as well as to others: it is only by bearing up with fortitude against these that he can securely place himself on the road to happiness. *True religion* is the art of advocating truth—of renouncing error—of contemplating reality—of drawing wisdom from experience—of cultivating man's nature to his own felicity, by teaching him to contribute to that of his associates; in short it is *reason, education*, and *legislation*, united to further the great end of human existence, by causing the passions of man to flow in a current genial to his own happiness.

Reason and *morals* cannot effect any thing on mankind if they do not point out to each individual that his true interest is attached to a conduct that is either useful to others or beneficial to himself; this conduct to be useful must conciliate for him the benevolence, gain for him the favor of these beings who are necessary to his happiness: it is then for the interest of mankind, for the happiness of the human race, it is for the esteem of himself, for the love of his fellows, for the advantages which ensue, that education in early life should kindle the imagination of the citizen; this is the true means of obtaining those happy results with which habit should familiarize him; which public opinion should render dear to his heart; for which example ought continually to rouse his faculties; after which he should be taught to search with unceasing attention. *Government* by the aid of recompences, ought to encourage him to follow this plan; by visiting crime with punishment it ought to deter those who are willing to interrupt it. Thus the hope of a true welfare, the fear of real evil, will be passions suitable to countervail those which by their impetuosity would injure society; these last will at least become very rare, if instead of feeding man's mind with unintelligible speculations, in lieu of vibrating on his ears words void of sense, he is only spoken to of realities, only shewn those interests which are in unison with truth.

Man is frequently so wicked, only, because he almost always feels himself interested in being so; let him be more enlightened, more familiarized with truth, more accustomed to virtue, he will be made more happy; he will necessarily become better. An equitable government, a vigilant administration, will presently fill the state with honest citizens; it will hold forth to them present reasons for benevolence; real advantages in truth; palpable motives to be virtuous; it will instruct them in their duties; it will foster them with its cares; it will allure them by the assurance of their own peculiar happiness; its promises faithfully fulfilled—its menaces regularly executed, will unquestionably have much more weight than those of a gloomy superstition, which never exhibits to their view other than illusory benefits, fallacious punishments, which the man hardened in wickedness will doubt every time he finds an interest in questioning them: present motives will tell more home to his heart than those which are distant and at best uncertain. The vicious and the wicked are so common upon the earth, so pertinacious in their evil courses, so attached to their irregularities, only because there are but few governments that make man feel the advantage of being just, the pleasure of being honest, the happiness of being benevolent on the contrary, there is hardly any place where the most powerful interests do not solicit him to crime, by favouring the propensities of a vicious organization; by countenancing those appetencies which nothing has attempted to rectify or lead towards virtue. A savage, who in his horde knows not the value of money, certainly would not commit a crime, if when transplanted into civilized society, he should presently learn to desire it, should make efforts to obtain it, and if he could without danger finish by stealing it; above all, if he had not been taught to respect the property of the beings who environ him. The savages and the child are precisely in the same state; it is the negligence of society, of those entrusted with their education, that renders both the one and the other wicked. The son of a noble, from his infancy learns to desire power, at a riper age he becomes ambitious; if he has the address to insinuate himself into favor, he perhaps becomes wicked, because in some societies he has been taught to know he may be so with impunity when he can command the ear of his sovereign. It is not therefore nature that makes man wicked, they are his institutions which determine him to vice. The infant brought up amongst robbers, can generally become nothing but a malefactor; if he had been reared with honest people, the chance is he would have been a virtuous man.

If the source be traced of that profound ignorance in which man is with respect to his morals, to the motives that can give volition to his will, it will be found in those false ideas which the greater number of speculators have formed to themselves, of human nature. The science of morals has become an enigma which it is impossible to unrevel; because man has made himself double; has distinguished his soul from his body; supposed it of a nature different from all known beings, with modes of action, with properties distinct from all other bodies, because he has emancipated this soul from physical laws, in order to submit it to capricious laws emanating from men who have pretended they are derived from imaginary regions, placed at very remote distances: metaphysicians seized upon these gratuitous suppositions, and by dint of subtilizing them, have rendered them completely unintelligible. These moralists have not perceived that motion is essential to the soul as well as to the living body; that both the one and the other are never moved but by material, by physical objects; that the want of each regenerate themselves unceasingly; that the wants of the soul, as well as those of the body are purely physical; that the most intimate, the most constant connection subsists between the soul and the body; or rather they have been unwilling to allow that they ate only the same thing considered under different points of view. Obstinate in their supernatural, unintelligible opinions, they have refused to open their eyes, which would have convinced them that the body in suffering rendered the soul miserable; that the soul afflicted undermined the body and brought it to decay; that both the pleasures and agonies of the mind have an influence over the body, either plunge it into sloth or give it activity: they have rather chosen to believe, that the soul draws its thoughts, whether pleasant or gloomy, from its own peculiar sources, while the fact is, that it derives its ideas only from material objects that strike on the physical organs; that it is neither determined to gaiety nor led on to sorrow, but by the actual state, whether permanent or transitory, in which the fluids and solids of the body are found. In short, they have been loath to acknowledge that the soul, purely passive, undergoes the same changes which the body experiences; is only moved by its intervention; acts only by its assistance, receives its sensations, its perceptions, forms its ideas, derives either its happiness or its misery from physical objects, through the medium of the organs of which the body is composed; frequently without its own cognizance, often in despite of itself.

By a consequence of these opinions, connected with marvellous systems, or systems invented to justify them, they have supposed the human soul to be a free agent; that is to say, that it has the faculty of moving itself; that it enjoys the privilege of acting independent of the impulse received from exterior objects, through the organs of the body; that regardless of these impulsions it can even resist them, and follow its own directions by its own energies; that it is not only different in its nature from all other beings, but has a separate mode of action; in other words, that it is an insolated point which is, not submitted to that uninterrupted chain of motion which bodies communicate to each other in a nature, whose parts are always in action. Smitten with their sublime notions, these speculators were not aware that in thus distinguishing the soul from the body and from all known beings, they rendered it an impossibility to form any true ideas of it, either to themselves or to others: they were unwilling to perceive the perfect analogy which is found between the manner of the soul's action and that by which the body is afflicted; they shut their eyes to the necessary and continual correspondence which is found between the soul and the body; they perhaps did not perceive that like the body it is subjected to the motion of attraction and repulsion; has an aptitude to be attracted, a disposition to repel, which is ascribable to qualities inherent in those physical subsistances, which give play to the organs of the body; that the volition of its will, the activity of its passions, the continual regeneration of its desires, are never more than consequences of that activity which is produced in the body by material objects which are not under its controul; that these objects render it either happy or miserable, active or languishing, contented or discontented, in despite of itself,—in defiance of all the efforts it is capable of making to render it otherwise; they have rather chosen to seek in the heavens for unknown powers to set it in motion; they have held forth to man distant, imaginary interests: under the pretext of procuring for him future happiness, he has been prevented from labouring to his present felicity, which has been studiously withheld from his knowledge: his regards have been fixed upon the heavens, that he might lose sight of the earth: truth has been concealed from him; and it has been pretended he would be rendered happy by dint of terrors, always at an immense distance; by means of shadows, with whose substances he could never come in contact; of chimeras formed by his own bewildered imagination, which changed nearly as often as the governments to which he was submitted. In short, hoodwinked by his fears, blinded by his own credulity, *he was only guided through the flexuous paths of life, by men blind as himself, where both the one and the other were frequently lost in the maze.*

CONCLUSION.

From every thing which has been hitherto said, it evidently results that all the errors of mankind, of whatever nature they may be, arise from man's having renounced reason, quitted experience, and refused the evidence of his senses that he might be guided by imagination, frequently deceitful; by authority, always suspicious. Man will ever mistake his true happiness as long as he neglects to study nature, to investigate her laws, to seek in her alone the remedies for those evils which are the consequence of his errors: he will be an enigma to himself, as long as he shall believe himself double; that he is moved by an inconceivable spiritual power, of the laws and nature of which he is ignorant; his intellectual, as well as his moral faculties, will remain unintelligible to him if he does not contemplate them with the same eyes as he does his corporeal qualities; if he does not view them as submitted in every thing to the same impulse, as governed by the same regulations. The system of his pretended free agency is without support; experience contradicts it every instant, and proves that he never ceases to be under the influence of necessity in all his actions; this truth, far from being dangerous to man, far from being destructive of his morals, furnishes him with their true basis by making him feel the necessity of those relations which subsists between sensible beings united in society: who have congregated with a view of uniting their common efforts for their reciprocal felicity. From the necessity of these relations, spring the necessity of his duties; these point out to him the sentiments of love, which he should accord to virtuous conduct; that aversion he should have for what is vicious; the horror he should feel for every thing criminal. From hence the true foundation of *Moral Obligation* will be obvious, which is only the necessity of talking means to obtain the end man proposes to himself by uniting in society; in which each individual for his own peculiar interest, his own particular happiness, his own personal security, is obliged to display dispositions requisite to conciliate the affections of his associates; to hold a conduct suitable to the preservation of the community; to contribute by his actions to the happiness of the whole. In a word, it is upon the necessary action and re-action of the human will upon the necessary attraction and repulsion of man's soul, that all his morals are bottomed: it is the unison of his will, the concert of his actions, that maintains society; it is rendered miserable by his discordance; it is dissolved by his want of union.

From what has been said, it may be concluded that the names under which man has designated the concealed causes acting in nature, and their various effects, are never more than *necessity* considered under different points of view, with the original cause of which—the great *cause of causes*—he must ever remain ignorant. It will be found that what he calls *order*, is a necessary consequence of causes and effects, of which he sees, or believes he sees, the entire connection, the complete routine, which pleases him as a whole, when he finds it conformable to his existence. In like manner it will be seen that what he calls *confusion*, is a consequence of like necessary causes and effects, of which he loses the concatenation, which he therefore thinks unfavourable to himself, or but little suitable to his being. That he has designated by the names of—

Intelligence, those necessary causes that necessarily operate the chain of events which he comprises under the term *order*:

Divinity, those necessary but invisible causes which give play to nature, in which every thing acts according to immutable and necessary laws:

Destiny or *fatality*, the necessary connection of those unknown causes and, effects which he beholds in the world:

Chance, those effects which he is not able to foresee, or of which he is ignorant of the necessary connection, with their causes:

Intellectual and *moral faculties*, those effects and those modifications necessary to an organized being, whom he has supposed to be moved by an inconceivable agent; who he has believed distinguished from his body, of a nature totally different from it, and which he has designated by the word SOUL. In consequence, he has believed this agent immortal; not dissoluble like the body. It has been shewn that the marvellous doctrine of another life, is founded upon gratuitous suppositions, contradicted by reflections, unsupported by experience, that may or may not be, without man's knowing any thing on the subject. It has been proved, that the hypothesis is not only useless to man's morals, but again, that it is calculated to palsy his exertions; to divert him from actively pursuing the true road to his own happiness; to fill him with romantic caprices; to inebriate him with opinions prejudicial to his tranquillity; in short, to lull to slumber the vigilance of legislators; by dispensing them from giving to education, to the institutions, to the laws of society, all that attention, which it is the duty and for his interest they should bestow. It must have been felt, that *politics* has unaccountably rested itself upon wrong opinions; upon ideas little capable of satisfying those passions, which every thing conspires to kindle in the heart of man; who ceases to view the future, while the present seduces and hurries him along. It has been shewn, that contempt of death is an advantageous sentiment, calculated to inspire man's mind with courage; to render him intrepid; to induce him to undertake that which may be truly useful to society; in short, from what has preceded, it will be obvious, what is competent to conduct man to happiness, and also what are the obstacles that error opposes to his felicity.

Let us not then, be accused of demolishing prejudice, without edifying the mind; with combating error without substituting truth; with underrating the power of the great *cause of causes*; with sapping at one and the same time the foundations of superstition and of sound morals. The last is necessary to man; it is founded upon his nature; its duties are certain, they must last as long as the human race remains; it imposes obligations on him, because, without it, neither individuals nor society could be able to subsist, either obtain or enjoy those advantages which nature obliges them to desire.

Listen then, O man! to those morals which are established upon, experience; which are grounded upon the necessity of things; do not lend thine ear to those superstitions founded upon reveries; rested upon imposture; built upon the capricious whims of a disordered imagination. Follow the lessons of those humane, those gentle morals, which conduct man to virtue, by the voice of happiness: turn a deaf ear to the inefficacious cries of superstition, which renders man really unhappy; which can never make him reverence VIRTUE; which renders truth hateful; which paints veracity in hideous colours; in short, let him see if REASON, without the assistance of a rival, who prohibits its use, will not more surely conduct him towards that great end, which is the object of his research, which is the natural tendency of all his views.

Indeed, what benefit has the human race hitherto drawn from those sublime, those supernatural notions with which superstition has fed mortals during so many ages? All those phantoms conjured—up by ignorance—brooded by imagination; all those hypothesis, subtile as they are irrational; from which experience is banished, all those words devoid of meaning with which languages are crowded; all those fantastical hopes; those panic terrors which have been brought to operate on the will of man; what have they done? Has any or the whole of them rendered him better, more enlightened to his duties, more faithful in their performance? Have those marvellous systems, or those sophistical inventions, by which they have been supported, carried conviction to his mind, reason into his conduct, virtue into his heart? Have they led him to the least acquaintance with the great *Cause of Causes?* Alas! it is a lamentable fact, that cannot be too often exposed, that all these things have done nothing more than plunge the human understanding into that darkness from which it is difficult to be withdrawn; sown in man's heart the most dangerous errors; of which it is scarcely possible to divest him; given birth to those fatal passions, in which may be found the true source of those evils, with which his species is afflicted: but have never enlightened his mind with truth, nor led him to that right healthy worship, which man best pays by a rational enjoyment of the faculties with which he is gifted.

Cease then, O mortal! to let thyself he disturbed with chimeras, to let thy mind be troubled with phantoms which thine own imagination has created, or to which arch imposture has given birth. Renounce thy vague hopes, disengage thyself from thine overwhelming fears, follow without inquietude the necessary routine which nature has marked out for thee; strew the road with flowers if thy destiny permits; remove, if thou art able, the thorns scattered over it. Do not attempt to plunge thy views into an impenetrable futurity; its obscurity ought to be sufficient to prove to thee, that it is either useless or dangerous to fathom. Think of making thyself happy in that existence which is known to thee: if thou wouldst preserve thyself, be temperate, be moderate, be reasonable: if thou seekest to render thy existence durable, be not prodigal of pleasure; abstain from every thing that can be hurtful to thyself, injurious to others: be truly intelligent; that is to say, learn to esteem thyself, to preserve thy being, to fulfil that end which at each moment thou proposest to thyself. Be virtuous, to the end that thou mayest render thyself solidly happy, that thou mayest enjoy the affections, secure the esteem, partake of the assistance of those by whom thou art surrounded; of those beings whom nature has made necessary to thine own peculiar felicity. Even when they should be unjust, render thyself worthy of their applause, of thine own love, and thou shalt live content, thy serenity shall not be disturbed, the end of thy career shall not slander thy life; which will be exempted from remorse: death will be to thee the door to a new existence, a new order, in which thou wilt be submitted, as thou art at present, to the eternal laws of nature, which ordains, that to LIVE HAPPY HERE BELOW, THOU MUST MAKE OTHERS HAPPY. Suffer thyself then, to be drawn gently along thy journey, until thou shalt sleep peaceable on that bosom which has given thee birth: if contrary to thine expectation, there should be another life of eternal felicity, thou canst not fail being a partaker.

For thou, wicked unfortunate! who art found in continual contradiction with thyself; thou whose disorderly machine can neither accord with thine own peculiar nature, nor with that of thine associates, whatever may be thy crimes, whatever may be thy fears of punishment in another life, thou art at least already cruelly punished in this? Do not thy follies, thy shameful habits, thy debaucheries, damage thine health? Dost thou not linger out life in disgust, fatigued with thine own excesses? Does not listlessness punish thee for thy satiated passions? Has not thy vigour, thy gaiety, thy content, already yielded to feebleness, crouched under infirmities, given place to regret? Do not thy vices every day dig thy grave? Every time thou hast stained thyself with crime, hast thou dared without horror to return into thyself, to examine thine own conscience? Hast thou not found remorse, error, shame, established in thine heart? Hast thou not dreaded the scrutiny of thy fellow man? Hast thou not trembled when alone; unceasingly feared, that truth, so terrible for thee, should unveil thy dark transgressions, throw into light thine enormous iniquities? Do not then any longer fear to part with thine existence, it will at least put an end to those richly merited torments thou hast inflicted on thyself; *Death, in delivering the earth from an incommodious burthen, will also deliver thee from thy most cruel enemy, thyself.*

END OF PART I.

THE SYSTEM OF NATURE
Volume 2

M. DE MIRABAUD

Paul Henri Thiery,
Baron d'Holbach

Introduction by
Robert D. Richardson, Jr.

MIRABAUD'S SYSTEM OF NATURE

Translated from the Original
BY SAMUEL WILKINSON

PART II.

ON THE DIVINITY:—PROOFS OF HIS EXISTENCE:—OF HIS ATTRIBUTES: OF HIS INFLUENCE OVER THE HAPPINESS OF MAN.

CHAP. I.

The Origin of Man's Ideas upon the Divinity.

If man possessed the courage, if he had the requisite industry to recur to the source of those opinions which are most deeply engraven on his brain; if he rendered to himself a faithful account of the reasons which make him hold these opinions as sacred; if he coolly examined the basis of his hopes, the foundation of his fears, he would find that it very frequently happens, those objects, or those ideas which move him most powerfully, either have no real existence, or are words devoid of meaning, which terror has conjured up to explain some sudden disaster; that they are often phantoms engendered by a disordered imagination, modified by ignorance; the effect of an ardent mind distracted by contending passions, which prevent him from either reasoning justly, or consulting experience in his judgment; that this mind often labours with a precipitancy that throws his intellectual faculties into confusion; that bewilders his ideas; that consequently he gives a substance and a form to chimeras, to airy nothings, which he afterwards idolizes from sloth, reverences from prejudice.

A sensible being placed in a nature where every part is in motion, has various feelings, in consequence of either the agreeable or disagreeable effects which he is obliged to experience from this continued action and re-action; in consequence he either finds himself happy or miserable; according to the quality of the sensations excited in him, he will love or fear, seek after or fly from, the real or supposed causes of such marked effects operated on his machine. But if he is ignorant of nature, if he is destitute of experience, he will frequently deceive himself as to these causes; for want of either capability or inclination to recur back to them, he will neither have a true knowledge of their energy, nor a clear idea of their mode of acting: thus until reiterated experience shall have formed his ideas, until the mirror of truth shall have shewn him the judgment he ought to make, he will be involved in trouble, a prey to incertitude, a victim to credulity.

Man is a being who brings with him nothing into the world save an aptitude to feeling in a manner more or less lively according to his individual organization: he has no innate knowledge of any of the causes that act upon him: by degrees his faculty of feeling discovers to him their various qualities; he learns to judge of them; time familiarizes him with their properties; he attaches ideas to them, according to the manner in which they have affected him; these ideas are correct or otherwise, in a ratio to the soundness of his organic structure: his judgment is faulty or not, as these organs are either well or ill-constituted; in proportion as they are competent to afford him sure and reiterated experience.

The first moments of man are marked by his wants; that is to say, the first impulse he receives is to conserve his existence; this he would not be able to maintain without the concurrence of many analogous causes: these wants in a sensible being, manifest themselves by a general languor, a sinking, a confusion in his machine, which gives him the consciousness of a painful sensation: this derangement subsists, is even augmented, until the cause suitable to remove it re-establishes the harmony so necessary to the existence of the human frame. Want, therefore, is the first evil man experiences; nevertheless it is requisite to the maintenance of his existence. Was it not for this derangement of his body, which obliges him to furnish its remedy, he would not be warned of the necessity of preserving the existence he has received. Without wants man would be an insensible machine, similar to a vegetable; like that he would be incapable of preserving himself; he would not be competent to using the means required to conserve his being. To his wants are to be ascribed his passions; his desires; the exercise of his corporeal functions; the play of his intellectual faculties: they are his wants that oblige him to think; that determine his will, that induce him to act; it is to satisfy them or rather to put an end to the painful sensations excited by their presence, that according to his capacity, to the natural sensibility of his soul, to the energies which are peculiar to himself, he gives play to his faculties, exerts the activity of his bodily strength, or displays the extensive powers of his mind. His wants being perpetual, he is obliged to labour without relaxation, to procure objects competent to satisfy them. In a word, it is owing to his multiplied wants that man's energy is kept in a state of continual activity: as soon as he ceases to have wants, he falls into inaction—becomes listless—declines into apathy— sinks into a languor that is incommodious to his feelings or prejudicial to his existence: this lethargic state of weariness lasts until new wants, by giving him fresh activity, rouse his dormant faculties—throw off his stupor—re-animate his vigour, and destroy the sluggishness to which he had become a prey.

From hence it will be obvious that evil is necessary to man; without it he would neither be in a condition to know that which injures him; to avoid its presence; or to seek his own welfare: without this stimulus, he would differ in nothing from insensible, unorganized beings: if those evanescent evils which he calls *wants*, did not oblige him to call forth his faculties, to set his energies in motion, to cull experience, to compare objects, to discriminate them, to separate those which have the capabilities to injure him, from those which possess the means to benefit him, he would be insensible to happiness— inadequate to enjoyment. In short, *without evil man would be ignorant of good*; he would be continually exposed to perish like the leaf on a tree. He would resemble an infant, who, destitute of experience, runs the risque of meeting his destruction at every step he takes, unguarded by his nurse. What the nurse is to the child, experience is to the adult; when either are wanting, these children of different lustres generally go astray: frequently encounter disaster. Without evil he would be unable to judge of any thing; he would have no preference; his will would be without volition, he would be destitute of passions; desire would find no place in his heart; he would not revolt at the most disgusting objects; he would not strive to put them away; he would neither have stimuli to love, nor motives to fear any thing; he would be an insensible automaton; he would no longer be a man.

If no evil had existed in this world, man would never have dreamt of those numerous divinities, to whom he has rendered such various modes of worship. If nature had permitted him easily to satisfy all his regenerating wants, if she had given him none but agreeable sensations, his days would have uninterruptedly rolled on in one perpetual uniformity; he would never have discovered his own nakedness; he would never have had motives to search after the unknown causes of things—to meditate in pain. Therefore man, always contented, would only have occupied himself with satisfying his wants; with enjoying the present, with feeling the influence of objects, that would unceasingly warn him of his existence in a mode that he must necessarily approve; nothing would alarm his heart; every thing would be analogous to his existence: he would neither know fear, experience distrust, nor have inquietude for the future: these feelings can only be the consequence of some troublesome sensation, which must have anteriorly affected him, or which by disturbing the harmony of his machine, has interrupted the course of his happiness; which has shewn him he is naked.

Independent of those wants which in man renew themselves every instant; which he frequently finds it impossible to satisfy; every individual experiences a multiplicity of evils—he suffers from the inclemency of the seasons—he pines in penury—he is infected with plague—he is scourged by war—he is the victim of famine—he is afflicted with disease—he is the sport of a thousand accidents, &c. This is the reason why all men are fearful; why the whole human race are diffident. The knowledge he has of pain alarms him upon all unknown causes, that is to say, upon all those of which he has not yet experienced the effect; this experience made with precipitation, or if it be preferred, by instinct, places him on his guard against all those objects from the operation of which he is ignorant what consequences may result to himself.

His inquietude is in proportion; his fears keep pace with the extent of the disorder which these objects produce in him; they are measured by their rarity, that is to say, by the inexperience he has of them; by the natural sensibility of the soul; and by the ardour of his imagination. The wore ignorant man is, the less experience he has, the more he is susceptible of fear; solitude, the obscurity of a forest, silence, and the darkness of night, desolate ruins, the roaring of the wind, sudden, confused noises, are objects of terror to all who are unaccustomed to these things. The uninformed man is a child whom every thing astonishes; who trembles at every thing he encounters: his alarms disappear, his fears diminish, his mind becomes calm, in proportion as experience familiarizes him, more or less, with natural effects; his fears cease entirely, as soon as he understands, or believes he understands, the causes that act; or when he knows how to avoid their effects. But if he cannot penetrate the causes which disturb him, if he cannot discover the agents by whom he suffers, if he cannot find to what account to place the confusion he experiences, his inquietude augments; his fears redouble; his imagination leads him astray; it exaggerates his evil; paints in a disorderly manner these unknown objects of his terror; magnifies their powers; then making an analogy between them and those terrific objects, with whom he is already acquainted, he suggests to himself the means he usually takes to mitigate their anger; to conciliate their kindness; he employs similar measures to soften the anger, to disarm the power, to avert the effects of the concealed cause which gives birth to his inquietudes, which fills him with anxiety, which alarms his fears. It is thus his weakness, aided by ignorance, renders him superstitious.

There are very few men, even in our own day, who have sufficiently studied nature, who are fully apprised of physical causes, or with the effects they must necessarily produce. This ignorance, without doubt, was much greater in the more remote ages of the world, when the human mind, yet in its infancy, had not collected that experience, taken that expansion, made those strides towards improvement, which distinguishes the present from the past. Savages dispersed, erratic, thinly scattered up and down, knew the course of nature either very imperfectly or not at all; society alone perfects human knowledge: it requires not only multiplied but combined efforts to unravel the secrets of nature. This granted, all natural causes were mysteries to our wandering ancestors; the entire of nature was an enigma to them; all its phenomena was marvellous, every event inspired terror to beings who were destitute of experience; almost every thing, they saw must have appeared to them strange, unusual, contrary to their idea of the order of things.

It cannot then furnish matter for surprise, if we behold men in the present day trembling at the sight of those objects which have formerly filled their fathers with dismay. *Eclipse, comets, meteors*, were, in ancient days, subjects of alarm to all the people of the earth: these effects, so natural in the eyes of the sound philosopher, who has by degrees fathomed their true causes, have yet the right, possess the power, to alarm the most numerous, to excite the fears of the least instructed part of modern nations. The people of the present day, as well as their ignorant ancestors, find something marvellous, believe there is a supernatural agency in all those objects to which their eyes are unaccustomed; they consider all those unknown causes as wonderful, that act with a force of which their mind has no idea it is possible the known agents are capable. The ignorant see wonders *prodigies, miracles*, in all those striking effects of which they are unable to render themselves a satisfactory account; all the causes which produce them they think *supernatural*; this, however, really implies nothing more than that they are not familiar to them, or that they have not hitherto witnessed natural agents, whose energy was equal to the production of effects so rare, so astonishing, as those with which their sight has been appalled.

Besides the ordinary phenomena to which nations were witnesses without being competent to unravel the causes, they have in times very remote from ours, experienced calamities, whether general or local, which filled them with the most cruel inquietude; which plunged them into an abyss of consternation. The traditions of all people, the annals of all nations, recal, even at this day, melancholy events, physical disasters, dreadful catastrophes, which had the effect of spreading universal terror among our forefathers, But when history should he silent on these stupendous revolutions, would not our own reflection on what passes under our eyes be sufficient to convince us, that all parts of our globe have been, and following the course of things, will necessarily be again violently agitated, overturned, changed, overflowed, in a state of conflagration? Vast continents have been inundated, seas breaking their limits have usurped the dominion of the earth; at length retiring, these waters have left striking, proofs of their presence, by the marine vestiges of shells, skeletons of sea fish, &c. which the attentive observer meets with at every step, in the bowels of those fertile countries we now inhabit—subterraneous fires have opened to themselves the most frightful volcanoes, whose craters frequently issue destruction on every side. In short, the elements unloosed, have at various times, disputed among themselves the empire of our globe; this exhibits evidence of the fact, by those vast heaps of wreck, those stupendous ruins spread over its surface. What, then, must have been the fears of mankind, who in those countries believed he beheld the entire of nature armed against his peace, menacing with destruction his very abode? What must have been the inquietude of a people taken thus unprovided, who fancied they saw nature cruelly labouring to their annihilation? Who beheld a world ready to be dashed into atoms; who witnessed the earth suddenly rent asunder; whose yawning chasm was the grave of large cities, whole provinces, entire nations? What ideas must mortals, thus overwhelmed with terror, form to themselves of the irresistible cause that could produce such extended effects? Without doubt they did not attribute these wide spreading calamities to nature; neither did they conceive they were mere physical causes; they could not suspect she was the author, the accomplice of the confusion she herself experienced; they did not see that these tremendous revolutions, these overpowering disorders, were the necessary result of her immutable laws; that they contributed to the general order by which she subsists; that, in point of fact, there was nothing more surprising in the inundation of large portions of the earth, in the swallowing up an entire nation, in a volcanic conflagration spreading destruction over whole provinces, than there is in a stone falling to the earth, or the death of a fly; that each equally has its spring in the necessity of things.

It was under these astounding circumstances, that nations, bathed in the most bitter tears, perplexed with the most frightful visions, electrified with terror, not believing there existed on this mundane ball, causes sufficiently powerful to operate the gigantic phenomena that filled their minds with dismay, carried their streaming eyes towards heaven, where their tremulous fears led them to suppose these unknown agents, whose unprovoked enmity destroyed, their earthly felicity, could alone reside.

It was in the lap of ignorance, in the season of alarm, in the bosom of calamity, that mankind ever formed his first notions of the *Divinity*. From hence it is obvious that his ideas on this subject are to be suspected, that his notions are in a great measure false, that they are always afflicting. Indeed, upon whatever part of our sphere we cast our eyes, whether it be upon the frozen climates of the north, upon the parching regions of the south, or under the more temperate zones, we every where behold the people when assailed by misfortunes, have either made to themselves national gods, or else have adopted those which have been given them by their conquerors; before these beings, either of their own creation or adoption, they have tremblingly prostrated themselves in the hour of calamity, soliciting relief; have ignorantly attributed to blocks of stone, or to men like themselves, those natural effects which were above their comprehension; the inhabitants of many nations, not contented with the national gods, made each to himself one or more gods, which he supposed presided exclusively over his own household, from whom he supposed he derived his own peculiar happiness, to whom he attributed all his domestic misfortunes. The idea of these powerful agents, these supposed distributors of good and evil, was always associated with that of terror; their name was never pronounced without recalling to man's wind either his own particular calamities or those of his fathers. In many places man trembles at this day, because his progenitors have trembled for thousands of years past. The thought of his gods always awakened in man the most afflicting ideas. If he recurred to the source of his actual fears, to the commencement of those melancholy impressions that stamp themselves in his mind when their name is announced, he would find it in the conflagrations, in the revolutions, in those extended disasters, that have at various times destroyed large portions of the human race; that overwhelmed with dismay those miserable beings who escaped the destruction of the earth; these in transmitting to posterity, the tradition of such afflicting events, have also transmitted to him their fears; have delivered down to their successors, those gloomy ideas which their bewildered imaginations, coupled with their barbarous ignorance of natural causes, had formed to them of the anger of their irritated gods, to which their alarm falsely attributed these sweeping disasters.

If the gods of nations had their birth in the bosom of alarm, it was again in that of despair that each individual formed the unknown power that he made exclusively for himself. Ignorant of physical causes, unpractised in their mode of action, unaccustomed to their effects, whenever he experienced any serious misfortune, whenever he was afflicted with any grievous sensation, he was at a loss how to account for it; he therefore attributed it to his household gods, to whom he made an immediate supplication for assistance, or rather for forbearance of further affliction: this disposition in man has been finely pourtrayed by Aesop in his fable of "the Waggoner and Hercules." The motion which in despight of himself was excited in his machine, his diseases, his troubles, his passions, his inquietude, the painful alterations his frame underwent, without his being able to fathom the true causes; at length death, of which the aspect in so formidable to a being strongly attached to existence, were effects he looked upon either as supernatural, or else he conceived they were repugnant to his actual nature; he attributed them to some mighty cause, which maugre all his efforts, disposed of him at each, moment. Thus palsied with alarm, benumbed with terror, he pensively meditated upon his sorrows; agitated with fear, he sought for means to avert the calamities that threatened him with destruction; his imagination, thus rendered desperate by his endurance of evils which he found inevitable, formed to him those phantoms which he called gods; before whom he trembled from a consciousness of his own weakness; thus disposed, he endeavoured by prostration, by sacrifices, by prayers, to disarm the anger of these imaginary beings to which his trepidation had given birth; whom he ignorantly imagined to be the cause of his misery, whom his fancy painted to him as endowed with the power of alleviating his sufferings: it was thus in the extremity of his grief, in the exacerbation of his mind, weighed down with misfortune, that unhappy man fashioned those chimeras which filled him with the most gloomy ideas, which he transmitted to his posterity, as the surest means of avoiding the evils to which he had been himself subjected.

Man never judges of those objects of which he is ignorant, but through the medium of those which come within his knowledge: thus man, taking himself for the model, ascribed will, intelligence, design, projects, passions; in a word, qualities analogous to his own, to all those unknown causes of which he experienced the action. As soon as a visible or supposed cause affects him in an agreeable manner, or in a mode favourable to his existence, he concludes it to be good, to be well intentioned towards him: on the contrary, he judges all those to be bad in their nature, evilly disposed, to have the intention of injuring him, which cause him any painful sensations. He attributes views, plans, a system of conduct like his own, to every thing which to his limited ideas appears of itself to produce connected effects; to act with regularity; to constantly operate in the same manner; that uniformly produces the same sensations in his own person. According to these notions, which he always borrows from himself, from his own peculiar mode of action, he either loves or fears those objects which have affected him; he in consequence approaches them with confidence or timidity; seeks after them or flies from them in proportion as the feelings they have excited are either pleasant or painful. Having travelled thus far, he presently addresses them; he invokes their aid; prays to them for succour; conjures them to cease his afflictions; to forbear tormenting him; as he finds himself sensible to presents, pleased with submission, he tries to win them to his interests by humiliation, by sacrifices; he exercises towards them the hospitality he himself loves; he gives them an asylum; he builds them a dwelling; he furnishes them with costly raiment; he makes their altars smoke with delicious food; he proffers to their acceptance the earliest flowers of spring; the finest fruits of autumn; the rich grain of summer; in short he sets before them all those things which he thinks will please them the most, because he himself places the highest value on them. These dispositions enable us to account for the formation of tutelary gods, of lares, of larvae, which every man makes to himself in savage and unpolished nations. Thus we perceive that weak superstitious mortals, ignorant of truth, devoid of experience, regard as the arbiters of their fate, as the dispensers of good and evil, animals, stones, unformed inanimate substances, which the effort of their heated imaginations transform into gods, whom they invest with intelligence, whom they clothe with desires, to whom they give volition.

Another disposition which serves to deceive the savage man, which will equally deceive those whom reason shall not enlighten on these subjects, is his attachment to omens; or the fortuitous concurrence of certain effects, with causes which have not produced them; the co-existence of these effects with certain causes, which have not the slightest connection with them, has frequently led astray very intelligent beings; nations who considered themselves very enlightened; who have either been disinclined or unable to disentangle the one from the other: thus the savage attributes bounty or the will to render him service, to any object whether animate or inanimate, such as a stone of a certain form, a rock, a mountain, a tree, a serpent, an owl, &c. if every time he encounters these objects in a certain position, it should so happen that he is more than ordinarily successful in hunting, that he should take an unusual quantity of fish, that he should be victorious in war, or that he should compass any enterprize whatever that he may at that moment undertake: the same savage will be quite as gratuitous in attaching malice, wickedness, the determination to injure him, to either the same object in a different position, or any others in a given posture, which way have met his eyes on those days when he shall have suffered some grievous accident, have been very unsuccessful in his undertakings, unfortunate in the chace, disappointed in his draught of fish: incapable of reasoning he connects these effects with causes, that reflection would convince him have nothing in common with each other; that are entirely due to physical causes, to necessary circumstances, over which neither himself nor his omens have the least controul: nevertheless he finds it much easier to attribute them to these imaginary causes; he therefore *deifies* them; looks upon them as either his guardian angels, or else as his most inveterate enemies. Having invested them with supernatural powers, he becomes anxious to explain to himself their mode of action; his self-love prevents his seeking elsewhere for the model: thus he assigns them all those motives that actuate himself; he endows them with passions; he gives them design—intelligence—will— imagines they can either injure him or benefit him, as be may render them propitious or otherwise to his views: he ends with worshipping them; with paying them divine honours; he appoints them priests; or at least always consults them before he undertakes any object of moment: such is their influence, that if they put on the evil position, he will lay aside the most important undertaking. The savage in this is never more than an infant, that is angry with the object that displeases him; just like the dog who gnaws the stone by which he has been wounded, without recurring to the hand by which it was thrown.

Such is the foundation of man's faith, in either happy or unhappy omens: devoid of experience, unaccustomed to reason with precision, fearing to call in the evidence of truth, he looks upon them either as gods themselves, or else as warnings given him by his other gods, to whom he attributes the faculties of sagacity and foresight, of which he is himself miserably deficient. Ignorance, when involved in disaster, when immersed in trouble, believes a stone, a reptile, a bird, much better instructed than himself. The slender observation of the ignorant only serves to render him more superstitious; he sees certain birds announce by their flight, by their cries, certain changes in the weather, such as cold, heat, rain, storms; he beholds at certain periods, vapours arise from the bottom of some particular caverns? there needs nothing further to impress upon him the belief, that these beings possess the knowledge of future events; enjoy the gifts of prophecy: he looks upon them as supernatural agents, employed by his gods: it is thus he becomes the dupe to his own credulity.

If by degrees the truth flashing occasionally on his mind, experience and reflection arrive at undeceiving him, with respect to the power, the intelligence, the virtues actually residing in these objects; he at least supposes them put in activity by some secret, some hidden cause; that they are the instruments, employed by some invisible agent, who is either friendly or inimical to his welfare. To this concealed agent, therefore, he addresses himself; pays him his vows; emplores his assistance; deprecates his wrath; seeks to propitiate him to his interests; is willing to soften his anger; for this purpose he employs the same means, of which he avails himself, either to appease or gain over the beings of his own species.

Societies in their origin, seeing themselves frequently afflicted by nature, supposed either the elements, or the concealed powers who regulated them, possessed a will, views, wants, desires, similar to their own. From hence, the sacrifices imagined to nourish them; the libations poured out to them; the steams, the incense to gratify their olfactory nerves. Their superstition led them to believe these elements or their irritated movers were to be appeased like irritated man, by prayers, by humiliation, by presents. Their imagination was ransacked to discover the presents that would be most acceptable in their eyes; to ascertain the oblations that would be most agreeable, the sacrifices that would most surely propitiate their kindness: as these did not make known their inclinations, man differed with his fellow on those most suitable; each followed his own disposition; or rather each offered what was most estimable in his own eyes; hence arose differences never to be reconciled the bitterest animosities; the most unconquerable aversions; the most, destructive jealousies! Thus some brought the fruits of the earth, others offered sheaves of corn: some strewed flowers over their fanes; some decorated them with the most costly jewels; some served them with meats; others sacrificed lambs, heifers, bulls; at length such was their delirium, such the wildness of their imaginations, that they stained their altars with human gore, made oblations of young children immolated virgins, to appease the anger of these supposed deities.

The old men, as having the most experience, were usually charged with the conduct of these peace-offerings, from whence, the name PRIEST; [Greek letters], *presbos*, in the Greek meaning an old man. These accompanied them with ceremonies, instituted rites, used precautions by consulting omens; adopted formalities, retraced to their fellow citizens the notions transmitted to them by their forefathers; collected the observations made by their ancestors; repeated the fables they had received; added commentaries of their own; subjoined supplications to the idols at whose shrine they were sacrificing. It is thus the sacerdotal order was established; thus that public worship was established; by degrees each community formed a body of tenets to be observed by the citizens; these were transmitted from race to race; held sacred out of reverence for their fathers; at length it was deemed sacrilege to doubt these pandects in any one particular; even the errors, that had crept into them with time, were beheld with reverential awe; he that ventured to reason upon them, was looked upon as an enemy to the commonwealth; as one whose impiety drew down upon them the vengeance of these adored beings, to which alone imagination had given birth; not contented with adopting the rituals, with following the ceremonies invented by themselves, one community waged war against another, to oblige it to receive their particular creeds; which the old men who regulated them, declared would infallibly win them the favor of their tutelary deities: thus very often to conciliate their favor, the victorious party immolated on the altars of their gods, the bodies of their unhappy captives; frequently they carried their savage barbarity the length of exterminating whole nations, who happened to worship gods different from their own: thus it frequently happened, that the friends of the serpent, when victorious, covered his altars with the mangled carcases of the worshippers of the stone, whom the fortune of war had placed in their hands: such were the unformed, the precarious elements of which rude nations every where availed themselves to compose their superstitions: they were always a system of conduct invented by imagination: conceived in ignorance, organized in misfortune, to render the unknown powers, to whom they believed nature was submitted, either favorable to their views, or to, induce them to cease those afflictions, which natural causes, for the wisest purposes, were continually heaping upon them; thus some irascible, at the same time placable being, was always chosen for the basis of the adopted superstition; it was upon these puerile tenets, upon these absurd notions, that the old men or the priests rested their doctrines; founded their rights; established their authority: it was to render these fanciful beings friendly to the race of man, that they erected, temples, raised altars, loaded them with wealth; in short, it was from such rude foundations, that arose the magnificent structure of superstition; under which man trembled for thousands of years: which governed the condition of society, which determined the actions of the people, gave the tone to the character, deluged the earth with blood, for such a long series of ages. But although these superstitions were originally invented by savages, they still have the power of regulating the fate of many civilized nations, who are not less tenacious of their chimeras, than their rude progenitors. These systems, so ruinous in their principles, have been variously modified by the human mind, of which it is the essence, to labour incessantly on unknown objects; it always, commences by attaching to these, a very first-rate importance, which it afterwards never dares coolly to examine.

Such was the course of man's imagination, in the successive ideas which he either formed to himself, or which he received from his fathers, upon the divinity. The first theology of man was grounded on fear, modelled by ignorance: either afflicted or benefitted by the elements, he adored these elements themselves; by a parity of reasoning, if reasoning it can be called, he extended his reverence to every material, coarse object; he afterwards rendered his homage to the agents he supposed presiding over these elements; to powerful genii; to inferior genii; to heroes; to men endowed with either great or striking qualities. Time, aided by reflection, with here and there a slight corruscation of truth, induced him in some places to relinquish his original ideas; he believed he simplified the thing by lessening the number of his gods, but he achieved nothing by this towards attaining to the truth; in recurring from cause to cause man finished by losing sight of every thing; in this obscurity, in this dark abyss, his mind still laboured, he formed new chimeras, he made new gods, or rather he formed a very complex machinery; still, as before, whenever he could not account for any phenomenon that struck his sight, he was unwilling to ascribe it to physical causes; and the name of his Divinity, whatever that might happen to be, was always brought in to supply his own ignorance of natural causes.

If a faithful account was rendered of man's ideas upon the Divinity, he would be obliged to acknowledge, that for the most part the word *Gods* has been used to express the concealed, remote, unknown causes of the effects he witnessed; that he applies this term when the spring of natural, the source of known causes ceases to be visible: as soon as he loses the thread of these causes, or as soon as his mind can no longer follow the chain, he solves the difficulty, terminates his research, by ascribing it to his gods; thus giving a vague definition to an unknown cause, at which either his idleness, or his limited knowledge, obliges him to stop. When, therefore, he ascribes to his gods the production of some phenomenon, the novelty or the extent of which strikes him with wonder, but of which his ignorance precludes him from unravelling the true cause, or which he believes the natural powers with which he is acquainted are inadequate to bring forth; does he, in fact, do any thing more than substitute for the darkness of his own mind, a sound to which he has been accustomed to listen with reverential awe? Ignorance may be said to be the inheritance of the generality of men; these attribute to their gods not only those uncommon effects that burst upon their senses with an astounding force, but also the most simple events, the causes of which are the most easy to be known to whoever shall be willing to meditate upon them. In short, man has always respected those unknown causes, those surprising effects which his ignorance prevented him from fathoming.

But does this afford us one single, correct idea of the *Divinity*? Can it be possible we are acting rationally, thus eternally to make him the agent of our stupidity, of our sloth, of our want of information on natural causes? Do we, in fact, pay any kind of adoration to this being, by thus bringing him forth on every trifling occasion, to solve the difficulties ignorance throws in our way? Of whatever nature this great cause of causes may be, it is evident to the slightest reflection that he has been sedulous to conceal himself from our view; that he has rendered it impossible for us to have the least acquaintance with him, except through the medium of nature, which he has unquestionably rendered competent to every thing: this is the rich banquet spread before man; he is invited to partake, with a welcome he has no right to dispute; to enjoy therefore is to obey; to be happy is to render that worship which must make him most acceptable; *to be happy himself is to make others happy; to make others happy is to be virtuous; to be virtuous he must revere truth: to know what truth is, he must examine with caution, scrutinize with severity, every opinion he adopts:* this granted, is it at all consistent with the majesty of the Divinity, is it not insulting to such a being to clothe him with our wayward passions; to ascribe to him designs similar to our narrow view of things; to give him our filthy desires; to suppose he can be guided by our finite conceptions; to bring him on a level with frail humanity, by investing him with our qualities, however much we may exaggerate them; to indulge an opinion that he can either act or think as we do; to imagine he can in any manner resemble such a feeble play-thing, as is the greatest, the most distinguished man? No! it is to degrade him in the eye of reason; to violate every regard for truth; to set moral decency at defiance; to fall back into the depth of cimmerian darkness. Let man therefore sit down cheerfully to the feast; let him contentedly partake of what he finds; but let him not worry the Divinity with his useless prayers, with his shallow-sighted requests, to solicit at his hands that which, if granted, would in all probability be the most injurious for himself; these supplications are, in fact, at once to say, that with our limited experience, with our slender knowledge, we better understand what is suitable to our condition, what is convenient to our welfare, than the mighty *Cause of all causes* who has left us in the hands of nature: it is to be presumptuous in the highest degree of presumption; it is impiously to endeavour to lift up a veil which it is evidently forbidden man to touch; that even his most strenuous efforts attempt in vain.

It remains, then, to inquire, if man can reasonably flatter himself with obtaining a perfect knowledge of the power of nature; of the properties of the beings she contains; of the effects which may result from their various combinations? Do we know why the magnet attracts iron? Are we better acquainted with the cause of polar attraction? Are we in a condition to explain the phenomena of light, electricity, elasticity? Do we understand the mechanism by which that modification of our brain, which we tall volition, puts our arm or our legs into motion? Can we render to ourselves an account of the manner in which our eyes behold objects, in which our ears receive sounds, in which our mind conceives ideas? All we know upon these subjects is, that they are so. If then we are incapable of accounting for the most ordinary phenomena, which nature daily exhibits to us, by what chain of reasoning do we refuse to her the power of producing other effects equally incomprehensible to us? Shall we be more instructed, when every time we behold an effect of which we are not in a capacity to develope the cause, we may idly say, this effect is produced by the power, by the will of God? Undoubtedly it is the great *Cause of causes* must have produced every thing; but is it not lessening the true dignity of the Divinity, to introduce him as interfering in every operation of nature; nay, in every action of so insignificant a creature as man? As a mere agent executing his own eternal, immutable laws; when experience, when reflection, when the evidence of all we contemplate, warrants the idea, that this ineffable being has rendered nature competent to every effect, by giving her those irrevocable laws, that eternal, unchangeable system, according to which all the beings she contains must eternally act? Is it not more worthy the exalted mind of the GREAT PARENT OF PARENTS, *ens entium*, more consistent with truth, to suppose that his wisdom in giving these immutable, these eternal laws to the macrocosm, foresaw every thing that could possibly be requisite for the happiness of the beings contained in it; that therefore he left it to the invariable operation of a system, which never can produce any effect that is not the best possible that circumstances however viewed will admit: that consequently the natural activity of the human mind, which is itself the result of this eternal action, was purposely given to man, that he might endeavour to fathom, that he might strive to unravel, that he might seek out the concatenation of these laws, in order to furnish remedies against the evils produced by ignorance. How many discoveries in the great science of natural philosophy has mankind progressively made, which the ignorant prejudices of our forefathers on their first announcement considered as impious, as displeasing to the Divinity, as heretical profanations, which could only be expiated by the sacrifice of the enquiring individuals; to whose labour their posterity owes such an infinity of gratitude? Even in modern days we have seen a SOCRATES destroyed, a GALLILEO condemned, whilst multitudes of other benefactors to mankind have been held in contempt by their uninformed cotemporaries, for those very researches into nature which the present generation hold in the highest veneration. *Whenever ignorant priests are permitted to guide the opinions of nations, science can make but a very slender progress:* natural discoveries will be always held inimical to the interest of bigotted superstitious men. It may, to the minds of infatuated mortals, to the shallow comprehension of prejudiced beings, appear very pious to reply on every occasion our gods do this, our gods do that; but to the contemplative philosopher, to the man of reason, to the real adorers of the great *Cause of causes*, it will never be convincing, that a sound, a mere word, can attach the reason of things; can have more than a fixed sense; can suffice to explain problems. The word GOD is for the most part used to denote the impenetrable cause of those effects which astonish mankind; which man is not competent to explain. But is not this wilful idleness? Is it not inconsistent with our nature? Is it not being truly impious, to sit down with those fine faculties we have received, and give the answer of a child to every thing we do not understand; or rather which our own sloth, or our own want of industry has prevented us from knowing? Ought we not rather to redouble our efforts to penetrate the cause of those phenomena which strike our mind? Is not this, in fact, the duty we owe to the great, the universal Parent? When we have given this answer, what have we said? nothing but what every one knows. Could the great *Cause of causes* make the whole, without also making its part? But does it of necessity follow that he executes every trifling operation, when he has so noble an agent as his own nature, whose laws he has rendered unchangeable, whose scale of operations can never deviate from the eternal routine he has marked out for her and all the beings she embraces? Whose secrets, if sought out, contain the true balsam of life—the sovereign remedy for all the diseases of man.

When we shall be ingenuous with ourselves, we shall be obliged to agree that it was uniformly the ignorance in which our ancestors were involved, their want of knowledge of natural causes, their unenlightened ideas on the powers of nature, which gave birth to the gods they worshipped; that it is, again, the impossibility which the greater part of mankind find to withdraw, themselves out of this ignorance, the difficulty they consequently find to form to themselves simple ideas of the formation of things, the labour that is required to discover the true sources of those events, which they either admire or fear, that makes them believe these ideas are necessary to enable them to render an account of those phenomena, to which their own sluggishness renders them incompetent to recur. Here, without doubt, is the reason they treat all those as irrational who do not see the necessity of admitting an unknown agent, or some secret energy, which for want of being acquainted with Nature, they have placed out of herself.

The phenomena of nature necessarily breed various sentiments in man: some he thinks favorable to him, some prejudicial, while the whole is only what it can be. Some excite his love, his admiration, his gratitude; others fill him with trouble, cause aversion, drive him to despair. According to the various sensations he experiences, he either loves or fears the causes to which he attributes the effects, which produce in him these different passions: these sentiments are commensurate with the effects he experiences; his admiration is enhanced, his fears are augmented, in the same ratio as the phenomena which strikes his senses are more or less extensive, more or less irresistible or interesting to him. Man necessarily makes himself the centre of nature; indeed he can only judge of things, as he is himself affected by them; he can only love that which he thinks favorable to his being; he hates, he fears every thing which causes him to suffer: in short, as we have seen in the former volume, he calls confusion every thing that deranges the economy of his machine; he believes all is in order, as soon as he experiences nothing but what is suitable to his peculiar mode of existence. By a necessary consequence of these ideas, man firmly believes that the entire of nature was made for him alone; that it was only himself which she had in view in all her works; or rather that the powerful cause to which this nature was subordinate, had only for object man and his convenience, in all the stupendous effects which are produced in the universe.

If there existed on this earth other thinking beings besides man, they would fall exactly into similar prejudices with himself; it is a sentiment founded upon that predilection which each individual necessarily has for himself; a predilection that will subsist until reason, aided by experience, in pointing out the truth, shall have rectified his errors.

Thus, whenever man is contented, whenever every thing is in order with respect to himself, he either admires or loves the causes to which he believes he is indebted for his welfare; when he becomes discontented with his mode of existence, he either fears or hates the cause which he supposes has produced these afflicting effects. But his welfare confounds itself with his existence; it ceases to make itself felt when it has become habitual, when it has been of long continuance; he then thinks it is inherrent to his essence; he concludes from it that he is formed to be always happy; he finds it natural that every thing should concur to the maintenance of his being. It is by no means the same when he experiences a mode of existence that is displeasing to himself: the man who suffers is quite astonished at the change which his taken place in his machine; he judges it to be contrary to the entire of nature, because it is incommodious to his own particular nature; he, imagines those events by which he is wounded, to be contrary to the order of things; he believes that nature is deranged every time she does not procure for him that mode of feeling which is suitable to his ideas: he concludes from these suppositions that nature, or rather that the agent who moves her; is irritated against him.

It is thus that man, almost insensible to good, feels evil in a very lively manner; the first he believes natural, the other he thinks opposed to nature. He is either ignorant, or forgets, that he constitutes part of a whole, formed by the assemblage of substances, of which some are analogous, others heterogeneous; that the various beings of which nature is composed, are endowed with a variety of properties, by virtue of which they act diversely on the bodies who find themselves within the sphere of their action; that some have an aptitude to attraction, whilst it is of the essence of others to repel; that even those bodies that attract at one distance, repel at another; that the peculiar attractions and repulsions of the particles of bodies perpetually oppose, invariably counteract the general ones of the masses of matter: he does not perceive that these beings, as destitute of goodness, as devoid of malice, act only according to their respective essences; follow the laws their properties impose upon them; without being in capacity to act otherwise than they do. It is, therefore, for want of being acquainted with these things, that he looks upon the great Author of nature, the great *Cause of causes*, as the immediate cause of those evils to which he is submitted; that he judges erroneously when he imagines that the Divinity is exasperated against him.

The fact is, man believes that his welfare is a debt due to him from nature; that when he suffers evil she does him an injustice; fully persuaded that this nature was made solely for himself, he cannot conceive she would make him, who is her lord paramount, suffer, if she was not moved thereto by a power who is inimical to his happiness; who has reasons with which he is unacquainted for afflicting, who has motives which he wishes to discover, for punishing him. From hence it will be obvious, that evil, much more than good, is the true motive of those researches which man has made concerning the Divinity—of those ideas which he has formed to himself—of the conduct he has held towards him. The admiration of the works of nature, or the acknowledgement of its goodness, seem never alone to have determined the human species to recur painfully by thought to the source of these things; familiarized at once with all those effects which are favourable to his existence, he does not by any means give himself the same trouble to seek the causes, that he does to discover those which disquiet him, or by which he is afflicted. Thus, in reflecting upon the Divinity, it was generally upon the cause of his evils that man meditated; his meditations were fruitless, because the evil he experiences, as well as the good he partakes, are equally necessary effects of natural causes, to which his mind ought rather to have bent its force, than to have invented fictitious causes of which he never could form to himself any but false ideas; seeing that he always borrowed them, from his own peculiar mariner of existing, acting, and feeling. Obstinately refusing to see any thing, but himself, he never became acquainted with that universal nature of which he constitutes such a very feeble part.

The slightest reflection, however, would have been sufficient to undeceive him on these erroneous ideas. Everything tends to prove that good and evil are modes of existence that depend upon causes by which a man is moved; that a sensible being is obliged to experience them. In a nature composed of a multitude of beings infinitely varied, the shock occasioned by the collision of discordant matter must necessarily disturb the order, derange the mode of existence of those beings who have no analogy with them: these act in every thing they do after certain laws, which are in themselves immutable; the good or evil, therefore, which man experiences, are necessary consequences of the qualities inherent to the beings, within whose sphere of action he is found. Our birth, which we call a benefit, is an effect as necessary as our death, which we contemplate as an injustice of fate: it is of the nature of all analogous beings to unite themselves to form a whole: it is of the nature of all compound beings to be destroyed, or to dissolve themselves; some maintain their union for a longer period than others; some disperse very quickly, as the ephemeron; some endure for ages, as the planets; every being in dissolving itself gives birth to new beings; these are destroyed in their turn; to execute the eternal, the immutable laws of a nature that only exists by the continual changes that all its parts undergo. Thus nature cannot be accused of malice, since every thing that takes place in it is necessary—is produced by an invariable system, to which every other being, as well as herself, is eternally subjected. The same igneous matter that in man is the principle of life, frequently becomes the principle of his destruction, either by the conflagration of a city, the explosion of a volcano, or his mad passion for war. The aqueous fluid that circulates through his machine, so essentially necessary to his actual existence, frequently becomes too abundant, and terminates him by suffocation; is the cause of those inundations which sometimes swallow up both the earth and its inhabitants. The air, without which he is not able to respire, is the cause of those hurricanes, of those tempests, which frequently render useless the labour of mortals. These elements are obliged to burst their bonds, when they are combined in a certain manner; their necessary but fatal consequences are those ravages, those contagions, those famines, those diseases, those various scourges, against which man, with streaming eyes and violent emotions, vainly implores the aid of those powers who are deaf to his cries: his prayers are never granted; but the same necessity which afflicted him, the same immutable laws which overwhelmed him with trouble, replaces things in the order he finds suitable to his species: a relative order of things which was, is, and always will be the only standard of his judgment.

 Man, however, made no such simple reflections: he either did not or would not perceive that every thing in nature acted by invariable laws; he continued stedfast in contemplating the good of which he was partaker, as a favor; in considering the evil he experienced, as a sign of anger in this nature, which he supposed to be animated by the same passions as himself or at least that it was governed by secret agents, who acted after his own manner, who obliged it to execute their will, that was sometimes favourable, sometimes inimical to the human species. It was to these supposed agents, with whom in the sunshine of his prosperity he was but little occupied, that in the bosom of his calamity he addressed his prayers; he thanked them, however, for their favours, fearing lest their ingratitude might farther provoke their fury: thus when assailed by disaster, when afflicted with disease, he invoked them with fervor: he required them to change in his favor the mode of acting which was the very essence of beings; he was willing that to make the slightest evil he experienced cease, that the eternal chain of things might be broken; and the unerring, undeviating course of nature might be arrested.

It was upon such ridiculous pretensions, that were founded those supplications, those fervent prayers, which mortals, almost always discontented with their fate, never in accord in their respective desires, addressed to their gods. They were unceasingly upon their knees before the altars, were ever prostrate before the power of the beings, whom they judged had the right of commanding nature; who they supposed to have sufficient energy to divert her course; who they considered to possess the means to make her subservient to their particular views; thus each hoped by presents, by humiliation, to induce them to oblige this nature, to satisfy the discordant desires of their race. The sick man, expiring in his bed, asks that the humours accumulated in his body should in an instant lose those properties which renders them injurious to his existence; that by an act of their puissance, his gods should renew or recreate the springs of a machine worn out by infirmities. The cultivator of a low swampy country, makes complaint of the abundance of rain with which his fields are inundated; whilst the inhabitant of the hill, raises his thanks for the favors he receives, solicits a continuance of that which causes the despair of his neighbour. In this, each is willing to have a god for himself, and asks according to his momentary caprices, to his fluctuating wants, that the invariable essence of things, should be continually changed in his favour.

From this it must be obvious, that man every moment asks a *miracle* to be wrought in his support. It is not, therefore, at all surprising that he displayed such ready credulity, that he adopted with such facility the relation of the marvellous deeds which were universally announced to him as the acts of the power, or the effects of the benevolence, of the various gods which presided over the nations of the earth: these wonderful tales, which were offered to his acceptance, as the most indubitable proofs of the empire of these gods over nature, which man always found deaf to his entreaties, were readily accredited by him; in the expectation, that if he could gain them over to his interest, this nature, which he found so sullen, so little disposed to lend herself to his views, would then be controuled in his own favor.

By a necessary consequence of these ideas, nature was despoiled of all power; she was contemplated only as a passive instrument, who acted at the will, under the influence of the numerous, all-powerful agents to whom the various superstitions had rendered her subordinate. It was thus for want of contemplating nature under her true point of view, that man has mistaken her entirely, that he believed her incapable of producing any thing by herself; that he ascribed the honor of all those productions, whether advantageous or disadvantageous to the human species, to fictitious powers, whom he always clothed with his own peculiar dispositions, only he aggrandized their force. In short, it was upon the ruins of nature, that man erected the imaginary colossus of superstition, that he reared the *altars of a Jupiter, the temples of an Apollo.*

If the ignorance of nature gave birth to such a variety of gods, the knowledge of this nature is calculated to destroy them. As soon as man becomes enlightened, his powers augment, his resources increase in a ratio with his knowledge; the sciences, the protecting arts, industrious application, furnish him assistance; experience encourages his progress, truth procures for him the means of resisting the efforts of many causes, which cease to alarm him as soon as he obtains a correct knowledge of them. In a word, his terrors dissipate in proportion as his mind becomes enlightened, because his trepidation is ever commensurate with his ignorance, and furnishes this great lesson, that *man, instructed by truth, ceases to be superstitious.*

CHAP. II.
Of Mythology, and Theology.

The elements of nature were, as we have shewn, the first divinities of man; he has generally commenced with adoring material beings; each individual, as we have already said, as may be still seen in savage nations, made to himself a particular god, of some physical object, which he supposed to be the cause of those events, in which he was himself interested; he never wandered to seek out of visible nature, the source either of what happened to himself, or of those phenomena to which he was a witness. As he every where saw only material effects, he attributed them to causes of the same genus; incapable in his infancy of those profound reveries, of those subtle speculations, which are the fruit of time, the result of leisure, he did not imagine any cause distinguished from the objects that met his sight, nor of any essence totally different from every thing he beheld.

The observation of nature was the first study of those who had leisure to meditate: they could not avoid being struck with the phenomena of the visible world. The rising and setting of the sun, the periodical return of the seasons, the variations of the atmosphere, the fertility and sterility of the earth, the advantages of irrigation, the damage caused by floods, the useful effects of fire, the terrible consequences of conflagration, were proper and suitable objects to occupy their thoughts. It was natural for them to believe that those beings they saw move of themselves, acted by their own peculiar energies; according as their influence over the inhabitants of the earth was either favorable or otherwise, they concluded them to have either the power to injure them, or the disposition to confer benefits. Those who first acquired the knowledge of gaining an ascendancy over man, then savage, wandering, unpolished, or dispersed in woods, with but little attachment to the soil, of which he had not yet learned to reap the advantage, were always more practised observers—individuals more instructed in the ways of nature, than the people, or rather the scattered hordes, whom they found ignorant and destitute of experience: their superior knowledge placed them in a capacity to render these services—to discover to them useful inventions, which attracted the confidence of the unhappy beings to whom they came to offer an assisting hand; savages who were naked, half famished, exposed to the injuries of the weather, obnoxious to the attacks of ferocious beasts, dispersed in caverns, scattered in forests, occupied with hunting, painfully labouring to procure themselves a very precarious subsistence, had not sufficient leisure to make discoveries calculated to facilitate their labour, or to render it less incessant. These discoveries are generally the fruit of society: isolated beings, detached families, hardly ever make any discoveries—scarcely ever think of making any. The savage is a being who lives in a perpetual state of infancy, who never reaches maturity unless some one comes to draw him out of his misery. At first repulsive, unsociable, intractable, he by degrees familiarizes himself with those who render him service; once gained by their kindness, he readily lends them his confidence; in the end he goes the length of sacrificing to them his liberty.

It was commonly from the bosom of civilized nations that have issued those personages who have carried sociability, agriculture, art, laws, gods, superstition, forms of worship, to those families or hordes as yet scattered; who united them either to the body of some other nations, or formed them into new nations, of which they themselves became the leaders, sometimes the king, frequently the high priest, and often their god. These softened their manners—gathered them together—taught them to reap the advantages of their own powers—to render each other reciprocal assistance—to satisfy their wants with greater facility. In thus rendering their existence more comfortable, thus augmenting their happiness, they attracted their love; obtained their veneration, acquired the right of prescribing opinions to them, made them adopt such as they had either invented themselves, or else drawn up in the civilized countries from whence they came. History points out to us the most famous legislators as men, who, enriched with useful knowledge they had gleaned in the bosom of polished nations, carried to savages without industry, needing assistance, those arts, of which, until then, these rude people were ignorant: such were the Bacchus's, the Orpheus's, the Triptolemus's, the Numa's, the Zamolixis's; in short, all those who first gave to nations their gods—their worship—the rudiments of agriculture, of science, of superstition, of jurisprudence, of religion, &c.

It will perhaps be enquired, If those nations which at the present day we see assembled, were all originally dispersed? We reply, that this dispersion may have been produced at various times, by those terrible revolutions, of which it has before been remarked our globe has more than once been the theatre; in times so remote, that history has not been able to transmit us the detail. Perhaps the approach of more than one comet may have produced on our earth several universal ravages, which have at each time annihilated the greater portion of the human species.

These hypotheses will unquestionably appear bold to those who have not sufficiently meditated on nature, but to the philosophic enquirer they are by no means inconsistent. There may not only have been one general deluge, but even a great number since the existence of our planet; this globe itself may have been a new production in nature; it may not always have occupied the place it does at present. Whatever idea may be adopted on this subject, if it is very certain that, independent of those exterior causes, which are competent to totally change its face, as the impulse of a comet may do, this globe contains within itself, a cause adequate to alter it entirely, since, besides the diurnal and sensible motion of the earth, it has one extremely slow, almost imperceptible, by which every thing must eventually be changed in it: this is the motion from whence depends the *precession* of the *equinoctial points*, observed by *Hipparchus* and other mathematicians, now well understood by astronomers; by this motion, the earth must at the end of several thousand years change totally: this motion will at length cause the ocean to occupy that space which at present forms the lands or continents. From this it will be obvious that our globe, as well as all the beings in nature, has a continual disposition to change. This motion was known to the ancients, and was what gave rise to what they called their great year, which the Egyptians fixed at thirty-six thousand five hundred and twenty-five years: the Sabines at thirty-six thousand four hundred and twenty-five, whilst others have extended it to one hundred thousand, some even to seven hundred and fifty-three thousand years. Again, to those general revolutions which our planet has at different times experienced, way he added those that have been partial, such as inundations of the sea, earthquakes, subterraneous conflagrations, which have sometimes had the effect of dispersing particular nations, and to make them forget all those sciences with which they were, before acquainted. It is also probable that the first volcanic fires, having had no previous vent, were more central, and greater in quantity, before they burst the crust of earth; as the sea washed the whole, it must have rapidly sunk down into every opening, where, falling on the boiling lava, it was instantly expanded into steam, producing irresistible explosion: whence it is reasonable to conclude, that the primaeval earthquakes wore more widely extended, and of much greater force, than those which occur in our days. Other vapours may be produced by intense heat, possessing a much greater elasticity, from substances that evaporate, such as mercury, diamonds, &c.; the expansive force of these vapours would be much greater than the steam of water, even at red hot heat consequently they, way have had sufficient energy to raise islands, continents, or even to have detached the moon from the earth; if the moon, as has been supposed by some philosophers, was thrown out of the great cavity which now contains the South Sea; the immense quantity of water flowing in from the, original ocean, and which then covered the earth, would much contribute to leave the continents and islands, which might be raised at the same time, above the surface of the water. In later days we have accounts of huge stones falling, from the firmament, which may have been thrown by explosion from some distant earthquake, without having been impelled with a force sufficient to cause them to circulate round the earth, and thus produce numerous small moons or satellites.

Those who were able to escape from the ruin of the world, filled with consternation, plunged in misery, were but little conditioned to preserve to their posterity a knowledge, effaced by those misfortunes, of which they had been both the victims and the witnesses: overwhelmed with dismay, trembling with fear, they were not able to hand down the history of their frightful adventures, except by obscure traditions; much less to transmit to us the opinions, the systems, the arts, the sciences, anterior to these petrifying revolutions of our sphere. There have been perhaps men upon the earth from all eternity; but at different periods they may have been nearly annihilated, together with their monuments, their sciences, and their arts; those who outlived these periodical revolutions, each time formed a new race of men, who by dint of time, labour, and experience, have by degrees withdrawn from oblivion the inventions of the primitive races. It is, perhaps, to these periodical revolutions of the human species, that is to be ascribed the profound ignorance in which we see man yet plunged, upon those objects that are the most interesting to him. This is, perhaps, the true source of the imperfection of his knowledge—of the vices of his political institutions—of the defect in his religion—of the growth of superstition, over which terror has always presided; here, in all probability, is the cause of that puerile inexperience, of those jejune prejudices, which almost every where keep man in a state of infancy, and which render him so little capable of either listening to reason or of consulting truth. To judge by the slowness of his progress, by the feebleness of his advance, in a number of respects, we should be inclined to say, the human race has either just quitted its cradle, or that he was never destined to attain the age of virility—to corroborate his reason.

However it may be with these conjectures, whether the human race may always have existed upon the earth, whether it may have been a recent production of nature, whether the larger animals we now behold were originally derived from the smallest microscopic ones, who have increased in bulk with the progression of time, or whether, as the Egyptian philosophers thought, mankind were originally hermaphrodites, who like the *aphis* produced the sexual distinction after some generations, which was also the opinion of Plato, and seems to have been that of Moses, who was educated amongst these Egyptians, as may be gathered from the 27th and 28th verses of the first chapter of GENESIS: "So God created man in his own image, in the image of God created be him; male and female created he them—And GOD blessed them, and GOD said unto them, be fruitful, and multiply, and replenish the earth, and subdue it: and have dominion over the fish of the sea, and over the fowl of the air, and over every living thing that moveth upon the earth:" it is not therefore presuming too much to suppose, as the Egyptians were a nation very fond of explaining their opinions by hieroglyphics, that that part which describes Eve as taken out of Adam's rib, was an hieroglyphic emblem: showing that mankind was in the primitive state of both sexes, united, who was afterwards divided into males and females. However, I say, this may be, it is extremely easy to recur to the origin of many existing nations: we shall find them always in the savage state; that is, to say, dispersed; composed of families detached from each other; of wandering, hordes; these were collected together, approximated at the voice of some missionary or legislator, from whom they received great benefits, who gave them gods, opinions, and laws. These personages, of whom the people newly congregated readily acknowledged the superiority, fixed the national gods, leaving to each individual, those which he had formed to himself, according to his own peculiar ideas, or else substituting others brought from those regions, from whence they themselves had emigrated.

The better to imprint their lessons on the minds of their new subjects, these men became the guides, the priests, the sovereigns, the masters of these infant societies; they formed discourses by which they spoke to the imagination of their willing auditors. POETRY seem best adapted to strike the mind of these rude people, to engrave on their memory those ideas with which they were willing to imbue them: its images, its fictions, its numbers, its rhyme its harmony, all conspired to please their fancy, to render permanent the, impressions it made: thus, the entire of nature, as well as all its parts, was personified, by its beautiful allegories: at its soothing voice, trees, stones, rocks, earth, air, fire, water, by imagination took intelligence, held conversation with man, and with themselves; the elements were deified by its songs, every thing was figuratively detailed in harmonious lays. The sky, which according to the then philosophy, was an arched concave, spreading over the earth, which was supposed to be a level plain; (for the doctrine of *antipodes* is of rather modern date) was itself made a god; was considered a more suitable residence, as making a greater distinction for these imaginary deities than the earth on which man himself resided. Thus the firmament was filled with deities.

Time, under the name of Saturn, was pictured as the son of heaven; or Coelus by earth, called Terra, or Thea; he was represented as an inexorable divinity—naturally artful, who devoured his own children— who revenged the anger of his mother upon his father; for which purpose she armed him with a scythe, formed of metals drawn from her own bowels, with which he struck Coelus, in the act of uniting himself to Thea, and so mutilated him, that he was ever after incapacitated to increase the number of his children: he was said to have divided the throne with Janus king of Italy, his reign seems to have been so mild, so beneficent, that it was called the *golden age*; human victims were sacrificed on his altars, until abolished by Hercules, who substituted small images of clay. Festivals in honor of this god, called Saturnalia, were instituted long antecedent to the foundation of Rome they were celebrated about the middle of December, either on the 16th, 17th, or 18th; they lasted in latter times several days, originally but one. Universal liberty prevailed at the celebration, slaves were permitted to ridicule their masters—to speak freely on every subject—no criminals were executed—war never declared; the priests made their human offerings with their heads uncovered; a circumstance peculiar to the Saturnalia, not adopted at other festivals.

The igneous matter, the etherial electric fluid, that invisible fire which vivifies nature, that penetrates all beings, that fertilizes the earth, which is the great principle of motion, the source of heat, was deified under the name of Jupiter: his combination with every being in nature was expressed by his metamorphoses—by the frequent adulteries imputed to him. He was armed with thunder, to indicate he produced meteors, to typify the electric fluid that is called lightning. He married the winds, which were designated under the name of Juno, therefore called the Goddess of the Winds, their nuptials were celebrated with great solemnity; all the gods, the entire brute creation, the whole of mankind attended, except one young woman named Chelone, who laughed at the ceremonies, for which impiety she was changed by Mercury into a tortoise, and condemned to perpetual silence. He was the most powerful of all the gods, and considered as the king and father both of gods and men: his worship was very extended, performed with greater solemnity, than that of any other god. Upon his altars smoked goats, sheep, and white bulls, in which he is said to have particularly delighted; the oak was rendered sacred to him, because he taught mankind to live upon acorns; he had many oracles where his precepts were delivered, the most celebrated of these were at Dodona and Ammon in Lybia; he was supposed to be invisible to the inhabitants of the earth; the Lacedemonians erected his statue with four heads, thereby indicating, that he listened readily to the solicitations of every quarter of the earth. Minerva is represented as having no mother, but to have come completely armed from his brains, when his head was opened by Vulcan; by which it is meant to infer that wisdom is the result of this ethereal fluid. Thus, following the same fictions, the sun, that beneficent star which has such a marked influence over the earth, became an Osiris, a Belus, a Mithras, an Adonis, an Apollo. Nature, rendered sorrowful by his periodical absence, was an Isis, an Astarte, a Venus, a Cybele. Astarte had a magnificent temple at Hieropolis served by three hundred priests, who were always employed in offering sacrifices. The priests of Cybele, called Corybantes, also Galli, were not admitted to their sacred functions without previous mutilation. In the celebration of their festivals these priests used all kinds of indecent expressions, beat drums, cymbals, and behaved just like madmen: his worship extended all over Phrygia, and was established in Greece under the name of *Eleusinian mysteries*. In short, every thing was personified: the sea was under the empire of Neptune; fire was adored by the Egyptians under the name of Serapis; by the Persians, under that of Ormus or Oromaze; and by the Romans, under that of Vesta and Vulcan.

Such was the origin of mythology: it may be said to be the daughter of natural philosophy, embellished by poetry; only destined to describe nature and its parts. If antiquity is consulted, it will be perceived without much trouble, that these famous sages, those legislators, those priests, those conquerors, who were the instructors of infant nations, themselves adored active nature, or the great whole considered relatively to its different operations or qualities; that this was what they caused the ignorant savages whom they had gathered together to adore. It was the great whole they deified; it was its various parts which they made their inferior gods; it was from the necessity of her laws they made fate. The Greeks called it Nature, a divinity who had a thousand names. Varro says, "I believe that God is the soul of the universe, and that the universe is God." Cicero says "that in the mysteries of Samothracia, of Lemnos, of Eleusis, it was nature much more than the gods, they explained to the initiated." Pliny says, "we must believe that the world, or that which is contained under the vast extent of the heavens, is the Divinity; even eternal, infinite, without beginning or end." It was these different modes of considering nature that gave birth to Polytheism, to idolatry. Allegory masqued its mode of action: it was at length parts of this great whole, that idolatry represented by statues and symbols.

To complete the proofs of what has been said; to shew distinctly that it was the great whole, the universe, the nature of things, which was the real object of the worship of Pagan antiquity, hardly any thing can be more decisive than the beginning of the hymn of Orpheus addressed to the god Pan.

"O Pan! I invoke thee, O powerful god! O universal nature! the heavens, the sea, the earth, who nourish all, and the eternal fire, because these are thy members, O all powerful Pan," &c. Nothing can be more suitable to confirm these ideas, than the ingenious explanation which is given of the fable of Pan, as well as of the figure under which he is represented. It is said, "Pan, according to the signification of his name, is the emblem by which the ancients have designated the great assemblage of things or beings: he represents the universe; and, in the mind of the wisest philosophers of antiquity, he passed for the greatest and most ancient of the gods. The features under which he is delineated form the portrait of nature, and of the savage state in which she was found in the beginning. The spotted skin of the leopard, which serves him for a mantle, imagined the heavens filled with stars and constellations. His person was compounded of parts, some of which were suitable to a reasonable animal, that is to say, to man; and others to the animal destitute of reason, such as the goat. It is thus," says he, "that the universe is composed of an intelligence that governs the whole, and of the prolific, fruitful elements of fire, water, earth, air. Pan, loved to drink and to follow the nymphs; this announces the occasion nature has for humidity in all her productions, and that this god, like nature, is strongly inclined to propagation. According to the Egyptians, and the most ancient Grecian philosophers, Pan had neither father nor mother; he came out of Demogorgon at the same moment with the Destinies, his fatal sisters; a fine method of expressing that the universe was the work of an unknown power, and that it was formed after the invariable relations, the eternal laws of necessity; but his most significant symbol, that most suitable to express the harmony of the universe, is his mysterious pipe, composed of seven unequal tubes, but calculated to produce the nicest, the most perfect concord. The orbs which compose the seven planets of our solar system, are of different diameters; being bodies of unequal mass, they describe their revolutions round the sun in various periods; nevertheless it is from the order of their motion that results the harmony of the spheres," &c.

Here then is the great macrocosm, the mighty whole, the assemblage of things adored and deified by the philosophers of antiquity; whilst the uninformed stopped at the emblem under which this nature was depicted; at the symbols under which its various parts, its numerous functions were personified; his narrow mind, his barbarous ignorance, never permitted him to mount higher; they alone were deemed worthy of being, initiated into the mysteries, who knew the realities masqued under these emblems. Indeed, it is not to be doubted for an instant, that the wisest among the Pagans adored nature; which ethnic theology designated under a great variety of nomenclature, under an immense number of different emblems. Apuleius, although a decided Platonist, accustomed to the mysterious, unintelligible notions of his master, calls "Nature the parent of all; the mother of the elements, the first offspring of the world;" again, "the mother of the stars, the parent of the seasons, and the governess of the whole world."—She was worshipped by many under the appellation of the *mother of the gods*. Indeed, the first institutors of nations, and their immediate successors in authority, only spoke to the people by fables, allegories, enigmas, of which they reserved to themselves the right of giving an explanation: this, in fact, constituted the mysteries of the various worship paid to the Pagan divinities. This mysterious tone they considered necessary, whether it was to mask their own ignorance, or whether it was to preserve their power over the uninformed, who for the most part only respect that which is above their comprehension. Their explications were generally dictated either by interest, or by a delirious imagination, frequently by imposture; thus from age to age, they did no more than render nature and its parts, which they bad originally depicted, more unknown, until they completely lost sight of the primitive ideas; these were replaced by a multitude of fictitious personages, under whose features this nature had primarily been represented to them. The people, either unaccustomed to think, or deeply steeped in ignorance, adored these personages, without penetrating into the true sense of the emblematical fables recounted to them. These ideal beings, with material figures, in whom they believed there resided a mysterious virtue, a divine power, were the objects of their worship, the source of their fears, the fountain of their hopes. The wonderful, the incredible actions ascribed to these fancied divinities, were an inexhaustible fund of admiration, which gave perpetual play to the fancy; which delighted not only the people of those days, but even the children of latter ages. Thus were transmitted from age to age, those marvellous accounts, which, although necessary to the existence of the power usurped by the ministers of these gods, did, in fact, nothing more than confirm the blindness of the ignorant: these never supposed that it was nature, its various operations, its numerous component parts—that it was the passions of man and his diverse faculties that lay buried under an heap of allegories; they did not perceive that the passions and faculties of human nature were used as emblems, because man was ignorant of the true cause of the phenomena he beheld. As strong passions seemed to hurry man along, in despite of himself, they either attributed these passions to a god, or deified them; frequently they did both: it was thus love became a deity; that eloquence, poetry, industry, were transformed into gods, under the names of Hermes, Mercury, Apollo; the stings of conscience were called the Furies: the people, bowed down in stupid ignorance, had no eyes but for these emblematical persons, under which nature was masked: they attributed to their influence the good, to their displeasure the evil, which they experienced: they entered into every kind of folly, into the most delirious acts of madness, to render them propitious to their views; thus, for want of being acquainted with the reality of things, their worship frequently degenerated into the most cruel extravagance, into the most ridiculous folly.

Thus it is obvious, that every thing proves nature and its various parts to have every where been the first divinities of man. Natural philosophers studied these deities, either superficially or profoundly, —explained some of their properties, detailed some of their modes of action. Poets painted them to the imagination of mortals, either in the most fascinating colours, or under the most hideous deformities; embodied them—furnished them with reasoning faculties—recounted their exploits—recorded their will. The statuary executed sometimes with the most enrapturing art, the ideas of the poets,—gave substance to their shadows—form to their airy nothings. The priest decorated these united works with a thousand marvellous qualities—with the most terrible passions—with the most inconceivable attributes; gave them, "a local habitation and a name." The people adored them; prostrated themselves before these gods, who were neither susceptible of love or hatred, goodness, or malice; they became persecuting, malevolent, cruel, unjust, in order to render themselves acceptable to powers generally described to them under the most odious features.

By dint of reasoning upon these emblems, by meditating upon nature, thus decorated, or rather disfigured, subsequent speculators no longer recollected the source from whence their predecessors had drawn their gods, nor the fantastic ornaments with which they had embellished them. Natural philosophers and poets were transformed by leisure into metaphysicians and theologians; tired with contemplating what they could have understood, they believed they had made an important discovery by subtilly distinguishing nature from herself—from her own peculiar energies—from her faculty of action. By degrees they made an incomprehensible being of this energy, which as before they personified, this they called the mover of nature, divided it into two, one congenial to man's happiness, the other inimical to his welfare; these they deified in the same manner as they had before done nature with her various parts. These abstract, metaphysical beings, became the sole object of their thoughts; were the subject of their continual contemplation; they looked upon them as realities of the highest importance: thus nature quite disappeared; she was despoiled of her rights; she was considered as nothing more than an unwieldy mass, destitute of power; devoid of energy, as an heap of ignoble matter purely passive: who, incapable of acting by herself, was not competent to any of the operations they beheld, without the direct, the immediate agency of the moving powers they had associated with her: which they had made the fulcrum necessary to the action of the lever. They either did not or would not perceive, that the *great Cause of causes, ens entium, Parent of parents*, had, in unravelling chaotic matter, with a wisdom for which man can never be sufficiently grateful, with a sagacity which he can never sufficiently admire, foreseen every thing that could contribute not only to his own individual happiness, but also to that of all the beings in nature; that he had given this nature immutable laws, according to which she is for ever regulated; after which she is obliged invariably to act; that he has described for her an eternal course, from which it is not permitted her to deviate, even for an instant; that she is therefore, rendered competent to the production of every phenomena, not only that he beholds, but of an infinity that he has never yet contemplated; that she needs not any exterior energy for this purpose, having received her powers from a hand far superior to any the feeble weak imagination of man is able to form; that when this nature appears to afflict him, it is only from the contraction of his own views, from the narrowness of his own ideas, that he judges; that, in fact, what he considers the evils of nature, are the greatest possible benefits he can receive, if he was but in a condition to be acquainted with previous causes, with subsequent effects. That the evils resulting to him from his own vices, have equally their remedies in this nature, which it is his duty to study; which if he does he will find, that the same omnipotent goodness, who gave her irrefragable laws, also planted in her bosom, balsams for all his maladies, whether physical or moral: but that it is not given him to know what this great, this universal cause is, for purposes of which he ought not to dispute the wisdom, when he contemplates the mighty wonders that surround him.

Thus man ever preferred an unknown power, to that of which he was enabled to have some knowledge, if he had only deigned to consult his experience; but he presently ceases to respect that which he understands; to estimate those objects which are familiar to him: he figures to himself something marvellous in every thing he does not comprehend; his mind, above all, labours to seize upon that which appears to escape his consideration; in default of experience, he no longer consults any thing, but his imagination, which feeds him with chimeras. In consequence, those speculators who have subtilly distinguished nature from her own powers, have successively laboured to clothe the powers thus separated with, a thousand incomprehensible qualities: as they did not see this power, which is only a mode, they made it a spirit—an intelligence—an incorporeal being; that is to say, of a substance totally different from every thing of which we have a knowledge. They never perceived that all their inventions, that all the words which they imagined, only served to mask their real ignorance; that all their pretended science was limited to saying, in what manner nature acted, by a thousand subterfuges which they themselves found it impossible to comprehend. Man always deceives himself for want of studying nature; he leads himself astray, every time he is disposed to go out of it; he is always quickly necessitated to return; he is even in error when he substitutes words which he does not himself understand, for things which he would much better comprehend if he was willing to look at them without prejudice.

Can a theologian ingenuously believe himself more enlightened, for having substituted the vague words spirit, incorporeal substance, &c. to the more intelligible terms nature, matter, mobility, necessity? However this may be, these obscure words once imagined, it was necessary to attach ideas to them; in doing this, he has not been able to draw them from any other source than the beings of this despised nature, which are ever the only beings of which he is enabled to have any knowledge. Man, consequently, drew them up in himself; his own soul served for the model of the universal soul, of which indeed according to some it only formed a portion; his own mind was the standard of the mind that regulated nature; his own passions, his own desires, were the prototypes of those by which he actuated this being; his own intelligence was that from which he formed that of the mover of nature; that which was suitable to himself, he called the order of nature; this pretended order was the scale by which he measured the wisdom of this being; in short, those qualities which he calls perfections in himself, were the archetypes in miniature, of the perfections of the being, he thus gratuitously supposed to be the agent, who operated the phenomena of nature. It was thus, that in despite of all their efforts, the theologians were, perhaps always will be, true Anthropomorphites. A sect of this denomination appeared in 359, in Egypt, they held the doctrine that their god had a bodily shape. Indeed it is very difficult, if not impossible to prevent man from making himself the sole model of his divinity. Montaigne says "man is not able to be other than he is, nor imagine but after his capacity; let him take what pains he may, he will never have a knowledge of any soul but his own." Xenophanes said, "if the ox or the elephant understood either sculpture or painting, they would not fail to represent the divinity under their own peculiar figure that in this, they would have as much reason as Polyclitus or Phidias, who gave him the human form." It was said to a very celebrated man that "God made man after his own image;" "man has returned the compliment," replied the philosopher. Indeed, man generally sees in his God, nothing but a man. Let him subtilize as he will, let him extend his own powers as he may, let him swell his own perfections to the utmost, he will have done nothing more than make a gigantic, exaggerated man, whom he will render illusory by dint of heaping together incompatible qualities. He will never see in such a god, but a being of the human species, in whom he will strive to aggrandize the proportions, until he has formed a being totally inconceivable. It is according to these dispositions that he attributes intelligence, wisdom, goodness, justice, science, power, to his divinity, because he is himself intelligent; because he has the idea of wisdom in some beings of his own species; because he loves to find in them ideas favourable to himself: because he esteems those who display equity; because he has a knowledge, which he holds more extensive in some individuals than himself; in short, because he enjoys certain faculties which depend on his own organization. He presently extends or exaggerates all these qualities in forming his god; the sight of the phenomena of nature, which he feels he is himself incapable of either producing or imitating, obliges him to make this difference between the being he pourtrays and himself; but he knows not at what point to stop; he fears lest he should deceive himself, if he should see any limits to the qualities he assigns, the word infinite, therefore, is the abstract, the vague term which he uses to characterize them. He says that his power is infinite, which signifies that when he beholds those stupendous effects which nature produces, he has no conception at what point his power can rest; that his goodness, his wisdom, his knowledge are infinite: this announces that he is ignorant how far these perfections ma be carried in a being whose power so much surpasses his own; that he is of infinite duration, because he is not capable of conceiving he could have had a beginning or can ever cease to be; because of this he considers a defect in those transitory beings of whom he beholds the dissolution, whom he sees are subjected to death. He presumes the cause of those effects to which he is a witness, of those striking phenomena that assail his sight, is immutable, permanent, not subjected to change, like all the evanescent beings whom he knows are submitted to dissolution, to destruction, to change of form. This mover of nature being always invisible to man, his mode of action being, impenetrable, he believes that, like his soul or the concealed principle which animates his own body, which he calls spiritual, a spirit, is the moving power of the universe; in consequence he makes a spirit the soul, the life, the principle of motion in nature. Thus when by dint of subtilizing, he has arrived at believing the principle by which his body is moved is a spiritual, immaterial substance, he makes the spirit of the universe immaterial in like manner: he makes it immense, although without extent; immoveable, although capable of moving nature: immutable, although he supposes him to be the author of all the changes, operated in the universe.

The idea of the unity of God, which cost Socrates his life, because the Athenians considered those Atheists who believed but in one, was the tardy fruit of human meditation. Plato himself did not dare to break entirely the doctrine of *Polytheism*; he preserved Venus, an all- powerful Jupiter, and a Pallas, who was the goddess of the country. The sight of those opposite, frequently contradictory effects, which man saw take place in the world, had a tendency to persuade him there must be a number of distinct powers or causes independent of each other. He was unable to conceive that the various phenomena he beheld, sprung from a single, from an unique cause; he therefore admitted many causes or gods, acting upon different principles; some of which he considered friendly, others as inimical to his race. Such is the origin of that doctrine, so ancient, so universal, which supposed two principles in nature, or two powers of opposite interests, who were perpetually at war with each other; by the assistance of which he explained, that constant mixture of good and evil, that blending of prosperity with misfortune, in a word, those eternal vicissitudes to which in this world the human being, is subjected. This is the source of those combats which all antiquity has supposed to exist between good and wicked gods, between an Osiris and a Typhoeus; between an

Orosmadis and an Arimanis; between a Jupiter and the Titanes; in these rencounters man for his own peculiar interest always gave the palm of victory to the beneficent deity; this, according to all the traditions handed down, ever remained in possession of the field of battle; it was so far right, as it is evidently for the benefit of mankind that the good should prevail over the wicked.

When, however, man acknowledged only one God, he generally supposed the different departments of nature were confided to powers subordinate to his supreme orders, under whom the sovereign of the gods discharged his care in the administration of the world. These subaltern gods were prodigiously multiplied; each man, each town, each country, had their local, their tutelary gods; every event, whether fortunate or unfortunate, had a divine cause; was the consequence of a sovereign decree; each natural effect, every operation of nature, each passion, depended upon a divinity, which a theological imagination, disposed to see gods every where, mistaking nature, either embellished or disfigured. Poetry tuned its harmonious lays, on these occasions, exaggerated the details, animated its pictures; credulous ignorance received the portraits with eagerness—heard the doctrines with submission.

Such is the origin of Polytheism: indeed the Greek word *Theos*, [Greek letters], is derived from *Theaomai*, [Greek letters], which implies to contemplate, or take a view of secret or hidden things. Such are the foundations, such the titles of the hierarchy, which man established between himself and his gods, because he generally believed he was incapable of the exalted privilege of immediately addressing himself to the incomprehensible Being whom he had acknowledged for the only sovereign of nature, without even having any distinct idea on the subject: such is the true genealogy of those inferior gods whom the uninformed place as, a proportional means between themselves and the first of all other causes. In consequence, among the Greeks and the Romans, we see the deities divided into two classes, the one were called great gods, because the whole world were nearly in accord in deifying the most striking parts of nature, such as the sun, fire; the sea, time, &c. these formed a kind of aristocratic order, who were distinguished from the minor gods, or from the multitude of ethnic divinities, who were entirely local; that is to say, were reverenced only in particular countries, or by individuals; as in Rome, where every citizen had his familiar spirit, called lares; and household god, called penates. Nevertheless, the first rank of these Pagan divinities, like the latter, were submitted to Fate, that is, to destiny, which obviously is nothing more than nature acting by immutable, rigorous, necessary laws; this destiny was looked upon as the god of gods; it is evident, that this was nothing more than necessity personified; that therefore it was a weakness in the heathens to fatigue with their sacrifices, to solicit with their prayers, those divinities whom they themselves believed were submitted to the decrees of an inexorable destiny, of which it was never possible for them to alter the mandates. *But man*, generally, *ceases to reason, whenever his theological notions are either brought into question, or are the subject of his inquiry.*

What has been already said, serves to show the common source of that multitude of intermediate powers, subordinate to the gods, but superior to man, with which he filled the universe: they were venerated under the names of nymphs, demi-gods, angels, daemons, good and evil genii, spirits, heroes, saints, &c. Among the Romans they were called *Dei medioxumi,* intermediate angels; they were looked upon as intercessors, as mediators, as powers whom it was necessary to reverence, in order either to obtain their favour, appease their anger, or divert their malignant intentions; these constitute different classes of intermediate divinities, who became either the foundation of their hopes, the object of their fears, the means of consolation, or the source of dread to those very mortals who only invented them when they found it impossible to form to themselves distinct, perspicuous ideas of the incomprehensible Being who governed the world in chief; or when they despaired of being able to hold communication with him directly.

Meditation and reflection diminished the number of those deities which composed the ethnic polytheism: some who gave the subject more consideration than others, reduced the whole to one all-powerful Jupiter; but still they painted this being in the most hideous colours, gave him the most revolting features, because they were still obstinately bent on making man, his action and his passions, the model: this folly led them into continual perplexities, because it heaped together contradictory, incompatible, extravagant qualities; it was quite natural it should do so: the limited views, the superficial knowledge, the irregular desires of frail, feeble mortals, were but little calculated to typify the mind of the real Divinity; of that great *Cause of causes,* that *Parent of parents,* from whom every thing must have emanated. Although they persuaded themselves it was sinning to give him rivals, yet they described him as a jealous monarch who could not bear a division of empire; thus taking the vanity of earthly princes for their emblem, as if it was possible such a being could have a competitor like a terrestrial monarch. Not having contemplated the immutable laws with which he has invested nature, to which every thing it contains is subjected, which are the result of the most perfect wisdom, they were puzzled to account for the contrariety of those effects which their weak minds led them to suppose as evils; seeing that sometimes those who fulfilled in the most faithful manner their duties in this life, were involved in the same ruin with the boldest, the most inconsiderate violaters: thus in making him the immediate agent, instead of the first author, the executive instead of the formative power, they caused him to appear capricious, as unreasonably vindictive against his creatures, when they ought to have known that his wisdom was unlimited, his kindness without bounds, when he infused into nature that power which produces these apparently contradictory effects; which, although they seem injurious to man's interests, are, if he was but capacitated to judge fairly, the most beneficial advantages that he can possibly derive. Thus they made the Divinity appear improvident, by continually employing him to destroy the work of his own hands: they, in fact, taxed him with impotence, by the perpetual non-performance of those projects of which their own imbecillity, their own erring judgment, had vainly supposed him to be the contriver.

To solve these difficulties, man created enemies to the Divinity, who although subordinate to the supreme God, were nevertheless competent to disturb his empire, to frustrate his views. Can any thing be worse conceived, can any thing be more truly derogatory to the great *Parent of parents*, than thus to make him resemble a king, who is surrounded with adversaries, willing to dispute with him his diadem? Such, however, is the origin of the *Fable of the Titanes*, or of the *rebellious angels*, whose presumption caused them to be plunged into the abyss of misery—who were changed into *demons*, or into evil genii: these according to their mythology, had no other functions, than to render abortive the projects of the Divinity; to seduce, to raise to rebellion, those who were his subjects. Miserable invention, feeble subterfuge, for the vices of mankind, although decorated with all the beauty of language. Can then sublimity of versification, the harmony of numbers, reconcile man to the idea that the puny offspring of natural causes is adequate for a single instant to dispute the commands, to thwart the desires, to render nugatory the decrees of a Being whose wisdom is of the most polished perfection; whose goodness is boundless; whose power must be more capacious than the human mind can possibly conceive?

In consequence of this *Fable of the Titanes*, the monarch of nature was represented as perpetually in a scuffle with the enemies he had himself created; as unwilling totally to subdue those with whom these fabulists have described him as dividing his authority—partaking his supreme power. This again was borrowed from the conduct of earthly monarchs, who, when they find a potent enemy, make a treaty with him; but this was quite unnecessary for the great *Cause of causes*; and only shows that man is utterly incapable of forming any other ideas than those which he derives from the situation of those of his own race, or of the beings by whom he is surrounded. According to this fable the subjects of the universal Monarch were never properly submitted to his authority; like an earthly king, he was in a continual state of hostility, and punished those who had the misfortune to enter into the conspiracies of the enemies of his glory: seeing that human legislators put forth laws, issued decrees, they established similar institutions for the Divinity; established oracles; his ministers pretended, through these mysterious mediums, to convey to the people his heavenly mandates, to unveil his concealed intentions: the ignorant multitude received these without examination, they did not perceive that it was man, and not the Divinity, who thus spoke to them; they did not feel that it must be impossible for weak creatures to act contrary to the will of God.

The *Fable of the Titanes, or rebellious angels*, is extremely ancient; very generally diffused over the world; it serves for the foundation of the theology of the Brachmins of Hindostan: according to these, all living bodies are animated by *fallen angels*, who under these forms expiate their rebellion. These contradictory notions were the basis of nearly all the superstitions of the world; by these means they imagined they accounted for the origin of evil—demonstrated the cause why the human species experience misery. In short, the conduct of the most arbitrary tyrants of the earth was but too frequently brought forth, too often acted upon, in forming the character of the Divinity, held forth to the worship of man: their imperfect jurisprudence was the source from whence they drew that which they ascribed to their god. Pagan theology was remarkable for displaying in the character of their divinities the most dissolute vices; for making them vindictive; for causing them to punish with extreme rigour those, crimes which the oracles predicted; to doom to the most lasting torments those who sinned without knowing their transgression; to hurl vengeance on those who were ignorant of their obscure will, delivered in language which set comprehension at defiance; unless it was by the priest who both made and fulminated it. It was upon these unreasonable notions, that the theologians founded the worship which man ought to render to the Divinity. Do not then let us be at all surprised if the superstitious man was in a state of continual alarm: if he experienced trances—if his mind was ever in the most tormenting dread; the idea of his gods recalled to him unceasingly, that of a pitiless tyrant who sported with the miseries of his subjects; who, without being conscious of their own wrong, might at each moment incur his displeasure: he could not avoid feeling that although they had formed the universe entirely for man, yet justice did not regulate the actions of these powerful beings, or rather those of the priests; but he also believed that their elevated rank placed them infinitely above the human species, that therefore they might afflict him at their pleasure.

It is then for want of considering good and evil as equally necessary; it is for want of attributing them to their true causes, that man has created to himself fictitious powers, malicious divinities, respecting whom it is found so difficult to undeceive him. Nevertheless, in contemplating nature, he would have been able to have perceived, that *physical evil* is a necessary consequence of the peculiar properties of some beings; he would have acknowledged that plague, contagion, disease, are due to physical causes under particular circumstances; to combinations, which, although extremely natural, are fatal to his species; he would have sought—in the bosom of nature herself the remedies suitable to diminish these evils, or to have caused the cessation of those effects under which he suffered: he would have seen in like manner that *moral evil* was the necessary consequence of defective institutions; that it was not to the Divinity, but to the injustice of his fellows he ought to ascribe those wars, that poverty, those famines, those reverses of fortune, those multitudinous calamities, those vices, those crimes, under which he so frequently groans. Thus to rid himself of these evils he would not have uselessly extended his trembling hands towards shadows incapable of relieving him; towards beings who were not the authors of his sorrows; he would have sought remedies for these misfortunes in a more rational administration of justice—in more equitable laws—in more I reasonable institutions— in a greater degree of benevolence towards his fellow man—in a more punctual performance of his own duties.

As these gods were generally depicted to man as implacable to his frailties as they denounced nothing but the most dreadful punishments against those who involuntarily offended, it is not at all surprising that the sentiment of fear prevailed over that of love: the gloomy ideas presented to his mind were calculated to make him tremble, without making him better; an attention to this truth will serve to explain the foundation of that fantastical, irrational, frequently cruel worship, which was paid to these divinities; he often committed the most cruel extravagancies against his own person, the most hideous crimes against the person of others, under the idea that in so doing, he disarmed the anger, appeased the justice, recalled the clemency, deserved the mercy of his gods.

In general, the superstitious systems of man, his human and other sacrifices, his prayers, his ceremonies, his customs; have had only for their object either to divert the fury of his gods, whom he believed he had offended; to render them propitious to his own selfish views; or to excite in them that good disposition towards himself, which his own perverse mode of thinking made him imagine they bestowed exclusively on others: on the other hand, the efforts, the subtilties of theology, have seldom had any other end, than to reconcile in the divinities it has pourtrayed, those discordant ideas which its own dogmas has raised in the minds of mortals. From what has preceded, it may fairly be concluded that ethnic theology undermined itself by its own inconsistencies; that the art of composing chimeras may therefore with great justice be defined to be that of combining those qualities which are impossible to be reconciled with each other.

CHAP. III.

Of the confused and contradictory Ideas of Theology.

Every thing that has been said, proves pretty clearly, that, in despite of all his efforts, man has never been able to prevent himself from drawing together from his own peculiar nature, the qualities he has assigned to the Being who governs the universe. The contradictions necessarily resulting from the incompatible assemblage of these human qualities, which cannot become suitable to the same subject, seeing that the existence of one destroys the existence of the other, have been shewn:—the theologians themselves have felt the insurmountable difficulties which their divinities presented to reason: they were so substantive, that as they felt the impossibility of withdrawing themselves out of the dilemma, they endeavoured to prevent man from reasoning, by throwing his mind into confusion—by continually augmenting the perplexity of those ideas, already so discordant, which they offered him of the gods. By these means they enveloped them in mystery, covered them with dense clouds, rendered them inaccessible to mankind: thus they themselves became the interpreters, the masters of explaining, according either to their fancy or their interest, the ways of those enigmatical beings they made him adore. For this purpose they exaggerated them more and more—neither time nor space, nor the entire of nature could contain their immensity—every thing became an impenetrable mystery. Although man has originally borrowed from himself the traits, the colours, the primitive lineaments of which he composed his gods; although he has made them jealous, powerful, vindictive monarchs, yet his theology, by force of dreaming, entirely lost sight of human nature. In order to render his divinities still more different from their creatures, it assigned them, over and above the usual qualities of man, properties so marvellous, so uncommon, so far removed from every thing of which his mind could form a conception, that he lost sight of them himself. From thence he persuaded himself these qualities were divine, because he could no longer comprehend them; he believed them worthy of his gods, because no man could figure to himself any one distinct idea of them. Thus theology obtained the point of persuading man he must believe that which he could not conceive; that he must receive with submission improbable systems; that he must adopt, with pious deference, conjectures contrary to his reason; that this reason itself was the most agreeable sacrifice he could make on the altars of his gods, who were unwilling he should use the gift they had bestowed upon him. In short, it had made mortals implicitly believe that they were not formed to comprehend the thing of all others the most important to themselves. Thus it is evident that superstition founded its basis upon the absurd principle that man is obliged to accredit firmly that which he is in the most complete impossibility of comprehending. On the other hand, man persuaded himself that the gigantic, the truly incomprehensible attributes which were assigned to these celestial monarchs, placed between them and their slaves a distance so immense, that these could not be by any means offended with the comparison; that these distinctions rendered them still greater; made them more powerful, more marvellous, more inaccessible to observation. Man always entertains the idea, that what he is not in a condition to conceive, is much more noble, much wore respectable, than that which he has the capacity to comprehend. The more a thing is removed from his reach, the more valuable it always appears.

These prejudices in man for the marvellous, appear to have been the source that gave birth to those wonderful, unintelligible qualities with which superstition clothed these divinities. The invincible ignorance of the human mind, whose fears reduced him to despair, engendered those obscure, vague notions, with which mythology decorated its gods. He believed he could never displease them, provided he rendered them incommensurable; impossible to be compared with any thing, of which he had a knowledge; either with that which was most sublime, or that which possessed the greatest magnitude, From hence the multitude of negative attributes with which ingenious dreamers have successively embellished their phantoms, to the end that they might more surely form a being distinguished from all others, or which possessed nothing in common with that which the human mind had the faculty of being acquainted with: they did not perceive that after all their endeavours, it was nothing wore than exaggerated human qualities, which they thus heaped together, with no more skill than a painter would display who should delineate all the members of the body of the same size, taking a giant for dimension.

The theological attributes with which metaphysicians decorated these divinities, were in fact nothing but pure negations of the qualities found in man, or in those beings of which he has a knowledge; by these attributes their gods were supposed exempted from every thing which they considered weakness or imperfection in him, or in the beings by whom he is surrounded: they called every quality infinite, which has been shewn is only to affirm, that unlike man, or the beings with whom he is acquainted, it is not circumscribed by the limits of space; this, however, is what he can never in any manner comprehend, because he is himself finite. Hobbes in his *Leviathan*, says, "whatsoever we imagine is finite. Therefore there is no idea, or conception of any thing we call infinite. No man can have in his mind an image of infinite magnitude, nor conceive infinite swiftness, infinite time, infinite force, or infinite power. When we say any thing is infinite, we signify only, that we are not able to conceive the ends and bound of the thing named, having no conception of the thing, but of our own inability." Sherlock says, "the word infinite is only a negation, which signifies that which has neither end, nor limits, nor extent, and, consequently, that which has no positive and determinate nature, and is therefore nothing;" he adds, "that nothing but custom has caused this word to be adopted, which without that, would appear devoid of sense, and a contradiction."

When it is said these gods are eternal, it signifies they have not had, like man or like every thing that exists, a beginning, and that they will never have an end: to say they are immutable, is to say, that unlike himself or every thing which he sees, they are not subject to change: to say they are immaterial, is to advance, that their substance or essence is of a nature not conceivable by himself, but which must from that very circumstance be totally different from every thing of which he has cognizance.

It is from the confused collection of these negative qualities, that has resulted the theological gods; those metaphysical wholes of which it is impossible for man to form to himself any correct idea. In these abstract beings every thing is infinity,—immensity,—spirituality,— omniscience,—order,—wisdom,—intelligence,—omnipotence. In combining these vague terms, or these modifications, the ethnic priests believed they formed something, they extended these qualities by thought, and they imagined they made gods, whilst they only composed chimeras. They imagined that these perfections or these qualities must be suitable to their gods, because they were not suitable to any thing of which they had a knowledge; they believed that incomprehensible beings must have inconceivable qualities. These were the materials of which theology availed itself to compose those inexplicable shadows before which they commanded the human race to bend the knee.

Nevertheless, experience soon proved that beings so vague, so impossible to be conceived, so incapable of definition, so far removed from every thing of which man could have any knowledge, were but little calculated to fix his restless views; his mind requires to be arrested by qualities which he is capacitated to ascertain; of which he is in a condition to form a judgment. Thus after it had subtilized these metaphysical gods, after it had rendered them so different in idea, from every thing that acts upon the senses, theology found itself under the necessity of again assimilating them to man, from whom it had so far removed them: it therefore again made them human by the moral qualities which it assigned them; it felt that without this it would not be able to persuade mankind there could possibly exist any relation between him and such vague, ethereal, fugitive, incommensurable beings; that it would never be competent to secure for them his adoration.

It began to perceive that these marvellous gods were only calculated to exercise the imagination of some few thinkers, whose minds were accustomed to labour upon chimerical subjects, or to take words for realities; in short it found, that for the greater number of the material children of the earth it was necessary to have gods more analogous to themselves, more sensible, more known to them. In consequence these divinities were re-clothed with human qualities; theology never felt the incompatibility of these qualities with beings it had made essentially different from man, who consequently could neither have his properties, nor be modified like himself. It did not see that gods who were immaterial, destitute of corporeal organs, were neither able to think nor to act as material beings, whose peculiar organizations render them susceptible of the qualities, the feelings the will, the virtues, that are found in them. The necessity it felt to assimilate the gods to their worshippers, to make an affinity between them, made it pass over without consideration these palpable contradictions—this want of keeping in their portrait: thus ethnic theology obstinately continued to unite those incompatible qualities, that discrepancy of character, which the human mind attempted in vain either to conceive or to reconcile: according to it, pure spirits were the movers of the material world; immense beings were enabled to occupy space, without however excluding nature; immutable deities were the causes of those continual changes operated in the world: omnipotent beings did not prevent those evils which were displeasing to them; the sources of order submitted to confusion: in short, the wonderful properties of these theological beings every moment contradicted themselves.

There is not less discrepancy, less incompatibility, less discordance in the human perfections, less contradiction in the moral qualities attributed to them, to the end that man might be enabled to form to himself some idea of these beings. These were all said to be *eminently* possessed by the gods, although they every moment contradicted each other: by this means they formed a kind of patch-work character, heterogeneous beings, discrepant phenomena, entirely inconceivable to man, because nature had never constructed any thing like them, whereby he was enabled to form a judgment. Man was assured they were eminently good—that it was visible in all their actions. Now goodness is a known quality, recognizable in some beings of the human species; this is, above every other, a property he is desirous to find in all those upon whom he is in a state of dependence; but he is unable to bestow the title of good on any among his fellows, except their actions produce on him those effects which he approves—that he finds in unison with his existence—in conformity with his own peculiar modes of thinking. It was evident, according to this reasoning, these ethnic gods did not impress him with this idea; they were said to be equally the authors of his pleasures, as of his pains, which were to be either secured or averted by sacrifices: thus when man suffered by contagion, when he was the victim of shipwreck, when his country was desolated by war, when he saw whole nations devoured by rapacious earthquakes, when he was a prey to the keenest sorrows, he at least was unable to conceive the bounty of those beings. How could he perceive the beautiful order which they had introduced into the world, while he groaned under such a multitude of calamities? How was he able to discern the beneficence of men whom he beheld sporting as it were with his species? How could he conceive the consistency of those who destroyed that which he was assured they had taken such pains to establish, solely for his own peculiar happiness? But had his mind been properly enlightened, had he been taught to know, that nature, acting by unerring laws, produces all the phenomena he beholds as a necessary consequence of her primitive impulse—that like the rest of nature he was himself subjected to the general operation— that no peculiar exemption had been made in his behalf— that sacrifices were useless—that the great *Parent of parents*, equally mindful of all his creatures, had set in action with the most consummate wisdom an invariable system, the apparent, casual evils of which were ever counterbalanced by the resulting good; that without repining, it was his duty, his interest, to submit; at the same time to examine with sedulity, to search with earnestness, into the recesses of this nature for remedies to the sorrows he endured. If he had been thus instructed, we should never behold him arraigning either the kindness, the wisdom, or the consistency of the gods; he would neither have ascribed his sufferings to the malicious interference of inferior deities, so derogatory to the divine majesty of the *Great Cause of causes*, nor would he have taxed with either inconsistency or unkindness, that nature which cannot act otherwise than she does. Perhaps of all the ideas that can be infused into the mind of man, none is more really subversive of his true happiness, none more incompatible with the reality of things, than that which persuades him he is himself a privileged being, the king of a nature where every thing is submitted to laws, the extent of which his finite mind cannot possibly conceive. Even admitting it should ultimately turn out to be a fact, he has yet no one positive evidence to justify the assumption; experience, which after all must always prove the best criterion for his judgment, daily proves, that in every thing he is subjected, like every other part of nature, to those invariable decrees from which nothing that he beholds is exempted.

Feeble monarch! of whom a grain of sand, some atoms of bile, some misplaced humours, destroy at once the existence and the reign: yet thou pretendest every thing was made for thee! Thou desirest that the entire of nature should be thy domain, and thou canst not even defend thyself from the slightest of her shocks! Thou makest to thyself a god for thyself alone; thou supposest that he unceasingly occupieth himself only for thy peculiar happiness; thou imaginest every thing was made solely for thy pleasure; and, following up thy presumptuous ideas, thou hast the audacity to call nature good or bad as thy weak intellect inclines: thou darest to think that the kindness exhibited towards thee, in common with other beings, is contradicted by the evil genii thy fancy has created! Dost thou not see that those beasts which thou supposest submitted to thine empire, frequently devour thy fellow-creatures; that fire consumeth them; that the ocean swalloweth them up; that those elements of which thou sometimes admirest the order, which sometimes thou accusest of confusion, frequently sweep them off the face of the earth; dost thou not see that all this is necessarily what it must be; that thou art not in any manner consulted in any of this phenomena? Indeed, according to thine own ideas, if thou wast to examine them with care, dost thou not admit that thy gods are the universal cause of all; that they maintain the whole by the destruction of its parts. Are they not then according to thyself, the gods of nature—of the ocean—of rivers—of mountains—of the earth, in which they occupiest, so very small a space—of all those other globes that thou seest roll in the regions of space—of those orbs that revolve round the sun that enlighteneth thee?—Cease, then, obstinately to persist in beholding nothing but thy sickly self in nature; do not flatter thyself that the human race, which reneweth itself, which disappeareth like the leaves on the trees, can absorb all the care, can ingross all the tenderness of that universal being, who, according to thyself, properly understood, ruleth the destiny of all things. Submit thyself in silence to mandates which thy unavailing prayers; can never change; to a wisdom which thy imbecility cannot fathom; to the unerring shafts of a fate, which nothing but thine own vanity, aided by thy perverse ignorance, could ever question, being the best possible good that can befall thee! which if thou couldst alter, thou wouldst with thy defective judgment render worse! What is the human race compared to the earth? What is this earth compared to the sun? What is our sun compared to those myriads of suns which at immense distances occupy the regions of space? not for the purpose of diverting thy weak eyes; not with a view to excite thy stupid admiration, as thou vainly imaginest; since multitudes of them are placed out of the range of thy visual organs: but to occupy the place which necessity hath assigned them. Mortal, feeble and vain! restore thyself to thy proper sphere; acknowledge every where the effect of necessity; recognize in thy benefits, behold in thy sorrows, the different modes of action of those various beings endowed with such a variety of properties, which surround thee; of which the macrocosm is the assemblage; and do not any longer suppose that this nature, much less its great cause, can possess such incompatible qualities as would be the result of human views or of visionary ideas, which have no existence but in thyself.

As long as theologians shall continue obstinately bent to make man the model of their gods; as long ask they shall pertinaciously undertake to explain the nature of these gods, which they will never be able to do, but after human ideas, although they may associate the most heterogeneous properties, the most discrepant functions; so long, I say, experience will contradict at every moment the beneficent views they, attach to their divinities; it will be in vain that they call them good: man, reasoning thus, will never be able to find good but in those objects which impel him in a manner favourable to his actual mode of existence; he always finds confusion in that which fills him with grievous sensations; he calls evil every thing that painfully affects him, even cursorily; those beings that produce in him two modes of feeling, so very opposite to each other, he will naturally conclude are sometimes favourable, sometimes unfavourable to him; at least, if he will not allow that they act necessarily, consequently are neither one nor the other, he will say that a world where he experiences so much evil cannot be submitted to men who are perfectly good; on the other hand, he will also assume that a world in which man receives so many benefits, cannot be governed by those who are without kindness. Thus he is obliged to admit of two principles equally powerful, who are in hostility with each other; or rather, he must agree that the same persons are alternately kind and unkind; this after all is nothing more than avowing they cannot be otherwise than they are; in this case it would be useless to sacrifice to them— to make solicitation; seeing it would be nothing but *destiny*—the necessity of things submitted invariable rules.

In order to justify these beings, constructed upon mortal principles, from injustice, in consequence of the evils the human species experience, the theologian is reduced to the necessity of calling them punishments inflicted for the transgressions of man. But then these general calamities include all men. Some, at least, may be supposed not to have offended. Thus he involves contradictions he finds it difficult to reconcile; to effectuate this he makes his *anthropomorphites* immaterial—incorporeal; that is, he says they are the negation of every thing of which he has a knowledge; consequently, beings who can have no relation with corporeal beings: and this avails him no better, as will be evident by reasoning on the subject. To offend any one, is to diminish the sum of his happiness; it is to afflict him, to deprive him of something, to make him experience a painful sensation. How is it possible man can operate on such beings; how can the physical actions of a material substance have any influence over an immaterial substance, devoid of parts, having no point of contact. How can a corporeal being make an incorporeal being experience incommodious sensations? On the other hand, *justice*, according to the only ideas man can ever form of it, supposes, a permanent disposition to render to each what is due to him; the theologian will not admit that the beings he has jumbled together owe any thing to man; he insists that the benefits they bestow are all the gratuitous effects of their own goodness; that they have the right to dispose of the work of their hands according to their own pleasure; to plunge it if they please into the abyss of misery; in short, that their volition is the only guide of their conduct. It is easy to see, that according to man's idea of justice, this does not even contain the shadow of it; that it is, in fact, the mode of action adopted by what he calls the most frightful tyrants. How then can he be induced to call men just who act after this manner? Indeed, while he sees innocence suffering, virtue in tears, crime triumphant, vice recompensed, and at the same time, is told the beings whom theology has invented are the authors, he will never be able to acknowledge them to have *justice*. But he will find no such contradictory qualities in nature, where every thing is the result of immutable laws: he will at once perceive that these transient evils produce more permanent good; that they are necessary to the conservation of the whole, or else result from modifications of matter, which it is competent for him to change, by altering his own mode of action; a lesson that nature herself teaches him when he is willing to receive her instructions. But to form gods with human passions, is to make them appear unjust; to say that such beings chastise their friends for their own I good, is at once to upset all the ideas he has either of kindness or unkindness: thus the incompatible human qualities ascribed to these beings, do in fact destroy their existence. If it be insisted they have the knowledge and power of man, only that they are more extended, then it becomes a very natural reply, to say, since they know every thing, they ought at least to restrain mischief; because this would be the observation of man upon the action of his fellows;—if it be urged these qualities are similar to the same qualities possessed by man, then it may be fairly asked in what do they differ?

To this, if any answer be given, be what it may, it will still be only changing the language: it will be invariably another method of expressing the same thing; seeing that man with all his ingenuity, will never be able to describe properties but after himself or those of the beings by whom he is surrounded.

Where is the man filled with kindness, endowed with humanity, who does not desire with all his heart to render his fellow creatures happy? If these beings, as the theologians assert, really have man's qualities augmented, would they not, by the same reasoning, exercise their infinite power to render them all happy? Nevertheless, in despite of these theologians, we scarcely find any one who is perfectly satisfied with his condition on earth: for one mortal that enjoys, we behold a thousand who suffer; for one rich man who lives in the midst of abundance, there are thousands of poor who want common necessaries: whole nations groan in indigence, to satisfy the passions of some avaricious princes, of some few nobles, who are not thereby rendered more contented—who do not acknowledge themselves more fortunate on that account. In short, under the dominion of these beings, the earth is drenched with the tears of the miserable. What must be the inference from all this? That they are either negligent of, or incompetent to, his happiness. But the mythologists will tell you coolly, that the judgments of his gods are impenetrable! How do we understand this term? Not to be taught—not to be informed—impervious—not to be pierced: in this case it would be an unreasonable question to inquire by what authority do you reason upon them? How do you become acquainted with these impenetrable mysteries? Upon what foundation do you attribute virtues which you cannot penetrate? What idea do you form to yourself of a justice that never resembles that of man? Or is it a truth that you yourself are not a man, but one of those impenetrable beings whom you say you represent?

To withdraw themselves from this, they will affirm that the justice of these idols are tempered with mercy, with compassion, with goodness: these again are human qualities: what, therefore, shall we understand by them? What idea do we attach to mercy? Is it not a derogation from the severe rules of an exact, a rigorous justice, which causes a remission of some part of a merited punishment? Here hinges the great incompatibility, the incongruity of those qualities, especially when augmented by the word *omni*; which shews how little suitable human properties are to the formation of divinities. In a prince, clemency is either a violation of justice, or the exemption from a too severe law: nevertheless, man approves of clemency in a sovereign, when its too great facility does not become prejudicial to society; he esteems it, because it announces humanity, mildness, a compassionate, noble soul; qualities he prefers in his governors to rigour, cruelty, inflexibility: besides, human laws are defective; they are frequently too severe; they are not competent to foresee all the circumstances of every case: the punishments they decree are not always commensurate with the offence: he therefore does not always think them just: but he feels very well, he understands distinctly, that when the sovereign extends his mercy, he relaxes from his justice—that if mercy he merited, the punishment ought not to take place—that then its exercise is no longer clemency, but justice: thus he feels, that in his fellow creatures these two qualities cannot exist at the same moment. How then is he to form his judgment of beings who are represented to possess both in the extremest degree? Is it not, in fact, announcing these beings to be men like ourselves, who act with our imperfections on an enlarged scale?

They then say, well, but in the next world these idols will reward you for all the evils you suffer in this: this, indeed, is something to look to, if it could be contemplated alone; unmixed with all they have formerly asserted: if we could also find that there was an unison of thinking on this point—if there was a reasonable comprehensible view of it held forth: but alas! here again human pleasures, human feelings, are the basis on which these rewards are rested; only they are promised in a way we cannot comprehend them; houris, or females who are to remain for ever virgins, notwithstanding the knowledge of man, are so opposed to all human comprehension, so opposite to all experience, are such mystic assertions, that the human mind cannot possibly embrace an idea of them: besides this is only promised by one class of these beings; others affirm it will be altogether different: in short, the number of modes in which this hereafter reward is promised to him, obliges man to ask himself one plain question, Which is the real history of these blissful abodes? At this question he staggers—he seeks for advice: each assures him that the other is in error—that his peculiar mode is that which will really have place; that to believe the other is a crime. How is he to judge now? Take what course he will, he runs the chance of being wrong; he has no standard whereby to measure the correctness of these contradictory assurances; his mind is held suspended; he feels the impossibility of the whole being right; he knows not that which he ought to elect! Again, they have positively asserted these beings owe nothing to man: how then is he to expect in a future life, a more real happiness than he enjoys in the present? This they parry, by assuring him it is founded upon their promises, contained in their revealed oracles. Granted: but is he quite certain these oracles have emanated from themselves? If they are so different in their detail, may there not be reasonable ground for suspecting some of them are not authentic? If there is, which are the spurious, which are the genuine? By what rule is he to guide himself in the choice; how, with his frail methods of judging, is he to scrutinize oracles delivered by such powerful beings— to discriminate the true from the false? The ministers of each will give you an infallible method, one that, is according to their own asseveration, cannot err; that is, by an implicit belief in the particular doctrine each promulgates.

Thus will be perceived the multitude of contradictions, the extravagant hypotheses which these human attributes, with which theology clothes its divinities, must necessarily produce. Beings embracing at one time so many discordant qualities will always be undefinable—can only present a train of ideas calculated to displace each other; they will consequently ever remain beings of the imagination. These beings, say their ministers, created the heavens, the earth, the creatures who inhabit it, to manifest their own peculiar glory; they have neither rivals, nor equals in nature; nothing which can be compared with them. Glory is, again, a human passion: it is in man the desire of giving his fellow- creatures an high opinion of him; this, passion is laudable when it stimulates him to undertake great projects—when it determines him to perform useful actions—but it is very frequently a weakness attached to his nature; it is nothing more than a desire to be distinguished from those beings with whom he compares himself, without exciting him to one noble, one generous act. It is easy to perceive that beings who are so much elevated above men, cannot be actuated by such a defective passion. They say these beings are jealous of their prerogatives. Jealousy is another human passion, not always of the most respectable kind: but it is rather difficult to conceive the existence of jealousy with profound wisdom, unlimited power, and the perfection of justice. Thus the theologians by dint of heaping quality on quality, aggrandizing each as is added, seem to have reduced themselves to the situation of a painter, who spreading all his colours upon his canvas together, after thus blending them into an unique mass, loses sight of the whole in the composition.

They will, nevertheless, reply to these difficulties, that goodness, wisdom, justice, are in these beings qualities so pre-eminent, so distinct, have so little affinity with these same qualities in man, that they are totally dissimilar—have not the least relation. Admit this to be the case, How then can he form to himself any idea of these perfections, seeing they are totally unlike those with which he is acquainted? They surely cannot mean to insinuate that they are the reverse of every thing he understands; because that would, in effect, bring them to a precise point which would not need any explanation; it is therefore a matter of certainty this cannot be the case: then if these qualities, when exercised by the beings they have described, are only human actions so obscured, so hidden, as not to be recognizable by man, How can weak mortals pretend to announce them, to have a knowledge of them, to explain them to others? Does then theology impart to the mind the ineffable boon of enabling it to conceive that which no man is competent to understand? Does it procure for its agents the marvellous faculty of having distinct ideas of beings composed of so many contradictory properties? Does it, in fact, make the theologian himself one of these incomprehensible beings.

They will impose silence, by saying the oracles have spoken; that through these mystical means they have made themselves known to mortals. The next question would naturally be, When, where, or to whom have these oracles spoken? Where are these oracles? An hundred voices raise themselves in the same moment; hands of Briaraeus are immediately stretched forth to shew them in a number of discordant collections, which each maintains, with an equal degree of vehemence, is the true code—the only doctrine man ought to believe: he runs them over, finds they scarcely agree in any one particular; but that in all the heaviest penalties are denounced against those who doubt the smallest part of any one of them. These beings of consummate wisdom are made to speak an obscure, irrational language; some of them, although their goodness is proclaimed, have been cruel and sanguinary; others, although their justice is held forth, have been partial, unjust, capricious; some, who are represented as all merciful, destine to the most hideous punishments the unhappy victims to their wrath: examine any one of them more closely, he will find that they have never in any two countries held literally the same language: that although they are said to have spoken in many places, that they have always spoken variously: What is the necessary result? The human mind, incapable of reconciling such manifest contradictions, unable to obtain from their ministers any corroborative evidence, that is not disputed by the others, falls into the strangest perplexity; is involved in doubts, entangled in a labyrinth to which no clue is to be found.

Thus the relations, which are supposed to exist between man and these theological idols, can only be founded on the moral qualities of these beings: if these are not known to him, if he cannot in any manner comprehend them, they cannot by any ingenuity of argument serve him for models. In order that they may be imitated, it is needful that these qualities were cognizable by the being who is to imitate them. How can he imitate that goodness, that justice, that mercy, which does not resemble either his own, or any thing he can conceive? If these beings partake in nothing of that which forms man—if the properties they do possess, although different, are not within the reach of his comprehension—if, he cannot embrace the most distant idea of them, which the theologian assures him he cannot, How is it possible he can set about imitating them? How follow a conduct suitable to please them —to render himself acceptable in their sight? What can in effect be the motive of that worship, of that homage, of that obedience, which these beings are said to exact—which he is informed he should offer at their altars, if he does not establish it upon their goodness—their veracity —their justice: in short, upon qualities which he is competent to understand? How can he have clear, distinct ideas of those qualities, if they are no longer of the same nature as those which he has learned to reverence in the beings of his own species?

To this they will reply, because none of them ever admit the least doubt of the rectitude of their own individual creed, that there can be no proportion between these idols and mortals, who are the work of their hands; that it is not permitted to the clay to demand of the potter who has formed it, "why ye have fashioned me thus;"—but if there can be no common measure between the workman and his work—if there can be no analogy between them, because the one is immaterial, the other corporeal, How do they reciprocally act upon each other? How can the gross organs of the one, comprehend the subtile quality of the other? Reasoning in the only way he is capable, and it surely will never be seriously argued that he is not to reason, will he not perceive that the earthen vase could only have received the form which it pleased the potter to give; that if it is formed badly, if it is rendered inadequate to the use for which it was designed, the vase is not in this instance to be blamed; the potter certainly has the power to break it; the vase cannot prevent him; it will neither have motives nor means to soften his anger; it will be obliged to submit to its destiny; but he will not be able to prevent his mind from thinking the potter harsh in thus punishing the vase, rather than by forming it anew, by giving it another figure, render it competent to the purposes he intended.

According to these notions the relations between man and these theological beings have no existence, they owe nothing to him, are dispensed from shewing him either goodness or justice; that man, on the contrary, owes them every thing: but contradictions appear at every step. If these have promised by their oracles any thing to man, it is rather difficult for him to believe, that what is so solemnly promised does not belong to him if he fulfils the condition of the promise. The difference a theologian may choose to find in these relations will hardly be convincing to a reasonable mind. The duties of man towards these beings can, according to their own shewing, have no other foundation than the happiness he expects from them: thus the relation has a reciprocity, it is founded upon their goodness, upon their justice, it demands obedience on his part, a conduct suitable to the benefits he receives. Thus, in whatever manner the theological system is viewed, it destroys itself. Will theology never feel that the more it endeavours to exaggerate the human qualities, the less it exalts the beings it pictures; the more incomprehensible it renders them, the more it contributes to swell its own ocean of contradictions; that to take human passions, mortal faculties at all, is perhaps the worst means it can pursue to form a perfect being; but that if it must persist in this method, then the further they remove them from man, the more they debase him, the more they weaken the relations subsisting between them: that in thus aggregating human properties, it should carefully abstain from associating in these pictures those qualities which man finds detestable in his fellows. Thus, despotism in man is looked upon as an unjust, unreasonable power; if it introduces such a quality into its portraits, it cannot rationally suppose them suitable to cultivate the esteem, to attract the voluntary homage of the human race: if, however, the canvas be examined, we shall frequently be struck, with perceiving this the leading feature; we shall equally find a want of keeping through the whole; that shadows are introduced, where lights ought to prevail; that the colouring is incongruous—the design without harmony.

The discrepancy of conduct which theology imputes to these idols, is not less remarkable than the contrariety of qualities it ascribes to them, or the inconsistency of the passions with which it invests them; sometimes, according to this, they are the friends to reason, desirous of the happiness of society; sometimes they are inimical to virtue; interdict the use of reason; flattered with seeing society disturbed, they sometimes afflict man without his being able to guess the cause of their displeasure; sometimes they are favourable to mankind—at others, indisposed towards the human species: sometimes they are represented as permitting crimes for the pleasure of punishing them—at others, they exert all their power to arrest crime in its birth; sometimes they elect a small number to receive eternal happiness, predestinating the rest to perpetual misery—to everlasting torments; at others, they throw open the gates of mercy to all who choose to enter them; sometimes they are pourtrayed as destroying the universe—at others, as establishing the most beautiful order in the planet we inhabit; sometimes they are held forth as countenancing deception—at others, as having the highest reverence for truth—as holding deceit in abomination. This, again, is the necessary result of the human faculties, the mortal passions, the frail qualities of which they compose the beings they hold forth to the admiration, to the worship, to the homage of the world.

Perhaps the most fatal consequences have arisen from founding the moral character of these divinities upon that of man. Those who first had the confidence to tell man that in these matters it was not permitted him to consult his reason, that the interests of society demanded its sacrifice, evidently proposed to themselves to make him the sport of their own wantonness—to make him the blind instrument of their own unworthiness. It is from this radical error that has sprung all those extravagances which the various superstitions have introduced upon the earth: from hence has flowed that sacred fury which has frequently deluged it with blood: here is the cause of those inhuman persecutions which have so often desolated nations: in short, all those horrid tragedies which have been acted on the vast theatre of the world, by command of the different ministers of the various systems, whose gods they have said ordained these shocking spectacles.

The theologians themselves have thus been the means, of calumniating the gods they pretended to serve, under the pretext of exalting their name— of covering them with glory; in this they may have been said to be true atheists, since they seem only to have been anxious to destroy the idols they themselves had raised, by the actions they have attributed to them —which has debased them in the eye of reason—rendered their existence more than doubtful to the man of humanity. Indeed, it would require more than human credulity to accredit the assertion that these beings ever could order the atrocities committed in their name. Every time they have been willing to disturb the harmony of mankind—whenever they have been desirous to render him unsociable, they have cried out that their gods ordained that he should be so. Thus they render mortals uncertain, make the ethical system fluctuate by founding it upon changeable, capricious idols, whom they represent much more frequently cruel and unjust, than filled with bounty and benevolence.

However it may be, admitting if they will for a moment that their idols possess all the human virtues in an infinite degree of perfection, we shall quickly be obliged to acknowledge that they cannot connect them with those metaphysical, theological, negative attributes, of which we have already spoken. If these beings are spirits that are immaterial, how can they be able to act like man, who is a corporeal being? Pure spirits, according to the only idea man can form of them, having no organs, no parts, cannot see any thing; can neither hear our prayers, attend to our solicitations, nor have compassion for our miseries. They cannot be immutable, if their dispositions can suffer change: they cannot be infinite, if the totality of nature, without being them, can exist conjointly with them: they cannot be omnipotent, if they either permit or do not prevent evil: they cannot be omnipresent, if they are not every where: they must therefore be in the evil as well as in the good. Thus in whatever manner they are contemplated, under whatever point of view they are considered, the human qualities which are assigned to them, necessarily destroy each other; neither can these same properties in any possible manner combine themselves with the supernatural attributes given to them by theology.

With respect to the revealed will of these idols, by means of their oracles, far from being a proof of their good will, of their commisseration for man, it would rather seem evidence of their ill-will. It supposes them capable of leaving mankind for a considerable season unacquainted with truths highly important to their interests; these oracles communicated to a small number of chosen men, are indicative of partiality, of predilections, that are but little compatible with the common Father of the human race. These oracles were ill imagined, since they tend to injure the immutability ascribed to these idols, by supposing that they permitted man to be ignorant at one time of their will, whilst at another time they were willing he should be instructed on the subject. Moreover, these oracles frequently predicted offences for which afterwards severe punishments were inflicted on those who did no more than fulfil them. This, according to the reasoning of man, would be unjust. The ambiguous language in which they were delivered, the almost impossibility of comprehending them, the inexplicable mysteries they contained, seemed to render them doubtful; at least they are not consistent with the ideas man is capable of forming of infinite perfection: but the fact clearly is, they were thus rendered capable of application to the contingency of events—could be made to suit almost any circumstances: this would render it not a very improbable conjecture, that these oracles were solely delivered by the priests themselves. It these were tried by the only test of which he has any knowledge—HIS REASON, it would naturally occur to the mind of man, that mystery could never, on any occasion, be used in the promulgation of substantive decrees meant to operate on the obedience, to actuate the moral conduct of man: it is quite usual with most legislators to render their laws as explicit as possible, to adapt them to the meanest understanding; in short, it would be reckoned want of good faith in a government, to throw a thick, mysterious veil over the announcement of that conduct which it wished its citizens to adopt; they would be apt to think such a procedure was either meant to cover its own peculiar ignorance, or else to entrap them into a snare; at best, it would be considered as furnishing a never-failing source of dispute, which a wise government would endeavour to avoid.

It will thus be obvious, that the ideas which theology has at various times, under various systems, held forth to man, have for the most part been confused, discordant, incompatible, and have had a general tendency to disturb the repose of mankind. The obscure notions, the vague speculations of these multiplied creeds, would be matter of great indifference, if man was not taught to hold them as highly important to his welfare—if he did not draw from them conclusions pernicious to himself—if he did not learn from these theologians that he must sharpen his asperity against those who do not contemplate them in the same point of view with himself: as he perhaps, then, will never have a common standard, a fixed rule, a regular graduated scale, whereby to form his judgment on these points—as all efforts of the imagination must necessarily assume divers shapes, undergo a variety of modifications, which can never be assimilated to each other, it was little likely that mankind would at all times be able to understand each other on this subject; much less that they would be in accord in the opinions they should adopt. From hence that diversity of superstitions which in all ages have given rise to the most irrational disputes; which have engendered the most sanguinary wars; which have caused the most barbarous massacres; which have divided man from his fellow by the most rancorous animosities, that will perhaps never be healed; because he has been impelled to consider the peculiar tenets he adopted, not only as immediately essential to his individual welfare, but also as intimately connected with the happiness, closely interwoven with the tranquillity of the nation of which he was a citizen. That such contrariety of sentiment, such discrepancy of opinion should exist, is not in the least surprising; it is, in fact, the natural result of those physical causes to which, as long as he exists, he is at all times submitted. The man of a heated imagination cannot accommodate himself to the god of a phlegmatic, tranquil being: the infirm, bilious, discontented, angry mortal, cannot view him under the same aspect as he who enjoys a sounder constitution,—as the individual of a gay turn, who enjoys the blessing of content, who wishes to live in peace. An equitable, kind, compassionate, tender-hearted man, will not delineate to himself the same portrait of his god, as the man who is of an harsh, unjust, inflexible, wicked character. Each individual will modify his god after his own peculiar manner of existing, after his own mode of thinking, according to his particular mode of feeling. A wise, honest, rational man will always figure to himself his god as humane and just.

Nevertheless, as fear usually presided at the formation of those idols man set up for the object of his worship; as the ideas of these beings were generally associated with that of terror as the recollections of sufferings, which he attributed to them, often made him tremble; frequently awakened in his mind the most afflicting, reminiscence; as it sometimes filled him with inquietude, sometimes inflamed his imagination, sometimes overwhelmed him with dismay, the experience of all ages proves, that these vague idols became the most important of all considerations—was the affair which most seriously occupied the human race: that they every where spread consternation—produced the most frightful ravages, by the delirious inebriation resulting from the opinions with which they intoxicated the mind. Indeed, it is extremely difficult to prevent habitual fear, which of all human passions is the most incommodious, from becoming a dangerous leaven; which in the long run will sour, exasperate, and give malignancy to the most moderate temperament.

If a misanthrope, in hatred of his race, had formed the project of throwing man into the greatest perplexity,—if a tyrant, in the plenitude of his unruly desire to punish, had sought out the most efficacious means; could either the one or the other have imagined that which was so well calculated to gratify their revenge, as thus to occupy him unceasingly with objects not only unknown to him, but which no two of them should ever see with precisely the same eyes; which notwithstanding they should be obliged to contemplate as the centre of all their thoughts—as the only model of their conduct—as the end of all their actions—as the subject of all their research—as a thing of more importance to them than life itself; upon which all their present felicity, all their future happiness, must necessarily depend? Could the gods themselves, in their solicitude to punish the impious Prometheus, for having stolen fire from the sun, have imagined a more certain method of executing their wishes? Was not Pandora's box, though stuffed with evils, trifling when compared with this? That at least left hope, to the unfortunate Epimetheus; this effectually cut it off.

If man was subjected to an absolute monarch, to a sultan who should keep himself secluded from his subjects; who followed no rule but his own desires; who did not feel himself bound by any duty; who could for ever punish the offences committed against him; whose fury it was easy to provoke; who was irritated even by the ideas, the thoughts of his subjects; whose displeasure might be incurred without even their own knowledge; the name of such a sovereign would assuredly be sufficient to carry trouble, to spread terror, to diffuse consternation into the very souls of those who should hear it pronounced; his idea would haunt them every where—would unceasingly afflict them—would plunge them into despair. What tortures would not their mind endure to discover this formidable being, to ascertain the secret of pleasing him! What labour would not their imagination bestow, to discover what mode of conduct might be able to disarm his anger! What fears would assail them, lest they might not have justly hit upon the means of assuaging his wrath! What disputes would they not enter into upon the nature, the qualities of a ruler, equally unknown to them all! What variety of means would not be adopted, to find favour in his eyes; to avert his chastisement!

Such is the history of the effects superstition has produced upon the earth. Man has always been panic-struck, because the systems adopted never enable him to form any correct opinion, any fixed ideas, upon a subject so material to his happiness; because every thing conspired either to give his ideas a fallacious turn, or else to keep his mind in the most profound ignorance; when he was willing to set himself right, when he was sedulous to examine the path which conducted to his felicity, when he was desirous of probing opinions so consequential to his peace, involving so much mystery, yet combining both his hopes and his fears, he was forbidden to employ the only proper method,—HIS REASON, guided by his experience; he was assured this would be an offence the most indelible. If he asked, Wherefore his reason had then been given him, since he was not to use it in matters of such high behest? he was answered, those were mysteries of which none but the initiated could be informed; that it sufficed for him to know, that the reason which he seemed so highly to prize, which he held in so much esteem, was his most dangerous enemy—his most inveterate, most determined foe. Where can be the propriety of such an argument? Can it really be that reason is dangerous? If so, the Turks are justified in their predilection for madmen: but to proceed, he is told that he must believe in the gods, not question the mission of their priests; in short, that he had nothing to do with the laws they imposed, but to obey them: when he then required that these laws might at least be made comprehensible to him; that he might be placed in a capacity to understand them; the old answer was returned, that they were *mysteries*; he must not inquire into them. But where is the necessity for mystery in points of such vast importance? He might, indeed, from time to time consult these oracles, when he was able to make the sacrifices demanded; he would then receive precepts for his conduct: these were always, however, given in such vague, indeterminate terms, that he had scarcely the chance of acting right. At different times the same oracles delivered different opinions: thus he had nothing, steady; nothing permanent, whereby to guide his steps; like a blind man left to himself in the streets, he was obliged to grope his way at the peril of his existence. This will serve to shew the urgent necessity there is for truth to throw its radiant lustre on systems big with so much importance; that are so calculated to corroborate the animosities, to confirm the bitterness of soul, between those whom nature intended should always act as brothers.

By the magical charms with which these idols were surrounded, the human species has remained either as if it was benumbed, in a state of stupid apathy, or else he has become furious with fanaticism: sometimes, desponding with fear, man cringed like a slave who bends under the scourge of an inexorable master, always ready to strike him; he trembled under a yoke made too ponderous for his strength: he lived in continual dread of a vengeance he was unceasingly striving to appease, without ever knowing when he had succeeded: as he was always bathed in tears, continually enveloped in misery—as he was never permitted to lose sight of his fears—as he was continually exhorted to nourish his alarm, he could neither labour for his own happiness nor contribute to that of others; nothing could exhilarate him; he became the enemy of himself, the persecutor of his fellow-creatures, because his felicity here below was interdicted; he passed his time in heaving the most bitter sighs; his reason being forbidden him, he fell into either a state of infancy or delirium, which submitted him to authority; he was destined to this servitude from the hour he quitted his mother's womb, until that in which he was returned to his kindred dust; tyrannical opinion bound him fast in her massive fetters; a prey to the terrors with which he was inspired, he appeared to have come upon the earth for no other purpose than to dream—with no other desire than to groan—with no other motives than to sigh; his only view seemed to be to injure himself; to deprive himself of every rational pleasure, to embitter his own existence; to disturb the felicity of others. Thus, abject, slothful, irrational, he frequently became wicked, under the idea of doing honour to his gods; because they instilled into his mind that it was his duty to avenge their cause, to sustain their honour, to propagate their worship.

Mortals were prostrate from race to race, before vain idols to which fear had given birth in the bosom of ignorance, during the calamities of the earth; they tremblingly adored phantoms which credulity had placed in the recesses of their own brain, where they found a sanctuary which time only served to strengthen; nothing could undeceive them; nothing was competent to make them feel, it was themselves they adored—that they bent the knee before their own work—that they terrified themselves with the extravagant pictures they had themselves delineated; they obstinately persisted in prostrating themselves, in perplexing themselves, in trembling; they even made a crime of endeavouring to dissipate their fears; they mistook the production of their own folly; their conduct resembled that of children, who having disfigured their own features, become afraid of themselves when a mirror reflects the extravagance they have committed. These notions so afflicting for themselves, so grievous to others, have their epoch from the calamities of man; they will continue, perhaps augment, until their mind, enlightened by discarded reason, illumined by truth, shall set in their true colours these various systems; until reflection guided by experience, shall attach no more importance to them, than is consistent with the happiness of society; until man, bursting the chains of superstition— recalling to mind the great end of his existence—taking a rational view of that which surrounds him, shall no longer refuse to contemplate nature under her true character; shall no longer persist in refusing to acknowledge she contains within herself the cause of that wonderful phenomena which strikes on the dazzled optics of man: until thoroughly persuaded of the weakness of their claim to the homage of mankind, he shall make one pious, simultaneous, mighty effort, and *overthrow the altars of Moloch and his priests*.

CHAP. IV.
Examination of the Proofs of the Existence of the Divinity, as given by CLARKE.

The unanimity of man in acknowledging the Divinity, is commonly looked upon as the strongest proof of his existence. There is not, it is said, any people on the earth who have not some ideas, whether true or false, of an all-powerful agent who governs the world. The rudest savages as well as the most polished nations, are equally obliged to recur by thought to the first cause of every thing that exists; thus it is affirmed, the cry of Nature herself ought to convince us of the existence of the Godhead, of which she has taken pains to engrave the notion in the minds of men: they therefore conclude, that the idea of God is innate.

Perhaps there is nothing of which man should be more sedulously careful than permitting a promiscuous assemblage of right with wrong—of suffering false conclusions to be drawn from true propositions; this will not improbably be found to be pretty much the case in this instance; the existence of the great *Cause of causes*, the *Parent of parents*, does not, I think, admit of any doubt in the mind of any one who has reasoned: but, if this existence did not rest upon better foundations than the unanimity of man on this subject, I am fearful it would not be placed upon so solid a rock as those who make this asseveration may imagine: the fact is, man is not generally agreed upon this point; if he was, superstition could have no existence; the idea of God cannot be *innate*, because, independent of the proofs offered on every side of the almost impossibility of innate ideas, one simple fact will set such an opinion for ever at rest, except with those who are obstinately determined not to be convinced by even their own arguments: if this idea was innate, it must be every where the same; seeing that that which is antecedent to man's being, cannot have experienced the modifications of his existence, which are posterior. Even if it were waived, that the same idea should be expected from all mankind, but that only every nation should have their ideas alike on this subject, experience will not warrant the assertion, since nothing can be better established than that the idea is not uniform even in the same town; now this would be an insuperable quality in an innate idea. It not unfrequently happens, that in the endeavour to prove too much, that which stood firm before the attempt, is weakened; thus a bad advocate frequently injures a good cause, although he may not be able to overturn the rights on which it is rested. It would, therefore, perhaps, come nearer to the point if it was said, "that the natural curiosity of mankind have in all ages, and in all nations, led him to seek after the primary cause of the phenomena he beholds; that owing to the variations of his climate, to the difference of his organization, the greater or less calamity he has experienced, the variety of his intellectual faculties, and the circumstances under which he has been placed, man has had the most opposite, contradictory, extravagant notions of the Divinity, but that he has uniformly been in accord in acknowledging both the existence, and the wisdom of his work—NATURE."

If disengaged from prejudice, we analyze this proof, we shall see that the universal consent of man, so diffused over the earth, actually proves little more than that he has been in all countries exposed to frightful revolutions, experienced disasters, been sensible to sorrows of which he has mistaken the physical causes; that those events to which he has been either the victim or the witness, have called forth his admiration or excited his fear; that for want of being acquainted with the powers of nature, for want of understanding her laws, for want of comprehending her infinite resources, for want of knowing the effects she must necessarily produce under given circumstances, he has believed these phenomena were due to some secret agent of which he has had vague ideas—to beings whom he has supposed conducted themselves after his own manner; who were operated upon by similar motives with himself.

The consent then of man in acknowledging a variety of gods, proves nothing, except that in the bosom of ignorance he has either admired the phenomena of nature, or trembled under their influence; that his imagination was disturbed by what he beheld or suffered; that he has sought in vain to relieve his perplexity, upon the unknown cause of the phenomena he witnessed, which frequently obliged him to quake with terror: the imagination of the human race has laboured variously upon these causes, which have almost always been incomprehensible to him; although every thing confessed his ignorance, his inability to define these causes, yet he maintained that he was assured of their existence; when pressed, he spoke of a spirit, (a word to which it was impossible to attach any determinate idea) which taught nothing but the sloth, which evidenced nothing but the stupidity of those who pronounced it.

It ought, however, not to excite any surprise that man is incapable of forming any substantive ideas, save of those things which act, or which have heretofore acted upon his senses; it is very evident that the only objects competent to move his organs are material,—that none but physical beings can furnish him with ideas,—a truth which has been rendered sufficiently clear in the commencement of this work, not to need any further proof. It will suffice therefore to say that the idea of God is not an innate, but an acquired notion; that it is the very nature of this notion to vary from age to age; to differ in one country from another; to be viewed variously by individuals. What do I say? It is, in fact, an idea hardly ever constant in the same mortal. This diversity, this fluctuation, this change, stamps it with the true character of an acquired opinion. On the other hand, the strongest proof that can be adduced that these ideas are founded in error, is, that man by degrees has arrived at perfectioning all the sciences which have any known objects for their basis, whilst the science of theology has not advanced; it is almost every where at the same point; men seem equally undecided on this subject; those who have most occupied themselves with it, have effected but little; they seem, indeed, rather to have rendered the primitive ideas man formed to himself on this head more obscure,—to have involved in greater mystery all his original opinions.

As soon as it is asked of man, what are the gods before whom he prostrates himself, forthwith his sentiments are divided. In order that his opinions should be in accord, it would be requisite that uniform ideas, analogous sensations, unvaried perceptions, should every where have given birth to his notions upon this subject: but this would suppose organs perfectly similar, modified by sensations which have a perfect affinity: this is what could not happen: because man, essentially different by his temperament, who is found under circumstances completely dissimilar, must necessarily have a great diversity of ideas upon objects which each individual contemplates so variously. Agreed in some general points, each made himself a god after his own manner; he feared him, he served him, after his own mode. Thus the god of one man, or of one nation, was hardly ever that of another man, or of another nation. The god of a savage, unpolished people, is commonly some material object, upon which the mind has exercised itself but little; this god appears very ridiculous in the eyes of a more polished community, whose minds have laboured more intensely upon the subject. A spiritual god, whose adorers despise the worship paid by the savage to a coarse, material object, is the subtle production of the brain of thinkers, who, lolling in the lap of polished society quite at their leisure, have deeply meditated, have long occupied themselves with the subject. The theological god, although for the most part incomprehensible, is the last effort of the human imagination; it is to the god of the savage, what an inhabitant of the city of Sybaris, where effiminacy and luxury reigned, where pomp and pageantry had reached their climax, clothed with a curiously embroidered purple habit of silk, was to a man either quite naked, or simply covered with the skin of a beast perhaps newly slain. It is only in civilized societies, that leisure affords the opportunity of dreaming—that ease procures the facility of reasoning; in these associations, idle speculators meditate, dispute, form metaphysics: the faculty of thought is almost void in the savage, who is occupied either with hunting, with fishing, or with the means of procuring a very precarious subsistence by dint of almost incessant labour. The generality of men, however, have not more elevated notions of the divinity, have not analyzed him more than the savage. A spiritual, immaterial God, is formed only to occupy the leisure of some subtle men, who have no occasion to labour for a subsistence. Theology, although a science so much vaunted, considered so important to the interests of man, is only useful to those who live at the expense of others; or of those who arrogate to themselves the privilege of thinking for all those who labour. This science becomes, in some polished societies, who are not on that account more enlightened, a branch of commerce extremely advantageous to its professors; equally unprofitable to the citizens; above all when these have the folly to take a very decided interest in their unintelligible system—in their discordant opinions.

What an infinite distance between an unformed stone, an animal, a star, a statue, and the abstracted Deity, which theology hath clothed with attributes under which it loses sight of him itself! The savage without doubt deceives himself in the object to which he addresses his vows; like a child he is smitten with the first object that strikes his sight —that operates upon him in a lively manner; like the infant, his fears are alarmed by that from which he conceives he has either received an injury or suffered disgrace; still his ideas are fixed by a substantive being, by an object which he can examine by his senses. The Laplander who adores a rock,—the negro who prostrates himself before a monstrous serpent, at least see the objects they adore. The idolater falls upon his knees before a statue, in which he believes there resides some concealed virtue, some powerful quality, which he judges may be either useful or prejudicial to himself; but that subtle reasoner, called a metaphysician, who in consequence of his unintelligible science, believes he has a right to laugh at the savage, to deride the Laplander, to scoff at the negro, to ridicule the idolater, doth not perceive that he is himself prostrate before a being of his own imagination, of which it is impossible he should form to himself any correct idea, unless, like the savage, he re-enters into visible nature, to clothe him with qualities capable of being brought within the range of his comprehension.

For the most part the notions on the Divinity, which obtain credit even at the present day, are nothing more than a general terror diversely acquired, variously modified in the mind of nations, which do not tend to prove any thing, save that they have received them from their trembling, ignorant ancestors. These gods have been successively altered, decorated, subtilized, by those thinkers, those legislators, those priests, who have meditated deeply upon them; who have prescribed systems of worship to the uninformed; who have availed themselves of their existing prejudices, to submit them to their yoke; who have obtained a dominion over their mind, by seizing on their credulity,—by making them participate in their errors,—by working on their fears; these dispositions will always be a necessary consequence of man's ignorance, when steeped in the sorrows of his heart.

If it be true, as asserted, that the earth has never witnessed any nation so unsociable, so savage, to be without some form of religious worship—who did not adore some god—but little will result from it respecting the Divinity. The word GOD, will rarely be found to designate more than the unknown cause of those effects which man has either admired or dreaded. Thus, this notion so generally diffused, upon which so much stress is laid; will prove little more than that man in all generations has been ignorant of natural causes,—that he has been incompetent, from some cause or other, to account for those phenomena which either excited his surprise or roused his fears. If at the present day a people cannot be found destitute of some kind of worship, entirely without superstition, who do not acknowledge a God, who have not adopted a theology more or less subtle, it is because the uninformed ancestors of these people have all endured misfortunes—have been alarmed by terrifying effects, which they have attributed to unknown causes—have beheld strange sights, which they have ascribed to powerful agents, whose existence they could not fathom; the details of which, together with their own bewildered notions, they have handed down to their posterity who have not given them any kind of examination.

It will readily be allowed, that the universality of an opinion by no means proves its truth. Do we not see a great number of ignorant prejudices, a multitude of barbarous errors, even at the present day, receive the almost universal sanction of the human race? Are not nearly all the inhabitants of the earth imbued with the idea of magic—in the habit of acknowledging occult powers—given to divination—believers in enchantment—the slaves to omens—supporters of witchcraft—thoroughly persuaded of the existence of ghosts? If some of the most enlightened persons are cured of these follies, they still find very zealous partizans in the greater number of mankind, who accredit them with the firmest confidence. It would not, however, be concluded by men of sound sense, in many instances not by the theologian himself, that therefore these chimeras actually have existence, although sanctioned with the credence of the multitude. Before Copernicus, there was no one who did not believe that the earth was stationary, that the sun described his annual revolution round it. Was, however, this universal consent of man upon a principle of astronomical science, which endured for so many thousand years, less an error on that account? Yet to have doubted the truth of such a generally-diffused opinion, one that had received the sanction of so many learned men—that was clothed with the sacred vestments of so many ages of credulity—that had been adopted by Moses, acknowledged by Solomon, accredited by the Persian magi—that Elijah himself had not refuted—that had obtained the fiat of the most respectable universities, the most enlightened legislators, the wisest kings, the most eloquent ministers; in short, a principle that embraced all the stability that could be derived from the universal consent of all ranks: to have doubted, I say, of this, would at one period have been held as the highest degree of profanation, as the most presumptuous scepticism, as an impious blasphemy, that would have threatened the very existence of that unhappy country from whose unfortunate bosom such a venomous, sacrilegious mortal could have arisen. It is well known what opinion was entertained of Gallileo for maintaining the existence of the antipodes. Pope Gregory excommunicated as atheists all those who gave it credit. Thus each man has his God: But do all these gods exist? In reply it will be said, somewhat triumphantly, each man hath his ideas of the sun, do all these suns exist? However narrow may be the pass by which superstition imagines it has thus guarded its favourite hypothesis, nothing will perhaps be more easy than the answer: the existence of the sun is a fact verified by the daily use of the senses; all the world see the sun; no one bath ever said there is no sun; nearly all mankind have acknowledged it to be both luminous and hot: however various may be the opinions of man, upon this luminary, no one has ever yet pretended there was more than one attached to our planetary system. But we may perhaps be told, there is a wide difference between that which can be contemplated by the visual organs, which can be understood by the sense of feeling, and that which does not come under the cognizance of any part of the organic structure of man. We must confess theology here has the advantage; that we are unable to follow it through its devious sinuosities; amidst its meandering labyrinths: but then it is the advantage of those who see sounds, over those who only hear them; of those who hear colours, over those who only see them; of the professors of a science, where every thing is built upon laws inverted from those common to the globe we inhabit; over those common understandings, who cannot be sensible to any thing that does not give an impulse to some of their organs.

If man, therefore, had the courage to throw aside his prejudices, which every thing conspires to render as durable as himself—if divested of fear he would examine coolly—if guided by reason he would dispassionately view the nature of things, the evidence adduced in support of any given doctrine; he would, at least, be under the necessity to acknowledge, that the idea of the Divinity is not innate— that it is not anterior to his existence—that it is the production of time, acquired by communication with his own species—that, consequently, there was a period when it did not actually exist in him: he would see clearly, that he holds it by tradition from those who reared him: that these themselves received it from their ancestors: that thus tracing it up, it will be found to have been derived in the last resort, from ignorant savages, who were our first fathers. The history of the world will shew that crafty legislators, ambitious tyrants, blood-stained conquerors, have availed themselves of the ignorance, the fears, the credulity of his progenitors, to turn to their own profit an idea to which they rarely attached any other substantive meaning than that of submitting them to the yoke of their own domination.

Without doubt there have been mortals who have dreamed they have seen the Divinity. Mahomet, I believe, boasted he had a long conversation with the Deity, who promulgated to him the system of the Mussulmans. But are there not thousands, even of the theologians, who will exhaust their breath, and fatigue their lungs with vociferating this man was a liar; whose object was to take advantage of the simplicity, to profit by the enthusiasm, to impose on the credulity of the Arabs; who promulgated for truths, the crazy reveries of his own distempered imagination? Nevertheless, is it not a truth, that this doctrine of the crafty Arab, is at this day the creed of millions, transmitted to them by their ancestors, rendered sacred by time, read to them in their mosques, adorned with all the ceremonies of superstitious worship; of which the inhabitants of a vast portion of the earth do not permit themselves for an instant to doubt the veracity; who, on the contrary, hold those who do not accredit it as dogs, as infidels, as beings of an inferior rank, of meaner capacities than themselves? Indeed that man, even if he were a theologian, would not experience the most gentle treatment from the infuriated Mahometan, who should to his face venture to dispute the divine mission of his prophet. Thus the ancestors of the Turk have transmitted to their posterity, those ideas of the Divinity which they manifestly received from those who deceived them; whose impositions, modified from age to age, subtilized by the priests, clothed with the reverential awe inspired by fear, have by degrees acquired that solidity, received that corroboration, attained that veteran stability, which is the natural result of public sanction, backed by theological parade.

The word God is, perhaps, among the first that vibrate on the ear of man; it is reiterated to him incessantly; he is taught to lisp it with respect; to listen to it with fear; to bend the knee when it is reverberated: by dint of repetition, by listening to the fables of antiquity, by hearing it pronounced by all ranks and persuasions, he seriously believes all men bring the idea with them into the world; he thus confounds a mechanical habit with instinct; whilst it is for want of being able to recal to himself the first circumstances under which his imagination was awakened by this name; for want of recollecting all the recitals made to him during the course of his infancy; for want of accurately defining what was instilled into him by his education; in short, because his memory does not furnish him with the succession of causes that have engraven it on his brain, that he believes this idea is really inherent to his being; innate in all his species. Iamblicus, indeed, who was a Pythagorean philosopher not in the highest repute with the learned world, although one of those visionary priests in some estimation with theologians, (at least if we may venture to judge by the unlimited draughts they have made on the bank of his doctrines) who was unquestionably a favourite with the emperor Julian, says, "that anteriorly to all use of reason, the notion of the gods is inspired by nature, and that we have even a sort of feeling of the Divinity, preferable to the knowledge of him." It is, however, uniformly by habit, that man admires, that he fears a being, whose name he has attended to from his earliest infancy. As soon as he hears it uttered, he without reflection mechanically associates it with those ideas with which his imagination has been filled by the recitals of others; with those sensations which he has been instructed to accompany it. Thus, if for a season man would be ingenuous with himself, he would concede that in the greater number of his race, the ideas of the gods, and of those attributes with which they are clothed, have their foundation, take their rise in, are the fruit of the opinions of his fathers, traditionally infused into him by education— confirmed by habit— corroborated by example—enforced by authority. That it very rarely happens he examines these ideas; that they are for the most part adopted by inexperience, propagated by tuition, rendered sacred by time, inviolable from respect to his progenitors, reverenced as forming part of those institutions he has most learned to value. He thinks he has always had them, because he has had them from his infancy; he considers them indubitable, because he is never permitted to question them— because he never has the intrepidity to examine their basis.

If it had been the destiny of a Brachman, or a Mussulman, to have drawn his first breath on the shores of Africa, he would adore, with as much simplicity, with as much fervour, the serpent reverenced by the Negroes, as he does the God his own metaphysicians have offered to his reverence. He would be equally indignant if any one should presumptuously dispute the divinity of this reptile, which he would have learned to venerate from the moment he quitted the womb of his mother, as the most zealous, enthusiastic fakir, when the marvellous wonders of his prophet should be brought into question; or as the most subtile theologian when the inquiry turned upon the incongruous qualities with which he has decorated his gods. Nevertheless, if this serpent god of the Negro should be contested, they could not at least dispute his existence. Simple as may be the mind of this dark son of nature, uncommon as may be the qualities with which he has clothed his reptile, he still may be evidenced by all who choose to exercise their organs of sight; not so with the theologian; he absolutely questions the existence of every other god but that which he himself has formed; which is questioned in its turn by his brother metaphysician. They are by no means disposed to admit the proofs offered by each other. Descartes, Paschal, and Doctor Samuel Clarke himself, have been accused of atheism by the theologians of their time. Subsequent reasoners have made use of their proofs, and even given them as extremely valid. Doctor Bowman published a work, in which he pretends all the proofs hitherto brought forward are crazy and fragile: he of course substitutes his own; which in their turn have been the subject of animadversion. Thus it would appear these theologians are not more in accord with themselves than they are with Turks or Pagans. They cannot even agree as to their proofs of existence: from age to age new champions arise, new evidence is adduced, the old discarded, or treated with contempt; profound philosophers, subtle metaphysicians, are continually attacking each other for their ignorance on a point of the very first importance. Amidst this variety of discussion, it is very difficult for simple winds, for those who steadily search after truth, who only wish to understand what they believe, to find a point upon which they can fix with reliance—a standard round which they may rally without fear of danger—a common measure that way serve them for a beacon to avoid the quicksands of delusion—the sophistry of polemics.

Men of very great genius have successively miscarried in their demonstrations; have been held to have betrayed their cause by the weakness of the arguments by which they have supported it; by the manner in which they have attempted to establish their positions. Thus many of them, when they believed they had surmounted a difficulty, had the mortification to find they had only given birth to an hundred others. They seem, indeed, not to be in a capacity to understand each other, or to agree among themselves, when they reason upon the nature and qualities of beings created by such a variety of imaginations, which each contemplates diversely, upon which the natural self-love of each disputant induces him to reject with vehement indignation every thing that does not fall in with his own peculiar mode of thinking—that does not quadrate either with his superstition or his ignorance, or sometimes with both.

The opponents of Clarke charge him with begging the question in his work on *The Being and Attributes of God*. They say he has pretended to prove this existence *a priori*, which they deem impossible, seeing there is nothing anterior to the first of causes; that therefore it can only be proved *a posteriori*, that is to say, by its effects. Law, in his *Inquiry into the Ideas of Space, Time, Immensity, &c.* has attacked him very triumphantly, for this manner of proof, which is stated to be so very repugnant to the school-men. His arguments have been treated with no more ceremony by Thomas D'Aquinas, John Scott, and others of the schools. At the present day I believe he is held in more respect—that his authority outweighs that of all his antagonists together. Be that as it may, those who have followed him have done nothing more than either repeat his ideas, or present his evidence under a new form. Tillotson argues at great length, but it would be rather difficult to understand which side of the question he adopts on this momentous subject; whether he is a Necessitarian, or among the opposers of Fatalism. Speaking of man, he says, "he is liable to many evils and miseries, which he can neither prevent or redress; he is full of wants, which he cannot supply, and compassed about with infirmities which he cannot remove, and obnoxious to dangers which he can never sufficiently provide against: he is apt to grieve for what he cannot help, and eagerly to desire what he is never able to obtain." If the proofs of Clarke, who has drawn them up in twelve propositions, are examined with attention, I think they may be fairly shielded from the reproach with which they have been loaded; it does not appear that he has proved his positions *a priori*, but *a posteriori*, according to rule. It seems clear, however, that he has mistaken the proof of the existence of the effects, for the proof of the existence of the cause: but here he seems to have more reason than his critics, who in their eagerness to prove that Clarke has not conformed to the rules of the schools, would entirely overlook the best, the surest foundation whereon to rest the existence of the *Great Cause of causes*, that *Parent of Parents*, whose wisdom shines so manifestly in nature, of which Clarke's work may be said to be such a masterly evidence. We shall follow, step by step, the different propositions in which this learned divine developes the received opinions upon the Divinity; which, when applied to nature, will be found to be so accurate, so correct, as to leave no further room to doubt either the existence or the wisdom of her great author, thus proved through her own existence. Dr. Clarke sets out with saying:

"*1st. Something has existed from all eternity.*"

This proposition is evident—hath no occasion for proofs. Matter has existed from all eternity, its forms alone are evanescent; matter is the great engine used by nature to produce all her phenomena, or rather it is nature herself. We have some idea of matter, sufficient to warrant the conclusion that this has always existed. First, that which exists, supposes existence essential to its being. That which cannot, annihilate itself, exists necessarily; it is impossible to conceive that that which cannot cease to exist, or that which cannot annihilate itself, could ever have had a beginning. If matter cannot be annihilated, it could not commence to be. Thus we say to Dr. Clarke, that it is matter, it is nature, acting by her own peculiar energy, of which no particle is ever in an absolute state of rest, which hath always existed. The various material bodies which this nature contains often change their form, their combination, their properties, their mode of action: but their principles or elements are indestructible—have never been able to commence. What this great scholar actually understands, when he makes the assertion "that an eternal duration is now actually past," is not quite so clear; yet he affirms, "that not to believe it would be a real and express contradiction." We may, however, safely admit his argument, "that when once any proposition is clearly demonstrated to, be true, it ought not to disturb us that there be perhaps some perplexing difficulties on the other side, which merely for want of adequate ideas of the manner of the existence of the things demonstrated, are not easily to be cleared."

2nd, "There has existed from eternity some one unchangeable and independent Being."

We may fairly inquire what is this Being? Is it independent of its own peculiar essence, or of those properties which constitute it such as it is? We shall further inquire, if this Being, whatever it may be, can make the other beings which it produces, or which it moves, act otherwise than they do, according to the properties which it has given them? And in this case we shall ask, if this Being, such as it way be supposed to be, does not act necessarily; if it is not obliged to employ indispensible means to fulfil its designs, to arrive at the end which it either has, or may be supposed to have in view? Then we shall say, that nature is obliged to act after her essence; that every thing which takes place in her is necessary; but that she is independent of her forms.

A man is said to be independent, when he is determined in his actions only by the general causes which are accustomed to move him; he is equally said to be dependent on another, when he cannot act but in consequence of the determination which this last gives him. A body is dependent on another body when it owes to it its existence, and its mode of action. A being existing from eternity cannot owe his existence to any other being; he cannot then be dependent upon him, except he owes his action to him; but it is evident that an eternal or self-existent Being contains in his own nature every thing that is necessary for him to act: then, matter being eternal, is necessarily independent in the sense we have explained; of course it hath no occasion for a mover upon which it ought to depend.

This eternal Being is also immutable, if by this attribute be understood that he cannot change his nature; but if it be intended to infer by it that he cannot change his mode of action or existence, it is without doubt deceiving themselves, since even in supposing an immaterial being, they would be obliged to acknowledge in him different modes of being, different volitions, different ways of acting; particularly if he was not supposed totally deprived of action, in which case he would be perfectly useless. Indeed it follows of course that to change his mode of action he must necessarily change his manner of being. From hence it will he obvious, that the theologians, in making their gods immutable, render them immoveable, consequently they cannot act. An immutable being, could evidently neither have successive volition, nor produce successive action; if this being hath created matter, or given birth to the universe, there must have been a time in which he was willing that this matter, this universe, should exist; and this time must have been preceded by another time, in which he was willing that it might not yet exist. If God be the author of all things, as well as of the motion and of the combinations of matter, he is unceasingly occupied in producing and destroying; in consequence, he cannot be called immutable, touching his mode of existing. The material world always maintains itself by motion, and the continual change of its parts; the sum of the beings who compose it, or of the elements which act in it, is invariably the same; in this sense the immutability of the universe is much more easy of comprehension, much more demonstrable than that of an other being to whom, they would attribute all the effects, all the mutations which take place. Nature is not more to be accused of mutability, on account of the succession of its forms, than the eternal Being is by the theologians, by the diversity of his decrees. Here we shall be able to perceive that, supposing the laws by which nature acts to be immutable, it does not require tiny of these logical distinctions to account for the changes that take place: the mutation which results, is, on the contrary, a striking proof of the immutability of the system which produces them; and completely brings mature under the range of this second proposition as stated by Dr. Clarke.

3dly, *"That unchangeable and independent Being which has existed from eternity without any eternal cause of its existence, must be self- existent, that is, necessarily existing."*

This proposition is merely a repetition of the first; we reply to it by inquiring, Why matter, which is indestructible, should not be self- existent? It is evident that a being who had no beginning, must be self- existent; if he had existed by another, he would have commenced to be; consequently he would not be eternal.

4thly, *"What the substance or essence of that Being which is self- existent, or necessarily existing, is, we have no idea; neither is it at all possible for us to comprehend it."*

Dr. Clarke would perhaps have spoken more correctly if he had said his essence is impossible to be known: nevertheless, we shall readily concede that the essence of matter is incomprehensible, or at least that we conceive it very feebly by the manner in which we are affected by it; but without this we should be less able to conceive the Divinity, who would then be impervious on any side. Thus it must necessarily be concluded, that it is folly to argue upon it, since it is by matter alone we can have any knowledge of him; that is to say, by which we can assure ourselves of his existence,—by which we can at all guess at his qualities. In short we must conclude, that every thing related of the Divinity, either proves him material, or else proves the impossibility in which the human mind will always find itself, of conceiving any being different from matter; without extent, yet omnipresent; immaterial, yet acting upon matter; spiritual, yet producing matter; immutable, yet putting every thing in activity, &c.

Indeed it must be allowed that the incomprehensibility of the Divinity does not distinguish him from matter; this will not be more easy of comprehension when we shall associate it with a being much less comprehensible than itself; we have some slender knowledge of it through some of its parts. We do not certainly know the essence of any being, if by that word we are to understand that which constitutes its peculiar nature. We only know matter by the sensations, the perceptions, the ideas which it furnishes; it is according to these that we judge it to be either favorable or unfavourable, following the particular disposition of our organs. But when a being does not act upon any part of our organic structure, it does not exist for us; we cannot, without exhibiting folly, without betraying our ignorance, without falling into obscurity, either speak of its nature, or assign its qualities; our senses are the only channel by which we could have formed the slightest idea of it; these not having received any impulse, we are, in point of fact, unacquainted with its existence. The incomprehensibility of the Divinity ought to convince man that it is a point at which he is bound to stop; indeed he is placed in a state of utter incapacity to proceed: this, however, would not suit with those speculators who are willing to reason upon him continually, to shew the depth of their learning,—to persuade the uninformed they understand that which is incomprehensible to all men; by which they expect to be able to submit him to their own views. Nevertheless, if the Divinity be incomprehensible, It would not be straining a point beyond its tension, to conclude that a priest, or metaphysician, did not comprehend him better than other men: it is not, perhaps, either the wisest or the surest way to become acquainted with him, to represent him to ourselves, by the imagination of a theologian.

5thly, *"Though the substance, or essence of the self-existent Being, is in itself absolutely incomprehensible to us, yet many of the essential attributes of his nature are strictly demonstrable, as well as his existence. Thus, in the first place, the self-existent Being must of necessity be eternal."*

This proposition differs in nothing from the first, except Dr. Clarke does not here understand that as the self-existent Being had no beginning, he can have no end. However this may be, we must ever inquire, Why this should not be matter? We shall further observe, that matter not being capable of annihilation, exists necessarily, consequently will never cease to exist; that the human mind has no means of conceiving how matter should originate from that which is not itself matter: is it not obvious, that matter is necessary; that there is nothing, except its powers, its arrangement, its combinations, which are contingent or evanescent? The general motion is necessary, but the given motion is not so; only during the season that the particular combinations subsist, of which this motion is the consequence, or the effect: we may be competent to change the direction, to either accelerate or retard, to suspend or arrest, a particular motion, but the general motion can never possibly be annihilated. Man, in dying, ceases to live; that is to say, he no longer either walks, thinks, or acts in the mode which is peculiar to human organization: but the matter which composed his body, the matter which formed his mind, does not cease to move on that account: it simply becomes susceptible of another species of motion.

6thly, "The self-existent Being must of necessity be infinite and omnipresent."

The word infinite presents only a negative idea—which excludes all bounds: it is evident that a being who exists necessarily, who is independent, cannot be limited by any thing which is out of himself; he must consequently be his own limits; in this sense we may say he is infinite.

Touching what is said of his omnipresence, it is equally evident that if there be nothing exterior to this being, either there is no place in which he must not be present, or that there will be only himself and the vacuum. This granted, I shall inquire if matter exists; if it does not at least occupy a portion of space? In this case, matter, or the universe, must exclude every other being who is not matter, from that place which the material beings occupy in space. In asking whether the gods of the theologians be by chance the abstract being which they call the vacuum or space, they will reply, no! They will further insist, that their gods, who are not matter, penetrate that which is matter. But it must be obvious, that to penetrate matter, it is necessary to have some correspondence with matter, consequently to have extent; now to have extent, is to have one of the properties of matter. If the Divinity penetrates matter, then he is material; by a necessary deduction he is inseparable from matter; then if he is omnipresent, he will be in every thing. This the theologian will not allow: he will say it is a mystery; by which I shall understand that he is himself ignorant how to account for his own positions; this will not he the case with making nature act after immutable laws; she will of necessity be every where, in my body, in my arm, in every other material being, because matter composes them all. The Divinity who has given this invariable system, will without any incongruous reasoning, without any subterfuge, be also present every where, inasmuch as the laws be has prescribed will unchangeably act through the whole; this does not seem inconsistent with reason to suppose.

7th, "The Self-existent Being must of necessity be but one."

If there he nothing exterior to a being who exists necessarily, it must follow that he is unique. It will be obvious that this proposition is the same with the preceding one; at least, if they are not willing to deny the existence of the material world.

8th, "The self-existent and original Cause of all things, must be an intelligent being."

Here Dr. Clarke most unquestionably assigneth a human quality: intelligence is a faculty appertaining to organized or animated beings, of which we have no knowledge out of these beings. To have intelligence, it is necessary to think; to think, it is requisite to have ideas; to have ideas, supposes senses; when senses exist they are material; when they are material, they cannot be a pure spirit, in the language of the theologian.

The necessary Being who comprehends, who contains, who produces animated beings, contains, includes, and produceth intelligence. But has the great whole a peculiar intelligence, which moveth it, which maketh it act, which determineth it in the mode that intelligence moves and determines animated bodies; or rather, is not this intelligence the consequence of immutable laws, a certain modification resulting from certain combinations of matter, which exists under one form of these combinations, but is wanting under another form? This is assuredly what nothing is competent absolutely, and demonstrably to prove. Man having placed himself in the first rank in the universe, has been desirous to judge of every thing after what he saw within himself, because he hath pretended that in order to be perfect it was necessary to be like himself. Here is the source of all his erroneous reasoning upon nature— the foundation of his ideas upon his gods. He has therefore concluded, perhaps not with the most polished wisdom, that it would be indecorous in himself, injurious to the Divinity, not to invest him with a quality which is found estimable in man—which he prizes highly—to which he attaches the idea of perfection—which he considers as a manifest proof of superiority. He sees his fellow-creature is offended when he is thought to lack intelligence; he therefore judges it to be the same with the Divinity. He denies this quality to nature, because he considers her a mass of ignoble matter, incapable of self-action; although she contains and produces intelligent beings. But this is rather a personification of an abstract quality, than an attribute of the Deity, with whose perfections, with whose mode of existence, he cannot by any possible means become acquainted according to the fifth proposition of Dr. Clarke himself. It is in the earth that is engendered those living animals called worms; yet we do not say the earth is a living creature. The bread which man eats, the wine that he drinks, are not themselves thinking substances; yet they nourish, sustain, and cause those beings to think, who are susceptible of this modification of their existence. It is likewise in nature, that is formed intelligent, feeling, thinking beings; yet it cannot be rationally said, that nature feels, thinks, and is intelligent after the manner of these beings, who nevertheless spring out of her bosom.

How! cries the metaphysician, the subtilizing philosopher, what! refuse to the Divinity, those qualities we discover in his creatures? Must, then, the work be more perfect than the workman? Shall God, who made the eye, not himself see? Shall God, who formed the ear, not himself hear! This at a superficial view appears insuperable: but are the questioners, however triumphantly they may make the inquiry, themselves aware of the length this would carry them, even if their queries were answered with the most unqualified affirmative? Have they sufficiently reflected on the tendency of this mode of reasoning? If this be admitted as a postulatum, are they prepared to follow it in all its extent? Suppose their argument granted, what is to be done with all those other qualities upon which man does not set so high a value? Are they also to be ascribed to the Divinity, because we do not refuse him qualities possessed by his creatures? By a parity of reasoning we should attach faculties that would be degrading to the Divinity. Thus it ever happens with those who travel out of the limits of their own knowledge; they involve themselves in perpetual contradictions which they can never reconcile; which only serve to prove that in arguing upon points, on which universal ignorance prevails, the result is constantly that all the deductions made from such unsteady principles, must of necessity be at war with each other, in hostility with themselves. Thus, although we cannot help feeling the profound wisdom, that must have dictated the system we see act with such uniformity, with such constancy, with such astonishing power, we cannot form the most slender idea of the particular nature of that wisdom; because if we were for an instant to assimilate it to our own, weak and feeble as it is, we should from that instant be in a state of contradiction; seeing we could not then avoid considering the evil we witness, the sorrow we experience, as a dereliction of this wisdom, which at least proves one great truth, *that we are utterly incapable of forming an idea of the Divinity*. But in contemplating things as our own experience warrants in whatever we do understand, in considering nature as acting by unchangeable laws, we find good and evil necessarily existing, without at all involving the wisdom of the great *Cause of causes*; who thus has no need to remedy that, which the further progress of the eternal system will regulate of itself, or which industry and patient research on our parts will enable us to discover the means of futurely avoiding.

9th, "*The self-existent and original Cause of all things, is not a necessary agent, but a being endued with liberty and choice.*"

Man is called free, when he finds within himself motives that determine him to action, or when his will meets no obstacle to the performance of that to which his motives have determined him. The necessary Being of which question is here made, doth he find no obstacles to the execution of the projects which are attributed to him? Is he willing, adopting their own hypothesis, that evil should be committed, or can he not prevent it? In this latter case he is not free; if his will does meet with obstacles, if he is willing to permit evil; then he suffers man to restrain his liberty, by deranging his projects; if he has not these projects, then they are themselves in error who ascribe them to him. How will the metaphysicians draw themselves out of this perplexing intricacy?

The further a theologian goes, whilst considering his gods as possessed of human qualities, as acting by mortal motives, the more he flounders— the greater the mass of contradiction he heaps together: thus if it be asked of him, can God reward crime, punish virtue, he will immediately answer, no! In this answer he will have truth: but then this truth, and the freedom which is ascribed to him, cannot, according to human ideas, exist together; because if this being cannot love vice, cannot hate virtue, and it is evident he cannot, he is in fact not more free than man himself. Again, God is said to have made a covenant with his creatures; now it is the very essence of a covenant to restrict choice; and that being must be considered a necessary agent who is under the necessity of fulfilling any given act. As it is impossible to suppose the Divinity can act irrationally, it must be conceded that as he made these laws, he is himself obliged to follow them: because if he was not, as we must again suppose he does nothing without a good reason, he would thereby imply, that the mode of action he adopted would be wiser; which would again involve a contradiction. The theologians fearing, without doubt, to restrain the liberty of the Divinity, have supposed it was necessary that he should not be bound by his own laws, in which they have shewn somewhat more ignorance of their subject than they imagined.

10th, *"The self-existent Being, the supreme Cause of all things, must of necessity have infinite power."*

As nature is adequate to produce every thing we see—as she contains the whole united power of the universe, her power has consequently no limits: the being who conferred this power cannot have less. But if the ideas of the theologians were adopted, this power would not appear quite so unlimited; since, according to them, man is a free agent, consequently has the means of acting contrary to this power, which at once sets a boundary to it. An equitable monarch is perhaps nothing less than he is a free agent; when he believes himself bound to act conformably to the laws, which he has sworn to observe, or which he cannot violate without wounding his justice. The theologian is a man who may be very fairly estimated neuter; because he destroys with one hand what he establishes with the other.

11th, *"The Supreme Cause and Author of all things, must of necessity be infinitely wise."*

As nature produces all things by certain immutable laws, it will require no great difficulty to allow that she may be infinitely wise: indeed, whatever side of the argument may be taken, this fact will result as a necessary consequence. It will hardly admit of a question that all things are produced by nature: if, therefore, we do not allow her wisdom to be first rate, it would be an insult to the Divinity, who gave her her system. If the theologian himself is to take the lead, he also admits that nature operates under the immediate auspices of his gods; whatever she does, must then, according to his own shewing, be executed with the most polished wisdom. But the theologian is not satisfied with going thus far: he will insist, not only that he knows what these things are, but also that he knows the end they have in view: this, unfortunately, is the rock he splits upon. According to his own admission, the ways of God are impenetrable to man. If we grant his position, what is the result? Why, that it is at random he speaks. If these ways are impenetrable, by what means did he acquire his knowledge of them? How did he discover the end proposed by the Deity? If they are not impenetrable, they then can be equally known to other men as to himself. The theologian would be puzzled to shew he has any more privileges in nature than his fellow mortals. Again, if he has asserted these things to be impenetrable, when they are not so, he is then in the situation that he has himself placed Mahomet: he is no longer worthy of being attended to, because he has swerved from veracity. It certainly is not very consistent with the sublime idea of the Divinity that he should be clothed with that weak, vain passion of man, called glory: the being who had the faculty of producing such a system as it operated in nature, could hardly be supposed to have such a frivolous passion as we know this to be in our fellows: and as we can never reason but after what we do know, it would appear nothing can be more inconsistent than thus continually heaping together our own feeble, inconsistent views, and then supposing the great *Cause of causes* acts by such futile rules.

12th, "*The supreme Cause and Author of all things must of necessity be a being of infinite goodness, justice, and truth, and all other moral perfections, such as become the supreme governor and judge of the world.*"

We must again repeat that these are human qualities drawn from the model of man himself; they only suppose a being of the human species, who should be divested of what we call imperfections: this is certainly the highest point of view in which our finite minds are capable of contemplating the Divinity: but as this being has neither species nor cause, consequently no fellow creatures, he must necessarily be of an order so different to man, that human faculties can in no wise be appropriately assigned to him. The idea of perfection, as man understands it, is an abstract, metaphysical, negative idea, of which he has no archetype whereby to form a judgment: he would call that a perfect being, who, similar to himself, was wanting in those qualities which he finds prejudicial to him; but such a being would after all be no wore than a man. It is always relatively to himself, to his own mode of feeling and of thinking, that a thing is either perfect or imperfect; it is according to this, that in his eyes a thing is more or less useful or prejudicial; agreeable or disagreeable. Justice includes all moral perfections. One of the most prominent features of justice, in the ideas of man, is the equity of the relations subsisting between beings, founded upon their mutual wants. According to the theologian, his gods owe nothing to man. How then does he measure out his ideas of justice? For a monarch to say he owed nothing to his subjects, would be considered, even by this theologian himself, as rank injustice; because he would expect the fulfilment of duties on their part, without exercising those which devolved upon himself. Duties, according to the only idea man can form of them, must he reciprocal. It is rather stretching the human capabilities, to understand the relations between a pure spirit and material beings—between finity and infinity—between eternal beings and those which are transitory: thus it is, that metaphysics hold forth an inconceivable being by the very attributes with which they clothe him; for either he has these attributes, or he has them not: whether he has them or has them not, man can only understand them after his own powers of comprehension. If he does at all understand them, he cannot have the slightest idea of justice unaccompanied by duties, which are the very basis, the superstructure, the pillars upon which this virtue rests. Whether we are to view it as self-love or ignorance in the theologian, that he thus dresses up his gods after himself, it certainly was not the happiest effort of his imagination to work by an inverse rule: for, according to himself, the qualities he describes are all the negation of what he calls them. Doctor Clarke himself stumbles a little upon these points; he insists upon free agency, and uses this extraordinary method to support his argument; he says, "God is, by necessity, a free agent: and be can no more possibly cease to be so, than he can cease to exist. He must of necessity, every moment choose to act, or choose to forbear acting; because two contradictories cannot possibly he true at once. Man also is by necessity, not in the nature of things, but through God's appointment, a free agent. And it is no otherwise in his power to cease to be such, than by depriving himself of life." Will Doctor Clarke permit us to put one simple question: If to be obliged to do a certain given thing, is to be free, what is it to be coerced? Or if two contradictories cannot be true at once, by what rule of logic are we to measure the idea of that freedom which arises out of necessity. Supposing necessity to be what Dr. Johnson, (using Milton as his authority) says it is, "compulsion," "fatality," would it be considered a man was less restrained in his actions because he was only compelled to do what was right? The restraint would undoubtedly he beneficial to him, but it would not therefore render him more a free agent. If the Divinity cannot love wickedness, cannot hate goodness, (and surely the theologians themselves will not pretend he can,) then the power of choice has no existence as far as these two things are concerned; and this upon Clarke's own principle, because two contradictories cannot be true at once. Nothing could, I think, appear a greater contradiction, than the idea that the *Great Cause of causes* could by any possibility love vice: if such a monstrous principle could for a moment have existence, there would be an end of all the foundations of religion.

    The Doctor is very little happier in reasoning upon *immateriality*. He says, by way of illustrating his argument, "that it is possible to infinite power to create an immaterial cogitative substance, endued with a power of beginning motion, and with a liberty of will or choice." Again, "that immaterial substances are not impossible; or, that a substance immaterial is not a contradictory notion. Now, whoever asserts that it is contradictory, must affirm that whatever is not matter is nothing; and that, to say any thing exists which is not matter, is saying that there exists something which is nothing, which in other words is plainly this,—that whatever we have not an idea of, is nothing, and impossible to be." It could, I am apt to believe, never have entered into any reasonable mind that a thing was impossible because he could have no idea of it:—many things, on the contrary, are possible, of which we have not the most slender notion: but it does not, I presume, flow consecutively out of this admission, that therefore every thing is, which is not impossible. Doctor Clarke then, rather begs the question on this occasion. In the schools it is never considered requisite to prove a negative; indeed, this is ranked by logicians amongst those things impossible to be, but it is considered of the highest importance to soundness of argument, to establish the affirmative by the most conclusive reasoning. Taking this for granted, we will apply the doctor's own reasoning. He says, "Nothing is that of which every thing, can truly be affirmed. So that the idea of nothing, if I may so speak, is absolutely the negative of all ideas; the idea, therefore, either of a finite or infinite nothing is a contradiction in terms." To affirm, of a thing with truth, it must be necessary to be acquainted with that thing. To have ideas, as we have already proved, it is necessary to have perceptions; to have perceptions, it is requisite to have sensations; to have sensations, requires organs. An idea cannot be, and not be, at the same moment: the idea of substance, it will scarcely be denied, is that of a thing solid, real, according to Dryden; capable of supporting accidents, according to Watts; something of which we can say that it is, according to Davies; body, corporeal nature, according to Newton; the idea of immaterial, according to Hooker, is incorporeal. How then am I to understand immaterial substance? Is it not, according to these definitions, that which cannot couple together? If a thing be immaterial, it cannot be a substance; if a substance, it cannot be immaterial: those I apprehend will not have many ideas, who do not see this is a complete negative of all ideas. If, therefore, on the outset, the doctor cannot find words, by which he can convey the idea of that of which he is so desirous to prove the existence, by what chain of reasoning does he flatter himself that he is to be understood? He will endeavour to draw out of this dilemma, by assuring as there are things which we can neither see nor touch, but which do not the less exist on that account. Granted: but from thence we can neither reason upon them, nor assign them qualities; we must at least either feel them or something like them, before we can have any idea of them: this, however, would not prove they were not substances, nor that substances can be immaterial. A thing may with great possibility exist of which we have no knowledge, and yet be material; but I maintain until we have a knowledge of it, it exists not for us, any more than colours exist for a man born blind; the man who has sight knows they do exist, can describe them to his dark neighbour; from this description the blind man may form some idea of them by analogy with what he himself already knows; or, perhaps, having a finer tact than his neighbour, he may be enabled to distinguish them by their surfaces; it would, therefore, be bad reasoning in the man born blind, to deny the existence of colours; because although these colours may have no relation with the senses in the absence of sight, they have with those who have it in their power to see and to know them: this blind man, however, would-appear a little ridiculous if he undertook to define them with all their gradations of shade; with all their variations under different masses of light. Again, if those who were competent to discriminate these modifications of matter called colours, were to define them to this blind man, as those modifications of matter called sound, would the blind man be able to have any conception of them? It certainly would not be wise in him to aver, that such a thing as colorific sound had no existence, was impossible; but at least he would be very justifiable in saying, they appeared contradictions, because he had some ideas of sound which did not at all aid him in forming those of colour; he would not, perhaps, be very inconclusive if he suspected the competency of his informer to the definition attempted, from his inability to convey to him in any distinct, understood terms, his own ideas of colours. The theologian is a blind man, who would explain to others who are also blind, the shades and colours of a portrait whose original he has not even stumbled upon in the dark. There is nothing incongruous in supposing that every thing which has existence is matter; but it requires the complete inversion of all our ideas, to conceive that which is immaterial; because, in point of fact, this would be a quality of which "nothing can with truth be affirmed."

It is, indeed true, that Plato, who was a great creator of chimeras, says, "those who admit nothing but what they can see and feel, are stupid ignorant beings, who refuse to admit the reality of the existence of invisible things." With all due deference to such an authority, we may still venture to ask, is there then no difference, no shade, no gradation, between an admission of possibilities and the proof of realities. Theology would then be the only science in which it is permitted to conclude that a thing is, as soon as it is possible to be. Will the assertion of either Clarke or Plato stand absolutely in place of all evidence? Would they themselves permit such to be convincing if used against them? The theologians evidently hold this Platonic, this dogmatical language; they have dreamed the dreams of their master; perhaps if they were examined a little, they would be found nothing more than the result of those obscure notions, those unintelligible metaphysics, adopted by the Egyptian, Chaldean, and Assyrian priests, among whom Plato drew up his philosophy. If, however, philosophy means that which we are led to suppose it does, by the great John Locke, it is "a system by which natural effects are explained." Taken in this sense we shall be under the necessity of agreeing, that the Platonic doctrines in no wise merit this distinction, seeing he has only drawn the human mind from the contemplation of visible nature, to plunge it into the unfathomable depths of invisibility—of intangibility—of suppositious speculation, where it can find little other food except chimeras or conjecture. Such a philosophy is rather fantastical, yet it would seem we are required to subscribe to its positions without being allowed to compare them with reason, to examine them through the medium of experience, to try the gold by the action of fire: thus we have in abundance the terms spirits, incorporeal substances, invisible powers, supernatural effects, innate ideas, mysterious virtues, possessed by demons, &c. &c. which render our senses entirely useless, which put to flight every thing like experience; while we are gravely told that "nothing is that, of which no thing can truly be affirmed." Whoever may be willing to take the trouble of reading the works of Plato and his disciples, such as Proclus, Iamblicus, Plotinus, and others, will not fail to find in them almost every doctrine, every metaphysical subject of the theologian; in fact, the theurgy of many of the modern superstitions, which for the most part seems to be little more than a slight variation of that adopted by the ethnic priests. Dreamers have not had that variety in their follies, that has generally been imagined. That some of these things should be extensively admitted, by no means affords proof of their existence. Nothing appears more facile than to make mankind admit the greatest absurdities, under the imposing name of mysteries; after having imbued him from his infancy with maxims calculated to hoodwink his reason—to lead him astray—to prevent him from examining that which he is told he must believe. Of this there cannot well exist a more decisive proof than the great extent of country, the millions of human beings who faithfully and without examination have adopted the idle dreams, the rank absurdities, of that arch impostor Mahomet. However this may be, we shall be obliged again to reply to Plato, and to those of his followers who impose upon us the necessity of believing that which we cannot comprehend, that, in order to know that a thing exists, it is at least necessary to have some idea of it; that this idea can only come to us by the medium of our senses; that consequently every thing of which our senses do not give us a knowledge, is in fact nothing for us; and can only rest upon our faith; upon that admission which is pretty generally, even by the theologian himself, considered as rather a sandy foundation whereon to erect the altar of truth: that if there be an absurdity in not accrediting the existence of that which we do not know, there is no less extravagance in assigning it qualities; in reasoning upon its properties; in clothing it with faculties, which may or may not be suitable to its mode of existence; in substituting idols of our own creation; in combining incompatible attributes, which will neither bear the test of experience nor the scrutiny of reason; and then endeavouring to make the whole pass current by dint of the word infinite, which we will now examine.

Infinite, according to Dennis, means "boundless, unlimited." Doctor Clarke thus describes it:—he says, "The self-existent being must be a most simple, unchangeable incorruptible being; without parts, figure, motion, divisibility, or any other such properties as we find in matter. For all these things do plainly and necessarily imply finiteness in their very notion, and are utterly inconsistent with complete infinity." Ingenuously, is it possible for man to form any true notion of such a quality? The theologians themselves acknowledge he cannot. Further, the Doctor allows, "That as to the particular manner of his being infinite, or every where present, in opposition to the manner of created things being present in such or such finite places, this is as impossible for our finite understandings to comprehend or explain, as it is for us to form an adequate idea of infinity." What is this, then, but that which no man can explain or comprehend? If it cannot be comprehended, it cannot be detailed; if it cannot be detailed, it is precisely "that of which nothing can with truth be affirmed;" and this is Dr. Clarke's own explanation of nothing. Indeed, is not the human mind obliged by its very nature to join limited quantities to other quantities, which it can only conceive as limited, in order to form to itself a sort of confused idea of something beyond its own grasp, without ever reaching the point of infinity, which eludes every attempt at definition? Then it would appear that it is an abstraction, a mere negation of limitation.

Our learned adversary seems to think it strange that the existence of incorporeal, immaterial substances, the essence of which we are not able to comprehend, should not be generally accredited. To enforce this belief, he says, "There is not so mean and contemptible a plant or animal, that does not confound the most enlarged understanding, upon earth: nay, even the simplest and plainest of all inanimate beings have their essence or substance hidden from us in the deepest and most impenetrable obscurity."

We shall reply to him,

First, That the idea of an immaterial substance; or being without extent, is only an absence of ideas, a negation of extent, as we have already shewn; that when we are told a being is not matter, they speak to us of that which is not, and do not teach us that which is; because by insisting that a being is such, that it cannot act upon any of our senses, they, in fact, inform us that we have no means of assuring ourselves whether such being exists or not.

Secondly, We shall avow without the least hesitation, that men of the greatest genius, of the most indefatigable research, are not acquainted with the essence of stones, plants, animals, nor with the secret springs which constitute some, which make others vegetate or act: but then at least we either feel them or see them; our senses have a knowledge of them in some respects; we can perceive some of their effects; we have something whereby to judge of them, either accurately or inaccurately; we can conceive that which is matter, however varied, however subtle, however minute, by analogy with other matter; but our senses cannot compass that which is immaterial on any side; we cannot by any possible means understand it; we have no means whatever of ascertaining its existence; consequently we cannot even form an idea of it; such a being is to us an occult principle, or rather a being which imagination has composed, by deducting from it every known quality. If we are ignorant of the intimate combination of the most material beings, we at least discover, with the aid of experience, some of their relations with ourselves: we have a knowledge of their surface, their extent, their form, their colour, their softness, their density; by the impressions they make on our senses, we are capable of discriminating them—of comparing them—of judging of them in some manner—of seeing them—

of either avoiding or courting them, according to the different modes in which we are affected by them; we cannot apply any of these tests to immaterial beings; to spirits; neither can those men who are unceasingly talking to mankind of these inconceivable things.

Thirdly, We have a consciousness of certain modifications in ourselves, which we call sentiment, thought, will, passions: for want of being acquainted with our own peculiar essence; for want of precisely understanding the energy of our own particular organization, we attribute these effects to a concealed cause, distinguished from ourselves; which the theologians call a spiritual cause, inasmuch as it appears to act differently from our body. Nevertheless, reflection, experience, every thing by which we are enabled to form any kind of judgment, proves that material effects can only emanate from material causes. We see nothing in the universe but physical, material effects, these can only be produced by analogous causes; it is, then certainly more rational to attribute them to nature herself, of which we may know something, if we will but deign to meditate her with attention, rather than to spiritual causes, of which we must for ever remain ignorant, let us study them as long as we please.

If incomprehensibility be not a sufficient reason for absolutely denying the possibility of immateriality, it certainly is not of a cogency to establish its existence; we shall always be less in a capacity to comprehend a spiritual cause, than one that is material; because materiality is a known quality; spirituality is an occult, an unknown quality; or rather it is a mode of speech of which we avail ourselves to throw a veil over our own ignorance. We are repeatedly told that our senses only bring us acquainted with the external of things; that our limited ideas are not capable of conceiving immaterial beings: we agree frankly to this position; but then our senses do not even shew us the external of these immaterial substances, Which the theologians will nevertheless attempt to define to us; upon which they unceasingly dispute among themselves; upon which even until this day they are not in perfect unison with each other. The great John Locke in his familiar letters, says, "I greatly esteem all those who faithfully defend their opinions; but there are so few persons who, according to the manner they do defend them, appear fully convinced of the opinions they profess, that I am tempted to believe there are more sceptics in the world than are generally imagined."

Abady, one of the most strenuous supporters of immaterialism, says, "The question is not what incorporeity is, but whether it be." To settle this disputable point, it were necessary to have some data whereon to form our judgment; but how assure ourselves of the existence of that, of which we shall never be competent to have a knowledge? If we are not told what this is; if some tangible evidence be not offered to the human mind; how shall we feel ourselves capacitated to judge whether or not its existence be even possible? How form an estimate of that picture whose colours elude our sight, whose design we cannot perceive, whose features have no means of becoming familiar to our mind, whose very canvas refuses itself to our all research, of which the artist himself can afford no other idea, no other description, but that it is, although he himself can neither shew us how or where! We have seen the ruinous foundations upon which men have hitherto erected this fanciful idea of immateriality; we have examined the proofs which they have offered, if proofs they can be called, in support of their hypothesis; we have sifted the evidence they have been willing to have accredited, in order to establish their position; we have pointed out the numberless contradictions that result from their want of union on this subject, from the irreconcileable qualities with which they clothe their imaginary system. What conclusion, then, ought fairly, rationally, consistently, to be drawn from the whole? Can we, or can we not admit their argument to be conclusive, such as ought to be received by beings who think themselves sane? Will it allow any other inference than that it has no existence; that immateriality is a quality hitherto unproved; the idea of which the mind of man has no means of compassing? Still they will insist, "there are no contradictions between the qualities which they attribute to these immaterial substances; but there is a difference between the understanding of man and the nature of these substances." This granted, are they nearer the point at which they labour? What standard is it necessary man should possess, to enable him to judge of these substances? Can they shew the test that will lead to an acquaintance with them? Are not those who have thus given loose to their imagination, who have given birth to this system, themselves men? Does not the disproportion, of which they speak with such amazing confidence, attach to themselves as well as to others? If it needs an infinite mind to comprehend infinity—to form an idea of incorporeity—can the theologian himself boast he is in a capacity to understand it? To what purpose then is it they speak of these things to others? Why do they attempt descriptions of that which they allow to be indescribable? Man, who will never be an infinite being, will never be able to conceive infinity; if, then, he has hitherto been incompetent to this perfection of knowledge, can he reasonably flatter himself he will ever obtain it; can he hope under any circumstances to conquer that which according to the shewing of all is unconquerable?

Nevertheless it is pretended, that it is absolutely necessary to know these substances: but how prove the necessity of having a knowledge of that which is impossible to be known? We are then told that good sense and reason are sufficient to convince us of its existence: this is taking new ground, when the old has been found untenable: for we are also told that reason is a treacherous guide; one that frequently leads us astray; that in religious matters it ought not to prevail: at least then they ought to shew us the precise time when we must resume this reason. Shall we consult it again, when the question is, whether what they relate is probable; whether the discordant qualities which they unite are consistently combined; whether their own arguments have all that solidity which they would themselves wish them to possess? But we have strangely mistaken them if they are willing that we should recur to it upon these points; they will instead, insist we ought blindly to be directed by that which they vouchsafe to inform us; that the most certain road to happiness is to submit in all things to that which they have thought proper to decide on the nature of things, of which they avow their own ignorance, when they assert them to be beyond the reach of mortals. Thus it would appear that when we should consent to accredit these mysteries, it would never arise of our own knowledge; seeing this can no otherwise obtain but by the effect of demonstrable evidence; it would never arise from any intimate conviction of our minds; but it would be entirely on the word of the theologian himself, that we should ground our faith; that we should yield our belief. If these things are to the human species what colours are to the man born blind, they have at least no existence with relation to ourselves. It will avail the blind man nothing to tell him these colours have no less existence, because he cannot see them. But what shall we say of that portrait whose colours the blind man attempts to explain, whose features he is willing we should receive upon his authority, whose proportions are to be taken from his description, merely because we know he cannot behold them?

The Doctor, although unwilling to relinquish his subject, removes none of the difficulty when he asks, "Are our five senses, by an absolute necessity in the nature of the thing, all and the only possible ways of perception? And is it impossible and contradictory there should be any being in the universe, indued with ways of perception different from these that are the result of our present composition? Or are these things, on the contrary, purely arbitrary; and the same power that gave us these, may have given others to other beings, and might, if he had pleased have given to us others in this present state?" It seems perfectly unnecessary to the true point of the argument to reason upon what can or cannot be done: I therefore reply, that the fact is, we have but five senses: by the aid of these man is not competent to form any idea whatever of immateriality; but he is also in as absolute a state of ignorance, upon what might be his capabilities of conception, if he had more senses. It is rather acknowledging a weakness in his evidence, on the part of the Doctor, to be thus obliged to rest it upon the supposition of what might be the case, if man was a being different to what he is; in other words, that they would be convincing to mankind if the human race were not human beings. Therefore to demand what the Divinity could have done in such a case, is to suppose the thing in question, seeing we cannot form an idea how far the power of the Divinity extends: but we may be reasonably allowed to use the theological argument in elucidation; these men very gravely insist, upon what authority must be best known to themselves, "that God cannot communicate to his works that perfection which he himself possesses;" at the same moment they do not fail to announce his omnipotence. Will it require any capacity, more than is the common lot of a child, to comprehend the absurd contradiction of the two assertions? As beings possessing but five senses, we must then, of necessity, regulate our judgment by the information they are capable of affording us: we cannot, by any possibility, have a knowledge of those, which confer the capacity to comprehend beings, of an order entirely distinguished from that in which we occupy a place. We are ignorant of the mode in which even plants vegetate, how then be acquainted with that which has no affinity with ourselves? A man born blind, has only the use of four senses; he has not the right, however, of assuming it as a fact, there does not exist an extra sense for others; but he may very reasonably, and with great truth aver, that he has no idea of the effects which would be produced in him, by the sense which he lacks: notwithstanding, if this blind man was surrounded by other men, whose birth had also left them devoid or sight, might he not without any very unwarrantable presumption, be authorized to inquire of them by what right, upon what authority, they spoke to him of a sense they did not themselves possess; how they were enabled to reason, to detail the minutiae of that sensation upon which their own peculiar experience taught them nothing?

In short, we can again reply to Dr. Clarke, and to the theologians, that following up their own systems, the supposition is impossible, and ought not to be made, seeing that the Divinity, who according to their own shewing, made man, was not willing that he should have more than five senses; in other words, that he should be nothing but what he actually is; they all found the existence of these immaterial substances upon the necessity of a power that has the faculty to give a commencement to motion. But if matter has always existed, of which there does not seem to exist a doubt, it has always had motion, which is as essential to it as its extent, and flows from its primitive properties. Indeed the human mind, with its five senses, is not more competent to comprehend matter devoid of motion, than it is to understand the peculiar quality of immateriality: motion therefore exists only in and by matter; mobility is a consequence of its existence; not that the great whole can occupy other parts of space than it actually does; the impossibility of that needs no argument, but all its parts can change their respective situations—do continually change them; it is from thence results the preservation, the life of nature, which is always as a whole immutable: but in supposing, as is done every day, that matter is inert, that is to say, incapable of producing any thing by itself, without the assistance of a moving power, which sets it in motion, are we by any means enabled to conceive that material nature receives this activity from an agent, who partakes in nothing of material substance? Can man really figure to himself, even in idea, that that which has no one property of matter, can create matter, draw it from its own peculiar source, arrange it, penetrate it, give it play, guide its course? Is it not, on the contrary, more rational to the mind, more consistent with truth, more congenial to experience, to suppose that the being who made matter is himself material: is there the smallest necessity to suppose otherwise? Can it make man either better or worse, that he should consider the whole that exists as material? Will it in any manner make him a worse subject to his sovereign; a worse father to his children; a more unkind husband; a more faithless friend?

Motion, then, is co-eternal with matter: from all eternity the particles of the universe have acted and reacted upon each other, by virtue of their respective energies; of their peculiar essences; of their primitive elements; of their various combinations. These particles must have combined in consequence of their affinity; they must have been either attracted or repelled by their respective relations with each other; in virtue of these various essences, they must have gravitated one upon the other; united when they were analagous; separated when that analogy was dissolved, by the approach of heterogeneous matter; they must have received their forms, undergone a change of figure, by the continual collision of bodies. In a material world the acting powers must be material: in a whole every part of which is essentially in motion, there is no occasion for a power distinguished from itself; the whole must be in perpetual motion by its own peculiar energy. The general motion, as we have elsewhere proved, has its birth from the individual motion, which beings ever active must uninterruptedly communicate to each other. Thus every cause produces its effect; this effect in its turn becomes a cause, which in like manner produces an effect; this constitutes the eternal chain of things, which although perpetually changing in its detail, suffers no change in its whole.

Theology, after all, has seldom done more than personify this eternal series of motion; the principle of mobility inherent to matter: it has clothed this principle with human qualities, by which it has rendered it unintelligible: in applying these properties, they have taken no means of understanding how far they were suitable or not: in their eagerness to make them assimilate, they have extended them beyond their own conception; they have heaped them together without any judgment; and they have been surprised when these qualities, contradictory in themselves, did not enable them satisfactorily to account for all the phenomena they beheld; from thence they have wrangled; accused each other of imbecility; yet infuriated themselves against whoever had the temerity to question that which they did not themselves understand; in short, they have acted like a man who should insist that all other men should have precisely the same vision that he himself had dreamed.

Be this as it may, the greater portion of what either Dr. Clarke or the theologians tell us, becomes, in some respects, sufficiently intelligible as soon as applied to nature—to matter: it is eternal, that is to say, it cannot have had a commencement, it never will have an end; it is infinite, that is to say, we have no conception of its limits. Nevertheless, human qualities, which must be always borrowed from ourselves, and with others we have a very slender acquaintance, cannot be well suitable to the entire of nature; seeing that these qualities are in themselves modes of being, or modes which appertain only to particular beings: not to the great whole which contains them.

Thus, to resume the answers which have been given to Dr. Clarke, we shall say: *First*, we can conceive that matter has existed from all eternity, seeing that we cannot conceive it to have been capable of beginning. *Secondly*, that matter is independent, seeing there is nothing exterior to itself; that it is immutable, seeing it cannot change its nature, although it is unceasingly changing its form and its combinations. *Thirdly*, that matter is self-existent, since not being able to conceive it can be annihilated, we cannot possibly conceive it can have commenced to exist. *Fourthly*, that we do not know the essence, or the true nature of matter, although we have a knowledge of some of its properties; of some of its qualities: according to the mode in which they act upon us. *Fifthly*, that matter not having had a beginning, will never have an end, although its numerous combinations, its various forms, have necessarily a commencement and a period. *Sixthly*, that if all that exists, or every thing our mind can conceive is matter, this matter is infinite; that is to say, cannot be limited by any thing; that it is omnipresent, seeing there is no place exterior to itself, indeed, if there was a place exterior to it, that would be a vacuum. *Seventhly*, that nature is unique, although its elements or its parts may be varied to infinity, indued with properties extremely opposite; with qualities essentially different. *Eighthly*, that matter, arranged, modified, and combined in a certain mode, produces in some beings what we call intelligence, which is one of its modes of being, not one of its essential properties, *Ninthly*, that matter is not a free agent, since it cannot act otherwise than it does, in virtue of the laws of its nature, or of its existence; that consequently, heavy bodies must necessarily fall; light bodies by the same necessity rise; fire must burn; man must experience good and evil, according to the quality of the beings whose action he experiences. *Tenthly*, that the power or the energy of matter, has no other bounds than those which are prescribed by its own existence. *Eleventhly*, that wisdom, justice, goodness, &c. are qualities peculiar to matter combined and modified, as it is found in some beings of the human species; that the idea of perfection is an abstract, negative, metaphysical idea, or mode of considering objects, which supposes nothing real to be exterior to itself. *Twelfthly*, that matter is the principle of motion, which it contains within itself: since matter alone is capable of either giving or receiving motion: this is what cannot be conceived of immateriality or simple beings destitute of parts, devoid of extent, without mass, having no ponderosity, which consequently cannot either move itself or other bodies.

CHAP. V.
Examination of the Proofs offered by DESCARTES, MALEBRANCHE, NEWTON, &c.

If the evidence of Clarke did not prove satisfactory—if the theologians of his day disputed the manner in which he handled his subject—if they were disposed to think he had not established his argument upon proper foundations, it did not seem probable that either the system of Descartes, the sublime reveries of Malebranche, or the more methodical mode adopted by Newton, were at all likely to meet with a better reception; the same objections will lie against them all, that they have not demonstrated the existence of their immaterial substances; although they have incessantly spoken of them, as if they were things of which they had the most intimate knowledge. Unfortunately this is a rock which the most sublime geniuses have not been competent to avoid: the most enlightened men have done little more than stammer upon a subject which they have all concurred in considering of the highest importance; which they unceasingly hold forth as the most necessary for man to know; without at the same time considering he is not in a condition to occupy himself with objects inaccessible to his senses—which his mind, consequently, can never grasp—which his utmost research cannot bring into that tangible shape by which alone he can be enabled to form a judgment.

To the end that we may be convinced of that want of solidity which the greatest men have not known how to give to the proofs they have offered, but which they have successively imagined has established their positions, let us briefly examine what the most celebrated philosophers, what the most subtile metaphysicians have said. For this purpose we will begin with Descartes, the restorer of philosophy among the moderns, to whose sublime errors we are indebted for the effulgent truths of the Newtonian system. This great man himself tells us, "All the strength of argument which I have hitherto used to prove the existence of immaterial substances, consists in this, that I acknowledge it would not be possible, my nature was such as it is, that is to say, that I should have in me the idea of immateriality, if this incorporeity did not truly exist; this same immateriality, of which the idea is in me, possesses all those high perfections of which our mind can have some slight idea, without however being able to comprehend them." In another place he says, "We must necessarily conclude from this alone, that because I exist, and have the idea of immateriality, that is to say, of a most perfect being, the existence is therefore most evidently demonstrated." There are not, perhaps, many except Descartes himself, to whom this would appear quite so conclusive; who would be impressed with the conviction which he seems to imagine is so very substantive.

First, We shall reply to Descartes, it is not a warrantable deduction, that because we have an idea of a thing, we must therefore conclude it exists; to give validity to such a mode of reasoning would be productive of the greatest mischief; would, in fact, tend to subvert all human institutions. Our imagination presents us with the idea of a sphinx, or of an hippogriff, besides a thousand other fantastical beings; are we, on that authority, to insist that these things really exist? Is the mere circumstance of our having an idea of various parts of nature, discrepantly jumbled together, without any other evidence as to the assemblage, a sufficient warrantry for calling upon mankind to accredit the existence of such heterogeneous masses? If a philosopher of the most consummate experience, of the greatest celebrity, one who enjoyed the confidence of mankind above every other, was to detail the faculties and perfections of these visionary beings, although he should hold them forth as the perfection of all natural combinations, would, I say, any reasonable being lend himself to the asseveration?

Secondly, It is obvious that the mere circumstance of existence, does not prove the absolute existence of any thing anterior to itself; although in man, as well as the other beings of nature, it is evidence that something has existed before him. If this argument was to be admitted, are they aware how far it, would carry them? To maintain that the existence of one being demonstrably proves the existence of an anterior being, would be, in fact, denying that any thing was self- existent. The fallacy of such a position is too glaring to need refutation.

Thirdly, It is not possible he should have a distinct, positive idea of immateriality, of which be, as well as the theologian, labours to prove the existence. It is impossible for man, for a material being, to form to himself a correct idea, or indeed any idea, of incorporeity; of a substance without extent, acting upon nature, which is corporeal; a truth which it may not be presuming too much to say we have already sufficiently proved.

Fourthly, It is equally impossible for man to have any clear, decided idea of perfection, of infinity, of immensity, and other theological attributes. To Descartes we must therefore reply as we have done to Dr. Clarke on his twelfth proposition.

Thus nothing can well be less conclusive than the proofs upon which Descartes rests the existence of immateriality. He gives it thought and intelligence, but how conceive these qualities without a subject to which they may adhere? He pretends that we cannot conceive it but "as a power which applies itself successively to the parts of the universe." Again, he says, "that an immaterial substance cannot be said to have extent, but as we say of fire contain in a piece of iron, which has not, properly speaking, any other extension than that of the iron itself" According to these notions we shall be justified in taxing him with having announced in a very clear, in a most unequivocal manner, that this is nature herself: this indeed is a pure Spinosism; it was decidedly on the principles of Descartes that Spinosa drew up his system; in fact it flows out of it consecutively.

We might, therefore, with great reason, accuse Descartes of atheism, seeing that he very effectually destroys the feeble proofs he adduces in support of his own hypothesis; we have solid foundation for insisting that his system overturns the idea of the creation, because if from the modification we subtract the subject, the modification itself disappears: and if, according to the Cartesians, this immateriality is nothing without nature, they are complete Spinosians, with another name. If incorporeity is the motive-power of this nature, it no longer exists independently; it, in fact, exists no longer than the subject to which it is inherent subsists. Thus no longer existing independently, it will exist only while the nature which it moves shall endure; without matter, without a subject to move, to preserve, what is to become of it, according to this doctrine, or rather according to this elucidation of a system which is in itself untenable?

It will be obvious from this, that Descartes, far from establishing on a rocky foundation the existence of this immateriality, totally destroys his own system. The same thing will necessarily happen to all those who reason upon his principles; they will always finish by confuting him, and by contradicting themselves. The same want of just inference, the same discrepancy, will obtrude themselves in the principles of the celebrated Father Malebranche; which, if considered with the slightest attention, appear to conduct directly to Spinosism; in fact, can any thing be more in unison with the language of Spinosa himself, than to say, as does Malebranche, "that the universe is only an emanation from God; that we see every thing in God, that every thing we see is only God; that God alone does every thing that is done; that all the action, with every operation that takes place in nature, is God himself; in a word, that God is every being and the only being." Is not this formally asserting that nature herself is God? Moreover, at the same time Malebranche assures us we see every thing in God, he pretends that it is not yet clearly demonstrated that matter and bodies have existence; that faith alone teaches us these mysteries, of which, without it, we should not have any knowledge whatever. In reply, it might be a very fair question, how the existence of the being who created matter can be demonstrated, if the existence of this matter itself be yet a problem? He himself acknowledges "that we can have no distinct demonstration of the existence of any other being than of that which is necessary;" he further adds, "that if it be closely examined, it will be seen, that it is not even possible to know with certitude, if God be or be not truly the creator of a material, of a sensible world." According to these notions, it is evident, that, following up the system of Malebranche, man has only his faith to guarantee the existence of the world; yet faith itself supposes its existence; if it be not, however, certain that it does exist, and the Bishop of Cloyne, Dr. Berkeley, has also held this in doubt, how shall we be persuaded that we must believe the oracles which have been delivered to a visionary world?

On the other hand, these notions of Malebranche completely overturns all the theological doctrines of free agency. How can the liberty of man's action be reconciled with the idea that it is the Divinity who is the immediate mover of nature; who actually gives impulse to matter and bodies, without whose immediate interference nothing takes place; who pre-determines his creatures to every thing they do? How can it be pretended, if this doctrine is to be accredited, that human souls have the faculty of forming thoughts—have the power of volition—are in a condition to move themselves—have the capacity to modify their existence? If it be supposed with the theologians, that the conservation of the creatures in the universe is a continued creation, must it not appear, that being thus perpetually recreated, they are enabled to commit evil? It will then be a self-evident fact, that, admitting the system of Malebranche, God does every thing, and that his creatures are no more than passive instruments in his hands. Under this idea they could not be answerable for their sins, because they would have no means of avoiding them. Under this notion they could neither have merit or demerit; they would be like a sharp instrument in their own hands, which whether it was applied to a good or to an evil purpose, it would attach to themselves, not to the instrument: this would annihilate all religion: it is thus that theology is continually occupied with committing suicide.

Let us now see, if the immortal Newton, the great luminary of science, the champion of astronomical truth, will afford us clearer notions, more distinct ideas, more certain evidence of the existence of immaterial substances. This great man, whose comprehensive genius unravelled nature, whose capacious mind developed her laws, seems to have bewildered himself, the instant he lost sight of them. A slave to the prejudices of his infancy, he had not the courage to hold the lamp of his own enlightened understanding to the agent theology has so gratuitously associated with nature; he has not been able to allow that her own peculiar powers were adequate to the production of that beautiful phenomena, he has with such masterly talents so luminously explained. In short, the sublime Newton himself becomes an infant when he quits physics, when he lays aside demonstration, to lose himself in the devious sinuosities, in the inextricable labyrinths, in the delusive regions of theology. This is the manner in which he speaks of the Divinity:

"This God," says he, "governs all, not as the soul of the world, but as the lord and sovereign of all things. It is in consequence of his sovereignty that he is called the Lord God, [Greek letters], *pantokrator*, the universal emperor. Indeed the word God is relative and relates itself with slaves; the Deity is the dominion or the sovereignty of God, not over his own body, as those think who look upon God as the soul of the world, but over slaves."

From this it will be seen that Newton, as well as the theologians, makes the Divinity a pure spirit, who presides over the universe as a monarch, as a lord paramount; that is to say, what man defines in earthly governors, despot, absolute princes, powerful monarchs, whose governments have no model but their own will, who exercise an unlimited power over their subjects, transformed into slaves; whom they usually compel to feel in a very grievous manner the weight of their authority. But according to the ideas of Newton, the world has not existed from eternity, the staves of God have been formed in the course of time; from this it would be a just inference, that before the creation of the world the god of Newton was a sovereign without subjects. Let us see if this truly great philosopher is more in unison with himself in the subsequent ideas which he delivers on this subject.

"The supreme God," he says, "is an eternal, infinite, and absolutely perfect being; but however perfect a being may be, if he has no sovereignty he is not the supreme God. The word God signifies Lord, but every lord is not god; it is the sovereignty of the spiritual Being which constitutes God; it is the true sovereignty which constitutes the true God; it is the supreme sovereignty which constitutes the supreme God; it is a false sovereignty which constitutes a false god. From true sovereignty, it follows, that the true God is living, intelligent, and powerful; and from his other perfections, it follows, that he is supremely or sovereignly perfect. He is eternal, infinite, omniscient; that is to say, he exists from eternity, and will never have an end; he governs all, and he knows every thing that is done, or that can be done. He is neither eternity nor infinity, but he is eternal and infinite; he is not space or duration, but he exists and is present." The term here used is *adest*, which appears to have been placed there to avoid saying that God is contained in space.

In all this unintelligible series, nothing is to be found but incredible efforts to reconcile the theological attributes, the abstract with the human qualities, which have been ascribed to the Divinity; we see in it negative qualities, which can no longer be suitable to man, given, however, to the Sovereign of nature, whom he has supposed a king. However it may be, this picture always supposes the Supreme God to have occasion for subjects to establish his sovereignty. It makes God stand in need of man for the exercise of his empire; without these, according to the text, he would not be a king; he could have had no empire when there was nothing: but if this description of Newton was just, if it really represented the Divinity, we might be very fairly permitted to ask, Does not this Spiritual King exercise his spiritual empire in vain, upon refractory beings, who do not at all times do that which he is willing they should; who are continually struggling against his power; who spread disorder in his states? This Spiritual Monarch, who is master of the minds, of the souls, of the wills, of the passions of his slaves, does he leave them the freedom of revolting against him? This infinite Monarch, who fills every thing with his immensity, who governs all, does he also govern the man who sins; does he direct his actions; is he in him when he offends his God? The devil, the false god, the evil principle, hath he not, according to this, a more extensive empire than the true God, whose projects, if we are to believe the theologians, he is unceasingly overturning? In earthly governments the true sovereign is generally considered to be him whose power in a state influences the greater number of his subjects. If, then, we could suppose him to be omnipresent, that is, present in all places, should we not say he was the sad witness to all the outrages committed against his authority, and we should not entertain a very exalted opinion of his power if he permitted them to continue. This, it is true, would be arguing upon a monarch of this world, still it would be the language held by observers.

Is the spirituality of the Divinity well supported by those who say he fills all space, who from that instant give him extent, ascribe to him volume, make him correspond with the various points of space? This is the very reverse of an immaterial substance.

"God is one," continues Newton, "and he is the same for ever, and every where, not only by his virtue alone, or by his energy, but also by his substance." But how are we to conceive that a being who is in continual activity, who produces all the changes which beings undergo, can always be himself the same? What is to be understood by either this virtue or this energy? These are relative terms, which do not present any clear, distinct idea to our mind, except as they apply to man: what are we, however, to understand by the divine substance? If this substance be spiritual, that is, devoid of extent, how can there exist in it any parts? How can it give impulse to matter, how set it in motion? How can it even be conceived by mortals?

Nevertheless Newton informs us, "that all things are contained in him, and are moved in him, but without reciprocity of action: God experiences nothing by the motion of bodies; these experience no resistance whatever by his omnipresence." It would here appear that he clothes the Divinity with that which bears the, character of vacuum—of nothing; without that, it would be almost impossible not to have a reciprocal action or relation between these substances, which are either penetrated or encompassed on all sides. It must be obvious, that in this instance our scientific author does not distinctly understand himself.

He proceeds, "It is an incontestible truth, that God exists necessarily, and the same necessity obliges to exist always and every where: from whence it follows, that he is in every thing similar to itself; he is all eyes, all ears, all brains, all arms, all feeling, all intelligence, all action; but in a mode by no means human, by no means corporeal, and which is totally unknown to us. In the same manner as a blind man has no idea of colours, it is that we have no idea of the mode in which God feels and understands." The necessary existence of the Divinity is precisely the thing in question; it is this existence that it was needful to have verified by proofs as clear, by evidence as distinct, by demonstration as strong, as gravitation and attraction. One would have hardly thought it possible the expansive capabilities of Newton would not have compassed it. But oh, unrivalled genius! so mighty, so powerful, so colossal, while yet you was a geometrician; so insignificant, so weak, so inconsistent; when you became a theologian; that is to say, when you reasoned upon that which can neither be calculated, nor submitted to experience; how could you think of speaking to us on a subject which, by your own confession is to you just what a picture is to a man born blind? Wherefore quit nature, which had already explained to you so much? Why seek in imaginary spaces those causes, those powers, that energy, which she would have distinctly pointed out to you, had you been willing to have consulted her with your usual sagacity? The gigantic, the intelligent Newton, suffers himself to be hoodwinked—to be blinded by prejudice; he has not courage to look a question fairly in the face, when that question involves notions which habit has rendered sacred to him; he turns his eyes from truth, he casts behind him his experience, he lulls to sleep his reason, when it becomes necessary to probe opinions full of contradictions, yet fraught with the best interests of humanity.

Let us, however, continue to examine how far the most transcendent genius is capable of leading himself astray, when once he abandons experience, when once he chains up his reason, when once he suffers himself to be guided by his imagination.

"God," continues the father of modern philosophy, "is totally destitute of body and of corporeal figure; here is the reason why he cannot be either seen, touched, or understood; and ought not to be adored under any corporeal form." What idea, however, can be formed of a being who is resembled by nothing of which we have any knowledge? What are the relations that can be supposed to exist between such very dissimilar beings? When man renders this being his adoration, does he not, in fact, in despite of himself, make him a being similar to his own species; does he not suppose that, like himself, he is sensible to homage—to be won by presents—gained by flattery; in short, he is treated like a king of the earth, who exacts the respect, demands the fealty, requires the obedience of all who are submitted to him. Newton adds, "we have ideas of his attributes, but we do not know that it is any one substance; we only see the figures and the colours of bodies; we only hear sounds; we only touch the exterior surfaces; we only scent odours; we only taste flavours: no one of our senses, no one of our reflections, can shew us the intimate nature of substances: we have still less ideas of God."

If we have an idea of the attributes of God, it is only because we clothe him with those which belong to ourselves; which we never do more than aggrandize, which we only augment or exaggerate; we then mistake them for those qualities with which we were at first acquainted. If in all those substances which are pervious to our senses, we only know them by the effects they produce on us, after which we assign them qualities, at least these qualities are something tangible, they give birth to clear and distinct ideas. This superficial knowledge, however slender it may be, with which our senses furnish us, is the only one we can possibly have; constituted as we are, we find ourselves under the necessity of resting contented with it, and we discover that it is sufficient for our wants; but we have not even the most superficial idea of immateriality, or a substance distinguished from all those with which we have the slightest acquaintance. Nevertheless, we hear men hourly reasoning upon it, disputing about its properties, advancing its faculties, as if they had the most demonstrable evidence of the fact; tearing each other in pieces, because the one does not readily admit what the other asserts, upon a subject which no man is competent to understand.

Our author goes on "We only have a knowledge of God by his attributes, by his properties, by the excellent and wise arrangement which he has given to all things, and by their FINAL CAUSES: we admire him in consequence of his perfections." I repeat, that we have no real knowledge of the Divinity; that we borrow his attributes from ourselves; but it is evident these cannot be suitable to the Universal Being, who neither can have the same nature nor the same properties as particular beings; it is nevertheless after ourselves that we assign him intelligence, wisdom, perfection, in subtracting from them what we call defects. As to the order, or the arrangement of the universe, man finds it excellent, esteems it the perfection of wisdom, as long as it is favorable to his species; or when the causes which are co-existent with himself do not disturb his own peculiar existence; otherwise he is apt to complain of confusion, and final causes vanish: he then attributes to an immutable God, motives equally borrowed from his own peculiar mode of action, for deranging the beautiful order he so much admires in the universe. Thus it is always in himself, that is, in his own individual mode of feeling, that he draws up the ideas of the order, the wisdom, the excellence, the perfection which he ascribes to the Deity; whilst the good as well as the evil which take place in the world, are the necessary consequence of the essence of things; of the general, immutable laws of nature; in short, of the gravitation, of the repulsion of matter; of those unchangeable laws of motion, which Newton himself has so ably thrown into light; but which he has by a strange fatuity forborne to apply when the question was concerning the cause of these phenomena, which prejudice has refused to the capabilities of nature. He goes on, "We revere, and we adore God, on account of his sovereignty: we worship him like his slaves; a God destitute of sovereignty, of providence, and of final causes, would be no more than nature and destiny." It is true that superstition enjoins man to adore its gods like ignorant slaves, who tremble under a master whom they know not; he certainly prays to them on all occasions, sometimes requesting nothing less than an entire change in the essence of things, to gratify his capricious desires, and it is perhaps well for him they are not competent to grant his request: in the origin, as we have shewn, these gods were nothing more than nature acting by necessary laws, clothed under a variety of fables; or necessity personified under a multitude of names. However this may be, we do not believe that true religion, that sterling worship which renders man grateful, whilst it exalts the majesty of the Divinity, requires any such meanness from man that he should act like a slave; he is rather expected to sit down to the banquet prepared for him, with all the dignity of an invited guest; under the cheering consciousness of a welcome that is never accorded to slaves; nothing is required at his hands, but that he should conduct himself temperately in the banquetting-house; that he should be grateful for the good cheer he receives; that he should have virtue; (which we have already sufficiently explained is to render himself useful, by making others happy); that he should not by pertinaciously setting up whimsical opinions, and insisting on their adoption by his neighbour, disturb the harmony of the feast; that he should be sufficiently intelligent to know when he is really felicitous, and not seek to put down the gaiety of his fellow guests; but that he should rise from the board satisfied with himself, contented with others; in short, to comprise the whole in a trite axiom of one of the Greek philosophers, he should learn the invaluable secret, "to *bear* and *forbear*."

But to proceed. Newton tells us, "that from a physical and blind necessity, which should preside every where, and be always the same, there could not emanate any variety in the beings; the diversity which we behold, could only have its origin in the ideas and in the will of a being which exists necessarily;" but wherefore should not this diversity spring out of natural causes, from matter acting upon matter; the action of which either attracts and combines various yet analogous elements, or else separates beings by the intervention of those substances which have not a disposition to unite? Is not bread the result of the combination of flour, yeast and water? As for the blind necessity, as it is elsewhere said, we must acknowledge it is that of which we are ignorant, either of its properties or its energies; of which being blind ourselves we have no knowledge of its mode of action. Philosophers explain all the phenomena that occur by the properties of matter; and though they feel the want of a more intimate acquaintance with natural causes, they do not therefore the less believe them deducible from these properties or these causes. Are, therefore, the philosophers atheists, because they do not reply, it is God who is the author of these effects? Is the industrious workman, who makes gunpowder, to be challenged as an atheist, because he says the terrible effects of this destructive material, which inspired the native Americans with such awe, which raised in their winds such wonder, are to be ascribed to the junction of the apparently harmless substances of nitre, charcoal and sulpher, set in activity by the accession of trivial scintillations, produced from the collision of steel with flint, merely because some bigoted *Priest of the Sun*, who is ignorant of the composition, chooses to think it is not possible such a striking phenomenon could be the work of any thing short of the secret agents, whom he has himself appointed to govern the world?

"It is allegorically said that God sees, hears, speaks, smiles, loves, hates, desires, gives, receives, rejoices, grows angry, fights, makes, or fashions, &c. because all that is said of God, is borrowed from the conduct of man, by an imperfect analogy." Man has not been able to act otherwise, for want of being acquainted with nature and her eternal course: whenever he has imagined a peculiar energy which he has not been able to fathom, he has given it the name of God; and he has then made him act upon the self-same principles, as he himself would adopt, according to which he would act if he was the master. It is from this proneness to *Theanthropy*, that has flowed all those absurd, and frequently dangerous ideas, upon which are founded the superstitions of the world; who all adore in their gods either natural causes of which they are ignorant, or else powerful mortals of whose malice they stand in awe. The sequel will shew the fatal effects that have resulted to mankind from the absurd ideas they have very frequently formed to themselves of the Divinity; that nothing could he more degrading to him, more injurious to themselves, than the idea of comparing him to an absolute sovereign, to a despot, to a tyrant. For the present let us continue to examine the proofs offered in support of their various systems.

It is unceasingly repeated that the regular action, the invariable order, which reigns in the universe, the benefits heaped upon mortals, announce a wisdom, an intelligence, a goodness, which we cannot refuse to acknowledge, in the cause which produces these marvellous effects. To this we must reply, that it is unquestionably true that not only these things, but all the phenomena he beholds, indicate the existence of something gifted very superiorly to erring man; the great question, however, is one that perhaps will never be solved, what is this being? Is this question answered by heaping together the estimable qualities of man? Speaking with relation to ourselves, which is all that the theologian really does, although in such numerous regions he pretends to do a great deal more, we can apply the terms goodness, wisdom, intelligence, the best with which we are acquainted, to this being for the want of having those that may be appropriate; but I maintain, this does not, in point of fact, afford us one single idea of the *Great Cause of causes*; we admire his works; and knowing that what we approve highly in our own species, we attribute to their being wise, we say the Divinity displays wisdom. So far it is well; but this, after all, is a human quality. If we consult experience, we shall presently be convinced that our wisdom does not bear the least affinity to the actions attributed to the Divinity. To get at this a little closer, we must endeavour to find out what we do not call wisdom in man; this will help us to form an estimate, how very incompetent we are to describe the qualities of a being that differs so very materially from ourselves. We most certainly should not call him a wise man, who having built a beautiful residence, should himself set it on fire; and thus destroy what he had laboured so much to bring to perfection: yet this happens every day in nature, without its being in any manner a warrantry for us to charge her with folly. If therefore we were to form our judgments after our own puny ideas of wisdom, what should we say? Why, in point of fact, just what the man does, who, thinking he has had too much rain, implores fine weather? Which, properly translated, is neither more nor less than giving the Divinity to understand he best knows what is proper for himself. The just, the only fair inference to be drawn from this, is, that we positively know nothing about the matter; that those who pretend they do, would, if it was upon any other subject, he suspected of having an unsound mind. We do not mean to insist that we are in the right, but we mean to aver that the object of this work is not so much either to build up new systems, or to put down old ones, as by shewing man the inconclusiveness of his reasonings upon matters not accessible to his comprehension—to induce him to be more tolerant to his neighbour—to invite him to be less rancorous against those who do not see with his eyes—to hold forth to him motives for forbearance, against those whose system of faith may not exactly harmonize with his own—to render him less ferocious in support of opinions, which, if he will but discard his prejudices, he may find not so solidly bottomed as he imagines. All we know is scarcely more than that the motion we witness in the universe is the necessary consequence of the laws of matter; that the uniformity of this motion is evidence of their immutability; that it is not too much to say it cannot cease to act in the manner it does, as long as the same causes operate, governed by the same circumstances. We evidently see that motion, however regular in our mind, that order, however beautiful to our admiring optics, yields to what we term disorder, to that which we designate frightful confusion, as soon as new causes, not analogous to the preceding, either disturb or suspend their action. We further know that a better knowledge of nature, the consequence of time, the result of patient, laborious, physical researches, with the comparison of facts and the application of experience, has enabled man in many instances to divert from himself the evil effects of inevitable causes, which anterior to these discoveries overwhelmed his unhappy progenitors with ruin. How far these salutary developements are to be carried by industry, what may be achieved by honesty, what light is to be gathered from the recession of prejudice, the wisest among men is not competent to decide. Certain it is, that phenomena which for ages were supposed to denounce the anger of the Deity against mankind, are now well understood to be common effects of natural causes.

Order, as we have elsewhere shewn, is only the effects which result to ourselves from a series of motion; there cannot be any disorder relatively to the great whole; in which all that takes place is necessary; in which every thing is determined by laws which nothing can change. The order of nature may he damaged or destroyed relatively to ourselves, but it is never contradicted relatively to herself, since she cannot act otherwise than she does: if we attribute to her the evils we sustain, we are equally obliged to acknowledge we owe to her the good we experience.

It in said, that animals furnish a convincing proof of the powerful cause of their existence; that the admirable harmony of their parts, the mutual assistance they lend each other, the regularity with which they fulfill their functions, the preservation of these parts, the conservation of such complicated wholes, announce a workman who unites wisdom with power; in short, whole tracts of anatomy and botany have been copied to prove nothing more than that these things exist, for of the power that produced them there cannot remain a doubt. We shall never learn more from these erudite tracts, save that there exists in nature certain elements with an aptitude to attraction; a disposition to unite, suitable to form wholes, to induce combinations capable of producing very striking effects. To be surprised that the brain, the heart, the arteries, the veins, the eyes, the ears of an animal, act as we see them—that the roots of plants attract juices, or that trees produce fruit, is to be surprised that a tree, a plant, or an animal exists at all. These beings would not exist, or would no longer be that which we know they are, if they ceased to act as they do: this is what happens when they die. If the formation, the combination, the modes of action, variously possessed by these beings, if their conservation for a season, followed by their destruction or dissolution, prove any thing, it is the immutability of those laws which operate in nature: we cannot doubt the power of nature; she produces all the animals we behold, by the combination, of matter, continually in motion; the harmony that subsists between the component parts of these beings, is a consequence of the necessary laws of their nature, and of that which results from their combination. As soon as this accord ceases, the animal is necessarily destroyed: from this we must conclude that every mutation in nature is necessary; is only a consequence of its laws; that it could not be otherwise than it is, under the circumstances in which it is placed.

Man, who looks upon himself as the *chef d'oeuvre*, furnishes more than any other production a proof of the immutability of the laws of nature: in this sensible, intelligent, thinking being, whose vanity leads him to believe himself the sole object of the divine predilection, who forms his God after his own peculiar model, we see only a more inconstant, a more brittle machine; one more subject to be deranged by its extreme complication, than the grosser beings: beasts destitute of our knowledge, plants that vegetate, stones devoid of feeling, are in many respects beings more highly favored than man: they are at least exempted from the sorrows of the mind—from the torments of reflection—from that devouring, chagrin to which he is so frequently a prey. Who is he who would not be a plant or a stone, every time reminiscence forces upon his imagination the irreparable loss of a beloved object? Would it not be better to be an inanimate mass, than a restless, turbulent, superstitious being, who does nothing but tremble under the imaginary displeasure of beings of his own creation; who to support his own gloomy opinions, immolates his fellow creatures at the shrine of his idol; who ravages the country, and deluges the earth with the blood of those who happen to differ from him on a speculative point of an unintelligible creed? Beings destitute of life, bereft of feeling, without memory, not having the faculties of thought, at least are not afflicted by the idea of either the past, the present, or the future; they do not at any rate believe themselves in danger of becoming eternally unhappy, because they way have reasoned badly; or because they happened to be born in a land where truth has never yet shed its refulgent beams on the darkened mind of perplexed mortals.

Let it not then be said that we cannot have an idea of a work, without also having an idea of the workman, as distinguished from his work: the savage, when he first beheld the terrible operation of gunpowder, did not form the most distant idea that it was the work of a man like himself. Nature is not to be contemplated as a work of this kind; she is self-existent. In her bosom every thing is produced: she is an immense elaboratory, provided with materials, who makes the instruments of which she avails herself in her operations. All her works are the effects of her own energies; of those agents which she herself produces; of those immutable laws by which she sets every thing in activity. Eternal, indestructible elements, ever in motion, combine themselves variously, and thus give birth to all beings, to all the phenomena which fill the weak eyes of erring mortals with wonder and dismay; to all the effects, whether good or bad, of which man experiences the influence; to all the vicissitudes he undergoes, from the moment of his birth until that of his death; to order and to confusion, which he never discriminates but by the various modes in which he is affected: in short, to all those miraculous spectacles with which he occupies his meditation—upon which he exercises his reason—which frequently spread consternation over the surface of the earth. These elements need nothing when circumstances favour their junction, save their own peculiar properties, whether individual or united, with the motion that is essential to them, to produce all those phenomena which powerfully striking the senses of mankind, either fill him with admiration, or stagger him with alarm.

But supposing for a moment that it was impossible to conceive the work, without also conceiving the workman, who watches over his work, where must we place this workman? Shall it be interior or exterior to his production? Is he matter and motion, or is he only space or the vacuum? In all these cases either he would be nothing, or he would be contained in nature: as nature contains only matter and motion, it must be concluded that the agent who moves it is material; that he is corporeal; if this agent be exterior to nature, then we can no longer form any idea of the place which he occupieth: neither can we better conceive an immaterial being; nor the mode in which a spirit without extent can act upon matter from which it is separated. These unknown spaces, which imagination has placed beyond the visible world, can have no existence for a being, who with difficulty sees down to his feet; he cannot paint to his mind any image of the power which inhabit them; but if he is compelled to form some kind of a picture, he must combine at random the fantastical colours which he is ever obliged to draw from the world he inhabits: in this case he will really do no more than reproduce in idea, part or parcels of that which he has actually seen; he will form a whole which perhaps has no existence in nature, but which it will be in vain he strives to distinguish from her; to place out of her bosom. When he shall be ingenuous with himself, When he shall be no longer willing to delude others, he will be obliged to acknowledge, that the portrait he has painted, although in its combination it resembles nothing in the universe, is nevertheless in all its constituent members an exact delineation of that which nature presents to our view. Hobbes in his *Leviathan* says, "The universe, the whole mass of things, is corporeal, that is to say, body; and hath the dimensions of magnitude, namely, length, breadth, and depth: also every part of body is likewise body, and hath the like dimensions; and consequently every part of the universe is body; and that which is not body, is no part of the universe; and because the universe is all, that which is no part of it is nothing; and consequently no where: nor does it follow from hence, that spirits are nothing, for they have dimensions, and are therefore really bodies; though that name in common speech be given to such bodies only as are visible, or palpable, that is, that have some degree of opacity: but for spirits they call them incorporeal; which is a name of more honour, and may therefore with more piety be attributed to God himself, in whom we consider not what attribute expresseth best his nature, which is incomprehensible; but what best expresseth our desire to honour him."

It will be insisted that if a statue or a watch were shewn to a savage, who had never before seen either, he would not be able to prevent himself from acknowledging that these things were the works of some intelligent agent of greater ability, possessing more industry than himself: it will be concluded from thence, that we are in like manner obliged to acknowledge that the universe, that man, that the various phenomena, are the works of an agent, whose intelligence is more comprehensive, whose power far surpasses our own. Granted: who has ever doubted it? the proposition is self-evident; it cannot admit of even a cavil. Nevertheless we reply, in the *first place*, that it is not to be doubted that nature is extremely powerful; diligently industrious: we admire her activity every time we are surprised by the extent, every time we contemplate the variety, every time we behold those complicated effects which are displayed in her works; or whenever we take the pains to meditate upon them: nevertheless, she is not really more industrious in one of her works than she is in another; she is not fathomed with more ease in those we call her most contemptible productions, than she is in her most sublime efforts: we no more understand how she has been capable of producing a stone or a metal, than the means by which she organized a head like that of the illustrious Newton. We call that man industrious who can accomplish things which we cannot; nature is competent to every thing: as soon therefore as a thing exists, it is a proof she has been capable of producing it: but it is never more than relatively to ourselves that we judge beings to be industrious: we then compare them to ourselves; and as we enjoy a quality which we call intelligence, by the assistance of which we accomplish things, by which we display our diligence, we naturally conclude from it, that those works which most astonish us, do not belong to her, but are to be ascribed to an intelligent being like ourselves, but in whom we make the intelligence commensurate with the astonishment these phenomena excite in us; that is to say, in other words, to our own peculiar ignorance, and the weakness incident to our nature.

In the *second place*, we must observe, that the savage, to whom either the statue or the watch is brought, will or will not have ideas of human industry: if he has ideas of it, he will feel that this watch or this statue, way be the work of a being of his own species, enjoying faculties of which he is himself deficient: if he has no idea of it, if he has no comprehension of the resources of human art, when he beholds the spontaneous motion of the watch, he will he impressed with the belief that it is an animal, which cannot be the work of man. Multiplied experience confirms this mode of thinking which is ascribed to the savage. The Peruvians mistook the Spaniards for gods, because they made use of gunpowder, rode on horseback, and came in vessels which sailed quite alone. The inhabitants of the island of Tenian being ignorant of fire before the arrival of Europeans, the first time they saw it, conceived it to be an animal who devoured the wood. Thus it is, that the savage, in the same manner as many great and learned men, who believe themselves much more acute, will attribute the strange effects that strike his organs, to a genius or to a spirit; that is to say, to an unknown power; to whom he will ascribe capabilities of which he believes the beings of his own species are entirely destitute: by this he will prove nothing, except that he is himself ignorant of what man is capable of producing. It is thus that a raw unpolished people raise their eyes to heaven, every time they witness some unusual phenomenon. It is thus that the people denominate all those strange effects, with the natural causes of which they are ignorant, miraculous, supernatural, divine; but these are not by reasonable persons therefore considered proofs of what they assert: as the multitude are generally unacquainted with the cause of any thing, every object becomes a miracle in their eyes; at least they imagine God is the immediate cause of the good they enjoy—of the evil they suffer. In short, it is thus that the theologians themselves solve every difficulty that starts in their road; they ascribe to God all those phenomena, of the causes of which either they are themselves ignorant, or else unwilling that man should be acquainted with the source.

In the *third place*, the savage, in opening the watch, and examining its parts, will perhaps feel, that this machinery announces a work which can only be the result of human labour. He will perhaps perceive, that they very obviously differ from the immediate productions of nature, whom he has not observed to produce wheels made of polished metal. He will further notice, perhaps, that these parts when separated, no longer act as they did when they were combined; that the motion he so much admired, ceases when their union is broken. After these observations, he will attribute the watch to the ingenuity of man; that is to say, to a being like himself, of whom he has some ideas, but whom he judges capable to construct machines to which he is himself utterly incompetent. In short, he will ascribe the honour of his watch to a being known to him in some respects, provided with faculties very far superior to his own; but he will be at an immense distance from the belief, that this material work, whose ingenuity pleases him so much, can be the effect of an immaterial cause; or of an agent destitute of organs, without extent; whose action upon material beings cannot be within, the sphere of his comprehension. Nevertheless, man, when he cannot embrace the causes of things, does not scruple to insist that they are impossible to be the production of nature, although he is entirely ignorant how far the powers of this nature extend; to what her capabilities are equal. In viewing the world, we must acknowledge material causes for many of those phenomena which take place in it; those who study nature are continually adding fresh discoveries to this list of physical causes; science, as she enriches the intellectual stores of human enjoyment, every day throws a broader light on the energies of nature, which *prejudice*, aided by its almost inseparable companion, *ignorance*, would for ever bind down in the fetters of impotence.

Let us not, however, he told, that pursuing this hypothesis, we attribute every thing to a blind cause—to the fortuitous concurrence of atoms—to chance. Those only are called blind causes of which we know not either the combination, the laws, or the power. Those effects are called fortuitous, with whose causes man is unacquainted; to which his experience affords him no clue; which his ignorance prevents him from foreseeing. All those effects, of which he does not see the necessary connection with their causes, he attributes to chance. Nature is not a blind cause; she never acts by chance; nothing that she does would ever be considered fortuitous, by him who should understand her mode of action—who had a knowledge of her resources—who was intelligent in her ways. Every thing that she produces is strictly necessary—is never more than a consequence of her eternal, immutable laws; all is connected in her by invisible bonds; every effect we witness flows necessarily from its cause, whether we are in a condition to fathom it, or whether we are obliged to let it remain hidden from our view. It is very possible there should be ignorance on our part; but the words spirit, intelligence, will not remedy this ignorance; they will rather redouble it, by arresting our research; by preventing us from conquering those impediments which obstruct us in probing the natural causes of the effects, with which our visual faculties bring us acquainted.

This may serve for an answer to the clamour of those who raise perpetual objections to the partizans of nature, by unceasingly accusing them with attributing every thing to chance. Chance is a word devoid of sense, which furnishes no substantive idea; at least it indicates only the ignorance of its employers. Nevertheless, we are triumphantly told, it is reiterated continually, that a regular work cannot be ascribed to the concurrence of chance. Never, we are informed, will it be possible to arrive at the formation of a poem such as the Iliad, by means of letters thrown together promiscuously or combined at random. We agree to it without hesitation; but, ingenuously, are the letters which compose a poem thrown with the hand in the manner of dice? It would avail as much to say, we could not pronounce a discourse with the feet. It is nature, who combines according to necessary laws, under given circumstances, a head organized in a mode suitable to bring forth a poem: it is nature who assembles the elements, which furnish man with a brain competent to give birth to such a work: it is nature, who, through the medium of the imagination, by means of the passions, in consequence of the temperament which she bestows upon man, capacitates him to produce such a masterpiece of fancy; such a never-fading effort of the mind: it is his brain modified in a certain manner, crowded with ideas, decorated with images, made fruitful by circumstances, that alone can become the matrix in which a poem can be conceived—in which the matter of it can be digested: this is the only womb whose activity could usher to an admiring world, the sublime stanzas which develope the story of the unfortunate Priam, and immortalize their author. A head organized like that of Homer, furnished with the same vigour, glowing with the same vivid imagination, enriched with the same erudition, placed under the same circumstances, would necessarily, and not by chance, produce the poem of the Iliad; at least, unless it be denied that causes similar in every thing must produce effects perfectly identical. We should without doubt be surprised, if there were in a dice-box a hundred thousand dice, to see a hundred thousand sixes follow in succession; but if these dice were all cogged or loaded, our surprise would cease: the particles of matter may be compared to cogged dice, that is to say, always producing certain determinate effects under certain given circumstances; these particles being essentially varied in themselves, countless in their combinations, they are cogged in myriads of different modes. The head of Homer, or of Virgil, was no more than an assemblage of particles, possessing peculiar properties; or if they will, of dice cogged by nature; that is to say, of beings so combined, of matter so wrought, as to produce the beautiful poems of the Iliad or the Aeneid. As much way be said of all other productions: indeed, what are men themselves but cogged dice—machines into which nature has infused the bias requisite to produce effects of a certain description? A man of genius produces a good work, in the same manner as a tree of a good species, placed in a prolific soil, cultivated with care, grafted with judgment, produces excellent fruit.

Then is it not either knavery or puerility, to talk of composing a work by scattering letters with the hand; by promiscuously mingling characters; or gathering together by chance, that which can only result from a human brain, with a peculiar organization, modified after a certain manner? The principle of human generation does not develope itself by chance; it cannot be nourished with effect, expanded into life, but in the womb of a woman: a confused heap of characters, a jumble of symbols, is nothing more than an assemblage of signs, whose proper arrangement is adequate to paint human ideas; but in order that these ideas may be correctly delineated, it is previously requisite that they should have been conceived, combined, nourished, connected, and developed in the brain of a poet; where circumstances make them fructify, mature them, and bring them forth in perfection, by reason of the fecundity, generated by the genial warmth and the peculiar energy of the matrix, in which these intellectual seeds shall have been placed. Ideas in combining, expanding, connecting, and associating themselves, form a whole, like all the other bodies of nature: this whole affords us pleasure, becomes a source of enjoyment, when it gives birth to agreeable sensations in the mind; when it offers to our examination pictures calculated to move us in a lively manner. It is thus that the history of the Trojan war, as digested in the head of Homer, ushered into the world with all the fascinating harmony of numbers peculiar to himself, has the power of giving a pleasurable impulse to heads, who by their analogy with that of this incomparable Grecian, are in a capacity to feel its beauties.

From this it will be obvious, that nothing can be produced by chance; that no effect can exist without an adequate cause for its existence; that the one must ever be commensurate with the other. All the works of nature grow out of the uniform action of invariable laws, whether our mind can with facility follow the concatenation of the successive causes which operate; or whether, as in her more complicated productions, we find ourselves in the impossibility of distinguishing the various springs which she sets in motion to give birth to her phenomena. To nature, the difficulty is not more to produce a great poet, capable of writing an admirable poem, than to form a glittering stone or a shining metal which gravitates towards a centre. The mode she adopts to give birth to these various beings, is equally unknown to us, when we have not meditated upon it; frequently the most sedulous attention, the most patient investigation affords us no information; sometimes, however, the unwearied industry of the philosopher is rewarded, by throwing into light the most mysterious operations. Thus the keen penetration of a Newton, aided by uncommon diligence, developed the starry system, which, for so many thousand years, had eluded the research of all the astronomers by whom he was preceded. Thus the sagacity of a Harvey giving vigour to his application, brought out of the obscurity in which for almost countless centuries it had been buried, the true course pursued by the sanguinary fluid, when circulating through the veins and arteries of man, giving activity to his machine, diffusing life through his system, and enabling him to perform those actions which so frequently strike an astonished world with wonder and regret. Thus Gallileo, by a quickness of perception, a depth of reasoning peculiar to himself, held up to an admiring world, the actual form and situation of the planet we inhabit; which until then had escaped the observation of the most profound geniuses—the most subtle metaphysicians—the whole host of priests; which when first promulgated was considered so extraordinary, so contradictory to all the then received opinions, either sacred or profane, that he was ranked as an atheist, as an impious blasphemer, to hold communion with whom, would secure to the communers a place in the regions of everlasting torment; in short, it was held an heresy of such an indelible dye, that notwithstanding the infallibility of his sacred function, Pope Gregory, who then filled the papal chair, excommunicated all those who had the temerity to accredit so abominable a doctrine.

Man is born by the necessary concurrence of those elements suitable to his construction; he increases in bulk, corroborates his system, expands his powers, in the same manner as a plant or a stone; which as well as himself, are augmented in their volume, invigorated in their capabilities, by the addition of homogeneous matter, that exists within the sphere of their attraction. Man feels, thinks, receives ideas, acts after a certain manner, that is to say, according to his organic structure, which is peculiar to himself; that renders him susceptible of modifications, of which the stone and the plant are utterly incapable. On the other hand, the organization of these beings is of a nature to enable them to receive other modifications, which man is not more capacitated to experience, than the stone or the plant are those which constitute him what he is. In consequence of this peculiar arrangement, the man of genius produces works of merit; the plant when it is healthy yields delicious fruits the stone when it is placed in a suitable matrix possesses a glittering brilliance which dazzles the eyes of mortals; each in their sphere of action both surprise and delight us; because we feel that they excite in us sensations, that harmonize with what we call order; in consequence of the pleasure they infuse, by the rarity, by the magnitude, and by the variety of the effects which they occasion us to experience. Nevertheless, that which is found most admirable in the productions of nature, that which is most esteemed in the actions of man, most highly valued in animals, most sought after in vegetation, most in request among fossils, is never more than the natural effects of the different particles of matter, diversely arranged, variously combined, submitted to numerous modifications; from matter thus united result organs, brains, temperament, taste, talents, all the multifarious properties, all the multitudinous qualities, which discriminate the beings whose multiplied activity make up the sum of what is designated animated nature.

Nature then produces nothing but what is necessary; it is not by fortuitous combinations, by chance throws, that she exhibits to our view the beings we behold; all her throws are sure, all the causes she employs have infallibly their effects. Whenever she gives birth to extraordinary, marvellous, rare beings, it is, that the requisite order of things the concurrence of the necessary productive causes, happens but seldom. As soon as those beings exist, they are to be ascribed to nature, equally with the most familiar of her productions; to nature every thing is equally possible, equally facile, when she assembles together the instruments or the causes necessary to act. Thus it seems presumption in man to set limits to the powers of nature, which he so very imperfectly understands. The combinations, or if they will, the throws that she makes in an eternity of existence, can easily produce all the beings that have existed: her eternal march must necessarily bring forth, again and again, the most astonishing circumstances; the most rare occurrences; those most calculated to rouse the wonder, to elicit the admiration of beings, who are only in a condition to give them a momentary consideration; who can get nothing more than a glimpse, without ever having either the leisure or the means to search into causes, which lie hid from their weak eyes, in the depths of Cimmerian obscurity. Countless throws during eternity, with elements and combinations varied almost to infinity, quite with relation to man, suffice to produce every thing of which he has a knowledge, with multitudes of other effects, of which he will never have the least conception.

Thus, we cannot too often repeat to the metaphysicians, to the supporters of immateriality, to the inconsistent theologians, who commonly ascribe to their adversaries the most ridiculous opinions, in order to obtain an easy, short-lived triumph in the prejudiced eyes of the multitude; or in the stagnant minds of those who never examine deeply; that chance is nothing but a word, as well as many other words, imagined solely to cover the ignorance of those to whom the course of nature is inexplicable—to shield the idleness of others who are too slothful to seek into the properties of acting causes. It is not chance that has produced the universe, it is self-existent; nature exists necessarily from all eternity: she is omnipotent because every thing is produced by her energies; she is omnipresent, because she fills all space; she is omniscient, because every thing can only be what it actually is; she is immovable, because as a whole she cannot be displaced; she is immutable, because her essence cannot change, although her forms may vary; she is infinite, because she cannot have any bounds; she is all perfect, because she contains every thing: in short, she has all the abstract qualities of the metaphysician, all the moral faculties of the theologian, without involving any contradiction, since that which is the assemblage of all, must of necessity contain the properties of all.

However concealed may be her ways, the existence of nature is indubitable; her mode of action is in some respects known to us. Experience amply demonstrates we might, if we were more industrious, become better acquainted with her secrets; but with an immaterial substance, with a pure spirit, the mind of man can never become familiar: he has no means by which he can picture to himself this incomprehensible, this inconceivable quality: in despite therefore of the roundness of assertion adopted by the theologian, notwithstanding all the subtilties of the metaphysician, it will always be for man, while he remains such as he now is, in the language of Doctor Samuel Clarke, that, *of which nothing can with truth be affirmed.*

CHAP. VI.
Of Pantheism; or of the Natural Ideas of the Divinity.

The false principle that matter is not self-existent; that by its nature it is in an impossibility to move itself; consequently incompetent to the production of those striking phenomena which arrest our wondering eyes in the wide expanse of the universe; it will be obvious, to all who seriously attend to what has preceded, is the origin of the proofs upon which theology rests the existence of immateriality. After these suppositions, as gratuitous as they are erroneous, the fallacy of which we have exposed elsewhere, it has been believed that matter did not always exist, but that its existence, as well as its motion, is a production of time; due to a cause distinguished from itself; to an unknown agent to whom it is subordinate. As man finds in his own species a quality which he calls intelligence, which presides over all his actions, by the aid of which he arrives at the end he proposes to himself; he has clothed this invisible agent with this quality, which he has extended beyond the limits of his own conception: be magnified it thus, because, having made him the author of effects of which he found himself incapable, he did not conceive it possible that the intelligence he himself possessed, unless it was prodigiously amplified, would be sufficient to account for those productions, to which his erring judgment led him to conclude the natural energy of physical causes were not adequate.

As this agent was invisible, as his mode of action was inconceivable, he made him a spirit, a word that really means nothing more than that he is ignorant of his essence, or that he acts like the breath of which he cannot trace the motion. Thus, in speaking of spirituality, he designated an occult quality, which he deemed suitable to a concealed being, whose mode of action was always imperceptible to the senses. It would appear, however, that originally the word spirit was not meant to designate immateriality; but a matter of a more subtile nature than that which acted coarsely on the organs: still of a nature capable of penetrating the grosser matter—of communicating to it motion—of instilling into it active life—of giving birth to those combinations— of imparting to them those modifications, which his organic structure rendered him competent to discover. Such was, as has been shewn, that all-powerful Jupiter, who in the theology of the ancients, was originally destined to represent the etherial, subtile matter that penetrates, vivifies, and gives activity to all the bodies of which nature is the common assemblage.

It would be grossly deceiving ourselves to believe that the idea of spirituality, such as the subtilty of dreaming metaphysicians present it in these days, was that which offered itself to our forefathers in the early stages of the human mind. This immateriality, which excludes all analogy with any thing but itself—which bears no resemblance to any thing of which man is capacitated to have a knowledge, was, as we have already observed, the slow, the tardy fruit of his imagination, after he had quitted experience, and renounced his reason. Men reared in luxurious leisure, unceasingly meditating, without the assistance of those natural helps with which attentive observation would have furnished them, by degrees arrived at the formation of this incomprehensible quality, which is so fugitive, that although man has been compelled to reverence it, to accredit it against all the evidence of his senses, they have never yet been enabled to give any other explanation of its nature, than by using a term to which it is impossible to attach any intelligible idea. Seraphis said, with tears in his eyes, "that in making him adopt the opinion of spirituality, they had deprived him of his God." Many fathers of the church have given a human form to the Divinity, and treated all those as heretics who made him spiritual. Thus by dint of reasoning, by force of subtilizing, the word spirit no longer presents any one image upon which the mind can fix itself; when they are desirous to speak of it, it becomes impossible to understand them, seeing that each visionary paints it after his own manner; and in the portrait he forms, consults only his own temperament, follows nothing but his own imagination, adopts nothing but his own peculiar reveries; the only point in which they are at all in unison, is in assigning to it inconceivable qualities, which they naturally enough believe are best suited to the incomprehensible beings they have delineated: from the incompatible heap of these qualities, generally resulted a whole, whose existence they thus rendered impossible. In short, this word, which has occupied the research of so many learned and intelligent men; which is considered of such importance to mankind, has been, in consequence of theological reveries, always fluctuating: these never bearing the least resemblance to each other, it has become destitute of any fixed sense, a mere sound, to which each who echoes it affixes his own peculiar ideas, which are never in harmony with those of his neighbour; which indeed are not even steady in himself, but like the camelion, assume the colour of every differing circumstance. This unintelligible word has been substituted for the more intelligible one of matter; man, when clothed with power, has entertained the most rancorous antipathies, pursued the most barbarous persecutions, against those who have not been enabled to contemplate this changeable idea under the same point of view with himself.

There have, however, been men who had sufficient courage to resist this torrent of opinion—to oppose themselves to this delirium; who have believed, that the object which was announced as the most important for mortals, as the sole object worthy of their thoughts, demanded an attentive examination; who apprehended that if experience could be of any utility, if judgment could afford any advantage, if reason was of any use whatever, it must, most unquestionably be, to consider this quality so opposed to every thing in nature, which was said to regulate all the beings which she contains. These quickly saw they could not subscribe to the general opinion of the uninformed, who never examine any thing, who take every thing upon the credit of others; much less was it consistent with sound sense to agree with their guides, who, either deceivers or deceived, forbade others to submit it to the scrutiny of reason; who were themselves frequently in an utter incapacity to pass it under such an ordeal.

Thus some thinkers, disgusted with the obscure and contradictory notions which others had through habit mechanically attached to this incomprehensible property, had the temerity to shake off the yoke which had been imposed upon them from their infancy: calling reason to their aid against those terrors with which they alarmed the ignorant, revolting at the hideous descriptions under which they attempted to defend their hypothesis, they had the intrepidity to tear the veil of delusion; to rend asunder the barriers of imposture; they considered with calm resolution, this formidable prejudice, contemplated with a serene eye this unsupported opinion, examined with cool deliberation this fluctuating notion, which had become the object of all the hopes, the source of all the fears, the spring of all the quarrels which distracted the mind, and disturbed the harmony of blind, confiding mortals.

The result of these inquiries has uniformly been, a conviction that no rational proof has ever been adduced in support of this hypothesis; that from the nature of the thing itself, none can be offered; that an incorporeity is inconceivable to corporeal beings; that these only behold nature acting after invariable laws, in which every thing is material; that all the phenomena of which the world is the theatre, spring out of natural causes; that man as well as all the other beings is the work or this nature, is only an instrument in her hand, obliged to accomplish the eternal decrees of an imperious necessity.

Whatever efforts the philosopher makes to penetrate the secrets of nature, he never finds more, as we have many times repeated, than matter; various in itself, diversely modified in consequence of the motion it undergoes. Its whole, as well as its parts, displays only necessary causes producing necessary effects, which flow necessarily one out of the other: of which the mind, aided by experience, is more or less competent to discover the concatenation. In virtue of their specific properties, all the beings that come under our review, gravitate towards a centre—attract analogous matter—repel that which is unsuitable to combination—mutually receive and give impulse—acquire qualities—undergo modifications which maintain them in existence for a season—are born and dissolved by the operation of an inexorable decree, that obliges every thing, we behold to pass into a new mode of existence. It is to these continued vicissitudes that are to be ascribed all the phenomena, whether trivial or of magnitude; ordinary or extraordinary; known or unknown; simple or complicated; which are operated in the universe. It is by these mutations alone that we have any knowledge of nature: she is only mysterious to those who contemplate her through the veil of prejudice: her course is always simple to those who look at her without prepossession.

To attribute the effects to which we are witnesses, to nature, to matter, variously combined with the motion that is inherent to it, is to give them an intelligible and known cause; to attempt to penetrate deeper, is to plunge ourselves into imaginary regions, where we find only a chaos of obscurities—where we are lost in an unfathomable abyss of incertitude. Let us then be content with contemplating nature, who, being self-existent, must in her essence possess motion; which cannot be conceived without properties, from which result perpetual action and re- action; or those continual efforts which give birth to such a numerous train of circumstances; in which a single molecule cannot be found, that does not necessarily occupy the place assigned to it, by immutable and necessary laws—that is for an instant in an absolute state of repose. What necessity can there exist to seek out of matter for a power to give it play, since its motion flows as necessarily out of its existence as its bulk, its form, its gravity, &c. since nature in inaction would no longer be nature?

If it be demanded, How can we figure to ourselves, that matter by its own peculiar energy can produce all the effects we witness? I shall reply, that if by matter it is obstinately determined to understand nothing but a dead, inert mass, destitute of every property, incapable of moving itself, we shall no longer have a single idea of matter; we shall no longer be able to account for any thing. As soon, however, as it exists, it must have properties; as soon as it has properties, without which it could not exist, it must act by virtue of those properties; since it is only by its action we can have a knowledge of its existence, be conscious of its properties. It is evident that if by matter be understood that which it is not, or if its existence be denied, those phenomena which strike our visual organs cannot be attributed to it. But if by nature be understood (that which she really is), an heap of existing matter, possessing various properties, we shall be obliged to acknowledge that nature must be competent to move herself; by the diversity of her motion, must have the capability, independent of foreign aid, to produce the effects we behold; we shall find that nothing can be made from nothing; that nothing is made by chance; that the mode of action of every particle of matter, however minute, is necessarily determined by its own peculiar, or by its individual properties.

We have elsewhere said, that that which cannot be annihilated—that which in its nature is indestructible—cannot have been inchoate, cannot have had a beginning to its existence, but exists necessarily from all eternity; contains within itself a sufficient cause for its own peculiar existence. It becomes then perfectly useless to seek out of nature a cause for her action which is in some respects known to us; with which indefatigable research may, judging of the future by the past, render us more familiar. As we know some of the general properties of matter; as we can discover some of its qualities, wherefore should we seek its motion in an unintelligible cause, of which we are not in a condition to become acquainted with any one of its properties? Can we conceive that immateriality could ever draw matter from its own source? Impossible; it is not within the grasp of human intellect. If creation is an eduction from nothing, there must have been a time when matter had not existence; there must consequently be a time when it will cease to be: this latter is acknowledged by many theologians themselves to be impossible. Do those who are continually talking of this mysterious act of omnipotence, by which a mass of matter has been, all at once, substituted to nothing, perfectly understand what they tell us? Is there a man on earth who conceives that a being devoid of extent can exist, become the cause of the existence of beings who have extent—act upon matter—draw it from his own peculiar essence—set it in motion? In truth, the more we consider theology, the more we must be convinced that it has invented words destitute of sense; substituted sounds to intelligible realities.

For want of consulting experience, for want or studying nature, for want of examining the material world, we have plunged ourselves into an intellectual vacuum, which we have peopled with chimeras, We have not stooped to consider matter, to study its different periods, to follow it through its numerous, changes. We have either ridiculously or knavishly confounded dissolution, decomposition, the separation of the elementary particles of bodies, with their radical destruction; we have been unwilling to see that the elements are indestructible; although the forms are fleeting, and depend upon transitory combination. We have not distinguished the change of figure, the alteration of position, the mutation of texture, to which matter is liable, from its annihilation, which is impossible; we have falsely concluded, that matter Was not a necessary being—that it commenced to exist—that this existence was derived from that which possessed nothing in common with itself—that that which was not substance, could give birth to that which is. Thus an unintelligible name has been substituted for matter, which furnishes us with true ideas of nature; of which at each instant we experience the influence, of which we undergo the action, of which we feel the power, and of which we should have a much better knowledge, if our abstract opinions did not continually fasten a bandage over our eyes.

Indeed the most simple notions of philosophy shew us, that, although bodies change and disappear, nothing is however lost in nature; the various produce of the decomposition of a body serves for elements, supplies materials, forms the basis, lays the foundation for accretions, contributes to the maintenance of other bodies. The whole of nature subsists, and is conserved only by the circulation, the transmigration, the exchange, the perpetual displacement of insensible atoms—the continual mutation of the sensible combinations of matter. It is by this palingenesia, this regeneration, that the great whole, the mighty macrocosm subsists; who, like the Saturn of the ancients, is perpetually occupied with devouring her own children.

It will not then be inconsistent with observation, repugnant to reason, contrary to good sense, to acknowledge that matter is self-existent; that it acts by an energy peculiar to itself; that it will never be annihilated. Let us then say, that matter is eternal; that nature has been, is, and ever will be occupied with producing and destroying; with doing and undoing; with combining and separating; in short, with following a system of laws resulting from its necessary existence. For every thing that she doth, she needs only to combine the elements of matter; these, essentially diverse, necessarily either attract or repel each other; come into collision, from whence results either their union or dissolution; by the same laws that one approximates, the other recedes from their respective spheres of action. It is thus that she brings forth plants, fossils, animals, men; thus she gives existence to organized, sensible, thinking beings, as well as to those who are destitute of either feeling or thought. All these act for the season of their respective duration, according to immutable laws, determined by their various properties; arising out of their configuration; depending on their masses; resulting from their ponderosity, &c. Here is the true origin of every thing which is presented to our view; this indicates the mode by which nature, according to her own peculiar powers, is in a state to produce all those astonishing effects which assail our wondering eyes; all that phenomena to which mankind is the witness; as well as all the bodies who act diversely upon the organs with which he is furnished, of which he can only judge according to the manner in which these organs are affected. He says they are good, when they are analogous to his own mode of existence—when they contribute to the maintenance of the harmony of his machine: he says they are bad, when they disturb this harmony. It is thus he ascribes views, ideas, designs, to the being he supposes to be the power by which nature is moved; although all the experience we are able to collect, unequivocally proves, that she acts after an invariable, eternal code of laws.

Nature is destitute of those views which actuate man; she acts necessarily, because she exists: her system is immutable, and founded upon the essence of things. It is the essence of the seed of the male, composed of primitive elements, which serve for the basis of an organized being, to unite itself with that of the female; to fructify it; to produce, by this combination, a new organized being; who, feeble in his origin, not having yet acquired a sufficient quantity of material particles to give him consistence, corroborates himself by degrees; strengthens himself by the daily accretion of analogous matter; is nourished by the modifications appropriate to his existence: matured by the continuation of circumstances calculated to give vigour to his frame; thus he lives, thinks, acts, engenders in his turn other organized beings similar to himself. By a consequence of his temperament and of physical laws, this generation does not take place, except when the circumstances necessary to its production find themselves united. Thus this procreation is not operated by chance; the animal does not fructify, but with an animal of his own species, because this is the only one analogous to himself, who unites the qualities, who combines the circumstances, suitable to produce a being resembling himself; without this he would not produce any thing, or he would only give birth to a being who would be denominated a monster, because it would be dissimilar to himself. It is of the essence of the grain of plants, to be impregnated by the pollen or seed of the stygma of the flower; in this state of copulation they in consequence develope themselves in the bowels of the earth; expand by the aid of water; shoot forth by the accession of heat; attract analogous particles to corroborate their system: thus by degrees they form a plant, a shrub, a tree, susceptible of that life, filled with that motion, capable of that action which is suitable to vegetable existence. It is of the essence of particular particles of earth, homogeneous in their nature, when separated by circumstances, attenuated by water, elaborated by heat, to unite themselves in the bosom of mountains, with other atoms which are analogous; to form by their aggregation, according to their various affinities, those bodies possessing more or less solidity; having more or less purity, which are called diamonds, chrystals, stones, metals, minerals. It is of the essence of exhalations raised by the heat of the atmosphere, to combine, to collect themselves, to dash against each other, and either by their union or their collision to produce meteors, to generate thunder. It is of the essence of some inflammable matter to gather itself together, to ferment in the caverns of the earth, to increase its active force by augmenting its heat, and then explode, by the accession of other matter suitable to the operation, with that tremendous force which we call earthquakes; by which mountains are destroyed; cities overturned; the inhabitants of the plains thrown into a state of consternation; these full of alarm, unused to meditate on natural effects, unconscious of the extent of physical powers, stretch forth their hands in dismay, heave the most desponding sighs, utter aloud their complaints, and earnestly implore a cessation of those evils, which nature, acting by necessary laws, obliges them to experience as necessarily as she does those benefits by which she fills them with the most extravagant joy. In short, it is of the essence of certain climates to produce men so organized, whose temperament is so modified, that they become either extremely useful or very prejudicial to their species, in the same manner as it is the property of certain portions of the land, to bring forth either delicious fruits or dangerous poisons.

In all this nature acts necessarily; she pursues an undeviating course, which we are bound to consider the perfection of wisdom; because she exists necessarily, has her modes of action determined by certain, invariable laws, which themselves flow out of the constituent properties of the various beings she contains, and those circumstances, which the eternal motion she is in must necessarily bring about. It is ourselves who have a necessary aim, which is our own conservation; it is by this that we regulate all the ideas we form to ourselves of the causes acting in nature; it is according to this standard we judge of every thing we see or feel. Animated ourselves, existing after a certain manner, possessing a soul endowed with rare and peculiar qualities, we, like the savage, ascribe a soul and animated life to every thing that acts upon us. Thinking and intelligent ourselves, we give these, faculties to those beings whom we suppose to be more powerful than mortals; but as we see the generality of matter incapable of modifying itself, we suppose it must receive its impulse from some concealed agent, some external cause, which our imagination pictures as similar to ourselves. Necessarily attracted by that which is advantageous to us, repelling by an equal necessity that which is prejudicial to our manner of existence; we cease to reflect that our modes of feeling are due to our peculiar organization, modified by physical causes: in this state, either of inattention or ignorance, we mistake the natural results of our own peculiar structure, for instruments employed by a being whom we clothe with our own passions—whom we suppose actuated by our own views—who, possessing our ideas, embraces a mode of thinking and acting similar to ourselves.

If after this it be asked, What is the end of nature? We shall reply that on this head we are ignorant; that it is more than probable no man will ever fathom the secret; but we shall also say, it is evidently to exist, to act, to conserve her whole. If then it be demanded, Wherefore she exists? We shall again reply, of this we know nothing at present, possibly never shall; but we shall also say, she exists necessarily, that her operations, her motion, her phenomena, are the necessary consequences of her necessary existence. There necessarily exists something; this is nature or the universe, this nature necessarily acts as she does. If it be wished to substitute any other word for nature, the question will still remain as it did, as to the cause of her existence; the end she has in view. It is not by changing of terms that a geometrician can solve problems; one word will throw no more light on a subject than another, unless that word carries a certain degree of conviction in the ideas which it generates. As long as we speak of matter, if we cannot develope all its properties, we shall at least have fixed, determinate ideas; something tangible, of which we have a slight knowledge, that we can submit to the examination of our senses: but from the moment we begin to talk of immateriality, of incorporeity, from thence our ideas become confused; we are lost in a labyrinth of conjecture—we have no one means of seizing the subject on any side—we are, after the most elaborate arguments, after the most subtle reasoning, obliged to acknowledge we cannot form the most slender opinion respecting it, that has any thing substantive for its support. In short, that it is precisely that thing "of which every thing may be denied, but of which nothing can with truth be affirmed." Let us clothe this incomprehensible being with whatever qualities we may, it will be always in ourselves we seek the model; they will be our own faculties that we delineate, our own passions that we describe. In like manner man, as long as he is ignorant, will always conjecture that it is for himself alone the universe was formed; not withstanding, he has nothing more to do, than to open his eyes in order to be undeceived. He will then see, that he undergoes a common destiny, equally partakes with all other beings of the benefits, shares with them without exception the evils of life; like them he is submitted to an imperious necessity, inexorable in its decrees; which is itself nothing more than the sum total of those laws which nature herself is obliged to follow.

Thus every thing proves that nature, or matter, exists necessarily; that it cannot in any moment swerve from those laws imposed upon it by its existence. If it cannot be annihilated, it cannot have been inchoate. The theologian himself agrees that it requires a miracle to annihilate an atom. But is it possible to derogate from the necessary laws of existence? Can that which exists necessarily, act but according to the laws peculiar to itself? Miracle is another word invented to shield our own sloth, to cover our own ignorance; it is that by which we wish to designate those rare occurrences, those solitary effects of natural causes, whose infrequency do not afford us means of diving into their springs. It is only saying by another expression, that an unknown cause hath by modes which we cannot trace, produced an uncommon effect which we did not expect, which therefore appears strange to us. This granted, the intervention of words, far from removing the ignorance in which we found ourselves with respect to the power and capabilities of nature, only serves to augment it, to give it more durability. The creation of matter becomes to our mind as incomprehensible, and appears as impossible as its annihilation.

Let us then conclude that all those words which do not present to the mind any determinate idea, ought to be banished the language of those who are desirous of speaking so as to be understood; that abstract terms, invented by ignorance, are only calculated to satisfy men destitute of experience; who are too slothful to study nature, too timid to search into her ways; that they are suitable only to content those enthusiasts, whose curious imagination pleases itself with making fruitless endeavours to spring beyond the visible world; who occupy themselves with chimeras of their own creation: in short, that these words are useful only to those whose sole profession it is to feed the ears of the uninformed with pompous sounds, that are not comprehended by themselves—upon the sense of which they are in a state of perpetual hostility with each other—upon the true meaning of which they have never yet been able to come to a common agreement; which each sees after his own peculiar manner of contemplating objects, in which there never was, nor probably never will be, the least harmony of feeling.

Man is a material being; he cannot consequently have any ideas, but of that which like himself is material; that is to say, of that which is in a capacity to act upon his organs, which has some qualities analogous with his own. In despite of himself, he always assigns material properties to his gods; the impossibility he finds in compassing them, has made him suppose them to be spiritual; distinguished from the material world. Indeed he, must be content, either not to understand himself, or he must have material ideas of the Divinity; the human mind may torture itself as long as it pleases, it will never, after all its efforts, be enabled to comprehend, that material effects can emanate from immaterial causes; or that such causes can have any relation with material beings. Here is the reason why man, as we have seen, believes himself obliged to give to his gods, these morals which he so much so highly esteems, in those beings of his race, who are fortunate enough to possess them: he forgets that a being who is spiritual, adopting the theological hypothesis, cannot from thence either have his organization, or his ideas; that it cannot think in his mode, nor act after his manner; that consequently it cannot possess what he calls intelligence, wisdom, goodness, anger, justice, &c. as he himself understands those terms. Thus, in truth, the moral qualities with which he has clothed the

Divinity, supposes him material, and the most abstract theological notions, are, after all, founded upon a direct, undeniable *Anthropomorphism.*

In despite of all their subtilties, the theologians cannot do otherwise; like all the beings of the human species, they have a knowledge of matter alone: they have no real idea of a pure spirit. When they speak of the intelligence, of the wisdom, of the designs of their gods, they are always those of men which they describe, that they obstinately persist in giving to beings, of which, according to their own shewing, to the evidence they themselves adduce, their essence does not render them susceptible; who if they had those qualities with which they clothe them, would from that very moment cease to be incorporeal; would be in the truest sense of the word, substantive matter. How shall we reconcile the assertion, that beings who have not occasion for any thing—who are sufficient to them selves—whose projects must be executed as soon as they are formed; can have volition, passions, desires? How shall we attribute anger to beings without either blood or bile? How can we conceive an omnipotent being (whose wisdom we admire in the striking order he has himself established in the universe,) can permit that this beautiful arrangement should be continually disturbed, either by the elements in discord, or by the crimes of human beings? In short, this being cannot have any one of the human qualities, which always depend upon the peculiar organization of man—upon his wants—upon his institutions, which are themselves always relative to the society in which he lives. The theologian vainly strives to aggrandize, to exaggerate in idea, to carry to perfection by dint of abstraction, the moral qualities of man; they are unsuitable to the Divinity; in vain it is asserted they are in him of a different nature from what they are in his creatures; that they are perfect; infinite; supreme; eminent; in holding this language, they no longer understand themselves; they can have no one idea of the qualities they are describing, seeing that man can never have a conception of them, but inasmuch as they bear an analogy to the same qualities in himself.

It is thus that by force of metaphysical subtilty, mortals have no longer any fixed, any determinate idea of the beings to which they have given birth. But little contented with understanding physical causes, with contemplating active nature; weary of examining matter, which experience proves is competent to the production of every thing, man has been desirous to despoil it of the energy which it is its essence to possess, in order to invest it in a pure spirit; in an immaterial substance; which he is under the necessity of re-making a material being, whenever he has an inclination either to form an idea of it to himself, or make it understood by others. In assembling the parts of man, which he does no more than enlarge, which he swells out to infinity, he believes he forms an immaterial being, who, for that reason, acquires the capability of performing all those phenomena, with the true causes of which he is ignorant; nevertheless those operations of which he does comprehend the spring, he as sedulously denies to be due to the powers of this being; time, therefore, according to these ideas, as he advances the progress of science, as he further developes the secrets of nature, is continually diminishing the number of actions ascribed to this being—is constantly circumscribing his sphere of action. It is upon the model of the human soul that he forms the soul of nature, or that secret agent from which she receives impulse. After having made himself double, he makes nature in like manner twofold, and then he supposes she is vivified by an intelligence, which he borrows from himself, Placed in an impossibility of becoming acquainted with this agent, as well as with that which he has gratuitously distinguished from his own body; he has invented the word spiritual to cover up his ignorance; which is only in other words avowing it is a substance entirely unknown to him. From that moment, however, he has no ideas whatever of what he himself has done; because he first clothes it with all the qualities he esteems in his fellows, and then destroys them by an assurance, that they in no wise resemble the qualities he has been so anxious to bestow. To remedy this inconvenience, he concludes this spiritual substance much more noble than matter; that its prodigious subtilty, which he calls simplicity, but which is only the effect of metaphysical abstraction, secures it from decomposition, from dissolution, from all those revolutions, to which material bodies, as produced by nature, are evidently exposed.

It is thus, that man always prefers the marvellous to the simple; the unintelligible to the intelligible; that which he cannot comprehend, to that which is within the range of his understanding; he despises those objects which are familiar to him; he estimates those alone with which he is incapable of having any intercourse: that of which he has only confused vague ideas, he concludes must contain something important for him to know—must have something supernatural in its construction. In short, he needs mystery to move his imagination—to exercise his mind— to feed his curiosity; which never labours harder, than when it is occupied with enigmas impossible to be guessed at; which from that very circumstance, he judges to be extremely worthy of his research. This, without doubt, is the reason he looks upon matter, which he has continually under his eyes, which he sees perpetually in action, eternally changing its form, as a contemptible thing—as a contingent being, that does not exist necessarily; consequently, that cannot exist independently: this is the reason why he has imagined a spirit, which he will never be able to conceive; which on that account he declares to be superior to matter; which he roundly asserts to be anterior to nature, and the only self-existent being. The human wind found food in these mystical ideas, they unceasingly occupied it; the imagination had play, it embellished them after its own manner: ignorance fed itself with the fables to which these mysteries gave rise; habit identified them with the existence of man himself: when each could ask the other concerning these ideas, without any one being in a capacity to return a direct answer, he felt himself gratified, he immediately concluded that the general impossibility of reply stamped them with the wondrous faculty of immediately interesting his welfare; of involving his most prominent interests, more than all the things put together, with which he had any possible means of becoming intimately acquainted. Thus they became necessary to his happiness; he believed he fell into a vacuum without them; he became the decided enemy to all those who endeavoured to lead him back to nature, which he had learned to despise; to consider only as an impotent mass, an heap of inert matter, not possessing any energy but what it received from causes exterior to itself; as a contemptible assemblage of fragile combinations, whose forms were continually subject to perish.

In distinguishing nature from her mover, man has fallen into the same absurdity as when he separated his soul from his body; life from the living being; the faculty of thought from the thinking being: deceived on his own peculiar nature, having taken up an erroneous opinion upon the energy of his own organs, he has in like manner been deceived upon the organization of the universe; he has distinguished nature from herself; the life of nature from living nature; the action of nature from active nature. It was this soul of the world—this energy of nature—this principle of activity, which man first personified, then separated by abstraction; sometimes decorated with imaginary attributes; sometimes with qualities borrowed from his own peculiar essence. Such were the aerial materials of which man availed himself to construct the incomprehensible, immaterial substances, which have filled the world with disputes—which have divided man from his fellow—which to this day he has never been able to define, even to his own satisfaction. His own soul was the model. Deceived upon the nature of this, he never had any just ideas of the Divinity, who was, in his mind, nothing more than a copy exaggerated or disfigured to that degree, as to make him mistake the prototype upon which it had been originally formed.

If, because man has distinguished himself from his own existence, it has been impossible for him ever to form to himself any true idea of his own nature; it is also because he has distinguished nature from herself, that both herself and her ways have been mistaken. Man has ceased to study nature, that he might, recur by thought to a substance which possesses nothing in common with her; this substance he has made the mover of nature, without which she would not be capable of any thing; to whom every thing that takes place in her system, must be attributed; the conduct of this being has appeared mysterious, has been held up as marvellous, because he seemed to be a continual contradiction: when if man had but recurred to the immutability of the laws of nature, to the invariable system she pursues, all would have appeared intelligible; every thing would have been reconciled; the apparent contrariety would have vanished. By thus taking a wrong view of things, wisdom and intelligence appeared to be opposed by confusion and disorder; goodness to be rendered nugatory by evil; while all is only just what it must inevitably be, under the given circumstances. In consequence of these erroneous opinions, in the place of applying himself to the study of nature, to discover the method of obtaining her favors, or to seek the means of throwing aside his misfortunes; in the room of consulting his experience; in lieu of labouring usefully to his own happiness; he has been only occupied with expecting these things by channels through which they do not flow; he has been disputing upon objects be never can understand, while he has totally neglected that which was within the compass of his own powers; which he might have rendered propitious to his views, by a more industrious application of his own talent; by a patient investigation, for the purpose of drawing at the fountain of truth, the limpid balsam that alone can heal the sorrows or his heart.

Nothing could be well more prejudicial to his race, than this extravagant theory; which, as we shall prove, has become the source of innumerable evils. Man has been for thousands of years trembling before idols of his own creation—bowing down before them with the most servile homage—occupied with disarming their wrath—sedulously employed in propitiating their kindness, without ever advancing a single step on the road he so much desires to travel. He will perhaps continue the same course for centuries to come, unless by some unlooked for exertion on his part, he shall happen to discard the prejudices which blind him; to lay aside his enthusiasm for the marvellous; to quit his fondness for the enigmatical; rally round the standard of his reason: unless, taking experience for his guide, he march undauntedly forward under the banner of truth, and put to the rout that host of unintelligible jargon, under the cumbrous load of which he has lost sight of his own happiness; which has but too frequently prevented him from seeking the only means adequate either to satisfy his wants, or to ameliorate the evils which he is necessarily obliged to experience.

Let us then re-conduct bewildered mortals to the altar of nature; let us endeavour to destroy that delusion which the ignorance of man, aided by a disordered imagination, has induced him to elevate to her throne; let us strive to dissipate that heavy mist which obscures to him the paths of truth; let us seek to banish from his mind those visionary ideas which prevent him from giving activity to his experience; let us teach him if possible not to seek out of nature herself, the causes of the phenomena he admires—to rest satisfied that she contains remedies for all his evils—that she has manifold benefits in store for those, who, rallying their industry, are willingly patiently to investigate her laws—that she rarely withholds her secrets from the researches of those who diligently labour to unravel them. Let us assure him that reason alone can render him happy; that reason is nothing more than the science of nature, applied to the conduct of man in society; that this reason teaches that every thing is necessary; that his pleasures as well as his sorrows are the effects of nature, who in all her works follows only laws which nothing can make her revoke; that his interest demands he should learn to support with equanimity of mind, all those evils which natural means do not enable him to put aside. In short, let us unceasingly repeat to him, it is in rendering his fellow creature happy, that he will himself arrive at a felicity he will in vain expect from others, when his own conduct refuses it to him.

Nature is self-existent; she will always exist; she produces every thing; contains within herself the cause of every thing; her motion is a necessary consequence of her existence; without motion we could form no conception of nature; under this collective name we designate the assemblage of matter acting by virtue of its peculiar energies. Every thing proves to us, that it is not out of nature man ought to seek the Divinity. If we have only an incomplete knowledge of nature and her ways—if we have only superficial, imperfect ideas of matter, how shall we be able to flatter ourselves with understanding or having any certain notions of immateriality, of beings so much more fugitive, so much more difficult to compass, even by thought, than the material elements; so much more shy of access than either the constituent principles of bodies, their primitive properties, their various modes of acting, or their different manner of existing? If we cannot recur to first causes, let its content ourselves with second causes, with those effects which we can submit to experience, let us collect the facts with which we have an acquaintance; they will enable us to judge of what we do not know: let us at least confine ourselves to the feeble glimmerings of truth with which our senses furnish us, since we do not possess means whereby to acquire broader masses of light.

Do not let us mistake for real sciences, those which have no other basis than our imagination; we shall find that such can at most be but visionary: let us cling close to nature which we see, which we feel, of which we experience the action; of which at least we understand the general laws. If we are ignorant of her detail, if we cannot fathom the secret principles she employs in her most complicated productions, we are at least certain she acts in a permanent, uniform, analogous, necessary manner. Let us then observe this nature; let us watch her movements; but never let us endeavour to quit the routine she prescribes for the beings of our species: if we do, we shall not only be obliged to return, but we shall also infallibly be punished with numberless errors, which will darken our mind, estrange us from reason; the necessary consequence will be countless sorrows, which we may otherwise avoid. Let us consider we are sensible parts of a whole, in which the forms are only produced to be destroyed; in which combinations are ushered into life, that they may again quit it, after having subsisted for a longer or a shorter season. Let us look upon nature as an immense elaboratory which contains every thing necessary for her action; who lacks nothing requisite for the production of all the phenomena she displays to our sight. Let us acknowledge her power to be inherent in her essence; amply commensurate to her eternal march; fully adequate to the happiness of all the beings she contains. Let us consider her as a whole, who can only maintain herself by what we call the discord of the elements; that she exists by the continual dissolution and re-union of her parts; that from this springs the universal harmony; that from this the general stability has its birth. Let us then re-establish omnipotent nature, so long mistaken by man, in her legitimate rights. Let us place her on that adamantine throne, which it is for the felicity of the human race she should occupy. Let us surround her with those ministers who can never deceive, who can never forfeit our confidence—*Justice and Practical Knowledge*. Let us listen to her eternal voice; she neither speaks ambiguously, nor in an unintelligible language; she may be easily comprehended by the people of all nations; because *Reason* is her faithful interpreter. She offers nothing to our contemplation but immutable truths. Let us then for ever impose silence on that enthusiasm which leads us astray; let us put to the blush that imposture which would riot on our credulity; let us discard that gloomy superstition, which has drawn us aside from the only worship suitable to intelligent beings. Above all, never let us forget that the temple of happiness can only be reached through the groves of virtue, which surround it on every side; that the paths which lead to these beautiful walks can only be entered by the road of experience, the portals of which are alone opened to those who apply to them the key of truth: this key is of very simple structure, has no complicated intricacy of wards, and is easily formed on the anvil of social intercourse, merely by *not doing unto others that which you would not wish they should do unto you.*

CHAP. VII.
Of Theism.—Of the System of Optimism.—Of final Causes.

Very few men have either the courage or the industry to examine opinions, which every one is in agreement to acknowledge; there is scarcely any one who ventures to doubt their truth, even when no solid arguments have been adduced in their support. The natural supineness of man readily receives them without examination upon the authority of others—communicates them to his successors in the season of their infancy; thus is transmitted from race to race, notions which once having obtained the sanction of time, are contemplated as clothed with a sacred character, although perhaps to an unprejudiced mind, who should be bent on searching into their foundation, no proofs will appear, that they ever were verified. It is thus with immateriality: it has passed current from father to son for many ages, without these having done any thing more than habitually consign to their brain those obscure ideas which were at first attached to it, which it is evident, from the admission even of its advocates, can never be removed, to admit others of a more enlightened nature. Indeed how can it possibly be, that light can be thrown upon an incomprehensible subject: each therefore modifies it after his own manner; each gives it that colouring that most harmonizes with his own peculiar existence; each contemplates it under that perspective which is the issue of his own particular vision: this from the nature of things cannot be the same in every individual: there must then of necessity be a great contrariety in the opinions resulting. It is thus also that each man forms to himself a God in particular, after his own peculiar temperament—according to his own natural dispositions: the individual circumstances under which he is found, the warmth of his imagination, the prejudices he has received, the mode in which he is at different times affected, have all their influence in the picture he forms. The contented, healthy man, does not see him with the same eyes as the man who is chagrined and sick; the man with a heated blood, who has an ardent imagination, or is subject to bile, does not pourtray him under the same traits as he who enjoys a more peaceable soul, who has a cooler fancy, who is of a more phlegmatic habit. This is not all; even the same individual does not view him in the same manner at different periods of his life: he undergoes all the variations of his machine—all the revolutions of his temperament—all those continual vicissitudes which his existence experiences. The idea of the Divinity is said to be innate; on the contrary, it is perpetually fluctuating in the mind of each individual; varies every moment in all the beings of the human species; so much so, that there are not two who admit precisely the same Deity; there is not a single one, who, under different circumstances, does not see him variously.

Do not then let us be surprised at the variety of systems adopted by mankind on this subject; it ought not to astonish us that there is so little harmony existing among men upon a point of such consequence; it ought not to appear strange that so much contradiction should prevail in the various doctrines held forth; that they should have such little consistency, such slender connection with each other; that the professors should dispute continually upon the rectitude of the opinions adopted by each: they must necessarily wrangle upon that which each contemplates so variously—upon which there is hardly a single mortal who is constantly in accord with himself.

All men are pretty well agreed upon those objects which they are enabled to submit to the test of experience; we do not hear any disputes upon the principles of geometry; those truths that are evident, that are easily demonstrable, never vary in our mind; we never doubt that the part is less than the whole; that two and two make four; that benevolence is an amiable quality; that equity is necessary to man in society. But we find nothing but perpetual controversy upon all those systems which have the Divinity for their object; they are full of incertitude; subject to continual variations: we do not see any harmony either in the principles of theology, or in the principles of its graduates. Even the proofs offered of his existence have been the subject of cavil; they have either been thought too feeble, have been brought forward against rule, or else have not been taken up with sufficient zeal to please the various reasoners who advocate the cause; the corollaries drawn from the premises laid down, are not the same in any two nations, scarcely in two individuals; the thinkers of all ages, in all countries, are perpetually in rivalry with each other; unceasingly quarrel upon all the points of religion; can never agree either upon their theological hypotheses, or upon the fundamental truths which should serve for their basis; even the attributes, the very qualities ascribed, are as warmly contested by some, as they are zealously defended by others.

These never-ending disputes, these perpetual variations, ought, at least, to convince the unprejudiced, that the ideas of the Divinity have neither the generally-admitted evidence, nor the certitude which are attributed to them; on the contrary, these contrarieties in the opinions of the theologians, if submitted to the logic of the schools, might be fatal to the whole of them: according to that mode of reasoning, which at least has the sanction of our universities, all the probabilities in the world cannot acquire the force of a demonstration; a truth is not made evident but when constant experience, reiterated reflection, exhibits it always under the same point of view; the evidence of a proposition cannot be admitted unless it carries with it a substantive demonstration; from the constant relation which is made by well constituted senses, results that evidence, that certitude, which alone can produce full conviction: if the major proposition of a syllogism should be overturned by the minor, the whole falls to the ground. Cicero, who is no mean authority on such a subject, says expressly, "No reasoning can render that false, which experience has demonstrated as evident." Wolff, in his Ontology, says; "That which is repugnant in itself, cannot possibly be understood; that those things which are in themselves contradictions, must always be deficient of evidence." St. Thomas says, "Being, is all that which is not repugnant to existence."

However it may be with these qualities, which the theologians assign to their immaterial beings, whether they may be irreconcileable, or whether they are totally incomprehensible, what can result to the human species in supposing them to have intelligence and views? Can an universal intelligence, whose care must be equally extended to every thing that exists, have more direct, more intimate relations with man, who only forms an insensible portion of the great whole? Can we seriously believe that it is to make joyful the insects, to gratify the ants of his garden, that the Monarch of the universe has constructed and embellished his habitation? Would our feeble eyes, therefore, become stronger—would our narrow views of things be enlarged—should we be better capacitated to understand his projects—could we with more certitude divine his plans, enter into his designs—would our exility of judgment be competent to measure his wisdom, to follow the eternal order he has established? Will those effects, which flow from his omnipotence, emanate from his providence—whether we estimate them as good, or whether we tax them as evil—whether we consider them beneficial, or view them as prejudicial—be less the necessary results of his wisdom, of his justice, of his eternal decrees? In this case can we reasonably suppose that a Being, so wise, so just, so intelligent, will derange his system, change his plan, for such weak beings as ourselves? Can we rationally believe we have the capacity to address worthy prayers, to make suitable requests, to point out proper modes of conduct to such a Being? Can we at all flatter ourselves that to please us, to gratify our discordant wishes, he will alter his immutable laws? Can we imagine that at our entreaty he will take from the beings who surround us their essences, their properties, their various modes of action? Have we any right to expect he will abrogate in our behalf the eternal laws of nature, that he will disturb her eternal march, arrest her everlasting course, which his wisdom has planned; which his goodness has conferred; which are, in fact, the admiration of mankind? Can we hope that in our favour fire will cease to burn, when we approximate it too closely; that fever shall not consume our habit, when contagion has penetrated our system; that gout shall not torment us, when an intemperate mode of life shall have amassed the humours that necessarily result from such conduct; that an edifice tumbling in ruins shall not crush us by its fall, when we are within the vortex of its action? Will our vain cries, our most fervent supplications, prevent a country from being unhappy, when it shall be devastated by an ambitious conqueror; when it shall be submitted to the capricious will of unfeeling tyrants, who bend it beneath the iron rod of their oppression?

If this infinite intelligence gives a free course to those events which his wisdom has prepared; if nothing happens in this world but after his impenetrable designs; we ought silently to submit; we have in fact nothing to ask; we should be madmen to oppose our own weak intellect to such capacious wisdom; we should offer an insult to his prudence if we were desirous to regulate them. Man must not flatter himself that he is wiser than his God; that he is in a capacity to make him change his will; with having power to determine him to take other means than those which he has chosen to accomplish his decrees. An intelligent Divinity can only have taken those measures which embrace complete justice; can only have availed himself of those means which are best calculated to arrive at his end; if he was capable of changing them, he could neither be called wise, immutable, nor provident. If it was to be granted, that the Divinity did for a single instant suspend those laws which he himself has given, if he was to change any thing in his plan, it would be supposing he had not foreseen the motives of this suspension; that he had not calculated the causes of this change; if he did not make these motives enter into his plan, it would be saying he had not foreseen the causes that render them necessary: if he has foreseen them without making them part of his system, it would be arraigning the perfection of the whole. Thus in whatever manner these things are contemplated, under whatever point of view they are examined, it is evident that the prayers which man addresses to the Divinity, which are sanctioned by the different modes of worship, always suppose he is supplicating a being whose wisdom and providence are defective; in fact, that his own is more appropriate to his situation. To suppose he is capable of change in his conduct, is to bring his omniscience into question; to vitally attack his omnipotence; to arraign his goodness; at once to say, that he either is not willing or not competent to judge what would be most expedient for man; for whose sole advantage and pleasure they will, notwithstanding, insist he created the universe: such are the inconsistent doctrines of theology; such the imbecile efforts of metaphysics.

It is, however, upon these notions, extravagant as they may appear, ill directed as they assuredly are, inconclusive as they must be acknowledged by unprejudiced minds, that are founded all the superstitions and many of the religions of the earth. It is by no means an uncommon sight, to see man upon his knees before an all-wise God, whose conduct he is endeavouring to regulate; whose decrees he wishes to avert; whose plan he is desirous to reform. These inconsistent objects he is occupied with gaining, by means equally repugnant to sound sense; equally injurious to the dignity of the Divinity: adopting his own sensations as the criterion of the feelings of the Deity; in some places he tries to win him to his interests by presents; sometimes we behold even the princes of the earth attempting to direct his views, by offering him splendid garments, upon which their own fatuity sets an inordinate value, merely because they have laboured at them themselves; some strive to disarm his justice by the most splendid pageantry; others by practices the most revolting to humanity; some think his immutability will yield to idle ceremonies; others to the most discordant prayers; it not unfrequently happens that to induce him to change in their favour his eternal decrees, those who have opposite interests to promote, each returns him thanks for that which the others consider as the greatest curse that can befal them. In short, man is almost every where prostrate before an omnipotent God, who, if we were to judge by the discrepancy of their requests, never has rendered his creatures such as they ought to be; who to accomplish his divine views has never taken the proper measures, who to fulfil his wisdom has continual need of the admonitions of man, conveyed either in the form of thanks or prayers.

We see, then, that superstition is founded upon manifest contradictions, which man must always fall into when he mistakes the natural causes of things—when he shall attribute the good or evil which he experiences to an intelligent cause, distinguished from nature, of which he will never be competent to form to himself any certain ideas. Indeed, man will always be reduced, as we have so frequently repeated, to the necessity of clothing his gods with his own imbecile qualities: as he is himself a changeable being, whose intelligence is limited; who, placed in divers circumstances, appears to be frequently in contradiction with himself; although he thinks he honours his gods in giving them his own peculiar qualities, he in fact does nothing more than lend them his own inconstancy, cover them with his own weakness, invest them with his own vices. It is thus that in reasoning, he is unable to account for the necessity of things—that he imagines there is a confusion which his prayers will have a tendency to remove—that he thinks the evils of life more than commensurate with the good: he does not perceive that an undeviating system, by operating upon beings diversely organized, whose circumstances are different, whose modes of action are at variance, must of necessity sometimes appear to be inimical to the interests of the individual, while it embraces the general good of the whole. The theologian may subtilize, exaggerate, render as unintelligible as he pleases, the attributes with which he clothes his divinities, he will never be able to remove the contradictions which arise from the discordant qualities which he thus heaps together; neither will he be able to give man any other mode of judging than what arises from the exercise of his senses, such as they are actually found. He will never be able to furnish the idea of an immutable being, while he shall represent this being as capable of being irritated and appeased by the prayers of mortals. He will never delineate the features of omnipotence under the portrait of a being who cannot restrain the actions of his inferiors. He will never hold up a standard of justice, while he shall mingle it with mercy, however amiable the quality; or while he shall represent it as punishing those actions, which the perpetrators were under the necessity of committing. Neither will he be able, under any circumstances, to make a finite mind comprehend infinity; much less when he shall represent this infinity as bounded by finity itself.

From this it will be obvious, that immaterial substances, such as are depicted by the theologians, can only be looked upon as the offspring of a metaphysical brain, unsupported by any of those proofs which are usually required to establish the propositions laid down among men; all the qualities which they ascribe to them, are only those which are suitable to material substances; all the abstract properties with which they invest them, are incomprehensible by material beings; the whole taken together, is one confused mass of contradictions: they have held forth to man, that it highly imported to his interests to know, to understand these substances; he has consequently set his intellect in action to discover some means of compassing an end, said to be so consequential to his welfare; he has, however, been unable to make any progress, because no clue could be offered to him of the road he must pursue; all was mere assertion unsupported by evidence; the whole was enveloped in complete darkness, into which the least scintillation of light could never penetrate. Notwithstanding, as soon as man believes himself greatly interested in knowing a thing, he labors to form to himself an idea of that, the knowledge of which be thinks so important; if insuperable obstacles impede his inquiries—if difficulties of a magnitude to alarm his industry intervene—if with immense labour he makes but little progress, then the slender success that attends his research, aided by a slothful disposition, while it wearies his diligence disposes him to credulity. It was thus, that a crafty ambitious Arab, subtle and knavish in his manners, insinuating in his address, profiting by this credulous inclination, made his countrymen adopt his own fanciful reveries as permanent truths, of which it was not permitted them for an instant to doubt; following up these opinions with enthusiasm, he stimulated them on to become conquerors; obliging the conquered to lend themselves to his system, he gave currency to a creed, invented solely for the purpose of enslaving mankind, which now spreads over immense regions inhabited by a numerous population, although like other systems it does not escape sectarianism, having above seventy branches. Thus ignorance, despair, sloth, the want of reflecting habits, place the human race in a state of dependance upon those who build up systems, while upon the objects which are the foundations, they have no one settled idea: once adopted, however, whenever these systems are brought into question, man either reasons in a very strange manner, or else is the dupe of very deceitful arguments: when they are agitated, and he finds it impossible to understand what is said concerning them when his mind cannot embrace the ambiguity of these doctrines, he imagines those who speak to him are better acquainted with the objects of their discourse than himself; these seizing the favourable opportunity, do not let it slip, they reiterate to him with Stentorian lungs, "That the most certain way is to agree with what they tell him; to allow himself to be guided by them;" in short, they persuade him to shut his eyes, that he may with greater perspicuity distinguish the road he is to travel: once arrived at this influence, they indelibly fix their lessons; irrevocably chain him to the oar; by holding up to his view the punishments intended for him by these imaginary beings, in case he refuses to accredit, in the most liberal manner, their marvellous inventions; this argument, although it only supposes the thing in question, serves to close his mouth—to put an end to his research; alarmed, confused, bewildered, he seems convinced by this victorious reasoning—attaches to it a sacredness that fills him with awe—blindly conceives that they have much clearer ideas of the subject than himself —fears to perceive the palpable contradictions of the doctrines announced to him, until, perhaps, some being, more subtle than those who have enslaved him, by labouring the point incessantly, attacking him on the weak side of his interest, arrives at throwing the absurdity of his system into light, and finally succeeds by inducing him to adopt that of another set of speculators. The uninformed man generally believes his priests have more senses than himself; he takes them for superior beings; for divine men. He only sees that which these priests inform him he must contemplate; to every thing else his eyes are completely hoodwinked; thus the authority of the priests frequently decides, without appeal, that which is useful perhaps only to the priesthood.

When we shall be disposed to recur to the origin of things, we shall ever find that it has been man's imagination, guided by his ignorance, under the influence of fear, which gave birth to his gods; that enthusiasm or imposture have generally either embellished or disfigured them; that credulity readily adopted the fabulous accounts which interested duplicity promulgated respecting them; that these dispositions, sanctioned by time, became habitual. Tyrants finding their advantage in sustaining them, have usually established their power upon the blindness of mankind, and the superstitious fears with which it is always accompanied. Thus, under whatever point of view it is considered, it will always be found that *error cannot be useful to the human species.*

Nevertheless, the happy enthusiast, when his soul is sensible of its enjoyments, when his softened imagination has occasion to paint to itself a seducing object, to which he can render thanks for the kindness he experiences, will ask, "Wherefore deprive me of a being that I see under the character of a sovereign, filled with wisdom, abounding in goodness? What comfort do I not find in figuring to myself a powerful, intelligent, indulgent monarch, of whom I am the favorite; who continually occupies himself with my welfare—unceasingly watches over my safety—who perpetually administers to my wants—who always consents that under him I shall command the whole of nature? I believe I behold him constantly showering his benefits on man; I see his Providence labouring for his advantage without relaxation; he covers the earth with verdure to delight him; he loads the trees with delicious fruits to gratify his palate; he fills the forests with animals suitable to his nourishment; he suspends over his head planets with innumerable stars, to enlighten him by day, to guide his erring steps by night; he extends around him the azure firmament to gladden his sight; he decorates the meadows with flowers to please his fancy; he causes crystal fountains to flow with limpid streams to slake his thirst; he makes rivulets meander through his lands to fructify the earth; he washes his residence with noble rivers, that yield him fish in abundance. Ah! suffer me to thank thee, Author of so many benefits: do not deprive me of my charming sensations. I shall not find my illusions so sweet, so consolatory in a severe destiny—in a rigid necessity—in a blind inanimate matter—in a nature destitute of intelligence, devoid of feeling."

"Wherefore," will say the unfortunate, from whom his destiny has rigorously withheld those benefits which have been lavished on so many others;

"wherefore ravish from me an error that is dear to me? Wherefore annihilate to me a being, whose consoling idea dries up the source of my tears—who serves to calm my sorrows? Wherefore deprive me of an object which I represent to myself as a compassionate, tender father; who reproves me in this world, but into whose arms I throw myself with confidence, when the whole of nature appears to have abandoned me? Supposing it no more than a chimera, the unhappy have occasion for it, to guarantee them against frightful despair: is it not cruel, is it not inhuman, to be desirous of plunging them into a vacuum, by seeking to undeceive them? Is it not an useful error, preferable to those truths which deprive the mind of every consolation, which do not hold forth any relief from its sorrows?"

Thus will equally reason the Negro, the Mussulman, the Brachman, and others. We shall reply to these enthusiasts, no! truth can never render you unhappy; it is this which really consoles us; it is a concealed treasure, much superior to all the superstitions ever invented by fear; it can cheer the heart; give it courage to support the burthens of life; make us smile under adversity; elevate the soul; render it active; furnishes it with means to resist the attacks of fate; to combat misfortunes with success. This will shew clearly that the good and evil of life are distributed with an equal hand, without respect to man's peculiar comforts; that all beings are equally regarded in the universe; that every thing is submitted to necessary laws; that man has no right whatever to think himself a being peculiarly favoured—who is exempted from the common operations of the eternal routine; that it is folly to think he is the only being considered—one for whose enjoyment alone every thing is produced; an attention to facts will suffice to put an end to this delusion, however pleasant may be the indulgence of such a notion; the most superficial glance of the eye will be sufficient to undeceive us in the idea, that he is the *final cause* of the creation— the constant object of the labours of nature, or of its Author. Let us seriously ask him, if he does not witness good constantly blended with evil? If he does not equally partake of them with the other beings in nature? To be obstinately bent to see only the evil, is as irrational as to be willing only to notice the good. Providence seems to be just as much occupied for one class of beings as for another. We see the calm succeed the storm; sickness give place to health; the blessings of peace follow the calamities of war; the earth in every country bring forth roots necessary for the nourishment of man, produce others suitable to his destruction. Each individual of the human species is a compound of good and bad qualities; all nations present a varied spectacle of virtues, growing up beside vices; that which gladdens one being, plunges another into sadness—no event takes place that does not give birth to advantages for some, to disadvantages for others. Insects find a safe retreat in the ruin of the palace, which crushes man in its fall; man by his death furnishes food for myriads of contemptible insects; animals are destroyed by thousands that he may increase his bulk; linger out for a season a feverish existence. We see beings engaged in perpetual hostility, each living at his neighbour's expence;

the one banquetting upon that which causes the desolation of the other; some luxuriously growing into flesh upon the misery which wears others into skeletons— profiting by misfortunes, rioting upon disasters, which ultimately, reciprocally destroy them. The most deadly poisons spring up beside the most wholesome fruits the earth equally nourishes the fatal steel which terminates man's career, and the fruitful corn that prolongs his existence; the bane and its antidote are near neighbours, repose on the same bosom, ripen under the same sun, equally court the hand of the incautious stranger. The rivers which man believes flow for no other purpose than to irrigate his residence, sometimes swell their waters, overtop their banks, inundate his fields, overturn his dwelling, and sweep away the flock and shepherd. The ocean, which he vainly imagines was only collected together to facilitate his commerce supply him with fish, and wash his shores; often wrecks his ships, frequently bursts its boundaries, lays waste his lands, destroys the produce of his industry, and commits the most frightful ravages. The halcyon, delighted with the tempest, voluntarily mingles with the storm; rides contentedly upon the surge; rejoiced by the fearful howlings of the northern blast, plays with happy buoyancy upon the foaming billows, that have ruthlessly dashed in pieces the vessel of the unfortunate mariner; who, plunged into an abyss of misery, with tremulous emotion clings to the wreck; views with horrific despair, the premature destruction of his indulged hopes; sighs deeply at the thoughts of home; with aching heart, thinks of the cherished friends his streaming eyes will never more behold in an agony of soul dwells upon the faithful affection of an adored wife, who will never again repose her drooping head upon his manly bosom; grows wild with the appalling remembrance of beloved children, his wearied arms will never more encircle with parental fondness; then sinks for ever, the unhappy victim of circumstances that fill with glee the fluttering bird, who sees him yield to the overwhelming force of the infuriate waves. The conqueror displays his military skill, fights a sanguinary battle, puts his enemy to the rout, lays waste his country, slaughters thousands of his fellows, plunges whole districts into tears, fills the land with the moans of the fatherless, the wailings of the widow, in order that the crows may have a banquet—that ferocious beasts may gluttonously gorge themselves with human gore—that worms may riot in luxury.

Thus when there is a question concerning an agent we see act so variously; whose motives seem sometimes to be advantageous, sometimes disadvantageous for the human race; at least each individual will judge after the peculiar mode in which he is himself affected; there will consequently be no fixed point, no general standard in the opinions men will form to themselves. Indeed our mode of judging will always be governed by our manner of seeing, by our way of feeling. This will depend upon our temperament, which itself springs out of our organization, and the peculiarity of the circumstances in which we are placed; these can never be the same for all the beings of our species. These individual modes of being affected, then, will always furnish the colours of the portrait which man may paint to himself of the Divinity; it must therefore be obvious they can never be determinate—can have no fixity—can never be reduced to any graduated scale; the inductions which they may draw from them, can never be either constant or uniform; each will always judge after himself, will never see any thing but himself or his own peculiar situation in the picture he delineates.

This granted, the man who has a contented, sensible soul, with a lively imagination, will paint the Divinity under the most charming traits; he will believe that he sees in the whole of nature nothing but proofs of benevolence, evidence of goodness, because it will unceasingly cause him agreeable sensations. In his poetical extacy he will imagine he every where perceives the impression of a perfect intelligence—of an infinite wisdom—of a providence tenderly occupied with the welfare of man; self- love joining itself to these exalted qualities, will put the finishing hand to his persuasion, that the universe is made solely for the human race; he will strive in imagination to kiss with transport the hand from which he believes he receives so many benefits; touched with his kindness, gratified with the perfume of roses whose thorns he does not perceive, or which his extatic delirium prevents him from feeling, he will think he can never sufficiently acknowledge the necessary effects, which he will look upon as indubitable testimony of the divine predilection for man. Completely inebriated with these feelings, this enthusiast will not behold those sorrows, will not notice that confusion of which the universe is the theatre: or if it so happens, be cannot prevent himself from being a witness, he will be persuaded that in the views of an indulgent providence, these calamities are necessary to conduct man to a higher state of felicity; the reliance which he has in the Divinity, upon whom he imagines they depend, induces him to believe, that man only suffers for his good; that this being, who is fruitful in resources, will know how to make him reap advantage from the evils which he experiences in this world: his mind thus pre-occupied, from thence sees nothing that does not elicit his admiration call forth his gratitude; excite his confidence; even those effects which are the most natural, the most necessary, appear in his eyes miracles of benevolence; prodigies of goodness: he shuts his eyes to the disorders which could bring these amiable qualities into question: the most cruel calamities, the most afflicting events, the most heart-rending circumstances, cease to be disorders in his eyes, and do nothing, more than furnish him with new proofs of the divine perfections; he persuades himself that what appears defective or imperfect, is only so in appearance; he admires the wisdom, acknowledges the bounty of the Divinity, even in those effects which are the most terrible for his race—most suitable to discourage his species—most fraught with misery for his fellow.

It is, without doubt, to this happy disposition of the human mind, in some beings of his order, that is to be ascribed the system of *Optimism*, by which enthusiasts, furnished with a romantic imagination, seem to have renounced the evidence of their senses: to find that even for man every thing is good in nature, where the good has constantly its concomitant evil, and where minds less prejudiced, less poetical, would judge that every thing is only that which it can be—that the good and the evil are equally necessary—that they have their source in the nature of things; moreover, in order to attribute any particular character to the events that take place, it would be needful to know the aim of the whole: now the whole cannot have an aim, because if it had a tendency, an aim, or end, it would no longer be the whole, seeing that that to which it tended would be a part not included.

It will be asserted by some, that the evils which we behold in this world are only relative, merely apparent; that they prove nothing against the good: but does not man almost uniformly judge after his own mode of feeling; after his manner of co-existing with those causes by which he is encompassed; which constitute the order of nature with relation to himself; consequently, he ascribes wisdom and goodness to all that which affects him pleasantly, disorder to that state of things by which he is injured. Nevertheless every thing which we witness in the world conspires to prove to us, that whatever is, is necessary; that nothing is done by chance; that all the events, good or bad, whether for us or for beings of a different order, are brought about by causes acting after certain and determinate laws; that nothing can he a sufficient warranty in us to clothe with any one of our human qualities, either nature or the motive-power which has been given to her.

With respect to those who pretend that supreme wisdom will know how to draw the greatest benefits for us, even out of the bosom of those calamities which it is permitted we shall experience in this world; we shall ask them, if they are themselves the confidents of the Divinity; or upon what they found these assertions so flattering to their hopes? They will, without doubt, tell us they judge by analogy; that from the actual proofs of goodness and wisdom, they have a just right to conclude in favour of future bounty. Would it not be a fair reply to ask, If they reason by analogy, and man has not been rendered completely happy in this world, what analogy informs them he will be so in another? If, according to their own shewing, man is sometimes made the victim of evil in his present existence, in order that he may attain a greater good, does not analogical reasoning, which they say they adopt, clearly warrant a deduction, that the same afflictions, for the same purposes, will be equally proper, equally requisite in the world to come?

Thus this language founds itself upon ruinous hypotheses, which have for their bases only a prejudiced imagination. It, in fact, signifies nothing more than that man once persuaded, without any evidence, of his future happiness, will not believe it possible he can be permitted to be unhappy: but might it not be inquired what testimony does he find, what substantive knowledge has he obtained of the peculiar good that results to the human species from those sterilities, from those famines, from those contagions, from those sanguinary conflicts, which cause so many millions of men to perish; which unceasingly depopulate the earth, and desolate the world we inhabit? Is there any one who has sufficient compass of comprehension to ascertain the advantages that result from the evils that besiege us on all sides? Do we not daily witness beings consecrated to misfortune, from the moment they quitted the womb of the parent who brought them into existence, until that which re-committed them to the earth, to sleep in peace with their fathers; who with great difficulty found time to respire; lived the constant sport of fortune; overwhelmed with affliction, immersed in grief, enduring the most cruel reverses? Who is to measure the precise quantity of misery required to derive a certain portion of good? Who is to say when the measure of evil will be full which it is necessary to suffer?

The most enthusiastic Optimists, the *Theists* themselves, the partizans of *Natural Religion*, as well as the most credulous and superstitious, are obliged to recur to the system of another life, to remedy the evils man is decreed to suffer in the present; but have they really any just foundation to suppose the next world will afford him a happiness denied him in this? If it is necessary to recur to a doctrine so little probable as that of a future existence, by what chain of reasoning do they establish their opinion, that when he shall no longer have organs, by the aid of which he is at present alone enabled either to enjoy or to suffer, he shall be able to compensate the evils he has endured; to enjoy a felicity, to partake of a pleasure this organic structure has refused him while on his pilgrimage through the land of his fathers.

From this it will be seen, that the proofs of a sovereign intelligence, or of a magnified human quality drawn from the order, from the harmony, from the beauty of the universe, are never more than those which are derived from men who are organized and modified after a certain mode; or whose cheerful imagination is so constructed as to give birth to agreeable chimeras which they embellish according to their fancy: these illusions, however, must be frequently dissipated even in themselves, whenever their machine becomes deranged; when sorrows assail them, when misfortune corrodes their mind; the spectacle of nature, which under certain circumstances has appeared to them so delightful, so seducing, must then give place to disorder, must yield to confusion. A man of melancholy temperament, soured by misfortunes, made irritable by infirmities, cannot view nature and her author under the same perspective, as the healthy man of a sprightly humour, who is contented with every thing. Deprived of happiness, the fretful man can only find disorder, can see nothing but deformity, can find nothing but subjects to afflict himself with; he only contemplates the universe as the theatre of malice, as the stage for tyrants to execute their vengeance; he grows superstitious, he gives way to credulity, and not unfrequently becomes cruel, in order to serve a master whom he believes he has offended.

In consequence of these ideas, which have their growth in an unhappy temperament, which originate in a peevish humour, which are the offspring of a disturbed imagination, the superstitious are constantly infected with terror, are the slaves to mistrust, the creatures of discontent, continually in a state of fearful alarm. Nature cannot have charms for them; her countless beauties pass by unheeded; they do not participate in her cheerful scenes; they look upon this world, so marvellous to the happy man, so good to the contented enthusiast, as a *valley of tears*, in which a vindictive fate has placed them only to expiate crimes committed either by themselves or by their fathers; they consider themselves as sent here for no other purpose than to be the sharers of calamity; the sport of a capricious fortune; that they are the children of sorrow, destined to undergo the severest trials, to the end that they may everlastingly arrive at a new existence, in which they shall be either happy or miserable, according to their conduct towards the ministers of a being who holds their destiny in his hands. These dismal notions have been the source of all the irrational systems that have ever prevailed; they have given birth to the most revolting practices, currency to the most absurd customs. History abounds with details of the most atrocious cruelties, under the imposing name of public worship; nothing has been considered either too fantastical or too flagitious by the votaries of superstition. Parents have immolated their children; lovers have sacrificed the objects of their affection; friends have destroyed each other: the most bloody disputes have been fomented; the most interminable animosities have been engendered, to gratify the whim of implacable priests, who by crafty inventions have obtained an influence over the people; to please blind zealots, who have never been able either to give fixity to their ideas, or to define their own feelings. Idle dreamers nourished with bile, intoxicated with theologic fury—atrabilarians, whose melancholic humour frequently disposes them to wickedness—visionaries, whose devious imaginations, heated with intemperate zeal, generally leads them to the extremes of fanaticism, working upon ignorance, whose usual bias is credulity, have incessantly disturbed the harmony of mankind, kindled the inextinguishable flame of discord, and in an almost uninterrupted succession, strewed the earth with the mangled carcasses of the multitudinous victims to mad-brained error, whose only crime has been their incapacity to dream according to the rules prescribed by these infuriate maniacs; although these have never been uniform—never assimilated in any two countries—never borne the same features in any two ages, nor even had the united concurrence of the persecuting contemporaries.

It is then in the diversity of temperament, arising from variety of organization—in the contrariety of passions, springing out of this miscellany, modified by the most opposite circumstances, that must be sought the difference we find in the opinions of the theist, the optimist, the happy enthusiast, the zealot, the devotee, the superstitious of all denominations; they are all equally irrational—the dupes of their imagination—the blind children of error. What one contemplates under a favorable point of view, the other never looks upon but on the dark side; that which is the object of the most sedulous research to one set, is that which the others most seek to avoid: each insists he is right; no one offers the least shadow of substantive proof of what he asserts; each points out the great importance of his mission, yet cannot even agree with his colleagues in the embassy, either upon the nature of their instructions, or the means to be adopted. It is thus whenever man sets forth a false supposition, all the reasonings he makes on it are only a long tissue of errors, which entail on him an endless series of misfortunes; every time he renounces the evidence of his senses, it is impossible to calculate the bounds at which his imagination will stop; when he once quits the road of experience, when he travels out of nature, when he loses sight of his reason, to strike into the labyrinths of conjecture, it is difficult to ascertain where his folly will lead him—into what mischievous swamps this *ignis fatuus* of the mind may beguile his wandering steps. It is certainly true, the ideas of the happy enthusiast will be less dangerous to himself, less baneful to others, than those of the atrabilarious fanatic, whose temperament may render him both cowardly and cruel; nevertheless the opinions of the one and of the other will not be less chimerical; the only difference will be, that of the first will produce agreeable, cheerful dreams; while that of the second will present the most appalling visions, terrific spectres, the fruit of a peevish transport of the brain: there will, however, never be more than a step between them all; the smallest revolution in the machine, a slight infirmity, an unforeseen affliction, suffices to change the course of the humours—to vitiate the temperament—to endanger the organization— to overturn the whole system of opinions of the happiest. As soon as the portrait is found disfigured, the beautiful order of things is overthrown relatively to himself; melancholy grapples him—pusillanimity benumbs his faculties—by degrees plunges, him into the rankest depths of gloomy superstition; he then degenerates into all those irregularities which are the dismal harvest of fanatic ignorance ploughed with credulity.

Those ideas, which have no archetype but in the imagination of man, must necessarily take their complexion from his own character; must be clothed with his own passions; must constantly follow the revolutions of his machine; be lively or gloomy; favourable or prejudicial; friendly or inimical; sociable or savage; humane or cruel; according as he whose brain they inhabit shall himself be disposed; in fact, they can never be more than the shadow of the substance he himself interposes between the light and the ground on which they are thrown. A mortal plunged from a state of happiness into misery, whose health merges into sickness, whose joy is changed into affliction, cannot in these vicissitudes preserve the same ideas; these naturally depend every instant upon the variations, which physical sensations oblige his organs to undergo. It will not therefore appear strange that these opinions should be fluctuating, when they depend upon the state of the nervous fluid, upon the greater or less portion of igneous matter floating in the sanguinary vessels.

Theism, or what is called *Natural Religion*, cannot have certain principles; those who profess it must necessarily be subject to vary in their opinions—to fluctuate in their conduct, which flows out of them. A system founded upon wisdom and intelligence, which can never contradict itself, when circumstances change will presently be converted into fanaticism; rapidly degenerate into superstition; such a system, successively meditated by enthusiasts of very distinct characters, must of necessity experience vicissitudes, and quickly depart from its primitive simplicity. The greater part of those philosophers who have been disposed to substitute theism for superstition, have not felt that it was formed to corrupt itself—to degenerate. Striking examples, however, prove this fatal truth. Theism is almost every where corrupted; it has by degrees given way to those superstitions, to those extravagant sects, to those prejudicial opinions with which the human species is degraded. As soon as man consents to acknowledge invisible powers out of nature, upon which his restless mind will never be able invariably to fix his ideas—which his imagination alone will be capable of painting to him; whenever he shall not dare to consult his reason relatively to those powers, it must necessarily be, that the first false step leads him astray, that his conduct as well as his opinions becomes in the long run perfectly absurd.

Those are usually called Theists, who, undeceived upon the greater number of grosser errors to which the uninformed, the superstitiously ignorant, tend the most determined support, simply hold the notion of unknown agents endowed with intelligence, wisdom, power and goodness, in short, full of infinite perfections, whom they distinguish from nature, but whom they clothe after their own fashion; to whom they ascribe their own limited views; whom they make act according to their own absurd passions. The religion of Abraham appears to have originally been a kind of theism, imagined to reform the superstition of the Chaldeans; Moses modified it, and gave it the Judaical form. Socrates was a theist, who lost his life in his attack on polytheism; his disciple Aristocles, or Plato, as he was afterwards called from his large shoulders, embellished the theism of his master, with the mystical colours which he borrowed from the Egyptian and Chaldean priests, which he modified in his own poetical brain, and preserved a remnant of polytheism. The disciples of Plato, such as Proclus, Ammonius, Jamblicus. Plotinus, Longinus, Porphyrus, and others, dressed it up still more fantastically, added a great deal of superstitious mummery, blended it with magic, and other unintelligible doctrines. The first doctors of Christianity were Platonists, who combined the reformed Judaism with the philosophy taught in Academia. Mahomet, in combating the polytheism of his country, seems to have been desirous of restoring the primitive theism of Abraham, and his son Ishmael; yet this has now seventy-two sects. Thus it will be obvious, that theism has no fixed point, no standard, no common measure more than other systems: that it runs from one supposition to another, to find in what manner evil has crept into the world. Indeed it has been for this purpose, which perhaps after all will never be satisfactorily explained, that the doctrine of free-agency was introduced; that the fable of Prometheus and the box of Pandora was imagined; that the history of the Titanes was invented; notwithstanding, it must be evident that these things as well as all the other trappings of superstition, are not more difficult of comprehension than the immaterial substances of the theists; the mind who can admit that beings devoid of parts, destitute of organs, without bulk, can move matter, think like man, have the moral qualities of human nature, need not hesitate to allow that ceremonies, certain motions of the body, words, rites, temples, statues, can equally contain secret virtues; has no occasion to withhold its faith from the concealed powers of magic, theurgy, enchantments, charms, talismans, &c.; can shew no good reason why it should not accredit inspirations, dreams, visions, omens, soothsayers, metamorphoses, and all the host of occult sciences: when things so contradictory to the dictates of reason, so completely opposed to good sense are freely admitted, there can no longer be an thing which ought to possess the right to make credulity revolt; those who give sanction to the one, may without much hesitation believe whatever else is offered to their credence. It would be impossible to mark the precise point at which imagination ought to arrest itself—the exact boundary that should circumscribe belief—the true dose of folly that may be permitted them; or the degree of indulgence that can with safety be extended to those priests who are in the habit of teaching so variously, so contradictorily, what man ought to think on the subjects they handle so advantageously to themselves; who when it becomes a question what remuneration is due from mankind for their unwearied exertions in his favour, are, in spite of all their other differences, in the most perfect union; except perhaps when they come to the division of the spoil: in this, indeed, the apple of discord sometimes takes a tremendous roll. Thus it will be clear that there can be no substantive grounds for separating the theists from the most superstitious; that it becomes impossible to fix the line of demarcation, which divides them from the most credulous of men; to shew the land-marks by which they can be discriminated from those who reason with the least conclusive persuasion. If the theist refuses to follow up the fanatic in every step of his cullibility, he is at least more inconsequent than the last, who having admitted upon hearsay an inconsistent, whimsical doctrine, also adopts upon report the ridiculous, strange means which it furnishes him. The first sets forth with an absurd supposition, of which he rejects the necessary consequences; the other admits both the principle and the conclusion. There are no degrees in fiction any more than in truth. If we admit the superstition, we are bound to receive every thing which its ministers promulgate, as emanating from its principle. None of the reveries of superstition embrace any thing more incredible than immateriality; these reveries are only corollaries drawn with more or less subtilty from unintelligible subjects, by those who have an interest in supporting the system. The inductions which dreamers have made, by dint of meditating on impenetrable materials, are nothing more than ingenious conclusions, which have been drawn with wonderful accuracy, from unknown premises, that are modestly offered to the sanction of mankind by enthusiasts, who claim an unconditional assent, because they assure us no one of the human race is in a capacity either to see, feel, or comprehend the object of their contemplation. Does not this somewhat remind us of what Rabelais describes as the employment of Queen Whim's officers, in his fifth book and twenty-second chapter?

Let us then acknowledge, that the man who is this most credulously superstitious, reasons in a more conclusive manner, or is at least more consistent in his credulity, than those, who, after having admitted a certain position of which they have no one idea, stop short all at once, and refuse to accredit that system of conduct which is the immediate, the necessary result of a radical and primitive error. As soon as they subscribe to a principle fatally opposed to reason, by what right do they dispute its consequences, however absurd they may be found? We cannot too often repeat, for the happiness of mankind, that the human mind, let it torture itself as much as it will, when it quits visible nature leads itself astray; for want of an intelligent guide it wanders in tracks that bewilder its powers, and is quickly obliged, to return into that with which it has at least some, acquaintance. If man mistakes nature and her energies, it is because he does not sufficiently study her—because he does not submit to the test of experience the phenomena he beholds; if he will obstinately deprive her of motion, he can no longer have any ideas of her. Does, he, however, elucidate his embarrassments, by submitting her action to the agency of a being of which he makes himself the model? Does he think he forms a god, when he assembles into one heterogeneous mass, his own discrepant qualities, magnified until his optics are no longer competent to recognize them, and then unites to them certain abstract properties of which he cannot form to himself any one conception? Does he, in fact, do more than collect together that which becomes, in consequence of its association, perfectly unintelligible? Yet, strange as it may appear, when he no longer understands himself—when his mind, lost in its own fictions, becomes inadequate to decipher the characters he has thus promiscuously assembled—when he has huddled together a heap of incomprehensible, abstract qualities, which he is obliged to acknowledge are the mere creatures of imagination, not within the reach of human intellect, he firmly persuades himself he has made a most accurate and beautiful portrait of the Divinity; he ostentatiously displays his picture, demands the eulogy of the spectator, and quarrels with all those who do not agree to adulate his creative powers, by adopting the inconceivable being he holds forth to their worship; in short, to question the existence of his extravaganza, rouses his most bitter reproaches; elicits his everlasting scorn; entails on the incredulous his eternal hatred.

On the other hand, what could we expect from such a being, as they have supposed him to be? What could we consistently ask of him? How make an immaterial being, who has neither organs, space, point, or contact, understand that modification of matter called voice? Admit that this is the being who moves nature—who establishes her laws—who gives to beings their various essences—who endows them with their respective properties; if every thing that takes place is the fruit of his infinite providence—the proof of his profound wisdom, to what end shall we address our prayers to him? Shall we solicit him to acknowledge that the wisdom and providence with which we have clothed him, are in fact erroneous, by entreating him to alter in our favour his eternal laws? Shall we give him to understand our wisdom exceeds his own, by asking, him for our pleasure to change the properties of bodies—to annihilate his immutable decrees—to trace back the invariable course of things—to make beings act in opposition to the essences with which he has thought it right to invest them? Will he at our intercession prevent a body ponderous and hard by its nature, such as a stone, for example, from wounding, in its fall a sensitive being such as the human frame? Again, should we not, in fact, challenge impossibilities, if the discordant attributes brought into union by the theologians were correct; would not immutability oppose itself to omnipotence; mercy to the exercise of rigid justice; omniscience, to the changes that might be required in foreseen plans? In physics, in consequence of the general research after a perpetual motion, science has drawn forth the discovery, that by amalgamating metals of contrary properties, the contractile powers of one kind, under given circumstances which cause the dilation of the other, by their opposite tendencies neutralize the actual effects of each, taken separately, and thus produce an equality in the oscillations, that, neither possessed individually.

It will perhaps, be insisted, that the infinite science of the Creator of all things, is acquainted with resources in the beings he has formed, which are concealed from imbecile mortals; that consequently without changing any thing, either in the laws of nature, or in the essence of things, he is competent to produce effects which surpass the comprehension of our feeble understanding; that these, effects will in no wise be contrary to that order which he himself has established in nature. Granted: but then I reply, *first*, that every thing which is conformable to the nature of things, can neither be called supernatural nor miraculous: many things are, unquestionably, above our comprehension; but then all that is operated in the world is natural— grows out of those immutable laws by which nature is regulated. In the *second* place, it will be requisite to observe, that by the word miracle an effect is designed, of which, for want of understanding nature, she is believed incapable. In the *third* place, it is worthy of remark, that the theologians, almost universally, insist that by miracle is meant not an extraordinary effort of nature, but an effect directly opposite to her laws, which nevertheless they equally challenge to have been prescribed by the Divinity. Buddaeus says, "a miracle is an operation by which the laws of nature, upon which depend the order and the preservation of the universe, are suspended." If, however, the Deity, in those phenomena that most excite our surprise, does nothing more than give play to springs unknown to mortals, there is, then, nothing in nature, which, in this sense, may not be looked upon as a miracle; because the cause by which a stone falls is as unknown to us, as that which makes our globe turn on its own axis. Thus, to explain the phenomena of nature by a miracle, is, in other words, to say we are ignorant of the actuating causes; to attribute them to the Divinity, is to agree we do not comprehend the resources of nature: it is little better than accrediting magic. To attribute to a sovereignly intelligent, immutable, provident, wise being, those miracles by which he derogates from his own laws, is at one blow to annihilate all these qualities: it is an inconsistency that would shame a child. It cannot be supposed that omnipotence has need of miracles to govern the universe, nor to convince his creatures, whose minds and hearts must be in his own hands. The last refuge of the theologian, when driven off all other ground, is the possibility of every thing he asserts, couched in the dogma, "that nothing is impossible to the Divinity." He makes this asseveration with a degree of self-complacency, with an air of triumph, that would almost persuade one he could not be mistaken; most assuredly, with those who dip no further than the surface, he carries complete conviction. But we must take leave to examine a little the nature of this proposition, and we do apprehend that a very slight degree of consideration will shew that it is untenable. In the *first* place, as we have before observed, the possibility of a thing by no means proves its absolute existence: a thing may be extremely possible, and yet not be. *Secondly*, if this was once to become an admitted argument, there would be, in fact, an end of all morality and religion. The Bishop of Chester, Doctor John Wilkins, says, "would not such men be generally accounted out of their wits, who could please themselves by entertaining actual hopes of any thing, merely upon account of the possibility of it, or torment themselves with actual fears of all such evils as are possible? Is there any thing imaginable more wild and extravagant amongst those in bedlam than this would be?" *Thirdly*, the impossibility would reasonably appear to be on the other side, so far from nothing being impossible, every thing that is erroneous would seem to be actually so; the Divinity could not possibly either love vice, cherish crime, be pleased with depravity, or commit wrong; this decidedly turns the argument against them; they must either admit the most monstrous of all suppositions, or retire from behind the shield with which they have imagined they rendered themselves invulnerable.

To those who may be inclined to inquire, whether it would not be better that all things were operated by a good, wise, intelligent Being, than by a blind nature, in which not one consoling quality is found; by a fatal necessity always inexorable to human intreaty? It may be replied, *first*, that our interest does not decide the reality of things, and that when this should be even more advantageous than it is pointed out, it would prove nothing. *Secondly*, that as we are obliged to admit some things are operated by nature, it is certainly on the side of probability that she performs the others; especially as her capabilities are more substantively proved by every age as it advances. *Thirdly*, that nature duly studied furnishes every thing necessary to render us as, happy as our essence admits. When, guided by experience, we shall consult her, with cultivated reason; she will discover to us our duties, that is to say, the indispensable means to which her eternal and necessary laws have attached our preservation, our own happiness, and that of society. It is decidedly in her bosom that we shall find wherewith to satisfy our physical wants; whatever is out of nature, can have no existence relatively to ourselves.

Nature, then, is not a step-mother to us; we do not depend upon an inexorable destiny. Let us therefore endeavour to become more familiar with her resources; she will procure us a multitude of benefits when we shall pay her the attention she deserves: when we shall feel disposed to consult her, she will supply us with the requisites to alleviate both our physical and moral evils: she only punishes us with rigour, when, regardless of her admonitions, we plunge into excesses that disgrace us. Has the voluptuary any reason to complain of the sharp pains inflicted by the gout, when experience, if he had but attended to its counsels, has so often warned him, that the grossness of sensual indulgence must inevitably amass in his machine those humours which give birth to the agony he so acutely feels? Has the superstitious bigot any cause for repining at the misery of his uncertain ideas, when an attentive examination of that nature, he holds of such small account, would have convinced him that the idols under whom he trembles, are nothing but personifications of herself, disguised under some other name? It is evidently by incertitude, discord, blindness, delirium, she chastises those who refuse to, acknowledge the justice of her claims.

In the mean time, it cannot be denied, that a pure Theism, or what is called Natural Religion, may not be preferable to superstition, in the same manner as reform has banished many of the abuses of those countries who have embraced it; but there is nothing short of an unlimited and inviolable liberty of thought, that can permanently assure the repose of the mind. The opinions of men are only dangerous when they are restrained, or when it is imagined necessary to make others think as we ourselves think. No opinions, not even those of superstition itself, would be dangerous, if the superstitious did not think themselves obliged to enforce their adoption, or had not the power to persecute those who refused. It is this prejudice, which, for the benefit of mankind, it is essential to annihilate; and if the thing be not achievable, then the next object which philosophy may reasonably propose to itself, will be to make the depositaries of power feel that they never ought to permit their subjects to commit evil for either superstitious or religious opinions. In this case, wars would be almost unheard of amongst men: instead of beholding the melancholy spectacle of man cutting the throat of his fellow man, because this cannot see with his eyes, we shall witness him essentially labouring to his own happiness by promoting that of his neighbour; cultivating the earth in peace; quietly bringing forth the productions of nature, instead of puzzling his brain with theological disputes, which can never be of the smallest advantage, except to the priests. It must be a self-evident truth, that an argument by men, upon that which is not accessible to man, *could only have been invented by knaves, who, like the professors of legerdemain, were determined to riot luxuriously on the ignorance and credulity of mankind.*

CHAP. VIII.
Examination of the Advantages which result from Man's Notions on the Divinity.—Of their Influence upon Mortals;—upon Politics;—upon Science;—upon the Happiness of Nations, and that of Individuals.

The slender foundation of those ideas which men form to themselves of their gods, must have appeared obvious in what has preceded; the proofs which have been offered in support of the existence of immaterial substances, have been examined; the want of harmony that exists in the opinions upon this subject, which all concur in agreeing to be equally impossible to be known to the inhabitants of the earth, has been shewn; the incompatibility of the attributes with which, theology has clothed incorporeity, has been explained. It has been proved, that the idols which man sets up for adoration, have usually had their birth, either in the bosom of misfortune, when ignorance was at a loss to account for the calamities of the earth upon natural principles, or else have been the shapeless fruit of melancholy, working upon an alarmed mind, coupled with enthusiasm and an unbridled imagination. It has been pointed out how these prejudices, transmitted by tradition from father to son, grafting themselves upon infant minds, cultivated by education, nourished by fear, corroborated by habit, have been maintained by authority; perpetuated by example. In short, every thing must have distinctly evidenced to us, that the ideas of the gods, so generally diffused over the earth, has been little more than an universal delusion of the human race. It remains now to examine if this error has been useful.

It needs little to prove error can never be advantageous for mankind; it is ever founded upon his ignorance, which is itself an acknowledged evil; it springs out of the blindness of his mind to acknowledged truths, and his want of experience, which it must be admitted are prejudicial to his interests: the more importance, therefore, he shall attach to these errors, the more fatal will be the consequences resulting from their adoption. Bacon, the illustrious sophist, who first brought philosophy out of the schools, had great reason when he said, "The worst of all things is deified error." Indeed, the mischiefs springing from superstition or religious errors, have been, and always will be, the most terrible in their consequences—the most extensive in their devastation. The more these errors are respected, the more play they give to the passions; the more value is attached to them, the more the mind is disturbed; the more they are insisted upon, the more irrational they render those, who are seized with the rage for proselytism; the more they are cherished, the greater influence they have on the whole conduct of our lives. Indeed, there can he but little likelihood that he who renounces his reason, in the thing which he considers as most essential to his happiness, will listen to it on any other occasion.

The slightest reflection will afford ample proof to this sad truth: in those fatal notions which man has cherished on this subject, are to be traced the true sources of all those prejudices, the fountain of all those sorrows, to which he is the victim. Nevertheless, as we have elsewhere said, utility ought to be the only standard, the uniform scale, by which to form a judgment on either the opinions, the institutions, the systems, or the actions of intelligent beings; it is according to the measure of happiness which these things procure for us, that we ought either to cover them with our esteem, or expose them to our contempt. Whenever they are useless it is our duty to despise them; as soon as they become pernicious, it is imperative to reject them; reason imperiously prescribes that our detestation should be commensurate with the evils which they cause.

Taking these principles for a land-mark, which are founded on our nature, which must appear incontestible to every reasonable being, with experience for a beacon, let us coolly examine the effects which these notions have produced on the earth. We have already, in more than one part of the work, given a glimpse of the doctrine of that morals, which having only for object the preservation of man, and his conduct in society, can have nothing, in common with imaginary systems: it has been shewn, that the essence of a sensitive, intelligent, rational being, properly meditated, would discover motives competent to moderate the fury of his passions—to induce him to resist his vicious propensities— to make him fly criminal habits—to invite him to render himself useful to those beings for whom his own necessities have a continual occasion; thus, to endear himself to his, fellow mortals, to become respectable in his own esteem. These motives will unquestionably be admitted to possess more solidity, to embrace greater, potency, to involve more truth, than those which are borrowed from systems that want stability; that assume more shapes than there are languages; that are not tangible to the tact of humanity; that must of necessity present a different perspective to all who shall view them through the medium of prejudice. From what has been advanced, it will be felt that education, which should make man in early life contract good habits, adopt favorable dispositions, fortified by a respect for public opinion, invigorated by ideas of decency, strengthened by wholesome laws, corroborated by the desire of meriting the friendship of others, stimulated by the fear of losing his own esteem, would be fully adequate to accustom him to a laudable conduct, amply sufficient to divert him from even those secret crimes, from which he is obliged to punish himself by remorse; which costs him the most incessant labour to keep concealed, by the dread of that shame, which must always follow their publicity. Experience demonstrates in the clearest manner, that the success of a first crime disposes him to commit a second; impunity leads on to the third, this to a lamentable sequel that frequently closes a wretched career with the most ignominious exhibition; thus the first delinquency is the commencement of a habit: there is much less distance from this to the hundredth, than from innocence to criminality: the man, however, who lends himself to a series of bad actions, under even the assurance of impunity, is most woefully deceived, because he cannot avoid castigating himself: moreover, he cannot know at what point of iniquity he shall stop. It has been shewn, that those punishments which society, for its own preservation, has the right to inflict on those who disturb its harmony, are more substantive, more efficacious, more salutary in their effects, than all the distant torments held forth by the priests; they intervene a more immediate obstacle to the stubborn propensities of those obdurate wretches, who, insensible to the charms of virtue, are deaf to the advantages that spring from its practice, than can he opposed by the denunciations, held forth in an hereafter existence, which he is at the same moment taught may be avoided by repentance, that shall only take place when the ability to commit further wrong has ceased. In short, one would be led to think it obvious to the slightest reflection, that politics, founded upon the nature of man, upon the principles of society, armed with equitable laws, vigilant over morals, faithful in rewarding virtue, constant in visiting crime, would be more suitable to clothe ethics with respectability, to throw a sacred mantle over moral goodness, to lend stability to public virtue, than any authority that can be derived from contested systems, the conduct of whose professors frequently disgrace the doctrines they lay down, which after all seldom do more than restrain those whose mildness of temperament effectually prevents them from running into excess; those who, already given to justice, require no coercion. On the other hand, we have endeavoured to prove that nothing can be more absurd, nothing actually more dangerous, than attributing human qualities to the Divinity which cannot but choose to find themselves in a perpetual contradiction.

Plato has said "that virtue consists in resembling God." But how is man to resemble a being, who, it is acknowledged, is incomprehensible to mankind—who cannot be conceived by any of those means, by which he is alone capable of having perceptions? If this being, who is shewn to man under such various aspects, who is said to owe nothing to his creatures, is the author of all the good, as well as all the evil that takes place, how can he be the model for the conduct of the human race living together in society? At most he can only follow one side of the character, because among his fellows, he alone is reputed virtuous who does not deviate in his conduct from justice; who abstains from evil; who performs with punctuality those duties he owes to his fellows. If it be taken up, and insisted he is not the author of the evil, only of the good, I say very well: that is precisely what I wanted to know; you thereby acknowledge he is not the author of every thing; we are no longer at issue; you are inconclusive to your own premises, consequently ought not to demand an implicit reliance on what you choose to assert.

But, replies the subtle theologian, that is not the affair; you must seek it in the creed I have set forth—in the religion of which I am a pillar. Very good: Is it then actually in the system of fanatics, that man should draw up his ideas of virtue? Is it in the doctrines which these codes hold forth, that he is to seek for a model? Alas! do they not pourtray their idols: under the most unwholesome colours; do they not represent them as following their caprice in every thing, who love or hate, who choose or reject, who approve or condemn according to their whim, who delight in carnage, who send discord amongst men, who act irrationally, who commit wantonness, who sport with their feeble subjects, who lay continual snares for them, who rigorously interdict the use of their reason? What, let us seriously ask, would become of morality, if men proposed to themselves such portraits for models!

It was, however, for the most part, systems of this temper that nations adopted. At was in consequence of these principles that what has been called religion in most countries, was far removed from being favourable to morality; on the contrary, it often shook it to its foundation— frequently left no vestige of its existence. It divided man, instead of drawing closer the bonds of union; in the place of that mutual love, that reciprocity of succour, which ought ever to distinguish human society, it introduced hatred and persecution; it made them seize every opportunity to cut each other's throat for speculative opinions, equally irrational; it engendered the most violent heart-burnings— the most rancorous animosities—the most sovereign contempt. The slightest difference in their received opinions rendered them the most mortal enemies; separated their interests for ever; made them despise each other; and seek every means to render their existence miserable. For these theological conjectures, nations become opposed to nations; the sovereign frequently armed himself against his subjects; subjects waged war with their sovereign; citizens gave activity to the most sanguinary hostility against each other; parents detested their offspring; children plunged the pointed steel, the barbed arrow, into the bosoms of those who gave them existence; husbands and wives disunited, became the scourges of each other; relations forgetting the ties of consanguinity, tore each other to pieces, or else reciprocally consigned them to oblivion; all the bonds of society were rent asunder; the social compact was broken up; society committed suicide: whilst in the midst of this fearful wreck—regardless of the horrid shrieks called forth by this dreadful confusion—unmindful of the havock going forward on all sides— each pretended that he conformed to the views of his idol, detailed to him by his priest—fulminated by the oracles. Far from making himself any reproach, for the misery he spread abroad, each lauded his own individual conduct; gloried in the crimes he committed in support of his sacred cause.

The same spirit of maniacal fury pervaded the rites, the ceremonies, the customs, which the worship, adopted by superstition, placed so much above all the social virtues. In one country, tender mothers delivered up their children to moisten with their innocent blood the altars of their idols; in another, the people assembled, performed the ceremony of consolation to their deities, for the outrages they committed against them, and finished by immolating to their anger human victims; in another, a frantic enthusiast lacerated his body, condemned himself for life to the most rigorous tortures, to appease the wrath of his gods. The Jupiter of the Pagans was a lascivious monster; the Moloch of the Phenicians was a cannibal; the savage idol of the Mexican requires thousands of mortals to bleed on his shrine, in order to satisfy his sanguinary appetite.

Such are the models superstition holds out to the imitation of man; is it then surprising that the name of these despots became the signal for madbrained enthusiasm to exercise its outrageous fury; the standard under which cowardice wreaked its cruelty; the watchword for the inhumanity of nations to muster their barbarous strength; a sound which spreads terror wherever its echo could reach; a continual pretext for the most barefaced breaches of public decorum; for the most shameless violation of the moral duties? It was the frightful character men gave of their gods, that banished kindness from their hearts—virtue from their conduct—felicity from their habitations—reason from their mind: almost every where it was some idol, who was disturbed by the mode in which unhappy mortals thought; this armed them with poignards against each other; made them stifle the cries of nature; rendered them barbarous to themselves; atrocious to their fellow creatures: in short, they became irrational, breathed forth vengeance, outraged humanity, every time that, instigated by the priest, they were inclined to imitate the gods of their idolatry, to display their zeal, to render themselves acceptable in their temples.

It is not, then, in such systems, man ought to seek either for models of virtue, or rules of conduct suitable to live in society. He needs human morality, founded upon his own nature; built upon invariable experience; submitted to reason. The ethics of superstition will always he prejudicial to the earth; cruel masters cannot be well served, but by those who resemble them: what then becomes of the great advantages which have been imagined resulted to man, from the notions which have been unceasingly infused into him of his gods? We see that almost <a name=054></a> all nations acknowledge them; yet, to conform themselves to their views, they trampled under foot the clearest rights of nature— the most evident duties of humanity; they appeared to act as if it was only by madness the most incurable—by folly the most preposterous—by the most flagitious crimes, committed with an unsparing hand, that they hoped to draw down upon themselves the favor of heaven—the blessings of the sovereign intelligence they so much boast of serving with unabated zeal; with the most devotional fervor; with the most unlimited obedience. As soon, therefore, as the priests give them to understand their deities command the commission of crime, or whenever there is a question of their respective creeds, although they are wrapt in the most impenetrable obscurity, they make it a duty with themselves to unbridle their rancour—to give loose to the most furious passions; they mistake the clearest precepts of morality; they credulously believe the remission of their own sins will be the reward of their transgressions against their neighbour. Would it not be better to be an inhabitant of Soldania in Africa, where never yet form of worship entered, or the name of God resounded, than thus to pollute the land with superstitious castigation—with the enmity of priests against each other?

Indeed, it is not generally in those revered mortals, spread over the earth to announce the oracles of the gods, that will be found the most sterling virtues. These men, who think themselves so enlightened, who call themselves the ministers of heaven, frequently preach nothing but hatred, discord, and fury in its name: the fear of the gods, far from having a salutary influence over their own morals, far from submitting them to a wholesome discipline, frequently do nothing more than increase their avarice, augment their ambition, inflate their pride, extend their covetousness, render them obstinately stubborn, and harden their hearts. We may see them unceasingly occupied in giving birth to the most lasting animosities, by their unintelligible disputes. We see them hostilely wrestling with the sovereign power, which they contend is subordinate to their own. We see them arm the chiefs of nations against the legitimate magistrates; distribute to the credulous multitude the most mortal weapons, to massacre each other in the prosecution of those futile controversies, which sacerdotal vanity clothes with the most interesting importance. Do these men, who advance the beauty of their theories, who menace the people with eternal vengeance, avail themselves of their own marvellous notions to moderate their pride—to abate their vanity—to lessen their cupidity—to restrain their turbulence—to bring their vindictive humours under control? Are they, even in those countries where their empire is established upon pillars of brass, fixed on adamantine rocks, decorated with the most curious efforts of human ingenuity—where the sacred mantle of public opinion shields them with impunity—where credulity, planted in the hot-bed of ignorance, strikes the roots of their authority into the very centre of the earth; are they, I would ask, the enemies to debauchery, the foes to intemperance, the haters of those excesses which they insist a severe God interdicts to his adorers? On the contrary, are they not seen to be emboldened in crime; intrepid in iniquity; committing the most shameful atrocities; giving free scope to their irregularities; indulging their hatred; glutting their vengeance; exercising the most savage cruelties on the miserable victims to their cowardly suspicion? In short, it may be safely advanced, without fear of contradiction, that scarcely any thing is more frequent, than that those men who announce these terrible creeds—who make men tremble under their yoke—who are unceasingly haranguing upon the eternity and dreadful nature of their punishments— who declare themselves the chosen ministers of their oracular laws—who make all the duties of morality centre in themselves; are those whom superstition least contributes to render virtuous; are men who possess the least milk of human kindness; the fewest feelings of tenderness; who are the most intolerant to their neighbours; the most indulgent to themselves; the most unsociable in their habits; the most licentious in their manners; the most unforgiving in their disposition. In contemplating their conduct, we should be tempted to accredit, that they were perfectly undeceived with respect to the idols whom they serve; that no one was less the dupe to those menaces which they so solemnly pronounce in their name, than themselves. In the hands of the priests of almost all countries, their divinities resembled the head of Medusa, which, without injuring him who shewed it, petrified all others. The priests are generally the most crafty of men, and many among them are substantively wicked.

Does the idea of these avenging, these remunerating systems, impose upon some princes of the earth, who found their titles, who rest their power upon them; who avail themselves of their terrific power to intimidate their subjects; to make the people, often rendered unhappy by their caprice, hold them in reverence? Alas! the theological, the supernatural ideas, adopted by the pride of some sovereigns, have done nothing more than corrupt politics—than metamorphose, them into an abject tyranny. The ministers of these idols, always tyrants themselves, or the cherishers of despots, are unceasingly crying out to monarchs that they are the images of the Divinity. Do they not inform the credulous multitude that heaven is willing they should groan under the most cruel bondage; writhe under the most multifarious injustice; that to suffer is their inheritance; that their princes have the indubitable right to appropriate the goods, dispose of the persons, coerce the liberty; command the lives of their subjects? Do not some of these chiefs of nations, thus poisoned in the name of deified idols, imagine that every indulgence of their wayward humour is freely permitted to them? At once competitors, representatives, and rivals of the celestial powers, do they not, in some instances, exercise after their example the most arbitrary despotism? Do they not, in the intoxication into which sacerdotal flattery has plunged them, think that like their idols, they are not accountable to man for their actions, that they owe nothing to the rest of mortals, that they are bound by no bonds but their own unruly will, to their miserable subjects?

Then it is evident that it is to theological notions, to the loose flattery of its ministers, that are to be ascribed the despotism, the tyrannical injustice, the corruption, the licentiousness of some princes, and the blindness of those people, to whom in heaven's name they interdict the love of liberty; who are forbid to labour effectually to their own happiness; to oppose themselves to violence, however flagrant; to exercise their natural rights, however conducive to their welfare. These intoxicated rulers, even while adoring their avenging gods, in the act of bending others to their worship, do not scruple to outrage them by their irregularities—by their want of moral virtue. What morality is this, but that of men who offer themselves as living images, as animated representatives of the Divinity? Are those monarchs, then, who are habitually unjust, who wrest without remorse the bread from the hands of a famished people, to administer to the profligacy of their insatiable courtiers—to pamper the luxury of the vile instruments of their enormities, atheists? Are, then, those ambitious conquerors, who not contented with oppressing their own slaves, carry desolation, spread misery, deal out death among the subjects of others, atheists? Do we not witness in some of those potentates who rule over nations by *divine right*, (a patent of power, which every usurper claims as his own) ambitious mortals, whose exterminating fury nothing can arrest; with hearts perfectly insensible to the sorrows of mankind; with minds without energy; with souls without virtue; who neglect their most evident duties, with which they do not even deign to become acquainted; powerful men, who insolently set themselves above the rules of equity; knaves who make a sport of honesty? Generally speaking, is there the least sincerity in the alliances which these rulers form among themselves? Do they ever last longer than for the season of their convenience? Do we find substantive virtues adorn those who most abjectly submit themselves to all the follies of superstition? Do they not tax each other as violators of property—as faithlessly aggrandizing themselves at the expence of their neighbour; in fact, do we not see them endeavouring to surprise, anxious to over-reach, ready to injure each other, without being arrested by the menaces of their creeds, or at all yielding to the calls of humanity? In general, they are too haughty to be humane; too inflated with ambition to be virtuous; they make a code for themselves, which they cannot help violating. Charles the Fifth used to say, "that being a warrior, it was impossible for him to have either conscience or religion." His general, the Marquis de Piscaire, observed, that "nothing was more difficult, than to serve at one and the same time, the god *Mars* and *Jesus Christ.*" Indeed, nothing can be more opposed to the true spirit of Christianity than the profession of arms; notwithstanding the Christian princes have the most numerous armies, and are in perpetual hostility with each other: perhaps the clergy themselves do not hold forth the most peaceable examples of the doctrine they teach; they sometimes wrangle for tithes, dispute for trifling enjoyments, quarrel for worldly opinion, with as much determined obstinacy, with as, much settled rancour, with as little charity, as could possibly inhabit the bosom of the most unenlightened Pagan, whose ignorance they despise—whose superstition they rank as the grossest effort of idolatrous debasement. It might almost admit of doubt whether they would be quite pleased to see the mild maxims of the Evangelists, the true Christian meekness, rigidly followed—whether they might not think the complete working of their own system would clash with their own immediate interests? Is it a demonstrable axiom that the ministers of the Christian faith do not think soldiers are beings extremely well calculated to give efficacy to their doctrine—solidity to their advantages—durability to their claims? Be this as it may, priests as well as monarchs have occasionally waged war for the most futile interests; impoverished a people from the anti-christian motives; wrested from each other with all the venom of furies, the bloody remnant of the nations they have laid waste; in fact, to judge by their conduct on certain occasions, it might have been a question if they were not disputing who should have the credit of making the greater number of miserable beings upon earth. At length, either wearied with their own fury, exhausted by their own devouring passions, or compelled by the stern hand of necessity, they have permitted suffering humanity to take breath; they have allowed the miseries concomitant on war, to cease for an instant their devastating havoc; they have made peace in the name of that God, whose decrees, as attested by themselves, they have been so wantonly outraging,—still ready, however, to violate their most solemn pledges, when the smallest interest could offer them a pretext.

Thus it will be obvious, in what manner the idea of the Divinity operates on the priest, as well as upon those who are called his images; who insist they have no account to render but to him alone. Among these representatives of the Divine Majesty, it is with difficulty during thousands of years we find some few who have equity, sensibility, virtue, or even the most ordinary talent. History points out some of these vicegerents of the Deity, who in the exacerbation of their delirious rage, have insisted upon displacing him, by exalting themselves into gods; and exacting the most obsequious worship; who have inflicted the most cruel torments on those who have opposed themselves to their madness, and refused to acknowledge the Divinity of their persons. These men, whose licentiousness knew no limits, from the impunity which attended their actions, notwithstanding they had learned to despise public opinion, to set decency at defiance, to indulge in the most shameless vice: in spite of the power they possessed; of the homage they received; of the terror they inspired: although they had learned to counterfeit, with great effect, the whole catalogue of human virtues; found it impossible, even with the addition of their enormous wealth, wrenched from the necessities of laborious honesty, to counterfeit the animating blush, which modest merit brings forth, when eulogized by some happy being whose felicity he has occasioned, by following the great law of nature—which says, "*love thy neighbour as thyself.*" On the contrary, we see them grow listless with satiety; disgusted with their own inordinate indulgences; obliged to recur to strange pleasures, to awaken their benumbed faculties; to run headlong into the most costly follies, in the fruitless attempt to keep up the activity of their souls, the spring of which they had for ever relaxed, by the profligacy of their enjoyment.

History, although it describes a multitude of vicious rulers, whose irregular propensities were of the most mischievous consequence to the human race, nevertheless, shews us but few who have been atheists. The annals of nations, on the contrary, offer to our view great numbers of superstitious princes, governed by their mistresses, led by unworthy favorites, leagued with priests, who passed their lives plunged in luxury; indulging the most effeminate pursuits; following the most childish pleasures; pleased with ostentatious show; slaves even to the fashion of the vestments that covered them; but strangers to every manly virtue; insensible to the sorrows of their subjects; although uniformly good to their hungry courtiers, invariably kind to those cringing sycophants who surrounded their persons, and poisoned their ears with the most fulsome flattery: in short, superstitious persecutors, who, to render themselves acceptable to their priests, to expiate their own shameful irregularities, added to all their other vices that of tyrannizing over the mind, of fettering the conscience, of destroying their subjects for their opinions, when they were in hostility with their own received doctrines. Indeed, superstition in princes frequently allied itself with the most horrid crimes; they have almost all professed religion, although very few of them have had a just knowledge of morality—have practiced any useful substantive virtue. Superstitious notions, on the contrary, often serve to render them more blind, to augment their evil inclinations; to set them at a greater distance from moral goodness. They for the most part believe themselves assured of the favor of heaven; they think they faithfully serve their gods, that the anger of their divinities is appeased, if for a short season they shew themselves attached to futile customs—lend themselves to absurd rites— perform some ridiculous duties, which superstition imposes on them, with a view to obtain their assistance in the prosecution of its own plans, very rarely in strict unison with their immediate interest. Nero, the cruel, sanguinary, matricidal Nero, his hands yet reeking with the blood of that unfortunate being who had borne him in her womb, who had, with agonizing pains, given the monster to the world that plunged the dagger in her heart, was desirous to be initiated into the *Eleusinian Mysteries*. The odious Constantine himself, found in the priests, accomplices disposed to expiate his crimes. The infamous Philip, whose ungovernable ambition caused him to be called the daemon of the south, whilst he assassinated his wife and son, caused the throats of the wretched Batavians to be cut for their religious opinions. It is thus, that the priests of superstition sometimes persuade sovereigns they can atone for crimes, by committing others of a more atrocious kind—of an increased magnitude.

It would be fair to conclude, from the conduct of so many princes, who had so much superstition, but so slender a portion of virtue, that the notion of their gods, far from being useful to them, only served to render them wore corrupt—to make them more abominable than they already were; that the idea of an avenging power, placed in the perspective of futurity, imposed but little restraint on the turbulence of deified tyrants, who were sufficiently powerful not to fear the reproaches of their subjects—who had the insensibility to be deaf to the censure of their fellows—who were gifted with an obduracy of soul, that prevented their having compassion for the miseries of mankind, from whom they fancied themselves so pre-eminently distinguished; which, in fact, they were, if crime can be allowed for the standard of distinction. Neither heaven nor earth furnishes a balsam of sufficient efficacy to heal the inveterate wounds of beings cankered to this degree: for such chronic diseases, there is "no balm in Gilead:" there is no curb sufficiently coercive to rein in the passions, to which superstition itself gives activity; which only makes them more unruly; renders them more inveterately rash. Whenever men flatter themselves with easily expiating their sins—when they soothe themselves with the consolatary idea of appeasing the anger of the gods by a show of earnestness, they then deliver themselves up, with the most unrestrained freedom, to the bent of their criminal pursuits. The most dissolute men are frequently in appearance extremely attached to superstition: it furnishes them with a means of compensating by ceremonies, that of which they are deficient in morals: it is much easier for them to adopt a faith, to believe in a doctrine, to conform themselves to certain rituals, than to renounce their habits, resist their passions, or relinquish the pursuit of that pleasure, which results to unprincipled minds from the prosecution of the most diabolical schemes.

Under chiefs, depraved even by superstition, nations continued necessarily to be corrupted. The great conformed themselves to the vices of their masters; the example of these distinguished men, whom the uninformed erroneously believe to be happy, was followed by the people; courts thus became the sinks from whence issued the epidemic contagion of licentious indulgence. The law only held forth pictures of honesty; the dispensers of jurisprudence were partial, partook of the mania of the times, were labouring under the general disease; Justice suffered her balance to rust, occasionally removed her bandage, although she always wore it in the presence of the poor; genuine ideas of equity had grown into disuse; distinct notions of right and wrong became troublesome and unfashionable; education was neglected; it served only to produce prejudiced beings, grounded in ignorance—devotees, always ready to injure themselves—fanatics, eager to shew their zeal ever willing to annoy their unfortunate neighbours. Superstition, sustained by tyranny, ousted every other feeling, hoodwinked its destined victims, rendered those tractable whom it had the intention to despoil. Whoever doubts of these truisms, has only to turn over the pages of history, he will find myriads of evidence to much more than is here stated. Machiavel, in his *Political Discourses upon Titus Livius*, labours the point hard, to shew the utility of superstition to the Roman Republic: unfortunately, however, the examples he brings forward in its support, incontestibly prove that none but the senate profited by the infatuation of the people, who availed itself of their blindness more effectually to bend them to its yoke.

Thus it was that nations, destitute of equitable laws, deficient in the administration of justice, submitted to irrational government, continued in slavery by the monarch, chained up in ignorance by the priest, for want of enlightened institutions, deprived of reasonable education, became corrupt, superstitious, and flagitious. The nature of man, the just interests of society, the real advantage of the sovereign, the true happiness of the people, once mistaken, were completely lost sight of; the morality of nature, founded upon the essence of man living in society, was equally unknown; lay buried under an enormous load of prejudice, that no common efforts were competent to remove. It was entirely forgotten that man has wants; that society was formed that he might, with greater security, facilitate the means of satisfying them; that government, to be legitimate, ought to have for object, the happiness—for end, the means of maintaining the indivisibility of the community; that consequently it ought to give activity to springs, full play to motives suitable to have a favorable influence over sensible beings. It was quite overlooked, that virtue faithfully rewarded, vice as regularly visited, had an elastic force, of which the public authorities could efficaciously avail themselves, to determine their citizens to blend their interests; to work out their own felicity, by labouring to the happiness of the body of which they were members. The social virtues were unknown, the *amor patriae* became a chimera. Men thus associated, thus blinded by their superstitious bias, credulously believed their own immediate interest consisted in injuring each other; they were solely occupied with meriting the favor of those men, who fatally accreditted the doctrine of clerical flatterers, of silver-toned courtiers, which taught that they wore distinctly interested in injuring the whole.

This is the mode in which the human heart has become perverted; here is the genuine source of moral evil; the hot-bed of that epidemical depravity, the cause of that hereditary corruption, the fountain of that inveterate delinquency, which pervaded the earth; rendering the abundance of nature nothing better than a curse; blasting the fairest prospects of humanity; degrading man below the beast of the forest; sinking his intellectual faculties in the most savage barbarity; rendering him the vile instrument of lawless ambition; the wretched tool by which the fetters of his species were firmly rivetted; obliging him to moisten his harvest with the bitter tears of the most abject slavery. For the purpose of remedying so many crying evils, grown insupportable, recourse was had to new superstitions. Notwithstanding this alone had produced them, it was still imagined, that the menaces of heaven would restrain passions which every thing conspired to rouse in all hearts; fatuity persuaded monarchs that ideal, metaphysical barriers, terrible fables, distant phantoms, would be competent to curb those inordinate desires, to rein in that impetuous propensity to crime, that rendered society incommodious to itself; credulity fancied that invisible powers would be more efficacious, than those visible motives that evidently invited mortals to the commission of mischief. Every thing was understood to be achieved, by occupying man's mind with gloomy chimeras, with vague, undefinable terrors, with avenging angels; and politics madly believed that its own interests grew out of the blind submission of its subjects, to the ministers of these delusive doctrines.

What was the result? Nations had only sacerdotal laws; theological morality; accommodated to the interests of the hierarchy—suitable to the views of subtle priests: who substituted reveries for realities, opinions for reason, rank fallacies for sterling truths; who made ceremonies supply the place of virtue; a pious blindness supersede the necessity of an enlightened understanding; undermined the sacredness of oaths, and placed fanaticism on the altars of sociability. By a necessary consequence of that confidence which the people were compelled to give to the ministers of superstition, two distinct authorities were established in each state, who were substantially at variance, in continual hostility with each other. The priest fought the sovereign with the formidable weapon of opinion; it generally proved sufficiently powerful to shake the most established thrones. Thus, although the hierarchy was unceasingly admonishing the people to submit themselves to the divine authority of their sovereigns, because it was derived immediately from heaven, yet, whenever it so happened that the monarch did not repay their advocacy, by blindly yielding his own authority to the supervisance of the priests, these made no scruple of threatening him with loss of his temporalities; fulminated their anathemas, interdicted his dominions, and sometimes went the length of absolving his subjects from allegiance. Superstition, in general, only upholds despotism, that it may with greater certainty direct its blows against its enemies; it overthrows it whenever it is found to clash with its interests. The ministers of invisible powers preach up obedience to visible powers, only when they find these humbly devoted to themselves. Thus the sovereign was never at rest, but when abjectly cringing to his priest, he tractably received his lessons—lent himself to his frantic zeal—and piously enabled him to carry on the furious occupation of proselytism. These priests, always restless, full of ambition, burning with intolerance, frequently excited the sovereign to ravage his own states—encouraged him to tyranny: when, pursuing this sacerdotal mania, he feared to have outraged humanity, to have incurred the displeasure of heaven, he was quickly reconciled to himself, upon promise of undertaking some distant expedition, for the purpose of bringing some unfortunate nation within the pale of their own particular creed. When the two rival powers united themselves, morality gained nothing by the junction; the people were neither more happy, nor more virtuous; their morals, their welfare, their liberty, were equally overwhelmed by the combined powers. Thus, superstitious princes always felt interested in the maintenance of theological opinions, which were rendered flattering to their vanity, favorable to their power. Like the grateful perfumes of Arabia, that are used to cover the ill scent of a deadly poison, the priest lulled them into security by administering to their sensualities; these, in return, made common cause with him: fully persuaded that the superstition which they themselves adopted, must be the most wholesome for their subjects, most conducive to their interests, those who refused to receive the boon, thus gratuitously forced upon them, were treated as enemies, held up to public scorn, and rendered the victims of punishment. The most superstitious sovereign became, either politically or through piety, the executioner of one part of his slaves; he was taught to believe it a sacred duty to tyrannize over the mind—to overwhelm the refractory—to crush the enemy of his priest, under an idea that he was therefore hostile to his own authority. In cutting the throats of these unfortunate sceptics, he imagined he at once discharged his obligations to heaven, and gave security to his own power. He did, not perceive, that by immolating victims to his priest, he in fact strengthened the arm of his most formidable foe—the real enemy to his authority—the rival of his greatness—the least subjected of his subjects.

But the prevalence of these false notions, with which both the minds of the sovereign and the people were prepossessed, it was found that every thing in society concurred to gratify the avidity, to bolster the pride, to glut the vengeance of the sacerdotal order: every where, it was to be observed, that the most turbulent, the most dangerous, the most useless men, were those who were the most amply rewarded. The strange spectacle presented itself, of beholding those who were born the bitterest enemies to sovereign power, cherished by its fostering care—honoured at its hands: the most rebellious subjects were looked upon as the pillars of the throne; the corrupters of the people were rendered the exclusive masters of education; the least laborious of the citizens were richly rewarded for their idleness—munificently remunerated for the most futile speculations—held in respect for their fatal discord—gorged with benefits for their inefficacious prayers: they swept off the fat of the land for their expiations, so destructive to morals, so calculated to give permanency to crime. Thus, by a strange fatuity, the viper that could, and frequently did, inflict the most deadly sting on the bosom of confiding credulity, was pampered and nourished by the unsuspecting hand of its destined victim.

For thousands of years, nations as well as sovereigns were emulously despoiling themselves to enrich the expounders of superstition; to enable them to wallow in abundance: they loaded them with honors, decorated them with titles, invested them with privileges, granted them immunities, for no other purpose than to make them bad citizens, unruly subjects, mischievous beings, who revenged upon society the advantages they had received. What was the fruit that kings and people gathered from their imprudent kindness? What was the harvest these men yielded to their labour? Did princes really become more powerful; were nations rendered more happy; did they grow more flourishing; did men become more rational? No! Unquestionably, the sovereign lost the greater portion of his authority; he was the slave of his priest; and when he wished to preserve the remnant that was left, or to recover some part of what had been wrested from him, he was obliged to be continually wrestling against the men his own indulgence, his own weakness, had furnished with means, to set his authority at defiance: the riches of society were lavished to support the idleness, maintain the splendour, satiate the luxury of the most useless, the most arrogant, the most dangerous of its members.

Did the morals of the people improve under the pastoral care of these guides, who were so liberally rewarded? Alas! the superstitious never knew them, their fanatic creed had usurped the place of every virtue; its ministers, satisfied with upholding the doctrines, with preserving the ceremonies so useful to their own interests, only invented fictitious crimes—multiplied painful penances—instituted absurd customs; to the end, that they might turn even the transgressions of their slaves to their own immediate profit. Every where they exercised a monopoly of expiatory indulgences; they made a lucrative traffic of pretended pardons from above; they established a tariff, according to which crime was no longer contraband, but freely admitted upon paying the customs. Those subjected to the heaviest impost, were always such as the hierarchy judged most inimical to its own stability; you might at a very easy rate obtain permission to attack the dignity of the sovereign, to undermine the temporal power, but it was enormously dear to be allowed to touch even the hem of the sacerdotal garments. Thus heresy, sacrilege, &c. were considered crimes of a much deeper dye, that fixed an indelible stain on the perpetrator, alarmed the mind of the priestly order, much more seriously than the most inveterate villainy, the most determined delinquency, which more immediately involved the true interests of society. Thence the ideas of the people were completely overturned, imaginary crimes terrified them, while real crimes had no effect upon their obdurate hearts. A man, whose opinions were at variance with the received doctrines, whose abstract systems did not harmonize with those of his priest, was more loathed than a corrupter of youth; more abhorred than an assassin; more hated than an oppressor; was held in greater contempt than a robber; was punished with greater rigor than the seducer of innocence. The acme of all wickedness, was to despise that which the priest was desirous should be looked upon as sacred. The celebrated Gordon says, "the most abominable of heresies, is to believe there is any other god than the clergy." The civil laws concurred to aid this confusion of ideas; they inflicted the most serious penalties, punished in the most atrocious manner those unknown crimes which imagination had magnified into the most flagitious actions; heretics, infidels, were brought to the stake, and publicly burnt with the utmost refinement of cruelty; the brain was tortured to find means of augmenting the sufferings of the unhappy victims to sacerdotal fury; whilst calumniators of innocence, adulterers, depredators of every description, knaves of all kinds, were at a trifling cost absolved from their past iniquity, and opened a new account of future delinquency.

Under such instructors what could become of youth? The period of juvenility was shamefully sacrificed to superstition. Man, from his earliest infancy, was poisoned with unintelligible notions; fed with mysteries; crammed with fables; drenched with doctrines, in which he was compelled to acquiesce without being able to comprehend. His brain was disturbed with phantoms, alarmed with chimeras, rendered frantic by visions. His genius was cramped with puerile pursuits, mechanical devotions, sacred trifles. Superstition at length so fascinated the human mind, made such mere automata of mankind, that the people consented to address their gods in a dialect they did not themselves understand: women occupied their whole lives in singing Latin, without comprehending a word of the language; the people assisted very punctually, without being competent to explain any part of the worship, under an idea that it was taken kindly they should thus weary themselves; that it was sufficient to shew their persons in the sacred temples, which were beautifully decorated to fascinate their senses. Thus man wasted his most precious moments in absurd customs; spent his life in idle ceremonies; his bead was crowded with sophisms, his mind was loaded with errors; intoxicated with fanaticism, he was the declared enemy to reason; for ever prepossessed against truth, the energy of his soul was resisted by shackles too ponderous for its elasticity; the spring gave way, and he sunk into sloth and wretchedness: from this humiliating state he could never again soar; he could no longer become useful either to himself or to his associates: the importance he attached to his imaginary science, or rather the systematic ignorance which served for its basis, rendered it impossible for the most fertile soil to produce any thing but thorns; for the best proportioned tree to yield any thing but crabs.

Does a superstitious, sacerdotal education, form intrepid citizens, intelligent fathers of families, kind husbands, just masters, faithful servants, loyal subjects, pacific associates? No! it either makes peevish enthusiasts or morose devotees, who are incommodious to themselves, vexatious to others: men without principle, who quickly pour the waters of Lethe over the terrors with which they have been disturbed; who know no moral obligation, who respect no virtue. Thus superstition, elevated above every thing else, held forth the fanatical dogma, "Better to obey the gods than men;" in consequence, man believed he must revolt against his prince, detach himself from his wife, detest his children, estrange himself from his friends, cut the throats of his fellow-citizens, every time they questioned the veracity of his faith: in short, a superstitious education, when it had its effect, only served to corrupt the juvenile heart—to fascinate youthful winds with its pageantry—to degrade the human soul—to make man mistake the duties he owed to himself, his obligations to society, his relations with the beings by whom he was surrounded.

What advantages might not nations have reaped, if they would have employed on useful objects, those riches, which ignorance has so shamefully lavished on the expounders of superstition; which fatuity has bestowed on the most useless ceremonies? What might not have been the progress of genius, if it had enjoyed those ample remunerations, granted during so many ages to those priests who at all times opposed its elevation? What perfection might not science have attained, what height might not the arts have reached, if they had had the same succours that were held forth with a prodigal hand to enthusiasm and futility? Upon what rocks might not morality have been rested, what solid foundations might not politics have found, with what majestic grandeur might not truth have illumined the human horizon, if they had experienced the same fostering cares, the same animating countenance, the same public sanction, which accompanied imposture—which was showered upon fanaticism—which shielded falsehood from the rude attack of investigation—which gave impunity to its ministers?

It is then obvious, that superstitious, theological notions, have not produced any of those solid advantages that have been held forth; if may be doubted whether they were not always, and ever will remain, contrary to healthy politics, opposed to sound morality; they frequently change sovereigns into restless, jealous, mischievous, divinities; they transform their subjects into envious, wicked slaves, who by idle pageantry, by futile ceremonies, by an exterior acquiescence in unintelligible opinions, imagine themselves amply compensated for the evil they commit against each other. Those who have never had the confidence to examine these sublimated opinions; those who feel persuaded that their duties spring out of these abstruse doctrines; those who are actually commanded to live in peace, to cherish each other, to lend mutual assistance, to abstain from evil, and to do good, presently lose sight of these sterile speculations, as soon as present interests, ungovernable passions, inveterate habits, or irresistible whims, hurry them away. Where are we to look for that equity, that union of interest, that peace, that concord, which these unsettled notions, supported by superstition, backed with the full force of authority, promise to the societies placed under their surveillance? Under the influence of corrupt courts, of time-serving priests, who, either impostors or fanatics, are never in harmony with each other, are only to be discerned vicious men, degraded by ignorance—enslaved by criminal habits—swayed by transient interests—guided by shameful pleasures— sunk in a vortex of dissipation; who do not even think of the Divinity. In despite of his theological ideas, the subtle courtier continues to weave his dark plots, labours to gratify his ambition, seeks to satisfy his avidity, to indulge his hatred, to wreak his vengeance, to give full swing to all the passions inherent to the perversity of his being: maugre that frightful hell, of which the idea alone makes her tremble, the woman of intrigue persists in her amours; continues her harlotry, revels in her adulteries. Notwithstanding their dissipated conduct, their dissolute manners, their entire want of moral principle, the greater part of those who swarm in courts, who crowd in cities, would recoil with horror, if the smallest doubt was exhibited of the truth of that creed which they outrage every moment, of their lives. What advantage, then, has resulted to the human race from those opinions, so universal, at the same time so barren? They seem rarely to have had any other kind of influence than to serve as a pretext for the most dangerous passions—as a mantle of security for the most criminal indulgences. Does not the superstitious despot, who would scruple to omit the least part of the ceremonies of his persuasion, on quitting the altars at which he has been sacrificing, on leaving the temple where they have been delivering the oracles and terrifying crime in the name of heaven, return to his vices, reiterate his injustice, increase his political crimes, augment his transgressions against society? Issuing from the sacred fane, their ears still ringing with the doctrines they have heard, the minister returns to his vexations, the courtier to his intrigues, the courtezan to her prostitution, the publican to his extortions, the merchant to his frauds, the trader to his tricks.

Will it be pretended that those cowardly assassins, those dastardly robbers, those miserable criminals, whom evil institutions, the negligence of government, the laxity of morals, continually multiply; from whom the laws, in many instances too sanguinary, frequently wrest their existence; will it, I say, be pretended that the malefactors who regularly furnish the gibbets, who daily crowd the scaffolds, are either incredulous or atheists? No! Unquestionably, these unfortunate beings, these wretched outcasts, these children of turpitude, firmly believe in God; his name has been repeated to them from their infancy; they have been informed of the punishment destined for sinners: they have been habituated in early life to tremble at his judgments; nevertheless they have outraged society; their unruly passions, stronger than their fears, not having been coerced by visible motives, have not, for much more cogent reasons, been restrained by those which are invisible: distant, concealed punishments will never be competent to arrest those excesses which present and assured torments are incapable of preventing.

In short, does not every day's experience furnish us the lesson, that men, persuaded that an all-seeing Deity views them, hears them, encompasses them, do not on that account arrest their progress when the furor exists, either for gratifying their licentious passions, or committing the most dishonest actions? The same individual who would fear the inspection of the meanest of his fellows, whom the presence of another man would prevent from committing a bad action, from delivering himself up to some scandalous vice, freely sins, cheerfully lends himself to crime, when he believes no eyes beholds him but those of his God. What purpose, then, does the conviction of the omniscience, the ubiquity, the omnipotence of the Divinity answer, if it imposes much less on the conduct of the human being, than the idea of being overlooked by the least of his fellow men? He who would not have the temerity to commit a crime, even in the presence of a child, will make no scruple of boldly committing it, when he shall have only his God for a witness. These facts, which are indubitable, ill serve for a reply to those who insist that the fear of God is more suitable to restrain the actions of men, than wholesome laws, with strict discipline. When man believes he has only his God to dread, he commonly permits nothing to interrupt his course.

Those persons who do not in the least suspect the power of superstitious notions, who have the most perfect reliance on their efficacy, very rarely, however, employ them, when they are desirous to influence the conduct of those who are subordinate to them; when they are disposed to re-conduct them to the paths of reason. In the advice which a father gives to his vicious, criminal son, he rather represents to him the present temporal inconveniencies to which his conduct exposes him, than the danger he encounters in offending an avenging God; he points out to him the natural consequences of his irregularities, his health damaged by debaucheries; the loss of his reputation by criminal pursuits; the ruin of his fortune by gambling; the punishments of society, &c. Thus the DEICOLIST himself, on the most important occasions of life, reckons more stedfastly upon the force of natural motives, than upon those supernatural inducements furnished by superstition: the same man, who vilifies the motives that an atheist can have to do good and abstain from evil, makes use of them himself on this occasion, because he feels they are the most substantive he can employ.

Almost all men believe in an avenging and remunerating God; yet nearly in all countries the number of the wicked bears a larger proportion than that of the good. If the true cause of this general corruption be traced, it will be more frequently found in the superstitious notions inculcated by theology, than in those imaginary sources which the various superstitions have invented to account for human depravity. Man is always corrupt wherever he is badly governed; wherever superstition deifies the sovereign, his government becomes unworthy: this perverted and assured of impunity, necessarily render his people miserable; misery, when it exceeds the point of endurance, as necessarily renders them wicked. When the people are submitted to irrational masters, they are never guided by reason. If they are blinded by priests, who are either deceived or impostors, their reason become useless. Tyrants, when combined with priests, have generally been successful in their efforts to prevent nations from becoming enlightened—from seeking after truth— from ameliorating their condition—from perfectioning their morals; and never has the union smiled upon liberty: the people, unable to resist the mighty torrent produced by the confluence of two such rivers, have usually sunk into the most abject slavery. It is only by enlightening the mass of mankind, by demonstrating truth, that we can promise to render him better; that we can indulge the hope of making him happy. It is by causing both sovereigns and subjects to feel their true relations with each other, that their actual interests will be improved; that their politics will be perfectioned: it will then be felt and accredited, that the true art of governing mortals, the sure method of gaining their affections, is not the art of blinding them, of deceiving them, or of tyrannizing over them. Let us, then, good humouredly consult reason, avail ourselves of experience, interrogate nature; we shall, perhaps, find what is requisite to be done, in order to labour efficaciously to the happiness of the human race. We shall most assuredly perceive, that error is the true source of the evils which embitter our existence; that it is in cheering the hearts, in dissipating those vain phantoms which alarm the ignorant, in laying the axe to the root of superstition, that we can peaceably seek after truth; that it is only in the conflagration of this baneful tree, we can ever expect to light the torch which shall illumine the road to felicity. Then let man study nature; observe her immutable laws; let him dive into his own essence; let him cure himself of his prejudices: these means will conduct him by a gentle declivity to that virtue, without which he must feel he can never be permanently happy in the world he inhabits.

If man could once cease to fear, from that moment he would he truly happy. Superstition is a domestic enemy which he always carries within himself: those who will seriously occupy themselves with this formidable phantom, must be content to endure continual agonies, to live in perpetual inquietude: if they will neglect the objects most worthy of interesting them, to run after chimeras, they will commonly pass a melancholy existence, in groaning, in praying, in sacrificing, in expiating faults, either real or imaginary, which they believe calculated to offend their priests; frequently in their irrational fury they will torment themselves, they will make it a duty to inflict on their own persons the most barbarous punishments: but society will reap no benefit from these mournful opinions—from the tortures of these pious irrationals; because their mind, completely absorbed by their gloomy reveries, their time dissipated in the most absurd ceremonies, will leave them no opportunity of being really advantageous to the community of which they are members. The most superstitions men are commonly misanthropists, quite useless to the world, and very injurious to themselves: if ever they display energy, it is only to devise means by which they can increase their own affliction; to discover new methods to torture their mind; to find out the most efficacious means to deprive themselves of those objects which their nature renders desirable. It is common in the world to behold penitents, who are intimately persuaded that by dint of barbarous inflictions on their own persons, by means of a lingering suicide, they shall merit the favor of heaven. Madmen of this species are to be seen every where; superstition has in all ages, in all places, given birth to the most cruel extravagances, to the most injurious follies.

If, indeed, these irrational devotees only injure themselves, and deprive society of that assistance which they owe to it, they without doubt do less mischief than those turbulent, zealous fanatics, who, infuriated with their superstitious ideas, believe themselves bound to disturb the world, to commit actual crimes, to sustain the cause of what they denominate the true faith. It not unfrequently happens that in outraging morality, the zealous enthusiast supposes he renders himself agreeable to his God. He makes perfection consist either in tormenting himself, or in rending asunder, in favour of his fanatical ideas, the most sacred ties that connect mortals with each other.

Let us, then, acknowledge, that the notions of superstition, are not more suitable to procure the welfare, to establish the content, to confirm the peace of individuals, than they are of the society of which they are members. If some peaceable, honest, inconclusive enthusiasts, find either comfort or consolation in them, there are millions who, more conclusive to their principles, are unhappy during their whole life; who are perpetually assailed by the most melancholy ideas; to whom their disordered imagination shews these notions, as every instant involving them in the most cruel punishments. Under such formidable systems, a tranquil, sociable devotee, is a man who has not reasoned upon them.

In short, every thing serves to prove, that superstitious opinions have the strongest influence over men; that they torment them unceasingly, divide them from their dearest connections, inflame their minds, envenom their passions, render them miserable without ever restraining their actions, except when their own temperament proves too feeble to propel them forward: all this holds forth one great lesson, that *superstition is incompatible with liberty, and can never furnish good citizens.*

CHAP. IX.
Theological Notions cannot be the Basis of Morality.—Comparison between Theological Ethics and Natural Morality.—Theology prejudicial to the human Mind.

Felicity is the great end of human existence; a supposition therefore, to be actually useful to man, should render him happy. By what parity of reasoning can he flatter himself that an hypothesis, which does not facilitate his happiness in his present duration, may one day conduct him to permanent bliss? If mortals only sigh, tremble, and groan in this world, of which they have a knowledge, upon what foundation is it they expect a more felicitous existence hereafter, in a world of which they know nothing? If man is every where the child of calamity, the victim to necessary evil, the unhappy sufferer under an immutable system, ought he reasonably to indulge a greater confidence in future happiness?

On the other hand, a supposition which should throw light on every thing, which should supply an easy solution to all the questions to which it could be applied, when even it should not be competent to demonstrate the certitude, would probably be true: but that system which should only obscure the clearest notions, render more insoluble the problems desired to be resolved by its means, would most assuredly be looked upon as fallacious; as either useless or dangerous. To be convinced of this principle, let us examine, without prejudice, if the theological ideas of the Divinity have ever given the solution to any one difficulty. Has the human understanding progressed a single step by the assistance of this metaphysical science? Has it not, on the contrary, had a tendency to obscure the wore certain science of morals? Has it not, in many instances, rendered the most essential duties of our nature problematical? Has it not in a great measure confounded the notions of virtue and vice, of justice and injustice? Indeed, what is virtue, in the eyes of the generality of theologians? They will instantly reply, "that which is conformable to the will of the incomprehensible beings who govern nature." But way it not be asked, without offence to the individual opinions of any one, what are these beings, of whom they are unceasingly talking, without having the capacity to comprehend them? How can we acquire a knowledge of their will? They will forthwith reply, with a confidence that is meant to strike conviction on uninformed minds, by recounting what they are not, without even attempting to inform us what they are. If they do undertake to furnish an idea of them, they will heap upon their hypothetical beings a multitude, of contradictory, incompatible attributes, with which they will form a whole, at once impossible for the human mind to conceive or else they will refer to oracles, by which they insist their intentions have been promulgated to mankind. If, however, they are requested to prove the authenticity of these oracles, which are at such variance with each other, they will refer to miracles in support of what they assert: these miracles, independent of the difficulty there must exist to repose in them our faith, when, as we have seen, they are admitted even by the theologians themselves, to be contrary to the intelligence, the immutability, to the omnipotency of their immaterial substances, are, moreover, warmly disputed by each particular sect, as being impositions, practised by the others for their own individual advantage. As a last resource, then, it will be necessary to accredit the integrity, to rely on the veracity, to rest on the good faith of the priests, who announce these oracles. On this again, there arises two almost insuperable difficulties, in the *first* place, who shall assure us of their actual mission? are we quite certain none of them may be mistaken? how shall we be justified in giving credence to their powers? are they not these priests themselves, who announce to us that they are the infallible interpreters of a being whom they acknowledge they do not at all know? In the *second* place, which set of these oracular developements are we to adopt? For to give currency to the whole, would, in point of fact, annihilate them entirely; seeing, that no two of them run in unison with each other. This granted, the priests, that is to say, men extremely suspicious, but little in harmony with each other, will be the arbiters of morality; they will decide (according to their own uncertain knowledge, after their various passions, in conformity to the different perspectives under which they view these things,) on the whole system of ethics; upon which absolutely rests the repose of the world—the sterling happiness of each individual. Would this be a desirable state? would it be that from which humanity has the best founded prospect of that felicity, which is the desired object of his research? Again; do we not see that either enthusiasm or interest is the only standard of their decisions? that their morals are as variable as their caprice? those who listen to them, very rarely discover to what line they will adhere. In their various writings, we have evidence of the most bitter animosities; we find continual contradictions; endless disputes upon what they themselves acknowledge to be the most essential points; upon those premises, in the substantive proof of which their whole system depends; the very beings they depict as their source of their various creeds, are pourtrayed as variable as themselves; as frequently changing their plans as these are their arguments. What results from all this to a rational man? It will be natural for him to conclude, that neither inconstant gods, nor vacillating priests, whose opinions are more fluctuating than the seasons, can be the proper models of a moral system, which should be as regular, as determinate, as invariable as the laws of nature herself; as that eternal march, from which we never see her derogate.

No! Arbitrary, inconclusive, contradictory notions, abstract, unintelligible speculations, can never be the sterling bases of the ethical science! They must be evident, demonstrable principles, deduced from the nature of man, founded upon his wants, inspired by rational education, rendered familiar by habit, made sacred by wholesome laws, that will flash conviction on our mind, render systems useful to mankind, make virtue dear to us—that will people nations with honest men—fill up the ranks with faithful subjects—crowd them with intrepid citizens. Incomprehensible beings can present nothing to our imagination, save vague ideas, which will never embrace any common point of union amongst those who shall contemplate them. If these beings are painted as terrible, the mind is led astray; if changeable, it always precludes us from ascertaining the road we ought to pursue. The menaces held forth by those, who, in despite of their own assertions, say they are acquainted with the views, with the determination of these beings, will seldom do more than render virtue unpleasant; fear alone will then make us practise with reluctance, that which reason, which our own immediate interest, ought to make us execute with pleasure. The inculcation of terrible ideas will only serve to disturb honest persons, without in the least arresting the progress of the profligate, or diverting the course of the flagitious: the greater number of men, when they shall be disposed to sin, to deliver themselves up to vicious propensities, will cease to contemplate these terrific ideas, will only behold a merciful God, who is filled with goodness, who will pardon the transgressions of their weakness. Man never views things but on that side which is most conformable to his desires.

The goodness of God cheers the wicked; his rigour disturbs the honest man. Thus, the qualities with which theology clothes its immaterial substances, themselves turn out disadvantageous to sound morality. It is upon this infinite goodness that the most corrupt men will have the audacity to reckon, when they are either hurried along by crime, or given up to habitual vice. If, then, they are reminded of their criminal courses, they reply, "God is good, his mercy is infinite, his clemency boundless:" thus it may be said that religion itself is pressed into the service of vice, by the children of turpitude. Superstition, above all, rather abets crime than represses it, by holding forth to mortals that by the assistance of certain ceremonies, the performance of certain rites, the repetition of certain prayers, aided by the payment of certain sums of money, they can appease the anger of their gods, assuage the wrath of heaven, wash out the stains of their sins, and be received with open arms into the happy number of the elect—be placed in the blissful abodes of eternity. In short, do not the priests of superstition universally affirm, that they possess infallible secrets, for reconciling the most perverse to the pale of their respective systems?

It must be concluded from this, that however these systems are viewed, in whatever manner they are considered, they cannot serve for the basis of morality, which in its very nature is formed to be invariably the same. Irascible systems are only useful to those who find an interest in terrifying the ignorance of mankind, that they may advantage themselves of his fears—profit by his expiations. The nobles of the earth, who are frequently men not gifted with the most exemplary morals—who do not on all occasions exhibit the most perfect specimens of self-denial—who would not, perhaps, be at all times held up as mirrors of virtue, will not see these formidable systems, when they shall be inclined to listen to their passions; to lend themselves to the indulgence of their unruly desires: they will, however, feel no repugnance to make use of them to frighten others, to the end that they may preserve unimpaired their superiority; that they may keep entire their prerogatives; that they may more effectually bind them to servitude. Like the rest of mankind, they will see their God under the traits of his benevolence; they will always believe him indulgent to those outrages they may commit against their fellows, provided they shew due respect for him themselves: superstition will furnish them with easy means to turn aside his Wrath; its ministers seldom omit a profitable opportunity, to expiate the crimes of human nature.

Morality is not made to follow the caprices of the imagination, the fury of the passions, the fluctuating interests of men: it ought to possess stability; to be at all times the same, for all the individuals of the human race; it ought neither to vary in one country, nor in one race from another: neither superstition nor religion, has a privilege to make its immutability subservient to the changeable laws of their systems. There is but one method to give ethics this solidity; it has been more than once pointed out in the course of this work: it is only to be founded upon the nature of man, bottomed upon his duties, rested upon the relations subsisting between intelligent beings, who are in love, with their happiness, who are occupied with their own preservation, who live together in society that they may With greater facility ascertain these ends. In short we must take for the basis of morality the necessity of things.

In weighing these principles, which are self evident, confirmed by constant experience, approved by reason, drawn from nature herself, we shall have an undeviating tone of conduct; a sure system of morality, that will never be in contradiction with itself. Man will have no occasion to recur to theological speculations to regulate his conduct in the visible world. We shall then be capacitated to reply to those who pretend that without them there can he no morality. If we reflect upon the long tissue of errors, upon the immense chain of wanderings, that flow from the obscure notions these various systems hold forth—of the sinister ideas which superstition in all countries inculcates; it would be much more conformable to truth to say, that all sound ethics, all morality, either useful to individuals or beneficial to society, is totally incompatible with systems which never represent their gods but under the form of absolute monarchs, whose good qualities are continually eclipsed by dangerous caprices. Consequently, we shall be obliged to acknowledge, that to establish morality upon a steady foundation, we must necessarily commence by at least quitting those chimerical systems upon which the ruinous edifice of supernatural morality has hitherto been constructed, which during such a number of ages, has been so uselessly preached up to a great portion of the inhabitants of the earth.

Whatever may have been the cause that placed man in his present abode, that gave him the faculties he possesses; whether the human species be considered as the work of nature, or whether it be supposed that he owes his existence to an intelligent being, distinguished from nature; the existence of man, such as he is, is a fact; we behold in him a being who thinks, who feels, who has intelligence, who loves himself, who tends to his own conservation, who in every moment of his duration strives to render his existence agreeable; who, the more easily to satisfy his wants and to procure himself pleasure, congregates in society with beings similar to himself; of whom his conduct can either conciliate the favour, or draw upon him the disaffection. It is, then, upon these general sentiments, inherent in his nature, which will subsist as long as his race shall endure, that we ought to found morality; which is only a science embracing, the duties of men living together in society.

These duties have their spring in our nature, they are founded upon our necessities, because we cannot reach the goal of happiness, if we do not employ the requisite means: these means constitute the moral science. To be permanently felicitous, we must so comport ourselves as to merit the affection, so act as to secure the assistance of those, beings with whom we are associated; these will only accord us their love, lend us their esteem, aid us in our projects, labour to our peculiar happiness, but in proportion as our own exertions shall be employed for their advantage. It is this necessity, flowing naturally out of the relations of mankind, that is called MORAL OBLIGATION. It is founded upon reflection, rested upon those motives competent to determine sensible, intelligent beings, to pursue that line of conduct, which in best calculated to achieve that happiness towards which they are continually verging. These motives in the human species, never can be other than the desire, always regenerating, of procuring good and avoiding evil. Pleasure and pain, the hope of happiness, or the fear of misery, are the only motives suitable to have an efficacious influence on the volition of sensible beings. To impel them towards this end, it is sufficient these motives exist and be understood to have a knowledge of them, it is only requisite to consider our own constitution: according to this, we shall find we can only love those actions, approve that conduct, from whence result actual and reciprocal utility; this constitutes VIRTUE. In consequence, to conserve ourselves, to make our own happiness, to enjoy security, we are compelled to follow the routine which conducts to this end; to interest others in our own preservation, we are obliged to display an interest in theirs; we must do nothing that can have a tendency to interrupt that mutual co-operation which alone can lead to the felicity desired. Such is the true establishment of moral obligation.

Whenever it is attempted to give any other basis to morality than the nature of man, we shall always deceive ourselves; none other can have the least stability; none can be more solid. Some authors, even of great integrity, have thought, that to give ethics more respectability in the eyes of man, to render more inviolable those duties which his nature imposes on him, it was needful to clothe them with the authority of a being whom they have made superior to nature—whom they have rendered more powerful than necessity. Theology, seizing on these ideas, with its own general want of just inference, has in consequence invaded morality; has endeavoured to connect it with its various systems. By some it has been imagined, this union would render virtue more sacred; that the fear attached to invisible powers, who govern nature, would lend more weight, would give more efficacy to its laws; in short, it has been believed that man, persuaded, of the necessity of the moral system, seeing it united with superstition, would contemplate superstition itself as necessary to his happiness. Indeed it is the supposition that these systems are essential to morality, that sustains the theological ideas— that gives permanency to the greater part of all the creeds on earth; it is erroneously imagined that without them man would neither understand nor practise the duties he owes to others. This prejudice once established, gives currency to the opinion that the vague ideas growing out of these systems are in such a manner connected with morality, are so linked with the actual welfare of society, that they cannot be attacked without overturning the social duties that bind man to his fellow. It is thought that the reciprocity of wants, the desire of happiness, the evident interests of the community, would be mere skeleton motives, devoid of all active energy, if they did not borrow their substance from these various systems; if they were not invested with the force derived from these numerous creeds; if they were not clothed with the sanction of those ideas which have been made the arbiters of all things.

Nothing, however, is more borne out by the evidence of experience, nothing has more thoroughly impressed itself on the minds of reflecting men, than the danger always arising from connecting truth with fiction; the known with the unknown; the delirium of enthusiasm, with the tranquillity of reason. Indeed what has resulted from the confused alliance, from the marvellous speculations, which theology has made with the most substantive realities? of mixing up its evanescent conjectures with the confirmed aphorisms of time? The imagination bewildered, has mistaken truth: superstition, by aid of its gratuitous suppositions, has commanded nature—made reason bow, under its bulky yoke,—submitted man to its own peculiar caprices; very frequently in the name of its gods obliged him to stifle his nature, to piously violate the most sacred duties of morality. When these superstitions have been desirous of restraining mortals whom they had previously hood-winked, whom they had rendered irrational, it gave them only ideal curbs, imaginary motives; it substituted unsubstantial causes, for those which were substantive; marvellous supernatural powers, for those which were natural, and well understood; it supplied actual realities, by ideal romances and visionary fables. By this inversion of principle, morality had no longer any fixed basis: nature, reason, virtue, demonstration, were laid prostrate before the most undefinable systems; were made to depend upon oracular promulgations, which never spake distinctly; indeed, they generally silenced reason, were often delivered by fanatics, which time proved to be impostors; by those who, always adopting the appellation of inspired beings, gave forth nothing but the wanderings of their own delirium, or else were desirous of profiting by the errors which they themselves instilled into mankind. Thus these men became deeply interested in preaching abject submission, non-resistance, passive- obedience, factitious virtues, frivolous ceremonies; in short, an arbitrary morality, conformable to their own reigning passions; frequently prejudicial to the rest of the human race.

It was thus, in making ethics flow from these various systems, they in point of fact submitted it to the dominant passions of men, who had a direct interest in moulding it to their own advantage. In being disposed to found it upon undemonstrated theories, they founded it upon nothing; in deriving it from imaginary sources, of which each individual forms to himself his own notion, generally adverse to that of his neighbour; in resting it upon obscure oracles, always delivered ambiguously, frequently interpreted by men in the height of delirium, sometimes by knaves, who had immediate interests to promote, they rendered it unsteady—devoid of fixed principle,—too frequently left it to the mercy of the most crafty of mankind. In proposing to man the changeable creeds of the theologians for a model, they weakened the moral system of human actions; frequently annihilated that which was furnished by nature; often substituted in its place nothing but the most perplexing incertitude; the most ruinous inconsistency. These systems, by the qualities which are ascribed, to them, become inexplicable enigmas, which each expounds as best suits himself; which each explains after his own peculiar mode of thinking; in which the theologian ever finds that which most harmonizes with his designs; which he can bend to his own sinister purposes; which he offers as irrefragible evidence of the rectitude of those actions, which at bottom have nothing but his own advantage in view. If they exhort the gentle, indulgent, equitable man, to be good, compassionate, benevolent; they equally excite the furious, who is destitute of these qualities, to be intolerant, inhuman, pitiless. The morality of these systems varies in each individual; differs in one country from another; in fact, those actions which some men look upon as sacred, which they have learned to consider meritorious, make others shudder with horror—fill them with the most painful recollections. Some see the Divinity filled with gentleness and mercy; others behold him as full of wrath and fury, whose anger is to be assuaged by the commission of the most shocking cruelties.

The morality of nature is clear, it is evident even to those who outrage it. It is not thus with superstitious morality; this is as obscure as the systems which prescribe it; or rather as fluctuating as the passions, as changeable as the temperaments, of those who expound them; if it was left to the theologians, ethics ought to be considered as the science of all others the most problematical, the most unsteady, the most difficult to bring to a point; it would require the most profound, penetrating genius, the most active, vigorous mind, to discover the principles of those duties man owes to himself, that he ought to exercise towards others; this would render the sources of the moral system attainable by a very small number of individuals; would effectually lock them up in the cabinets of the metaphysicians; place them under the treacherous guardianship of priests: to derive it from those systems, which are in themselves undefinable, with the foundations of which no one is actually acquainted, which each contemplates after his own mode, modifies after his own peculiar ideas, is at once to submit it to the caprice of every individual; it is completely to acknowledge, we know not from whence it is derived, nor whence it has its principles. Whatever may be the agent upon whom they make nature, or the beings she contains, to depend; with whatever power they way suppose him invested, it is very certain that man either does, or does not exist; but as soon as his existence is acknowledged, as soon as it is admitted to be what it actually is, when he shall be allowed to be a sensible being living in society, in love with his own felicity, they cannot without either annihilating him, or new modelling him, cause him to exist otherwise than he does. Therefore, according to his actual essence, agreeable to his absolute qualities, conformable to those modifications which constitute him a being, of the human species, morality becomes necessary to him, and the desire of conserving himself will make him prefer virtue to vice, by the same necessity that he prefers pleasure to pain. If, following up the doctrine of the theologians, "that man hath occasion for supernatural grace to enable him to do good," it must be very injurious to sound principles of morality; because he will always wait for "the call from above," to exercise that virtue, which is indispensable to his welfare. Tertullian, nevertheless says expressly, "wherefore will ye trouble yourselves, seeking after the law of God, whilst ye have that which is common to all the world, and which is written on the tablets of nature?"

To say, that man cannot possess any moral sentiments without embracing the discordant systems offered to his acceptance, is, in point of fact, saying, that he cannot distinguish virtue from vice; it is to pretend that without these systems, man would not feel the necessity of eating to live, would not make the least distinction, would be absolutely without choice in his food: it is to pretend, that unless he is fully acquainted with the name, character, and qualities of the individual who prepares a mess for him, he is not competent to discriminate whether this mess be agreeable or disagreeable, good or bad. He who does not feel himself satisfied what opinions to adopt, upon the foundation and moral attributes of these systems, or who even formally denies them, cannot at least doubt his own existence-his own functions—his own qualities—his own mode of feeling—his own method of judging; neither can he doubt the existence of other organized beings similar to himself; in whom every thing discovers to him qualities analogous with his own; of whom he can, by certain actions, either gain the love or incur the hatred—secure the assistance or attract the ill-will—merit the esteem or elicit the contempt; this knowledge is sufficient to enable him to distinguish moral good and evil. In short, every man enjoying a well- ordered organization, possessing the faculty of making true experience, will only need to contemplate himself in order to discover what he owes to others: his own nature will enlighten him much more effectually upon his duties, than those systems in which he will consult either his own unruly passions, those of some enthusiast, or those of an impostor. He will allow, that to conserve himself, to secure his own permanent welfare, he is frequently obliged to resist the blind impulse of his own desires; that to conciliate the benevolence of others, he must act in a mode conformable to their advantage; in reasoning thus, he will find out what virtue actually is; if he puts his theory into practice, he will be virtuous; he will be rewarded for his conduct by the harmony of his own machine; by the legitimate esteem of himself, confirmed by the good opinion of others, whose kindness he will have secured: if he acts in a contrary mode, the trouble that will ensue, the disorder of his frame, will quickly warn him that nature, thwarted by his actions, disapproves his conduct, which is injurious to himself; to which he will be obliged to add the condemnation of others, who will hate him. If the wanderings of his mind prevent him from seeing the more immediate consequences of his irregularities, neither will he perceive the distant rewards, the remote punishments, which these systems hold forth; because they will never speak to him so distinctly as his conscience, which will either reward or punish him on the spot. Theology has never yet known how to give a true definition of virtue: according to it, it is an effort of grace, that disposes man to do that which is agreeable to the Divinity. But what is this grace? How doth it act upon man? How shall we know what is agreeable to a Divinity who is incomprehensible to all men?

Every thing that has been advanced evidently proves, that superstitious morality is an infinite loser when compared with the morality of nature, with which, indeed, it is found in perpetual contradiction. Nature invites man to love himself, to preserve his existence, to incessantly augment the sum of his happiness: superstition teaches him to be in love only with formidable doctrines, calculated to generate his dislike; to detest himself; to sacrifice to his idols his most pleasing sensations— the most legitimate pleasures of his heart. Nature counsels man to consult reason, to adopt it for his guide; superstition pourtrays this reason as corrupted, as a treacherous director, that will infallibly lead him astray. Nature warns him to enlighten his understanding, to search after truth, to inform himself of his duties; superstition enjoins him not to examine any thing, to remain in ignorance, to fear truth; it persuades him there are no relations so important to his interest, as those which subsist between himself and systems which he can never understand. Nature tells the being who is in love with his welfare, to moderate his passions, to resist them when they are found destructive to himself, to counteract them by substantive motives collected from experience; superstition desires a sensible being to have no passions, to be an insensible mass, or else to combat his propensities by motives borrowed from the imagination, which are as variable as itself. Nature exhorts man to be sociable, to love his fellow creatures, to be just, peaceable, indulgent, benevolent, to permit his associates to freely enjoy their opinions; superstition admonishes him to fly society, to detach himself from his fellow mortals, to hate them when their imagination does not procure them dreams conformable to his own; to break through the most sacred bonds, to maintain his own opinions, or to frustrate those of his neighbour; to torment, to persecute, to massacre, those who will not be mad after his own peculiar manner. Nature exacts that man in society should cherish glory, labour to render himself estimable, endeavour to establish an imperishable name, to be active, courageous, industrious; superstition tells him to be abject, pusillanimous, to live in obscurity, to occupy himself with ceremonies; it says to him, be useless to thyself, and do nothing for others. Nature proposes to the citizen, for his model, men endued with honest, noble, energetic souls, who have usefully served their fellow citizens; superstition recommends to his imitation mean, cringing sycophants; extols pious enthusiasts, frantic penitents, zealous fanatics, who for the most ridiculous opinions have disturbed the tranquility of empires. Nature urges the husband to be tender, to attach himself to the company of his mate, to cherish her in his bosom; superstition makes a crime of his susceptibility, frequently obliges him to look upon the conjugal bonds as a state of pollution, as the offspring of imperfection. Nature calls to the father to nurture his children, to cherish their affection, to make them useful members of society; superstition advises him to rear them in fear of its systems, to hoodwink them, to make them superstitious, which renders them incapable of actually serving society, but extremely well calculated to disturb its repose. Nature cries out to children to honor their parents, to listen to their admonitions, to be the support of their old age; superstition says, prefer the oracles; in support of the systems of which you are an admitted member, trample father and mother under your feet. Nature holds out to the philosopher that he should occupy himself with useful objects, consecrate his cares to his country, make advantageous discoveries, suitable to perfect the condition of mankind; superstition saith, occupy thyself with useless reveries; employ thy time in endless dispute; scatter about with a lavish hand the seeds of discord, calculated to induce the carnage of thy fellows; obstinately maintain opinions which thou thyself canst never understand. Nature points out to the perverse man, that he should blush for his vices, that he should feel sorrow for his disgraceful propensities, that he should be ashamed of crime; it shews him, that his most secret irregularities will necessarily have an influence over his own felicity; superstition crieth to the most corrupt men, to the most flagitious mortals, "do not irritate the gods, whom thou knowest not; but if, peradventure, against their express command, thou dost deliver thyself up to crime, remember that their mercy is infinite, that their compassion endureth for ever, that therefore they may be easily appeased; thou hast nothing more to do than to go into their temples, prostrate thyself before their altars, humiliate thyself at the feet of their ministers; expiate thy transgressions by largesses, by sacrifices, by offerings, by ceremonies, and by prayer; these things done with a willing spirit, and a contrite heart, will pacify thine own conscience, and cleanse thee in the eyes of heaven."

The rights of the citizen, or the man in society, are not less injured by superstition, which is always in contradiction with sound politics. Nature says distinctly to man, "thou art free; no power on earth can justly deprive thee of thy rights, without thine own consent; and even then, thou canst not legitimately make thyself a slave to thy like." Superstition tells him he is a slave, condemned to groan all his life under the iron rod of the representatives of its system. Nature commands man to love the country which gave him birth, to serve it faithfully, to blend his interests with it, to unite against all those who shall attempt to injure it; superstition generally orders him to obey without murmur the tyrants who oppress it, to serve them against its best interests, to merit their favors by contributing to enslave their fellow citizens to their ungovernable caprices: notwithstanding these general orders, if the sovereign be not sufficiently devoted to the priest, superstition quickly changes its language, it then calls upon subjects to become rebels; it makes it a duty in them to resist their masters; it cries out to them, "it is better to obey the gods than men." Nature acquaints princes that they are men: that it is not by their capricious whims that they can decide what is just; that it is not their wayward humours that can mark what is unjust; that the public will maketh the law. Superstition often insinuates to them that they are gods, to whom nothing in this world ought to offer resistance; sometimes, indeed, it transforms them into tyrants, whom enraged heaven is desirous should be immolated to its wrath.

Superstition corrupts princes; these corrupt the law, which, like themselves, becomes unjust; from thence institutions are perverted; education only forms men who are worthless, blinded with prejudice, smitten with vain objects, enamoured of wealth, devoted to pleasures, which they must obtain by iniquitous means: thus nature, mistaken, is disdained; virtue is only a shadow quickly sacrificed to the slightest interest, while superstition, far from remedying these evils to which it has given birth, does nothing more than render them still more inveterate; or else engenders sterile regrets which it presently effaces: thus, by its operation, man is obliged to yield to the force of habit, to the general example, to the stream of those propensities, to those causes of confusion, which conspire to hurry all his species, who are not willing to renounce their own welfare, on to the commission of crime.

Here is the mode by which superstition, united with politics, exert their efforts to pervert, abuse, and poison the heart of man; the generality of human institutions appear to have only for their object to abase the human character, to render it more flagitiously wicked. Do not then let us be at all astonished if morality is almost every where a barren speculation, from which every one is obliged to deviate in practice, if he will not risk the rendering himself unhappy. Men can only have sound morals, when, renouncing his prejudices, he consults his nature; but the continued impulse which his soul is every moment receiving, on the part of more powerful motives, quickly compels him to forget those ethical rules which nature points out to him. He is continually floating between vice and virtue; we behold him unceasingly in contradiction with himself; if, sometimes, he justly appreciates the value of an honest, upright conduct, experience very soon shews him, that this cannot lead him to any thing, which he has been taught to desire, on the contrary, that it may be an invincible obstacle to the happiness which his heart never ceases for an instant to search after. In corrupt societies it is necessary to become corrupt, in order to become happy.

Citizens, led astray at the same time both by their spiritual and temporal guides, neither knew reason nor virtue. The slaves both of their superstitious systems, and of men like themselves, they had all the vices attached to slavery; kept in a perpetual state of infancy, they had neither knowledge nor principles; those who preached virtue to them, knew nothing of it themselves, and could not undeceive them with respect to those baubles in which they had learned to make their happiness consist. In vain they cried out to them to stifle those passions which every thing conspired to unloose: in vain they made the thunder of the gods roll to intimidate men whose tumultuous passions rendered them deaf. It was soon discovered that the gods of the heavens were much less feared than those of the earth; that the favour of the latter procured a much more substantive welfare than the promises of the former; that the riches of this world were more tangible than the treasures reserved for favorites in the next; that it was much more advantageous for men to conform themselves to the views of visible powers than to those of powers who were not within the compass of their visual faculties.

Thus society, corrupted by its priests, guided by their caprice, could only bring forth a corrupt offspring. It gave birth to avaricious, ambitious, jealous, dissolute citizens, who never saw any thing happy but crime; who beheld meanness rewarded; incapacity honoured; wealth adored; debauchery held in esteem; who almost every where found talents discouraged; virtue neglected; truth proscribed; elevation of soul crushed; justice trodden under foot; moderation languishing in misery; liberality of mind obligated to groan under the ponderous bulk of haughty injustice.

In the midst of this disorder, in this confusion of ideas, the precepts of morality could only be vague declamations, incapable of convincing any one. What barrier could superstition, with its imaginary motives, oppose to the general corruption? When it spake reason, it could not be heard; its gods themselves were not sufficiently powerful to resist the torrent; its menaces failed of effect, on those hearts which every thing hurried along to crime; its distant promises could not counterbalance present advantages; its expiations, always ready to cleanse mortals from their sins, emboldened them to persevere in their criminal pursuits; its frivolous ceremonies calmed their consciences; its zeal, its disputes, its caprices, only multiplied the evils, with which society found itself afflicted; only gave them an inveteracy that rendered them more widely mischievous; in short, in the most vitiated nations there was a multitude of devotees, and but very few honest men. Great and small listened to the doctrines of superstition, when they appeared favorable to their dominant passions; when they were desirous to counteract them, they listened no longer. Whenever superstition was conformable to morality, it appeared incommodious, it was only followed when it either combatted ethics or destroyed them. The despot himself found it marvellous, when it assured him he was a god upon earth; that his subjects were born to adore him alone, to administer to his phantasms. He neglected it when it told him to be just; from thence he saw it was in contradiction with itself, that it was useless to preach equity to a deified mortal; besides, he was assured the gods would pardon every thing, as soon as he should consent to recur to his priests, always ready to reconcile them; the most wicked of their subjects reckoned in the same manner upon their divine assistance: thus superstition, far from restraining vice, assured its impunity; its menaces could not destroy the effects which its unworthy flattery had produced in princes; these same menaces could not annihilate the hope which its expiations had furnished to all. Sovereigns, either inflated with pride, or always confident of washing out their crimes by timely sacrifices, no longer actually feared their gods; become gods themselves, they believed they were permitted any thing against poor pitiful mortals, whom they no longer considered under any other light than as playthings destined for their earthly amusement.

If the nature of man was consulted in his politics which supernatural ideas have so woefully depraved, it would completely rectify those false notions that are entertained equally by sovereigns and by subjects; it would contribute more amply than all the superstitions existing, to render society happy, powerful, and flourishing under rational authority. Nature would teach man, it is for the purpose of enjoying a greater portion of happiness, that mortals live together in society; that it is its own preservation, its own immediate felicity, that society should have for its determinate, unchangeable object: that without equity, a nation only resembles a congregation of enemies; that his most cruel foe, is the man who deceives him in order that he may enslave him; that the scourges most to be feared, are those priests who corrupt his chiefs, who, in the name of the gods assure them of impunity for their crimes: she would prove to him that association is a misfortune under unjust, negligent, destructive governments.

This nature, interrogated by princes, would teach them they are men and not gods; that their power is only derived from the consent of other men; that they themselves are citizens, charged by other citizens, with the care of watching over the safety of the whole; that the law ought to be only the expression of the public will; that it is never permitted them to counteract nature, or to thwart the invariable end of society. This nature would make monarchs feel, that to be truly great, to be decidedly powerful, they ought to command elevated, virtuous souls; not minds degraded by despotism, vitiated by superstition. This nature would teach sovereigns, that in order to be cherished by their subjects, they ought to afford them succour; to cause them to enjoy those benefits which their wants render imperative, that they should at all times maintain them, inviolably, in the possession of their rights, of which they are the appointed defenders—of which they are the constituted guardians. This nature would prove to all those princes who should deign to consult her, that it is only by good actions, by kindness, they can either merit the love, or secure the attachment of the people; that oppression does nothing more than raise up enemies against them; that violence only makes their power unsteady; that force, however brutally used, cannot confer on them any legitimate right; that beings essentially in love with happiness, must sooner or later finish by revolting against an authority that establishes itself by injustice; that only makes itself felt by the outrage it commits: this is the manner in which nature, the sovereign of all beings, in whose system all are equal, would speak to one of these superb monarchs, whom flattery has deified:—"Untoward, headstrong child! Pigmy, so proud of commanding pigmies! Have they then assured thee that thou art a god? Have they flattered thee that thou art something supernatural? Know there is nothing superior to myself. Contemplate thine own insignificance, acknowledge thine impotence against the slightest of my blows. I can break thy sceptre; I can take away thine existence; I can level thy throne with the dust; I can scatter thy people; I can destroy even the earth which thou inhabitest; and yet thou hast the folly to believe thou art a god. Be then, again, thyself; honestly avow that thou art a man, formed to submit to my laws equally with the meanest of thy subjects. Learn then, and never let it escape thy memory, that thou art the man of thy people; the minister of thy nation; the interpreter of its laws; the executer of its will; the fellow-citizen of those whom thou hast the right of commanding, only because they consent to obey thee, in view of that well being which thou promisest to procure for them. Reign, then, on these conditions; fulfil thy sacred engagements. Be benevolent: above all, equitable. If thou art willing to have thy power assured to thee, never abuse it; let it be circumscribed by the immovable limits of eternal justice. Be the father of thy people, and they will cherish thee as thy children. But, if unmindful of thy duties, thou neglectest them; if negligent of thine own interest, thou separatest them from those of thy great family, if thou refusest to thy subjects that happiness which thou owest them; if, heedless of thy own security, thou armest thyself against them; thou shall be like all tyrants, the slave to gloomy care, the bondman of alarm, the vassal of cruel suspicion: thou wilt become the victim to thine own folly. Thy people, reduced to despair, shorn of their felicity, will no longer acknowledge thy divine rights. In vain, then, thou wouldst sue for aid to that superstition which hath deified thee; it can avail nothing with thy people, whom sharp misery had rendered deaf; heaven will abandon thee to the fury of those enemies to which thy frenzy shall have given birth. Superstitious systems can effect nothing against my irrevocable decrees, which will that man shall ever irritate himself against the cause of his sorrows."

In short, every thing would make known to rational princes, that they have no occasion for superstition to be faithfully obeyed on earth; that all the powers contained in these systems will not sustain them when they shall act the tyrant; that their true friends are those who undeceive the people in their delusions; that their real enemies are those who intoxicate them with flattery—who harden them in crime—who make the road to heaven too easy for them—

who feed them with fanciful, chimerical doctrines, calculated to make them swerve from those cares, to divert them from those sentiments, which they justly owe to their nations.

It is then, I repeat it, only by re-conducting man to nature, that we can procure him distinct notions, evident opinions, certain knowledge; it is only by shewing him his true relations with his fellows, that we can place him on the road to happiness. The human mind, blinded by theology, has scarcely advanced a single step. Man's superstitious systems have rendered him sceptical on the most demonstrable truths. Superstition, while it pervaded every thing, while it had an universal influence, served to corrupt the whole: philosophy, dragged in its train, although it swelled its triumphant procession, was no longer any thing but an imaginary science: it quitted the real world to plunge into the sinuosities of the ideal, inconceivable labyrinths of metaphysics; it neglected nature, who spontaneously opened her book to its examination, to occupy itself with systems filled with spirits, with invisible powers, which only served to render all questions more obscure; which, the more they were probed, the more inexplicable they became; which took delight in promulgating that which no one was competent to understand. In all difficulties it introduced the Divinity; from thence things only became more and more perplexed, until nothing could be explained. Theological notions appear only to have been invented to put man's reason to flight; to confound his judgment; to deceive his mind; to overturn his clearest ideas in every science. In the hands of the theologian, logic, or the art of reasoning, was nothing more than an unintelligible jargon, calculated to support sophism, to countenance falsehood, to attempt to prove the most palpable contradictions. Morality, as we have seen, became wavering and uncertain, because it was founded on ideal systems, never in harmony with themselves, which, on the contrary, were continually contradicting their own most positive assertions. Politics, as we have elsewhere said, were cruelly perverted by the fallacious ideas given to sovereigns of their actual rights. Jurisprudence was determinately submitted to the caprices of superstition, which shackled labour, chained down human industry, controuled activity, and fettered the commerce of nations. Every thing, in short, was sacrificed to the immediate interests of these theologians: in the place of every rational science, they taught nothing but an obscure, quarrelsome metaphysics, which but too often caused the blood of those unhappy people to flow copiously who were incapable of understanding its hallucinations.

Born an enemy to experience, theology, that supernatural science, was an invincible obstacle to the progress of the natural sciences, as it almost always threw itself in their way. It was not permitted to experimental philosophy, to natural history, to anatomy, to see any thing but through the jaundiced eye of superstition. The most evident facts were rejected with disdain, proscribed with horror, when ever they could not be made to quadrate with the idle hypotheses of superstition. Virgil, the Bishop of Saltzburg, was condemned by the church, for having dared to maintain the existence of the antipodes; Gallileo suffered the most cruel persecutions, for asserting that the sun did not make its revolution round the earth. Descartes was obliged to die in a foreign land. Priests, indeed, have a right to be the enemies to the sciences; the progress of reason must, sooner or later, annihilate superstitious ideas. Nothing that is founded upon nature, that is bottomed upon truth, can ever be lost; while the systems of imaginations, the creeds of imposture, must be overturned. Theology unceasingly opposed itself to the happiness of nations—to the progress of the human mind—to useful researches—to the freedom of thought; it kept man in ignorance; all his steps being guided by it, he was no more than a tissue of errors. Indeed, is it resolving a question in natural philosophy, to say that an effect which excites our surprise, that an unusual phenomenon, that a volcano, a deluge, a hurricane, a comet, &c. are either signs of divine wrath, or works contrary to the laws of nature? In persuading nations, as it has done, that the calamities, whether physical or moral, which they experience, are the effects of the divine anger, or chastisements which his power inflicts on them, has it not, in fact, prevented them from seeking after remedies for these evils? Would it not have been more useful to have studied the nature of things, to have sought in nature herself, or in human industry, for succours against those sorrows with which mortals are afflicted, than to attribute the evil which man experiences to an unknown power, against whose will it cannot be supposed there exists any relief? The study of nature, the search after truth, elevates the soul, expands the genius, is calculated to render man active, to make him courageous. Theological notions appear to have been made to debase him, to contract his mind, to plunge him into despondence. In the place of attributing to the divine vengeance those wars, those famines, those sterilities, those contagions, that multitude of calamities, which desolate the earth; would it not have been more useful, more consistent with truth, to have shewn man that these evils were to be ascribed to his own folly, or rather to the unruly passions, to the want of energy, to the tyranny of some princes, who sacrifice nations to their frightful delirium? The irrational people, instead of amusing themselves with expiations for their pretended crimes, seeking to render themselves acceptable to imaginary powers; should they not rather have sought in a more healthy administration, the true means of avoiding those scourges, to which they were the victims? Natural evils demand natural remedies: ought not experience then long since to have convinced mortals of the inefficacy of supernatural remedies, of expiatory sacrifices, of fastings, of processions, &c. which almost all the people of the earth have vainly opposed to the disasters which they experienced?

Let us then conclude, that theology with its notions, far from being useful to the human species, is the true source of all those sorrows which afflict the earth of all those errors by which man is blinded; of those prejudices which benumb mankind; of that ignorance which renders him credulous; of those vices which torment him; of those governments which oppress him. Let us be fully persuaded that those theological, supernatural ideas, with which man is inspired from his infancy, are the actual causes of his habitual folly; are the springs of his superstitious quarrels; of his sacred dissensions; of his inhuman persecutions. Let us, at length, acknowledge, that they are these fatal ideas which have obscured morality; corrupted polities; retarded the progress of the sciences; annihilated happiness; banished peace from the bosom of mankind, Then let it be no longer dissimulated, that all those calamities, for which man turns his eyes towards heaven, bathed in tears, have their spring in the imaginary systems he has adopted: let him, therefore, cease to expect relief from them; let him seek in nature, let him search in his own energies, those resources, which superstition, deaf to his cries, will never procure for him. Let him consult the legitimate desires of his heart, and he will find that which he oweth to himself, also that which he oweth to others; let him examine his own essence, let him dive into the aim of society, from thence he will no longer be a slave; let him consult experience, he will find truth, and he will discover, that *error can never possible render him happy.*

CHAP. X.
Man can form no Conclusion from the Ideas which are offered him of the Divinity.—Of their want of just Inference.—Of the Inutility of his Conduct.

It has been already stated, that ideas to be useful, must be founded upon truth; that experience must at all times demonstrate their justice: if, therefore, as we have proved, the erroneous ideas which man has in almost all ages formed to himself of the Divinity, far from being of utility, are prejudicial to morality, to politics, to the happiness of society, to the welfare of the individuals who compose it, in short, to the progress of the human understanding; reason, and our interest, ought to make us feel the necessity of banishing from our mind these illusive, futile opinions, which can never do more than confound it—which can only disturb the tranquillity of our hearts. In vain should we flatter ourselves with arriving at the correction of theological notions; erroneous in their principles, they are not susceptible of reform. Under whatever shape an error presents itself, as soon as man shall attach an undue importance to it, it will, sooner or later, finish by producing consequences dangerous in proportion to their extent. Besides, the inutility of those researches, which in all ages have been made after the true nature of the Divinity, the notions that have hitherto been entertained, have done little more than throw it into greater obscurity, even to those who have most profoundly meditated on the subject; then, ought not this very inutility to convince us that this subject is not within the reach of our capacity that this being will not be better known to us, or by our descendants, than it hath been to our ancestors, either the most savage or the most ignorant? The object, which of all others man has at all times reasoned upon the most, written upon the most, nevertheless remains the least known; far from progressing in his research, time, with the aid of theological ideas, has only rendered it more impossible to be conceived. If the Divinity be such as dreaming theology depicts, he must himself be a Divinity who is competent to form an idea of him. We know little of man, we hardly know ourselves, or our own faculties, yet we are disposed to reason upon a being inaccessible to our senses. Let us, then, travel in peace over the line described for us by nature, without having a wish to diverge from it, to hunt after vague systems; let us occupy ourselves with our true happiness; let us profit of the benefits spread before us; let us labour to multiply them, by diminishing the number of our errors; let us quietly submit to those evils we cannot avoid, and not augment them by filling our mind with prejudices calculated to lead us astray. When we shall give it serious reflection, every thing will clearly prove that the pretended science of theology is, in truth, nothing but presumptuous ignorance, masked under pompous, unintelligible words. In short, let us terminate unfruitful researches; be content at least to acknowledge our invincible ignorance; it will clearly be more substantively advantageous, than an arrogant science, which has hitherto done little more than sow discord on the earth—affliction in the heart of man.

In supposing a sovereign intelligence who governs the world; in supposing a Divinity who exacts from his creatures that they should have a knowledge of him, that they should understand his attributes, his wisdom, his power; who is desirous they should render him homage; it must be allowed, that no man on earth in this respect completely fulfils the views of providence. Indeed, nothing is more demonstrable than the impossibility in which the theologians find themselves, to form to their mind any idea whatever of the Divinity. Procopius, the first bishop of the Goths, says in the most solemn manner: "I esteem it a very foolish temerity to be disposed to penetrate into the knowledge of the nature of God;" and further on he acknowledges, "that he has nothing more to say of him, except that he is perfectly good. He who knoweth more, whether he be ecclesiastic or layman, has only to tell it." The weakness, the obscurity of the proofs offered, of the systems attributed to him, the manifest contradictions into which they fall, the sophisms, the begging of the question, which are employed, evidently prove they are themselves in the greatest incertitude upon the nature of that being with whom it is their profession to occupy their thoughts: even the author of *A New View of Society* acknowledges, "that up to this moment it is, not possible yet to say which is right or which is wrong: that had any one of the various opposing systems which until this day have governed the world, and disunited man from man, been true, without any mixture of error; that system, very speedily after its public promulgation, would have pervaded society, and compelled all men to have acknowledged its truth." But granting that they have a knowledge of this being, that his essence, his attributes, his systems, were so fully demonstrated to them, as no longer to leave any doubt in their mind, do the rest of the human race enjoy the same advantages? Are they, in fact, in a condition to be charged with this knowledge? Ingenuously, how many persons are to be found in the world, who have the leisure, the capacity, the penetration, necessary to understand what is meant to be designated under the name of an immaterial being—of a pure spirit, who moveth matter without being himself matter; who is the motive of all the powers of nature, without being contained in nature—without being able to touch it? Are there, in the most religious societies, many persons who are competent to follow their spiritual guides, in the subtle proofs which they adduce in evidence of their creeds, upon which they bottom their systems of theology?

Without question very few men are capable of profound, connected meditation; the exercise of intense thought is, for the greater number, a species of labour as painful as it is unusual. The people, obliged to toil hard, in order to obtain subsistence, are commonly incapable of reflection; nobles, men of the world, women, young people, occupied with their own immediate affairs, taken up with gratifying their passions, employed in procuring themselves pleasure, as rarely think deeply as the uninformed. There are not, perhaps, two men in an hundred thousand, who have seriously asked themselves the question, *What it is they understand by the word God?* Whilst it is extremely rare to find persons to whom the nature of God is a problem. Nevertheless, as we have said, conviction supposes that evidence alone has banished doubt from the mind. Where, then, are the web who are convinced of the rectitude of these systems? Who are those in whom we shall find the complete certitude of these truths, so important to all? Who are the persons, who have given themselves an accurate account of the ideas they have formed upon the Divinity, upon his attributes, upon his essence? Alas! throughout the whole world, are only to be seen some speculators, who, by dint of occupying themselves with the idea, have, with great fatuity, believed they have discovered something decisive in the confused, unconnected wanderings of their own imagination; they have, in consequence, endeavoured to form a whole, which, chimerical as it is, they have accustomed themselves to consider as actually existing: by force of musing upon it, they have sometimes persuaded themselves they, saw it distinctly; these have not unfrequently succeeded in making others believe, their reveries, although they may not have mused upon it quite so much as themselves.

It is seldom more than hearsay, that the mass of the people adopt either the systems of their fathers, or of their priests: authority, confidence, submission, habit, take place of conviction—supersede proof; they prostrate themselves before idols, lend themselves to different creeds, because their ancestors have taught them to fall down, and worship; but never do they inquire wherefore they bend the knee: it is only because, in times far distant, their legislators, their guides, have imposed it upon them as a duty; these have said, "adore and believe those gods, whom ye cannot comprehend; yield yourselves in this instance to our profound wisdom; we know more than ye do respecting the Divinity." But wherefore, it might be inquired, should I take this system upon your authority? It is, they will reply, because the gods will have it thus; because they will punish you, if you dare to resist. But are not these gods the thing in question? Nevertheless, man has always been satisfied with this circle of errors; the idleness of his mind made him find it most easy to yield to the judgment of others. All superstitions are uniformly founded upon error, established by authority; equally forbid examination; are equally indisposed to permit that man should reason upon them; it is power that wills he should unconditionally accredit them: they are rested solely upon the influence of some few men, who pretend to a knowledge of things, which they admit are incomprehensible for all their species; who, at the same time, affirm they are sent as missionaries to announce them to the inhabitants of the earth: these inconceivable systems, formed in the brain of some enthusiastic persons, have most unquestionably occasion for men to expound them to their fellows. Man is generally credulous as a child upon those objects which relate to superstition; he is told he must believe them; as he generally understands nothing of the matter, he imagines he runs no risk in joining sentiments with his priest, whom he supposes has been competent to discover what he himself is not able to comprehend. The most rational people argue thus: "What shall I do? What interest can so many persons have to deceive?" But, seriously, does this prove that they do not deceive? They may do it from two motives: either because they are themselves deceived, or because they have a great interest in deceiving. By the confession of the theologians themselves, man is, for the greater part, without *religion*: he has only *superstition*. Superstition, according to them, "is a worship of the Divinity, either badly understood or irrational," or else, "worship rendered to a false Divinity." But where are the people or the clergy who will allow, either that their Divinity is false, or their worship irrational? How shall it be decided who is right, or who is wrong? It is evident that in this affair great numbers must be wrong. Indeed, Buddaeus, in his *Treatise on Atheism*, tells us, "in order that a religion may be true, not only the object of the worship must be true, but we must also have a just idea of it. He, then, who adoreth God without knowing him, adoreth him in a perverse and corrupt manner, and is generally guilty of superstition." This granted, would it not be fair to demand of the theologians, if they themselves can boast of having a *just idea* or real knowledge of the Divinity?

Admit for a moment they have, would it not then be evident, that it is for the priest, for the inspired, for the metaphysician, that this idea, which is said to be so necessary for the whole human race, is exclusively reserved? If we examine, however, we shall not find any harmony among the theological notions of these various inspired men, or of that hierarchy which is scattered over the earth: even those who make a profession of the same system, are not in unison upon the leading points. Are they ever contented with the proofs offered by their colleagues? Do they unanimously subscribe to each other's ideas? Are they agreed upon the conduct to be adopted; upon the manner of explaining their texts; upon the interpretation of the various oracles? Does there exist one country upon the whole earth, where the science of theology is actually perfectioned?—where the ideas of the Divinity are rendered so clear, as not to admit of cavil? Has this science obtained any of that steadiness, any of that consistency, any of that uniformity, which is found attached to other branches of human knowledge; even to the most futile arts, or to those trades which are most despised? Has the multitude of subtle distinctions, with which theology in some countries is filled throughout; have the words spirit, immateriality, incorporeity, predestination, grace, with other ingenious inventions, imagined by sublime thinkers, who during so many ages have succeeded each other, actually had any other effect than to perplex things; to render the whole obscure; decidedly unintelligible? Alas! do, they not offer practical demonstration, that the science held forth as the most necessary to man, has not, hitherto, been able to acquire the least degree of stability; has remained in the most determined state of indecision; has entirely failed in obtaining solidity? For thousands of years the most idle dreamers have been relieving each other, meditating on systems, diving into concealed ways, inventing hypothesis suitable to develope this important enigma. Their slender success has not at all discouraged theological vanity; the priests have always spoken of it as of a thing with which they were most intimately acquainted;

they have disputed with all the pertinancy of demonstrated argument; they have destroyed each other with the most savage barbarity; yet, notwithstanding, to this moment, this sublime science remains entirely unauthenticated; almost unexamined. Indeed, if things were coolly contemplated, it would be obvious that these theories are not formed for the generality of mankind, who for the most part are utterly incompetent to comprehend the aerial subtilities upon which they rest. Who is the man, that understandeth any thing of the fundamental principles of these systems? Whose capacity embraces spirituality, immateriality, incorporeity, or the mysteries of which he is every day informed? Are there many persons who can boast of perfectly understanding the state of the question, in those theological disputations, which have frequently had the potency to disturb the repose of mankind? Nevertheless, even women believe themselves obliged to take part in the quarrels excited by these idle speculators, who are of less actual utility, to society, than the meanest artizan.

Man would, perhaps, have been too happy, if confining himself to those visible objects which interest him, he had employed half that energy which he has wasted in researches after incomprehensible systems, upon perfecting the real sciences; in giving consistency to his laws; in establishing his morals upon solid foundations; in spreading a wholesome education among his fellows. He would, unquestionably, have been much wiser, more fortunate, if he had agreed to let his idle, unemployed guides quarrel among themselves unheeded; if he had permitted them to fathom those depths calculated to astound the mind, to amaze the intellect, without intermeddling with their irrational disputes. But it is the essence of ignorance, to attach great importance to every thing which it doth not understand. Human vanity makes the mind bear up against difficulties. The more an object eludes our inquiry, the more efforts we make to compass it; because from thence our pride is spurred on, our curiosity is set afloat, our passions are irritated, and it assumes the character of being highly interesting to us. On the other hand, the more continued, the more laborious our researches have been, the more importance we attach to either our real or our pretended discoveries; the more we are desirous not to have wasted our time; besides, we are always ready warmly to defend the soundness of our own judgment. Do not let us then be surprised at the interest that ignorant persons have at all times taken in the discoveries of their priests; nor at the obstinate pertinacity which they have ever manifested in their disputes. Indeed, in combating for his own peculiar system, each only fought for the interests of his own vanity, which of all human passions is the most quickly alarmed, the most calculated to lead man on to the commission of great follies.

Theology is truly the vessel of the Danaides. By dint of contradictory qualities, by means of bold assertions, it has so shackled its own systems as to render it impossible they should act. Indeed, when even we should suppose the existence of these theological systems, the reality of codes so discordant with each other and with themselves, we can conclude nothing from them to authorize the conduct, or sanction the mode of worship which they prescribe. If their gods are infinitely good, wherefore should we dread them? If they are infinitely wise, what reason have we to disturb ourselves with our condition? If they are omniscient, wherefore inform them of our wants, why fatigue them with our requests? If they are omnipresent, of what use can it be to erect temples to them? If they are lords of all, why make sacrifices to them; why bring them offerings of what already belongs to them? If they are just, upon what foundation believe that they will punish those creatures whom they have filled with imbecility? If their grace works every thing in man, what reason can there be why he should be rewarded? If they are omnipotent, how can they be offended; how can we resist them? If they are rational, how can the enrage themselves against blind mortals, to whom they have left the liberty of acting irrationally? If they are immutable, by what right shall we pretend to make them change their decrees? If they are inconceivable, wherefore should we occupy ourselves with them? If the knowledge of these systems be the most necessary thing, wherefore are they not more evident, more consistent, more manifest?

This granted, he who can undeceive himself on the afflicting notions of these theories, hath this advantage over the credulous, trembling, superstitious mortal—that he establishes in his heart a momentary tranquility, which, at least, rendereth him happy in this life. If the study of nature hath banished from his mind, those chimeras with which the superstitions man is infested, he, at least, enjoys a security of which this sees himself deprived. In consulting this nature, his fears are dissipated, his opinions, whether true or false, acquire a steadiness of character; a calm succeeds the storm, which panic terror, the result of wavering notions, excite in the hearts of all men who occupy themselves with these systems. If the human soul, cheered by philosophy, had the boldness to consider things coolly; it would no longer behold the universe submitted to implacable systems, under which man is continually trembling. If he was rational, he would perceive that in committing evil he did not disturb nature; that he either injureth himself alone, or injures other beings capable of feeling the effects of his conduct, from thence he would know the line of his duties; he would prefer virtue to vice, for his own permanent repose: he would, for his own satisfaction, for his own felicity in this world, find himself deeply interested in the practice of moral goodness; in rendering virtue habitual; in making it dear to the feeling of his heart: his own immediate welfare would be concerned in avoiding vice, in detesting crime, during the short season of his abode among intelligent, sensible beings, from whom he expects his happiness. By attaching himself to these rules, he would live contented with his own conduct; he would be cherished by those who are capable of feeling the influence of his actions; he would expect without inquietude the term when his existence should have a period; he would have no reason to dread the existence which *might* follow the one he at present enjoys: he would not fear to be deceived in his reasonings. Guided by demonstration, led gently along by honesty, he would perceive, that he could have nothing to dread from a beneficent Divinity, who would not punish him for those involuntary errors which depend upon the organization, which without his own consent he has received.

Such a man so conducting himself, would have nothing to apprehend, whether at the moment of his death, he falls asleep for ever; or whether that sleep is only a prelude to another existence, in which he shall find himself in the presence of his God. Addressing himself to the Divinity, he might with confidence say,

"O God! Father, who hath rendered thyself invisible to thy child! Inconceivable, hidden Author of all, whom I could not discover! Pardon me, if my limited understanding hath not been able to know thee, in a nature, where every thing hath appeared to me to be necessary! Excuse me, if my sensible heart hath not discerned thine august traits among those numerous systems which superstitious mortals tremblingly adore: if, in that assemblage of irreconcileable qualities, with which the imagination hath clothed thee, I could only see a phantom. How could my coarse eyes perceive thee in nature, in which all my senses have never been able to bring me acquainted but with material beings, with, perishable forms? Could I, by the aid of these senses, discover thy spiritual essence, of which no one could furnish me any idea? Could my feeble brain, obliged to form its judgments after its own capacity, discern thy plans, measure thy wisdom, conceive thine intelligence, whilst the universe presented to my view a continued mixture of order and confusion—of good and evil—of formation and destruction? Have I been able to render homage to the justice of thy priests, whilst I so frequently beheld crime triumphant, virtue in tears? Could I possibly acknowledge the voice of a being filled with wisdom, in those ambiguous, puerile, contradictory oracles, published in thy name in the different countries of the earth I have quitted? If I have not known thy peculiar existence, it is because I have not known either what thou couldst be, where thou couldst be placed, or the qualities which could be assigned thee. My ignorance is excusable, because it was invincible: my mind could not bend itself under the authority of men, who acknowledged they were as little enlightened upon thine essence as myself; who were for ever disputing among themselves; who were in harmony only in imperiously crying out to me, to sacrifice to them that reason which thou hadst given to me; But, oh God! If thou cherishest thy creatures, I also, like thee, have cherished them; I have endeavoured to render them happy, in the sphere in which I have lived. If thou art the author of reason, I have always listened to it—have ever endeavoured to follow it; if virtue pleaseth thee, my heart hath always honoured it; I have never willingly outraged it: when my powers have permitted me, I have myself practised it; I was an affectionate husband, a tender father, a sincere friend, a faithful subject, a zealous citizen; I have held out consolation to the afflicted; and if the foibles of my nature have been either injurious to myself or incommodious to others, I have not at least made the unfortunate groan under the weight of my injustice. I have not devoured the substance of the poor—I have not seen without pity the widow's tears; I have not heard without commiseration the cries of the orphan. If thou didst render man sociable, if thou was disposed that society should subsist, if thou wast desirous the community might be happy, I have been the enemy to all who oppressed him, the decided foe to all those who deceived him, in order that they might advantage themselves of his misfortunes.

"If I have not thought properly of thee, it is because my understanding could not conceive thee; if I have spoken ill of thy systems, it is because my heart, partaking too much of human nature, revolted against the odious portrait under which they depicted thee. My wanderings have been the effect of the temperament which thou hast given me; of the circumstances in which, without my consent, thou hast placed me; of those ideas, which in despite of me, have entered into my mind. As thou art good, as thou art just, (as we are assured thou art) thou wilt not punish me for the wanderings of mine imagination; for faults caused by my passions, which are the necessary consequence of the organization which I have received from thee. Thus I cannot doubt thy justice, I cannot dread the condition which thou preparest for me. Thy goodness cannot have permitted that I should incur punishment for inevitable errors. Thou wouldst rather prevent my being born, than have called me into the rank of intelligent beings, there to enjoy the fatal liberty of rendering myself eternally unhappy."

It is thus that a disciple of nature, who, transported all at once into the regions of space, should find himself in the presence of his God, would be able to speak, although he should not have been in a condition to lend himself to all the abstract systems of theology which appear to have been invented for no other purpose than to overturn in his mind all natural ideas. This illusory science seems bent an forming its systems in a manner the most contradictory to human reason; notwithstanding we are obliged to judge in this world according to its dictates; if, however, in the succeeding world, there is nothing conformable to this, what can be of more inutility, than to think of it or reason upon it? Besides, wherefore should we leave it to the judgment of men, who are, themselves, only enabled to act after our manner?

Without a very marked derangement of our organs, our sentiments hardly ever vary upon those objects which either our senses experience, or which reason has clearly demonstrated, In whatever circumstances we are found, we have no doubt either upon the whiteness of snow, the light of day, or the utility of virtue. It is not so with those objects which depend solely upon our imagination—which are not proved to us by the constant evidence of our senses; we judge of them variously, according to the dispositions in which we find ourselves. These dispositions fluctuate by reason of the involuntary impulse which our organs every instant receive, on the part of an infinity of causes, either exterior to ourselves, or else contained within our own frame. These organs are, without our knowledge, perpetually modified, either relaxed or braced by the density, more or less, of the atmosphere; by heat and by cold; by dryness and by humidity; by health and by sickness; by the heat of the blood; by the abundance of bile; by the state of the nervous system, &c. These various causes have necessarily an influence upon the momentary ideas, upon the instantaneous thoughts, upon the fleeting opinions of man, He is, consequently, obliged to see under a great variety of hues, those objects which his imagination presents to him; without it all times having the capacity to correct them by experience: to compare them by memory. This, without doubt, is the reason why man is continually obliged to view his gods, to contemplate his superstitious systems, under such a diversity of aspects, in different periods of his existence. In the moment, when his fibres find themselves disposed to he tremulous, he will be cowardly, pusillanimous; he will think of these systems only with fear and trembling. In the moment, when these same fibres shall have more tension, he will possess more firmness, he will then view these systems with greater coolness. The theologian will call his pusillanimity, "inward feeling;" "warning from heaven;" "secret inspiration;" but he who knoweth man, will say that this is nothing more than a mechanical motion, produced by a physical or natural cause. Indeed, it is by a pure physical mechanism, that we can explain all the revolutions that take place in the system, frequently from one minute to another; all the fluctuations in the opinions of mankind; all the variations of his judgment: in consequence of which we sometimes see him reasoning justly, sometimes in the most irrational manner.

This is the mode by which, without recurring to grace, to inspirations, to visions, to supernatural notions, we can render ourselves an account of that uncertain, that wavering state into which we sometimes behold persons fall, when there is a question respecting their superstition, who are otherwise extremely enlightened. Frequently, in despite of all reasoning, momentary dispositions re-conduct them to the prejudices of their infancy, upon which on other occasions they appear to be entirely undeceived. These changes are very apparent, especially under infirmities, in sickness, or at approach of death. The barometer of the understanding is then frequently obliged to fall. Those chimeras which he despised, or which in a state of health, he set down at their true value, are then realized. He trembles, because his machine is enfeebled; he is irrational because his brain is incapable of fulfilling its functions with exactitude. It is evident these are the actual causes of those changes which the priests well know how to make use of against what they call incredulity; from which they draw proofs of the reality of their sublimated opinions. Those conversions, or those alterations, which take place, in the ideas of man, have always their origin in some derangement of his machine; brought on either by chagrin or by some other natural or known cause.

Submitted to the continual influence of physical causes, our systems invariably follow the variations of the body; we reason well when the body is healthy—when it is soundly constituted; we reason badly when the corporeal faculties are deranged; from thence our ideas become disconnected, we are no longer equal to the task of associating them with precision; we are incapable of finding principles, or to draw from them just inferences; the brain, in fact, is shaken; we no longer contemplate any thing under its actual point of view. It is a man of this kind, who does not see things in frosty weather, under the same traits as when the season is cloudy, or when it is rainy; he does not view them in the same manner in sorrow as in gaiety; when in company as when alone. Good sense suggests to us, that it is when the body is sound, when the mind is undisturbed by any mist, that we can reason with accuracy; this state can furnish us with a general standard, calculated to regulate our judgment; even to rectify our ideas, when unexpected causes shall make them waver.

If the opinions even of the same individual, are fluctuating, subject to vaccillate, how many changes must they experience in the various beings who compose the human race? If there do not, perhaps, exist two persons who see a physical object under the same exact form or colour, what much greater variety must they not have in their mode of contemplating those things which have existence only in their imagination? What an infinity of combinations, what a multitude of ideas, must not minds essentially different, form to themselves when they endeavour to compose an ideal being, which each moment of their existence must present to them under a different aspect? It would, then, be a most irrational enterprise, to attempt to prescribe to man what he ought to think of superstition, which is entirely under the cognizance of his imagination; for the admeasurement of which, as we have very frequently repeated, mortals will never have any common standard. To oppugn the superstitious opinions of man, is to commence hostilities with his imagination—to attack his fancy—to be at war with his organization—to enter the lists with his habits, which are of themselves sufficient to identify with his existence, the most absurd, the most unfounded ideas. The more imagination man has, the greater enthusiast he will be in matters of superstition; reason will have the less ability to undeceive him in his chimeras. In proportion as his fancy is powerful, these chimeras themselves will become food necessary to its ardency. In fine, to battle with the superstitious notions of man, is to combat the passions he usually indulges for the marvellous; it is to assail him on that side where he is least vulnerable; to force him in that position where he unites all his strength—where he keeps the most vigilant guard. In despite of reason, those persons who have a lively imagination, are perpetually re-conducted to those chimeras which habit renders dear to them, even when they are found troublesome; although they should prove fatal. Thus a tender soul hath occasion for a God that loveth him; the happy enthusiast needeth a God who rewardeth him; the unfortunate visionary wants a God who taketh part in his sorrows; the melancholy devotee requireth a God who chastiseth him, who maintaineth him in that trouble which has become necessary to his diseased organization; the frantic penitent exacteth a God, who imposes upon him an obligation to be inhuman towards himself; whilst the furious fanatic would believe himself unhappy, if he was deprived of a God who commanded him to make others experience the effect of his inflamed humours, of his unruly passions.

He is, without question, a less dangerous enthusiast who feeds himself with agreeable illusions, than he whose soul is tormented with odious spectres. If a placid, tender soul, does not commit ravages in society, a mind agitated by incommodious passions, cannot fail to become, sooner or later, troublesome to his fellow creatures. The God of a Socrates, or a Fenelon, may be suitable to souls as gentle as theirs; but he cannot be that of a whole nation, in which it is extremely rare men of their temper are found: if honest men only view their gods as fitted with benefits; vicious, restless, inflexible individuals, will give them their own peculiar character, from thence will authorize themselves to indulge, a free course to their passions. Each will view his deities with eyes only open to his own reigning prejudice; the number of those who will paint them as afflicting will always be greater, much more to be feared, than those who shall delineate them under seducing colors: for one mortal that those ideas will render happy, there will be thousands who will be made miserable; they will, sooner or later, become an inexhaustible source of contention; a never failing spring of extravagant folly; they will disturb the mind of the ignorant, over whom impostors will always gain ascendancy—over whom fanatics will ever have an influence: they will frighten the cowardly, terrify the pussillanimous, whose imbecility will incline them to perfidy, whose weakness will render them cruel; they will cause the most upright to tremble, who, even while practising virtue, will fear incurring the divine displeasure; but they will not arrest the progress of the wicked, who will easily cast them aside, that they may the more commodiously deliver themselves up to crime; or who will even take advantage of these principles, to justify their transgression. In short, in the hands of tyrants, these systems will only serve to crush the liberty of the people; will be the pretext for violating, with impunity, all equitable rights. In the hands of priests they will become talismans, suitable to intoxicate the mind; calculated to hoodwink the people; competent to subjugate equally the sovereign as the subject; in the hands of the multitude, they will be a two-edged sword, with which they will inflict, at the same moment, the most dreadful wounds on themselves—the most serious injuries on their associates.

On the other hand, these theological systems, as we have seen, being only an heap of contradictions, which represent the Divinity under the most incompatible characters, seem to doubt his wisdom, when they invite mortals to address their prayers to him, for the gratification of their desires; to pray to him to grant that which he has not thought it proper to accord to them. Is it not, in other words, to accuse him with neglecting his creatures? Is it not to ask him to alter the eternal decrees of his justice; to change the invariable laws which he hath himself determined? Is it not to say to him, "O, my God! I acknowledge thy wisdom, thine omniscience, thine infinite goodness; nevertheless, thou forgettest thy servant; thou losest sight of thy creature; thou art ignorant, or thou feignest ignorance, of that which he wanteth: dost thou not see that I suffer from the marvellous arrangement, which thy wise laws have made in the universe? Nature, against thy commands, actually renders my existence painful: change then, I beseech thee, the essence which thy will has given to all beings. Grant that the elements, at this moment, lose in my favor their distinguishing properties; so order it, that heavy bodies shall not fall, that fire shall not burn, that the brittle frame which I have received at thine hands, shall not suffer those shocks which it every instant experiences. Rectify, I pray thee, for my happiness, the plan which thine infinite prudence hath marked out from all eternity." Such is very nearly the euchology which man adopts; such are the discordant, absurd requests which he continually puts up to the Divinity, whose wisdom he extols; whose intelligence he holds forth to admiration; whose providence he eulogizes; whose equity he applauds; whilst he is hardly ever contented with the effects of the divine perfections.

Man is not more consequent in those thanksgivings which he believes himself obliged to offer to the throne of grace. Is it not just, he exclaims, to thank the Divinity for his kindness? Would it not be the height of ingratitude to refuse our homage to the Author of our existence; to withhold our acknowledgements from the Giver of every thing that contributes to render it agreeable? But does he not frequently offer up his thanksgivings for actions that overwhelm his neighbour with misery? Does not the husbandman on the hill, return thanks for the rain that irrigates his lands parched with drought, whilst the cultivator of the valley is imploring a cessation of those showers which deluge his fields—that render useless the labour of his hands? Thus each becomes thankful for that which his own limited views points out to him as his immediate interest, regardless of the general effect produced by those circumstances on the welfare of his fellows. Each believes that it is either a peculiar dispensation of providence in his own favor, or a signal of the heavenly wrath directed against himself; whilst the slightest reflection would clearly evince it to be nothing more than the inevitable order of things, which take place without the least regard to his individual comforts. From this it will be obvious, that these systems do not teach their votaries, practically, to love their neighbour as themselves. But in matters of superstition, mortals never reason; they only follow the impulse of their fears; the direction of their imagination; the force of their temperament; the bent of their own peculiar passions; or those of the guides, who have acquired the right of controling their understanding. Fear has generally created these systems; terror unceasingly accompanies them; it is impossible to reason while we tremble.

We do not, however, flatter ourselves that reason will be capable, all at once, to deliver the human race from those errors with which so many causes united have contributed to poison him. The vainest of all projects would be the expectation of curing, in an instant, those epidemical follies, those hereditary fallacies, rooted during so many ages; continually fed by ignorance; corroborated by custom; borne along by the passions made inveterate by interest; grounded upon the fears, established upon the ever regenerating calamities of nations. The ancient disasters of the earth gave birth to the first systems of theology, new revolutions would equally produce others; even if the old ones should chance to be forgotton. Ignorant, miserable, trembling beings, will always either form to themselves systems, or else adopt those which imposture shall announce—which fanaticism shall be disposed to give them.

It would therefore be useless to propose more than to hold out reason to those who are competent to understand it; to present truth to those who can sustain its lustre; who can with serenity contemplate its refulgent beauty; to undeceive those who shall not be inclined to oppose obstacles to demonstration; to enlighten those who shall not desire pertinaciously to persist in error. Let us, then, infuse courage into those who want power to break with their illusions; let us cheer up the honest man, who is much more alarmed by his fears than the wicked, who, in despite of his opinions, always follows the rule of his passions: let us console the unfortunate, who groans under a load of prejudices which he has not examined: let us dissipate the incertitude of those whose doubts render them unhappy; who ingenuously seek after truth, but who find in philosophy itself only wavering opinions little calculated to determine their fluctuating minds. Let us banish from the man of genius those chimerical speculations which cause him to waste his time; let us wrest his gloomy superstition from the intimidated mortal, who, duped by his vain fears, becomes useless to society; let us remove from the atrabilarious being those systems that afflict him, that exasperate his mind, that do nothing more than kindle his anger against his incredulous neighbour; let us tear from the fanatic those terrible ideas which arm him with poniards against the happiness of his fellows; let us pluck from tyrants, let us snatch from impostors, those opinions which enable them to terrify, to enslave, and to despoil the human species. In removing from honest men their formidable notions let us not encourage those of the wicked, who are the enemies of society; let us deprive the latter of those illegitimate sources, upon which they reckon to expiate their transgressions; let us substitute actual, present terrors, to those which are distant and uncertain to those which do not arrest the most licentious excesses; let us make the profligate blush at beholding themselves what they really are; let the ministers of superstition tremble at finding their conspiracies discovered; let them dread the arrival of the day, when mortals, cured of those errors with which they have abused them, will no longer be enslaved by their artifice.

If we cannot induce nations to lay aside their inveterate prejudices, let us, at least, endeavour to prevent them from relapsing into those excesses, to the commission of which superstition has so frequently hurried them; let mankind form to himself chimeras, if he cannot do without them; let him think as he may feel inclined, provided his reveries do not make him forget that he is a man; that he does not cease to remember that a sociable being is not formed to resemble the most ferocious animals. Let us try to balance the fictitious interests of superstition, by the more immediate advantages of the earth. Let sovereigns, as well as their subjects, at length acknowledge that the benefits resulting from truth, the happiness arising from justice, the tranquillity springing out of wholesome laws, the blessings to be derived from a rational education, the superiority to be obtained from a physical, peaceable morality, are much more substantive than those they vainly expect from their respective superstitious systems, Let them feel, that advantages so tangible, benefits so precious, ought not to be sacrificed to uncertain hopes, so frequently contradicted by experience. In order to convince themselves of these truths, let every rational man consider the numberless crimes which superstition has caused upon our globe; let them study the frightful history of theology: let them read over the biography of its more odious ministers, who have too often fanned the spirit of discord—kindled the flame of fury—stirred up the raging fire of madness: let the prince and the people, at least, sometimes learn to resist the demoniacal passions of these interpreters of unintelligible systems, which they acknowledge they do not themselves at all understand, especially when they shall invoke them to be inhuman; when they shall preach up intolerance; when they invite them to barbarity; above all, when they shall command them, in the name of their gods, to stifle the cries of nature; to put down the voice of equity; to be deaf to the remonstrances of reason; to be blind to the interest of society.

Feeble mortals! led astray by error, how long will ye permit your imagination, so active, so prompt to seize on the marvellous, to continue to seek out of the universe pretexts to render you baneful to yourselves, injurious to the beings with whom ye live in society? Wherefore do ye not follow in peace, the simple, easy route marked out for ye by nature? To what purpose do ye scatter thorns on the road of life? What avails it, that ye multiply those sorrows to which your destiny exposes ye? What advantages can ye derive from systems with which the united efforts of the whole human species have not been competent to bring ye acquainted? Be content, then, to remain ignorant of that, which the human mind is not formed to comprehend; which human intellect is not adequate to embrace: occupy yourselves with truth; learn the invaluable art of living happy; perfection your morals; give rationality to your governments; simplify your laws, and rest them on the pillars of justice; watch over education, and see that it is of an invigorating quality; give attention to agriculture, and encourage beneficial improvements; foster those sciences which are actually useful, and place their professors in the most honorable stations; labor with ardour, and munificently reward those whose assiduity promotes the general welfare; oblige nature by your industry to open her immense stores, to become propitious to your exertions; do these things, and the gods will oppose nothing to your felicity. Leave to idle thinkers, to soporific dreamers, to waking visionaries, to useless enthusiasts, the unproductive task, the unfruitful occupation, of fathoming depths, from which ye ought sedulously to divert your attention; enjoy with moderation, the benefits attached to your present existence; augment their number when reason sanctions the multiplication; but never attempt to spring yourselves forward, beyond the sphere destined for your action. If you must have chimeras, permit your fellow creatures to have theirs also; but never cut the throats of your brethren, when, they cannot rave in your own manner. If ye will have unintelligible systems, if ye cannot be contented without marvellous doctrines, if the infirmities of your nature require an invisible crutch, adopt such as may best suit with your humour; select those which you may think most calculated to support your tottering frame; if ye can, let your own imagination give birth to them; but do not insist on your neighbours making the same choice with yourself: do not suffer these imaginary theories to infuriate your mind: let them not so far intoxicate your understandings, as to make ye mistake the duties ye owe to the real beings with whom ye are associated. Always remember, that amongst these duties, the foremost, the most consequential, the most immediate in its bearing upon the felicity of the human race, stands, *a reasonable indulgence for the foibles of others.*

CHAP. XI.
Defence of the Sentiments contained in this Work.—Of Impiety.—Do there exist Atheists?

What has been said in the course of this work, ought sufficiently to undeceive those who are capable of reasoning on the prejudices to which they attached so much importance. But the most evident truths frequently crouch under fear; are kept at bay by habit; prove abortive against the force of enthusiasm. Nothing is more difficult to remove from its resting place than error, especially when long prescription has given it full possession of the human mind. It is almost unassailable when supported by general consent; when it is propagated by education; when it has acquired inveteracy by custom: it commonly resists every effort to disturb it, when it is either fortified by example, maintained by authority, nourished by the hopes, or cherished by the fears of a people, who have learned to look upon these delusions as the most potent remedies for their sorrows. Such are the united forces which sustain the empire of unintelligible systems over the inhabitants of this world; they appear to give stability to their throne; to render their power immoveable; to make their reign as lasting as the human race.

We need not, then, be surprised at seeing the multitude cherish their own blindness; encourage their superstitious notions; exhibit the most sensitive fear of truth. Every where we behold mortals obstinately attached to phantoms from which they expect their happiness; notwithstanding these fallacies are evidently the source of all their sorrows. Deeply smitten with the marvellous, disdaining the simple, despising that which is easy of comprehension, but little instructed in the ways of nature, accustomed to neglect the use of their reason, the uninformed, from age to age, prostrate themselves before those invisible powers which they have been taught to adore. To these they address their most fervent prayers; implore them in their misfortunes, offer them the fruits of their labour; they are unceasingly occupied either with thanking their vain idols for benefits they have not received at their bands, or else in requesting from them favors which they can never obtain. Neither experience nor reflection can undeceive them; they do not perceive these idols, the work of their own hands, have always been deaf to their intreaties; they ascribe it to their own conduct; believe them to be violently irritated: they tremble, groan out the most dismal lamentations; sigh bitterly in their temples; strew their altars with presents; load their priests with their largesses; it never strikes their attention that these beings, whom they imagine so powerful, are themselves submitted to nature; are never propitious to their wishes, but when nature herself is favourable. It is thus that nations are the accomplices of those who deceive them; are themselves as much opposed to truth as those who lead them astray.

In matters of superstition, there are very few persons who do not partake, more or less, of the opinions of the illiterate. Every man who throws aside the received ideas, is generally considered a madman; is looked upon as a presumptuous being, who insolently believes himself much wiser than his associates. At the magical sound of superstition, a sudden panic, a tremulous terror takes possession of the human species: whenever it is attacked, society is alarmed; each individual imagines he already sees the celestial monarch lift his avenging arm against the country in which rebellious nature has produced a monster with sufficient temerity to brave these sacred opinions. Even the most moderate persons tax with folly, brand with sedition, whoever dares combat with these imaginary systems, the rights of which good sense has never yet examined. In consequence, the man who undertakes to tear the bandeau of prejudice, appears an irrational being—a dangerous citizen; his sentence is pronounced with a voice almost unanimous; the public indignation, roused by fanaticism, stirred up by imposture, renders it impossible for him to be heard in his defence; every one believes himself culpable, if he does not exhibit his fury against him; if he does not display his zeal in hunting him down; it is by such means man seeks to gain the favor of the angry gods, whose wrath is supposed to be provoked. Thus the individual who consults his reason, the disciple of nature, is looked upon as a public pest; the enemy to superstition is regarded as the enemy to the human race; he who would establish a lasting peace amongst men, is treated as the disturber of society; the man who would be disposed to cheer affrighted mortals by breaking those idols, before whom prejudice has obliged them to tremble, is unanimously proscribed as an atheist. At the bare name of atheist the superstitious man quakes; the deist himself is alarmed; the priest enters the judgement chair with fury glaring in his eyes; tyranny prepares his funeral pile, the vulgar applaud the punishments which irrational, partial laws, decree against the true friend of the human species.

Such are the sentiments which every man must expect to excite, who shall dare to present his fellow creatures with that truth which all appear to be in search of, but which all either fear to find, or else mistake what we are disposed to shew it to them. But what is this man, who is so foully calumniated as an atheist? He is one who destroyeth chimeras prejudicial to the human race; who endeavours to re-conduct wandering mortals back to nature; who is desirous to place them upon the road of experience; who is anxious that they should actively employ their reason. He is a thinker, who, having meditated upon matter, its energies, its properties, its modes of acting, hath no occasion to invent ideal powers, to recur to imaginary systems, in order to explain the phenomena of the universe—to develope the operations of nature; who needs not creatures of the imagination, which far from making him better understand nature, do no more than render it wholly inexplicable, an unintelligible mass, useless to the happiness of mankind.

Thus, the only men who can have pure, simple, actual ideas of nature, are considered either as absurd or knavish speculators. Those who form to themselves distinct, intelligible notions of the powers of the universe, are accused of denying the existence of this power: those who found every thing that is operated in this world, upon determinate, immutable laws, are accused with attributing every thing to chance; are taxed with blindness, branded with delirium, by those very enthusiasts themselves, whose imagination, always wandering in a vacuum, regularly attribute the effects of nature to fictitious causes, which have no existence but in their own heated brain; to fanciful beings of their own creation; to chimerical powers, which they obstinately persist in preferring to actual, demonstrable causes. No man in his proper senses can deny the energy of nature, or the existence of a power by virtue of which matter acts; by which it puts itself in motion; but no man can, without renouncing his reason, attribute this power to an immaterial substance; to a power placed out of nature; distinguished from matter; having nothing in common with it. Is it not saying, this power does not exist, to pretend that it resides in an unknown being, formed by an heap of unintelligible qualities, of incompatible attributes, from whence necessarily results a whole, impossible to have existence? Indestructible elements, the atoms of Epicurus, of which it is said the motion, the collision, the combination, have produced all beings, are, unquestionably, much more tangible than the numerous theological systems, broached in various parts of the earth. Thus, to speak precisely, they are the partizans of imaginary theories, the advocates of contradictory beings, the defenders of creeds, impossible to be conceived, the contrivers of substances which the human mind cannot embrace on any side, who are either absurd or knavish; those enthusiasts, who offer us nothing but vague names, of which every thing is denied, of which nothing is affirmed, are the real *Atheists*; those, I say, who make such beings the authors of motion, the preservers of the universe, are either blind or irrational. Are not those dreamers, who are incapable of attaching any one positive idea to the causes of which they unceasingly speak, true deniers? Are not those visionaries, who make a pure nothing the source of all beings, men really groping in the dark? Is it not the height of folly to personify abstractions, to organize negative ideas, and then to prostrate ourselves before the figments of our own brain?

Nevertheless, they are men of this temper who regulate the opinions of the world; who hold up to public scorn, those who are consistent to principle; who expose to the most infuriate vengeance, those who are more rational than themselves. If you will but accredit those profound dreamers, there is nothing short of madness, nothing on this side the most complete derangement of intellect, that can reject a totally incomprehensible motive-power in nature. Is it, then, delirium to prefer the known to the unknown? Is it a crime to consult experience, to call in the evidence of our senses, in the examination of that which we are informed is the most important to be understood? Is it a horrid outrage to address ourselves to reason; to prefer its oracles to the sublime decisions of some sophists, who themselves acknowledge they do not comprehend any thing of the systems they announce? Nevertheless, according to these men, there is no crime more worthy of punishment— there is no enterprize more dangerous to morals—no treason more substantive against society, than to despoil these immaterial substances, which they know nothing about, of those inconceivable qualities which these learned doctors ascribe to them—of that equipage with which a fanatical imagination has furnished them—of those miraculous properties with which ignorance, fear, and imposture have emulated each other in surrounding them: there is nothing more impious than to call forth man's reason upon superstitious creeds; nothing more heretical than to cheer up mortals against systems, of which the idea alone is the source of all their sorrows; there is nothing more pious, nothing more orthodox, than to exterminate those audacious beings who have had sufficient temerity to attempt to break an invisible charm that keeps the human species benumbed in error: if we are to put faith in the asseverations of the hierarchy, to be disposed to break man's chains is to rend asunder his most sacred bonds.

In consequence of these clamours, perpetually renovated by the disciples of imposture, kept constantly afloat by the theologians, reiterated by ignorance, those nations, which reason, in all ages, has sought to undeceive, have never dared to hearken to its benevolent lessons: they have stood aghast at the very name of physical truth. The friends of mankind were never listened to, because they were the enemies to his superstition—the examiners of the doctrines of his priest. Thus the people continued to tremble; very few philosophers had the courage to cheer them; scarcely any one dared brave public opinion; completely inoculated by superstition, they dreaded the power of imposture, the menaces of tyranny, which always sought to uphold themselves by delusion. The yell of triumphant ignorance, the rant of haughty fanaticism, at all time stifled the feeble voice of the disciple of nature; his lessons were quickly forgotten; he was obliged to keep silence; when he even dared to speak, it was frequently only in an enigmatical language, perfectly unintelligible to the great mass of mankind. How should the uninformed, who with difficulty compass the most evident truths, those that are the most distinctly announced, be able to comprehend the mysteries of nature, presented under half words, couched under intricate emblems.

In contemplating the outrageous language which is excited among theologians, by the opinions of those whom they choose to call atheists; in looking at the punishments which at their instigation were frequently decreed against them, should we not be authorized to conclude, that these doctors either are not so certain as they say they are, of the infallibility of their respective systems; or else that they do not consider the opinions of their adversaries so absurd as they pretend? It is always either distrust, weakness, or fear, frequently the whole united, that render men cruel; they have no anger against those whom they despise; they do not look upon folly as a punishable crime. We should be content with laughing at an irrational mortal, who should deny the existence of the sun; we should not think of punishing him, unless we had, ourselves, taken leave of our senses. Theological fury never proves more than the imbecility of its cause. Lucian describes Jupiter, who disputing with Menippus, is disposed to strike him to the earth with his thunder; upon which the philosopher says to him, "Ah! thou vexest thyself, thou usest thy thunder! then thou art in the wrong." The inhumanity of these men-monsters, whose profession it was to announce chimerical systems to nations, incontestibly proves, that they alone have an interest in the invisible powers they describe; of which they successfully avail themselves to terrify, mortals: they are these tyrants of the mind, however, who, but little consequent to their own principles, undo with one hand that which they rear up with the other: they are these profound logicians who, after having formed a deity filled with goodness, wisdom and equity, traduce, disgrace, and completely annihilate him, by saving he is cruel, capricious, unjust, and despotic: this granted, these men are truly impious; decidedly heretical.

He who knoweth not this system, cannot do it any injury, consequently cannot be called impious. "To he impious," says Epicurus, "is not to take away from the illiterate the gods which they have; it is to attribute to these gods the opinions of the vulgar." To be impious is to insult systems which we believe; it is knowingly to outrage them. To be impious, is to admit a benevolent, just God, at the same time we preach up persecution and carnage. To be impious, is to deceive men in the name of a Deity, whom we make use of as a pretext for our own unworthy passions. To be impious, is to speak falsely on the part of a God, whom we suppose to be the enemy of falsehood. In fine, to be impious, is to make use of the name of the Divinity in order to disturb society—to enslave it to tyrants—to persuade man that the cause of imposture is the cause of God; it is to impute to God those crimes which would annihilate his divine perfections. To be impious, and irrational, at the same time, is to make, by the aggregation of discrepant qualities, a mere chimera of the God we adore.

On the other hand, to be pious, is to serve our country with fidelity; it is to be useful to our fellow creatures; to labour to the welfare of society. Every one can put in his claim to this piety, according to his faculties; he who meditates can render himself useful, when he has the courage to announce truth—to attack error—to battle those prejudices which everywhere oppose themselves to the happiness of mankind; it is to be truly useful, it is even a duty, to wrest from the hands of mortals those homicidal weapons which wretched fanatics so profusely distribute among them; it is highly praiseworthy to deprive imposture of its influence; it is loving our neighbour as ourself to despoil tyranny of its fatal empire over opinion, which at all times it so successfully employs to elevate knaves at the expence of public happiness; to erect its power upon the ruins of liberty; to establish unruly passions upon the wreck of public security. To be truly pious, is religiously to observe the wholesome laws of nature; to follow up faithfully those duties which she prescribes to us; in short, to be pious is to be humane, equitable, benevolent: it is to respect the rights of mankind. To be pious and rational at the same time, is to reject those reveries which would be competent to make us mistake the sober counsels of reason.

Thus, whatever fanaticism, whatever imposture may say, he who denieth the solidity of systems which have no other foundation than an alarmed imagination; he who rejecteth creeds continually in contradiction with themselves; he who banisheth from his heart, doctrines perpetually wrestling with nature, always in hostility with reason, ever at war with the happiness of man; he, I repeat, who undeceiveth himself on such dangerous chimeras, when his conduct shall not deviate from those invariable rules which sound morality dictates, which nature approves, which reason prescribes, may be fairly reputed pious, honest, and virtuous. Because a man refuseth to admit contradictory systems, as well as the obscure oracles, which are issued in the name of the gods, does it then follow, that such a man refuses to acknowledge the evident, the demonstrable laws of nature, upon which he depends, of which he in obliged to fulfil the necessary duties, under pain of being punished in this world; whatever he may be in the in the next? It is true, that if virtue could by any chance consist in an ignominious renunciation of reason, in a destructive fanaticism, in useless customs, the atheist, as he is called, could not pass for a virtuous being: but if virtue actually consists in doing to society all the good of which we are capable, this miscalled atheist may fairly lay claim to its practice: his courageous, tender soul, will not be found guilty, for hurling his legitimate indignation against prejudices, fatal to the happiness of the human species.

Let us listen, however, to the imputations which the theologians lay upon those men they falsely denominate atheists; let us coolly, without any peevish humour, examine the calumnies which they vomit forth against them: it appears to them that atheism, (as they call differing in opinion from themselves,) is the highest degree of delirium that can assail the human mind; the greatest stretch of perversity that can infect the human heart; interested in blackening their adversaries, they make incredulity the undeniable offspring of folly; the absolute effect of crime. "We do not," say they to us, "see those men fall into the horrors of atheism, who have reason to hope the future state will be for them a state of happiness." In short, according to these metaphysical doctors, it is the interest of their passions which makes them seek to doubt systems, at whose tribunals they are accountable for the abuses of this life; it is the fear of punishment which is alone known to atheists; they are unceasingly repeating the words of a Hebrew prophet, who pretends that nothing but folly makes men deny these systems; perhaps, however, if he had suppressed his negation, he would have more closely aproximated the truth. Doctor Bentley, in his *Folly of Atheism*, has let loose the whole Billingsgate of theological spleen, which he has scattered about with all the venom of the most filthy reptiles: if he and other expounders are to be believed, "nothing is blacker than the heart of an atheist; nothing is more false than his mind. Atheism," according to them, "can only be the offspring of a tortured conscience, that seeks to disengage itself from the cause of its trouble. We have a right", says Derham, "to look upon an atheist as a monster among rational beings; as one of those extraordinary productions which we hardly ever meet with in the whole human species; and who, opposing himself to all other men, revolts not only against reason and human nature, but against the Divinity himself."

We shall simply reply to all these calumnies by saying, it is for the reader to judge if the system which these men call atheism, be as absurd as these profound speculators (who are perpetually in dispute on the uninformed, ill organized, contradictory, whimsical productions of their own brain) would have it believed to be! It is true, perhaps, that the system of naturalism hitherto has not been developed in all its extent: unprejudiced persons however, will, at least, be enabled to know whether the author has reasoned well or ill; whether or not he has attempted to disguise the most important difficulties; distinctly to see if he has been disingenuous; they will be competent to observe if, like unto the enemies of human reason, he has recourse to subterfuges, to sophisms, to subtle discriminations, which ought always to make it suspected of those who use them, either that they do not understand or else that they fear the truth. It belongs then to candour, it is the province of disinterestedness, it is the duty of reason to judge, if the natural principles which have been here ushered to the world be destitute of foundation; it is to these upright jurisconsults that a disciple of nature submits his opinions: he has a right to except against the judgment of enthusiasm; he has the prescription to enter his caveat against the decision of presumptuous ignorance; above all, he is entitled to challenge the verdict of interested knavery. Those persons who are accustomed to think, will, at least find reasons to doubt many of those marvellous notions, which appear as incontestable truths only to those, who have never assayed them by the standard of good sense.

We agree with Derham, that atheists are rare; but then we also say, that superstition has so disfigured nature, so entangled her rights— enthusiasm has so dazzled the human mind-terror has so disturbed the heart of man— imposture has so bewildered his imagination—tyranny has so enslaved his thoughts: in fine, error, ignorance, and delirium have so perplexed and confused the clearest ideas, that nothing is more uncommon than to find men who have sufficient courage to undeceive themselves on notions which every thing conspires to identify with their very existence. Indeed, many theologians in despite of those bitter invectives with which they attempt to overwhelm the men they choose to call atheists, appear frequently to have doubted whether any ever existed in the world. Tertullian, who, according to modern systems, would be ranked as an atheist, because he admitted a corporeal God, says, "Christianity has dissipated the ignorance in which the Pagans were immersed respecting the divine essence, and there is not an artizan among the Christians who does not see God, and who does not know him." This uncertainty of the theologic professors was, unquestionably, founded upon those absurd ideas, which they ascribe to their adversaries, whom they have unceasingly accused with attributing every thing to chance—to blind causes—to dead, inert matter, incapable of self-action. We have, I think, sufficiently justified the partizans of nature against these ridiculous accusations; we have throughout the whole proved, and we repeat it, that chance is a word devoid of sense, which as well as all other unintelligible words, announces nothing but ignorance of actual causes. We have demonstrated that matter is not dead; that nature, essentially active and self-existent, has sufficient energy to produce all the beings which she contains—all the phenomena we behold. We have, throughout, made it evident that this cause is much more tangible, more easy of comprehension, than the inconceivable theory to which theology assigns these stupendous effects. We have represented, that the incomprehensibility of natural effects was not a sufficient reason for assigning to them a system still more incomprehensible than any of those of which, at least, we have a slight knowledge. In fine, if the incomprehensibility of a system does not authorize the denial of its existence, it is at least certain that the incompatibility of the attributes with which it is clothed, authorizes the assertion, that those which unite them cannot be any thing more than chimeras, of which the existence is impossible.

This granted, we shall be competent to fix the sense that ought to be attached to the name of atheist; which, notwithstanding, the theologians lavish on all those who deviate in any thing from their opinions. If, by atheist, be designated a man who denieth the existence of a power inherent in matter, without which we cannot conceive nature, and if it be to this power that the name of God is given, then there do not exist any atheists, and the word under which they are denominated would only announce fools. But if by atheists be understood men without enthusiasm; who are guided by experience; who follow the evidence of their senses; who see nothing in nature but what they actually find to have existence, or that which they are capacitated to know; who neither do, nor can perceive any thing but matter essentially active, moveable, diversely combined, in the full enjoyment of various properties, capable of producing all the beings who display themselves to our visual faculties, if by atheists be understood natural philosophers, who are convinced that without recurring to chimerical causes, they can explain every thing, simply by the laws of motion; by the relation subsisting between beings; by their affinities; by their analogies; by their aptitude to attraction; by their repulsive powers; by their proportions; by their combinations; by their decomposition: if by atheists be meant these persons who do not understand what *Pneumatology* is, who do not perceive the necessity of spiritualizing, or of rendering incomprehensible, those corporeal, sensible, natural causes, which they see act uniformly; who do not find it requisite to separate the motive- power from the universe; who do not see, that to ascribe this power to an immaterial substance, to that whose essence is from thenceforth totally inconceivable, is a means of becoming more familiar with it: if by atheists are to be pourtrayed those men who ingenuously admit that their mind can neither receive nor reconcile the union of the negative attributes and the theological abstractions, with the human and moral qualities which are given to the Divinity; or those men who pretend that from such an incompatible alliance, there could only result an imaginary being; seeing that a pure spirit is destitute of the organs necessary to exercise the qualities, to give play to the faculties of human nature: if by atheists are described those men who reject systems, whose odious and discrepant qualities are solely calculated to disturb the human species—to plunge it into very prejudicial follies: if, I repeat it, thinkers of this description are those who are called atheists, it is not possible to doubt their existence; and their number would be considerable, if the light of sound natural philosophy was more generally diffused; if the torch of reason burnt more distinctly; or if it was not obscured by the theological bushel: from thence, however, they would be considered neither as irrational; nor as furious beings, but as men devoid of prejudice, of whose opinions, or if they prefer it, whose ignorance, would be much more useful to the human race, than those ideal sciences, those vain hypotheses, which for so many ages have been the actual causes of all man's tribulation.

Doctor Cudworth, in his *Intellectual System*, reckons four species of atheists among the ancients.

First.—The disciples of Anaximander, called *Hylopathians*, who attributed every thing to matter destitute of feeling. His doctrine was, that men were born of earth united with water, and vivified by the beams of the sun; his crime seems to have been, that he made the first geographical maps and sun-dials; declared the earth moveable and of a cylindrical form.

Secondly.—The *Atomists*, or the disciples of Democritus, who attribute every thing, to the concurrence of atoms. His crime was, having first taught that the milky way was occasioned by the confused light from a multitude of stars.

Thirdly.—The *Stoics*, or the disciples of Zeno, who admitted a blind nature acting after certain laws. His crime appears to be, that he practised virtue with unwearied perseverance, and taught that this quality alone would render mankind happy.

Fourthly.—The *Hylozoists*, or the disciples of Strato, who attributed life to matter. His crime consisted in being one of the most acute natural philosophers of his day, enjoying high favour with Ptolemy Philadelphus, an intelligent prince, whose preceptor be was.

If, however, by atheists, are meant those men, who are obliged to avow, that they have not one idea of the system they adore, or which they announce to others; who cannot give any satisfactory account, either of the nature or of the essence of their immaterial substances; who can never agree amongst themselves on the proofs which they adduce in support of their System; on the qualities or on the modes of action of their incorporeities, which by dint of negations they render a mere nothing; who either prostrate themselves, or cause others to bow down, before the absurd fictions of their own delirium: if, I say, by atheists, be denominated men of this stamp, we shall be under the necessity of allowing, that the world is filled with them: we shall even be obliged to place in this number some of the most active theologians, who are unceasingly reasoning upon that Which they do not understand; who are eternally disputing upon points which they cannot demonstrate; who by their contradictions very efficaciously undermine their own systems; who annihilate all their own assertions of perfection, by the numberless imperfections with which they clothe them; who rebel against their gods by the atrocious character under which they depict them. In short, we shall be able to consider as true atheists, those credulous, weak persons, who upon hearsay and from tradition, bend the knee before idols, of whom they have no other ideas, than those which are furnished them by their spiritual guides, who themselves acknowledge that they comprehend nothing about the matter.

What has been said amply proves that the theologians themselves have not always known the sense they could affix to the word atheist; they have vaguely attacked, in an indistinct manner, calumniated with it, those persons whose sentiments and principles were opposed to their own. Indeed, we find that these sublime professors, always infatuated with their own particular opinions, have frequently been extremely lavish in their accusations of atheism, against all those whom they felt a desire to injure; whose characters it was their pleasure to paint in unfavourable colours; whose doctrines they wished to blacken; whose systems they sought to render odious: they were certain of alarming the illiterate, of rousing the antipathies of the silly, by a loose imputation, or by a word, to which ignorance attaches the idea of horror, merely because it is unacquainted with its true sense. In consequence of this policy, it has been no uncommon spectacle to see the partizans of the same sect, the adorers of the same gods, reciprocally treat each other as atheists, in the fervour of their theological quarrels; to be an atheist, in this sense, is not to have, in every point, exactly the same opinions as those with whom we dispute, either on superstitious or religious subjects. In all times the uninformed have considered those as atheists, who did not think upon the Divinity precisely in the same manner as the guides whom they were accustomed to follow. Socrates, the adorer of a unique God, was no more than an atheist in the eyes of the Athenian people.

Still more, as we have already observed, those persons have frequently been accused of atheism, who have taken the greatest pains to establish the existence of the gods, but who have not produced satisfactory proofs: when their enemies wished to take advantage of them, it was easy to make them pass for atheists, who had wickedly betrayed their cause, by defending it too feebly. The theologians have frequently been very highly incensed against those who believed they had discovered the most forcible proof of the existence of their gods, because they were obliged to discover that their adversaries could make very contrary inductions from their propositions; they did not perceive that it was next to impossible not to lay themselves open to attack, in establishing principles visibly founded upon that which each man sees variously. Thus Paschal says, "I have examined if this God, of whom all the world speaks, might not have left some marks of himself. I look every where, and every where I see nothing but obscurity. Nature offers one nothing, that may not be a matter of doubt and inquietude. If I saw nothing in nature which indicated a

Divinity, I should determine with myself, to believe nothing about it. If every where I saw the sign of a creator, I should repose myself in peace, in the belief of one. But seeing too much to deny, and too little to assure me of his existence, I am in a situation that I lament, and in which I have an hundred times wished, that if a God doth sustain nature, he would give unequivocal marks of it, and that if the signs which he hath given be deceitful, that he would suppress them entirely; that he said all or nothing, to the end that I might see which side I ought to follow."

In a word, those who have most vigorously taken up the cause of the theological systems, have been taxed with atheism and irreligion; the most zealous partizans have been looked upon as deserters, have been contemplated as traitors; the most orthodox theologians have not been able to guarantee themselves from this reproach; they have mutually bespatered each other; prodigally lavished, with malignant reciprocity, the most abusive terms: nearly all have, without doubt, merited these invectives, if in the term atheist be included those men who have not any idea of their various systems, that does not destroy itself, whenever they are willing to submit it to the touchstone of reason. From whence we may conclude, without subjecting ourselves to the reproach of being hasty, that error will not stand the test of investigation; that it will not pass the ordeal of comparison; that it is in its hues a perfect chamelion; that consequently it can never do more than lead to the most absurd deductions: that the most ingenious systems, when they have their foundations in hallucination, crumble like dust under the rude band of the assayer; that the most sublimated doctrines, when they lack the substantive quality of rectitude, evaporate under the scrutiny of the sturdy examiner, who tries them in the crucible; that it is not by levelling abusive language against those who investigate sophisticated theories, they will either be purged of their absurdities, acquire solidity, or find an establishment to give them perpetuity; that moral obliquities, can never be made rectilinear by the mere application of unintelligible terms, or by the inconsiderate jumble of discrepant properties, however gaudy the assemblage: in short, that the only criterion of truth is, *that it is ever consistent with itself.*

CHAP. XII.
Is what is termed Atheism compatible with Morality?

After having proved the existence of those whom the superstitious bigot, the heated theologian, the inconsequent theist, calls *atheists*, let us return to the calumnies which are so profusely showered upon them by the deicolists. According to Abady, in his *Treatise on the Truth of the Christian Religion*, "an atheist cannot be virtuous: to him virtue is only a chimera; probity no more than a vain scruple; honesty nothing but foolishness;—he knoweth no other law than his interest: where this sentiment prevails, conscience is only a prejudice; the law of nature only an illusion; right no more than an error; benevolence hath no longer any foundation; the bonds of society are loosened; the ties of fidelity are removed; friend is ready to betray friend; the citizen to deliver up his country; the son to assassinate his father, in order to enjoy his inheritance, whenever they shall find occasion, and that authority or silence shall shield them from the arm of the secular power, which alone is to be feared. The most inviolable rights, and most sacred laws, must no longer be considered, except as dreams and visions." Such, perhaps, would be the conduct, not of a feeling, thinking, reflecting being, susceptible of reason; but of a ferocious brute, of an irrational wretch, who should not have any idea of the natural relations which subsist between beings, reciprocally necessary to each other's happiness. Can it actually be supposed, that a man capable of experience, furnished with the faintest glimmerings of sound sense, would lend himself to the conduct which is here ascribed to the atheist; that is to say, to a man who is conversant with the evidence of facts; who ardently seeks after truth; who is sufficiently susceptible of reflection, to undeceive himself by reasoning upon those prejudices which every one strives to shew him as important; which all voices endeavour to announce to him as sacred? Can it, I repeat, be supposed, that any enlightened, any polished society, contains a citizen so completely blind, not to acknowledge his most natural duties; so very absurd, not to admit his dearest interests; so completely besotted not to perceive the danger he incurs in incessantly disturbing his fellow creatures; or in following no other rule, than his momentary appetites? Is not every human being who reasons in the least possible manner, obliged to feel that society is advantageous to him; that he hath need of assistance; that the esteem of his fellows is necessary to his own individual happiness; provoked, that he has every thing to fear from the wrath of his associates; that the laws menace whoever shall dare to infringe them? Every man who has received a virtuous education, who has in his infancy experienced the tender cares of a parent; who has in consequence tasted the sweets of friendship; who has received kindness; who knows the worth of benevolence; who sets a just value upon equity; who feels the pleasure which the affection of our fellow creatures procures for us; who endures the inconveniences which result from their aversion who smarts under the sting which is inflicted by their scorn, is obliged to tremble at losing, by his measures, such manifest advantages—at incurring such, imminent danger. Will not the hatred of others, the fear of punishment, his own contempt of himself, disturb his repose every time that, turning, inwardly upon his own conduct, he shall contemplate it under the same perspective as does his neighbour? Is there then no remorse but for those who believe in incomprehensible systems? Is the idea that we are tinder the eye of beings of whom we have but vague notions, more forcible than the thought that we are viewed by our fellow men; than the fear of being detected by ourselves; than the dread of exposure; than the cruel necessity of becoming despicable in our own eyes; than the wretched alternative, to be constrained to blush guiltily, when we reflect on our wild career, and the sentiments which it must infallibly inspire?

This granted, we shall reply deliberately to this Abady, that an atheist is a man who understands nature, who studies her laws; who knows his own nature; who feels what it imposes upon him. An atheist hath experience; this experience proves to him every moment that vice can injure him; that his most concealed faults, his most secret dispositions, may be detected—may display his character in open day; this experience proves to him that society is useful to his happiness; that his interest authoritatively demands he should attach himself to the country that protects him, which enables him to enjoy in security the benefits of nature; every thing shews him that in order to be happy he must make himself beloved; that his parent is for him the most certain of friends; that ingratitude would remove him from his benefactor; that justice is necessary to the maintenance of every association; that no man, whatever way he his power, can be content with himself, when he knows he is an object of public hatred. He who has maturely reflected upon himself, upon his own nature, upon that of his associates, upon his own wants, upon the means of procuring them, cannot prevent himself from becoming acquainted with his duties—from discovering the obligations he owes to himself, as well as those which he owes to others; from thence he has morality, he has actual motives to confirm himself to its dictates; he is obliged to feel, that these duties are imperious: if his reason be not disturbed by blind passions, if his mind be not contaminated by vicious habits, he will find that virtue is the surest road to felicity. The atheists, as they are styled, or the fatalists, build their system upon necessity: thus, their moral speculations, founded upon the nature of things, are at least much more permanent, much more invariable, than those which only rest upon systems that alter their aspect according to the various dispositions of their adherents—in conformity with the wayward passions of those who contemplate, them. The essence of things, and the immutable laws of nature, are not subject to fluctuate; it is imperative with the atheist, as he is facetiously called by the theologian, to call whatever injures himself either vice or folly; to designate that which injures others, crime; to describe all that is advantageous to society, every thing which contributes to its permanent happiness, virtue.

It will be obvious, then, that the principles of the miscalled atheist are much less liable to be shaken, than those of the enthusiast, who shall have studied a baby from his earliest Infancy; who should have devoted not only his days, but his nights, to gleaning the scanty portion of actual information that he scatters through his volumes; they will have a much more substantive foundation than those of the theologian, who shall construct his morality upon the harlequin scenery of systems that so frequently change, even in his own distempered brain. If the atheist, as they please to call those who differ in opinion with themselves, objects to the correctness, of—their systems, he cannot deny his own existence, nor that of beings similar to himself, by whom he is surrounded; he cannot doubt the reciprocity of the relations that subsist between them; he cannot question the duties which spring out of these relations; Pyrrhonism, then, cannot enter his mind upon the, actual principles of morality; which is nothing more than the science of the relations of beings living together in society.

If, however, satisfied with a barren, speculative knowledge of his duties, the atheist of the theologian should not apply them in his conduct—if, hurried along by the current of his ungovernable passions— if, borne forward by criminal habits—if, abandoned to shameful vices- if, possessing a vicious temperament, which he has not been sedulous to correct—if, lending himself to the stream of outrageous desires, he appears to forget his moral obligations, it by no means follows, either that he hath no principles, or that his principles are false: it can only be concluded from such conduct, that in the intoxication of his passions, in the delirium of his habits, in the confusion of his reason, he does not give activity to doctrines grounded upon truth; that he forgets to give currency to ascertained principles; that he may follow those propensities which lead him astray. In this, indeed, he will have dreadfully descended to the miserable level of the theologian, but he will nevertheless find him the partner of his folly—the partaker of his insanity—the companion of his crime.

Nothing is, perhaps, more common among men, than a very marked discrepancy between the mind and the heart; that is to say, between the temperament, the passions, the habits the caprices, the imagination, and the judgment, assisted by reflection. Nothing is, in fact, more rare, than to find these harmoniously running upon all fours with each other; it is, however, only when they do, that we see speculation influence practice. The most certain virtues are those which are founded upon the temperament of man. Indeed, do we not every day behold mortals in contradiction with themselves? Does not their more sober judgment unceasingly condemn the extravagancies to which their undisciplined passions deliver them up? In short, doth not every thing prove to us hourly, that men, with the very best theory, have sometimes the very worst practice; that others with the most vicious theory, frequently adopt the most amiable line of conduct? In the blindest systems, in the most atrocious superstitions, in those which are most contrary to reason, we meet with virtuous men, the mildness of whose character, the sensibility of whose hearts, the excellence of whose temperament, re conducts them to humanity, makes them fall back upon the laws of nature, in despite of their furious theories. Among the adorers of the most cruel, vindictive, jealous gods, are found peaceable, souls, who are enemies to persecution; who set their faces against violence; who are decidedly opposed to cruelty: among the disciples of a God filled with mercy, abounding in clemency, are seen barbarous monsters; inhuman cannibals: nevertheless, both the one and the other acknowledge, that their gods ought to serve them for a model. Wherefore, then, do they not in all things conform themselves? It is because the most wicked systems cannot always corrupt a virtuous soul; that those which are most bland, most gentle in their precepts, cannot always restrain hearts driven along by the impetuosity of vice. The organization will, perhaps, be always more potential than either superstition or religion. Present objects, momentary interests, rooted habits, public opinion, have much more efficacy than unintelligible theories, than imaginary systems, which themselves depend upon the organic structure of the human frame.

The point in question then is, to examine if the principles of the atheist, as he is erroneously called, be true, and not whether his conduct be commendable? An atheist, having an excellent theory, founded upon nature, grafted upon experience, constructed upon reason, who delivers himself up to excesses, dangerous to himself, injurious to society, is, without doubt, an inconsistent man. But he is not more to be feared than a superstitious bigot; than a zealous enthusiast; or than even a religious man who, believing in a good, confiding in an equitable, relying on a perfect God, does not scruple to commit the most frightful devastations in his name. An atheistical tyrant would assuredly not be more to be dreaded than a fanatical despot. An incredulous philosopher, however, is not so mischievous a being as an enthusiastic priest, who either fans the flame of discord among his fellow subjects, or rises in rebellion against his legitimate monarch. Would, then, an atheist clothed with power, be equally dangerous as a persecuting priest-ridden king; as a savage inquisitor; as a whimsical devotee; or, as a morose bigot? These are assuredly more numerous in the world than atheists, as they are ludicrously termed, whose opinions, or whose vices are far from being in a condition to have an influence upon society; which is ever too much hoodwinked by the priest, too much blinded by prejudice, too much the slave of superstition, to be disposed to give them a patient hearing.

An intemperate, voluptuous atheist, is not more dangerous to society than a superstitions bigot, who knows how to connect licentiousness, punic faith, ingratitude, libertinism, corruption of morals, with his theological notions. Can it, however, be ingeniously imagined, that a man, because he is falsely termed an atheist, or because he does not subscribe to the vengeance of the most contradictory systems, will therefore he a profligate debaucheé, malicious, and persecuting; that he will corrupt the wife of his friend; will turn his own wife adrift; will consume both his time and his money in the most frivolous gratifications; will be the slave to the most childish amusements; the companion of the most dissolute men; that he will discard all his old friends; that he will select his bosom confidents from the brazen betrayers of their native land—from among the hoary despoilers of connubial happiness—from out of the ranks of veteran gamblers; that he will either break into his neighbour's dwelling, or cut his throat; in short, that he will lend himself to all those excesses, the most injurious to society, the most prejudicial to himself, the most deserving public castigation? The blemishes of an atheist, then, as the theologian styles him, have not any thing more extraordinary in them than those of the superstitious man; they possess nothing with which his doctrine can he fairly reproached. A tyrant, who should he incredulous, would not be a more incommodious scourge to his subjects, than a theological autocrat, who should wield his sceptre to the misery of his people. Would the nation of the latter feel more happy, from the mere circumstance that the tyger who governed it believed in the most abstract systems, heaped the most sumptuous presents on the priests, and humiliated himself at their shrine? At least it must be acknowledged, according to the shewing of the theologian himself, that under the dominion of the atheist, a nation would not have to apprehend superstitious vexations; to dread persecutions for opinion; to fear proscriptions for ill-digested systems; neither would it witness those strange outrages that have sometimes been Committed for the interests of heaven, even under the mildest monarchs. If it was the victim to the turbulent passions of an unbelieving prince, the sacrifice to the folly of a sovereign who should be an infidel, it would not, at least, suffer from his blind infatuation, for theological systems which he does not understand; nor from his fanatical zeal, which of all the passions that infest monarchs, is ever the most destructive, always the most dangerous. An atheistical tyrant, who should persecute for opinions, would be a man not consistent with his own principles; he could not exist; he would not, indeed, according to the theologian, be an atheist at most, he would only furnish one more example, that mortals much more frequently follow the blind impulse of their passions, the more immediate stimulus of their interest, the irresistible torrent of their temperament, than their speculations, however grave, however wise. It is, at least, evident, that an atheist has one pretext less than a credulous prince, for exercising his natural wickedness.

Indeed, if men condescended to examine things coolly, they would find that on this earth the name of God is but too frequently made use of as a motive to indulge the worst of human passions. Ambition, imposture, and tyranny, have often formed a league to avail themselves of its influence, to the end that they might blind the people, and bend them beneath a galling yoke: the monarch sometimes employs it to give a divine lustre to his person—the sanction of heaven to his rights—the confidence of its votaries to his most unjust, most extravagant whims. The priest frequently uses it to give currency to his pretensions, to the end that he may with impunity gratify his avarice, minister to his pride, secure his independence. The vindictive, enraged, superstitious being, introduces the cause of his gods, that he may give free scope to his fury, which he qualifies with zeal. In short, superstition becomes dangerous, because it justifies those passions, lends legitimacy to those crimes, holds forth as commendable those excesses, of which it does not fail to gather the fruit: according to its ministers, every thing is permitted to revenge the most high: thus the name of the Divinity is made use of to authorize the most baneful actions, to palliate the most injurious transgressions. The atheist, as he is called, when he commits crimes, cannot, at least, pretend that it is his gods who command them, or who clothe them with the mantle of their approval, this is the excuse the superstitious being offers for his perversity; the tyrant for his persecutions; the priest for his cruelty, and for his sedition; the fanatic for the ebullition of his boiling passions; the penitent for his inutility.

"They are not," says Bayle, "the general opinions of the mind, but the passions, which determine us to act." Atheism, as it is called, is a system which will not make a good man wicked but it may, perhaps, make a wicked man good. "Those," says the same author, "who embraced the sect of Epicurus, did not become debaucheés because they had adopted the doctrine of Epicurus; they only lent themselves to the system, then badly understood, because they were debaucheés." In the same manner, a perverse man may embrace atheism, because he will flatter himself, that this system will give full scope to his passions: he will nevertheless be deceived. Atheism, as it is called, if well understood, is founded upon nature and upon reason, which never can, like superstition, either justify or expiate the crimes of the profligate.

From the diffusion of doctrines which make morality depend upon unintelligible, incomprehensible systems, that are proposed to man for a model, there has unquestionably resulted very great inconvenience. Corrupt souls, in discovering, how much each of these suppositions are erroneous or doubtful, give loose to the rein of their vices, and conclude there are not more substantive motives for acting well; they imagine that virtue, like these fragile systems, is merely chimerical; that there is not any cogent solid reason for practising it in this world. Nevertheless, it must be evident, that it is not as the disciples of any particular tenet, that we are bound to fulfil the duties of morality; it is as men, living together in society, as sensible beings seeking to secure to ourselves a happy existence, that we should feel the moral obligation. Whether these systems maintain their ground, or whether the do not, our duties will remain the same; our nature, if consulted, will incontestibly prove, that *vice is a decided evil, that virtue is an actual, a substantial good.*

If, then, there be found atheists who have denied the distinction of good and evil, or who have dared to strike at the foundations of morality; we ought to conclude, that upon this point they have reasoned badly; that they have neither been acquainted with the nature of man, nor known the true source of his duties; that they have falsely imagined that ethics, as well as theology, was only an ideal science; that the fleeting systems once destroyed, there no longer remained any bonds to connect mortals. Nevertheless, the slightest reflection would have incontestibly proved, that morality is founded upon immutable relations subsisting between sensible, intelligent, sociable beings; that without virtue, no society can maintain itself; that without putting the curb on his desires, no mortal can conserve himself: man is constrained from his nature to love virtue, to dread crime, by the same necessity that obliges him to seek happiness, and fly from sorrow: thus nature compels him to place a distinction between those objects which please, and those objects Which injure him. Ask a man, who is sufficiently irrational to deny the difference between virtue and vice, if it would be indifferent to him to be beaten, robbed, calumniated, treated with ingratitude, dishonoured by his wife, insulted by his children, betrayed by his friend? His answer will prove to you, that whatever he may say, he discriminates the actions of mankind; that the distinction between good and evil, does not depend either upon the conventions of men, or upon the ideas which they may have of particular systems; upon the punishments or upon the recompenses which attend mortals in a future existence.

On the contrary, an atheist, as he is denominated, who should reason with justness, would feel himself more interested than another in practising those virtues to which he finds his happiness attached in this world. If his views do not extend themselves beyond the limits of his present existence, he must, at least, desire to see his days roll on in happiness and in peace. Every man, who during the calm of his passions, falls back upon himself, will feel that his interest invites him to his own preservation; that his felicity rigorously demands he should take the necessary means to enjoy life peaceably that it becomes an imperative duty to himself to keep his actual abode free from alarm; his mind untainted by remorse. Man oweth something to man, not merely because he would offend any particular system, if he was to injure his fellow creature; but because in doing him an injury he would offend a man; would violate the laws of equity; in the maintenance of which every human being finds himself interested.

We every day see persons who are possessed of great talents, who have very extensive knowledge, who enjoy very keen penetration, join to these advantages a very corrupt heart; who lend, themselves to the most hideous vices: their opinions may be true in some respects, false in a great many others; their principles may be just, but their inductions are frequently defective; very often precipitate. A man may embrace sufficient knowledge to detect some of his errors, yet command too little energy to divest himself of his vicious propensities. Man is a being whose character depends upon his organization, modified by habit— upon his temperament, regulated by education—upon his propensities, marshalled by example—upon his; passions, guided by his government; in short, he is only what transitory or permanent circumstances make him: his superstitious ideas are obliged to yield to this temperament; his imaginary systems feel a necessity to accommodate themselves to his propensities; his theories give way to his interests. If the system which constitutes man an atheist in the eyes of this theologic friend, does not remove him from the vices with which he was anteriorly tainted, neither does it tincture him with any new ones; whereas, superstition furnishes its disciples with a thousand pretexts for committing evil without repugnance; induces them even to applaud themselves for the commission of crime. Atheism, at least, leaves men such as they are; it will neither increase a man's intemperance, nor add to his debaucheries, it will not render him more cruel than his temperament before invited him to be: whereas superstition either lacks the rein to the most terrible passions, gives loose to the most abominable suggestions, or else procures easy expiations for the most dishonourable vices. "Atheism," says Chancellor Bacon, "leaves to man reason, philosophy, natural piety, laws, reputation, and every thing that can serve to conduct him to virtue; but superstition destroys all these things, and erects itself into a tyranny over the understandings of men: this is the reason why atheism never disturbs the government, but renders man more clear-sighted, as seeing nothing beyond the bounds of this life." The same author adds, "that the times in which men have turned towards atheism, have been the most tranquil; whereas superstition has always inflamed their minds, and carried them on to the greatest disorders; because it infatuates the people with novelties, which wrest from and carry with them all the authority of government."

Men, habituated to meditate, accustomed to make study a pleasure, are not commonly dangerous citizens: whatever may be their speculations, they never produce sudden revolutions upon the earth. The winds of the people, at all times susceptible to be inflamed by the marvellous, their dormant passions liable to be aroused by enthusiasm, obstinately resist the light of simple truths; never heat themselves for systems that demand a long train of reflection—that require the depth of the most acute reasoning. The system of atheism, as the priests choose to denominate it, can only be the result of long meditation; the fruit of connected study; the produce of an imagination cooled by experience: it is the child of reason. The peaceable Epicurus never disturbed Greece; his philosophy was publicly taught in Athens during many centuries; he was in incredible favour with his countrymen, who caused statues to be erected to him; he had a prodigious number of friends, and his school subsisted for a very long period. Cicero, although a decided enemy to the Epicureans, gives a brilliant testimony to the probity both of Epicurus and his disciples, who were remarkable for the inviolable friendship they bore each other. In the time of Marcus Aurelius, there was at Athens a public professor of the philosophy of Epicurus, paid by that emperor, who was himself a stoic. Hobbes did not cause blood to flow in England, although in his time, religious fanaticism made a king perish on the scaffold. The poem of Lucretius caused no civil wars in Rome; the writings of Spinosa did not excite the same troubles in Holland as the disputes of Gomar and D'Arminius. In short, we can defy the enemies to human reason to cite a single example, which proves in a decisive manner that opinions purely philosophical, or directly contrary to superstition, have ever excited disturbances in the state. Tumults have generally arisen from theological notions, because both princes and people have always foolishly believed they ought to take a part in them. There is nothing so dangerous as that empty philosophy, which the theologians have combined with their systems. It is to philosophy, corrupted by priests, that it peculiarly belongs to blow up the embers of discord; to invite the people to rebellion; to drench the earth with human blood. There is, perhaps, no theological question, which has not been the source of immense mischief to man; whilst all the writings of those denominated atheists, whether ancient or modern, have never caused any evil but to their authors; whom dominant imposture has frequently immolated at his deceptive shrine.

The principles of atheism are not formed for the mass of the people, who are commonly under the tutelage of their priests; they are not calculated for those frivolous capacities, not suited to those dissipated minds, who fill society with their vices, who hourly afford evidence of their own inutility; they will not gratify the ambitious; neither are they adapted to intriguers, nor fitted for those restless beings who find their immediate interest in disturbing the harmony of the social compact: much less are they made for a great number of persons, who, enlightened in other respects, have not sufficient courage to divorce themselves from the received prejudices.

So many causes unite themselves to confirm man in those errors which he draws in with his mother's milk, that every step that removes him from these endeared fallacies, costs him uncommon pain. Those persons who are most enlightened, frequently cling on some side to the general prepossession. By giving up these revered ideas, we feel ourselves, as it were, isolated in society: whenever we stand alone in our opinions, we no longer seem to speak the language of our associates; we are apt to fancy ourselves placed on a barren, desert island, in sight of a populous, fruitful country, which we can never reach: it therefore requires great courage to adopt a mode of thinking that has but few approvers. In those countries where human knowledge has made some progress; where, besides, a certain freedom of thinking is enjoyed, may easily be found a great number of deicolists, theists, or incredulous beings, who, contented with having trampled under foot the grosser prejudices of the illiterate, have not dared to go back to the source— to cite the more subtle systems before the tribunal of reason. If these thinkers did not stop on the road, reflection would quickly prove to them that those systems which they have not the fortitude to examine, are equally injurious to sound ratiocination, fully as revolting to good sense, quite as repugnant to the evidence of experience, as any of those doctrines, mysteries, fables, or superstitious customs, of which they have already acknowledged the futility; they would feel, as we have already proved, that all these things are nothing more than the necessary consequences of those primitive errors which man has indulged for so many ages in succession; that in admitting these errors, they no longer have any rational cause to reject the deductions which the imagination has drawn from them. A little attention would distinctly shew them, that it is precisely these errors that are the true cause of all the evils of society; that those endless disputes, those sanguinary quarrels, to which superstition and the spirit of party every instant give birth, are the inevitable effects of the importance they attach to errors which possess all the means of distraction, that scarcely ever fail to put the mind of man into a state of combustion. In short, nothing is more easy than to convince ourselves that imaginary systems, not reducible to comprehension, which are always painted under terrific aspects, must act upon the imagination in a very lively manner, must sooner or later produce disputes—engender enthusiasm—give birth to fanaticism—end in delirium.

Many persons acknowledge, that the extravagances to which superstition lends activity, are real evils; many complain of the abuse of superstition, but there are very few who feel that this abuse, together with the evils, are the necessary consequences of the fundamental principles of all superstition; which are founded upon the most grievous notions, which rest themselves on the most tormenting opinions. We daily see persons undeceived upon superstitious ideas, who nevertheless pretend that this superstition "is salutary for the people;" that without its supernatural magic, they could not he kept within due bounds; in other words, could not be made the voluntary slaves of the priest. But, to reason thus, is it not to say, poison is beneficial to mankind, that therefore it is proper to poison them, to prevent them from making an improper use of their power? Is it not in fact to pretend it is advantageous to render them absurd; that it is a profitable course to make them extravagant; wholesome to give them an irrational bias; that they have need of hobgoblins to blind them; require the most incomprehensible systems to make them giddy; that it is imperative to submit them either to impostors or to fanatics, who will avail themselves of their follies to disturb the repose of the world? Again, is it an ascertained fact, does experience warrant the conclusion, that superstition has a useful influence over the morals of the people? It appears much more evident, is much better borne out by observation, falls more in with the evidence of the senses, that it enslaves them without rendering them better; that it constitutes an herd of ignorant beings, whom panic terrors keep under the yoke of their task-masters; whom their useless fears render the wretched instruments of towering ambition—of rapacious tyrants; of the subtle craft of designing priests: that it forms stupid slaves, who are acquainted with no other virtue, save a blind submission to the most futile customs, to which they attach a much more substantive value than to the actual virtues springing out of the duties of morality; or issuing from the social compact which has never been made known to them. If by any chance, superstition does restrain some few individuals, it has no effect on the greater number, who suffer themselves to be hurried along by the epidemical vices with which they are infected: they are placed by it upon the stream of corruption, and the tide either sweeps them away, or else, swelling the waters, breaks through its feeble mounds, and involves the whole in one undistinguished mass of ruin. It is in those countries where superstition has the greatest power, that will always be found the least morality. Virtue is incompatible with ignorance; it cannot coalesce with superstition; it cannot exist with slavery: slaves can only be kept in subordination by the fear of punishment; ignorant children are for a moment intimidated by imaginary terrors. But freemen, the children of truth, have no fears but of themselves; are neither to be lulled into submission by visionary duties, nor coerced by fanciful systems; they yield ready obedience to the evident demonstrations of virtue; are the faithful, the invulnerable supporters of solid systems; cling with ardour to the dictates of reason; form impenetrable ramparts round their legitimate sovereigns; and fix their thrones on an immoveable basis, unknown to the theologian; that cannot be touched with unhallowed hands; whose duration will be commensurate with the existence of time itself. To form freemen, however, to have virtuous citizens, it is necessary to enlighten them; it is incumbent to exhibit truth to them; it is imperative to reason with them; it is indispensable to make them feel their interests; it is paramount to learn them to respect themselves; they must be instructed to fear shame; they must be excited to have a just idea of honour; they must be made familiar with the value of virtue, they must be shewn substantive motives for following its lessons. How can these happy effects ever he expected from the polluted fountains of superstition, whose waters do nothing more than degrade mankind? Or how are they to be obtained from the ponderous, bulky yoke of tyranny, which proposes nothing more to itself, than to vanquish them by dividing them; to keep them in the most abject condition by means of lascivious vices, and the most detestable crimes?

The false idea, which so many persons have of the utility of superstition, which they, at least, judge to be calculated to restrain the licentiousness of the illiterate, arise from the fatal prejudice that it is a useful error; that truth may be dangerous. This principle has complete efficacy to eternize the sorrows of the earth: whoever shall have the requisite courage to examine these things, will without hesitation acknowledge, that all the miseries of the human race are to be ascribed to his errors; that of these, superstitious error must he the most prejudicial, from the importance which is usually attached to it; from the haughtiness with which it inspires sovereigns; from the worthless condition which it prescribes to subjects; from the phrenzy which it excites among the vulgar. We shall, therefore, be obliged to conclude, that the superstitious errors of man, rendered sacred by time, are exactly those which for the permanent interest of mankind, for the well-being of society, for the security of the monarch himself, demand the most complete destruction; that it is principally to their annihilation, the efforts of a sound philosophy ought to be directed. It is not to be feared, that this attempt will produce either disorders or revolutions: the more freedom shall accompany the voice of truth, the more convincing it will appear; although the more simple it shall be, the less it will influence men, who are only smitten with the marvellous; even those individuals who most sedulously seek after truth, who pursue it with the greatest ardour, have frequently an irresistible inclination, that urges them on, and incessantly disposes them to reconcile error with its antipode. That great master of the art of thinking, who holds forth to his disciples such able advice, says, with abundant reason, "that there is nothing but a good and solid philosophy, which can, like another Hercules, exterminate those monsters called popular errors: it is that alone which can give freedom to the human mind."

Here is, unquestionably, the true reason why atheism, as it is called, of which hitherto the principles have not been sufficiently developed, appears to alarm even those persons who are the most destitute of prejudice. They find the interval too great between vulgar superstition and an absolute renunciation of it; they imagine they take a wise medium in compounding with error; they therefore reject the consequences, while they admit the principle; they preserve the shadow and throw away the substance, without foreseeing that, sooner or later, it must, by its obstetric art, usher into the world, one after another, the same follies which now fill the heads of bewildered human beings, lost in the labyrinths of incomprehensible systems. The major part of the incredulous, the greater number of reformers, do no more than prune a cankered tree, to whose root they dare not apply the axe; they do not perceive that this tree will in the end produce the same fruit. Theology, or superstition, will always be an heap of combustible matter: brooded in the imagination of mankind, it will always finish by causing the most terrible explosions. As long as the sacerdotal order shall have the privilege of infecting youth—of habituating their minds to tremble before unmeaning words—of alarming nations with the most terrific systems, so long will fanaticism be master of the human mind; imposture will, at its pleasure, cast the apple of discord among the members of the state. The most simple error, perpetually fed, unceasingly modified, continually exaggerated by the imagination of man, will by degrees assume a collossal figure, sufficiently powerful to upset every institution; amply competent to the overthrow of empires. Theism is a system at which the human mind cannot make a long sojourn; founded upon error, it will, sooner or later, degenerate into the most absurd, the most dangerous superstition.

Many incredulous beings, many theists, are to be met with in those countries where freedom of opinion reigns; that is to say, where the civil power has known how to balance superstition. But, above all, atheists as they are termed, will be found in those nations where, superstition, backed by the sovereign authority, most enforces the ponderosity of its yoke; most impresses the volume of its severity; imprudently abuses its unlimited power. Indeed, when in these kind of countries, science, talents, the seeds of reflection, are not entirely stifled, the greater part of the men who think, revolt at the crying abuses of superstition; are ashamed of its multifarious follies; are shocked at the corruption of its professors; scandalized at the tyranny of its priests: are struck with horror at those massive chains which it imposes on the credulous. Believing with great reason, that they can never remove themselves too far from its savage principles, the system that serves for the basis of such a creed, becomes as odious as the superstition itself; they feel that terrific systems can only be detailed by cruel ministers; these become detestable objects to every enlightened, to every honest mind, in which either the love of equity, or the sacred fire of freedom resides; to every one who is the advocate of humanity—the indignant spurner of tyranny. Oppression gives a spring to the soul; it obliges man to examine closely into the cause of his sorrows; misfortune is a powerful incentive, that turns the mind to the side of truth. How formidable a foe must not outraged reason be to falsehood? It at least throws it into confusion, when it tears away its mask; when it follows it into its last entrenchment; when it proves, beyond contradiction, that *nothing is so dastardly as delusion detected, or tyrannic power held at bay.*

CHAP. XIII.

Of the motives which lead to what is falsely called Atheism.—Can this System be dangerous?—Can it be embraced by the Illiterate?

The reflections, as well as the facts which have preceded, will furnish a reply to those who inquire what interest man has in not admitting unintelligible systems? The tyrannies, the persecutions, the numberless outrages committed under these systems; the stupidity, the slavery, into which their ministers almost every where plunge the people; the sanguinary disputes to which they give birth; the multitude of unhappy beings with which their fatal notions fill the world; are surely abundantly sufficient to create the most powerful, the most interesting motives, to determine all sensible men, who possess the faculty of thought, to examine into the authenticity of doctrines, which cause so many serious evils to the inhabitants of the earth.

A theist, very estimable for his talents, asks, "if there can be any other cause than an evil disposition, which can make men atheists?" I reply to him, yes, there are other causes. There is the desire, a very laudable one, of having a knowledge of interesting truths; there is the powerful interest of knowing what opinions we ought to hold upon the object which is announced to us as the most important; there is the fear of deceiving ourselves upon systems which are occupied with the opinions of mankind, which do not permit he should deceive himself respecting them with impunity. But when these motives, these causes, should not subsist, is not indignation, or if they will, an evil disposition, a legitimate cause, a good and powerful motive, for closely examining the pretensions, for searching into the rights of systems, in whose name so many crimes are perpetrated? Can any man who feels, who thinks, who has any elasticity in his soul, avoid being incensed against austere theories, which are visibly the pretext, undeniably the source, of all those evils, which on every side assail the human race? Are they not these fatal systems which are at once the cause and the ostensible reason of that iron yoke that oppresses mankind; of that wretched slavery in which he lives; of that blindness which hides from him his happiness; of that superstition, which disgraces him; of those irrational customs which torment him; of those sanguinary quarrels which divide him; of all the outrages which he experiences? Must not every breast in which humanity is not extinguished, irritate itself against that theoretical speculation, which in almost every country is made to speak the language of capricious, inhuman, irrational tyrants?

To motives so natural, so substantive, we shall join those which are still more urgent, more personal to every reflecting man: namely, that benumbing terror, that incommodious fear, which must be unceasingly nourished by the idea of capricious theories, which lay man open to the most severe penalties, even for secret thoughts, over which he himself has not any controul; that dreadful anxiety arising out of inexorable systems, against which he may sin without even his own knowledge; of morose doctrines, the measure of which he can never be certain of having fulfilled; which so far from being equitable, make all the obligations lay on one side; which with the most ample means of enforcing restraint, freely permit evil, although they hold out the most excruciating punishments for the delinquents? Does it not then, embrace the best interests of humanity, become of the highest importance to the welfare of mankind, of the greatest consequence to the quiet of his existence, to verify the correctness of these systems? Can any thing be more rational than to probe to the core these astounding theories? Is it possible that any thing can be more just, than to inquire rigorously into the rights, sedulously to examine the foundations, to try by every known test, the stability of doctrines, that involve in their operations, consequences of such colossal magnitude; that embrace, in their dictatory mandates, matters of such high behest; that implicate the eternal felicity of such countless millions in the vortex of their action? Would it not be the height of folly to wear such a tremendous yoke without inquiry; to let such overwhelming notions pass current unauthenticated; to permit the soi-disant ministers of these terrific systems to establish their power, without the most ample verification of their patents of mission? Would it, I repeat, be at all wonderful, if the frightful qualities of some of these systems, as exhibited by their official expounders, whom the accredited functionaries of similar systems, do not scruple, in the face of day, to brand as impostors, should induce rational beings to drive them entirely from their hearts; to shake off such an intolerable burden of misery; to even deny the existence of such appalling doctrines, of such petrifying systems, which the superstitious themselves, whilst paying them their homage, frequently curse from the very bottom of their hearts?

The theist, however, will not fail to tell the atheist, as he calls him, that these systems are not such as superstition paints them; that the colours are coarse, too glaring, ill assorted, the perspective out of all keeping; he will then exhibit his own picture, in which the tints are certainly blended with more mellowness, the colouring of a more pleasing hue, the whole more harmonious, but the distances equally indistinct: the atheist, in reply, will say, that superstition itself, with all the absurd prejudices, all the mischievous notions to which it gives birth, are only corollaries drawn from the fallacious ideas, from those obscure principles, which the deicolist himself indulges. That his own incomprehensible system authorizes the incomprehensible absurdities, the inconceivable mysteries, with which superstition abounds; that they flow consecutively from his own premises; that when once the mind of mortals is bewildered in the dark, inextricable mazes of an ill-directed imagination, it will incessantly multiply its chimeras. To assure the repose of mankind, fundamental errors must be annihilated; that he may understand his true relations, be acquainted with his imperative duties, primary delusions must be rectified; to procure him that serenity of soul, without which there can be no substantive happiness, original fallacies must be undermined. If the systems of the superstitious be revolting, if their theories be gloomy, if their dogmas are unintelligible, those of the theist will always be contradictory; will prove fatal, when he shall be disposed to meditate upon them; will become the source of illusions, with which, sooner or later, imposture will not omit to abuse his credulity. Nature alone, with the truths she discovers, is capable of lending to the human mind that firmness which falsehood will never be able to shake; to the human heart that self- possession, against which imposture will in vain direct its attacks.

Let us again reply to those who unceasingly repeat that the interest of the passions alone conduct man to what is termed atheism: that it is the dread of future punishment that determines corrupt individuals to make the most strenuous efforts to break up a system they have reason to dread. We shall, without hesitation, agree that it is the interest of man's passions which excites him to make inquiries; without interest, no man is tempted to seek; without passion, no man will seek vigorously. The question, then, to be examined, is, if the passions and interests, which determine some thinkers to dive into the stability or the systems held forth to their adoption, are or are not legitimate? These interests have, already been exposed, from which it has been proved, that every rational man finds in his inquietudes, in his fears, reasonable motives to ascertain, whether or not it be necessary to pass his life in perpetual dread; in never ceasing agonies? Will it be said, that an unhappy being, unjustly condemned to groan in chains, has not the right of being willing to render them asunder; to take some means to liberate himself from his prison; to adopt some plan to escape from those punishments, which every instant threaten him? Will it be pretended that his passion for liberty has no legitimate foundation, that he does an injury to the companions of his misery, in withdrawing himself from the shafts of tyrannical infliction; or in furnishing, them also with means to escape from its cruel strokes? Is, then, an incredulous man, any thing more than one who has taken flight from the general prison, in which despotic superstition detains nearly all mankind? Is not an atheist, as he is called, who writes, one who has broken his fetters, who supplies to those of his associates who have sufficient courage to follow him, the means of setting themselves free from the terrors that menace them? The priests unceasingly repeat that it is pride, vanity, the desire of distinguishing himself from the generality of mankind, that determines man to incredulity. In this they are like some of those wealthy mortals, who treat all those as insolent who refuse to cringe before them. Would not every rational man have a right to ask the priest, where is thy superiority in matters of reasoning? What motives can I have to submit my reason to thy delirium? On the other hand, way it not be said to the hierarchy, that it is interest which makes them priests; that it is interest which renders them theologians; that it is for the interest of their passions, to inflate their pride, to gratify their avarice, to minister to their ambition, &c. that they attach themselves to systems, of which they alone reap the benefits? Whatever it may be, the priesthood, contented with exercising their power over the illiterate, ought to permit those men who do think, to be excused from bending the knee before their vain, illusive idols.

We also agree, that frequently the corruption of morals, a life of debauchery, a licentiousness of conduct, even levity of mind, may conduct man to incredulity; but is it not possible to be a libertine, to be irreligious, to make a parade of incredulity, without being on that account an atheist? There is unquestionably a difference between those who are led to renounce belief in unintelligible systems by dint of reasoning, and those who reject or despise superstition, only because they look upon it as a melancholy object, or an incommodious restraint. Many persons, no doubt, renounce received prejudices, through vanity or upon hearsay; these pretended strong minds have not examined any thing for themselves; they act upon the authority of others, whom they suppose to have weighed things more maturely. This kind of incredulous beings, have not, then, any distinct ideas, any substantive opinions, and are but little capacitated to reason for themselves; they are indeed hardly in a state to follow the reasoning of others. They are irreligious in the same manner as the majority of mankind are superstitious, that is to say, by credulity like the people; or through interest like the priest. A voluptuary devoted to his appetites; a debaucheé drowned in drunkenness; an ambitious mortal given up to his own schemes of aggrandizement; an intriguer surrounded by his plots; a frivolous, dissipated mortal, absorbed by his gewgaws, addicted to his puerile pursuits, buried in his filthy enjoyments; a loose woman abandoned to her irregular desires; a choice spirit of the day: are these I say, personages, actually competent to form a sound judgment of superstition, which they have never examined? Are they in a condition to maturely weigh theories that require the utmost depth of thought? Have they the capabilities to feel the force of a subtle argument; to compass the whole of a system: to embrace the various ramifications of an extended doctrine? If some feeble scintillations occasionally break in upon the cimmerian darkness of their minds; if by any accident they discover some faint glimmerings of truth amidst the tumult of their passions; if occasionally a sudden calm, suspending, for a short season, the tempest of their contending vices, permits the bandeau of their unruly desires by which they are blinded, to drop for an instant from their hoodwinked eyes, these leave on them only evanescent traces; scarcely sooner received than obliterated. Corrupt men only attack the gods when they conceive them to be the enemies to their vile passions. Arrian says, "that when men imagine the gods are in opposition to their passions, they abuse them, and overturn their altars." The Chinese, I believe, do the same. The honest man makes war against systems which he finds are inimical to virtue—injurious to his own happiness—baneful to that of his fellow mortals—contradictory to the repose, fatal to the interests of the human species. The bolder, therefore, the sentiments of the honest atheist, the more strange his ideas, the more suspicious they appear to other men, the more strictly he ought to observe his own obligations; the more scrupulously he should perform his duties; especially if he be not desirous that his morals shall calumniate his system; which duly weighed, will make the necessity of sound ethics, the certitude of morality, felt in all its force; but which every species of superstition tends to render problematical, or to corrupt.

Whenever our will is moved by concealed and complicated motives, it is extremely difficult to decide what determines it; a wicked man may be conducted to incredulity or to scepticism by those motives which he dare not avow, even to himself; in believing he seeks after truth, he may form an illusion to his mind, only to follow the interest of his passions; the fear of an avenging system will perhaps determine him to deny their existence without examination; uniformly because he feels them incommodious. Nevertheless, the passions sometimes happen to be just; a great interest carries us on to examine things more minutely; it may frequently make a discovery of the truth, even to him who seeks after it the least, or who is only desirous to be lulled to sleep, who is only solicitous to deceive himself. It is the same with a perverse man who stumbles upon truth, as it is with him, who flying from an imaginary danger, should encounter in his road a dangerous serpent, which in his haste he should destroy; he does that by accident, without design, which a man, less disturbed in his mind, would have done with premeditated deliberation.

To judge properly of things, it is necessary to be disinterested; it is requisite to have an enlightened mind, to have connected ideas to compass a great system. It belongs, in fact, only to the honest man to examine the proofs of systems—to scrutinize the principles of superstition; it belongs only to the man acquainted with nature, conversant with her ways, to embrace with intelligence the cause of the SYSTEM OF NATURE. The wicked are incapable of judging with temper; the ignorant are inadequate to reason with accuracy; the honest, the virtuous, are alone competent judges in so weighty an affair. What do I say? Is not the virtuous man, from thence in a condition to ardently desire the existence of a system that remunerates the goodness of men? If he renounces those advantages, which his virtue confers upon him the right to hope, it is, undoubtedly, because he finds them imaginary. Indeed, every man who reflects will quickly perceive, that for one timid mortal, of whom these systems restrain the feeble passions, there are millions whose voice they cannot curb, of whom, on the contrary, they excite the fury; for one that they console, there are millions whom they affright, whom they afflict; whom they make unhappy: in short, he finds, that against one inconsistent enthusiast, which these systems, which are thought so excellent, render happy, they carry discord, carnage, wretchedness into vast countries; plunge whole nations into misery; deluge them with tears.

However this may be, do not let us inquire into motives which may determine a man to embrace a system; let us rather examine the system itself; let us convince ourselves of its rectitude; if we shall find that it is founded upon truth, we shall never, be able to esteem it dangerous. It is always falsehood that is injurious to man; if error be visibly the source of his sorrows, reason is the true remedy for them; this is the panacea that can alone carry consolation to his afflictions. Do not let us farther examine the conduct of a man who presents us with a system; his ideas, as we have already said, may be extremely sound, when even his actions are highly deserving of censure. If the system of atheism cannot make him perverse, who is not so by his temperament, it cannot render him good, who does not otherwise know the motives that should conduct him to virtue. At least we have proved, that the superstitious man, when he has strong passions, when he possesses a depraved heart, finds even in his creed a thousand pretexts more than the atheist, for injuring the human species. The atheist has not, at least, the mantle of zeal to cover his vengeance; he has not the command of his priest to palliate his transports; he has not the glory of his gods to countenance his fury; the atheist does not enjoy the faculty of expiating, at the expence of a sum of money, the transgressions of his life; of availing himself of certain ceremonies, by the aid of which he may atone for the outrages he may have committed against society; he has not the advantage of being able to reconcile himself with heaven, by some easy custom; to quiet the remorse of his disturbed conscience, by an attention to outward forms: if crime has not deadened every feeling of his heart, he is obliged continually to carry within himself an inexorable judge, who unceasingly reproaches him for his odious conduct; who forces him to blush for his own folly; who compels him to hate himself; who imperiously obliges him to fear examination, to dread the resentment of others. The superstitious man, if he be wicked, gives himself up to crime, which is followed by remorse; but his superstition quickly furnishes him with the means a getting rid of it; his life is generally no more than a long series of error and grief, of sin and expiation, following each other in alternate succession; still more, he frequently, as we have seen, perpetrates crimes of greater magnitude, in order to wash away the first. Destitute of any permanent ideas on morality, he accustoms himself to look upon nothing as criminal, but that which the ministers, the official expounders of his system, forbid him to commit: he considers actions of the blackest dye as virtues, or as the means of effacing those transgressions, which are frequently held out to him as faithfully executing the duties of his creed. It is thus we have seen fanatics expiate their adulteries by the most atrocious persecutions; cleanse their souls from infamy by the most unrelenting cruelty; make atonement for unjust wars by the foulest means; qualify their usurpations by outraging every principle of virtue; in order to wash away their iniquities, bathe themselves in the blood of those superstitious victims, whose infatuation made them martyrs.

An atheist, as he is falsely called, if he has reasoned justly, if he has consulted nature, hath principles more determinate, more humane, than the superstitious; his system, whether gloomy or enthusiastic, always conducts the latter either to folly or cruelty; the imagination of the former will never be intoxicated to that degree, to make him believe that violence, injustice, persecution, or assassination are either virtuous or legitimate actions. We every day see that superstition, or the cause of heaven, as it is called, hoodwinks even those persons who on every other occasion are humane, equitable, and rational; so much so, that they make it a paramount duty to treat with determined barbarity, those men who happen to step aside from their mode of thinking. An heretic, an incredulous being, ceases to be a man, in the eyes of the superstitious. Every society, infected with the venom of bigotry, offers innumerable examples of juridical assassination, which the tribunals commit without scruple, even without remorse. Judges who are equitable on every other occasion, are no longer so when there is a question of theological opinions; in steeping their hands in the blood of their victims, they believe, on the authority of the priests, they conform themselves to the views of the Divinity. Almost every where the laws are subordinate to superstition; make themselves accomplices in its fanatical fury; they legitimate those actions most opposed to the gentle voice of humanity; they even transform into imperative duties, the most barbarous cruelties. The president Grammont relates, with a satisfaction truly worthy of a cannibal, the particulars of the punishment of Vanini, who was burned at Thoulouse, although he had disavowed the opinions with which he was accused; this president carries his demoniac prejudices so far, as to find wickedness in the piercing cries, in the dreadful howlings, which torment wrested from this unhappy victim to superstitious vengeance. Are not all these avengers of the gods miserable men, blinded by their piety, who, under the impression of duty, wantonly immolate at the shrine of superstition, those wretched victims whom the priests deliver over to them? Are they not savage tyrants, who have the rank injustice to violate thought; who have the folly to believe they can enslave it? Are they not delirious fanatics, on whom the law, dictated by the most inhuman prejudices, imposes the necessity of acting like ferocious brutes? Are not all those sovereigns, who to gratify the vanity of the priesthood, torment and persecute their subjects, who sacrifice to their anthropophagite gods human victims, men whom superstitious zeal has converted into tygers? Are not those priests, so careful of the soul's health, who insolently break into the sacred sanctuary of man's mind, to the end that they may find in his opinions motives for doing him an injury, abominable knaves, disturbers of the public repose, whom superstition honours, but whom virtue detests? What villains are more odious in the eyes of humanity, what depredators more hateful to the eye of reason, than those infamous inquisitors, who by the blindness of princes, by the delirium of monarchs, enjoy the advantage of passing judgment on their own enemies; who ruthlessly commit them to the charity of the flames? Nevertheless, the fatuity of the people makes even these monsters respected; the favour of kings covers them with kindness; the mantle of superstitious opinion shields them from the effect of the just execration of every honest man. Do not a thousand examples prove, that superstition has every where produced the most frightful ravages: that it has continually justified the most unaccountable horrors? Has it not a thousand times armed its votaries with the dagger of the homicide; let loose passions much wore terrible than those which it pretended to restrain; broken up the most sacred bonds by which mortals are connected with each other? Has it not, under the pretext of duty, under the colour of faith, under the semblance of zeal, under the sacred name of piety, favoured cupidity, lent wings to ambition, countenanced cruelty, given a spring to tyranny? Has it not legitimatized murder; given a system to perfidy; organized rebellion; made a virtue of regicide? Have not those princes who have been foremost as the avengers of heaven, who have been the lictors of superstition, frequently themselves become its victims? In short, has it not been the signal for the most dismal follies, the most wicked outrages, the most horrible massacres? Has not its altars been drenched with human gore? Under whatever form it has been exhibited, has it not always been the ostensible cause of the most bare-faced violation—of the sacred rights of humanity?

Never will an atheist, as he is called, as called, as he enjoys his proper senses, persuade himself that similar actions can be justifiable; never will he believe that he who commits them can be an estimable man; there is no one but the superstitious, whose blindness makes him forget the most evident principles of morality, whose callous soul renders him deaf to the voice of nature, whose zeal causes him to overlook the dictates of reason, who can by any possibility imagine the most destructive crimes are the most prominent features of virtue. If the atheist be perverse, he, at least, knows that he acts wrong; neither these systems, nor their priests, will be able to persuade him that he does right: one thing, however, is certain, whatever crimes he may allow himself to commit, he will never be capable of exceeding those which superstition perpetrates without scruple; that it encourages in those whom it intoxicates with its fury; to whom it frequently holds forth wickedness itself, either as expiations for offences, or else as orthodox, meritorious actions.

Thus the atheist, however wicked he may be supposed, will at most be upon a level with the devotee, whose superstition encourages him to commit crimes, which it transforms into virtue. As to conduct, if he be debauched, voluptuous, intemperate, adulterous, the atheist in this differs in nothing from the most credulously superstitious, who frequently knows how to connect these vices with his credulity, to blend with his superstition certain atrocities, for which his priests, provided he renders due homage to their power, especially if he augments their exchequer, will always find means to pardon him. If he be in Hindoostan, his brahmins will wash him in the sacred waters of the Ganges, while reciting a prayer. If he be a Jew, upon making an offering, his sins will be effaced. If he be in Japan, he will be cleansed by performing a pilgrimage. If he be a Mahometan, he will be reputed a saint, for having visited the tomb of his prophet; the Roman pontiff himself will sell him indulgences; but none of them will ever censure him for those crimes he may have committed in the support of their several faiths.

We are constantly told, that the indecent behaviour of the official expounders of superstition, the criminal conduct of the priests, or of their sectaries, proves nothing against the goodness of their systems. Admitted: but wherefore do they not say the same thing of the conduct of those whom they call atheists, who, as we have already proved, way have a very substantive, a very correct system of morality, even while leading a very dissolute life? If it be necessary to judge the opinions of mankind according to their conduct, which is the theory that would bear the scrutiny? Let us, then, examine the opinion of the atheist, without approving his conduct; let us adopt his mode of thinking, if we find it marked by the truth; if it shall appear useful; if it shall be proved rational; but let us reject his mode of action, if that should be found blameable. At the sight of a work performed with truth, we do not embarrass ourselves with the morals of the workman: of what importance is it to the universe, whether the illustrious Newton was a sober, discreet citizen, or a debauched intemperate man? It only remains for us to examine his theory; we want nothing more than to know whether he has reasoned acutely; if his principles be steady; if the parts of his system are connected; if his work contains more demonstrable truths, than bold ideas? Let us judge in the same manner of the principles of the atheist; if they appear strange, if they are unusual, that is a solid reason for probing them more strictly; if he has spoken truth, if he has demonstrated his positions, let us yield to the weight of evidence; if he be deceived in some parts, let us distinguish the true from the false; but do not let us fall into the hacknied prejudice, which on account of one error in the detail, rejects a multitude of incontestible truisms. Doctor Johnson, I think, says in his preface to his Dictionary, "when a man shall have executed his task with all the accuracy possible, he will only be allowed to have done his duty; but if he commits the slightest error, a thousand snarlers are ready to point it out." The atheist, when he is deceived, has unquestionably as much right to throw his faults on the fragility of his nature, as the superstitious man. An atheist may have vices, may be defective, he may reason badly; but his errors will never have the consequences of superstitious novelties; they will not, like these, kindle up the fire of discord in the bosom of nations; the atheist will not justify his vices, defend his wanderings by superstition; he will not pretend to infallibility, like those self-conceited theologians who attach the Divine sanction to their follies; who initiate that heaven authorizes those sophisms, gives currency to those falsehoods, approves those errors, which they believe themselves warranted to distribute over the face of the earth.

It will perhaps be said, that the refusal to believe in these systems, will rend asunder one of the most powerful bonds of society, by making the sacredness of an oath vanish. I reply, that perjury is by no means rare, even in the most superstitious nations, nor even among the most religious, or among those who boast of being the most thoroughly convinced of the rectitude of their theories. Diagoras, superstitious as he was, and it was not well possible to be more so, it is said became an atheist, on seeing that the gods did not thunder their vengeance on a man who had taken them as evidence to a falsity. Upon this principle, how many atheists ought there to be? From the systems that have made invisible unknown beings the depositaries of man's engagements, we do not always see it result that they are better observed; or that the most solemn contracts have acquired a greater solidity. If history was consulted, it would now and then be in evidence, that even the conductors of nations, those who have said they were the images of the Divinity, who have declared that they held their right of governing immediately from his hands, have sometimes taken the Deity as the witness to their oaths, have made him the guarantee of their treaties, without its having had all the effect that might have been expected, when very trifling interests have intervened; it would appear, unless historians are incorrect, that they did not always religiously observe those sacred engagements they made with their allies, much less with their subjects. To form a judgment from these historic documents, we should be inclined to say, there have been those who had much superstition, joined with very little probity; who made a mockery both of gods and men; who perhaps blushed when they reviewed their own conduct: nor can this be at all surprising, when it not unfrequently happened that superstition itself absolved them from their oaths. In fact, does not superstition sometimes inculcate perfidy; prescribe violation of plighted faith? Above all, when there is a question of its own interests, does it not dispense with engagements, however solemn, made with those whom it condemns? It is, I believe, a maxim in the Romish church, that *"no faith is to be held with heretics."* The general council of Constance decided thus, when, notwithstanding the emperor's passport, it decreed John Hus and Jerome of Prague to be burnt. The Roman pontiff has, it is well known, the right of relieving his sectaries from their oaths; of annulling their vows: this same pontiff has frequently arrogated to himself the right of deposing kings; of absolving their subjects from their oaths of fidelity. Indeed, it is rather extraordinary that oaths should be prescribed, by the laws of those nations which profess Christianity, seeing that Christ has expressly forbidden the use of them. If things were considered attentively, it would be obvious that under such management, superstition and politics are schools of perjury. They render it common: thus knaves of every description never recoil, when it is necessary to attest the name of the Divinity to the most manifest frauds, for the vilest interests. What end, then, do oaths answer? They are snares, in which simplicity alone can suffer itself to be caught: oaths, almost every where, are vain formalities, that impose nothing upon villains; nor do they add any thing to the sacredness of the engagements of honest men; who would neither have the temerity nor the wish to violate them; who would not think themselves less bound without an oath. A perfidious, perjured, superstitious being, has not any advantage over an atheist, who should fail in his promises: neither the one nor the other any longer deserves the confidence of their fellow citizens nor the esteem of good men; if one does not respect his gods, in whom he believes, the other neither respects his reason, his reputation, nor public opinion, in which all rational men cannot refuse to believe. Hobbes says, "an oath adds nothing to the obligation. For a covenant, if lawful, binds in the sight of God, without the oath, as much as with it: if unlawful, bindeth not at all: though it be confirmed with an oath." The heathen form was, "let Jupiter kill me else, as I kill this beast." Adjuration only augments, in the imagination of him who swears, the fear of violating an engagement, which he would have been obliged to keep, even without the ceremony of an oath.

It has frequently been asked, if there ever was a nation that had no idea of the Divinity: and if a people, uniformly composed of atheists, would be able to subsist? Whatever some speculators may say, it does not appear likely that there ever has been upon our globe, a numerous people who have not had an idea of some invisible power, to whom they have shewn marks of respect and submission: it has been sometimes believed that the Chinese were atheists: but this is an error, due to the Christian missionaries, who are accustomed to treat all those as atheists, who do not hold opinions similar with their own upon Divinity. It always appears that the Chinese are a people extremely addicted to superstition, but that they are governed by chiefs who are not so, without however their being atheists for that reason. If the empire of China be as flourishing as it is said to be, it at least furnishes a very forcible proof that those who govern have no occasion to be themselves superstitious, in order to govern with propriety a people who are so. It is pretended that the Greenlanders have no idea of the Divinity. Nevertheless, it is difficult to believe it of a nation so savage. Man, inasmuch as he is a fearful, ignorant animal, necessarily becomes superstitious in his misfortunes: either he forms gods for himself, or he admits the gods which others are disposed to give him; it does not then appear, that we can rationally suppose there may have been, or that there actually is, a people on the earth a total stranger to some Divinity. One will shew us the sun, the moon, or the stars; the other will shew us the sea, the lakes, the rivers, which furnish him his subsistence, the trees which afford him an asylum against the inclemency of the weather; another will shew us a rock of an odd form; a lofty mountain; or a volcano that frequently astonishes him by its emission of lava; another will present you with his crocodile, whose malignity he fears; his dangerous serpent, the reptile to which he attributes his good or bad fortune. In short, each individual will make you behold his phantasm or his tutelary or domestic gods with respect.

But from the existence of his gods, the savage does not draw the same inductions as the civilized, polished man: the savage does not believe it a duty to reason continually upon their qualities; he does not imagine that they ought to influence his morals, nor entirely occupy his thoughts: content with a gross, simple, exterior worship, he does not believe that these invisible powers trouble themselves with his conduct towards his fellow creatures; in short, he does not connect his morality with his superstition. This morality is coarse, as must be that of all ignorant people; it is proportioned to his wants, which are few; it is frequently irrational, because it is the fruit of ignorance; of inexperience; of the passions of men but slightly restrained, or to say thus, in their infancy. It is only numerous, stationary, civilized societies, where man's wants are multiplied, where his interests clash, that he is obliged to have recourse to government, to laws, to public worship, in order to maintain concord. It is then, that men approximating, reason together, combine their ideas, refine their notions, subtilize their theories; it is then also, that those who govern them avail themselves of invisible powers, to keep them within bounds, to render them docile, to enforce their obedience, to oblige them to live peaceably. It was thus, that by degrees, morals and politics found themselves associated with superstitious systems. The chiefs of nations, frequently, themselves, the children of superstition, but little enlightened upon their actual interests; slenderly versed in sound morality; with an extreme exilty of knowledge on the actuating motives of the human heart; believed they had effected every thing requisite for the stability of their own authority; as well as achieved all that could guarantee the repose of society, that could consolidate the happiness of the people, in rendering their subjects superstitious like themselves; by menacing them with the wrath of invisible powers; in treating them like infants who are appeased with fables, like children who are terrified by shadows. By the assistance of these marvellous inventions, to which even the chiefs, the conductors of nations, are themselves frequently the dupes; which are transmitted as heirlooms from race to race; sovereigns were dispensed from the trouble of instructing themselves in their duties; they in consequence neglected the laws, enervated themselves in luxurious ease, rusted in sloth; followed nothing but their caprice: the care of restraining their subjects was reposed in their deities; the instruction of the people was confided to their priests, who were commissioned to train them to obedience, to make them submissive, to render them devout, to teach them at an early age to tremble under the yoke of both the visible and invisible gods.

It was thus that nations, kept by their tutors in a perpetual state of infancy, were only restrained by vain, chimerical theories. It was thus that politics, jurisprudence, education, morality, were almost every where infected with superstition; that man no longer knew any duties, save those which grew out of its precepts: the ideas of virtue were thus falsely associated with those of imaginary systems, to which imposture generally gave that language which was most conducive to its own immediate interests: mankind thus fully persuaded, that without these marvellous systems, there could not exist any sound morality, princes, as well as subjects, equally blind to their actual interests, to the duties of nature, to their reciprocal rights, habituated themselves to consider superstition as necessary to mortals—as indispensibly requisite to govern men—as the most effectual method of preserving power—as the most certain means of attaining happiness.

It is from these dispositions, of which we have so frequently demonstrated the fallacy, that so many persons, otherwise extremely enlightened, look upon it as an impossibility that a society formed of atheists, as they are termed, could subsist for any length of time. It does not admit a question, that a numerous society, who should neither have religion, morality, government, laws, education, nor principles, could not maintain itself; that it would simply congregate beings disposed to injure each other, or children who would follow nothing but the blindest impulse; but then is it not a lamentable fact, that with all the superstition that floats in the world, the greater number of human societies are nearly in this state? Are not the sovereigns of almost every country in a continual state of warfare with their subjects? Are not the people, in despite of their superstition, not withstanding the terrific notions which it holds forth, unceasingly occupied with reciprocally injuring each other; with rendering themselves mutually unhappy? Does not superstition itself, with its supernatural notions, unremittingly flatter the vanity of monarchs, unbridle the passions of princes, throw oil into the fire of discord, which it kindles between those citizens who are divided in their opinion? Could those infernal powers, who are supposed to be ever on the alert to mischief mankind, be capable of inflicting greater evils upon the human race than spring from fanaticism, than arise out of the fury to which theology gives birth? Could atheists, however irrational they may be supposed, if assembled together in society, conduct themselves in a more criminal manner? In short, is it possible they could act worse than the superstitious, who, saturated with the most pernicious vices, guided by the most extravagant systems, during so many successive ages, have done nothing more than torment themselves with the most cruel inflictions; savagely cut each other's throats, without a shadow of reason; make a merit of mutual extermination? It cannot be pretended they would. On the contrary, we boldly assert, that a community of atheists, as the theologian calls them, because they cannot fall in with his mysteries, destitute of all superstition, governed by wholesome laws, formed by a salutary education, invited to the practice of virtue by instantaneous recompences, deterred from crime by immediate punishments, disentangled from illusive theories, unsophisticated by falsehood, would be decidedly more honest, incalculably more virtuous, than those superstitious societies, in which every thing contributes to intoxicate the mind; where every thing conspires to corrupt the heart.

When we shall be disposed usefully to occupy ourselves with the happiness of mankind, it is with superstition that the reform must commence; it is by abstracting these imaginary theories, destined to affright the ignorant, who are completely in a state of infancy, that we shall be able to promise ourselves the desirable harvest of conducting man to a state of maturity. It cannot be too often repeated, there can be no morality without consulting the nature of man, without studying his actual relations with the beings of his own species; there can be no fixed principle for man's conduct, while it is regulated upon unjust theories; upon capricious doctrines; upon corrupt systems; there can be no sound politics without attending to human temperament, without contemplating him as a being associated for the purpose of satisfying his wants, consolidating his happiness, and assuring its enjoyment. No wise government can found itself upon despotic systems; they will always make tyrants of their representatives. No laws can be wholesome, that do not bottom themselves upon the strictest equity; which have not for their object the great end of human society. No jurisprudence can be advantageous for nations, if its administration be regulated by capricious systems, or by human passions deified. No education can be salutary, unless it be founded upon reason; to be efficacious to its proposed end, it must neither be construed upon chimerical theories, nor upon received prejudices. In short, there can be no probity, no talents, no virtue, either under corrupt masters, or under the conduct of those priests who render man the enemy to himself—the determined foe to others; who seek to stifle in his bosom the germ of reason; who endeavour to smother science, or who try to damp his courage.

It will, perhaps, be asked, if we can reasonably flatter ourselves with ever reaching the point to make a whole people entirely forget their superstitious opinions; or abandon the ideas which they have of their gods? I reply, that the thing appears utterly impossible; that this is not the end we can propose to ourselves. These ideas, inculcated from the earliest ages, do not appear of a nature to admit eradication from the mind of the majority of mankind: it would, perhaps be equally arduous to give them to those persons, who, arrived at a certain time of life, should never have heard them spoken of, as to banish them from the minds of those, who have been imbued with them from their tenderest infancy. Thus, it cannot be reckoned possible to make a whole nation pass from the abyss of superstition, that is to say, from the bosom of ignorance, from the ravings of delirium, into absolute naturalism, or as the priests of superstition would denominate it, into atheism; which supposes reflection—requires intense study—demands extensive knowledge—exacts a long series of experience—includes the habit of contemplating nature—the faculty of observing her laws; which, in short, embraces the expansive science of the causes producing her various phenomena; her multiplied combinations, together with the diversified actions of the beings she contains, as well as their numerous properties. In order to be an atheist, or to be assured of the capabilities of nature, it is imperative to have meditated her profoundly: a superficial glance of the eye will not bring man acquainted with her resources; optics but little practised on her powers, will unceasingly be deceived; the ignorance of actual causes will always induce the supposition of those which are imaginary; credulity will, thus re-conduct the natural philosopher himself to the feet of superstitious phantoms, in which either his limited vision, or his habitual sloth, will make him believe he shall find the solution to every difficulty.

Atheism, then, as well as philosophy, like all profound abstruse sciences, is not calculated for the vulgar; neither is it suitable to the great mass of mankind. There are, in all populous, civilized nations, persons whose circumstances enable them to devote their time to meditation, whose easy finances afford them leisure to make deep researches into the nature of things, who frequently make useful discoveries, which, sooner or later, after they have been submitted to the infallible test of experience, when they have passed the fiery ordeal of truth, extend widely their salutary effects, become extremely beneficial to society, highly advantageous to individuals. The geometrician, the chemist, the mechanic, the natural philosopher, the civilian, the artizan himself, are industriously employed, either in their closets, or in their workshops, seeking the means to serve society, each in his sphere: nevertheless, not one of their sciences or professions are familiar to the illiterate; not one of the arts with which they are respectively occupied, are known to the uninitiated: these, however, do not fail, in the long run, to profit by them, to reap substantive advantages from those labours, of which they themselves have no idea. It is for the mariner, that the astronomer explores his arduous science; it is for him the geometrician calculates; for his use the mechanic plies his craft: it is for the mason, for the carpenter, for the labourer, that the skilful architect studies his orders, lays down well-proportioned elaborate plans. Whatever may be the pretended utility of Pneumatology, whatever may be the vaunted advantages of superstitious opinions, the wrangling polemic, the subtle theologian, cannot boast either of toiling, of writing, or of disputing for the advantage of the people, whom, notwithstanding, he contrives to tax, very exorbitantly, for those systems they can never understand; from whom he levies the most oppressive contributions, as a remuneration for the detail of those mysteries, which under any possible circumstances, cannot, at any time whatever, be of the slightest benefit to them. It is not, then, for the multitude that a philosopher should propose to himself, either to write or to meditate: the Code of Nature, or the principles of atheism, as the priest calls it, are not, as we have shewn, even calculated for the meridian of a great number of persons, who are frequently too much prepossessed in favour of the received prejudices, although extremely enlightened on other points. It is extremely rare to find men, who, to an enlarged mind, extensive knowledge, great talents, join either a well regulated imagination, or the courage necessary to successfully oppugn habitual errors; triumphantly to attack those chimerical systems, with which the brain has been inoculated from the first hour of its birth. A secret bias, an invincible inclination, frequently, in despite of all reasoning, re-conducts the most comprehensive, the best fortified, the most liberal minds, to those prejudices which have a wide-spreading establishment; of which they have themselves taken copious draughts during the early stages of life. Nevertheless, those principles, which at first appear strange, which by their boldness seem revolting, from which timidity flies with trepidation, when they have the sanction of truth, gradually insinuate themselves into the human mind, become familiar to its exercise, extend their happy influence on every side, and finally produce the most substantive advantages to society. In time, men habituate themselves to ideas which originally they looked upon as absurd; which on a superficial glance they contemplated as either noxious or irrational: at least, they cease to consider those as odious, who profess opinions upon subjects on which experience makes it evident they may be permitted to have doubts, without imminent danger to public tranquillity.

Then the diffusion of ideas among mankind is not an event to be dreaded: if they are truths, they will of necessity be useful: by degrees they will fructify. The man who writes, must neither fix his eyes upon the time in which he lives, upon his actual fellow citizens, nor upon the country he inhabits. He must speak to the human race; he must instruct future generations; he must extend his views into the bosom of futurity; in vain he will expect the eulogies of his contemporaries; in vain will he flatter himself with seeing his reasoning adopted; in vain he will soothe himself with the pleasing reflection, that his precocious principles will be received with kindness; if he has exhibited truisms, the ages that shall follow will do justice to his efforts; unborn nations shall applaud his exertions; his future countrymen shall crown his sturdy attempts with those laurels, which interested prejudice withholds from him in his own days; it must therefore be from posterity, he is to expect the need of applause due to his services; the present race is hermetically sealed against him: meantime let him content himself with having done well; with the secret suffrages of those few friends to veracity who are so thinly spread over the surface of the earth. It is after his death, that the trusty reasoner, the faithful writer, the promulgator of sterling principles, the child of simplicity, triumphs; it is then that the stings of hatred, the shafts of envy, the arrows of malice, either exhausted or blunted, enable mankind to judge with impartiality; to yield to conviction; to establish eternal truth upon its own imperishable altars, which from its essence must survive all the error of the earth. It is then that calumny, crushed like the devouring snail by the careful gardener, ceases to besmear the character of an honest man, while its venomous slime, glazed by the sun, enables the observant spectator to trace the filthy progress it had made.

It is a problem with many people, *if truth may not be injurious?* The best intentioned persons are frequently in great doubt upon this important point. The fact is, *it never injures any but those who deceive mankind*: this has, however, the greatest interest in being undeceived. Truth may be injurious to the individual who announces it, but it can never by any possibility harm the human species; never can it be too distinctly presented to beings, always either little disposed to listen to its dictates, or too slothful to comprehend its efficacy. If all those who write to publish important truths, which, of all others, are ever considered the most dangerous, were sufficiently ardent for the public welfare to speak freely, even at the risk of displeasing their readers, the human race would be much more enlightened, much happier than it now is. To write in ambiguous terms, is very frequently to write to nobody. The human mind is idle; we must spare it, as much as possible, the trouble of reflection; we must relieve it from the embarrassment of intense thinking. What time does it not consume, what study does it not require, at the present day, to unravel the amphibological oracles of the ancient philosophers, whose actual sentiments are almost entirely lost to the present race of men? If truth be useful to human beings, it is an injustice to deprive them of its advantages; if truth ought to be admitted, we must admit its consequences, which are also truths. Man, taken generally, is fond of truth, but its consequences often inspire him with so much dread, so alarm his imbecility, that, frequently, he prefers remaining in error, of which a confirmed habit prevents him from feeling the deplorable effects. Besides, we shall say with Hobbes, "that we cannot do men any harm by proposing truth to them; the worst mode is to leave them in doubt, to let them remain in dispute." If an author who writes be deceived, it is because he may have reasoned badly. Has he laid down false principles? It remains to examine them. Is his system fallacious? Is it ridiculous? It will serve to make truth appear with the greatest splendor: his work will fall into contempt; the writer, if he be witness to its fall, will be sufficiently punished for his temerity; if he be defunct, the living cannot disturb his ashes. No man writes with a design to injure his fellow creatures; he always proposes to himself to merit their suffrages, either by amusing them, by exciting their curiosity, or by communicating to them discoveries, which he believes useful. Above all, no work can be really dangerous, if it contains truth. It would not be so, even if it contained principles evidently contrary to experience—opposed to good sense. Indeed, what would result from a work that should now tell us the sun is not luminous; that parricide is legitimate; that robbery is allowable; that adultery is not a crime? The smallest reflection would make us feet the falsity of these principles; the whole human race would protest against them. Men would laugh at the folly of the author; presently his book, together with his name, would be known only by its ridiculous extravagancies. There is nothing but superstitious follies that are pernicious to mortals; and wherefore? It is because authority always pretends to establish them by violence; to make them pass for substantive virtues; rigorously punishes those who shall he disposed to smile at their inconsistency, or examine into their pretensions. If man was more rational, he would examine superstitious opinions as he examines every thing else; he would look upon theological theories with the same eyes that he contemplates systems of natural philosophy, or problems in geometry: the latter never disturbs the repose of society, although they sometimes excite very warm disputes in the learned world. Theological quarrels would never be attended with any evil consequences, if man could gain the desirable point of making those who exercise power, feel that the disputes of persons, who do not themselves understand the marvellous questions upon which they never cease wrangling, ought not to give birth to any other sensations than those of indifference; to rouse no other passion than that of contempt.

It is, at least, this indifference not speculative theories, so just, so rational, so advantageous for states, that sound philosophy may propose to introduce, gradually, upon the earth. Would not the human race be much happier—if the sovereigns of the world, occupied with the welfare of their subjects, leaving to superstitious theologians their futile contests, making their various systems yield to healthy politics; obliged these haughty ministers to become citizens; carefully prevented their disputes from interrupting the public tranquillity? What advantage might there not result to science; what a start would be given to the progress of the human mind, to the cause of sound morality, to the advancement of equitable jurisprudence, to the improvement of legislation, to the diffusion of education, from an unlimited freedom of thought? At present, genius every where finds trammels; superstition invariably opposes itself to its course; man, straitened with bandages, scarcely enjoys the free use of any one of his faculties; his mind itself is cramped; it appears continually wrapped up in the swaddling clothes of infancy. The civil power, leagued with spiritual domination, appears only disposed to rule over brutalized slaves, shut up in a dark prison, where they reciprocally goad each other with the efferverscence of their mutual ill humour. Sovereigns, in general, detest liberty of thought, because they fear truth; this appears formidable to them, because it would condemn their excesses; these irregularities are dear to them, because they do not, better than their subjects, understand their true interests; properly considered, these ought to blend themselves into one uniform mass.

Let not the courage of the philosopher, however, be abated by so many united obstacles, which would appear for ever to exclude truth from its proper dominion; to banish reason from the mind of man; to spoil nature of her imprescriptible rights. The thousandth part of those cares which are bestowed to infect the human mind, would be amply sufficient to make it whole. Let us not, then, despair of the case: do not let us do man the injury to believe that truth is not made for him; his mind seeks after it incessantly; his heart desires it faithfully; his happiness demands it with an imperious voice; he only either fears it, or mistakes it, because superstition, which has thrown all his ideas into confusion, perpetually keeps the bandeau of delusion fast bound over his eyes; strives, with an almost irresistible force, to render him an entire stranger to virtue.

Maugre the prodigious exertions that are made to drive truth from the earth; in spite of the extraordinary pains used to exile reason—of the uninterrupted efforts to expel true science from the residence of mortals; time, assisted by the progressive knowledge of ages, may one day be able to enlighten even those princes who are the most outrageous in their opposition to the illumination of the human mind; who appear such decided enemies to justice, so very determined against the liberties of mankind. Destiny will, perhaps, when least expected, conduct these wandering outcasts to the throne of some enlightened, equitable, courageous, generous, benevolent sovereign, who, smitten with the charms of virtue, shall throw aside duplicity, frankly acknowledge the true source of human misery, and apply to it those remedies with which wisdom has furnished him: perhaps he may feel, that those systems, from whence it is pretended he derives his power, are the true scourges of his people; the actual cause of his own weakness: that the official expounders of these systems are his most substantial enemies—his most formidable rivals; he may find that superstition, which he has been taught to look upon as the main support to his authority, in point of fact only enfeebles it—renders it tottering: that superstitious morality, false in its principles, is only calculated to pervert his subjects; to break down their intrepidity; to render them perfidious; in short, to give them the vices of slaves, in lieu of the virtues of citizens. A prince thus disentangled from prejudice, will perhaps behold, in superstitious errors, the fruitful source of human sorrows, and commiserations, the condition of his race, it may be, will generously declare, that they are incompatible with every equitable administration.

Until this epoch, so desirable for humanity, shall arrive, the principles of naturalism will be adopted only by a small number of liberal-minded men, who shall dive below the surface; these cannot flatter themselves either with making proselytes, or having a great number of approvers: on the contrary, they will meet with zealous adversaries, with ardent contemners, even in those persons who upon every other subject discover the most acute minds; display the most consummate knowledge. Those men who possess the greatest share of ability, as we have already observed, cannot always resolve to divorce themselves completely from their superstitious ideas; imagination, so necessary to splendid talents, frequently forms in them an insurmountable obstacle to the total extinction of prejudice; this depends much more upon the judgment than upon the mind. To this disposition, already so prompt to form illusions to them, is also to be joined the force of habit; to a great number of men, it would he wresting from them a portion of themselves to take away their superstitious notions; it would be depriving them of an accustomed aliment; plunging them into a dreadful vacuum: obliging their distempered minds to perish for want of exercise. Menage remarks, "that history speaks of very few incredulous women, or female atheists:" this is not surprising; their organization renders them fearful; their nervous system undergoes periodical variations; the education they receive disposes them to credulity. Those among them who have a sound constitution, who have a well ordered imagination, have occasion for chimeras suitable to occupy their leisure; above all, when the world abandons them, then superstitious devotion, with its attractive ceremonies, becomes either a business or an amusement.

Let us not be surprised, if very intelligent, extremely learned men, either obstinately shut their eyes, or run counter to their ordinary sagacity, every time there is a question respecting an object which they have not the courage to examine with that attention they lend to many others. Lord Chancellor Bacon pretends, "that a little philosophy disposes men to atheism, but that great depth re-conducts them to religion." If we analyze this proposition, we shall find it signifies, that even moderate, indifferent thinkers, are quickly enabled to perceive the gross absurdities of superstition; but that very little accustomed to meditate, or else destitute of those fixed principles which could serve them for a guide, their imagination presently replaces them in the theological labyrinth, from whence reason, too weak for the purpose, appeared disposed to withdraw them: these timid souls, who fear to take courage, with minds disciplined to be satisfied with theological solutions, no longer see in nature any thing but an inexplicable enigma; an abyss which it is impossible for them to fathom: these, habituated to fix their eyes upon an ideal, mathematical point, which they have made the centre of every thing, whenever they lose sight of it, find the universe becomes an unintelligible jumble to them; then the confusion in which they feel themselves involved, makes them rather prefer returning to the prejudices of their infancy, which appear to explain every thing, than to float in the vacuum, or quit a foundation which they judge to be immoveable. Thus the proposition of Bacon should seem, to indicate nothing, except it be that the most experienced persons cannot at all times defend themselves against the illusions of their imagination; the impetuosity of which resists the strongest reasoning.

Nevertheless, a deliberate study of nature is sufficient to undeceive every man who will calmly consider things: he will discover that the phenomena of the world is connected by links, invisible to superficial notice, equally concealed from the too impetuous observer, but extremely intelligible to him who views her with serenity. He will find that the most unusual, the most marvellous, as well as the most trifling, or ordinary effects, are equally inexplicable, but that they all equally flow from natural causes; that supernatural causes, under whatever name they way be designated, with whatever qualities they may be decorated, will never do more than increase difficulties; will only make chimeras multiply. The simplest observation will incontestibly prove to him that every thing is necessary; that all the effects he perceives are material; that they can only originate in causes of the same nature, when he even shall not be able to recur to them by the assistance of his senses. Thus his mind, properly directed, every where show him nothing but matter, sometimes acting in a manner which his organs permit him to follow, at others in a mode imperceptible by the faculties he possesses: he will see that all beings follow constant invariable laws, by which all combinations are united and destroyed; he will find that all forms change, but that, nevertheless, the great whole ever remains the same. Thus, cured of the idle notions with which he was imbued, undeceived in those erroneous ideas, which from habit be attached to imaginary systems, he will cheerfully consent to be ignorant of whatever his organs do not enable him to compass; he will know that obscure terms, devoid of sense, are not calculated to explain difficulties; guided by reason, be will throw aside all hypothesis of the imagination; the champion of rectitude, he will attach himself to realities, which are confirmed by experience, which are evidenced by truth.

The greater number of those who study nature, frequently do not consider, that prejudiced eyes will never discover more than that which they have previously determined to find: as soon as they perceive facts contrary to their own ideas, they quickly turn aside, and believe their visual organs have deceived them; if they return to the task, it is in hopes to find means by which they may reconcile the facts to the notions with which their own mind is previously tinctured. Thus we find enthusiastic philosophers, whose determined prepossession shews them what they denominate incontestible evidences of the systems with which they are pre-occupied, even in those things, that most openly contradict their hypothesis: hence those pretended demonstrations of the existence of theories, which are drawn from final causes—from the order of nature—from the kindness evinced to man, &c. Do these same enthusiasts perceive disorder, witness calamities? They induct new proofs of the wisdom, fresh evidence of the intelligence, additional testimony to the bounty of their system, whilst all these occurrences as visibly contradict these qualities, as the first seem to confirm or to establish them. These prejudiced observers are in an ecstacy at the sight of the periodical motions of the planets; at the order of the stars; at the various productions of the earth; at the astonishing harmony in the component parts of animals: in that moment, however, they forget the laws of motion; the powers of gravitation; the force of attraction and repulsion; they assign all these striking phenomena to unknown causes, of which they have no one substantive idea. In short, in the fervor of their imagination they place man in the centre of nature; they believe him to be the object, the end, of all that exists; that it is for his convenience every thing is made; that it is to rejoice his mind, to pleasure his senses, that the whole was created; whilst they do not perceive, that very frequently the entire of nature appears to be loosed against his weakness; that the elements themselves overwhelm him with calamity; that destiny obstinately persists in rendering him the most miserable of beings. The progress of sound philosophy will always be fatal to superstition, whose notions will he continually contradicted by nature.

Astronomy has caused judiciary astrology to vanish; experimental philosophy, the study of natural history and chemistry, have rendered it impossible for jugglers, priests or sorcerers, any longer to perform miracles. Nature, profoundly studied, must necessarily cause the overthrow of those chimerical theories, which ignorance has substituted to her powers.

Atheism, as it is termed, is only so rare, because every thing conspires to intoxicate man with a dazzling enthusiasm, from his most tender age; to inflate him from his earliest infancy, with systematic error, with organized ignorance, which of all others is the most difficult to vanquish, the most arduous to root out. Theology is nothing more than a science of words, which by dint of repetition we accustom ourselves to substitute for things: as soon as we feel disposed to analyze them, we are astonished to find they do not present us with any actual sense. There are, in the whole world, very few men who think deeply: who render to themselves a faithful account of their own ideas; who have keen penetrating minds. Justness of intellect is one of the rarest gifts which nature bestows on the human species. It is not, however, to be understood by this, that nature has any choice in the formation of her beings; it is merely to be considered, that the circumstances very rarely occur which enable the junction of a certain quantity of those atoms or parts, necessary to form the human machine in such due proportions, that one disposition shall not overbalance the others; and thus render the judgment erroneous, by giving it a particular bias. We know the general process of making gunpowder;

nevertheless, it will sometimes happen that the ingredients have been so happily blended, that this destructive article is of a superior quality to the general produce of the manufactory, without, however, the chemist being on that account entitled to any particular commendation; circumstances have been decidedly favorable, and these seldom occur. Too lively an imagination, an over eager curiosity, are as powerful obstacles to the discovery of truth, as too much phlegm, a slow conception, indolence of mind, or the want of a thinking habit: all men have more or less imagination, curiosity, phlegm, bile, indolence, activity: it is from the happy equilibrium which nature has observed in their organization, that depends that invaluable blessing, correctness of mind. Nevertheless, as we have heretofore said, the organic structure of man is subject to change; the accuracy of his mind varies with the mutations of his machine: from hence may be traced those almost perpetual revolutions that take place in the ideas of mortals; above all when there is a question concerning those objects, upon which experience does not furnish any fixed basis whereon to rest their merits.

To search after right, to discover truth, requires a keen, penetrating, just, active mind; because every thing strives to conceal from us its beauties: it needs an upright heart, one in good faith with itself, joined to an imagination tempered with reason, because our habitual fears make us frequently dread its radiance, sometimes bursting like a meteor on our darkened faculties; besides, it not unfrequently happens, that we are actually the accomplices of those who lead us astray, by an inclination we too often manifest to dissimilate with ourselves on this important measure. Truth never reveals itself either to the enthusiast smitten with his own reveries; to the fellifluous fanatic enslaved by his prejudices; to the vain glorious mortal puffed up with his own presumptuous ignorance; to the voluptuary devoted to his pleasures; or to the wily reasoner, who, disingenuous with himself, has a peculiar spontaneity to form illusions to his mind. Blessed, however, with a heart, gifted with a mind such as described, man will surely discover this *rara avis:* thus constituted, the attentive philosopher, the geometrician, the moralist, the politician, the theologian himself, when he shall sincerely seek truth, will find that the corner-stone which serves for the foundation of all superstitious systems, is evidently rested upon fiction. The philosopher will discover in matter a sufficient cause for its existence; he will perceive that its motion, its combination, its modes of acting, are always regulated by general laws, incapable of variation. The geometrician, without quiting nature, will calculate the active force of matter; it will then become obvious to him, that to explain its phenomena, it is by no means necessary to have recourse to that which is incommensurable with all known powers. The politician, instructed in the true spring which can act upon the mind of nations, will feel distinctly, that it is not imperative to recur to imaginary theories, whilst there are actual motives to give play to the volition of the citizens; to induce them to labour efficaciously to the maintenance of their association; he will readily acknowledge that fictitious systems are calculated either to slaken the exertions, or to disturb the motion of so complicated a machine an human society. He who shall more honor truth than the vain subtilities of theology, will quickly perceive that this pompous science is nothing more than an unintelligible jumble of false hypothesis; that it continually begs its principles; is full of sophisms; contains only vitiated circles; embraces the most subdolous distinctions; is ushered to mankind by the most disingenuous arguments, from which it is not possible, under any given circumstances, there should result any thing but puerilities—the most endless disputes. In short, all men who have sound ideas of morality, whose notions of virtue are correct, who understand what is useful to the human being in society, whether it be to conserve himself individually, or the body of which he is a member, will acknowledge, that in order to discover his relations, to ascertain his duties, he has only to consult his own nature; that he ought to be particularly careful neither to found them upon discrepant systems, nor to borrow them from models that never can do more than disturb his mind; that will only render his conduct fluctuating; that will leave him for ever uncertain of its proper character.

Thus, every rational thinker, who renounces his prejudices, will be enabled to feel the inutility, to comprehend the fallacy of so many abstract systems; he will perceive that they have hitherto answered no other purpose than to confound the notions of mankind; to render doubtful the clearest truths. In quitting the regions of the empyreum, where his mind can only bewilder itself, in re-entering his proper sphere, in consulting reason, man will discover that of which he needs the knowledge; he will be able to undeceive himself upon those chimerical theories, which enthusiasm has substituted for actual natural causes; to detect those figments, by which imposture has almost every where superseded the real motives that can give activity in nature; out of which the human mind never rambles, without going woefully astray; without laying the foundation of future misery.

The Deicolists, as well as the theologians, continually reproach their adversaries with their taste for paradoxes—with their attachment to systems; whilst they themselves found all their reasoning upon imaginary hypothesis— upon visionary theories; make a principle of submitting their understanding to the yoke of authority; of renouncing experience; of setting down as nothing the evidence of their senses. Would it not be justifiable in the disciples of nature, to say to these men, who thus despise her, "We only assure ourselves of that which we see; we yield to nothing but evidence; if we have a system, it is one founded upon facts; we perceive in ourselves, we behold every where else, nothing but matter; we therefore conclude from it that matter can both feel and think: we see that the motion of the universe is operated after mechanical laws; that the whole results from the properties, is the effect of the combination, the immediate consequence of the modification of matter; thus, we are content, we seek no other explication of the phenomena which nature presents. We conceive only an unique world, in which every thing is connected;

where each effect is linked to a natural cause, either known or unknown, which it produces according to necessary laws; we affirm nothing that is not demonstrable; nothing that you are not obliged to admit as well as ourselves: the principles we lay down are distinct: they are self-evident: they are facts. If we find some things unintelligible, if causes frequently become arduous, we ingenuously agree to their obscurity; that is to say, to the limits of our own knowledge. But in order to explain these effects, we do not imagine an hypothesis; we either consent to be for ever ignorant of them, or else we wait patiently until time, experience, with the progress of the human mind, shall throw them into light: is not, then, our manner of philosophizing consistent with truth? Indeed, in whatever we advance upon the subject of nature, we proceed precisely in the same manner as our opponents themselves pursue in all the other sciences, such as natural history, experimental philosophy, mathematics, chemistry, &c. We scrupulously confine ourselves to what comes to our knowledge through the medium of our senses; the only instruments with which nature has furnished us to discover truth. What is the conduct of our adversaries? In order to expound things of which they are ignorant, they imagine theories still more incomprehensible than what they are desirous to explain; theories of which they themselves are obliged to acknowledge they have not the most slender notion. Thus they invert the true principles of logic, which require we should proceed gradually from that which is most known, to that with which we are least acquainted. Again, upon what do they found the existence of these theories, by whose aid they pretend to solve all difficulties? It is upon the universal ignorance of mankind; upon the inexperience of man; upon his fears; upon his disordered imagination; upon a pretended *intimate sense*, which in reality is nothing more than the effect of vulgar prejudice; the result of dread; the consequence of the want of a reflecting habit, which induces them to crouch to the opinions of others; to be guided by the mandates of authority, rather than take the trouble to examine for their own information. Such, O theologians! are the ruinous foundations upon which you erect the superstructure of your doctrine. Accordingly, you find it impossible to form to yourselves any distinct idea of those theories which serve for the basis of your systems; you are unable to comprehend either their attributes, their existence, the nature of their localities, or their mode of action. Thus, even by your own confession, ye are in a state of profound ignorance, on the primary elements of that which ye constitute the cause of all that exists: of which, according to your own account, it is imperative to have a correct knowledge. Under whatever point of view, therefore, ye are contemplated, it must be admitted ye are the founders of aerial systems; of fanciful theories: of all systematizers, ye are consequently the most absurd; because in challenging your imagination to create a cause, this cause, at least, ought to diffuse light over the whole; it would be upon this condition alone that its incomprehensibility could be pardonable; but to speak ingenuously, does this cause serve to explain any thing? Does it make us conceive more clearly the origin of the world; bring us more distinctly acquainted with the actual nature of man; does it more intelligibly elucidate the faculties of the soul; or point out with more perspicuity the source of good and evil? No! unquestionably: these subtle theories explain nothing, although they multiply to infinity their own difficulties; they, in fact, embarrass elucidation, by plunging into greater obscurity those matters in which they are interposed. Whatever may be the question agitated, it becomes complicated: as soon as these theories are introduced, they envelope the most demonstrable sciences with a thick, impenetrable mist; render the most simple notions complex; give opacity to the most diaphanous ideas; turn the most evident opinions into insolvable enigmas. What exposition of morality does the theories, upon which ye found all the virtue, present to man? Do not all your oracles breathe inconsistency? Does not your doctrines embrace every gradation of character, however discrepant: every known property, however opposed. All your ingenious systems, all your mysteries, all the subtilties which ye have invented, are they capable of reconciling that discordant assemblage of amiable and unamiable qualities, with which ye have dressed up your figments? In short, is it not by these theories that ye disturb the harmony of the universe; is it not in their name ye follow up your barbarous proscriptions; in their support, that ye so inhumanly exterminate all who refuse to subscribe to your organized reveries; who withhold assent to those efforts of the imagination which ye have collectively decorated with the pompous name of religion; but which, individually, ye brand as superstition, always excepting that to which ye lend yourselves. Agree, then, O Theologians! Acknowledge, then, ye subtle metaphysicians! Consent, then, ye organizers of fanciful theories! that not only are ye systematically absurd, but also that ye finish by being atrocious; because whenever ye obtain the ascendancy one over the other, your unfortunate pre-eminence is distinguished by the most malevolent persecution; your domination is ushered in with cruelty; your career is described with blood: from the importance which your own interest attaches to your ruinous dogmas; from the pride with which ye tumble down the less fortunate systems of those who started with you for the prize of plunder; *from that savage ferocity, under which ye equally overwhelm human reason, the happiness of the individual, and the felicity of nations.*"

CHAP. XIV.
A Summary of the Code of Nature.

Truth is the only object worthy the research of every wise man; since that which is false cannot be useful to him: whatever constantly injures him cannot be founded upon truth; consequently, ought to be for ever proscribed. It is, then, to assist the human mind, truly to labour for his happiness, to point out to him the clew by which he may extricate himself from those frightful labyrinths in which his imagination wanders; from those sinuosities whose devious course makes him err, without ever finding a termination to his incertitude. Nature alone, known through experience, can furnish him with this desirable thread; her eternal energies can alone supply the means of attacking the Minotaur; of exterminating the figments of hypocrisy; of destroying those monsters, who during so many ages, have devoured the unhappy victims, which the tyranny of the ministers of Moloch have exacted as a cruel tribute from affrighted mortals. By steadily grasping this inestimable clew, rendered still more precious by the beauty of the donor, man can never be led astray—will never ramble out of his course; but if, careless of its invaluable properties, for a single instant he suffers it to drop from his hand; if, like another Theseus, ungrateful for the favour, he abandons the fair bestower, he will infallibly fall again into his ancient wanderings; most assuredly become the prey to the cannibal offspring of the White Bull. In vain shall he carry his views above his head, to find resources which are at his feet; so long as man, infatuated with his superstitious notions, shall seek in an imaginary world the rule of his earthly conduct, he will be without principles; while he shall pertinaciously contemplate the regions of a distempered fancy, so long he will grope in those where he actually finds himself; his uncertain steps will never encounter the welfare he desires; never lead him to that repose after which he so ardently sighs, nor conduct him to that surety which is so decidedly requisite to consolidate his happiness.

But man, blinded by his prejudices; rendered obstinate in injuring his fellow, by his enthusiasm; ranges himself in hostility even against those who are sincerely desirous of procuring for him the most substantive benefits. Accustomed to be deceived, he is in a state of continual suspicion; habituated to mistrust himself, to view his reason with diffidence, to look upon truth as dangerous, he treats as enemies even those who most eagerly strive to encourage him; forewarned in early life against delusion, by the subtilty of imposture, he believes himself imperatively called upon to guard with the most sedulous activity the bandeau with which they have hoodwinked him; he thinks his eternal welfare involved in keeping it for ever over his eyes; he therefore wrestles with all those who attempt to tear it from his obscured optics. If his visual organs, accustomed to darkness, are for a moment opened, the light offends them; he is distressed by its effulgence; he thinks it criminal to be enlightened; he darts with fury upon those who hold the flambeau by which he is dazzled. In consequence, the atheist, as the arch rogue from whom he differs ludicrously calls him, is looked upon as a malignant pest, as a public poison, which like another Upas, destroys every thing within the vortex of its influence; he who dares to arouse mortals from the lethargic habit which the narcotic doses administered by the theologians have induced passes for a perturbator; he who attempts to calm their frantic transports, to moderate the fury of their maniacal paroxysms, is himself viewed as a madman, who ought to be closely chained down in the dungeons appropriated to lunatics; he who invites his associates to rend their chains asunder, to break their galling fetters, appears only like an irrational, inconsiderate being, even to the wretched captives themselves: who have been taught to believe that nature formed them for no other purpose than to tremble: only called them into existence that they might be loaded with shackles. In consequence of these fatal prepossessions, the *Disciple of Nature* is generally treated as an assassin; is commonly received by his fellow citizens in the same manner as the feathered race receive the doleful bird of night, which as soon as it quits its retreat, all the other birds follow with a common hatred, uttering a variety of doleful cries.

No, mortals blended by terror! The friend of nature is not your enemy; its interpreter is not the minister of falsehood; the destroyer of your vain phantoms is not the devastator of those truths necessary to your happiness; the disciple of reason is not an irrational being, who either seeks to poison you, or to infect you with a dangerous delirium. If he is desirous to wrest the thunder from those terrible theories that affright ye, it is that ye way discontinue your march, in the midst of storms, over roads that ye can only distinguish by the sudden, but evanescent glimmerings of the electric fluid. If he breaks those idols, which fear has served with myrrh and frankencense—which superstition has surrounded by gloomy despondency—which fanaticism has imbrued with blood; it is to substitute in their place those consoling truths that are calculated to heal the desperate wounds ye have received; that are suitable to inspire you with courage, sturdily to oppose yourselves to such dangerous errors; that have power to enable you to resist such formidable enemies. If he throws down the temples, overturns the altars, so frequently bathed with the bitter tears of the unfortunate, blackened by the most cruel sacrifices, smoked with servile incense, it is that he may erect a fane sacred to peace; a hall dedicated to reason; a durable monument to virtue, in which ye may at all times find an asylum against your own phrenzy; a refuge from your own ungovernable passions; a sanctuary against those powerful dogmatists, by whom ye are oppressed. If he attacks the haughty pretensions of deified tyrants, who crush ye with an iron sceptre, it is that ye may enjoy the rights of your nature; it is to the end that ye may be substantively freemen, in mind as well as in body; that ye may not be slaves, eternally chained to the oar of misery; it is that ye may at length be governed by men who are citizens, who may cherish their own semblances, who way protect mortals like themselves, who may actually consult the interests of those from whom they hold their power. If he battles with imposture, it is to re- establish truth in those rights which have been so long usurped by fiction. If he undermines the base of that unsteady, fanatical morality, which has hitherto done nothing more than perplex your minds, without correcting your hearts; it is to give to ethics an immovable basis, a solid foundation, secured upon your own nature; upon the reciprocity of those wants which are continually regenerating in sensible beings: dare, then, to listen to his voice; you will find it much more intelligible than those ambiguous oracles, which are announced to you as the offspring of capricious theories; as imperious decrees that are unceasingly at variance with themselves. Listen then to nature, she never contradicts her own eternal laws.

"O thou!" cries this nature to man, "who, following the impulse I have given you, during your whole existence, incessantly tend towards happiness, do not strive to resist my sovereign law. Labour to your own felicity; partake without fear of the banquet which is spread before you, with the most hearty welcome; you will find the means legibly written on your own heart. Vainly dost thou, O superstitious being! seek after thine happiness beyond the limits of the universe, in which my hand hath placed thee: vainly shalt thou search it in those inexorable theories, which thine imagination, ever prone to wander, would establish upon my eternal throne: vainly dost thou expect it in those fanciful regions, to which thine own delirium hath given a locality and a shame: vainly dost thou reckon upon capricious systems, with whose advantages thou art in such ecstasies; whilst they only fill thine abode with calamity—thine heart with dread—thy mind with illusions—thy bosom with groans. Know that when thou neglectest my counsels, the gods will refuse their aid. Dare, then, to affranchise thyself from the trammels of superstition, my self-conceited, pragmatic rival, who mistakes my rights; renounce those empty theories, which are usurpers of my privileges; return under the dominion of my laws, which, however severe, are mild in comparison with those of bigotry. It is in my empire alone that true liberty reigns. Tyranny is unknown to its soil; equity unceasingly watches over the rights of all my subjects, maintains them in the possession of their just claims; benevolence, grafted upon humanity, connects them by amicable bonds; truth enlightens them; never can imposture blind them with his obscuring mists. Return, then, my child, to thy fostering mother's arms! Deserter, trace back thy wandering steps to nature! She will console thee for thine evils; she will drive from thine heart those appalling fears which overwhelm thee; those inquietudes that distract thee; those transports which agitate thee; those hatreds that separate thee from thy fellow man, whom thou shouldst love as thyself. Return to nature, to humanity, to thyself! Strew flowers over the road of life: cease to contemplate the future; live to thine own happiness; exist for thy fellow creatures; retire into thyself, examine thine own heart, then consider the sensitive beings by whom thou art surrounded: leave to their inventors those systems which can effect nothing towards thy felicity. Enjoy thyself, and cause others also to enjoy, those comforts which I have placed with a liberal hand, for all the children of the earth; who all equally emanate from my bosom: assist them to support the sorrows to which necessity has submitted them in common with thyself. Know, that I approve thy pleasures, when without injuring thyself, they are not fatal to thy brethren, whom I have rendered indispensably necessary to thine own individual happiness. These pleasures are freely permitted thee, if thou indulgest them with moderation; with that discretion which I myself have fixed. Be happy, then, O man! Nature invites thee to participate in it; but always remember, thou canst not be so alone; because I invite all mortals to happiness as well as thyself; thou will find it is only in securing their felicity that thou canst consolidate thine own. Such is the decree of thy destiny: if thou shalt attempt to withdraw thyself from its operation, recollect that hatred will pursue thee; vengeance overtake thy steps; and remorse be ever ready at hand to punish the infractions of its irrevocable mandates.

"Follow then, O man! in whatever station thou findest thyself, the routine I have described for thee, to obtain that happiness to which thou hast an indispensable right to challenge pretension. Let the sensations of humanity interest thee for the condition of other men, who are thy fellow creatures; let thine heart have commisseration for their misfortunes: let thy generous hand spontaneously stretch forth to lend succour to the unhappy mortal who is overwhelmed by his destiny; always bearing in thy recollection, that it may fall heavy upon thyself, as it now does upon him. Acknowledge, then, without guile, that every unfortunate has an inalienable right to thy kindness. Above all, wipe from the eyes of oppressed innocence the trickling crystals of agonized feeling; let the tears of virtue in distress, fall upon thy sympathizing bosom; let the genial glow of sincere friendship animate thine honest heart; let the fond attachment of a mate, cherished by thy warmest affection, make thee forget the sorrows of life: be faithful to her love, responsible to her tenderness, that she may reward thee by a reciprocity of feeling; that under the eyes of parents united in virtuous esteem, thy offspring may learn to set a proper value on practical virtue; that after having occupied thy riper years, they may comfort thy declining age, gild with content thy setting sun, cheer the evening of thine existence, by a dutiful return of that care which thou shalt have bestowed on their imbecile infancy.

"Be just, because equity is the support of human society! Be good, because goodness connects all hearts in adamantine bonds! Be indulgent, because feeble thyself, thou livest with beings who partake of thy weakness! Be gentle, because mildness attracts attention! Be thankful, because gratitude feeds benevolence, nourishes generosity! Be modest, because haughtiness is disgusting to beings at all times well with themselves. Forgive injuries, because revenge perpetuates hatred! Do good to him who injureth thee, in order to shew thyself more noble than he is; to make a friend of him, who was once thine enemy! Be reserved in thy demeanor, temperate in thine enjoyment, chaste in thy pleasures, because voluptuousness begets weariness, intemperance engenders disease; forward manners are revolting: excess at all times relaxes the springs of thy machine, will ultimately destroy thy being, and render thee hateful to thyself, contemptible to others.

"Be a faithful citizen; because the community is necessary to thine own security; to the enjoyment of thine own existence; to the furtherance of thine own happiness. Be loyal, but be brave; submit to legitimate authority; because it is requisite to the maintenance of that society which is necessary to thyself. Be obedient to the laws; because they *are*, or *ought to be*, the expression of the public will, to which thine own particular will ought ever to be subordinate. Defend thy country with zeal; because it is that which renders thee happy, which contains thy property, as well as those beings dearest to thine heart: do not permit this common parent of thyself, as well as of thy fellow citizens, to fall under the shackles of tyranny; because from thence it will be no more than thy common prison. If thy country, deaf to the equity of thy claims, refuses thee happiness—if, submitted to an unjust power, it suffers thee to be oppressed, withdraw thyself from its bosom in silence, but never disturb its peace.

"In short, be a man; be a sensible, rational being; be a faithful husband; a tender father; an equitable master; a zealous citizen; labour to serve thy country by thy prowess; by thy talents; by thine industry; above all, by thy virtues. Participate with thine associates those gifts which nature has bestowed upon thee; diffuse happiness, among thy fellow mortals; inspire thy fellow citizens with content; spread joy over all those who approach thee, that the sphere of thine actions, enlivened by thy kindness, illumined by thy benevolence, may react upon thyself; be assured that the man who makes others happy cannot himself be miserable. In thus conducting thyself, whatever may be the injustice of others, whatever may be the blindness of those beings with whom it is thy destiny to live, thou wilt never be totally bereft of the recompense which is thy due; no power on earth be able to ravish from thee that never failing source of the purest felicity, inward content; at each moment thou wilt fall back with pleasure upon thyself; thou wilt neither feel the rankling of shame, the terror of internal alarm, nor find thy heart corroded by remorse. Thou wilt esteem thyself; thou wilt be cherished by the virtuous, applauded and loved by all good men, whose suffrages are much more valuable than those of the bewildered multitude. Nevertheless, if externals occupy thy contemplation, smiling countenances will greet thy presence; happy faces will express the interest they have in thy welfare; jocund beings will make thee participate in their placid feelings. A life so spent, will each moment be marked by the serenity of thine own soul, by the affection of the beings who environ thee; will be made cheerful by the friendship of thy fellows; will enable thee to rise a contented, satisfied guest from the general feast; conduct thee gently down the declivity of life, lead thee peaceably to the period of thy days; for die thou must: but already thou wilt survive thyself in thought; thou wilt always live in the remembrance of thy friends; in the grateful recollection of those beings whose comforts have been augmented by thy friendly attentions; thy virtues will, beforehand have erected to thy fame an imperishable monument: if heaven occupies itself with thee, it will feel satisfied with thy conduct, when it shall thus have contented the earth.

"Beware, then, how thou complainest of thy condition; be just, be kind, be virtuous, and thou canst never be wholly destitute of felicity. Take heed how thou enviest the transient pleasure of seductive crime; the deceitful power of victorious tyranny; the specious tranquillity of interested imposture; the plausible manners of venal justice; the shewy, ostentatious parade of hardened opulence. Never be tempted to increase the number of sycophants to an ambitious despot; to swell the catalogue of slaves to an unjust tyrant; never suffer thyself to be allured to infamy, to the practice of extortion, to the commission of outrage, by the fatal privilege of oppressing thy fellows; always recollect it will be at the expence of the most bitter remorse thou wilt acquire this baneful advantage. Never be the mercenary accomplice of the spoilers of thy country; they are obliged to blush secretly whenever they meet the public eye.

"For, do not deceive thyself, it is I who punish, with an unerring hand, all the crimes of the earth; the wicked may escape the laws of man, but they never escape mine. It is I who have formed the hearts, as well an the bodies of mortals; it is I who have fixed the laws which govern them. If thou deliverest thyself up to voluptuous enjoyment, the companions of thy debaucheries may applaud thee; but I shall punish thee with the most cruel infirmities; these will terminate a life of shame with deserved contempt. If thou givest, thyself up to intemperate indulgences, human laws may not correct thee, but I shall castigate thee severely by abridging thy days. If thou art vicious, thy fatal habits will recoil on thine own head. Princes, those terrestrial divinities, whose power places them above the laws of mankind, are nevertheless obliged to tremble under the silent operation of my decrees. It is I who chastise them; it is I who fill their breasts with suspicion; it is I who inspire them with terror; it is I who make them writhe under inquietude; it is I who make them shudder with horror, at the very name of august truth; it is I who, amidst the crowd of nobles who surround them, make them feel the inward workings of shame; the keen anguish of guilt; the poisoned arrows of regret; the cruel stings of remorse; it is I who, when they abuse my bounty, diffuse weariness over their benumbed souls; it is I who follow uncreated, eternal justice; it is I who, without distinction of persons, know how to make the balance even; to adjust the chastisement to the fault; to make the misery bear its due proportion to the depravity; to inflict punishment commensurate with the crime. The laws of man are just, only when they are in conformity with mine; his judgements are rational, only when I have dictated them: my laws alone are immutable, universal, irrefragable; formed to regulate the condition of the human race, in all ages, in all places, under all circumstances.

"If thou doubtest mine authority, if thou questionest the irresistible power I possess over mortals, contemplate the vengeance I wreak on all those who resist my decrees. Dive into the recesses of the hearts of those various criminals, whose countenances, assuming a forced smile, cover souls torn with anguish. Dost thou not behold ambition tormented day and night, with an ardour which nothing can extinguish? Dost not thou see the mighty conquerer become the lord of devastated solitudes; his victorious career, marked by a blasted cultivation, reign sorrowfully over smoking ruins; govern unhappy wretches who curse him in their hearts; while his soul, gnawed by remorse, sickens at the gloomy aspect of his own triumphs? Dost thou believe that the tyrant, encircled with his flatterers, who stun him with their praise, is unconscious of the hatred which his oppression excites; of the contempt which his vices draw upon him; of the sneers which his inutility call forth; of the scorn which his debaucheries entail upon his name? Dost thou think that the haughty courtier does not inwardly blush at the galling insults he brooks; despise, from the bottom of his soul, those meannesses by which he is compelled to purchase favours; feel at his heart's core the wretched dependence in which his cupidity places him.

"Contemplate the indolent child of wealth, behold him a prey to the lassitude of unmeasured enjoyment, corroded by the satiety which always follows his exhausted pleasures. View the miser with an emaciated countenance, the consequence of his own penurious disposition, whose callous heart is inaccessible to the calls of misery, groaning over the accumulating load of useless treasure, which at the expense of himself, he has laboured to amass. Behold the gay voluptuary, the smiling debauchee, secretly lament the health they have so inconsiderately damaged so prodigally thrown away: see disdain, joined to hatred, reign between those adulterous married couples, who have reciprocally violated the sacred vows they mutually pledged at the altar of Hymen; whose appetencies have rendered them the scorn of the world; the jest of their acquaintance; polluted tributaries to the surgeon. See the liar deprived of all confidence; the knave stript of all trust; the hypocrite fearfully avoiding the penetrating looks of his inquisitive neighbour; the impostor trembling at the very name of formidable truth. Bring under your review the heart of the envious, uselessly dishonored; that withers at the sight of his neighbour's prosperity. Cast your eyes on the frozen soul of the ungrateful wretch, whom no kindness can warm, no benevolence thaw, no beneficence convert into a genial fluid. Survey the iron feelings of that monster whom the sighs of the unfortunate cannot mollify. Behold the revengeful being nourished with venemous gall, whose very thoughts are serpents; who in his rage consumes himself. Envy, if thou canst, the waking slumbers of the homicide; the startings of the iniquitous judge; the restlessness of the oppressor of innocence; the fearful visions of the extortioner; whose couches are infested with the torches of the furies. Thou tremblest without doubt at the sight of that distraction which, amidst their splendid luxuries, agitates those farmers of the revenue, who fatten upon public calamity—who devour the substance of the orphan—who consume the means of the widow—who grind the hard earnings of the poor: thou shudderest at witnessing the remorse which rends the souls of those reverend criminals, whom the uninformed believe to be happy, whilst the contempt which they have for themselves, the unerring shafts of secret upbraidings, are incessantly revenging an outraged nation. Thou seest, that content is for ever banished the heart; quiet for ever driven from the habitations of those miserable wretches on whose minds I have indelibly engraved the scorn, the infamy, the chastisement which they deserve. But, no! thine eyes cannot sustain the tragic spectacle of my vengeance. Humanity obliges thee to partake of their merited sufferings; thou art moved to pity for these unhappy people, to whom consecrated errors renders vice necessary; whose fatal habits make them familiar with crime. Yes; thou shunnest them without hating them; thou wouldst succour them, if their contumacious perversity had left thee the means. When thou comparest thine own condition, when thou examinest thine own soul, thou wilt have just cause to felicitate thyself, if thou shalt find that peace has taken up her abode with thee; that contentment dwells at the bottom of thine own heart. In short, thou seest accomplished upon them, as well as, upon thyself, the unalterable decrees of destiny, which imperiously demand, that crime shall punish itself, that virtue never shall be destitute Of remuneration."

Such is the sum of those truths which are contained in the *Code of Nature*; such are the doctrines, which its disciples can announce. They are unquestionably preferable to that supernatural superstition which never does any thing but mischief to the human species. Such is the worship that is taught by that sacred reason, which is the object of contempt with the theologian; which meets the insult of the fanatic; who only estimates that which man can neither conceive nor practise; who make his morality consist in fictitious duties; his virtue in actions generally useless, frequently pernicious to the welfare of society; who for want of being acquainted with nature, which is before their eyes, believe themselves obliged to seek in ideal worlds imaginary motives, of which every thing proves the inefficacy. The motive which the morality of nature employs, is the self-evident interest of each individual, of each community, of the whole human species, in all times, in every country, under all circumstances. Its worship is the sacrifice of vice, the practise of real virtues; its object is the conservation of the human race, the happiness of the individual, the peace of mankind; its recompences are affection, esteem, and glory; or in their default, contentment of mind, with merited self-esteem, of which no power will ever be able to deprive virtuous mortals; its punishments, are hatred, contempt, and indignation; which society always reserves for those who outrage its interests; from which even the most powerful can never effectually shield themselves.

Those nations who shall be disposed to practise a morality so wise, who shall inculcate it in infancy, whose laws shall unceasingly confirm it, will neither have occasion for superstition, nor for chimeras. Those who shall obstinately prefer figments to their dearest interests, will certainly march forward to ruin. If they maintain themselves for a season, it is because the power of nature sometimes drives them back to reason, in despite of those prejudices which appear to lead them on to certain destruction. Superstition, leagued with tyranny, for the waste of the human species, are themselves frequently obliged to implore the assistance of a reason which they contemn; of a nature which they disdain; which they debase; which they endeavour to crush under the ponderous bulk of artificial theories. Superstition, in all times so fatal to mortals, when attacked by reason, assumes the sacred mantle of public utility; rests its importance on false grounds, founds its rights upon the indissoluble alliance which it pretends subsists between morality and itself; notwithstanding it never ceases for a single instant to wage against it the most cruel hostility. It is, unquestionably, by this artifice, that it has seduced so many sages. In the honesty of their hearts, they believe it useful to politics; necessary to restrain the ungovernable fury of the passions; thus hypocritical superstition, in order to mask to superficial observers, its own hideous character, like the ass with the lion's skin, always knows how to cover itself with the sacred armour of utility; to buckle on the invulnerable shield of virtue; it has therefore, been believed imperative to respect it, notwithstanding it felt awkward under these incumbrances; it consequently has become a duty to favor imposture, because it has artfully entrenched itself behind the altars of truth; its ears, however, discover its worthlessness; its natural cowardice betrays itself; it is from this intrenchment we ought to drive it; it should be dragged forth to public view; stripped of its surreptitious panoply; exposed in its native deformity; in order that the human race may become acquainted with its dissimulation; that mankind may have a knowledge of its crimes; that the universe may behold its sacrilegious hands, armed with homicidal poniards, stained with the blood of nations, whom it either intoxicates with its fury, or immolates without pity to the violence of its passions.

The MORALITY OF NATURE is the only creed which her interpreter offers to his fellow citizens; to nations; to the human species; to future races, weaned from those prejudices which have so frequently disturbed the felicity of their ancestors. The friend of mankind cannot be the friend of delusion, which at all times has been a real scourge to the earth. The APOSTLE OF NATURE will not be the instrument of deceitful chimeras, by which this world is made only an abode of illusions; the adorer of truth will not compromise with falsehood; he will make no covenant with error; conscious it must always be fatal to mortals. He knows that the happiness of the human race imperiously exacts that the dark unsteady edifice of superstition should be razed to its foundations; in order to elevate on its ruins a temple suitable to peace—a fane sacred to virtue. He feels it is only by extirpating, even to the most slender fibres, the poisonous tree, that during so many ages has overshadowed the universe, that the inhabitants of this world will be able to use their own optics—to bear with steadiness that light which is competent to illumine their understanding—to guide their wayward steps—to give the necessary ardency to their souls. If his efforts should be vain; if he cannot inspire with courage, beings too much accustomed to tremble; he will, at least, applaud himself for having dared the attempt. Nevertheless, he will not judge his exertions fruitless, if he has only been enabled to make a single mortal happy: if his principles have calmed the conflicting transports of one honest soul; if his reasonings have cheered up some few virtuous hearts. At least he will have the advantage of having banished from his own mind the importunate terror of superstition; of having expelled from his own heart the gall which exasperates zeal; of having trodden under foot those chimeras with which the uninformed are tormented. Thus, escaped from the peril of the storm, he will calmly contemplate from the summit of his rock, those tremendous hurricanes which superstition excites; he will hold forth a succouring hand to those who shall be willing to accept it; he will encourage them with his voice; he will second them with his best exertions, and in the warmth of his own compassionate heart, he will exclaim:

O NATURE; sovereign of all beings! and ye, her adorable daughters, VIRTUE, REASON, and TRUTH! remain for ever our revered protectors: it is to you that belong the praises of the human race; to you appertains the homage of the earth. Shew, us then, O NATURE! that which man ought to do, in order to obtain the happiness which thou makest him desire. VIRTUE! Animate him with thy beneficent fire. REASON! Conduct his uncertain steps through the paths of life. TRUTH! Let thy torch illumine his intellect, dissipate the darkness of his road. Unite, O assisting deities! your powers, in order to submit the hearts of mankind to your dominion. Banish error from our mind; wickedness from our hearts; confusion from our footsteps; cause knowledge to extend its salubrious reign; goodness to occupy our souls; serenity to dwell in our bosoms. Let imposture, confounded, never again dare to shew its head. Let our eyes, so long, either dazzled or blindfolded, be at length fixed upon those objects we ought to seek. Dispel for ever those mists of ignorance, those hideous phantoms, together with those seducing chimeras, which only serve to lead us astray. Extricate us from that dark abyss into which we are plunged by superstition; overthrow the fatal empire of delusion; crumble the throne of falsehood; wrest from their polluted hands the power they have usurped. Command men, without sharing your authority with mortals: break the chains that bind them down in slavery: tear away the bandeau by which they are hoodwinked; allay the fury that intoxicates them; break in the hands of sanguinary, lawless tyrants, that iron sceptre with which they are crushed to exile: the imaginary regions, from whence fear has imported them, those theories by which they are afflicted. Inspire the intelligent being with courage; infuse energy into his system, that, at length, he may feel his own dignity; that he may dare to love himself; to esteem his own actions when they are worthy; that a slave only to your eternal laws, he may no longer fear to enfranchise himself from all other trammels; that blest with freedom, he may have the wisdom to cherish his fellow creature; and become happy by learning to perfection his own condition; instruct him in the great lesson, that the high road to felicity, is prudently to partake himself, and also to cause others to enjoy, the rich banquet which thou, O Nature! hast so bountifully set before him. Console thy children for those sorrows to which their destiny submits them, by those pleasures which wisdom allows them to partake; teach them to be contented with their condition; to banish envy from their mind; to yield silently to necessity. Conduct them without alarm to that period which all beings must find; *let them learn that time changes all things, that consequently they are made neither to avoid its scythe nor to fear its arrival.*

[TRANSLATOR'S APPENDIX]

A BRIEF SKETCH
OF THE
LIFE AND WRITINGS
OF
M. DE. MIRABAUD.

At a time when we are on the eve of an important change in our political affairs, which must evidently lead either to the recovery and re- establishment of our liberties, or to a military despotism, those who are connected with the press ought to use every exertion to enlighten their fellow-citizens, and to assert their right of canvassing, in the most free and unrestrained manner, every subject connected with the happiness of man.

The priesthood have ever been convenient tools in the hands of tyrants, to keep the bulk of the people in a degraded servility. By the superstitious and slavish doctrines which they infuse into their minds, they prevent them from thinking for themselves and asserting their own independence. At a moment when national schools are erecting in every quarter of the country, not with a sincere desire of enlightening the rising generation, but with the insidious design of instilling into their minds the doctrines of "Church and King," in order to bolster up a little longer the present rotten, tottering, and corrupt system: at a moment, too, when thousands of fanatic preachers are traversing the country, with a view to subjugate the human mind to the baleful empire of visionary enthusiasm and sectarian bigotry to the utter extinction of every noble, manly, liberal, and pilanthropic principle;—at such a moment as this, we thought that the "SYSTEM OF NATURE" could not fail to render essential service to the cause both of civil and religious liberty. No work, ancient or modern, has surpassed it, in the eloquence and sublimity of its language, or in the facility with which it treats the most abtruse and difficult subjects. It is, without exception, the boldest effort the human mind has yet produced, in the investigation of morals and theology—in the destruction of priestcraft and superstition —and in developing the sources of all those passions and prejudices which have proved so fatal to the tranquillity of the world.

The republic of letters has never produced an author whose pen was so well calculated to emancipate mankind from all those trammels with which the nurse, the schoolmaster and the priest have successively locked up their noblest faculties, before they were capable of reasoning and judging for themselves. The frightful apprehensions of the gloomy bigot, and all the appalling terrors of superstition, are here utterly annihilated, to the complete satisfaction of every unbiassed and impartial person.—These we considered as necessary observations to make, previous to any attempt at the biography of the author.

Biography may be reckoned among the most interesting of literary productions. Its intrinsic value is such, that, though capable of extraordinary embellishment from the hand of genius, yet no inferiority of execution can so degrade it, as to deprive it of utility. Whatever relates even to man in general, considered only as an aggregate of active and intelligent beings, has a strong claim upon our notice; but that which relates to our author, as distinguished from the rest of his species, moving in a more exalted sphere, and towering above them by the resplendent excellencies of his mind, seems to me to be peculiarly calculated for our contemplation, and ought to form the highest pleasure of our lives. There is a principle of curiosity implanted in us, which leads us, in an especial manner, to investigate our fellow creatures; the eager inquisitiveness with which the mechanic seeks to know the history of his fellow-workmen and the ardour with which the philosopher, the poet, or the historian hunts for details that may familiarize him with, a Descartes or a Newton, with a Milton, a Hume, or a Gibbon— spring from the same source. Their object, however, may perhaps vary; for, in the former, it may be for the sake of detraction, invidious cavil, or malice; in the latter, it is a sweet homage paid by the human heart to the memory of departed genius.

It has been repeatedly observed that the life of a scholar affords few materials for biography. This is only negatively true;—could every scholar have a Boswell, the remark would vanish; or were every scholar a Rousseau, a Gibbon, or a Cumberland it would be equally nugatory. What can present higher objects of contemplation—what can claim more forcibly our attention—where can we seek for subjects of a more precious nature, than in the elucidation of the operations of mind, the acquisition of knowledge, the gradual expansion of genius; its application, its felicities, its sorrows, its wreaths of fame, its cold, undeserved neglect? Such scenes, painted by, the artist himself, are a rich bequest to mankind: even when traced by the hand of friendship or the pencil of admiration, they possess a permanent interest in our hearts. I cannot conceive a life more worthy of public notice, more important, more interesting to human nature, than the life of a literary man, were it executed according to the ideas I have formed of it: did it exhibit a faithful delineation of the progress of intellect, from the cradle upwards; did it portray, in accurate colors, the production of what we call genius: by what accident it was first awakened; what were its first tendencies; how directed to a particular object; by what means it was nourished and unfolded; the gradual progress of its operation in the production of a work; its hopes and fears; its delights; its miseries; its inspirations; and all the thousand fleeting joys that so often invest its path but for a moment, and then fade like the dews of the morning. Let it contain too a transcript of the many nameless transports that float round the heart, that dance in the gay circle before the ardent gazing eye, when the first conception of some future effort strikes the mind; how it pictures undefined delights of fame and popular applause; how it anticipates the bright moments of invention, and dwells with prophetic ecstasy on the felicitous execution of particular parts, that already start into existence by the magic touch of a heated imagination. Let it depict the tender feelings of solitude, the breathings of midnight silence, the scenes of mimic life, of imaged trial, that often occupy the musing mind; let it be such a work, so drawn, so coloured, and who shall pronounce it inferior? Who rather will not confess that it presents a picture of human nature, where every heart may find some corresponding harmony? When, therefore, it is said, that the life of a scholar is barren, it is so only because it has never been properly delineated; because those parts only have been selected which are common, and fail to distinguish him from the common man; because we have never penetrated into his closet, or into his heart; because we have drawn him only as an outward figure, and left unnoticed that internal structure that would delight, astonish, and improve. And then, when we compare the life of such a man with the more active one of a soldier, a statesman, or a lawyer, we pronounce it insipid, uninteresting. True;—the man of study has not fought for hire—he has not slaughtered at the command of a master: he would disdain to do so. Though unaccompanied with the glaring actions of public men, which confound and dazzle by their publicity, but shrink from the estimation of moral truth, it would present a far nobler picture; yes, and a more instructive one:—the calm disciple of reason meditates in silence; he walks his road with innoxious humility; he is poor, but his mind is his treasure; he cultivates his reason, and she lifts him to the pinnacle of truth; he learns to tear away the veil of self-love, folly, pride, and prejudice, and bares the human heart to his inspection; he corrects and amends; he repairs the breaches made by passion; the proud man passes him by, and looks upon him with scorn; but he feels his own worth, that ennobling consciousness which swells in every vein, and inspires him with true pride—with manly independence: to such a man I could sooner bow in reverence, than to the haughtiest, most successful candidate for the world's ambition. But of such men, for the reason I have already mentioned, our information is scanty. While of others, who have commanded a greater share of public notoriety, venal or mistaken admiration has given more than we wished to know. Among these respected individuals of human nature, may be placed Mirabaud. Had Mirabaud been an Englishman, who doubts but that we should have possessed at least ample details of the usual subjects of biographical notice; while all that has been collected among his own countrymen, is a scanty memoir in a common dictionary. That we are doomed to remain ignorant of the life of such men, speaks a loud disgrace.—I lament it.

JOHN BAPTISTE MIRABAUD, was born at Paris in the year 1674. He prosecuted his infantile studies under the direction of his parents, and was afterwards entered a member of the *Congregation of the Priests of the Oratory*, where he passed several years, and produced some very bold writings, which were never intended for publication.

He was subsequently appointed tutor to the princesses of the House of Orleans, and then took the resolution of destroying the greater part of the manuscripts that he produced while a member of the *Congregation*; but the treachery of some of his friends, to whom he had confided his manuscripts, rendered this precaution useless, for some of his works were published during the time he remained the preceptor to his royal pupils; among which number may be reckoned his "New Liberties of Thought," a work but little calculated for gaining him friends in the purlieus of the Court of Orleans. The "Origin and Antiquity of the World," in three parts, was also published at this period, and from the publication of this work, may be dated the resolution of M. de Mirabaud to quit his office of preceptor, which he relinquished, having become more independent; he now gave himself up entirely to his philosophical studies, and produced the "System of Nature," with which he was assisted by Diderot, D'Alembert, Baron D'Olbac, and others.

The profound metaphysical knowledge displayed throughout the System of Nature, and the doctrines which are therein advanced, warrants the conclusion, that it is at once the most decisive, boldest, and most extraordinary work, that the human understanding ever had the courage to produce. The study of metaphysics his generally been considered the most terrific to the indolent mind; but the clear and perspicuous reasoning of a Mirabaud, who has united the most profound argument, with the most fascinating eloquence, charm and instruct us at the same time. But it was not, to be expected that such doctrines as are contained in the System of Nature, would he advanced without meeting with some opposition from the superficial and bigoted metaphysicians, who feel an interest in upholding a system of delusion and superstition. No! certainly not, Their interest was threatened, and their *craft* in danger, and the consequence was, that the *Atheist* or *Disciple of Nature*, has been abused with every scurrilous epithet, "full of sound and fury, signifying nothing."

Atheism is stigmatized with having "opened a wide door for libertinism, destroying the social and moral compact; and striking a deadly blow at religion. It is asserted that the atheist, who by his opinions has deprived himself of the hope and consolation of a future life, has no motive for the practise of virtue, or to contribute to the well being of society. Deprived of a chimera which religion every where presents him, he wanders through the cheerless gloom of scepticism, regardless of the consequences of an abandoned life. Without a God, he acknowledges no benefactor; without divine laws, he knows no rule for the conduct of life, and submits to no law but his passions. An enemy to all social order, he spurns at human laws, and breaks through every barrier opposed to his wickedness." Under such colours is an atheist painted: a short digression must be suffered to examine this picture, and to disprove the assertions so sweepingly made.

I admit that atheism strikes a deadly blow at religion; because under the cloak of religion, mankind have been oppressed in all ages; but that it encourages libertinism, or destroys the "social and moral compact," I have yet to learn. In all organized governments, men are restrained from crime and compelled to submission by laws supposed to be made for the general benefit.

These laws are the effect of the first formation of society for mutual preservation. Here then is a sufficient motive for the one as well as the other, to contribute to the well-being of society. The laws of Nature are the same in effect on the atheist and the religionist. If man be led captive by his passions, and gives himself to debauchery and voluptuousness, nature will punish him with bodily infirmities and a debilitated mind. If he be intemperate, she will shorten his days and bring him to the grave with the most poignant remorse. The fatal effects of his vicious propensities will fall upon his own head. A disturber of social order will live in continual fear of the vengeance of society, and that very fear is a more dreadful punishment than the just vengeance which perhaps he escapes. It renders life burdensome, and makes a man hateful to himself. Can men have stronger motives for the practise of virtue? The atheist is in full possession of these motives, and the religionist is most completely swayed by them, whatever may be his pretensions to others derived from religion. But we are assured he has other motives; more powerful incentives, in the promise of future rewards and punishments. This, like all other chimerical doctrines, cannot be maintained if we look at the general practise of mankind. Let us trace the effects of this doctrine, or rather let us examine the actions, conduct, and character of men professing it, and we shall see how little influence it has over them. The bulk of society believe they shall answer in a future life for the deeds done in the present. Nay, I hardly think one in a hundred thousand will say they doubt it. What then is its effect? With this dreadful sentence, *"Thou shalt go into everlasting punishment,"* continually sounded in their ears, do we not daily see the greatest enormities committed? Are not the most horrid crimes perpetrated in all parts of the world? The most vicious propensities and the most extravagant follies are almost indiscriminately gratified. Is not vice frequently triumphant, and virtue compelled to seek her own reward in retirement? The laws of society are broken by the most flagrant injustice, and the laws of nature outraged by the most shocking depravity. All this evil exists in nations believing themselves to be accountable beings after death. Where then are the beneficial effects arising, to mankind from the promulgation of this doctrine? Men who cannot be restrained from doing evil by human laws, have no dread of any other. Their whole lives and conduct confirm this. Others who live in submission to the laws of society, give themselves up to those vicious habits, (without fear of divine laws) which the law does not take cognizance of. Men, not wholly depraved, or not without the pale of society, generally respect the laws, and fear the bad opinion of others. Hence we observe, when interest or passion leads them into secret vices, they invariably play the hypocrite; and although they are aware of the denunciations of their God, whom they acknowledge is a witness to all their actions, while they preserve their fair fame they still persevere. In fact, they live as if they disbelieved in his existence; and yet the greatest criminal, the most depraved wretch, would shudder at being told there is no God. The atheist, as a man, is liable to commit the same crimes, and fall into the same vices as the believer; but because he is an atheist, is he a worse criminal than the other? In one respect, I conceive he is not so bad. He only acts in defiance of *human* laws,—he only offends men; the other infringes *both divine* and *human*;—he defies both God and man. Both are injurious to society and themselves, and both are actuated by the came motives.

Again we are told, that the well disposed part of mankind are rendered more virtuous, and the vicious less vicious by this doctrine. How are we to know that? If the virtuous man acts uprightly, does good to his fellow creatures, restrains his passions, and returns good for evil, experience teaches him it is his interest so to do. Those who are viciously disposed are only deterred from crime by penal laws. Societies cannot long exist, where evil has the ascendency. Without social laws, this would really be the case, notwithstanding the threats of an avenging God. If men were told they would not be answerable for the evil committed in this life to human laws, but that God would punish them after death, it is evident the human race would soon be exterminated. On the other hand, tell them their crimes will never be punished by God, or, in other words, there is no other God than NATURE, but that the laws of men will avenge the offences against society; so long as those laws are administered with justice and impartiality, so long will such society continue to improve. Hence it is evident that the system which will maintain order in society by itself, must be the best and most rational. A good government without religion would be more solid and lasting, and tend more to the preservation of mankind, than all the theocratical or ecclesiastical governments that ever the world was subject to.—Thus much for the opponents of atheism.

It has been asserted with a perverse obstinacy, by the advocates for the existence of a deity, that the SYSTEM OF NATURE was never written by the author whose name it bears.—It is granted that it was not published during his life: but that circumstance forms no reason why such a conclusion should be drawn. The persecutions which the atheists have endured, were a sufficient excuse for the work not appearing in any form during the life time of its venerable author. The Athenians sought to try Diagoras the Melian, for atheism; but he fled from Athens, and a price was offered for his head. Protagoras was banished from Athens, and his books burnt, because he ventured to assert, that he knew nothing of the gods. Stephen Dolet was burnt at Paris for atheism. Giordano Bruno was burnt by the Inquisitors in Italy. Lucilio Vanini was burnt at Thoulouse, through the kind offices of an Attorney-General. Bayle was under the necessity of fleeing to Holland. Casimio Liszynski was executed at Grodno;—and Akenhead at Edinborough. And the body of the eloquent and erudite Hume, was obliged to be watched many nights by his friends, lest it should be taken up by the fanatics, who considered him one of the greatest monsters of iniquity, because he did not happen to believe as they believed.—With these pictures of Christian persecution before his eyes, is it surprising that M. de Mirabaud should adopt the resolution of suffering the SYSTEM OF NATURE to appear as a posthumous work? That the same fate would have attended him, the most devout Christian will not undertake to deny.

However the sentiments of M. de Mirabaud may be condemned by the fanatics, all those who knew him bear the most brilliant testimony of his integrity, candour, and the soundness of his understanding; in a word, to his social virtues, and the innocence of his manners. He died universally regretted, at Paris, the twenty-fourth of June, 1760, in the eighty-sixth year of his age.

The following works, written by him at different periods, were never published:—*The Life of Jesus Christ. Impartial Reflections on the Gospel. The Morality of Nature. An Abridged History of the Priesthood; Ancient and Modern. The Opinions of the Ancients concerning the Jews.* A wretched mutilated edition of this last work was published at Amsterdam, in 1740, in two small volumes, under the title of *Miscellaneous Dissertations.*

FINIS.

www.ingramcontent.com/pod-product-compliance
Lightning Source LLC
Chambersburg PA
CBHW060314230426
43663CB00009B/1694